ACCA

Advanced Performance Management (APM)

Practice & Revision Kit

For exams in September 2021, December 2021, March 2022 and June 2022

First edition 2007
Fifteenth edition February 2021

ISBN 9781 5097 3756 7
(previous ISBN 9781 5097 8397 7)
e-ISBN 9781 5097 3854 0

Cataloguing-in-Publication Data
A catalogue record for this book is available
from the British Library

Published by

BPP Learning Media Ltd
BPP House, Aldine Place
London W12 8AA

www.bpp.com/learningmedia

Printed in the United Kingdom

Your learning materials, published by BPP
Learning Media Ltd, are printed on paper
obtained from traceable, sustainable sources.

The contents of this book are intended as a
guide and not professional advice. Although
every effort has been made to ensure that the
contents of this book are correct at the time of
going to press, BPP Learning Media makes no
warranty that the information in this book is
accurate or complete and accept no liability for
any loss or damage suffered by any person
acting or refraining from acting as a result of
the material in this book.

We are grateful to the Association of Chartered
Certified Accountants for permission to
reproduce past examination questions. The
suggested solutions in the practice answer bank
have been prepared by BPP Learning Media Ltd,
unless otherwise stated.

Contents

Finding questions

Question index

The headings in this checklist/index indicate the main topics of questions, but questions often cover several different topics. Past exam questions are designated with the date of the exam in which they featured, although some have been amended to reflect subsequent changes to the syllabus or in the format of the exam. Prior to September 2018, Advanced Performance Management (APM) was known as P5 Advanced Performance Management.

Since September 2015 there have been four exam sittings per year, but ACCA generally only publish two exams' worth of questions per year. These releases are compiled from questions selected from the preceding sessions. These compilation exams are denoted as 'Mar/Jun' and 'Sept/Dec' in the index below.

		Time allocation (Mins)	Page number	
Part A: Strategic planning and control	**Marks**		**Question**	**Answer**
1 ENT Entertainments (P5, 6/11, amended)	25	49	3	113
2 BPC (P5, 12/07, amended)	25	49	4	116
3 CRC (APM, Mar/Jun 19)	25	49	5	119
4 Drinks Group (P5, 12/12, amended)	25	49	7	122
5 Godel (P5, 6/14, amended)	25	49	9	127
6 Perkin (P5, Sept/Dec 15)	25	49	10	131
7 Jolt (APM, Sept 18)	25	49	12	135
8 Booxe (P5, 6/14)	25	49	13	138
9 PLX Refinery (P5, 2013 Pilot Exam)	25	49	14	142
10 Alflonnso (P5, Sept/Dec 16)	25	49	16	146

Part B: Impact of risk and uncertainty				
11 Sberry (APM, Sept/Dec 18)	25	49	18	150
12 Sweet Cicely (P5, Sept/Dec 17)	25	49	19	154
13 Turing (P5, 6/14)	25	49	20	157

BPP
LEARNING
MEDIA

50-mark (Section A) Questions	Marks	Time allocation (Mins)	Page number Question	Answer
54 Lopten (P5, 12/13, amended)	50	98	79	313
55 Chiven (APM, Mar/Jun 18)	50	98	81	319
56 Folt (APM, 3/19)	50	98	83	326
57 Flack (P5, Mar/Jun 16)	50	98	85	331
58 Cantor (P5, 6/14)	50	98	88	337
59 Boltzman Machines (P5, 12/14, amended)	50	98	91	346
60 Merkland Sportswear (P5, 6/15)	50	98	94	353
61 Monza Pharma (P5, Sept/Dec 16)	50	98	97	361
62 Dargeboard Services (P5, Mar/Jun 17)	50	98	100	368
63 Thyme Engine Products (P5, Sept/Dec 17)	50	98	103	373
64 Fearties (APM, Sept 18)	50	98	105	380
65 Rezillos (APM, Dec 18)	50	98	108	385

Mock exam 1

Mock exam 2 (APM Specimen Exam)

Mock exam 3 (APM, Sep/Dec 2019 Exams, Sample questions)

Mock exam 4 (APM Sep/Dec 2020 Exams, Sample questions)

Topic index

Listed below are the key APM syllabus topics and the numbers of the questions in this Kit covering those topics. We have also included a reference to the relevant Chapter of the BPP APM Workbook, the companion to the BPP APM Practice and Revision Kit, in case you wish to revise the information on the topic you have covered.

If you need to concentrate your practice and revision on certain topics or if you want to attempt all available questions that refer to a particular subject, you will find this index useful.

Syllabus topic	Question numbers	Workbook chapter
Accountability and responsibility accounting	24, 35(b)(ii)	8
Activity-based costing	10, 31, 48(a)	13
Activity-based management	45, 46, 48, Mock 3 Qn2	13
Appraisals and performance management	8(c), 64(iv)	12
Balanced scorecard	39, 40, 41, 59(d), 61(i), 64(i) Mock 1 Qn 1	13
Benchmarking	21, 59(b), 65	1
BCG matrix	1	1
Big Data	20, 55(iv)	6
Budgeting and types of budget	3, 4, 5, 6, Mock 1 Qn 2, Mock 3 Qn 3	3
Building Blocks model (Fitzgerald and Moon)	44, 62(iv), Mock 1 Qn 1	12, 13
Business process re-engineering (BPR)	7, 8, 37(a)	4
Business structure (and performance measurement)	50	14
Corporate failure	2(c), 51, 52, 53, Mock 1 Qn 3, Mock 2 Qn 2	15
Costs of quality	31(b), 32(a), 56, 61(iv), 63(iv)	11
Critical success factors (CSFs)	23(a), 54, 56(a), Mock 2 Qn 1, Mock 4 Qn 1	2
Divisional performance measures	24	8
Economic value added (EVA™)	24, 25, 38, 43, 46, 47, 58(iii), Mock 2 Qn 1	8
Environmental management accounting	9, 10	4
Enterprise resource planning systems (ERPS)	15, Mock 2 Qn 1(iv), Mock 4 Qn 2b	6
External environment (and impact on organisations)	11, 12, 54	1, 4
Financial performance	21, 61(ii & iii)	7
Five forces (Porter)	2, Mock 2 Qn 3	1

Syllabus topic	Question numbers	Workbook chapter
Information systems and IT systems	14a, 56(d), 57(v), Mock 2 Qn 1	6
Integrated Reporting	19, 63(ii)	6
JIT	30(a), 32, 59(c), Mock 2 Qn 1(iii; iv)	11
Joint ventures	13, 14b, Mock 4 Q2a	14
Kaizen costing	32, 33, Mock 2 Qn 1(iii; iv)	11
Key performance indicators (KPIs)	23(a), 54, 56 (a), 62, 64(i), Mock 2 Qn 1ii, Mock 4 Qn 1i	2
League tables	26, 28(b), Mock 4 Qn 1iv	9
Lean information systems	15, 17, 18, 61(v)	6
Management accounting and information systems	14a, 57(v), Mock 2 Qn 1,	6
Management and control styles	29(c), 36(b), 38(c), 64(iii)	12
McKinsey 7S	Mock 4 Qn 2a	4
Mission statements	57(i), 58(v), 62(i)	2
Mistakes and misconceptions in the use of numerical data	65(ii)	6
Non-financial performance indicators	27, 29(a), 34(a), Mock 4 Qn 1iii	10
Performance management in complex business structures	13, 14, 50	14
Performance management information systems	14, 15, 16, 17, 47b	6
Performance measures	21(a), 55, (ii), 57(ii–iv)	7
Performance pyramid (Lynch & Cross)	42, 49	13
Performance reports	55, 57(i), 58(i), 63(i), 65(a)	6
Problems of performance measurement	42	12
Public sector organisations	19(a), 26, 27, 28, 29	9
Qualitative data	64(ii)	10
Quality	30(b), 31(b), 34, 35, 56 (c, d), 61(iv), 63(iv), Mock 3 Qn1 (iii),(iv)	11
Responsibility and controllability	24, 36	3, 8
Reward and remuneration schemes	1(c), 24, 36, 37(b), 40(c), 62(v), 64(iv), Mock 1 Qn 1(v)	12
RFID technology	17	6
Risk and uncertainty	11, 12, 13, 60(iii)	5
Service organisations	44, Mock 1 Qn 1	4
Six Sigma	34, 35, 50c	11

Syllabus topic	Question numbers	Workbook chapter
Stakeholders	25(b), 39(b), 59, Mock 4 Q3b	4
SWOT analysis	60	1
Target costing	33, 56 (b), 63(iii), Mock 3 Qn 1ii	11
Total quality management (TQM)	32(d), 63(iii), Mock 2 Qn 1(iii; iv)	11
Transfer pricing	22, 23	8
Value-based management	43, 46, 47, 58(iv)	13
Value chain	55(iii), 60(v)	4
Value for money	27(b), 28, 29(b), Mock 4 Qn 1ii	9
Virtual organisations	50	14

The exam

Computer-based exams

With effect from the March 2020 sitting, ACCA have commenced the launch of computer-based exams (CBEs) for this exam with the aim of rolling out into all markets internationally over a short period. BPP materials have been designed to support you, whichever exam format you are studying towards. For more information on these changes and when they will be implemented, please visit the ACCA website.

Approach to examining the syllabus

The technical articles section on ACCA's website include one called 'Advanced Performance Management Examiner's approach'. This article outlines the way the syllabus will be tested, and the qualities candidates should demonstrate when answering APM questions. The article also addresses the five main syllabus areas for APM in turn, and identifies what qualities candidates should demonstrate under each. We reproduce the main points here.

(1) **The application of strategic planning and control models in performance management.** The models stress the need to take a holistic view of the factors that affect a business and to consider them when giving strategic advice on performance. Good candidates often distinguish themselves by being able to synthesise disparate detailed points into an overall, strategic approach for an organisation.

(2) **Factors external to the business, and the impact of risk and uncertainty on organisational performance.** Candidates need to move beyond the internal factors associated with traditional management accounting to consider the information needs of the strategic level of management as well as the operational and tactical levels.

(3) **The information that management require and the systems that are needed for its delivery.** Candidates are expected to be aware of the effect of information technologies on performance management decision making rather than the detail of these technologies. Candidates will not be required to have detailed technical knowledge of hardware and software, but they should be conversant with the broad hardware and software trends and issues, and how these interact with the provision of performance information throughout the organisation. In particular, candidates need to recognise the impact that technology (and developments in technology) can have on performance management and decision making in an organisation.

(4) and (5) **The fourth capability** is the **application** of the techniques and assumed knowledge to specific scenarios. You shouldn't simply discuss theories and models in general terms; you need to apply them specifically to the scenario identified in the question, in order to evaluate an organisation's performance and identify potential ways to improve organisational performance. **The fifth capability**, which builds directly on the fourth, is being able to take performance measurement information and turn it into **advice which is commercially valuable for strategic decision makers.** This capability also requires the candidate to be able to recognise and advise on situations where the organisation is in danger of failing.

Candidates also need to present their answers in a professional manner. There will be four **professional marks** available in the Section A question, and it should be possible for a well-prepared student to score most of these. For example, the effective use of appropriate introductions and conclusions, and helpfully breaking the document into properly headed sub-sections, will help to demonstrate a professional approach to writing a report. However, it should be stressed that the approach taken will vary from question to question and the exam tests the candidates' ability to apply their knowledge of professional presentation. In order to score full professional marks, the answer will have to be tailored to the specifics of the scenario in the question recognising the needs of the readers of the document.

Presentation points. First: on rounding. At this final level, candidates should use their own judgment about the level of detail to which they round figures – the basic rule is that there should be enough detail to make a useful conclusion without obscuring it with insignificant figures. However, it is also very important that you round correctly (ie up or down) according to the underlying figures.

Second, short paragraphs are usually clear but single sentence paragraphs are often insufficient and unable to get to the depth required at Strategic Professional level, where APM sits. Bullet points are useful for lists, but are not sufficient if an analysis or evaluation is required.

Finally, reading model solutions is not a substitute for actually writing out your own answers.

Summarising the advice ACCA's examining team gives for APM:

Candidates should do the following:

- Understand the objectives of the exam as explained in the syllabus and prepare the detailed topics in the Study Guide.

- Be very comfortable with the areas tested in *Performance Management* (at Applied Skills level) which constitute brought forward knowledge for APM.

- Ensure that their preparation for the exam has been based on a programme of study set for the required syllabus and exam structure.

- Use an ACCA-approved study materials for APM. They are structured around the syllabus and ACCA's examining team reviews them so that they give an effective coverage of what is examinable.

- Practise questions under exam conditions in order to improve speed and presentation skills, ensuring these test discursive, computational and analytic abilities.

- Study all the technical articles relevant to APM that are published on ACCA's website.

- Be able to clearly communicate understanding and application of knowledge in the context of a business scenario.

The questions tend to be wide-ranging, as the examining team wants to link topics and mix ideas up. So you are better knowing something about every part of the syllabus than a lot of detail about a few areas only.

Format of the exam

The Advanced Performance Management syllabus is assessed by a **3 hour 15 minute exam**. The pass mark is **50%**. All questions in the exam are **compulsory**.

The format of the exam is:

		Number of marks
Section A:	One 50 mark case study question	50
Section B:	Two questions worth 25 marks each	50
		100

Section A will contain **one case study question** worth **50 marks in total**, but comprising four or five requirements relating to the same scenario information. The detail of the requirements will (from September 2019 onwards) be **embedded in the scenario**. The 'requirements' at the end of the scenario then ask you to respond as you have been instructed in the scenario. Therefore, you need to refer back to the detailed requirements in the scenario in order to answer each part of the question.

The case study scenario will be based on an organisation in a particular business context, and will include the organisation's mission and strategic objectives. Candidates will be expected to assess the methods by which the organisation is controlling, managing and measuring performance in order to achieve its objectives. This assessment could include an evaluation of the organisation's performance report, its information systems, new strategies or projects, and its performance management and measurement systems. Candidates could be expected to undertake calculations, draw comparisons against relevant information where appropriate, and be prepared to offer recommendations as needed.

Candidates should expect to see Section A of the exam focus on a **range of issues from across syllabus sections A, C and D**, although the issues will vary depending on the business context of the organisation in the scenario.

Professional marks will be available in Section A for the candidate's approach to the format requested for the answer (eg a report to the Board of Directors).

Section B will comprise a further two 25-mark questions.

These questions are more likely to assess a range of discrete subject areas from the main syllabus section headings. However, they will still require evaluation and synthesis of information contained within a scenario, and the application of this information to the question requirements.

Although one subject area is likely to be emphasised in each Section B question, candidates should not assume that questions will be solely about content from that area.

One of the Section B questions will come mainly from **syllabus section E**. The other question can come from **any other syllabus section**.

The **pass mark** for the APM exam is 50%.

Exams prior to 2018

Prior to September 2018, there was a degree of choice in the exam. Although the 50 mark Section A question was compulsory, candidates had a choice of 2 questions from 3 in Section B. However, from September 2018, is no longer any choice. All the questions are now compulsory.

Analysis of past exams

The table below provides details of when each element of the syllabus has been examined in the ten most recent sittings, and whether it was examined as part of a Section A or Section B question. We have also included a reference to the relevant Chapter of the BPP APM Workbook, the companion to the BPP APM Practice and Revision Kit, in case you need to revise the information on the topic covered.

Note that in exams prior to September 2018 there were three questions in Section B (of which two had to be answered) so that four questions in total are referenced for those exams.

Since September 2015, ACCA have generally been issuing two sample exams each year, one after the December exam session, the other after the June sitting. These exams will be compiled from questions selected from the two preceding sessions, eg in December 2017 the sample questions were compiled from the September 2017 and December 2017 exams.

Workbook chapter		Sept/Dec 2020	Mar/June 2020	Sept/Dec 2019	Mar/June 2019	Dec 2018	Sept 2018	Mar/June 2018	Sept/Dec 2017	Mar/June 2017	Sept/Dec 2016
	STRATEGIC PLANNING AND CONTROL										
1	Strategic management accounting					A, B			B		
2	Performance hierarchy	A		A	A		A			A	A, B
3	Performance management and control				B					B	B
4	Organisational change, environmental and ethical issues	B		A			B	A			B
	IMPACT OF RISK AND UNCERTAINTY ON ORGANISATIONAL PERFORMANCE										
5	Impact of risk and uncertainty			B		B			B		
	PERFORMANCE MEASUREMENT SYSTEMS AND DESIGN										
6	Performance management systems and design	B	A*	A		A	B	A, B	A	A, B	A
	STRATEGIC PERFORMANCE MEASUREMENT										
7	Strategic performance measures in the private sector		A*	A					B	A, B	A
8	Divisional performance and transfer pricing issues		B					B			B
9	Not-for-profit organisations	A							B		
10	Non-financial performance indicators	A					A				
11	The role of quality in performance management systems		B		A	B			A	B	A
12	Performance management and strategic HR issues						A		B	A	

Workbook chapter		Sept/ Dec 2020	Mar/ June 2020	Sept/ Dec 2019	Mar/ June 2019	Dec 2018	Sept 2018	Mar/ June 2018	Sept/ Dec 2017	Mar/ June 2017	Sept/ Dec 2016
	PERFORMANCE EVALUATION AND CORPORATE FAILURE										
13	Alternative views of performance measurement and management		B	B	B	B	A	B		A	A, B
14	Strategic performance issues in complex business structures	B						B			
15	Predicting and preventing corporate failure						B	B			

* the March 2020 50 mark question contained an area that is no longer in the APM syllabus; for this reason this question has not been included in this practice and revision kit.

IMPORTANT!

The table above gives a broad idea of how frequently major topics in the syllabus are examined. It should **not be used to question spot** and predict, for example, that a certain topic will not be examined because it has been examined in the last two sittings. The examining team's report indicate that they are well aware that some students try to question spot. The examining team avoid predictable patterns and may, for example, examine the same topic two sittings in a row. Equally, just because a topic has not been examined for a long time, this does not necessarily mean it will be examined in the next exam!

Syllabus and Study Guide

The complete APM syllabus and study guide can be found by visiting the exam resource finder on the ACCA website.

Helping you with your revision

BPP Learning Media – ACCA Approved Content Provider

As an ACCA **Approved Content Provider**, BPP Learning Media gives you the **opportunity** to use revision materials reviewed by the ACCA examining team. By incorporating the ACCA examining team's comments and suggestions regarding the depth and breadth of syllabus coverage, the BPP Learning Media Practice & Revision Kit provides excellent, **ACCA-approved** support for your revision.

These materials are reviewed by the ACCA examining team. The objective of the review is to ensure that the material properly covers the syllabus and study guide outcomes, used by the examining team in setting the exams, in the appropriate breadth and depth. The review does not ensure that every eventuality, combination or application of examinable topics is addressed by the ACCA Approved Content. Nor does the review comprise a detailed technical check of the content as the Approved Content Provider has its own quality assurance processes in place in this respect.

BPP Learning Media do everything possible to ensure the material is accurate and up to date when sending to print. In the event that any errors are found after the print date, they are uploaded to the following website: www.bpp.com/learningmedia/Errata.

The structure of this Practice & Revision Kit

The 25 mark questions in the exam typically focus on one main syllabus area. The 25 mark questions in this Kit have been grouped according to the section of the syllabus (Parts A-E) to which they mainly relate.

The 50 mark questions in the exam cover a number of different syllabus areas, so the 50 mark questions in this Kit are found in a single bank of questions.

There are also four mock exams which provide you the opportunity to refine your knowledge and skills as part of your final exam preparations.

Question practice

Question practice under timed conditions is absolutely vital. We strongly advise you to create a revision study plan which focuses on question practice. This is so that you can get used to the pressures of answering exam questions in limited time, develop proficiency in the Specific APM skills and the Exam success skills. Ideally, you should aim to cover all questions in this Kit, and very importantly, all four mock exams.

Selecting questions

To help you plan your revision, we have provided a full topic index which maps the questions to topics in the syllabus (see page viii).

Making the most of question practice

At BPP Learning Media we realise that you need more than just questions and model answers to get the most from your question practice.

- Our **Top tips**, included for all questions, provide essential advice on tackling questions, presenting answers and the key points that answers need to include.

- We include **marking guides** to show you what the examining team rewards

- We include **comments from the examining team** to show you where students struggled or performed well in the actual exam

Attempting mock exams

There are four mock exams, including the ACCA Specimen Exam, which provide practice at coping with the pressures of the exam day. We strongly recommend that you attempt them under exam conditions. All the mock exams reflect the question styles and syllabus coverage of the exam.

Topics to revise

ACCA's Study Guide for APM highlights that 'candidates should expect to see Section A of the exam focus on a range of issues from across syllabus sections A, C and D'. The Study Guide also notes that 'one of the Section B questions will come mainly from syllabus section E' while 'the other Section B question can come from any other syllabus section'.

Taken together though, these points mean that the questions in your exam could cover any area of the syllabus. Moreover, because **all the questions in the APM exam are compulsory**, it is essential to learn the **entire syllabus** to maximise your chances of passing. There are no shortcuts – trying to spot topics to be examined is dangerous and will significantly reduce the likelihood of success. As this is an advanced ('Strategic Professional') level exam, it also assumes knowledge of topics covered in *Performance Management* at Applied Skills level.

That said, the **main capabilities** in the syllabus (which is shown on ACCA's website) take you through what the examining team expects you to be able to do when you have completed your studies:

- Use strategic planning and control models to plan and monitor organisational performance

- Assess the impact of risk and uncertainty on organisational performance

- Identify and evaluate the design features of effective performance management information and monitoring systems and recognise the impact of developments in technology on performance measurement and management systems

- Apply appropriate strategic performance measurement techniques in evaluating and improving organisational performance

- Advise clients and senior management on strategic business performance evaluation and on recognising vulnerability to corporate failure

These five areas are the syllabus areas covered in the syllabus for *Advanced Performance Management*.

However, whilst it is important that you work through your way through the Workbook and cover all the different syllabus areas, it is also important to try and think how the areas might relate to each other, and how they could be used to help managers in an organisation control and improve the performance of that organisation. Remember, this exam is about performance **management**, as well as performance **measurement**; and you should treat both of these aspects (measurement and management) with equal importance as you are studying for your APM exam.

Remember to come out of the detail once you have finished a chapter and practised some questions. Take some time to reflect on how the chapter has covered the syllabus and how it feeds back into the capabilities which you will need to display in order to pass the APM exam.

Gaining the easy marks

Your technical knowledge (including knowledge brought forward from *Performance Management*) should enable you to score a small number of relatively easy marks. There are likely to be some marks available in certain requirements for **definitions** or **explanations** that don't have to be related to the scenario. However, don't assume that you can ignore all the scenarios and still pass! The level of marks available in APM for knowledge alone (without application) is around 20-30% and so is nowhere near enough to pass the exam.

There are **professional marks** available in the Section A question, and some of these should be easy to obtain. For example, there are likely to be marks available for presenting your answer in the format, style and tone, requested (eg a report).

Reports should always have an appropriate title. They should be **formally written**, with an **introductory paragraph** setting out the aims of the report. You should use **short paragraphs** and **appropriate headings**, with a brief summary of findings as a conclusion.

Essential skill areas

There are three areas you should develop in order to achieve exam success in the Advanced Performance Management (APM):

(1) Knowledge application
(2) Specific APM skills
(3) Exam success skills

At the revision and final exam preparation phases these **should be developed together as part of a comprehensive study plan of focused question practice**.

Take some time to revisit the Specific **APM skills and Exam success skills**. These are shown in the diagram below and followed by tutorial guidance of how to apply them.

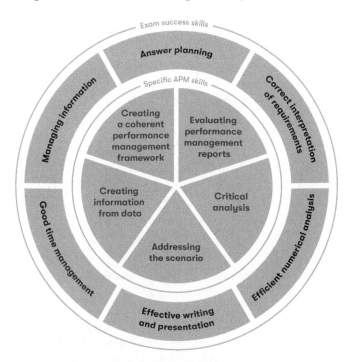

Specific APM skills

These are the skills specific to APM that we think you need to develop in order to pass the exam.

In the BPP Workbook for APM there are five **Skills Checkpoints** which define each skill and show how it is applied in answering a question. A brief summary of each skill is given below.

Skill 1: Creating information from data

One of the themes in the APM syllabus is that accountants are increasingly expected to act as 'internal business consultants'. An important aspect of this role is in interpreting the **meaning** of data, ie **creating information from data.**

In any part of the exam you may be given data (or calculations) that have already been prepared by a more junior accountant and your role will be to analyse that data and interpret what it means for the organisation in the scenario.

ACCA's examining team have noted (in past exams) that where data has been provided for analysis, **candidates have often failed to add any value in their analysis of that data.**

A step-by-step technique for ensuring that **analysis of data creates useful information**, and therefore **adds value**, is outlined below:

Step 1	Consider the 'big picture'; ie the **main issues** facing the organisation as presented in the scenario of the question.
Step 2	Plan to categorise your analysis into a **small number** of **relevant categories**. When relevant, plan to use ratio analysis to add meaning to the data provided.
Step 3	Complete your answer by discussing the data and any further numerical analysis (eg ratios) by reference to the 'big picture' issues identified in Step 1. **Avoid statements that simply describe the data**, without adding any value in terms of analysis.

Skills Checkpoint 1 in the BPP Workbook for APM covers this technique in detail through application to an exam-standard question. Consider revisiting Skills Checkpoint 1 to improve this skill.

Skill 2: Creating a coherent performance management framework

In the exam, it is highly like you will need to assess the methods by which an organisation is controlling, managing and measuring performance, in order to achieve its objectives.

An important part of this could be in assessing whether the organisation has a coherent performance management framework (for example, whether the key performance indicators it measures will help it achieve its mission and objectives) and recommend ways the framework could be improved.

Key steps in developing and applying this skill are outlined below:

Step 1	Identify an organisation's mission and/or objectives in the question scenario, to get an understanding of the aspects of performance which are important to the organisation.
Step 2	Identify whether the aspects of performance being measured/monitored (eg CSFs; KPIs) relate to key areas of performance, and help to support the organisation in achieving its mission and objectives. (Could the measures used be improved?)
Step 3	If you are asked to recommend KPIs or CSFs, make sure these relate to mission, objectives etc. and make use of data provided in the scenario.

Skills Checkpoint 2 in the BPP Workbook for APM covers this technique in detail through application to an exam-standard question. Consider revisiting Skills Checkpoint 2 to specifically improve this skill.

Skill 3: Evaluating performance management reports

An important element of creating a coherent performance management framework is ensuring that performance reports show how well an organisation is performing in the areas which are strategically significant for it. Exam questions can often require you to evaluate a performance report, and this requires you to assess the report to see if it provides relevant information about appropriate areas of performance, in a way that is easy for users to understand, and which enables them to take effective control action.

A step-by-step technique for evaluating performance management reports is outlined below.

Step 1	Where a question includes a significant table of data, read the requirements carefully to make sure that you understand clearly whether a question requires you to analyse the performance of an **organisation**, or of the **performance report** itself.
Step 2	Where a question requires analysis of the performance report, make sure that you clearly understand the mission, strategy and objectives of a company (from the main body of the scenario) and carefully consider the degree to which the performance report gives visibility to these strategic factors.
Step 3	Also consider other practical factors such as the structure, clarity and level of detail of the report, and whether it distorts the meaning of data. Where relevant to the requirement, look for positive as well as negative features of the report.
Step 4	Complete your answer plan and write up your answer. If you are asked to recommend improvements, make sure these relate specifically to the organisation in the scenario and its context, rather than being generic points.

Skills Checkpoint 3 in the BPP Workbook for APM covers this technique in detail through application to an exam-standard question. Consider revisiting Skills Checkpoint 3 to specifically improve this skill.

Skill 4: Critical analysis

The overall aim of the APM syllabus highlights that candidates should be able to exercise professional judgement in selecting and applying strategic management accounting techniques in different business contexts. As such, it is important to critically analyse the techniques that you study, for example to consider whether a certain technique would be appropriate for an organisation to use in a certain situation or not.

This skill requires you not only to understand the techniques, but also to appreciate their potential advantages or disadvantages. Just because an organisation in a question scenario is thinking about introducing a new technique does not necessarily mean that technique is appropriate for the organisation.

The skill of critical analysis can potentially be applied to any syllabus area in APM, and can be an important ingredient in developing a discussion that addresses the question scenario in a way that adds value.

A step-by-step technique for critical analysis is outlined below.

Step 1	Analyse the scenario and requirements. Ensure that you recognise the possibility that using a critical approach in your analysis can be a useful way of 'adding value'.
Step 2	Plan your answer. Without adopting a hyper-critical approach, ensure your answer is balanced, in terms of identifying the potential benefits **and** limitations of techniques that are being used or recommended.
Step 3	As you write your answer, try wherever possible to apply your analysis to the scenario, instead of simply writing about criticisms (or benefits) in generic, technical terms.

Skills Checkpoint 4 in the BPP Workbook for APM covers this technique in detail through application to an exam-standard question. Consider revisiting Skills Checkpoint 4 to specifically improve this skill.

Skill 5: Addressing the scenario

All of the questions in the APM exam will be scenario-based.

It is **vital** that you use the information in the scenario to ensure that the discussion points that you are making in your answer are 'relevant'. The discussion parts of a question – applying your knowledge to the scenario – will normally account for the majority of the marks available.

Although you need to have a good underlying knowledge of a number of theories and frameworks, in the APM exam you will primarily be tested on your **ability to apply** your theoretical knowledge to the scenario in question, not your ability to simply recite it. The APM ACCA Examining Team often comment that candidates who repeat memorised material 'will probably score only between 20% and 30%...'

A good, professional-level answer needs to go beyond the mere repetition of how a technique works and focus on relating it to the entity's specific environment, as identified in the question scenario.

The skill of addressing the scenario is the most important of the APM specific sills. It is relevant to every syllabus area, and **every question** in the APM exam.

A step-by-step technique for addressing the scenario is outlined below.

Step 1	Allow at least 20% of your allotted time for analysing the scenario and the requirements. Begin by analysing the requirements so that you know what you are looking for when you read the scenario.
Step 2	Prepare an answer plan using key words from the requirements as headings. Complete your answer plan by working through each paragraph of the question identifying specific points that are relevant to the scenario and requirement, to make sure you generate enough points to score a pass mark.
Step 3	As you write your answer, explain what you mean – in one (or two) sentence(s) – and then explain **why this matters in the given scenario**. This should result in a series of short paragraphs that address the specific context of the scenario. Avoid quoting theory at length.

Skills Checkpoint 5 in the BPP Workbook for APM covers this technique in detail through application to an exam-standard question. Consider revisiting Skills Checkpoint 5 to specifically improve this skill.

Exam success skills

Passing the APM exam requires more than applying syllabus knowledge and demonstrating the specific APM skills; it also requires the development of excellent exam technique through question practice.

We consider the following six skills, or exam techniques, to be vital for exam success. These skills were introduced in the BPP Workbook for APM and you can revisit the five Skills Checkpoints in the Workbook for tutorial guidance on how to apply each of the six Exam success skills in your question practice and in the exam.

Try to consider your performance in all six Exam success skills during your revision stage question practice, and reflect on your particular strengths, and your weaker areas, which you can then work on.

Exam success skill 1

Managing information

Questions in the exam will present you with a lot of information. The skill is how you handle this information to make the best use of your time. The key is determining how you will approach the exam and then actively reading the questions.

Advice on developing this skill

To avoid being overwhelmed by the quantity of information provided, you must take an **active approach** to reading each question.

Active reading means focussing on the question's requirements first, highlighting key verbs such as 'evaluate', 'analyse', 'explain', 'discuss', to ensure you answer the question properly. Then, now that you have an understanding of what the question will require you to do, read the rest of the question, highlighting important and relevant information, and making notes of any relevant technical information you think you will need.

Computer-based exam

In a computer-based exam (CBE) the **highlighter tool** provided in the toolbar at the top of the screen offers a range of colours:

,

This allows you to choose **different colours to answer different aspects to a question**. For example, if a question asked you to discuss the pros and cons of an issue then you could choose a different colour for highlighting pros and cons within the relevant section of a question.

The **strikethrough function** allows you to delete areas of a question that you have dealt with – this can be useful in managing information if you are dealing with numerical questions because it can allow you to ensure that all numerical areas have been accounted for in your answer (although this is of limited use in the APM exam).

The CBE also allows you to **resize windows** by clicking on the bottom right-hand corner of the window as highlighted in the following section:

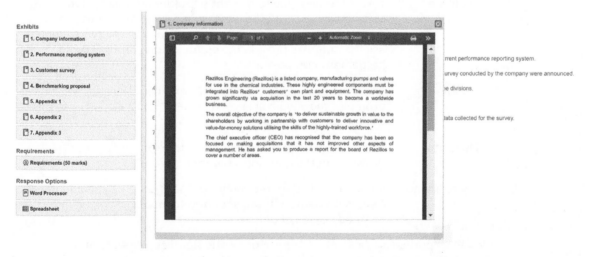

This functionality allows you to **display a number of windows at the same time**, so this could allow you review:

- the question requirements and the exhibit relating to that requirement, at the same time; or

- the window containing your answer (whether a word processing or spreadsheet document) and the exhibit relating to that requirement, at the same time.

Exam success skill 2

Correct interpretation of the requirements

The active verb used often dictates the approach that written answers should take (eg 'explain', 'discuss', 'evaluate'). It is important you identify and use the verb to define your approach. The **correct interpretation of the requirements** skill means correctly producing only what is being asked for by a requirement. Anything not required will not earn marks.

Advice on developing this skill

This skill can be developed by analysing question requirements and applying this process:

Step 1	Read the requirement
	Firstly, read the requirement a couple of times slowly and carefully, and **highlight the active verbs**. Use the active verbs to define what you plan to do. Make sure you identify any sub-requirements within a requirement, this is **often signalled by the use of the word 'and'** within a requirement.
	Important active verbs for APM include the following:

Verb	Meaning
Advise	This requires you to provide someone with useful information, or to **tell them what you think they should do** based on a consideration of the issues presented in a scenario.
Analyse	This requires you **break an issue into separate parts** and discuss, examine, or interpret each part.
	This may require you to **give reasons for** the current situation or what has happened.
Apply	This requires you to put a concept into action by applying it **to the scenario** in a relevant way.
Assess	This requires you to **judge the importance** or estimate the nature, quality or significance of an issue.
Discuss	This will require you to consider and debate/argue about the **pros and cons** of an issue.
Evaluate	This will require you to present a **'balanced' discussion** of an issue looking at both the positive and negative issues. Where numbers feature in a question, an evaluation will require you to use the numbers provided to create a value from which **a judgement** can be made.
Explain	This involves making an idea clear and could require you to, for example, show logically how a concept is developed or to **give the reason for** an event.
Illustrate	This will require you to **give concrete examples**, normally drawn from the question's scenario.
Recommend	If you are asked to **'recommend'** then you are expected to **use details presented in the scenario** to create a logical and **justified** course of action.

In APM – particularly in Section A questions – **the detailed aspects of a requirement are often embedded in the scenario.** For example, in the scenario, the CEO may ask you analyse or evaluate something, and then the requirement will ask you to respond to the CEO's instruction. Therefore, the initial requirement by itself may not provide a complete understanding of a question's requirement (although it is a useful starting point).

Step 2	Read the rest of the question
	By reading the requirement first, you will have an idea of what you are looking out for as you read through the case overview and exhibits. This is a great time saver and means you don't end up having to read the whole question in full twice. You should do this in an active way – see Exam success skill 1: Managing Information.

Step 3	Read the requirement again
	Read the requirement again to remind yourself of the exact wording before starting your written answer. This will capture any misinterpretation of the requirements or any missed requirements entirely. This should become a habit in your approach and, with repeated practice, you will find the focus, relevance and depth of your answer plan will improve.

Exam success skill 3

Answer planning: Priorities, structure and logic

This skill requires the planning of the key aspects of an answer which accurately and completely responds to the requirement.

Advice on developing this skill

Everyone will have a preferred style for an answer plan. For example, it may be a mind map, bullet-pointed lists or simply annotating the questions. Choose the approach that you feel most comfortable with, or, if you are not sure, try out different approaches for different questions until you have found your preferred style.

For a discussion question, annotating the questions is likely to be insufficient. It would be better to draw up a separate answer plan in the format of your choosing (eg a mind map or bullet-pointed lists).

In a **computer-based exam** you can use the copy and paste functions to **copy the question requirements to the beginning of your answer**. This will allow you to ensure that your answer plan addresses all parts of the question requirements.

You can also **copy the question requirements to the main body of your answer.** This will allow you to create sub-headings for your answer, again ensuring that your answer addresses all parts of the question requirements.

Copying and pasting simply involves highlighting the relevant information and either right clicking to access the copy and paste functions, or alternatively using Ctrl C to copy and Ctrl V to paste.

Exam success skill 4

Efficient numerical analysis

This skill aims to maximise the marks awarded by making clear to the marker the process of arriving at your answer. This is achieved by laying out an answer such that, even if you make a few errors, you can still score subsequent marks for follow-on calculations. It is vital that you do not lose marks purely because the marker cannot follow what you have done.

Advice on developing this skill

This skill can be developed by applying the following process:

Step 1	Use a standard proforma working where relevant
	If answers can be laid out in a standard proforma then always plan to do so. This will help the marker to understand your working and allocate the marks easily. It will also help you to work through the figures in a methodical and time-efficient way.

Step 2	**Show your workings**
	Keep your workings as clear and simple as possible and ensure they are cross-referenced to the main part of your answer. Where it helps, provide brief narrative explanations to help the marker understand the steps in the calculation. This means that if a mistake is made you do not lose any subsequent marks for follow-on calculations.
Step 3	**Keep moving!**
	It is important to remember that, in an exam situation, it can sometimes be difficult to get every number 100% correct. The key is therefore ensuring you do not spend too long on any single calculation. If you are struggling with a solution then make a sensible assumption, state it and move on.

In a **computer-based exam** (CBE) it is important to **show the marker where numbers have come from,** ie it is not sensible to perform the calculations on a calculator and then manually transfer them to the spreadsheet. The marker also needs to be able to see **what the numbers are intended to mean**. For example in the following spreadsheet the marker can see that the highlighted calculation in cell K9 is calculated as I9/G2 because this is what is recorded in the spreadsheet cell (as shown in the first row), and can also see from the headings in cells C9 and K4 that this is meant to be a measure of the appraisal costs as a percentage of sales.

	A	B	C	D	E	F	G	H	I	J	K	L	M	N
1		Cost of quality report												
2					Sales		4500							
3														
4		Cost of conformance					$000s		$000s		% sales			
5			Prevention costs											
6					Maintenance		8		8		0.18%			
7														
8					Quality audit		2							
9			Appraisal costs		QC supervisor		35		37		0.82%			
10												1.00%		

K9 — fx =I9/G2

If the workings are visible in the cell, as shown here, then there is **less need to show detailed workings.** It will still sometimes be helpful to produce workings because they can reduce the likelihood of errors being made (if calculations are complex).

In a **computer-based exam** (CBE) you can also use useful spreadsheet short-cuts to improve the efficiency of numerical analysis. For APM useful short-cuts, these include the ability to calculate totals and averages and also to calculate NPV, IRR and MIRR.

Further details are given below:

Function	Guidance & examples
Sum	=SUM(A1:A10) adds all the numbers in spreadsheet cells A1 to A10.
Average	=AVERAGE(A1:A10) averages the numbers in spreadsheet cells A1 to A10.
NPV	Net present value is based on future cash flows, assuming that the first cash flow is in one year's time.
	For example, if the future cash flows from a project arise over five years and need to be discounted at 10% then the formula could be as follows:
	=NPV(0.1, B10:F10)
	This would give the present value of cash flows from time period 1-5; the cash outflow in time 0 would then need to be deducted to calculate the net present value.

IRR	Internal rate of return is based on future cash flows, looking at cash outflows and inflows in each year of a project, from time 0 onwards.
	For example, to identify the internal rate of return of the future cash flows from a project arising over five years then the formula could be as follows:
	=IRR(A10:F10)
MIRR	Modified internal rate of return is based on future cash flows (looking at cash outflows and inflows) in each year of a project, from time 0 onwards.
	The formula is =MIRR (values, finance rate, reinvestment rate). The finance rate and reinvestment rate will normally be the same.
	For example, to identify the MIRR of the future cash flows from a project arising over five years (involving time periods 0-5), where the cost of capital to be applied to cash outflows (the finance rate) and cash inflows (reinvestment rate) is 10%, then the formula could be as follows:
	=MIRR (A10:F10, 0.1, 0.1)

Where numerical calculations require commentary then this can be provided in a word processing document with a **reference to calculations provided within the spreadsheet**.

Exam success skill 5

Effective writing and presentation

Written answers should be presented so that the marker can clearly see the points you are making, presented in the format specified in the question. The skill is to provide efficient written answers with sufficient breadth of points that answer the question, in the right depth, in the time available.

Advice on developing this skill

Step 1	**Use headings**
	Using the headings and sub-headings from your answer plan will give your answer structure, order and logic. This will ensure your answer links back to the requirement and is clearly signposted, making it easier for the marker to understand the different points you are making. Underlining your headings will also help the marker.
Step 2	**Write your answer in short, but full, sentences**
	Use short, punchy sentences with the aim that every sentence should say something different and generate marks. Write in full sentences, ensuring your style is professional.

For APM there are four professional marks in question 1 of the exam:

These can be obtained by:

1. A suitable, simple, heading to the answer (eg a simple report format) and use of headings / sub-headings (eg linked to the requirements) throughout the report: 1 mark is normally given for this

2. A short introduction paragraph outlining the structure of the report: 1 mark is normally given for this

3. A clear well-structured answer (eg referencing spreadsheet calculations where appropriate) presented in a concise, practical (as opposed to academic) way that adds value and addresses the given requirements: 2 marks are normally given for this

Exam success skill 6

Good time management

This skill means planning your time across all the requirements so that all tasks have been attempted at the end of the 3 hours 15 minutes available and actively checking on time during your exam. This is so that you can flex your approach and prioritise requirements which, in your judgement, will generate the maximum marks in the available time remaining.

Advice on developing this skill

The exam is 3 hours 15 minutes long, which translates to 1.95 minutes per mark. Therefore a 10-mark requirement should be allocated a maximum of 20 minutes to complete your answer before you move on to the next task. At the beginning of a question, work out the amount of time you should be spending on each requirement and write the finishing time next to each requirement on your exam. If you take the approach of spending 10–15 minutes reading and planning at the start of the exam, adjust the time allocated to each question accordingly; eg if you allocate 15 minutes to reading, then you will have 3 hours remaining, which is 1.8 minutes per mark.

In APM it is **crucial to spend time planning before starting to write your answer**. This allows time for a candidate to immerse themselves in the question scenarios.

Planning time can be built into time management by amending the 1.95 minutes per mark approach to allow for planning time. The total time for planning your answer should be about 20% of the total time you would allocate to a question. This means that for a section A question planning time would be 50 marks × 1.95 × 0.2 = (approximately) 20 minutes and for a section B question planning time would be 25 marks × 1.95 × 0.2 = 10 minutes.

Allowing 20% of time for planning means allocating 80% of the time for writing so the 1.95 minutes per mark approach becomes ie 0.8 × 1.95 = 1.56 minutes per mark for writing your answer.

Keep an eye on the clock

Aim to attempt all requirements, but be ready to be ruthless and move on if your answer is not going as planned. The challenge for many is sticking to planned timings. Be aware this is difficult to achieve in the early stages of your studies and be ready to let this skill develop over time.

If you find yourself running short on time and know that a full answer is not possible in the time you have, consider recreating your plan in overview form and then add key terms and details as time allows. Remember, some marks may be available, for example, simply stating a conclusion which you don't have time to justify in full.

Question practice

Question practice is a core part of learning new topic areas. When you practise questions, you should focus on improving the Exam success skills – personal to your needs – by obtaining feedback or through a process of self-assessment.

If sitting this exam as a computer-based exam, practising as many exam-style questions as possible in the ACCA CBE practice platform will be the key to passing this exam. You should attempt questions under **timed conditions** and ensure you produce full answers to the discussion parts as well as doing the calculations. Also ensure that you attempt all mock exams under exam conditions.

ACCA have launched a free on-demand resource designed to mirror the live exam experience, helping you to become more familiar with the exam format. You can access the platform via the Study Support Resources section of the ACCA website navigating to the CBE question practice section and logging in with your myACCA credentials.

Questions

Advanced Performance Management (APM)

STRATEGIC PLANNING AND CONTROL

Questions 1 to 10 cover strategic planning and control, the subject of Part A of the syllabus for *Advanced Performance Management* (APM).

1 ENT Entertainments (6/11, amended)   **49 mins**

Company background and objectives

ENT Entertainment Co (ENT) is a large, diversified entertainment business based in Teeland. The company's objective is the maximisation of shareholder wealth for its family owners. It has four divisions:

(1)   Restaurants
(2)   Cafés
(3)   Bars
(4)   Dance clubs

Recently, ENT's board has identified that there are problems in managing such a diversified company. They have employed consultants who have recommended that they should perform a Boston Consulting Group (BCG) analysis to understand whether they have the right mix of businesses. The chief executive officer (CEO) has questioned whether using this analysis is helpful in managing the group's performance.

A business analyst has prepared information on each division, and this is shown in Appendix 1.

Economic context

In Teeland, the economy is generally growing at about 2% per annum. The restaurant, café and bar sectors are all highly fragmented with many small operators. Consequently, a market share of more than 3.0% is considered large as that is comparable to the share of the largest operators in each sector. There are fewer small late night dance club operators and the market leader currently holds a 15.0% market share. There have not been many new developments within the divisions except for a new wine bar format launched by the Bars Division which has surprised the board by its success.

Divisional performance

Each division's performance is measured by economic value added (EVA™). The divisional managers have a remuneration package that is made up in two equal parts by a salary set according to industry norms and a bonus element which is based on achieving the cost budget numbers set by the company board. The Chairman of the board has been examining the consistency of the overall objective of the business, the divisional performance measure and the remuneration packages at divisional level. He has expressed the worry that these are not properly aligned and that this might lead to dysfunctional behaviour by the divisional management.

Required

(a)   Perform a BCG analysis of ENT's business and use this to evaluate the company's
      performance.   **(7 marks)**

(b)   Critically evaluate this BCG analysis as a performance management system at ENT.

                                                                                    (7 marks)

(c)   (i)   Evaluate the divisional managers' remuneration packages in the light of the
                 divisional performance systems and your BCG analysis.   **(6 marks)**

      (ii)   Explain the implications of the BCG analysis and divisional performance systems on
                 the management styles which might be appropriate at ENT.   **(5 marks)**

                                                                        (Total = 25 marks)

APPENDIX 1

Revenue information for each division

Revenue	Actual 20X0 $m	Actual 20X1 $m	Forecast 20X2 $m	Forecast 20X3 $m
Restaurants				
ENT	54	56	59	62
Market sector	10,752	10,860	10,968	10,968
Cafés				
ENT	31	34	41	47
Market sector	3,072	3,348	3,717	4,051
Bars				
ENT	349	342	336	336
Market sector	9,984	9,784	9,491	9,206
Dance clubs				
ENT	197	209	219	241
Market sector	1,792	1,900	2,013	2,195

2 BPC (12/07, amended)   49 mins

The directors of Blaina Packaging Co (BPC), a well-established manufacturer of cardboard boxes, are currently considering whether to enter the cardboard tube market. Cardboard tubes are purchased by customers whose products are wound around tubes of various sizes, ranging from large tubes around which carpets are wound to small tubes around which films and paper products are wound. The cardboard tubes are usually purchased in very large quantities by customers. On average, the cardboard tubes comprise between 1% and 2% of the total cost of the customers' finished product.

The directors have gathered the following information:

(1)   The cardboard tubes are manufactured on machines which vary in size and speed. The lowest cost machine is priced at $30,000 and requires only one operative for its operation. A one-day training course is required in order that an unskilled person can then operate such a machine in an efficient and effective manner.

(2)   The cardboard tubes are made from specially formulated paper which, at times during recent years, has been in short supply.

(3)   At present, four major manufacturers of cardboard tubes have an aggregate market share of 80%. The current market leader has a 26% market share. The market shares of the other three major manufacturers, one of which is JOL Co, are equal in size. The product ranges offered by the four major manufacturers are similar in terms of size and quality. The market has grown by 2% per annum during recent years.

(4)   A recent report on the activities of a foreign-based multinational company revealed that consideration was being given to expanding operations in their Packaging Division overseas. The division possesses large-scale automated machinery for the manufacture of cardboard tubes of any size.

(5)   Another company, Plastic Tubes Co (PTC), produces a narrow, but increasing, range of plastic tubes which are capable of housing small products such as film and paper-based products. At present, these tubes are on average 30% more expensive than the equivalent sized cardboard tubes sold in the marketplace.

Required

(a)   Using Porter's five forces model, assess the attractiveness of the option to enter the market for cardboard tubes as a performance improvement strategy for BPC.   **(10 marks)**

(b)   Discuss the limitations of Porter's five forces model as a technique for assessing how attractive an industry is to enter.   **(5 marks)**

(c) JOL Co was the market leader with a share of 30% three years ago. The managing director of JOL Co stated at a recent meeting of the board of directors that: 'our loss of market share during the last three years might lead to the end of JOL Co as an organisation and therefore we must address this issue immediately'.

Required

Discuss the statement of the managing director of JOL Co and discuss six performance indicators, other than decreasing market share, which might indicate that JOL Co might fail as a corporate entity. **(10 marks)**

(Total = 25 marks)

3 CRC (Mar/Jun 19)   **49 mins**

Cortinas Retail Clothing (CRC): Company information

CRC started as a clothing retailer 20 years ago with one store. The business expanded steadily and had 10 stores after 18 years of trading. Since then, the rate of expansion has increased rapidly with an average of four stores opening per year.

CRC is planning to open its first large out of town store soon and is also considering the acquisition of a food retailing business. Both of these will be supplied with items using CRC's existing central warehouse.

Introduction of RFID system

At the beginning of the 20X5 accounting year, to cope with this rapid growth, CRC acquired a RFID (radio frequency identification device) system at its single central warehouse. This was to help manage inventory more effectively and speed up the processes for receiving items from suppliers and despatching them to stores. Items are still moved manually by staff in the CRC warehouse where there is little automation compared to competitors. There has been some resistance from staff to the RFID system, which they find difficult to use. CRC is currently trying to reduce the number of suppliers it has to help increase efficiency in the warehouse.

Budgeting system

The budget setting process has remained unchanged since CRC was formed. All managers prepare draft budgets using spreadsheets and submit them to the CRC board for approval. Managers use the previous year results as a starting point when drafting the budgets and increase the variable costs in line with any anticipated growth in volumes. For example, when preparing the budget for the year ending 30 June 20X6, the manager of the central warehouse used the actual costs of running the warehouse from the previous year and increased them all by the same percentage. This was to reflect an anticipated increase in volumes in 20X6 over 20X5. Managers are appraised on their performance against the approved budgets.

CRC has needed all its financial resources to fund its expansion and so it has only old and basic IT systems, which are not enterprise resource planning systems, unified databases or networked systems.

It has been suggested to the CRC board that the current system of budgeting is no longer suitable and that the business should move to activity-based budgeting (ABB). The CEO has asked you to evaluate the potential introduction of ABB at CRC.

Central warehouse activity in July 20X5

The board has never seen an activity-based budget before and is unsure how it could be used to explain variances between actual and budgeted performance in the central warehouse. As an example, they would like to see how an activity-based budget for the year ending 30 June 20X6 could be used to explain variances from the actual results for the month of July 20X5.

The two key activities which drive costs in the central warehouse are receipts of items into the goods inwards section and despatches of items from the goods outwards section. A receipt into good inwards involves accepting a delivery of items from a supplier, tagging those items and putting them away in the warehouse. Receipts from suppliers contain variable numbers of individual items. Despatches of items from goods outwards are to CRC's own retail stores. Cost driver rates for these two activities will be used to set monthly cost budgets for the warehouse.

The board asked an analyst to prepare an activity-based budget for the central warehouse for the year ending 30 June 20X6. The analyst has collected relevant information on the costs for the year needed to prepare the activity-based budget and has begun the work (Appendix 1).

The total annual cost relating to goods inwards needs to be determined. This should be used to calculate the budgeted cost of each receipt into goods inwards, in order to explain the variance between the budgeted cost and the actual cost of receipts of goods inwards for the month of July 20X5. The analyst has already correctly included the costs of the warehouse manager's salary and the lease of the RFID system into the incomplete activity-based budget in Appendix 1. The board has asked you to complete the analyst's work.

To enable you to complete your calculations, you are told that in July 20X5 there were 650 receipts into goods inwards. These receipts contained 100,000 items, which is the same as the budgeted number of items for the month. The actual total cost of activities driven by receipts into goods inwards for the month was $18,000.

It is now 1 September 20X5.

Required

(a) Evaluate whether CRC should move from its current budgeting system to ABB.

(13 marks)

(b) Complete the analyst's work in Appendix 1 as required by the board and explain the variance between the budgeted cost and the actual cost for each receipt into goods inwards for July 20X5.

(12 marks)

(Total = 25 marks)

APPENDIX 1

Analyst's incomplete activity-based budget for the central warehouse for YE 30 June 20X6.

	Total $	Goods inwards $	Goods outwards $	Other $
Warehouse manager's salary (1)	55,000	–	–	55,000
Lease of RFID system (2)	75,000	45,000	30,000	–
RFID tagging (3)				
Warehouse staff wages (4)				
Heating and lighting (5)				

Sub-total cost of activities driven by the receipt of goods inwards

Analyst's notes

Relevant information on costs in the central warehouse for the year ending 30 June 20X6

(1) The cost of the warehouse manager's salary relates to all sections of the warehouse and cannot be apportioned directly to goods inwards or goods outwards.

(2) The cost for the RFID system is invoiced by a lease company. 60% of this cost is allocated to goods inwards and the remainder relates to goods outwards.

(3) The cost of RFID tagging is the wages cost for specially trained staff, known as taggers. Their only job is to attach RFID tags to items when they are received, before the items are put away in the warehouse. All items received are RFID tagged and the costs of tagging are allocated entirely to the cost of goods inwards. Each tagger can attach 35,000 tags per month and is paid an annual salary of $24,000. The cost of each individual RFID tag is negligible.

(4) There were 12 full-time warehouse staff throughout the year to 30 June 20X5 who were each paid an annual salary of $22,500. Two more staff will be recruited at the beginning of the new budget year. 50% of the warehouse staff work in goods inwards and 50% in goods outwards.

(5)   The cost of heating and lighting relates to all sections of the warehouse and cannot be apportioned directly to goods inwards or goods outwards. The actual heating and lighting cost for last year was $10,000, and the warehouse manager has proposed a budget of $10,500 for the coming year. The general cost of inflation though is expected to be zero.

(6)   The annual number of receipts into goods inwards expected is 9,000, containing a total of 1,200,000 items. These are expected to occur evenly over the year.

4 Drinks Group (12/12, amended)   49 mins

Company background

The Drinks Group (DG) has been created over the last three years by merging three medium-sized family businesses. These businesses are all involved in making fruit drinks. Fizzy (F) makes and bottles healthy, fruit-based sparkling drinks. Still (S) makes and bottles fruit-flavoured non-sparkling drinks and Healthy (H) buys fruit and squeezes it to make basic fruit juices. The three companies have been divisionalised within the group structure. A fourth division called Marketing (M) exists to market the products of the other divisions to various large retail chains. Marketing has only recently been set up in order to help the business expand. All of the operations and sales of DG occur in Nordland, which is an economically well-developed country with a strong market for healthy non-alcoholic drinks.

The group has recruited a new finance director (FD), who was asked by the board to perform a review of the efficiency and effectiveness of the Finance Department as her first task on taking office. The FD has just presented her report to the board regarding some problems at DG.

Extract from FD's report to the board:

'The main area for improvement, which was discussed at the last board meeting, is the need to improve profit margins throughout the business. There is no strong evidence that new products or markets are required but that the most promising area for improvement lies in better internal control practices.

Control

As DG was formed from an integration of the original businesses (F, S, H), there was little immediate effort put into optimising the control systems of these businesses. They have each evolved over time in their own way. Currently, the main method of central control that can be used to drive profit margin improvement is the budget system in each business. The budgeting method used is to take the previous year's figures and simply increment them by estimates of growth in the market that will occur over the next year. These growth estimates are obtained through a discussion between the financial managers at group level and the relevant divisional managers. The management at each division are then given these budgets by head office and their personal targets are set around achieving the relevant budget numbers.

Divisions

H and S Divisions are in stable markets where the levels of demand and competition mean that sales growth is unlikely, unless by acquisition of another brand. The main engine for prospective profit growth in these divisions is through margin improvements. The managers at these divisions have been successful in previous years and generally keep to the agreed budgets. As a result, they are usually not comfortable with changing existing practices.

F is faster growing and seen as the star of the Group. However, the Group has been receiving complaints from customers about late deliveries and poor quality control of the F products. The F managers have explained that they are working hard within the budget and capital constraints imposed by the board and have expressed a desire to be less controlled.

The Marketing Division has only recently been set up and the intention is to run each marketing campaign as an individual project which would be charged to the division whose products are benefiting from the campaign. The managers of the manufacturing divisions are very doubtful of the value of M, as each believes that they have an existing strong reputation with their customers that does not require much additional spending on marketing. However, the board decided at the last meeting that there was scope to create and use a marketing budget effectively at DG, if its costs were carefully controlled. Similar to the other divisions, the Marketing Division budgets are set by taking the previous year's actual spend and adding a percentage increase. For M, the increase corresponds to the previous year's growth in group turnover.'

End of extract

Budgeting methods

At present, the FD is harassed by the introduction of a new information system within the Finance Department which is straining the resources of the department. However, she needs to respond to the issues raised above at the board meeting and so is considering using different budgeting methods at DG. She has asked you, the management accountant at the Group, to do some preliminary work to help her decide whether and how to change the budget methods. The first task that she believes would be useful is to consider the use of rolling budgets. She thinks that fast-growing F may prove the easiest division in which to introduce new ideas.

F's incremental budget for the current year is given below. You can assume that cost of sales and distribution costs are variable and administrative costs are fixed.

	Q1 $'000	Q2 $'000	Q3 $'000	Q4 $'000	Total $'000
Revenue	17,520	17,958	18,407	18,867	72,752
Cost of sales	9,636	9,877	10,124	10,377	40,014
Gross profit	7,884	8,081	8,283	8,490	32,738
Distribution costs	1,577	1,616	1,657	1,698	6,548
Administration costs	4,214	4,214	4,214	4,214	16,856
Operating profit	2,093	2,251	2,412	2,578	9,334

The actual figures for Quarter 1 (which has just completed) are:

	$'000
Revenue	17,932
Cost of sales	9,863
Gross profit	8,069
Distribution costs	1,614
Administration costs	4,214
Operating profit	2,241

On the basis of the Q1 results, sales volume growth of 3% per quarter is now expected.

The FD has also heard you talking about bottom-up budgeting and wants you to evaluate its use at DG.

Required

(a) Evaluate the suitability of incremental budgeting at each division. **(8 marks)**

(b) Recalculate the budget for Fizzy Division (F) using rolling budgeting and assess the use of rolling budgeting at F. **(8 marks)**

(c) Recommend, with reasons, a suitable budgeting method which could be used at the Marketing Division (M). **(3 marks)**

(d) Analyse and recommend the appropriate level of participation in budgeting at Drinks Group (DG). **(6 marks)**

(Total = 25 marks)

5 Godel (6/14, amended)   49 mins

Company background and strategy

Godel Goodies (Godel) manufactures a variety of own-label sweets for the two largest supermarket chains in Seeland. The business makes several different flavours of the same basic product. The strategy of the business has been to be a cost leader in order to win the supermarkets' business. The sales of Godel vary up and down from quarter to quarter depending on the state of the general economy and competitive forces. Most of the sweet manufacturers have been in business for decades and so the business is mature with little scope to be innovative in new product development. The supermarkets prefer to sign suppliers to long-term contracts and so it is difficult for new entrants to gain a foothold in this market. The management style at Godel is very much command and control which fits with the strategy and type of business. Indeed, most employees have been at Godel for many years and have expressed their liking for the straightforward nature of their work.

Variance analysis

The chief executive officer (CEO) of Godel has asked your firm of accountants to advise him as his finance director (FD) will be absent for several months due to a recently diagnosed illness. As the CEO is preparing for the next board meeting, he has obtained the operating statement and detailed variance analysis from one of the junior accountants (Appendix 1).

The CEO is happy with the operating statement but wants to understand the detailed operational and planning variances, given in Appendix 1, for the board meeting. He needs to know what action should be taken as a result of these specific variances.

Budgeting process

The FD had been looking at the budgeting process before she fell ill. The CEO has decided that you should help him by answering some questions on budgeting at Godel.

Currently, the budget at Godel is set at the start of the year and performance is measured against this. The company uses standard costs for each product and attributes overheads using absorption costing based on machine hours. No variations are allowed to the standard costs during the year. The standard costs and all budget assumptions are discussed with the relevant operational manager before being set. However, these managers grumble that the budget process is very time consuming and that the results are ultimately of limited value from their perspective. Some of them also complain that they must frequently explain that the variances are not their fault. The CEO wants to know your views on whether this way of budgeting is appropriate and whether the managers' complaints are justified. He is satisfied that there is no dysfunctional behaviour at Godel which may lead to budget slack or excessive spending and that all managers are working in the best interests of the company.

Shortly before she fell ill, the FD had suggested that in order to stop managers complaining about having to explain variances that were not their fault, the managers should produce their own draft budgets, which would then be reviewed and consolidated centrally. The CEO is not sure what impact this change could have, and wants you to evaluate it before he makes any changes to Godel's current budgeting system.

Required

(a)   Advise the CEO on the implications for performance management at Godel of analysing variances into the planning and operational elements as shown in Appendix 1.   **(6 marks)**

(b)   Evaluate the budgeting system at Godel.   **(12 marks)**

(c)   Evaluate the FD's proposal to introduce a bottom-up approach to budgeting.   **(7 marks)**

(Total = 25 marks)

APPENDIX 1

(Note. You may assume that all figures in this appendix are correct.)

Operating statement for Godel

Period: May 20X4 (last month)

			$	$	
Budgeted profit				214,200	
Budget fixed production costs				264,180	
Budgeted contribution				478,380	
Sales variances	volume		20,100		Adverse
	price		8,960		Adverse
				29,060	Adverse
Actual sales minus standard cost of sales				449,320	

		Favourable	Adverse
		$	$
Variable cost variance			
Material	price		4,200
	usage	3,500	
Labour	rate	1,100	
	efficiency	24,480	
	idle time		5,600
Variable overhead	expenditure		1,080
	efficiency	3,060	
		32,140	10,880

		$	
		21,260	Favourable
Actual contribution		470,580	
Budgeted fixed production overhead	271,728		
Expenditure variance	18,696		Adverse
Actual fixed production overhead		290,424	
Actual profit		180,156	

Detailed variances

Total variable cost variances		$	
	Planning	20,680	Favourable
	Operational	580	Favourable
Sales price variances			
	Planning	15,600	Adverse
	Operational	6,640	Favourable

6 Perkin (Sep/Dec 15, amended)   49 mins

Company background and objectives

Perkin manufactures electronic components for export worldwide, from factories in Ceeland, for use in smartphones and handheld gaming devices. These two markets are supplied with similar components by two divisions, Phones Division (P) and Gaming Division (G). Each division has its own selling, purchasing, IT and research and development (R&D) functions, but separate IT systems. Some manufacturing facilities, however, are shared between the two divisions.

Perkin's corporate objective is to maximise shareholder wealth through innovation and continuous technological improvement in its products. The manufacturers of smartphones and gaming devices, who use Perkin's components, update their products frequently and constantly compete with each other to launch models which are technically superior.

Budgeting process

Perkin has a well-established incremental budgeting process. Divisional managers forecast sales volumes and costs months in advance of the budget year. These divisional budgets are then scrutinised by the main board, and revised significantly by them in line with targets they have set for the business. The finalised budgets are often approved after the start of the accounting year. Under pressure to deliver consistent returns to institutional shareholders, the board does not tolerate failure by either division to achieve the planned net profit for the year once the budget is approved. Last year's results were poor compared to the annual budget. Divisional managers, who are appraised on the financial performance of their own division, have complained about the length of time that the budgeting process takes and that the performance of their divisions could have been better but was constrained by the budgets which were set for them.

In P Division, managers had failed to anticipate the high popularity of a new smartphone model incorporating a large screen designed for playing games, and had not made the necessary technical modifications to the division's own components. This was due to the high costs of doing so, which had not been budgeted for. Based on the original sales forecast, P Division had already committed to manufacturing large quantities of the existing version of the component and so had to heavily discount these in order to achieve the planned sales volumes.

A critical material in the manufacture of Perkin's products is silver, which is a commodity which changes materially in price according to worldwide supply and demand. During the year supplies of silver were reduced significantly for a short period of time and G Division paid high prices to ensure continued supply. Managers of G Division were unaware that P Division held large inventories of silver which they had purchased when the price was much lower.

Initially, G Division accurately forecasted demand for its components based on the previous years' sales volumes plus the historic annual growth rate of 5%. However, overall sales volumes were much lower than budgeted. This was due to a fire at the factory of their main customer, which was then closed for part of the year. Reacting to this news, managers at G Division took action to reduce costs, including closing one of the three R&D facilities in the division.

However, when the customer's factory reopened, G Division was unwilling to recruit extra staff to cope with increased demand; nor would P Division reallocate shared manufacturing facilities to them, in case demand increased for its own products later in the year. As a result, Perkin lost the prestigious preferred supplier status from its main customer who was unhappy with G Division's failure to effectively respond to the additional demand. The customer had been forced to purchase a more expensive, though technically superior, component from an alternative manufacturer.

The institutional shareholders' representative, recently appointed to the board, has asked you as a performance management expert for your advice. 'We need to know whether Perkin's budgeting process is appropriate for the business, and how this contributed to last year's poor performance.'

However, the shareholder representative did also acknowledge that external factors had contributed to Perkin's poor performance in the last year, and suggested that it would be useful if Perkin's performance reports distinguished between variances which had resulted from its own operational performance as opposed to external circumstances which could not have been anticipated when the budgets were produced. You noted that many organisations address this issue by analysing variances into planning and operational elements.

Required

(a)   Evaluate the weaknesses in Perkin's current budgeting system and whether it is suitable for the environment in which Perkin operates.   **(14 marks)**

(b)   Evaluate the extent to which Perkin's poor performance for the last year can be attributed to external factors.   **(6 marks)**

(c)   Discuss the potential benefits to Perkin of analysing variances into planning and operational elements.   **(5 marks)**

(Total = 25 marks)

7 Jolt (Sept 18)   49 mins

Company information

Jolt manufactures high quality swimwear and cycling clothing in its only factory, which employs 1,000 manufacturing staff and 200 support staff. Its products are used by both amateur and professional sports players in its home country. Jolt is known for its high ethical standards towards its workers, suppliers and the environment, and has voluntarily published a corporate sustainability report for many years.

Jolt is organised into traditional functional departments such as procurement, finance and sales, most of which have their own unreliable spreadsheet-based systems for planning and reporting. As a result, Jolt often fails to produce accurate, timely and consistent data to monitor its own performance, which contributes to failures in achieving the performance targets set by its retail customers.

Developments in Jolt's market

Jolt's market is seasonal and competitive. Retailers, who are Jolt's customers, for both swimwear and cycling clothing have two key demands: they want lower prices to pass on to consumers and they also require suppliers to meet performance targets relating to lead times and quality.

To help them comply with the retailers' demands, Jolt's competitors have closed down all of their own manufacturing facilities and outsourced all production to overseas suppliers, who have much larger factories and lower costs. To mitigate the cost of shipping goods over long distances, Jolt's competitors have invested in sophisticated software to consolidate orders so that each shipping container is completely full before being dispatched from their suppliers. Purchase invoice processing is also automated by the integration of information systems into the suppliers' bespoke systems.

Business process re-engineering proposal

In order to reduce costs, it has been proposed to outsource the manufacture of swimwear, which is 50% of Jolt's total output, to a supplier 17,000 km away. A comparison of the cost of manufacturing and the cost of outsourcing swimwear is given in Appendix 1.

This will mean that staff from Jolt's functional departments will re-organise into multi-disciplinary teams, each serving major customer accounts. Each team will perform all aspects of account management, from taking sales orders and procurement, through to arranging shipping and after sales service. Team members dealing with customers will work in Jolt's home country, while those managing quality and supplier audits will work close to the manufacturing site. Teams will be given greater autonomy to set selling prices to reflect market conditions. Many support staff will work in unfamiliar roles, or be offered new jobs overseas after the re-organisation.

A consultant has advised Jolt that the outsourcing and re-organisation proposal has characteristics of re-engineered processes, and could be described as business process re-engineering (BPR). She advised that, as well as evaluating how BPR will improve its business performance in meeting its customers' demands and requirements, Jolt should take into account any development in information systems which may be required, as well as the ethical aspects of the proposed changes.

Required

(a)   Evaluate how the BPR proposal could improve Jolt's performance in relation to its retail customers' two key demands.   (11 marks)

(b)   Advise Jolt on the development of its information systems which would be required for the BPR proposal to deliver performance improvements.   (6 marks)

(c)   Assess the potential impact of Jolt's high ethical standards on the BPR proposal and consequently on business performance.   (8 marks)

(Total = 25 marks)

APPENDIX 1

Comparison of the average cost of manufacturing and outsourcing swimwear production

	Manufacturing $	Outsourcing $[1]
Average cost per unit		
Material cost	1.85	–
Labour cost	2.20	–
Factory overhead	0.95	–
Purchase cost from supplier[2]	–	3.50
Total	5.00	3.50

Notes

1   Purchase cost of outsourced products is translated into $ from the supplier's home currency.

2   In addition to the purchase cost from the supplier, Joly must pay for shipping costs at the rate of $5,000 for each large, standard sized shipping container, regardless of the number of units in it. Each contains holds 10,000 units when fully loaded.

3   Due to changes in international trade tariffs expected in the near future, swimwear imports in to Jolt's home country will be subject to 10% import duty on the cost of imports excluding shipping cost.

8 Booxe (6/14)   49 mins

Company background

Booxe is a furniture manufacturing company based in the large, developed country of Teeland. Booxe is the largest furniture manufacturer in Teeland supplying many of the major retail chains with their own-brand furniture and also making furniture under its own brand (Meson). In a highly competitive market such as Teeland, Booxe has chosen a strategy of cost leadership.

Booxe has been in business for more than 70 years and there is a strong sense of tradition and appreciation of craft skills in the workforce. The average time which an employee has worked for the firm is 18 years. This has led to a bureaucratic culture; for example, the company's information systems are heavily paper based. In addition, and in line with this traditional culture, the organisation is divided into a set of functional departments, such as production, warehousing, human resources and finance.

Business process re-engineering project

In order to drive down costs, the chief executive officer (CEO) decided to re-engineer the processes at Booxe. She decided that there should be a small pilot project to demonstrate the potential of business process re-engineering (BPR) to benefit Booxe and she selected the goods receiving activity in the company's warehousing operations for this.

The CEO has asked you as a performance management expert to complete the post-implementation review of the pilot project by assessing what it has delivered in financial terms. The project identified that ten of the warehouse staff spend about half their time matching goods delivered documents to purchase orders and dealing with subsequent problems. It was noted that 25% of all such matches failed and the staff then had to identify the issue and liaise with the Purchasing Department in order to get the goods returned to the supplier and a suitable credit note issued. The project introduced a new information system to replace the existing paper-based system. The new system allowed purchase orders to be entered by the Purchasing Department and then checked online to the goods delivered as they arrived at the warehouse. This allowed warehouse staff to reject incorrect deliveries immediately.

 BPP LEARNING MEDIA

The following are further details provided in relation to the project:

Notes relating to old system:

1   Average staff wage in warehouse $25,000 p.a.
2   Purchasing staff time in handling delivery queries 8.5 days per week
3   Average staff wage in purchasing is $32,000 p.a. for working a five-day week

Notes relating to new system:

New IT system costs:

		$
4	Hardware for warehouse and purchasing depts	220,000
5	Software total cost	275,000
6	Ongoing servicing cost (p.a.)	22,500
7	It is expected that the new system will last for eight years.	

The CEO now plans to apply BPR across Booxe and, as well as completing the post-implementation review, she needs to know how BPR will change the accounting information systems and the culture at Booxe. Booxe's current accounting system is a traditional one of overhead absorption based on labour hours with variances to budget used as control indicators. She has heard that an activity-based approach using enterprise resource planning (ERP) systems is fairly common and wants to know how these ideas might link to BPR at Booxe.

The CEO is concerned that middle management unrest may be a problem at Booxe. For example, the warehouse manager was uncomfortable with the cultural change required in the BPR project and decided to take early retirement before the project began. As a result, a temporary manager was put in place to run the warehouse during the project.

Appraisal process

The CEO has also begun to reconsider the human resources system at Booxe and she wants your advice on how the staff appraisal process can improve performance in the company. The existing system of manager appraisal is for the staff member to have an annual meeting with their line superior to review the previous year's work and discuss generally how to improve their efforts. Over the years, it has become common for these meetings to be informal and held over lunch at the company's expense. The CEO wants to understand the purpose of a staff appraisal system and how the process can improve the performance of the company. She also wants comments on the appropriate balance between control and staff development as this impacts on staff appraisal at Booxe.

Required

(a)   Assess the financial impact of the pilot BPR project in the warehousing operations.

(6 marks)

(b)   Assess the impact of BPR on the culture and management information systems at Booxe.

(11 marks)

(c)   Advise on the appraisal process at Booxe as instructed by the CEO.   (8 marks)

(Total = 25 marks)

9 PLX Refinery (2013 Pilot Exam)   49 mins

Company background

PLX Refinery Co is a large oil refinery business in Kayland. Kayland is a developing country with a large and growing oil exploration and production business which supplies PLX with crude oil. Currently, the refinery has the capacity to process 200,000 barrels of crude oil per day and makes profits of $146m per year. It employs about 2,000 staff and contractors. The staff are paid $60,000 each per year on average (about twice the national average pay in Kayland).

The government of Kayland has been focused on delivering rapid economic growth over the last 15 years. However, there are increasing signs that the environment is paying a large price for this growth, with public health suffering. There is now a growing environmental pressure group, Green

Kayland (GK), which is organising protests against the companies that they see as being the major polluters.

Environmental concerns

Kayland's government wishes to react to the concerns of the public and the pressure groups. It has requested that companies involved in heavy industry contribute to a general improvement in the treatment of the environment in Kayland.

As a major participant in the oil industry with ties to the nationalised oil exploration company (Kayex), PLX believes it will be strategically important to be at the forefront of environmental developments. It is working with other companies in the oil industry to improve environmental reporting since there is a belief that this will lead to improved public perception and economic efficiency of the industry. PLX has had a fairly good compliance record in Kayland, with only two major fines (of $1m each) being levied in the last eight years for safety breaches and river pollution. However, the main focus of PLX's performance measures remains on financial performance.

Information systems

The existing information systems within PLX also focus on financial performance. They support financial reporting obligations and allow monitoring of key performance metrics such as earnings per share and operating margins. Recent publications on environmental accounting have suggested there are a number of techniques (such as input/output analysis, activity-based costing (ABC) and a lifecycle view) that may be relevant in implementing improvements to these systems.

Capital expenditure and new product development

PLX is considering a major capital expenditure programme to enhance capacity, safety and efficiency at the refinery. This will involve demolishing certain older sections of the refinery and building on newly acquired land adjacent to the site. Overall, the refinery will increase its land area by 20%.

Part of the refinery extension will also manufacture a new plastic, Kayplas. Kayplas is expected to have a limited market life of five years after which it will be replaced by Kayplas2. The refinery accounting team have forecast the following data associated with this product and calculated PLX's traditional performance measure of product profit for the new product:

All figures are in $m.

	20X2	20X3	20X4	20X5	20X6
Revenue	25.0	27.5	30.1	33.2	33.6
Costs					
Production costs	13.8	15.1	16.6	18.3	18.5
Marketing costs	5.0	4.0	3.0	3.0	2.0
Development costs	5.6	3.0	0.0	0.0	0.0
Product profit	0.6	5.4	10.5	11.9	13.1

Subsequently, the following environmental costs have been identified from PLX's general overheads as associated with the production of Kayplas.

	20X2	20X3	20X4	20X5	20X6
Waste filtration	1.2	1.4	1.5	1.9	2.1
Carbon dioxide exhaust extraction	0.8	0.9	0.9	1.2	1.5

Additionally, other costs associated with closing down and recycling the equipment in Kayplas production are estimated at $18m in 20X6.

The board wishes to consider how it can contribute to the oil industry's performance in environmental accounting, how it can implement the changes that this might require, and how these changes will benefit the company.

Required

(a) Discuss and illustrate four different cost categories that would aid transparency in environmental reporting both internally and externally at PLX. **(6 marks)**

(b) Explain, and evaluate, how the three environmental accounting techniques mentioned can assist in managing the environmental and strategic performance of PLX. **(9 marks)**

(c) Assess the impact of implementing and input/output analysis on the information systems used at PLX. **(3 marks)**

(d) Evaluate the costing approach used for Kayplas's performance compared to a life cycle costing approach, performing appropriate calculations. **(7 marks)**

(Total = 25 marks)

10 Alflonnso (Sept/Dec 16)   49 mins

Alflonnso is a large producer of industrial chemicals, with divisions in 25 countries. The Agrochemicals Division produces a chemical pesticide, known internally as 'ALF', to control pests in a crop which is of worldwide significance, economically and for food production. Pesticides such as ALF only remain effective for a limited time, after which pests become resistant to them and a replacement product needs to be found. A scientific study has shown that the current variant, ALF6, is becoming ineffective in controlling pests, and in some places it has accumulated in the soil to levels which may significantly reduce crop yields in the future if it is continued to be used. The Agrochemicals Division is evaluating three new products to find one replacement for ALF6.

ALF7

ALF7 is produced by a small chemical modification to the existing product and requires little research and development (R&D) resources to develop it. As it is closely related to the current variant, it is only expected to remain effective, and in use, for three years. It is unclear whether ALF7 will accumulate in the soil in the same way as ALF6 does.

Red

Red is a new type of pesticide which will incur large amounts of R&D expenditure to develop a commercial version. In addition, the Agrochemicals Division will have to fund a long-term scientific study into the effect of Red on the environment at a cost of $4m for each of the 15 years that the product will be in use, and for five years afterwards.

Production of Red generates large amounts of toxic by-products which must be treated in the division's waste treatment facility. The production plant used to produce Red must also be decommissioned for cleaning, at an estimated cost of $45m, at the end of the life of the product.

Green

Green is a form of a naturally occurring chemical, thought to be safe and not to accumulate in the environment. It is expected to remain in use for eight years. Production of Green requires relatively large amounts of energy. Significant R&D expenditure is also needed to produce an effective version, as Green remains active in the environment for only a short time. Because of this, Green is unsuitable for use in climates where crop production is already difficult.

The Global Food Production Organisation (GFPO) is a non-governmental organisation which funds new ways to increase global crop production, especially in regions where food for human consumption is already scarce. The GFPO has agreed to make a significant contribution to the R&D costs of producing a replacement for ALF6, but will be unwilling to contribute to the R&D costs for Green because it cannot be used in every region. Similarly, a number of governments, in countries where Alflonnso has licences to operate its other chemical businesses, have warned the company of the potential public disapproval should the Agrochemical Division choose to replace ALF6 with a product unsuitable for use in areas where food production is scarce.

The newly appointed chief financial officer (CFO) for the Agrochemicals Division has asked you, as a performance management consultant, for your advice.

One of our analysts in the Agrochemicals Division,' she said, 'has produced a single period statement of profit or loss (Appendix 1) to show the profitability of the three new products we are considering as replacements for ALF6.

I think the analyst's calculations are too simplistic,' she continued. 'The costs of the waste treatment are apportioned based on the expected revenue of the new products. This is consistent with Alflonnso's traditional group accounting policy, but I don't think this gives an accurate costing for the new products. Also, I watched a presentation recently about the use of life cycle costing and also how environmental management accounting (EMA) can help reduce costs in the categories of conventional, contingent and reputation costs, and as a result improve performance.

Required

(a) (i)   Explain how activity-based costing may help the Agrochemicals Division in assessing the profitability of the three new products. **(5 marks)**

     (ii) Using activity-based costing, and excluding the value of the grant from the GFPO, calculate the total waste treatment costs and R&D costs of the three new products. **(3 marks)**

(b) Using your answers from part (a) (ii), calculate the average net profit per litre of each of the three alternative new products over their expected life cycles and comment on the results. **(9 marks)**

(c) Advise how EMA may help improve the performance of the Agrochemicals Division. **(8 marks)**

(Total = 25 marks)

APPENDIX 1

Single period statement of profit or loss for the replacement products for ALF6 (Note 1)

	ALF7	Red	Green
Revenue per litre ($)	8.00	13.00	11.00
Quantity sold and produced (million litres)	100	85	75
	$m	$m	$m
Revenue	800	1,105	825
Direct material, labour and energy	(524)	(724)	(565)
Factory overheads	(80)	(122)	(74)
Environmental study	–	(4)	–
Waste treatment of toxic by-products (Note 2)	(54)	(63)	(71)
Net profit (Note 3)	142	192	115
Average profit per litre ($)	1.42	2.26	1.53

Notes to the statement of profit or loss

1 All figures exclude the contribution from the GFPO towards the R&D costs of the new product.

2 Waste treatment is an overhead cost incurred in the division's waste treatment facility. Currently, costs of waste treatment are apportioned to products according to expected revenue. The total annual cost of the waste treatment facility, which processes a total of 55 million litres of waste each year, is $300m. Any waste treatment capacity not used by any of the three new products can be used to treat waste created during the manufacture of other products in the division. One litre of waste by-product is produced for every 12.5 litres of ALF7 produced, for every 2.5 litres of Red produced, and for every 100 litres of Green.

3 R&D costs are incurred in the division's R&D facility. In accordance with the group's accounting policy, R&D expenditure is not currently apportioned to individual products. The annual cost of the R&D facility is $60m and has a total of 30,400 R&D hours available, of which 800 hours would be required to develop ALF7, 8,500 hours to develop Red, and 4,000 hours to develop Green.

IMPACT OF RISK AND UNCERTAINTY

Questions 11 to 13 cover the impact of risk and uncertainty on organisational performance, the subject of Part B of the syllabus for *Advanced Performance Management* (APM).

11 Sberry (Sep/Dec 18)   49 mins

Sberry: Company information

Sberry manufactures products which have a short lifecycle due to technological obsolescence. It aims to keep each product in production for at least 18 months so that it can recover the high cost of product development and make an acceptable profit before the product becomes obsolete. Sberry has always manufactured its products in its home country of Deeland, from where all materials are also sourced.

Sales opportunity in Kayland

An opportunity has been identified to export one of three newly developed products – Red, Blue and Green – to Kayland, due to citizens' increasing levels of income there. The rate of technological obsolescence is slower in Kayland than in Deeland. The estimated levels of demand, selling prices and costs of the three products are shown in Appendix 1.

Stakeholders' views on the risks of the Kayland opportunity

Three of Sberry's key stakeholder groups – employees, directors and shareholders – have been consulted for their views on the proposal to export to Kayland and, in particular, on which of the three newly developed products to export there.

The employees have a cautious approach to the proposal following the recent failure of another product launch. That product was withdrawn as it breached poorly understood safety regulations and a number of employees lost their jobs as a result.

The directors, all of whom are individually wealthy, have served on the board for many years and are keen to earn the large bonus which is currently offered solely on the total profit made by the new product over its lifecycle.

The shareholders neither avoid nor seek risk, but they are keen that the company considers the external environment in Kayland in order to maximise performance there, whichever of the products is chosen to be exported. They have asked for a PEST* analysis of the environment in Kayland to be produced. A first draft of this has indicated that the exchange rate between the Deeland dollar (D$) and the Kayland dollar (K$) is a key economic factor which may affect performance.

*Political, economic, socio-cultural and technological

Required

(a)   Advise which of the three newly developed products each of the three key stakeholder groups would choose to export to Kayland based on their respective risk appetites.

(14 marks)

(b)   Explain the problems of using the risk and uncertainty analysis techniques which you have used in part (a).   (5 marks)

(c)   Advise the shareholders how analysing the external environment in Kayland using a PEST analysis can help Sberry maximise its performance there. You are **NOT** required to produce a PEST analysis.   (6 marks)

(Total = 25 marks)

APPENDIX 1

Estimated levels of demand, selling prices and costs (Note 1) of the three newly developed products

	Red	Blue	Green
Total demand (units) (Note 2)	50,000	60,000	160,000
Selling price (K$) (Note 3)	8.00	9.00	6.00
Total unit cost (D$) (Note 4)	2.40	3.00	2.50

Notes to the appendix:

1 Development costs are sunk costs and can be ignored.

2 The estimated product life of each of the three products is the same and the total demand is for the whole life of the product.

3 The current exchange rate between the D$ and the K$ is D$1.00 = K$2.00. Sberry's finance director has estimated that over the life of the product there is a 75% probability that the average exchange rate of the D$ will strengthen by 10% against the K$, and a 25% probability that the average exchange rate of the D$ will weaken by 10% against the K$.

4 At the current exchange rate, 50% of the total costs for each product is for materials which are imported from Kayland and invoiced in K$. There will be no opening or closing inventory, whichever of the three new products is chosen.

12 Sweet Cicely (Sept/Dec 17)   49 mins

Company background

Sweet Cicely (SC) manufactures sweets and confectionery and has delivered stable but modest increases to the shareholder wealth for many years. Following a change in ownership, the new shareholders are keen to increase the long-term performance of the business and are prepared to accept a high level of risk to achieve this.

New chocolate factory

SC is considering setting up a factory to manufacture chocolate bars. There are three options (1, 2 and 3) for the size and output capacity of the new chocolate factory. SC must choose a size most suited to the expected demand for its products. As well as the impact of the quality, branding and pricing of its products, demand for SC chocolate bars will be influenced by external factors such as consumer tastes for chocolate over other sweets, and even the suggested health benefits of certain types of chocolate.

A high-cost ingredient in chocolate bars is cocoa, a commodity traded on international markets. The market price of cocoa fluctuates with worldwide demand. Due to economic growth, chocolate consumption is rising in many countries, where it was once considered a luxury. In some countries, however, governments are considering introducing additional taxes on products containing sugar in order to reduce the consumption of chocolate and confectionery products. Being derived from an agricultural crop, the availability and price of cocoa is also influenced by climatic conditions, soil erosion, and disease. Conflicts and political instability in cocoa growing regions can also restrict its availability. Recent technological advances in the production of cocoa, such as the use of genetically modified crops, promise higher yields from cocoa plants in the near future.

Planning and decision making

You have been asked to help SC choose one of the three options for the new chocolate factory. One board member told you:

> The board proposed expanding into cake manufacturing several years ago. With hindsight, our planning on that proposal was poor. We sold only slightly fewer cakes than expected, but hadn't realised how sensitive our operating profit would be to a small change in demand. The previous shareholders thought problems in the cake business would put their

BPP
LEARNING
MEDIA

dividends at risk, so SC stopped manufacturing cakes, barely a year after it started. The board does not want to repeat these mistakes. We want to minimise the opportunity cost of making the wrong decision about the size of the new chocolate factory.

Appendix 1 shows the net present values for the three options discounted at SC's current cost of capital. Appendix 2 shows the expected operating profit generated by the three options in the first year of the project, according to the market price of cocoa, and assuming an annual demand of 70 million chocolate bars.

Required

(a)   Advise SC why decisions, such as what size of chocolate factory to build, must include consideration of risk and uncertainty, and evaluate the use of PEST analysis in managing the risk and uncertainty surrounding the project. **(14 marks)**

(b)   Using the data in Appendix 1, explain which of the three options for the new chocolate factory would be preferred by the board and the new shareholders according to their respective risk appetites. **(6 marks)**

(c)   Using the data in Appendix 2, recommend which of the three options for the new chocolate factory a risk neutral investor would choose, and explain any problems with the approach used to make the choice. **(5 marks)**

(Total = 25 marks)

APPENDIX 1

Net present values for the three options discounted at SC's current cost of capital

Annual demand for chocolate bars	Option 1 $m	Option 2 $m	Option 3 $m
50 million	4.0	(8.0)	(32.0)
60 million	6.0	16.0	(24.0)
70 million	6.0	16.0	17.0

APPENDIX 2

Expected operating profit generated by the three options in the first year of the project, assuming an annual demand of 70 million chocolate bars

Probability	Market price of cocoa $ per ton	Option 1 $m	Option 2 $m	Option 3 $m
0.3	2,500	3.0	5.0	7.0
0.4	3,000	0.5	2.0	1.5
0.3	3,500	(2.0)	(1.0)	(2.0)

13 Turing (6/14)   49 mins

Joint venture: TandR

Turing Aerodynamics (Turing) has formed a joint venture (JV) with Riemann Generators (Riemann) in order to design and manufacture high-performance wind turbines which generate electricity. The JV is called TandR with each party owning 50%. Turing will design and build the pylons, housing and turbine blades while Riemann will supply the generators to be fitted inside the housing.

Turing

Turing is a medium-sized firm known for its blade design skills. It is owned by three venture capital firms (VCs) (each holding 30% of the shares), with the remaining 10% being given to management to motivate them. The VCs each have a large portfolio of business investments and accept that some of these investments may fail provided that some of their investments show large gains. Management is an ambitious group who enjoys the business and technical challenges of introducing new products.

Riemann

On the other hand, Riemann is a large, family-owned company working in the highly competitive electricity generator sector. The shareholders of Riemann see the business as mature and want it to offer a stable, long-term return on capital. However, recently, Riemann had to seek emergency refinancing (debt and equity) due to its thin profit margins and tough competition, both of which are forecast to continue. As a result, Riemann's shareholders and management are concerned for the survival of the business and see TandR as a way to generate some additional cash flow. Unlike at Turing, the management of Riemann does not own significant shareholdings in the company which has preferred to pay fixed salaries.

Choice of design for the turbines

TandR is run by a group of managers made up from each of the JV partners. They are currently faced with a decision about the design of the product. There are three design choices depending on the power which the wind turbines can generate (measured in megawatts (MW)):

Design	Description
8 MV	A large 8 MW unit
3 MW	A 3 MW unit
1 MW	A basic 1 MW unit

The engineering for the 1 MW and 3 MW units is well understood and so design is much simpler than for the 8 MW unit which would be world leading if completed.

The demand for the different types of units will depend on government subsidies of the electricity price charged by the electricity generating companies which will buy the wind turbines and the planning regulations for building such large structures. It is believed that there will be orders for either 1,000, 1,500 or 2,000 units but there is no clear picture yet of which demand level is more likely than the others.

The estimated costs and prices for the units are:

Type	Variable cost per unit $m	Fixed costs $m	Price per unit $m
8 MW	10.4	7,500.0	20.8
3 MW	4.8	820.0	9.6
1 MW	1.15	360.0	4.6

Notes

1   The fixed costs cover the initial design, development and testing of the units.

2   The costs and prices are in real terms with the 8 MW unit likely to take more years to develop than the others.

Required

(a)   Assess the risk appetites of the two firms in the JV and provide a justified recommendation for each firm of an appropriate method of decision making under uncertainty to assess the different types of wind turbines.   **(9 marks)**

(b)   Evaluate the choice of turbine design types using your recommended methods from part (a) above.   **(8 marks)**

(c)   Discuss the problems encountered in managing performance in a JV such as TandR.
                    (8 marks)

                    (Total = 25 marks)

PERFORMANCE MEASUREMENT SYSTEMS AND DEVELOPMENTS IN TECHNOLOGY

Questions 14 to 20 cover performance measurement systems and developments in technology, the subject of Part C of the syllabus for APM.

14 Luvij (Mar/Jun 18)   49 mins

Company background

Luvij manufactures high quality, luxury women's footwear. It sells its products on its own website and also to small independent retailers.

Data collection and performance analysis

In order to monitor performance and aid decision making, Luvij collects sales data on all of its footwear ranges and feedback on its designs from customers and retailers. In addition, to ensure that prices remain competitive, Luvij has a team of staff to monitor the prices of similar products on competitors' websites and to identify design trends in the market, which change frequently, and from season to season. Generating new footwear designs consistent with changing market trends is a critical success factor for Luvij. The large volume of data collected is entered into a complex spreadsheet by one data entry clerk.

Luvij operates a functional structure with different departments for sales, production, purchasing and design. The spreadsheet is sent by email to the senior manager of each of these departments at the end of each quarter. The senior manager for the sales, production and buying departments are expected to generate the relevant sales, production and purchasing forecasts by analysing information contained in the spreadsheet. The senior manager of the design department uses the information to generate new footwear designs consistent with market trends.

Potential joint venture

Luvij has a strategic objective to become the market leader in the sale of high quality, children's footwear to small independent footwear retailers. It has already invested heavily in market research and developing innovative designs. To reduce the risks of not achieving this strategic objective, for example, by having insufficient capacity to produce a larger range of footwear styles, the board is considering entering into a joint venture with Shirville.

Shirville is a large manufacturer of exclusively children's footwear. Its advanced manufacturing machinery and production techniques mean that it can produce the high volumes required to supply supermarkets and chain stores* found on the main streets of most towns and cities. Shirville's objective for the joint venture is to utilise spare production capacity it has in a factory which it holds on a lease which expires in three years.

Director's concerns

One recently appointed board member at Luvij has commented,

> I believe that the external information on market trends and competitors' prices compiled in the quarterly spreadsheet is of limited usefulness as I have heard complaints from managers that they have difficulty understanding the large volume of data given to them, and that they often receive this too late. The company I worked for in my previous job used a unified corporate database to share information in real time across all parts of the business. A similar unified corporate database may be useful for Luvij. I am also concerned about the potential problems of measuring and managing the performance of the joint venture with Shirville. The fact that the two businesses have different objectives is just one example of why these problems may occur, though there will also be other reasons.

*Chain stores are large retailers with multiple stores based in different locations.

Required

(a)   Explain the factors which might limit the usefulness of the external information currently used by Luvij, and evaluate how the use of a unified corporate database could help to overcome these limitations. **(15 marks)**

(b)   Advise the board on the potential problems with the measurement and management of the performance of the joint venture with Shirville. **(10 marks)**

(Total = 25 marks)

15 TREN engine components   49 mins

TREN manufactures standard engine components. It operates a costing system based on absorption costing and standard costs, and the management control system is based on monthly variance analysis reports.

TREN has recently appointed a new chief executive officer (CEO), who has begun to introduce changes to the manufacturing systems. He believes in lean manufacturing principles, and has begun to establish a just-in-time manufacturing system, with a focus on reducing inventories and production cycle times, and eliminating waste. Discussions are in progress with major suppliers to introduce just-in-time purchasing arrangements.

The CEO has informed the management accountant that changes will be needed to the company's internal accounting systems, and has indicated that TREN will need a lean management accounting system to support its lean manufacturing system. The CEO is dissatisfied with many of the features of the current management accounting system. There are many errors in data capture for the cost accounting system, and monthly variance reports are not produced until two weeks after the end of each month. He also considers that the wrong information is being reported.

Required

(a)   Explain the main principles of a lean information system and discuss why an organisation may not experience the improvements in productivity and profitability they expect if they implement a lean information system. **(11 marks)**

(b)   Discuss the reasons why TREN's current cost and management accounting systems do not fulfil the requirements of lean information systems. **(6 marks)**

(c)   Identify the changes that should be made to TREN's management accounting system in order to turn it into a lean information system. **(8 marks)**

(Total = 25 marks)

16 Forion Electronics (6/15)   49 mins

Company background

Forion Electronics (Forion) manufactures a range of electronic goods. Its business has grown rapidly over the last ten years and is now complex and international. Forion manufactures over 100 different products, selling into 25 different countries. There is a supplier base of over 200 companies from which Forion sources. As the business has become more complex, the board has found it difficult to pull together all the information that it requires in order to make decisions.

Information systems

The current information systems are developed in-house and are based in the functional departments (such as purchasing, manufacturing, warehousing and delivery, selling and marketing). The organisation uses the financial system as a means of bringing together information for an overview of corporate performance.

There have been a number of examples of problems encountered with information in Forion:

- There are inefficiencies arising from ordering the wrong amount of subcomponents.

- There are often stock-outs or obsolescence of unsold goods in the warehouses, although the Marketing Department prepares good sales forecasts.

- Sometimes, there are insufficient delivery vehicles available to meet customer deadlines.

The board of Forion believes the problems arise from poor information sharing within the company. It is considering the purchase of an enterprise resource planning system (ERPS) to be the single information system for the whole organisation.

Potential strategic alliance

Also, Forion is planning to launch a smartphone. However, in order to make it competitive they need to have high-visibility, durable screens. As the cost of screen development is considerable, it has been decided to form a strategic alliance with a well-known screen manufacturer to provide this key component for the new smartphone. Bon Accord Screens (BAS) has been chosen as the strategic ally, as it has a strong reputation for its quality of manufacturing and new product development. BAS has been trying to break into the smartphone market for several years.

The alliance agreement has stipulated three critical areas of performance for BAS's supply to Forion:

(1) Quality of manufacturing, measured by fault rates of screens supplied being within agreed tolerances (so that they fit Forion's phone bodies)

(2) Time of delivery, measured by the number of times a shipment is more than one day overdue

(3) The ability to provide technical upgrades to the screens as the market demands

The service level agreement will be based on these three points and there will be financial penalties built into the agreement if BAS fails to meet these.

Required

(a) Discuss the integration of information systems in an ERPS and how the ERPS may impact on performance management issues at Forion. **(10 marks)**

(b) Evaluate, from Forion's viewpoint, the usefulness of the three critical areas in the alliance agreement for measuring the performance of BAS. **(8 marks)**

(c) Evaluate the relative reliability of financial and non-financial data from internal and external sources in the context of the alliance between Forion and BAS. **(7 marks)**

(Total = 25 marks)

17 Quark Healthcare (12/13)   49 mins

Organisational background

Quark Healthcare (Quark) runs a number of large hospitals which provide general medical care for the people of Veeland. Veeland is an advanced economy and healthcare is considered to be a high skill, high technology and high status industry. It is compulsory for the people of Veeland to purchase health insurance and then the insurance companies reimburse the healthcare providers for services delivered. The insurance companies audit the healthcare providers and grade them for value for money. As there are a number of hospital chains (such as Quark), the insurers will encourage their insured customers to use those which are most efficient. The ultimate sanction for a healthcare provider is for an insurance company to remove them from the list of acceptable providers.

Quark has large amounts of capital tied up in expensive medical equipment and a drug inventory. The existing systems for accounting for these items are traditional ones aimed at avoiding theft and obsolescence. Quark has an inventory system which requires regular (weekly) physical checks of the drugs in inventory in order to update it. It is important that the right drugs must be in easily accessible stores (located throughout the hospital) in order to act quickly in case of a medical emergency. Also, the accounting staff at Quark maintain a non-current asset register (NCAR) which logs the location of all major assets including medical equipment. The problem with the NCAR is that it is often out of date as doctors will take equipment in time of emergency and not properly log its new location. This often leads to equipment lying unused in one area of the hospital while being searched for in another area, to the detriment of patient care.

Radio-frequency identification devices (RFID)

Quark has recently instituted a tagging project where radio-frequency identification devices (RFID) will be attached to the most valuable pieces of equipment used in treatment and also to batches of high-value drugs. The hospitals are fitted with WiFi networks which can pick up the RFID signal so that the RFID tags will be detectable throughout a hospital. The tags will identify the object which they are attached to by a unique identification number and will give its location. The identifier number will link to the inventory system which will identify the product, the quantity initially delivered in that batch and the date of delivery. The RFID information will be accessible through the computer terminals throughout the hospitals.

The chief financial officer (CFO) of Quark has asked you to advise him on the impact of this new system on performance management at Quark. He has suggested that you look at the costs and benefits which will be associated with producing the information from the RFID system, the impact of the nature of the information supplied, the changes to performance management reporting and how the new information could be used for improved control at the hospital. He is keen to be seen to be at the forefront of accounting and management developments and has been reading about cost control techniques. Recently, he has heard about 'lean' systems, so wants to know how the RFID system and its impact on the hospital fit with this concept. Given the importance of the medical staff in running the hospital, he also wants to know how their behaviour will be affected by the control information from the RFID system. There is a very strict social order among these staff (in increasing order of skills: nurses, general doctors and specialist doctors) which regularly causes friction when one group feels it is not given its due status. For example, recently, the general doctors agreed to a new method for nurses to record drugs administered to patients but this new system has not been fully implemented due to complaints by the nurses and specialist doctors who were not consulted on the change.

Required

(a) Assess the impact of the RFID system on the performance management at Quark as suggested by the CFO. **(12 marks)**

(b) Evaluate whether the overall management of the hospital can be considered to be 'leaner' as a result of the RFID information system. **(7 marks)**

(c) Evaluate how the medical staff's attitudes will influence the design and implementation of the RFID system and how it might be used to promote responsibility and accountability at the hospital.

(6 marks)

(Total = 25 marks)

18 Nelson, Jody & Nigel (Mar/Jun 17) 49 mins

Nelson, Jody and Nigel (NJN) operates a warehouse and distribution centre, storing and distributing 5,000 product lines on behalf of its client, an overseas sports equipment manufacturer.

Warehouse information system

NJN receives goods in shipping containers, which should include a packing list of the items they contain. Sometimes, packing lists are lost in transit and the manufacturer is asked for duplicates. Packing lists are manually input into NJN's warehouse information system (WIS) in batches, usually within 48 hours of the goods being received. Goods are first unpacked into a sorting area, and later moved to wherever there is available warehouse space once the packing list has been input. The WIS records the location within the warehouse where each item is located. The client's customers, who are retail stores, place orders by email, and do not currently have access to real-time inventory levels in NJN's warehouse.

Each morning picking lists are printed in the warehouse office. These lists show the quantities of items to be picked and the items' 12-digit product codes. Staff use these codes to retrieve items from the warehouse locations for despatch to retailers. In 8% of picking lists, at least one item is not in the location or does not have the quantity specified by the WIS. As a result, the item is not despatched, or the wrong item is picked. A small team investigates these discrepancies, using special reports which the warehouse manager extracts from the WIS. The team manually reconciles quantities of missing items in the warehouse to the sports equipment manufacturer's own records of the items which should be in inventory. If missing items cannot be found, the customer is informed via an email that they are unavailable.

Recent issues

The sports equipment manufacturer has a service level agreement with NJN, covering the accuracy of picking and the proportion of customers' orders successfully fulfilled. NJN's performance on these has deteriorated, especially when there is increased seasonal demand for certain products. At these times staff are under increased pressure to pick items quickly, and so picking accuracy deteriorates and absenteeism increases. There have also been accidents where goods have not been safely placed or safely picked from warehouse locations at busy times. These accidents have resulted in minor injuries to some employees.

The sports equipment manufacturer has threatened to end NJN's contract if performance does not improve. In response, NJN has recruited more staff to investigate discrepancies between items physically in warehouse locations, and those shown on the WIS at busy periods. It has also begun a series of cyclical inventory counts where every product line is counted every month to correct the quantities and locations shown on the WIS. NJN has rented an additional nearby warehouse in which to sort incoming items before they are put away.

Lean principles

NJN has hired a management consultant who is an expert in 'lean' principles and the application of these to management information systems. She believes that the WIS is wasteful, not adding value to the business or to its customers, and has suggested that NJN would benefit from the application of lean principles to this system.

She has suggested three proposals – that NJN:

- Reorganise the warehouse by storing high volume items close to the despatch area,
- Shut down the additional warehouse, and;
- Discontinue the cyclical inventory counts.

To help with the adoption of lean principles in the warehouse reorganisation, the management consultant recommends NJN apply the '5Ss'* of lean principles, and she has suggested performance metrics which can be used to evaluate NJN's progress towards adopting these (Appendix 1).

*: Structurise, Systemise, Sanitise, Standardise, Self-discipline.

Required

(a)   Assess whether NJN's existing warehouse information system (WIS) is effective in reducing waste and adding value in NJN's workflow.   **(10 marks)**

(b)   Advise whether the three proposals suggested by the management consultant will help to eliminate the different types of waste identified under lean principles.   **(6 marks)**

(c)   Evaluate whether the application of each of the 5Ss following the warehouse reorganisation at NJN is adequately measured by the performance metrics in Appendix 1.

(9 marks)

(Total = 25 marks)

APPENDIX 1

Performance measures for 5ss relating to warehouse reorganisation

(1) Warehouse manager's daily assessment of the tidiness of the warehouse on a scale of 1–10.

(2) The proportion of inventory not stored in order of its alphabetical description with products with names beginning with 'A' nearest the despatch area and 'Z' furthest away.

(3) The number of accidents caused by goods being incorrectly stored or picked.

19 Great National Trains   49 mins

In contrast to many other countries, the railway system in Pecoland remains nationalised, and services are operated by Great National Trains (GNT). The Chairman of the GNT Railways Board reports to senior civil servants in the Ministry of Transport. However, Pecoland also has a rail regulator who has the power to make recommendations directly to the Minister of Transport in relation to all issues relating to the operation and performance of GNT.

The Rail Regulator's role is to ensure that the rail service in Pecoland is delivered in a safe and efficient manner, and in a way which provides high levels of satisfaction to all rail users. GNT's overall strategic objective is to deliver reliable, punctual and safe rail services to customers efficiently and cost effectively, while continuing to reduce its level of carbon emissions.

The Government views cost effectiveness as the key aspect of all public sector services in Pecoland, and it has also imposed the overriding financial objective that GNT should at least cover its operating costs from the revenue it earns.

Over the last ten years, GNT has made a significant investment in its rail network and its trains. Diesel trains are being replaced by electric trains following the electrification of the network.

There are three subsidiary companies within GNT:

(1) Passenger Co runs passenger rail services, which include express services between the major towns and cities, as well as slower services to more remote locations. (The number of services on some rural routes has been reduced significantly in recent years, due to the relatively low number of passengers using them. However, these cutbacks provoked strong opposition from groups of local residents who relied on the railways for their transport.)

(2) Freight Co runs freight services, transporting bulk goods such as coal and oil, and industrial products such as steel and cars, and a range of retail products for supermarkets and other retailers. Across the majority of the rail network, freight trains run on the same tracks as passenger trains, although there are a few lines (for example, to power stations) which are used exclusively by freight trains.

(3) Track Co is responsible for managing, and upgrading, the track, signalling and property; for example, station buildings.

The majority of Passenger Co's locomotives are now electric as the lines between all the major cities in Pecoland have already been electrified. Most of Freight Co's trains are hauled by diesel locomotives, but it has recently invested in a number of electric engines which are less harmful to the environment. Passenger Co contributes about 50% of GNT's total revenue.

Freight Co contributes about 40% of GNT's total revenue. Its share of the freight haulage market in Pecoland is approximately 10%, and the majority of freight is transported by road. However, the amount of freight carried by rail has begun to increase in recent years due to worsening congestion on Pecoland's roads.

A number of retailers in Pecoland are currently considering the impact of their supply chains on the environment and looking for ways to reduce the impacts of their supply chain. They are currently evaluating the environmental benefits of switching more of their deliveries from road to rail freight. However, the retailers, like many companies in Pecoland, also value the convenience of road freight, which allows goods to be delivered directly to their premises.

Key performance indicators (KPIs)

Each of the three subsidiary companies measures their performance against a range of KPIs, based upon meeting GNT's overall strategic objectives. Examples of the KPIs include:

Passenger Co

- The number of customer complaints received
- The percentage of trains arriving at their destination on time
- The number of signals passed at danger

Freight Co

- Train capacity utilisation (the actual load capacity as a proportion of the total available load capacity for a journey)

- The percentage of trains arriving at their destination on time

- Carbon emissions generated (per tonne transported per kilometre travelled)

- The number of signals passed at danger

Track Co

- The number of delays to services per month due to signalling failure
- The number of complaints per month relating to station cleanliness

In recent years, there have been suggestions that GNT is not providing a value for money service for rail users, and that the rail services in Pecoland should be privatised. The minister of transport and the Rail Regulator both oppose privatisation, however, and believe that retaining GNT under national control provides the best way of creating value from Pecoland's rail system over the medium and long term.

GNT produces an annual report, which summarises its financial and operating performance for the year, including statistics showing actual performance against target for the KPIs. The group management accountant collates all these figures for the annual report. The annual report also describes the governance structures within the organisation.

However, the rail regulator has recently recommended that GNT should produce an integrated report, because this would help to focus attention on the organisation's ability to create value in the medium and long term, as well as on its short-term performance. GNT's board is sceptical of the idea, feeling that the costs involved in producing the amount of non-financial information required for an integrated report will outweigh the benefits of doing so.

Required

(a) Discuss the difficulties faced by GNT, as a public sector organisation, in setting and measuring strategic objectives. **(10 marks)**

(b) Discuss the additional information which GNT would provide to its stakeholders in an integrated report, compared to its current annual report. **(6 marks)**

(c) Evaluate the potential impact on the amount and type of information prepared by the group management accountant if GNT starts to produce integrated reports, and the issues the management accountant could face in preparing that information. **(9 marks)**

(Total = 25 marks)

20 Amal (6/12, amended)

Company background and objectives

Amal Airline (Amal) is the national airline of Jayland. The airline's objective is to be the best premium global airline.

Recent events

Amal provides long- and short-haul services all over the world and is based at its hub at Jaycity airport. Amal has been hit by a worldwide reduction in air travel due to poor economic conditions. The most recent financial results show a loss and this has caused the board to reconsider its position and take action to address the changed environment.

Amal has cut its dividend in order to conserve cash and it is trying to rebuild profitability by reducing costs by 14%. The airline is capital intensive as it needs to maintain a large fleet of modern aircraft. The two major costs for the airline are staff and fuel. In trying to renegotiate working conditions and pay, the management have angered the unionised workforce. There has already been some strike action by the unions representing the aircraft crew and ground staff and more is threatened.

Additionally, the board is pushing forward a large project to improve the design of the company website in order to increase the number of passengers who check in online and so would not require as much assistance at the airport. The new design is also aiming to increase the number of passengers who book their tickets through the company's website rather than other resellers' websites or at booking agents.

The board has also been considering taking advantage of new technology in aircraft engines by making a large investment ($450m) in new low-noise, fuel-efficient aircraft in an effort to reduce the environmental complaints surrounding air travel and also cut costs.

Performance analysis

The chief executive officer (CEO) has provided the data for Amal and two of its main competitors (shown in Appendix 1). Kayland Air is a government-owned and run airline in the neighbouring country of Kayland. It has a similar mix of business to Amal and targets a similar market. Cheapo Air is currently one of the most successful of the new privately owned airlines that have gained significant market share over the last 15 years by offering a cheap but basic short-haul service to customers in and around Jayland. Cheapo Air subcontracts many of its activities in order to remain flexible. The CEO wants you to calculate some suitable performance measures and explain the results.

Big Data

The CEO believes that Amal could be making more use of Big Data. He has recently returned from a conference about 'Big Data in the Airline Industry' where one of the speakers talked about the benefits of Big Data in relation to four key areas:

- Identifying trends in passenger demand and using this to set prices

- Understanding and influencing the customer's selection process (in particular reducing the number of potential customers who start booking a flight online but do not go on to complete the transaction)

- Boosting revenue from in-flight sales by optimising the on-board store for individual flights

- Understanding customer sentiment and improving customer satisfaction

Amal currently offers the same selection of in-flight products on all its flights.

The CEO has asked you to explain how using Big Data in these four areas could help Amal improve its performance. However, he also wants to understand the potential implications that using Big Data could have for Amal's management information systems, given that a number of Amal's IT staff are already working on the website upgrade project.

Required

(a)   Using the data provided, analyse the three airlines using appropriate performance
        indicators and comment on your results.   **(12 marks)**

(b)   Explain how Big Data could be used to help Amal's performance, in relation to the four key
        areas identified at the conference.   **(8 marks)**

(c)   Discuss the potential implications of Big Data for Amal's management information systems.
                                                                                    (5 marks)

                                                                            (Total = 25 marks)

APPENDIX 1

Data provided by the CEO:

Data for the most recent calendar year

	Amal	Kayland Air	Cheapo Air
Passengers ('000)	23,649	38,272	35,624
Passenger kilometres (millions)	79,618	82,554	40,973
Revenue ($m)	5,430	7,350	2,170
Costs			
Fuel ($m)	1,480	1,823	535
Staff ($m)	1,560	2,998	238
Staff numbers	32,501	56,065	5,372
Operating profit ($m)	630	54	127
Number of aircraft	182	361	143
Average aircraft size (seats)	195	163	125
Seat kilometres (millions)	100,654	105,974	46,934

Note. A seat kilometre is generated for every one kilometre flown by an **available** seat on the
company's aircraft.

21 Chicory (Sept/Dec 17)   49 mins

Assume it is now December 20X7.

Company background

Chicory operates a chain of depots in Deeland, supplying and fitting tyres and other vehicle parts to lorries, buses and agricultural vehicles. Chicory's objective is to maximise shareholder wealth. Due to a slowdown in the Deeland economy, Chicory's recent performance has been weak. An unsuccessful acquisition has also caused cash flow problems and a write-off of goodwill of $24.7m in the year to 30 June 20X7.

Benchmarking exercise

The board has commissioned a benchmarking exercise to help improve Chicory's performance. This exercise will involve comparison of a range of financial and other operational performance indicators against Fennel, a similar business in Veeland. Fennel has agreed to share some recently available performance data with Chicory as they operate in different countries. The reason Fennel was chosen as a benchmark is that as well as supplying and fitting tyres and parts to heavy vehicles, a large part of Fennel's business involves supplying electricity to charging points to recharge electric cars. Fennel installs and operates the charging points in public places, and users pay Fennel for the electricity they use. The board of Chicory intends to follow a similar business model as the use of electric cars is increasing in Deeland.

The Veeland economy is growing strongly. Electric car use there has increased rapidly in the last two years, encouraged by tax incentives for businesses, like Fennel, to install and operate charging points. The Veeland government has also underwritten loans taken out by businesses to finance this technology, which has enabled Fennel to borrow funds for the significant capital investment required. The cost of components used in the charging points is falling rapidly. Capitalisation of development costs related to this technology is permitted in Veeland, but not in Deeland. In 20X5, Fennel invested heavily in IT systems which significantly improved performance by increasing the availability of parts in its depots, and reducing inventories.

Chicory uses return on average capital employed (ROCE) as its main financial performance indicator, and this is to be benchmarked against Fennel. One board member suggested that, though it may have some disadvantages, EBITDA (earnings before interest, tax, depreciation and amortisation) could have advantages as a performance measure over the existing measure, and should also be included in the benchmarking exercise.

You have been given the most recently available financial data for both businesses in Appendix 1, with the data for Fennel being converted into dollars ($) from its home currency.

Required

(a)   Evaluate the relative financial performance of Chicory against Fennel using the two financial performance measures identified in the benchmarking exercise and evaluate their use as performance measures in this situation.

(i)   ROCE   (6 marks)
(ii)   EBITDA   (10 marks)

(b)   Advise Chicory on the problems of using the benchmarking exercise with Fennel as a way to improve performance.   (9 marks)

(Total = 25 marks)

Benchmark data

Extract from statement of financial position

	30 June 20X7 Chicory $m	31 December 20X5 Fennel[1] $m
End of year		
Total assets	140.0	296.0
Current liabilities	(81.0)	(120.0)
Beginning of year (Note 1)		
Total assets	138.0	290.0
Current liabilities	(60.0)	(120.0)

Income statement

	30 June 20X7 Chicory $m	31 December 20X5 Fennel $m
Revenue	175.1	350.0
Cost of sales	(130.1)	(299.0)
Gross profit	45.0	51.0
Administrative expenses	(11.0)	(25.0)
Write off of goodwill	(24.7)	–
Operating profit (Note 2)	9.3	26.0
Interest payable	(1.8)	(8.0)
Profit before tax	7.5	18.0
Tax	(3.0)	(1.0)
Net profit	4.5	17.0

Notes

1     $6m of new capital was introduced into Fennel on 31 March 20X5. Normally, new net investment is spread evenly over the year.

2   Operating profit is after charging depreciation of non-current assets of $18m in Chicory, and $25m in Fennel.

22 Landual Lamps (6/13)   **49 mins**

Company background and organisational structure

Landual Lamps (Landual) manufactures and delivers floor and table lamps for homes and offices in Beeland. The company sells through its website and uses commercial logistics firms to deliver its products. The markets for its products are highly competitive. The company has traditionally relied on the high quality of its designs to drive demand for its products.

The company is divided into two divisions (components and assembly), plus a head office that provides design, administrative and marketing support. The manufacturing process involves:

(1)   The Components Division making the housing components and electrical components for the lamp. This is an intricate process as it depends on the specific design of the lamp and so serves as a significant source of competitive advantage for Landual.

(2)   The Assembly Division assembling the various components into a finished lamp ready for shipment. This is a simple process.

The finance director (FD) of Landual is currently overloaded with work due to changes in financial accounting policies that are being considered at board level. As a result, she has been unable to look at certain management accounting aspects of the business and has asked you to do a review of the transfer pricing policy between the Components and Assembly Divisions.

Transfer pricing policy

The current transfer pricing policy at Landual is as follows:

- Market prices for electrical components are used as these are generic components for which there is a competitive external market.

- Prices for housing components based on total actual production costs to the Components Division are used as there is no external market for these components since they are specially designed for Landual's products.

Currently, the Components Division produces only for the Assembly Division in order to meet overall demand without the use of external suppliers for housing and electrical components. If the Components Division were to sell its electrical components externally, then additional costs of $269,000 would arise for transport, marketing and bad debts.

Potential changes

The FD is considering two separate changes within Landual: one to the transfer pricing policy, and a second one to the divisional structure.

First, the transfer pricing policy for housing components would change to use variable cost to the Components Division. The FD wants to know the impact of the change in transfer pricing policy on the existing results of the two divisions and the company. (No change is proposed to the transfer price of the electrical components.)

Second, as can be seen from the divisional performance report below, the two divisions are currently treated as profit centres. The FD is considering splitting the Components Division into two further separate divisions: an Electrical Components Division and a Housing Components Division. If the board agrees to this proposal, then the Housing Components Division will be treated as a cost centre only, charging its total production cost to the Assembly Division. The Electrical Components and Assembly Divisions will remain as profit centres.

The FD needs to understand the impact of this proposed new divisional structure on divisional performance assessment and on the company as a whole. She has asked that, in order to keep the discussion on the new divisional structure simple, you use the existing transfer pricing policy to do illustrative calculations. She stated that she would reallocate head office costs to the two new components divisions in proportion to their cost of sales.

Financial and other information for Landual is provided in Appendix 1.

Required

(a) Evaluate the current system of transfer pricing at Landual, using illustrative calculations as appropriate. **(10 marks)**

(b) Advise the FD on the impact of changing the transfer pricing policy for housing components as suggested by the FD and comment on your results, using illustrative calculations as appropriate. **(6 marks)**

(c) Evaluate the impact of the change in proposed divisional structure on the profit in the divisions and the company as directed by the FD. **(9 marks)**

(Total = 25 marks)

APPENDIX 1

ACTUAL DATA FOR LANDUAL FOR THE YEAR ENDED 31 MARCH 20X3

	Components Division $'000	Assembly Division $'000	Landual $'000
Sales:			
Electrical	1,557		
Housing	8,204		
Sub-total	9,761	15,794	15,794
Cost of sales:			
Electrical	804	1,557	
Housing	6,902	8,204	
Sub-total	7,706	9,761	7,706
Fixed production costs:			
Electrical	370		
Housing	1,302		
Sub-total	1,672	1,268	2,940
Allocated head office costs	461	2,046	2,507
Profit	(78)	2,719	2,641

Note. The Components Division has had problems meeting budgets recently, with an adverse variance of $575,000 in the last year. This variance arises in relation to the cost of sales for housing component production.

23 Laudan Advertising Agency (Sep/Dec 16)   49 mins

Company background, and objectives

Laudan Advertising Agency (LAA) is based in Geeland and has three autonomous subsidiaries: A, B and C. All three subsidiaries are profit centres and LAA seeks to maximise the long-term wealth of its shareholders. A is based in Geeland, while both B and C are located in other parts of the world. LAA is a highly respected advertising agency, which in the last five years has created advertising campaigns for 25 of the world's top 100 most recognised brands.

LAA's four key objectives published on its website are to:

- Delight our clients by the quality of our work
- Provide excellent value for money to our clients
- Give our clients access to specialist and local knowledge
- Ensure our clients return to us time after time

There are three main functions within LAA:

(1) Campaign management, which involves researching and understanding clients' requirements and budgets and designing a suitable advertising campaign for them

(2) Creative design, which is where the visual appearance of the advert and graphics are created

(3) Media buying, which negotiates prices with, and buys advertising time and space from, magazine and newspaper publishers, internet search engines and TV companies

Each subsidiary has its own department for campaign management and for media buying. Only A, however, has a creative design department.

The directors at LAA believe that without visually appealing design, any advertising campaign is unlikely to be successful and meet the expectations of the client. They identified the importance of being able to produce high quality creative design as a critical success factor for the business.

Two years ago, they decided to concentrate all of LAA's creative design at a 'centre of design excellence' within A. The intention was to improve the quality of creative design within the business by giving staff access to the latest design technology, and by attracting the most talented designers to work there.

Additional key performance indicator

To encourage the three subsidiaries to use the internal creative design department within A, instead of external third-party design agencies, the directors created a new additional key performance indicator on which to appraise the performance of all subsidiaries and of subsidiary managers:

- All subsidiaries, including A, must purchase at least 90% of creative design work internally from A.

Prior to the introduction of this performance indicator, 40% of creative design work in each of the three subsidiaries was purchased from external design agencies.

The directors of LAA have become concerned that the introduction of the new key performance indicator may be causing managers to operate in ways which are not helping to meet LAA's stated objectives. They have asked for comments from subsidiary managers (Appendix 1) about whether they have met the 90% target in the most recent period and, if not, to explain why this is.

Required

(a)   Evaluate how the following help LAA to manage performance in order to achieve its stated objectives:

   (i)   Identifying the critical success factor of producing high quality creative design; and

   (ii)   Setting the key performance indicator for the requirement to purchase 90% of design work internally.   **(8 marks)**

(b)   Assess the need for a formal transfer pricing policy at LAA.   **(9 marks)**

(c)   Advise the directors whether LAA should use a market value transfer price as suggested by the manager of Subsidiary C.   **(8 marks)**

(Total = 25 marks)

APPENDIX 1

Subsidiary managers' comments on achievement of KPI for 90% creative design work purchased internally

Subsidiary A

'A purchased 86% of design work from our internal design department in the period. It would have been almost 100%, but we won a large order for a new client who operates in a specialised industry of which we have no experience. As a result, we had to use the services of a specialised external design agency, which was much more expensive than using our in-house team.'

Subsidiary B

'B purchased 62% of design work internally in the period. Though the quality of the designs is very good, they were more appealing to consumers in Geeland than here in Veeland, where B operates. The internal design department did not seem to understand consumer preferences in Veeland, and many of their designs were rejected by a key client of ours. As a result, an important advertising campaign missed key deadlines, by which time the internal design department had insufficient capacity to finish the work and we had to use an external agency.

As there is no formal transfer pricing policy in place at LAA, the basis of the transfer price charged by the internal design department is also unclear to us. It appears to be based on full cost of the design work, including apportioned overheads and an allowance for bad debts and marketing expenses, plus a very substantial mark-up. We have spent a long time trying to negotiate this price with A, which is much more expensive than external designers. Furthermore, we are currently being investigated by the tax authorities here in Veeland who have indicated that the prices charged by A for design do seem well in excess of market rates.'

BPP
LEARNING
MEDIA

Subsidiary C

'C purchased 91% of design work from the internal design department in the period, as well as achieving all our other performance targets. A key client of ours ran a major advertising campaign during the period. We used the internal design department for the first time for this campaign, instead of the usual external agency that we have used in the past for work for this client. The client was very unhappy with the extra cost that this incurred, as the number of design hours and the hourly rate was much higher than for previous campaigns. The internal design department refused to reduce the price after long negotiations and we had to give a large discount to the client before they would settle our invoice. As a result, our gross profit margin for the period was significantly reduced.

It would be much fairer if the transfer price charged by A was based on the market price of the services provided.'

24 Jenson, Lewis and Webb (Mar/Jun 17)   49 mins

Company background and objectives

Jenson, Lewis and Webb (JLW) manufactures tubes of acrylic paint for sale to artists and craft shops in Kayland and Seeland. JLW has two divisions, Domestic Division and Export Division, both based in Kayland. All costs are incurred in Kayland dollars ($KL). Domestic Division is an investment centre and sells only to customers in Kayland. Export Division is a profit centre and exports all its products to Seeland, where customers are invoiced in Seeland pounds (£SL), at prices fixed at the start of the year. The objective of JLW is to maximise shareholder wealth.

Capital expenditure

At the beginning of the year ended 31 December 20X6, the head office at JLW purchased new production machinery for Export Division for $KL2.5m, which significantly increased the production efficiency of the division. Managers at Domestic Division were considering purchasing a similar machine, but decided to delay the purchase until the beginning of the following financial year. On 30 June 20X6 the $KL weakened by 15% against the £SL, after which the exchange rate between the two currencies has remained unchanged.

Performance appraisal

The managers of the two divisions are currently appraised on the performance of their own divisions, and are awarded a large bonus if the net profit margin of their division exceeds 8% for the year. Extracts from the management accounts for the year ended 31 December 20X6 for both divisions are given in Appendix 1. On being told that she would not be receiving a bonus for the financial year, the manager of Export division has commented that she has had difficulty in understanding the bonus calculations for her division as it is not based on traceable profit, which would consider only items which relate directly to the division. She also does not believe it is appropriate that the net profit margin used to appraise her performance is the same as 'that which is used to evaluate the performance of Export division itself'. She has asked for a meeting with the directors to discuss this further.

JLW's directors intend to award divisional managers' bonuses on the basis of net profit margin achieved in 20X6 as planned, but have asked you as a performance management consultant for your advice on the comments of the export division manager in advance of their meeting with her. One director has also suggested that, in future, economic value added (EVA™) may be a good way to evaluate and compare the performance of the two divisions. You are asked for your advice on this too, but you have been specifically asked not to attempt a calculation of EVA™.

Required

(a) Evaluate the comments of the export division manager that the net profit margin used to appraise her own performance should be different from that used to appraise the performance of the Export Division itself.   **(7 marks)**

(b) Recommend, using appropriate calculations, whether the manager of the Export Division should receive her bonus for the year.   **(8 marks)**

(c)   Advise whether the use of economic value added (EVA™) is an appropriate measure of performance of the divisions. You are not required to perform an EVA™ calculation. **(10 marks)**

(Total = 25 marks)

APPENDIX 1 – EXTRACTS FROM MANAGEMENT ACCOUNTS FOR YEAR ENDED 31 DECEMBER 20X6

	Export Division $KL'000	Domestic Division $KL'000
Revenue (Note 1)	8,000	12,000
Cost of sales	(4,800)	(7,800)
Gross profit	3,200	4,200
Depreciation	(395)	(45)
Allocated head office costs	(360)	(540)
Other overheads (Note 2)	(1,900)	(2,300)
Net profit	545	1,315
Net profit margin on revenue	6.8%	11.0%
Capital employed (Note 3)	6,500	8,500

Notes

1   Revenue accrues evenly over the financial year.

2   Other overheads for Domestic Division include the creation of a bad debt provision equivalent to $KL75,000 for a wholesale customer who had financial difficulties during the year, and $KL90,000 for advertising a new range of paints launched at the end of the year.

3   JLW is financed in equal proportions by debt and equity. The cost of equity is 8% and the after tax cost of debt is 5%.

25 Stillwater Services (12/12, amended)   49 mins

Company background

Stillwater Services (SS) is a listed water utility company providing water and sewage services to the public and businesses of a region of Teeland. The company was formed when the government-owned Public Water Company of Teeland was broken up into regional utility companies (one of which was SS) and sold into private ownership over four years ago.

Industry regulator

As a vital utility for the economy of Teeland, water services are a government-regulated industry. The regulator is principally concerned that SS does not abuse its monopoly position in the regional market to unjustifiably increase prices. The majority of services (80%) are controlled by the regulator who sets an acceptable return on capital employed (ROCE) level and ensures that the pricing of SS within these areas does not breach this level. The remaining services, such as a bottled water operation and a contract repairs service, are unregulated and SS can charge a market rate for these. The regulator calculates its ROCE figure based on its own valuation of the capital assets being used in regulated services and the operating profit from those regulated services.

The target pre-tax ROCE set by the regulator is 6%. If SS were to breach this figure, then the regulator could fine the company. In the past, other such companies have seen fines amounting to millions of dollars.

Economic value added (EVA™)

The board of SS is trying to drive the performance for the benefit of the shareholders. This is a new experience for many at SS, having been in the public sector until four years ago. In order to try to better communicate the objective of maximising shareholder wealth, the board has decided to introduce economic value added (EVA™) as the key performance indicator.

BPP LEARNING MEDIA

The finance director has asked you to calculate EVA™ for the company, based on the following financial information for the year ending 30 September 20X2:

Stillwater Services

	Regulated $m	Non-regulated $m	20X2 total $m
Revenue	276.0	69.0	345.0
Operating costs	230.0	47.0	277.0
Operating profit	46.0	22.0	68.0
Finance charges			23.0
Profit before tax			45.0
Tax at 25%			9.5
Profit after tax			35.5

Capital employed:	20X2 $m	20X1 $m
Measured from published accounts	657.0	637.0
Measured by regulator (for regulated services only)	779.0	761.0

Notes

1   Total operating costs include:

	20X2 $m	20X1 $m
Depreciation	59	57
Provision for doubtful debts	2	0.5
Research and development	12	–
Other non-cash items	7	6

2   Economic depreciation is assessed to be $83m in 20X2.

   Economic depreciation includes any appropriate amortisation adjustments.

   In previous years, it can be assumed that economic and accounting depreciation were the same.

3   Tax is the cash paid in the current year ($9m) and an adjustment of $0.5m for deferred tax provisions. There was no deferred tax balance prior to 20X2.

4   The provision for doubtful debts was $4.5m on the 20X2 statement of financial position.

5   Research and development is not capitalised in the accounts.

   It relates to a new project that will be developed over five years and is expected to be of long-term benefit to the company. 20X2 is the first year of this project.

6   Cost of capital of SS

   Equity   16%
   Debt (pre-tax)   5%

7   Gearing of SS

   40% equity
   60% debt

Required

(a)   Evaluate the performance of SS using EVA™.   **(13 marks)**

(b)   With reference to the issues involved in managing different stakeholder groups, analyse the potential influence of the regulator, the directors, and the shareholders on performance management at SS.   **(5 marks)**

(c)   Assess whether SS meets its regulatory ROCE target and comment on the impact of such a constraint on performance management at SS.   **(7 marks)**

(Total = 25 marks)

26 Essland Police Forces (12/13)   49 mins

You are a performance management expert brought in by the chief executive officer (CEO) of the Department of the Interior for the country of Essland. The department is a branch of the Essland Government which handles security, policing, immigration and border control. The CEO is a civil servant and he reports to the Minister for the Interior. The Minister for the Interior is an elected politician selected by the Prime Minister of Essland, who leads its government.

League tables

The newly elected Minister for the Interior has instructed the CEO to implement his policy for improving the regional police forces' performance by copying the method used for schools. In a recent initiative by the School's Ministry, a league table for the hundreds of schools in Essland was created, showing the best and worst in terms of examination performance only, in order to motivate senior school managers to improve. The league table was used to create targets for assessing the schools' and their managers' performance. Additionally, parents in Essland have the right to choose which school their children attend and so often base their selection on league table performance. Therefore, the Minister has had a policy review body draw up a method of creating a league table for the police forces.

The CEO has requested your help to clarify his own thinking on this new policy for the four regional police forces in Essland (Cashire (C), Dashire (D), Eshire (E) and Fashire (F)). The CEO needs you to assess the use of the league table using the policy review body's suggested method and has collected the data and calculation of the league table given in Appendix 1 to assist you. He also wants to assess whether the table will help in meeting the Department's aim and goals for the police.

Aim and goals

The overall aim of the Department (and its police forces) is 'to provide a value-for-money service to ensure that the community can live in safety with confidence in their physical and legal security'. The detailed goals of the Department are to:

- Tackle the underlying causes of crime and achieve long-term sustainable solutions
- Bring perpetrators to justice
- Provide protection and support for individuals and communities at risk of harm
- Respond to community needs by being accessible and engaging with their concerns

The CEO warned you, 'I'm not interested in the performance of the forces. I'm interested in the method of assessment, so don't waste time with your ideas on how to improve actual policing.'

The CEO also wishes to understand the strengths and weaknesses of the use of a league table, its link to targets and the likely reaction of employees to this system of performance management, especially as there is a strong union representing the police. He is worried about the employees' attitude to the introduction of the system and its effects on their behaviour and their sense of accountability. He is also concerned about importing the use of a league table from the schools sector, as it might not be appropriate here.

Required

(a) Evaluate the method of calculating and measuring the force scores for use in the league table in achieving the Department of the Interior's aims and goals. **(14 marks)**

(b) Discuss the merits of league tables in performance management and address the CEO's concerns over their use in managing the performance of Essland's police forces. **(11 marks)**

(Total = 25 marks)

APPENDIX 1

The appendix defines the policy review body's method for scoring each force, provides the basic data for each force and then calculates the current force score placing the forces into a league table:

Force score = Rank 1 × 0.25 + Rank 2 × 0.25 + Rank 3 × 0.25 + Rank 4 × 0.25

Where each rank is the ranking from 4 to 1 which each force gets for each of the following variables (4 is best, 1 is worst):

- Rank 1 is based on the number of crimes per 10,000 of population.
- Rank 2 is based on the solution rate for crimes reported in the year.
- Rank 3 is based on the user satisfaction score (based on a survey of the population).
- Rank 4 is based on the percentage of calls to police answered within ten seconds.

For example, a force which was top ranked in each of the ranks would get a force score of 4 (= 4 × 0.25 + 4 × 0.25 + 4 × 0.25 + 4 × 0.25).

Data by region:
For the calendar year 20X2

	C	D	E	F
Population	1,250,000	900,000	1,700,000	1,500,000
Number of crimes reported in year	62,500	47,250	83,300	63,000
Number of crimes solved in year	31,250	22,680	45,815	33,390
User satisfaction score	71%	80%	73%	68%
Percentage of calls to police answered within ten seconds	92%	93%	91%	94%
Number of police force employees	6,200	4,400	8,500	7,900
Cost of police force for year ($m)	404	298	572	510

Calculation of force score:

	C	D	E	F
Number of reported crimes per 10,000 of population	500	525	490	420
Rank 1	2	1	3	4
Solution rate for crimes reported in year	50%	48%	55%	53%
Rank 2	2	1	4	3
Rank 3 (user satisfaction)	2	4	3	1
Rank 4 (call handling)	2	3	1	4
Force score	2	2.25	2.75	3

The league table for 20X2 is:

	Force	Score
1.	F	3.00
2.	E	2.75
3.	D	2.25
4.	C	2.00

Note. You should assume that the calculations in Appendix 1 are accurate.

27 Beeshire Local Authority (12/14)   49 mins

Waste collection in Beeshire

Beeshire Local Authority (BLA) is a local government body which provides a range of services for the area of Beeshire within the country of Seeland. Beeshire is a wealthy area within the country with many tourist attractions. One of BLA's tasks is to ensure that waste is collected from the homes and businesses in Beeshire. The goal for BLA's Waste Management Department is 'to maintain Beeshire as a safe, clean and environmentally friendly place where people and businesses want to both stay in and return to'. The need for waste collection is linked to public health concerns, the desire to keep the streets clean and attractive and the desire to increase the amount of rubbish which is recycled. BLA is funded through a single local tax and does not charge its residents or businesses separately for most of its services, including waste collection. There is no public or political appetite for outsourcing services such as waste management.

Waste collection is performed by the workforce using a fleet of vehicles. The waste is either taken to recycling plants or else to landfill sites for burying. BLA obtains revenues from all the recycled waste but this only just covers the cost of running the recycling facilities.

Against a background estimate that waste will increase by 1% p.a. in the future, the national Government has ordered local authorities, such as BLA, to promote the recycling of waste and has set a target of 40% of all waste to be recycled by 2015. In order to discourage the creation of non-recyclable waste, the Government has imposed a levy per tonne of waste buried in landfill sites and has stated that this levy will rise over the next five years in order to encourage continuing improvement in the amount of recycled waste.

Performance measures

Currently, Seeland is in a long recession and so local authority revenues have fallen as tax revenues reflect the poor state of the economy. Along with other local authorities, BLA has tried to cut costs and so has focused on financial measures of performance. In a recent, private meeting, the chief executive of BLA was heard to say 'keep costs under control and we will worry about quality of service only when complaint levels build to an unacceptable level'. As one of the area's largest employers, cutting staff numbers has been very difficult for BLA due to the impact on the local economy and the reaction of the residents.

The current performance indicators used at BLA are drawn from the existing information systems with national figures given for comparison. Those relating to waste collection for the year ending 31 March 20X4 are shown in Appendix 1.

Required

(a) Explain why non-financial indicators are particularly useful for public sector organisations, illustrating your answer with brief examples relevant to BLA. **(6 marks)**

(b) Explain how the value for money provision of waste services by BLA should be assessed by suggesting and calculating justified performance indicators using the information in the scenario. **(12 marks)**

(c) Discuss the difficulties of measuring qualitative factors of performance, suggesting appropriate solutions for BLA. **(7 marks)**

(Total = 25 marks)

APPENDIX 1

BLA – Performance information for year ending 31 March 20X4

			BLA	National total
Total cost	($m)		250	2,850
Volume of waste				
	landfilled	(tonnes)	1,250,000	13,750,000
	recycled	(tonnes)	950,000	9,500,000
	total	(tonnes)	2,200,000	23,250,000
No. of staff			3,500	39,900
Staff cost	($m)		110	1,190
No. of households			2,380,952	26,190,476
No. of complaints about waste uncollected			18,250	200,750

	BLA	National average
Frequency of waste collections (days)	14	12

Notes on BLA data

1   Cost data and number of households comes from BLA's financial systems.

2   Waste data comes from weighing lorries at the landfill sites and recycling facilities.

3   Staff data is collected from BLA's HR system.

4   Complaints data is based on numbers of letters and phone calls to the Waste Management Department.

5   Frequency of collection data is obtained from the department's vehicle schedules.

28 Teeland Universities (Mar/Jun 16)   49 mins

Objectives

Universities in Teeland have three stated objectives:

(1)   To improve the overall standard of education of citizens in Teeland

(2)   To engage in high quality academic research

(3)   To produce well-qualified university graduates to meet the needs of the graduate jobs market in Teeland

Government funding

Each university is funded by a fixed sum of money from the Teeland Government according to the number of students studying there. In addition, universities receive extra funds from the Government and also from other organisations, such as large businesses and charities. These funds are used to support academic research.

Following the onset of an economic recession, the Teeland Government has stated its intention to reduce spending on publicly funded services such as the universities.

Proposal to introduce league tables

One senior politician, following his recent visit to neighbouring Veeland, was controversially quoted as saying:

> The universities in Veeland offer much better value for money for the citizens there compared to our universities here in Teeland. There are 25 students for each member of academic staff in Veeland, whereas in Teeland, the average number is 16, and yet, the standard of education of citizens is much higher in Veeland. The Veeland Government sets targets for many aspects of the services delivered by all the universities in Veeland. Furthermore, league tables of the performance of individual universities are published on the internet, and university leaders are given bonuses if their university falls within the top quarter of the league table. In Veeland, the system of performance measurement of the universities is considered so important that there is a special government department of 150 staff just to measure it.

He went on to add:

> I want to see a similar system of league tables, targets and bonuses for university leaders being introduced here in Teeland. To appear near the top of the league tables, I think we should expect each university to increase the number of graduates entering graduate jobs by at least 5% each year. I would also like to see other steps taken to increase value for money, such as reducing the number of academic staff in each university and reducing the salary of newly recruited academic staff.

You have been asked to advise the Teeland Government on the measurement of value for money of the universities and the proposed introduction of league tables for comparing their performance.

Appendix 1 contains details and existing performance data relating to four of the best known universities in Teeland.

Northcity University is famous for its high teaching standards and outstanding academic research in all subjects. As such, it attracts the most able students from all parts of the world to study there.

Southcity University is a large university in the capital city of Teeland and offers courses in a wide range of subjects, though most of the funding it receives for academic research is for science and technology, in which it is particularly successful.

Eastcity University is a small university specialising in the teaching of arts and humanities subjects such as history and geography.

Westcity University currently offers less strict entry standards to attract students from more diverse backgrounds, who may not normally have the opportunity of a university education.

Required

(a) Advise the Teeland Government how it could assess the value for money of the universities in Teeland, using the performance data in Appendix 1. **(12 marks)**

(b) Assess the potential benefits of league tables for improving the performance of universities in Teeland and discuss the problems of implementing the proposal to introduce league tables. **(13 marks)**

(Total = 25 marks)

APPENDIX 1

Existing university performance data

	North	South	East	West
Number of students	17,600	30,400	5,200	11,200
Number of academic staff	1,750	2,400	485	625
Entry requirements (Note 1)	100	77	72	48
Total annual payroll cost of academic staff	$109m	$149m	$20m	$37m
Graduate jobs filled each year (Note 2)	4,180	6,555	1,154	1,750
Funds received for academic research	$491m	$474m	$26m	$14m
TSOR survey rating (Note 3)	84%	76%	73%	90%
Position in league table (Note 4)	1	11	14	21

Key to performance data

Notes

1. Entry requirements represent students' average attainment in examinations prior to entering university. The entry requirement of the highest ranking university is scored as 100, with the score of all other universities being in proportion to that score.

2. The number of graduates each year who go on to further study or who begin jobs normally undertaken by university graduates. In Teeland, students attend university for an average of 3.2 years.

3. The Teeland students overall satisfaction rating (TSOR) survey is undertaken by the Teeland Government to assess students' overall satisfaction with the standard of teaching, the social and support aspects of university life and their optimism for their own future job prospects.

4. The Education Department of the Teeland Government has produced a provisional league table ranking the overall performance of each of the 45 universities in Teeland, with 1 being the highest ranking university. This has been compiled using a number of performance measures, weighted according to what the Government believes are the most important of these measures.

BPP
LEARNING
MEDIA

29 Tosemary and Rhyme Hospital (Sept/Dec 17) 49 mins

Organisational background

Tosemary and Rhyme Hospital (TRH) is a small hospital for the treatment of patients with only minor injuries. Patients arriving at TRH with more serious injuries are referred to a larger hospital nearby. Those with minor injuries are admitted into TRH and wait to be seen by a doctor. After treatment, most patients leave the hospital and need not return. If their treatment has failed, however, they are re-admitted for additional treatment.

Patients do not have to pay for treatment at TRH, which is a not-for-profit, public sector hospital. It is funded entirely by the government from taxation and a fixed level of funding is received from the government each year. It is up to TRH to allocate its funding to different areas, such as doctors' salaries, medicines and all other costs required to run a hospital.

Objectives

TRH's objectives are:

- To give prompt access to high quality medical treatment for patients

- To provide value for money for the taxpayer, as measured by the '3Es' framework of economy, efficiency and effectiveness

- To contribute to medical science by developing innovative ways to deliver treatment to patients

Concerns about performance measurement systems

It has been suggested to TRH that the hospital has inadequate performance measurement systems in place to assess whether it is achieving its objectives, and that insufficient attention is given to the importance of non-financial performance indicators. You have been asked for your advice, and have met with some of the doctors to get their opinions.

One senior doctor has told you:

> I think TRH always delivers value for money. We've always achieved our total financial budgets. Doctors here work much longer hours than colleagues in other hospitals, often without being paid for working overtime. There is not enough government funding to recruit more doctors. At busy times, we've started referring more patients arriving at TRH to the larger hospital nearby. This has helped reduce average waiting times. Patients arriving at TRH are now seen by a doctor within 3 hours 50 minutes rather than 4 hours as was previously the case. So, we're already doing all we can. I don't know how much time we spend developing innovative ways to deliver treatment to patients though, as most of the performance data we doctors receive relates to financial targets.

Recent performance data for TRH and national average information has been provided in Appendix 1. This is indicative of the data which the doctors at TRH receive.

Required

(a) Explain why non-financial performance indicators are particularly important to measure the performance of not-for-profit organisations such as TRH.   **(5 marks)**

(b) Justify one performance measure for each of the components of the value for money framework used at TRH and, using the measure, evaluate whether TRH is delivering value for money.   **(10 marks)**

(c) Evaluate the extent to which the management style at TRH can be said to be budget constrained and advise on the implications of this approach for managing TRH's performance.   **(10 marks)**

(Total = 25 marks)

APPENDIX 1

Data for the year ended 31 August 20X7

	TRH	National average (Note 1)
Number of doctors	25	24
Total doctors' salaries including overtime	$3.75m	$4.20m
Total doctors' salaries budget including overtime	$3.75m	$3.20m
Number of patients treated	24,375	20,000
Average staff satisfaction rating (Note 2)	9%	89%
Number of patients re-admitted	1,830	300

Notes

1   National average for other public sector minor injuries hospitals.

2   Staff satisfaction rating was obtained by conducting a survey of all 25 doctors. A survey score of 100% represents 'totally satisfied', and a score of 0% represents totally unsatisfied.

30 Coruisk (3/20)   49 mins

Exhibit 1: Company information

Coruisk is a clothing manufacturer in Teeland which produces a range of dresses that it sells to Ericht. The range of dresses are the only products which Coruisk produces and Ericht is its only customer.

Ericht is a well-known retailer in Teeland. Ericht has recently been affected by changes in consumer purchasing preferences to buying clothes online and, as a result, is keen to reduce its inventory holding as a way of reducing its costs. Ericht is also finding that it has an excess of goods which it has to discount as consumer tastes appear to change more quickly than in the past.

Exhibit 2: Current purchasing policy

Coruisk currently obtains its raw material from four suppliers. Each of these suppliers operates differently in terms of the processes and procedures which they adopt in trading with Coruisk. Coruisk has been agreeable to this, as the quality of the raw material supplied has generally been acceptable.

More recently, however, Coruisk has found reason to question the accuracy and quality of the raw material delivered from one supplier. Additionally, another supplier now only despatches material to Coruisk in full-load quantities, as it wishes to optimise the use of its delivery vehicles.

Exhibit 3: Current production methods

The performance metric at Coruisk for production efficiency is the number of dresses produced per period. Coruisk's method of production is to produce individual dresses in long production runs, which has helped in maximising output.

Staff working in the production department have their bonus based on this metric. Goods which have not been produced to the required standard have traditionally been rejected at the end of the production process. Coruisk's production control manager has indicated to you that the current production methods have been successful, as the company only has 5% of its goods returned from Ericht due to poor quality.

Exhibit 4: JIT and costs of quality

Ericht would like to move to a just-in-time (JIT) system of purchasing its goods from Coruisk. The board of Coruisk has asked you for help, as a management consultant, to advise it as to how the company may have to change its approach to the areas of purchasing and production to prepare itself for producing to JIT principles.

The chief executive officer (CEO) does not believe that the company will encounter any problems in adapting to Ericht's requirements and has told you:

> We have very good quality control practices and procedures in place and are confident that we are consistently supplying goods which are required at an acceptable price and at high quality. Our practice of testing goods at the final stage of production, and before they leave the factory, supports this.

Coruisk's CEO has also made available to you a list of costs which she believes address all relevant costs of quality. These costs are detailed in Appendix 1. The headings for a cost of quality report are also supplied in this appendix. She indicated that some of these costs have never been measured before and have been given financial values to help you give advice. She also told you that Coruisk's current revenue is $4.5m.

Required

It is now 1 September 20X5.

(a) Assess the changes which Coruisk will have to make in the areas of purchasing and production in order to supply goods to Ericht on a JIT basis. **(13 marks)**

(b) Prepare a cost of quality report for Coruisk based on the information in Appendix 1 and comment on potential quality cost changes in light of the proposed move to JIT.

(12 marks)

(Total = 25 marks)

Exhibit 5: APPENDIX 1

CEO's estimates of quality related costs

	$'000
Estimated costs of handling complaints from Ericht	135
Material costs	2,000
Scrap (cannot be reworked)	58
Quality control supervisor's salary (employed full time)	35
Rework cost	72
Machine downtime	38
Product recalls and cost of goods returned	180
Labour cost of production	800
Quality audit	2
Foregone contribution from lost sales (estimated)*	85
Routine maintenance	8

Cost of quality report headings

Costs of conformance:

Prevention costs

Appraisal costs

Costs of non-conformance:

Internal failure costs

External failure costs

* The foregone contribution from lost sales is an estimate made by the CEO of potential sales lost to Ericht due to problems related to production and delivery experienced by Coruisk.

31 Navier Aerials (6/13)   49 mins

Company background

Navier Aerials Co (Navier) manufactures satellite dishes for receiving satellite television signals. Navier supplies the major satellite TV companies which install standard satellite dishes for their customers. The company also manufactures and installs a small number of specialised satellite dishes to individuals or businesses with specific needs resulting from poor reception in their locations.

Cost reduction programme

The chief executive officer (CEO) wants to initiate a programme of cost reduction at Navier. His plan is to use activity-based management (ABM) to allocate costs more accurately and to identify non value adding activities. The first department to be analysed is the Customer Care Department, as it has been believed for some time that the current method of cost allocation is giving unrealistic results for the two product types.

At present, the finance director (FD) absorbs the cost of customer care into the product cost on a per unit basis using the data in Table 1 in the Appendix. He then tries to correct the problem of unrealistic costing, by making rough estimates of the costs to be allocated to each product based on the operations director's impression of the amount of work of the department. In fact, he simply adds $100 above the standard absorbed cost to the cost of a specialised dish to cover the assumed extra work involved at customer care.

The cost accountant has gathered information for the Customer Care Department in Table 2 (in the Appendix) from interviews with the finance and customer care staff. She has used this information to correctly calculate the total costs of each activity using activity-based costing in Table 3 (in the Appendix). The CEO wants you, as a senior management accountant, to complete the work required for a comparison of the results of the current standard absorption costing to activity-based costing for the standard and specialised dishes.

Once this is done, the CEO wants you to consider the implications for management of the customer care process of the costs of each activity in that department. The CEO is especially interested in how this information may impact on the identification of non value added activities and quality management at Navier.

Required

(a) Evaluate the impact of using activity-based costing, compared to the existing costing system for customer care, on the cost of both types of product.   **(13 marks)**

(b) Assess how the information on each activity can be used and improved upon at Navier in assisting cost reduction and quality management in the Customer Care Department.

Note. There is no need to make comments on the different product types here.   **(12 marks)**

(Total = 25 marks)

APPENDIX

Navier Dishes: Information for the year ending 31 March 20X3

Customer care (CC) Department

Table 1: Existing costing data

	$'000
Salaries	400
Computer time	165
Telephone	79
Stationery and sundries	27
Depreciation of equipment	36
	707

Note. CC cost is currently allocated to each dish based on 16,000 orders a year, where each order contains an average of 5.5 dishes.

Table 2: Activity-costing data

Activities of CC dept	Staff time	Comments
Handling enquiries and preparing quotes for potential orders	40%	Relates to 35,000 enquiries/quotes per year
Receiving actual orders	10%	Relates to 16,000 orders in the year
Customer credit checks	10%	Done once an order is received
Supervision of orders through manufacture to delivery	15%	
Complaints handling	25%	Relates to 3,200 complaints per year

Notes

1   Total department cost is allocated using staff time as this drives all of the other costs in the department.

2   90% of both enquiries and orders are for standard dishes. The remainder are for specialised dishes.

3   Handling enquiries and preparing quotes for specialised dishes takes 20% of staff time allocated to this activity.

4   The process for receiving an order, checking customer credit and supervision of the order is the same for both a specialised dish order and a standard dish order.

5   50% of the complaints received are for specialised dish orders.

6   Each standard dish order contains an average of six dishes.

7   Each specialised dish order contains an average of one dish.

Table 3: Activity-based costs

	Total $	Standard $	Specialised $
Handling enquiries and preparing quotes	282,800	226,240	56,560
Receiving actual orders	70,700	63,630	7,070
Customer credit checks	70,700	63,630	7,070
Supervision of order through manufacture to delivery	106,050	95,445	10,605
Complaints handling	176,750	88,375	88,375
Total	707,000	537,320	169,680

32 Tench (12/11, amended)   49 mins

Company and industry background

Tench Cars (Tench) is a large national car manufacturing business. It is based in Essland, a country that has recently turned from state communism to democratic capitalism. The car industry had been heavily supported and controlled by the bureaucracy of the old regime. The Government had stipulated production and employment targets for the business but had ignored profit as a performance measure. Tench is now run by a new generation of capitalist businesspeople intent on rejuvenating the company's fortunes.

The company has a strong position within Essland, which has a population of 200 million and forms the majority of Tench's market. However, the company has also traditionally achieved a good market share in six neighbouring countries due to historic links and shared culture between them and Essland. All of these markets are experiencing growing car ownership as political and market reforms lead to greater wealth in a large proportion of the population. Additionally, the new Government in Essland is deregulating markets and opening the country to imports of foreign vehicles.

Current plans

Tench's management recognises that it needs to make fundamental changes to its production approach in order to combat increased competition from foreign manufacturers. Tench's cars are now being seen as ugly and pollutive and having poor safety features in comparison to the foreign competition. Management plans to address this by improving the quality of its cars through the use of quality management techniques. It plans to improve financial performance through the use of Kaizen costing and just-in-time purchasing and production. Tench's existing performance reporting system uses standard costing and budgetary variance analysis in order to monitor and control production activities.

The chief financial officer (CFO) of Tench has commented that he is confused by the terminology associated with quality management and needs a clearer understanding of the different costs associated with quality management. The CFO also wants to know the impact of including quality costs and using the Kaizen costing approach on the traditional standard costing approach at Tench.

Required

In response to the CFO's comments:

(a) Discuss the impact of the collection and use of quality costs on the current costing systems at Tench. **(6 marks)**

(b) Discuss and evaluate the impact of the Kaizen costing approach on the costing systems and employee management at Tench. **(8 marks)**

(c) Briefly evaluate the effect of moving to just-in-time purchasing and production, noting the impact on performance measures at Tench. **(6 marks)**

(d) Explain why the adoption of total quality management (TQM) is particularly important within a just-in-time (JIT) production environment. **(5 marks)**

(Total = 25 marks)

33 Pitlane (Mar/Jun 17)   49 mins

Company background

Pitlane Electronic Components (Pitlane) manufactures components for use in the electricity distribution network in Deeland. Demand from Pitlane's biggest customer, to replace identical but worn out components, has been constant for many years. Pitlane has recently renewed an exclusive long-term supply agreement with this customer, who has always agreed to buy the components for their total standard cost plus a fixed profit margin of 15%. Variances between standard and actual costs of the components are negligible. Pitlane runs several production lines in two factories located in different areas of Deeland. The factories' layout is poorly designed and the production process requires components to be transported around and between the factories.

Government incentives

The Deeland Government wants to encourage renewable electricity generation. It is offering a three-year subsidy scheme, beginning in 20X8, for consumers to have solar panels installed on the roofs of their homes. As an added incentive, businesses will be exempt from tax on profits made on the sale of solar panels and related components.

New product development

To take advantage of this scheme, Pitlane has built a prototype of a new electrical component, known as the 'Booster', which increases the output from domestic solar panels. The Booster will be sold to installers of solar panels and not directly to consumers. Pitlane's marketing department has estimated market data for the duration of the scheme based on a similar scheme in Veeland (Appendix 1). As a result of its products being unchanged for many years, Pitlane has little recent experience of developing new products and estimating costs and potential revenues from them. It is expected that many competitor products will be launched during the scheme, at the end of which demand is expected to fall greatly, and production of the Booster will discontinue.

Pitlane's shareholders insist that for the Booster project to go ahead, it must meet the financial performance objective of achieving a 15% net profit margin, after all costs, for the duration of the scheme.

The Booster's total fixed costs during the scheme are estimated to be $10m, including $2.8m upfront development costs to enable the Booster to communicate the amount of solar energy generated directly to consumers' smartphones via an app. The product development team at Pitlane believes this feature, and the use of highest quality packaging, will allow it to charge 10% more that the average price of its competitors. The marketing team, however, has questioned the overall value of these two features and whether customers would be prepared to pay extra for them, as most of the Deeland population do not yet own smartphones.

Pitlane has estimated the direct costs for the Booster (Appendix 2). The largest direct cost is for the four main sub-components. These are bought in bulk from six different suppliers in Deeland, though all are readily available from suppliers worldwide. The sub-components are fragile. During production of the Booster prototype, many sub-components were found to be damaged during the production process by workers incorrectly assembling them. This resulted in the completed prototype Boosters being scrapped after testing by the Quality Control Department. The manufacturing director is concerned that the incorrect assembly of sub-components by workers may mean that it may not be profitable for Pitlane to start full scale production of Boosters. To counteract these quality problems, Pitlane will employ more highly skilled workers, who are paid around 30% more than most other workers in the business which is accounted for in the cost estimate given in Appendix 2. Pitlane staff have never been encouraged to suggest any ways to improve the manufacturing process.

Pitlane's directors are concerned that the Booster project will not meet the shareholders' financial performance objective. They have asked you, as a consultant experienced in target costing, Kaizen costing and other Japanese business practices, for your advice.

Required

(a) Calculate the cost gap per unit in each of the three years of the Booster's life, taking into account all estimated costs. **(6 marks)**

(b) Advise on the extent to which target costing would help Pitlane to achieve the financial performance objective set by the shareholders. **(12 marks)**

(c) Advise Pitland how Kaizen costing may be used to help the Booster project achieve the financial performance objective set by the shareholders. **(7 marks)**

(Total = 25 marks)

APPENDIX 1 – ESTIMATED MARKET DATA FOR BOOSTER

	20X8	20X9	20Y0
Total market size (units)	600,000	500,000	460,000
Average price of competitors products ($/unit)	180	170	160
Booster market share of total market	10%	15%	20%

APPENDIX 2 – ESTIMATED UNIT DIRECT COST OF BOOSTER

	$
Sub-components	94
Assembly labour	21
Packaging	10
Distribution	2
Internal transport and handling	7
Total	134

34 Thebe (6/12, amended)

49 mins

Company background

Thebe Telecom (Thebe) is a large national telephone business in Fayland. Thebe provides telephone services to more than 11 million customers through its fixed line and mobile services. Thebe has three strategic business units: mobile; fixed line telephone (incorporating broadband); and corporate services (serving other businesses' telephone needs). It has become the largest mobile operator in Fayland through a series of acquisitions of competitors and operating licences.

Thebe's chief executive officer (CEO) has won many awards for being an innovative businessman who recognises the rapid changes in technology, regulation and competitor action that occur in the sector. Thebe's major competitor in Fayland is the original nationalised telephone company, FayTel, which was privatised 20 years ago but which retains many of the features of a monopoly supplier including a massive infrastructure. As a result, Thebe's CEO realised long ago that competition on the basis of price and volume would not work against such a large competitor and so he has focused on customer service as the key to growing the business.

Improving service quality

In order to improve the company's competitive position, the CEO decided that the company should consider a Six Sigma initiative to give an immediate step change improvement to the service quality at Thebe. The initiative involved a number of projects, including one to improve the quality of customers' bills. FayTel was publicly criticised by the Government's consumer advocate who pointed to occasional misallocations of call minutes to the wrong numbers and also, more frequently, the application of incorrect tariffs in calculating the costs of calls. Thebe's CEO is aware that all telephone businesses (including Thebe) have these problems but this is an area in which Thebe can gain a competitive advantage and has taken a special interest in this project by championing it himself.

The project is focused on improving the accuracy of customers' bills and the handling of complaints. Within the Billing Department, the company divided activities into normal money collection, credit control on overdue payments and managing complaints. Process diagrams were created for each of these areas and then data was sourced from customer feedback at the various points of interaction with Thebe employees (such as complaint handling) and internal measurables created. The project team was formed from line managers from all three strategic business units and the Billing Department.

The CEO's involvement in the projects to improve service quality at Thebe made him realise that the performance summary prepared for the monthly board papers does not include any non-financial aspects of performance, and Thebe's key performance indicators also focus solely on financial performance.

Required

(a) Evaluate the benefits of Thebe's board monitoring non-financial aspects of performance as well as financial ones. **(8 marks)**

(b) Explain how the general way in which Six Sigma is implemented helps improve the quality of performance, illustrating your answer with reference to Thebe. **(8 marks)**

(c) Explain and illustrate how the DMAIC method for the implementation of Six Sigma could be applied at Thebe. **(9 marks)**

(Total = 25 marks)

35 Posie (Sep/Dec 15)

49 mins

Company background and structure

Posie is a large business which manufactures furniture. It is made up of two autonomous divisions in Deeland.

The Manufacturing Division purchases raw materials from external suppliers, and performs all manufacturing and packaging operations. All sales are made through the Retail Division which has 95 retail stores in Deeland, as well as through Posie's own well-developed website. Posie has retail operations in eight other countries as well as in Deeland. These overseas businesses operate as independent subsidiaries within the Retail Division, each with their own IT and accounting functions.

The furniture is sold in boxes for customers to assemble themselves. About 10% of the products sold by Posie are purchased already packaged from other manufacturers. All deliveries are outsourced through a third-party distribution company.

Customer returns and complaints

Posie's corporate objective is to maximise shareholder wealth by producing 'attractive, functional furniture at low prices'. This is how customers generally perceive the Posie brand. The chief executive officer (CEO) of Posie is concerned about increasing levels of returns made by customers and increasing numbers of consumers complaining on online forums about products purchased from Posie.

Concerned about the impact on the Posie brand and the cost-leadership strategy, the CEO has asked you, as a performance management expert, to help Posie implement the Six Sigma technique to reduce the number of products returned and in particular to define customers' requirements and measure Posie's existing performance. The production director has been appointed to sponsor the project and you will be supported by a small team of managers who have recently received training in Six Sigma. The board member responsible for manufacturing quality recently resigned because she thought it was unfair that the Manufacturing Division was being held responsible for the increased level of customer returns.

You have been given access to some information concerning the reasons why customers return goods to help you measure existing performance in this area (Appendix 1). This is an extract from the management reporting pack presented to the board at their monthly meetings. The returns data, however, are only compiled every six months due to the lengthy analysis required of data from Posie's overseas retail operations. It is included twice a year in the board report along with the key performance indicators (KPIs) for customer satisfaction. The last time this information was produced 93% of customers indicated they **were satisfied with the quality of the manufacture of Posie's products.**

Information requirements

The CEO has heard that Six Sigma requires 'large amounts of facts and data'. He suggested that the returns data contain insufficient detail and that as part of your project you may need to do more analysis; for example, on why customers are not satisfied with the manufacturing quality.

He also added, 'I'm not sure that our current IT systems are capable of generating the data we need to identify which responsibility centres within the Manufacturing Division are the root causes of the problem of customer returns. We are planning to change the designation of the overseas retail businesses from profit centres to revenue centres, but again we need to know first how this will affect the information requirements of the business and any potential problems with doing so.'

Required

(a) Advise the board how the Six Sigma project at Posie to reduce returns from customers could be implemented using DMAIC methodology.   **(15 marks)**

(b) Evaluate the impact on Posie's information requirements arising from:

   (i)   The need to identify and improve on the level of customer returns   **(6 marks)**

   (ii) The proposed re-designation of the overseas subsidiaries from profit centres to revenue centres   **(4 marks)**

(Total = 25 marks)

APPENDIX 1

Reasons given by customers for returning goods

Category	Reason for return of goods	% responses
1	Difficult to assemble or pieces missing	48
2	Goods arrived damaged	14
3	Goods were not as described or were defective	25
4	Goods were of poor quality or no longer wanted	11
5	Arrived late	2
Total		100

36 Albacore (2013 Pilot Exam)   49 mins

Company background

Albacore Chess Stores (Albacore) is a chain of 12 shops specialising in selling items associated with the game of chess: boards, pieces, clocks, software and books. Three years ago, the company was the subject of a venture capital buyout from a larger group. A new senior management team was put in place after the buyout. They have the aim of running the business in order to maximise profits.

Budgeting process

The chief financial officer (CFO), along with the other members of senior management, sets the annual budget and uses a standard costing approach with variance analysis in order to control individual shop performance. The head office handles all capital purchases and brand marketing. All inventory purchasing is done centrally and the shop opening times are set as standard across the company. As an illustration of senior management attitude, the CFO had set the budget for staff costs for 20X1 at $7 per hour for part-time staff, and this was rigorously observed in the period.

Each shop is run by a manager who reports their financial results to head office. The shop managers recruit and manage the staffing of their shop. They have some autonomy in setting prices locally and have been given authority to vary prices by up to 10% from a master list produced by the CFO. They also have a local marketing budget agreed each year by the shop's manager and the marketing director as part of the annual appraisal process.

Performance appraisal and reward systems

The shop managers have approached the Chairman of Albacore to complain about the way that they are managed and their remuneration. They feel that their efforts are unrecognised by senior management. One manager commented:

> I have had a successful year in hard economic circumstances. I have run a number of promotions in the shop that have been well received by the customers. However, the budgets that are set are impossible to achieve and as a result I have not been paid any bonus although I feel that I have done everything in my power to bring in good profits.

The shop managers at Albacore are paid a basic salary of $27,000 with bonuses of up to 30% of basic salary dependent on two factors: performance above budget and the operational director's performance assessment. The budget for the next year is prepared by the CFO and presented at the shop manager's annual appraisal.

The Chairman has come to you to ask if you can consider the system of performance assessment for the shop managers and give an independent perspective on the reward systems at Albacore. She has heard of variance analysis but is unsure about what would be relevant in this situation. She has provided the following illustrative information from the previous year for one shop:

ALBACORE CHESS STORES

TUNNY BRANCH YEAR TO SEPTEMBER 20X1

	Budget $	Actual $	Variance $
Sales	266,000	237,100	−28,900
Cost of sales	106,400	94,840	11,560
Gross profit	159,600	142,260	−17,340
Marketing	12,000	11,500	500
Staff costs: manager	27,000	27,000	0
part-time staff	38,000	34,000	4,000
Property costs	26,600	26,600	0
Shop profit	56,000	43,160	−12,840

Notes

1   Property costs includes heating, lighting and rental.

2   Positive variances are favourable.

The manager of this shop commented at the appraisal meeting that she felt that the assessment was unfair since her failure to make budget was due to general economic conditions. The industry as a whole saw a 12% fall in revenues during the period and the budget for the period was set to be the same as the previous period. She was not paid a bonus for the period.

Required

(a)   Evaluate the suitability of the existing branch information given as a means of assessing the shop manager's performance and draft an improved branch report with justifications for changes.   **(13 marks)**

(b)   Analyse the performance management style and evaluate the performance appraisal system at Albacore. Suggest suitable improvements to its reward system for the shop managers.   **(12 marks)**

(Total = 25 marks)

37 Cuthbert (Mar/Jun 16)   **49 mins**

Company background

Cuthbert is based in Ceeland and manufactures jackets for use in very cold environments by mountaineers and skiers. It also supplies the armed forces in several countries with variants of existing products, customised by the use of different coloured fabrics, labels and special fastenings for carrying equipment. Cuthbert incurs high costs on design and advertising in order to maintain the reputation of the brand.

Each jacket is made up of different shaped pieces of fabric called 'components'. These components are purchased by Cuthbert from an external supplier. The external supplier is responsible for ensuring the quality of the components and the number of purchased components found to be defective is negligible. The cost of the components forms 80% of the direct cost of each jacket, and the prices charged by Cuthbert's supplier for the components are the lowest in the industry.

Production process

There are three stages to the production process of each jacket, which are each located in different parts of the factory:

Stage 1 – Sewing

The fabric components are sewn together by a machinist. Any manufacturing defects occurring after sewing has begun cannot be rectified, and finished garments found to be defective are heavily discounted or, in the case of bespoke variants, destroyed.

Stage 2 – Assembly

The garments are filled with insulating material and sewn together for the final time.

Stage 3 – Finishing

Labels, fastenings and zips are sewn to the finished garments. Though the process for attaching each of these is similar, machinists prefer to work only on labels, fastenings or zips to maximise the quantity which they can sew each hour.

Jackets are produced in batches of a particular style in a range of sizes. Throughout production, the components required for each batch of jackets are accompanied by a paper batch card which records the production processes which each batch has undergone. The batch cards are input into a production spreadsheet so that the stage of completion of each batch can be monitored and the position of each batch in the factory is recorded.

There are 60 machinists working in the Sewing Department, and 40 in each of the Assembly and Finishing Departments. All the machinists are managed by 10 supervisors whose duties include updating the batch cards for work done and inputting this into a spreadsheet, as well as checking the quality of work done by machinists. The supervisors report to the factory manager, who has overall responsibility for the production process.

Machinists are paid an hourly wage and a bonus according to how many items they sew each week, which usually comprises 60% of their total weekly wages.

Supervisors receive an hourly wage and a bonus according to how many items their team sews each week. The Factory Manager receives the same monthly salary regardless of production output. All employees are awarded a 5% annual bonus if Cuthbert achieves its budgeted net profit for the year.

Recent problems and issues

Recently, a large emergency order of jackets for the Ceeland army was cancelled by the customer as it was not delivered on time due to the following quality problems and other issues in the production process:

- A supervisor had forgotten to input several batch cards and as a result batches of fabric components were lost in the factory and replacements had to be purchased.

- There were machinists available to sew buttons onto the jackets, but there was only one machinist available who had been trained to sew zips. This caused further delay to production of the batch.

- When the quality of the jackets was checked prior to despatch, many of them were found to be sewn incorrectly as the work had been rushed. By this time the agreed delivery date had already passed, and it was too late to produce a replacement batch.

This was the latest in a series of problems in production at Cuthbert, and the directors have decided to use business process re-engineering (BPR) in order to radically change the production process.

BPR and changes to the production process

The proposal being considered as an application of BPR is the adoption of 'team working' in the factory, the three main elements of which are as follows:

(1) Production lines would reorganise into teams, where all operations on a particular product type are performed in one place by a dedicated team of machinists.

(2) Each team of machinists would be responsible for the quality of the finished jacket and, for the first time, machinists would be encouraged to bring about improvements in the production process. There would no longer be the need to employ supervisors and the existing supervisors would join the teams of machinists.

(3) The number of batches in production would be automatically tracked by the use of radio frequency identification (RFID) tags attached to each jacket. This would eliminate the need for paper batch cards, which are currently input into a spreadsheet by the supervisors.

BPP
LEARNING
MEDIA

You have been asked as a performance management consultant to advise the board on whether BPR could help Cuthbert overcome the problems in its production process.

Required

(a) Advise how the proposed use of BPR would influence the operational performance of Cuthbert. **(14 marks)**

(b) Evaluate the effectiveness of the current reward systems at Cuthbert, and recommend and justify how these systems would need to change if the BPR project goes ahead. **(11 marks)**

(Total = 25 marks)

38 Beach Foods (6/15) 49 mins

Company background and structure

Beach Foods (Beach) is a family-owned business which has grown strongly over its 100-year history. The objective of the business is to maximise the family's wealth through their shareholdings. Beach has three divisions. It manufactures a variety of foods in two of the divisions: Beach Baby Foods (Baby) and Beach Chocolate Foods (Chocolate). Each of these divisions knows its own market and sets prices accordingly. The third division (R&D) researches new products on the instructions of the other divisions and is considered to be vital to the survival and growth of Beach. The board of Beach has been considering the impact of using a divisional structure and has come to you as a performance management consultant to ask for your advice.

Divisional performance measures

There is disagreement at board level about the correct choice of divisional performance measure to be used in the two manufacturing divisions. Currently, the business uses EVA™ but two directors have been questioning its value, complaining that it is complicated to understand. These directors have been promoting the use of either residual income (RI) or return on investment (ROI) as alternatives. The board wants to use the same measure for each division. As well as qualitatively evaluating these different measures, the board needs an assessment of the impact of a change in performance measure on their perception of these divisions' performance. Therefore, as an example, they require you to calculate and discuss the use of ROI and RI at Baby Division, given the data in Appendix 1.

Divisional control and management style

The chief executive officer (CEO) of Beach has engaged a business analyst to perform a study of the portfolio of manufacturing businesses which make up Beach. This has been completed in Appendix 2. The CEO wants your comments (based on the categorisation given in Appendix 2) on how this work will impact on the performance management of the divisions. Specifically, the CEO has asked for your recommendations on how to control each division; that is, whether each division should be treated as a cost/profit/investment centre and also the appropriate management style to use for handling staff in each division. The CEO commented to you:

> I have heard of different approaches to the use of budget information in assessing performance: budget-constrained, profit-conscious and also a non-accounting style. I need to know how these approaches might apply to each division given your other comments.

Managers' concerns

All of this work has been partly prompted by complaints from the divisional managers. The Chocolate divisional managers complain that they had to wait for a year to get approval to upgrade their main production line. This production line upgrade has reduced wastage and boosted Chocolate's profit margin by 10 percentage points. The Baby Division has been very successful in using the ideas of the Research and Development (R&D) Division, although Baby's managers do complain about the recharging of R&D costs to their division. Head office managers are worried about Chocolate as it has seemed to be drifting recently with a lack of strategic direction. Chocolate's managers are considered to be good but possibly not sufficiently focused on what benefits Beach as a whole.

Required

(a) Assess the use of EVA™ as a divisional performance measure for the manufacturing divisions at Beach. **(8 marks)**

(b) Using Appendix 1, calculate the ROI and RI for Baby and assess the impact of the assumptions made when calculating these metrics on the evaluation of the performance of this division and its management. **(7 marks)**

(c) Provide justified recommendations for each division's control and management style as requested by the CEO. **(10 marks)**

(Total = 25 marks)

APPENDIX 1

Figures from Beach management accounts for year ended 31 March:

Baby Division	20X5
	$m
Revenue	220
Costs	
Divisional operating costs	121
R&D costs recharged	11
Allocated head office management fees	28
Profit before tax	60
Capital employed	424

Notes

1 Baby launched a new product with a large publicity campaign during the year.

2 The notional cost of capital for Baby is estimated by the chief financial officer at 11%. Weighted average cost of capital (WACC) for Beach is 7.5%.

3 ROI for similar entities is 20%.

4 EVA™ for Baby is calculated as $35m.

APPENDIX 2

Star Baby: Market growth 18% Relative market share 105%	Question mark
Cash cow Chocolate: Market growth 3% Relative market share 120%	Dog

Relative market share is the market share of the division compared to that of the market leader. If an organisation is a market leader, then its market share is compared to the next largest competitor.

Note. You may assume that the calculations and this categorisation are accurate.

PERFORMANCE EVALUATION AND CORPORATE FAILURE

Questions 39 to 53 cover performance evaluation and corporate failure, the subject of Part E of the syllabus for APM.

39 Pharmaceutical Technologies (2013 Pilot Exam)
49 mins

Company background

Pharmaceutical Technologies Co (PT) is a developer and manufacturer of medical drugs in Beeland. It is one of the 100 largest listed companies on the national stock exchange. The company focuses on buying prospective drugs (which have shown initial promise in testing) from small bio-engineering companies. PT then leads these drugs through three regulatory stages to launch in the general medical market.

The three stages are:

(1) To confirm the safety of the drug (does it harm humans?), in small-scale trials;
(2) To test the efficacy of the product (does it help cure?), again in small-scale trials; and
(3) Finally, large-scale trials to definitively decide on the safety and efficacy of the product.

The drugs are then marketed through the company's large sales force to healthcare providers and end users (patients). The healthcare providers are paid by either health insurance companies or the national government dependent on the financial status of the patient.

Industry regulator

The Beeland Drug Regulator (BDR) oversees this testing process and makes the final judgement about whether a product can be sold in the country.

Its objectives are to protect, promote and improve public health by ensuring that:

*   Medicines have an acceptable balance of benefit and risk;
*   The users of these medicines understand this risk-benefit profile; and
*   New beneficial product development is encouraged.

The regulator is governed by a board of trustees appointed by the Government. It is funded directly by the Government and also through fees charged to drug companies when granting licences to sell their products in Beeland.

Balanced scorecard

PT has used share price and earnings per share as its principal measures of performance to date. However, the share price has underperformed the market, and the health sector, in the last two years. The chief executive officer (CEO) has identified that these measures are too narrow and is considering implementing a balanced scorecard approach to address this problem.

A working group has drawn up a suggested balanced scorecard. It began by identifying the objectives from the board's medium-term strategy:

*   Create shareholder value by bringing commercially viable drugs to market.
*   Improve the efficiency of drug development.
*   Increase shareholder value by innovation in the drug approval process.

The working group then considered the stakeholder perspectives:

*   Shareholders want a competitive return on their investment.

*   Payers/purchasers (governments, insurers and patients) want to pay a reasonable price for the drugs.

*   Regulators want an efficient process for the validation of drugs.

*   Doctors want safe and effective drug products.

*   Patients want to be cured.

Finally, this leads to the proposed scorecard of performance measures:

- Financial – share price and earnings per share

- Customer – number of patients using PT products

- Internal business process – exceed industry standard on design and testing; time to regulatory approval of a product

- Learning and growth – training days undertaken by staff; time to market of new product; percentage of drugs bought by PT that gain final approval

The balanced scorecard now needs to be reviewed to ensure that it will address the company's objectives and the issues that it faces in its business environment.

Required

(a) Evaluate the performance measures proposed for PT's balanced scorecard. **(10 marks)**

(b) Briefly describe a method of analysing stakeholder influence and analyse the influence of four different external stakeholders on the regulator (BDR). **(8 marks)**

(c) Using your answer from part (b), describe how the application of the balanced scorecard approach at BDR would differ from the approach within PT. **(7 marks)**

(Total = 25 marks)

40 Victoria-Yeeland Logistics (6/15)   49 mins

Company background and objectives

Victoria-Yeeland Logistics (Victoria) is a logistics support business, which operates a fleet of lorries to deliver packages of goods on behalf of its customers within the country of Yeeland. Victoria collects packages from its customers' manufacturing sites or from the customers' port of importation and delivers to the final user of the goods. The lorries are run and maintained from a set of depots spread throughout Yeeland.

The overall objective of Victoria is to maximise shareholder wealth. The delivery business in Yeeland is dominated by two international companies and one other domestic business and profit margins are extremely tight. The market is saturated by these large operators and a number of smaller operators. The cost base of Victoria is dominated by staff and fuel, with fuel prices being highly volatile in the last few years.

Balanced scorecard

In order to improve performance measurement and management at Victoria, the chief financial officer (CFO) plans to use the balanced scorecard (BSC). However, she has been pulled away from this project in order to deal with an issue with refinancing the business's principal lending facility. The CFO has already identified some suitable metrics but needs you, as her assistant, to complete her work and address any potential questions which might arise when she makes her presentation on the BSC to the board. The CFO has completed the identification of metrics for three of the perspectives (Appendix 1) but has yet to complete the work on the metrics for the customer perspective. This should be done using the data given in Appendix 2.

Reward management issues

Additionally, two issues have arisen in the reward management system at Victoria, one in relation to senior management and the other for operational managers. Currently, senior management gets a fixed salary supplemented by an annual bonus awarded by the board. Shareholders have been complaining that these bonuses are not suitable. The operational managers also get bonuses based on their performance as assessed by their management superiors. The operational managers are unhappy with the system. In order to address this, it has been suggested that they should be involved in bonus target setting as otherwise there is a sense of demotivation from such a system. The CFO wants an evaluation of this system of rewards in light of the introduction of the BSC and best practice.

Required

(a) Discuss how Victoria's success in the customer perspective may impact on the metrics given in the financial perspective. **(5 marks)**

(b) Recommend, with justification, and calculate a suitable performance metric for each customer perspective success factor. Comment on the problems of using customer complaints to measure whether packages are delivered safely and on time. **(11 marks)**

(c) Advise Victoria on the reward management issues outlined by the CFO. **(9 marks)**

(Total = 25 marks)

APPENDIX 1

Financial perspective

(How do we appear to our shareholders?)
Return on capital employed
Profit margin
Revenue growth

Customer perspective

(How do we appear to our customers?)
Success factors:
Ability to meet customers' transport needs
Ability to deliver packages quickly
Ability to deliver packages on time
Ability to deliver packages safely

Internal process perspective

(What business processes must excel?)
Time taken to load and unload
Lorry capacity utilisation

Learning and growth perspective

(How do we sustain and improve our ability to grow?)
Leadership competence (qualitative judgement)
Training days per employee

APPENDIX 2

The process: A customer makes a transport request for a package to be collected and delivered to a given destination. The customer is supplied with a time window in which the delivery will occur. Packages are then loaded onto lorries and delivered according to a route specified by the depot's routing manager.

Total number of customer transport requests	610,000
Total number of packages transported	548,000
Total number of lorry journeys	73,000
Total package kilometres	65,760,000
Total package minutes	131,520,000
Number of delivery complaints from customers:	
from damaged packages	8,220
from late delivery (outside agreed time window)	21,920

Notes

1 All figures are for the last financial year.
2 A package kilometre is defined as a kilometre travelled by one package.
3 A package minute is defined as a minute spent in transit by one package.

41 Soup (Sep/Dec 15)

Company background

Soup operates passenger rail services in Deeland, a technologically advanced country, with high demand for fast, reliable rail travel from business and leisure passengers. Many passengers choose train travel because they see it as less harmful to the environment than other forms of transport.

Operating license and government warning

Soup's main objective is to maximise shareholder wealth. Since becoming licensed to operate routes in Regions A and B by the Deeland Government five years ago, Soup has consistently delivered increased dividends and share prices for investors. In its initial appraisal of the licensing opportunity, Soup expected to operate the routes for at least 15 years; however, its licence may not be renewed when it expires in three years' time. The Government has warned Soup it 'is unhappy about high returns to shareholders while there are many reports of poor passenger service, overcrowded trains and unreliable services on certain routes and at busy times'.

Soup owns its fleet of diesel powered trains. Each train in Region A has seven coaches with 70 passenger seats available per coach. In the less busy Region B, each train has six coaches, each with 70 seats. As a condition of the licence, Soup runs a set number of services at both busy and quieter times in both regions. Soup has two larger rivals, both operating electric trains, which cause less harm to the environment than diesel powered trains. They run on the same routes in both regions.

The Government regulates fares charged to passengers, which are the same per distance travelled for every operator in that region. The railway track, stations and other infrastructure are managed by the Government which charges the operators a fee. There are several stations along the route which are only used by Soup trains and others where Soup trains do not stop at all.

Soup's trains are 25 years old, originally purchased cheaply from an operator whose licence was withdrawn by the Government. Soup believes the low price it paid is a key competitive advantage enabling it to steadily increase its return on capital employed, the company's main performance measure, to a level well in excess of its rivals. The shareholders are pleased with the growth in passenger numbers over the last five years, which is the other performance measure Soup uses.

Soup's ageing trains spend increasing time undergoing preventative maintenance, safety checks or repairs. A recent television documentary also showed apparently poor conditions on board, such as defective heating and washroom facilities and dirty, torn seating. Passengers complained in the programme of difficulties finding a seat, the unreliability of accessing wireless internet services and even that the menu in the on-board café had not changed for five years.

Soup's chief executive officer (CEO) responded that unreliable internet access arose from the rapid growth in passengers expecting to access the internet on trains. She said Soup had never received any formal complaints about the lack of choice in the on-board café, nor had she heard of a recent press report that Soup's trains were badly maintained, so causing harm to the environment.

Performance measures

The CEO has asked you, as chief management accountant, for your advice. 'In view of the Government's warning, we must develop performance measures balancing the needs of passengers with the requirements of the shareholders,' she has said. 'I don't want to know how to improve the actual performance of the business – that is the job of the operational managers – nor do I just want a list of suggested performance measures. Instead I need to know why these performance measures will help to improve the performance of Soup.'

The following data applies to Soup:

	Region A	Region B
Number of services per day		
Peak times	4	4
Other times	6	8
Number of passengers per day		
Peak times	2,500	1,400
Other times	2,450	1,850

Required

(a) Advise the CEO on how the use of the balanced scorecard could improve the performance management system of Soup. **(10 marks)**

(b) Using the performance data given, evaluate the comments of the Deeland Government that Soup's trains are overcrowded. **(7 marks)**

(c) Assess the problems Soup may encounter in selecting and interpreting performance measures when applying the balanced scorecard to its performance management system. **(8 marks)**

(Total = 25 marks)

42 Graviton (12/13)   49 mins

Company background

Graviton Clothing (Graviton) is a listed manufacturer of clothing with a strong reputation for producing desirable, fashionable products which can attract high selling prices. The company's objective is to maximise shareholder wealth. Graviton's products are sold through its own chain of stores. Graviton's markets demand designs which are in tune with current fashion trends which can alter every few weeks. Therefore, the business's stated aim is to focus production on these changing market trends by maintaining flexibility to adapt to that market demand through close control of all stages of the supply chain (design, manufacture and distribution).

Performance measurement system

The chief executive officer (CEO) is unhappy with the current performance measurement system at Graviton. The system was created about five years ago by the finance director who has subsequently retired. The aim of the system was to provide the company with a list of measures which would cover performance at the strategic, tactical and operational levels of management. An example of the most recent performance report is given in Appendix 1.

Recent events

Recent press reports about Graviton have been mixed, with positive comments about the innovative new designs and much admiration over the growth of sales which the business has achieved. However, there has been some criticism from customers of the durability of Graviton's clothes and from institutional investors that the dividend growth is not strong.

The CEO believes that there are major gaps in the current list of key metrics used by Graviton. She wants an evaluation of the current system and suggestions for improvements. However, she has warned you that the board wants a reasoned argument for each measure to be included in the list in order to avoid overloading each level of management with too much data.

Although rapidly growing, Graviton has had some problems in the last few years which have appeared on recent internal audit reports. It was found that a senior manager at factory site 1 has been delaying invoicing for completed orders in order to ensure that profit targets are met in both the current and the next accounting period. At factory site 2, there has been excellent return on a low capital employed figure although there is a significant adverse variance in the equipment repairs account.

Problems with performance measures

The board is dominated by long-serving executives who are sceptical of change, given Graviton's growth over the past three years. At a recent board meeting, they have shared the CEO's concern about data overload and also have pointed out a variety of problems with the use of performance measures. They presented the CEO with a list of three common problems (myopia, gaming, ossification) and argued that the current good performance of the business did not justify changing the performance measurement system. The CEO needs to know if these problems apply to Graviton and if they do, then what can be done to manage them.

Required

(a) Evaluate the current performance measurement system using the performance pyramid of Lynch and Cross. **(15 marks)**

(b) Assess whether the three problems listed by the board apply to Graviton and suggest appropriate performance management solutions to them. **(10 marks)**

(Total = 25 marks)

APPENDIX 1

GRAVITON PERFORMANCE DASHBOARD REPORT FOR THE YEAR TO SEPTEMBER 20X3

	20X3	20X2	20X1	Change 20X3/20X2
Financial				
Revenue ($m)	1,723	1,570	1,413	9.7%
Operating profit ($m)	320	314	308	1.9%
ROCE	15.8%	15.9%	15.9%	
Design				
Design awards won	3	2	3	50.0%
Manufacture				
Average time to market (days)	22.2	22.3	22.1	−0.4%
Distribution				
Deliveries on time	87.0%	86.8%	87.3%	0.2%

Commentary:

- The revenue growth of the business remains strong in a difficult market.

- Return on capital employed matches the industry average of about 16%.

- Time to market for new designs has been maintained at 22 days by paying overtime to designers in order to meet production schedules.

43 Totaig (3/20)   49 mins

Exhibit 1: Company information

Totaig manufactures high quality and innovative small electrical appliances such as hairdryers and vacuum cleaners. All of the board of directors, who are the strategic decision makers, have always worked in the business and are members of the Totaig family. Most of the operational managers joined as factory workers when the business started and have taken on more responsibilities as the business has grown.

Totaig has basic and outdated IT systems for a business of its complexity and has always used traditional financial performance measures such as return on investment (ROI) and operating profit margin.

Totaig has historically had few competitors and the directors have focused on improving financial results from one year to the next, with little long-term planning. A number of overseas competitors have, however, recently entered Totaig's market. It is estimated that, within one year, these competitors will be able to produce at a similar unit cost to Totaig and that within three to five years, the quality of the competitors' products will be comparable to the current quality of

Totaig's products. Totaig may have to invest heavily in product development and make acquisitions in the future in order to compete effectively.

Exhibit 2: Value based management (VBM)

A consultant has recently told the directors that implementing VBM may help Totaig to respond to the increase in competition over the next one to five years. The consultant has defined VBM as 'the alignment of the business strategy, management processes and culture on maximising shareholder wealth by focusing on key drivers of value'. The directors have accepted this as a reasonable definition of VBM and most of them now agree that VBM would be useful, though others are not yet convinced.

The directors have, however, asked you for further advice on one aspect of the implementation of VBM at Totaig. At her recent presentation, the consultant presented a slide (Appendix 1) showing the four steps in implementing VBM. The directors want your advice on how to implement Step 2, which is defining performance targets. Your advice should focus on the following four areas:

(1)   Selection of appropriate measures and targets

(2)   Timescales to which the targets should relate

(3)   Management levels (strategic and operational) in the business to which the targets should relate

(4)   Difficulties in measuring and managing performance using VBM

Exhibit 3: Measuring value

The directors are unsure of a suitable financial performance indicator for them to use to measure whether Totaig is creating value. As an illustration, they have asked you to evaluate, by calculating economic value added (EVA™), whether Totaig has generated value for the year to 30 June 20X5. You should use the financial information given in Appendix 2, and advise on the difficulties of using EVA™ as a performance indicator at Totaig.

Required

It is now 1 September 20X5.

(a)   Advise the directors on the implementation of Step 2 of VBM as requested.   **(15 marks)**

(b)   Evaluate both whether Totaig has created value and the difficulties of using EVA™ as a performance indicator at Totaig.   **(10 marks)**

(Total = 25 marks)

Exhibit 4: APPENDIX 1

Four steps in implementing VBM

Step 1	Produce a strategy for maximising value
Step 2	Define performance targets
Step 3	Create a plan to achieve the targets
Step 4	Set up measurement and reward systems

Exhibit 5: APPENDIX 2

Income statement for the year to 30 June 20X5

	$'000
Operating profit	10,000
Interest expense	(1,500)
Profit before tax	8,500
Tax at 22%	(1,870)
Profit after tax	6,630

Notes:

1   During the year, $450,000 of advertising cost which will generate sales in future periods was expensed to the income statement.

2   The allowance for doubtful debts at the end of the period was $300,000, a reduction of $200,000 from the beginning of the period.

3   The capital employed at the beginning of the period was $88,944,000.

4   Totaig's after-tax weighted average cost of capital (WACC) is currently 9%. The company is financed by a mixture of equity and fixed and floating rate loans.

5   The directors are considering changing Totaig's policies for the depreciation of non-current assets for the year ending 30 June 20X6.

44 APX Accountancy (6/11, amended)   49 mins

Company background

APX Accountancy (APX) is an accountancy partnership with 12 branches covering each of the main cities of Emland. The business is well established, having organically grown over the last 40 years to become the second largest non-international practice in Emland. The accountancy market is mature and expands and contracts along with the general economic performance of Emland.

APX offers accountancy, audit, tax and business advisory services. The current business environment in Emland is dominated by a recession and the associated insolvency work is covered within the business advisory area of APX.

Performance management

At present, the practice collects the following information for strategic performance evaluation:

	Audit	Tax	Business advisory	Total
Revenue ($m)				
APX	69.1	89.2	64.7	223.0
Accounting industry	557.0	573.0	462.0	1,592.0
Change in revenue on previous year				
APX	3.0%	8.0%	22.0%	10.0%
Accounting industry	2.5%	4.5%	16.0%	6.8%
Profit margin at APX	6.4%	7.8%	10.5%	8.1%
Customer service score (1 to 5, with 5 being excellent)				
APX	3.4	3.9	4.1	

The figures shown are for the most recent financial year and illustrate the metrics used by APX. Equivalent monthly figures are produced for each of the monthly partner meetings which review practice performance.

The staff are remunerated based on their grade, with non-partners obtaining a bonus of up to 10% of basic salary based on their line managers' annual review. The partners receive a fixed salary with a share of profit which depends on their contractual responsibilities within the partnership.

BPP
LEARNING
MEDIA

The managing partner of APX is dissatisfied with the existing performance management system, as she is not convinced that it is helping to achieve the long-term goal of expanding and ultimately floating the business on the national stock exchange. Therefore, she has asked you to consider the impact of applying Fitzgerald and Moon's building block approach to performance management in the practice.

In addition, the marketing manager at APX believes that the firm as a whole doesn't pay enough attention to customer service. At the last management meeting he said that, in his opinion, the customer service score(*) was the most important figure out of the performance metrics currently used by APX, and he said he felt it was no coincidence that the area of the business with the highest customer service score had also performed best financially.

* Customer service scores reflect ratings given by customers in relation to the level of service they feel they have received from APX.

Required

(a)   Briefly describe Fitzgerald and Moon's building block model of performance management.
(4 marks)

(b)   Evaluate the existing performance management system at APX by applying the building block model. **(8 marks)**

(c)   Explain the main improvements the introduction of a building block approach to performance management could provide, and suggest specific improvements to the existing system of performance measures at APX in light of the introduction of the building block model. **(8 marks)**

(d)   Briefly evaluate the marketing manager's statement about the customer service score.
(5 marks)

(Total = 25 marks)

45 Vunderg (3/19)   49 mins

Vunderg: Company information

Vunderg manufactures windows and related products. The overheads in the business are high and primarily relate to procurement, customer administration and product design. Procurement and customer administration overheads relate to all of Vunderg's product groups. Design overheads currently relate to only two product groups, glasshouses and conservatories. Vunderg's current costing system has been in use for a long time and absorbs overheads into product costs on a direct labour hours basis. The current costing system does not involve identifying the factors which drive the costs of the company's activities and allocating overheads to products based on their usage of those factors.

Current product range

Windows

For many years, Vunderg has manufactured UPVC window frames used for residential house building. Vunderg buys the glass from an external supplier, inserts it into a frame and sells the completed window units to a small number of large construction companies. These window units all have standard designs, specifications and sizes. This market is very competitive, and Vunderg must offer a complete range of windows for sale to the construction companies.

Glasshouses

Five years ago, Vunderg developed a range of small garden glasshouses, for non-commercial use, made of attractive and high quality materials. After initial quality problems due to the use of materials and manufacturing methods new to Vunderg, glasshouse production is now efficient, quality is high and the glasshouses now command premium prices.

The glasshouses are sold nationwide through 40 retailers, who vary significantly in the size of orders they place and the level of customer support and trade discounts which they receive from Vunderg. As a result, the profitability of selling to different retailers, or types of retailer, varies significantly.

Conservatories

More recently, Vunderg began manufacturing conservatories* using the same materials as its glasshouse range. These conservatories are expensive and are made to measure for individual customers' houses. There are a wide range of finishes and options available to choose from. Conservatories which match garden glasshouses have become popular with customers who can afford them. Unlike Vunderg's other products, these are sold directly to individual home owners.

*Conservatories are structures made mainly of glass, which are attached to the side of residential houses. They form an additional room in a house and are popular in cool climates.

Future product development

Vunderg is looking to move into another new market soon, as the market for making windows for houses is now saturated. This new market will be the manufacture and design of large windows to be installed in the entrance halls of large, prestigious commercial buildings. These will be bespoke items, designed and manufactured to customers' own specifications.

Recent performance

The CEO is concerned by a recent fall in overall net profit margin, despite modest revenue growth and good control of direct costs. In particular, he has said:

> The conservatories part of the business may not be as profitable as its positive contribution (Appendix 1) may suggest. For example, our procurement department spends a lot of time sourcing special materials and finishes requested by customers. Many conservatories have leaked in the rain so we have to rectify these faults and work on a new design to prevent this happening. As we have only basic information systems, it is unclear how much some of these activities are costing. Over 20% of our factory space is dedicated to manufacturing conservatories. We may be better off discontinuing these products.

The CEO has some experience of activity based costing (ABC) in a previous role and believes that activity based management (ABM) could help to improve Vunderg's strategic performance. He is keen to know what the limitations are of using the ABM method for Vunderg's products and customer types, and the problems with its implementation before he makes a decision to implement it.

It is now 1 September 20X5.

Required

(a) Advise the CEO how activity based management (ABM) could help improve the strategic performance of Vunderg. **(13 marks)**

(b) As required by the CEO, assess the limitations of using the ABM method for Vunderg's products and customer types, and the problems with its implementation. **(12 marks)**

(Total = 25 marks)

APPENDIX 1

Contribution by product type for the year ended 30 June 20X5

Product type	No. of units sold	Total contribution ($'000)
Windows	175,000	9,800
Glasshouses	3,800	969
Conservatories	650	910

46 LOL cards (12/10, amended) 49 mins

LOL Co (LOL) is a chain of shops selling cards and gifts throughout its country. It has been listed on the stock exchange for ten years and enjoys a fairly high profile in the retail sector of the national economy. You have been asked by the chief executive officer (CEO) to advise the company on value-based management (VBM) as a different approach to performance management. The CEO has read about this method as a way of focusing on shareholder interests and in the current tough economic climate, she thinks that it may be a useful development for LOL.

The company has traditionally used earnings per share (EPS) growth and share price in order to assess performance. The changes being proposed are considered significant and the CEO wants to be briefed on the implications of the new analysis and also how to convince both the board and the major investors of the benefits.

Financial data for LOL

	20X9 $m	20Y0 $m
Profit before interest and tax	50.7	43.5
Interest paid	4.0	7.8
Profit after interest and tax	35.0	26.8
Average number of shares in issue (millions)	160	160

Capital employed at the end of the year was	$m
20X8	99.2
20X9	104.1
20Y0	97.8

LOL aims for a capital structure of 50:50 debt to equity.

Costs of capital were

	20X9	20Y0
Equity	12.70%	15.30%
Debt (post-tax cost)	4.20%	3.90%

Corporation tax is at the rate of 25%.

Stock market information

	20X9	20Y0
Stock market all-share index	2,225.4	1,448.9
Retailing sector index	1,225.6	907.1
LOL (average share price) ($)	12.20	10.70

The fall in profits can, in part at least, be attributed to an increase in costs. The CFO has advised that LOL needs to focus on cost reduction rather than cost containment. She proposes to achieve this through the introduction of activity-based management.

Required

(a) Explain to the CEO what VBM involves and how it can be used to focus the company on shareholder interests. **(4 marks)**

(b) Perform an assessment of the financial performance of LOL using economic value added (EVA™) and evaluate your results compared with those of EPS growth and share price performance. You should state any assumptions made. **(12 marks)**

(c) Evaluate VBM measures against traditional profit-based measures of performance. **(3 marks)**

(d) Discuss how activity-based management (ABM) differs from traditional cost allocation systems, and how ABM seeks to achieve cost reduction. **(6 marks)**

(Total = 25 marks)

47 Bazeele (Mar/Jun 18) 49 mins

Organisational background

Bazeele hires out plant and machinery to small firms working in the construction industry. Bazeele's senior managers, including the chief executive officer (CEO), have worked in the business since it was established 30 years ago, and they own the majority of the shares. During that time, Bazeele has acquired many smaller plant hire businesses. Of these business units, those which have underperformed after acquisition have either been sold on or restructured, for example, to increase their operating margins. Bazeele has recently diversified by hiring out large items of plant to large construction firms working on major infrastructure projects. These projects can last for up to ten years. Strong growth in the general economy has increased the number of these large projects and has also led to a predicted large increase in bank interest rates.

The shareholders' objective is for Bazeele to maintain its historic return on capital employed (ROCE). Managers at business units are given the objective of maintaining net profit margins of their own business units. Similarly, managers at individual branches of business units are given the same objective according to their own areas of responsibility.

Following two years of poor performance, it has been suggested to the CEO that Bazeele would benefit from adopting a value-based management (VBM) approach.

The CEO requires your advice and has said:

> The shareholders are unsure what VBM is, whether it will benefit Bazeele, and what changes the business would need to make if it were to adopt it. All managers in the business are already clear what their objectives are. For example, one business unit manager recently postponed some expensive staff training on improving customer satisfaction, which I believe was the correct decision. Our recent poor performance has meant we cannot afford this sort of expenditure, especially as we have no information on what levels of customer satisfaction actually are. Personally, I dislike change, but would not object to the adoption of VBM if it was thought to be beneficial for Bazeele. The shareholders have heard that economic value added (EVA™) can be used to measure whether Bazeele has created or destroyed value for its shareholders, but this has not yet been calculated.

Details of the company's recent performance are given in Appendix 1.

Required

(a) Evaluate whether a value-based management approach is appropriate for Bazeele.

(7 marks)

(b) Explain to the CEO what changes Bazeele would need to make to its performance measurement and performance management systems if it were to adopt a value-based management approach. (7 marks)

(c) Using the information in Appendix 1, advise the CEO whether Bazeele has generated economic value for its shareholders. (11 marks)

(Total = 25 marks)

APPENDIX 1

Notes from Bazeele's management accounts for the most recent year end:

1   Net profit after tax for the year: $10m

2   Capital employed at the start of the year: $250m

3   The interest charge for the year was $15m on a variable rate loan with an interest rate of 10%. Bazeele is funded 60% by debt and 40% by equity. The cost of equity is 12%. Bazeele pays tax at a rate of 20%.

4   The depreciation charge for non-current assets for the year was $6.0m; the economic depreciation of which was $14.0m. At the start of the period, the accumulated economic depreciation of non-current assets exceeded its accounting depreciation by $16.0m.

5   Brought forward at the start of the year was a provision of $4.8m which was made in respect of a debt owed by a customer who has since repaid it.

6   Within the current profit or loss account there is an expense for $0.6m for advertising in trade magazines. This led to several enquiries from new customers involved in large infrastructure projects, which has resulted in Bazeele signing at least two large contracts after the end of the accounting period.

48 Dibble (Mar/Jun 16) 49 mins

Dibble is formed of two autonomous divisions, Timber and Steel, and manufactures components for use in the construction industry. Dibble has always absorbed production overheads to the cost of each product on the basis of machine hours.

Timber Division

Timber Division manufactures timber frames used to support the roofs of new houses. The timber, which is purchased pre-cut to the correct length, is assembled into the finished frame by a factory worker who fastens the components together. Timber Division manufactures six standard sizes of frame which is sufficient for use in most newly built houses.

Steel Division

Steel Division manufactures steel frames and roof supports for use in small commercial buildings such as shops and restaurants. There is a large range of products, and many customers also specify bespoke designs for short production runs or one-off building projects. Steel is cut and drilled using the division's own programmable computer aided manufacturing machinery (CAM), and is bolted together or welded by hand.

Steel Division's strategy is to produce novel bespoke products at a price comparable to the simpler and more conventional products offered by its competitors. For example, many of Steel Division's customers choose to have steel covered in one of a wide variety of coloured paints and other protective coatings at the end of the production process. This is performed off-site by a subcontractor, after which the product is returned to Steel Division for despatch to the customer. Customers are charged the subcontractor's cost plus a 10% mark-up for choosing this option. The board of Steel Division has admitted that this pricing structure may be too simplistic, and that it is unsure of the overall profitability of sales of some groups of products or sectors of the market.

Recently, several customers have complained that incorrectly applied paint has flaked off the steel after only a few months' use. More seriously, a fast food restaurant has commenced litigation with Dibble after it had to close for a week while steel roof frames supplied by Steel Division were repainted. Following this, the Production Manager has proposed increasing the number of staff inspecting the quality of coating on the frames, and purchasing expensive imaging machinery to make inspection more efficient.

Activity-based costing and activity-based management

The chief executive officer (CEO) at Dibble has approached you as a performance management expert for your advice. 'At a conference recently,' he told you, 'I watched a presentation by a CEO at a similar business to ours talking about the advantages and disadvantages of using activity-based costing (ABC) and how over several years the adoption of activity-based management (ABM) had helped them to improve both strategic and operational performance.'

'I don't want you to do any detailed calculations at this stage, but I'd like to know more about ABC and ABM, and know whether they would be useful for Dibble,' he said.

You are provided with extracts of the most recent management accounts for Timber and Steel Divisions:

Division	Timber	Steel
	$'000	$'000
Revenue	25,815	20,605
Materials	12,000	10,100
Direct labour	4,500	850
Subcontract costs	75	650
Analysis of production overheads		
Set-up time for CAM machinery	–	575
Machining time	–	2,777
Storage of goods awaiting or returned from subcontractors	120	395
Transfer of goods to and from subcontractors	50	300
Inspection and testing	35	425
Total production overheads	205	4,472
Gross profit	9,035	4,533

Required

(a) (i) Advise the CEO how ABC could be implemented. **(4 marks)**

(ii) Assess whether it may be more appropriate to use ABC in Timber and Steel Divisions than the costing basis currently used. **(8 marks)**

(b) Advise the CEO how ABM could be used to improve business performance in Dibble.

(13 marks)

(Total = 25 marks)

49 Zones (Sep/Dec 18) 49 mins

Zones: Company information

Zones is an overnight parcel delivery business. Since it was founded by the current CEO, it has grown rapidly due to a boom in online shopping. It now operates 1,000 delivery vehicles of various sizes. Recently, financial performance and market share have deteriorated. Zones has had no clear corporate vision, an excessive focus on financial objectives and inadequate systems to measure and manage performance of the underlying processes driving its financial performance.

Business model

Zones' collection and delivery service uses delivery vehicles to transport parcels to and from local depots and individual addresses. Vehicles may also pick up parcels from the addresses to which they deliver. Each time the vehicle calls to pick up or deliver parcels is known as a stop, and the time of day for each stop is booked in advance. At the end of each day, vehicles, along with any parcels not delivered, return to the depot. Regardless of who pays for the service, Zones regards anyone to whom it delivers, or from whom it picks up parcels, as a customer. In the long term, the requirements of both of these groups for a competitively priced, reliable and flexible service will be similar.

Performance improvement proposals

The CEO believes that reductions in customer satisfaction and flexibility, caused by a decline in operational performance, may have led to the recent deterioration in financial performance and market share. It has been suggested that Zones use the Lynch and Cross performance pyramid (Appendix 1) to reverse this deterioration, and three new measures for operational performance have been suggested in Appendix 2. The CEO has stated that Zones' corporate vision should be:

'To increase shareholder wealth by becoming the leading overnight parcel delivery business, providing quality, reliability and value for customers.'

It is also proposed to use the DMAIC (define, measure, analyse, improve and control) method to implement the Six Sigma methodology to improve the quality of delivery. Two measures have been defined in Appendix 3 which may help improve Zones' delivery performance.

Required

(a) Advise the CEO how the Lynch and Cross performance pyramid can help Zones achieve its corporate vision. **(7 marks)**

(b) Using the performance pyramid, evaluate the extent to which the suggested new measures in Appendix 2 can be used to measure and manage operational performance at Zones. **(9 marks)**

(c) Advise whether the two measures defined in Appendix 3 are suitable for use in the DMAIC method to implement the Six Sigma methodology in order to improve delivery performance. **(9 marks)**

(Total = 25 marks)

APPENDIX 1

Lynch and Cross performance pyramid

APPENDIX 2

Suggested new measures for operational performance

Measure	Description
Vehicle utilisation	Average utilisation of all vehicle capacity. This is measured by taking the average of vehicle load as a percentage of capacity when the vehicle leaves the depot at the beginning of each day and the vehicle load as a percentage of capacity when the vehicle returns to the depot at the end of each day. Capacity is measured either according to the internal volume or the length of the vehicle, depending on the type of vehicle being used.
Fuel consumption	Average litres of fuel per kilometre travelled for all vehicles.
On-time stops	Percentage of stops made within 30 minutes* of the booked time.

* Zones receives complaints from customers relating to deliveries not made on time. Of these, less than 0.0001% relate to deliveries made within 30 minutes of the booked time.

APPENDIX 3

Suggested new measures for improving quality of delivery using the DMAIC methodology

Measure	Description
On-time stops	Percentage of stops made within 10 minutes of the booked time.
Failed deliveries	Percentage of deliveries which cannot be made due to the customer being unavailable to take the delivery, or by parcels being incorrectly addressed. Currently, 5% of deliveries are failed and have to be returned to the depot.

50 Callisto (6/12, amended)　　　　　　　49 mins

Company background

Callisto Retail (Callisto) is an online reseller of local craft products related to the historic culture of the country of Callistan. The business started ten years ago as a hobby of two brothers, Jeff and George. The brothers produced humorous, short video clips about Callistan which were posted on its website and became highly popular. They decided to use the website to try to sell Callistan merchandise and good initial sales made them believe that they had a viable business idea.

Callisto has gone from strength to strength and now boasts sales of $120m per annum, selling anything related to Callistan. Callisto is still very much the brothers' family business. They have gathered around themselves a number of strategic partners into what Jeff describes as a virtual company. Callisto has the core functions of video clip production, finance and supplier relationship management. The rest of the functions of the organisation (warehousing, delivery and website development) are outsourced to strategic partners.

The brothers work from their family home in the rural North of Callistan while other Callisto employees work from their homes in the surrounding villages and towns. These employees are involved in video editing, system maintenance, handling customer complaints and communication with suppliers and outsourcers regarding inventory. The employees log in to Callisto's systems via the national internet infrastructure. The outsourced functions are handled by multinational companies of good reputation which are based around the world. The brothers have always been fascinated by information technology and so they depend on email and electronic data interchange to communicate with their product suppliers and outsourcing partners.

Recent issues

Recently, there have been emails from regular customers of the Callisto website complaining about slow or non-delivery of orders that they have placed. George has commented that this represents a major threat to Callisto as the company operates on small profit margins, relying on volume to drive the business. He believes that sales growth will drive the profitability of the business due to its cost structure.

Contracts and service level agreements

Jeff handles the management of outsourcing and has been reviewing the contracts that exist between Callisto and its strategic partner for warehousing and delivery, RLR Logistics. The current contract for warehousing and delivery is due for renewal in two months and currently has the following service level agreements (SLAs):

(1)　　RLR agrees to receive and hold inventory from Callisto's product suppliers.

(2)　　RLR agrees to hold 14 days' inventory of Callisto's products.

(3)　　RLR agrees to despatch from its warehouse any order passed from Callisto within three working days, inventory allowing.

(4)　　RLR agrees to deliver to customers anywhere in Callistan within two days of despatch.

Breaches in these SLAs incur financial penalties on a sliding scale depending on the number and severity of the problems. Each party to the contract collects their own data on performance and this has led to disagreements in the past over whether service levels have been achieved, although no penalties have been triggered to date. The most common disagreement arises over inventory levels held by RLR, with RLR claiming that it cannot be expected to deliver products that are late in arriving to inventory due to the product suppliers' production and delivery issues.

Required

(a)　　Assess the difficulties of performance measurement and performance management in complex business structures such as Callisto, especially in respect of the performance of their employees and strategic partners.　　　　　　　　　**(17 marks)**

(b) George has also been increasingly concerned about the length of time it is taking for customer complaints to be addressed, and the damage which delays in replying to customer complaints could have on Callisto's reputation. In this respect, he is also worried that Callisto's employees are not working as productively as they could be.

Consequently, he has designed a daily report which lists all the employees in alphabetical order, and then shows four columns of data for each employee:

(1) How long they have been logged on to Callisto's system
(2) How many videos they have edited
(3) How many complaints they have handled
(4) How many suppliers or outsourcers they have contacted

Required

Evaluate the usefulness of George's proposed report, and suggest ways the output report could be improved.   **(8 marks)**

(Total = 25 marks)

51 Coal Creek (12/12, amended)   49 mins

Company background

Coal Creek Nursing Homes (CCNH) is a company operating residential care homes for the elderly in Geeland.

The residents at CCNH are those elderly people who can no longer care for themselves at home and whose family are unable to look after them. There are 784 homes with about 30,000 residents under the care of the company. There are about 42,500 staff, who range from head office staff, through home managers, to the care staff and cleaners and caterers.

The company is a private company which aims to make a suitable return to its shareholders. It had revenues of $938m in the last year and is one of the largest providers of residential care places in Geeland.

The company is split into two divisions: General Care (GC) which handles ordinary elderly residents and Special Care (SC), which is a newer operation that handles residents who need intensive care and attention due to physical or mental ailments.

CCNH does not own its homes but rents them from a number of large commercial landlords. It has taken on a large number of new homes recently in order to cope with the expansion of SC, which has proved successful with 24% p.a. revenue growth over the last two years. GC is a mature business with little growth in a sector that is now fully supplied. GC has seen volumes and margins falling as price pressure comes from its main customers (public sector health organisations which contract out this part of their care provision).

Recent events

A new chief executive officer (CEO) has just taken over at CCNH. She was appointed because the board of CCNH believed that the company was in difficulty. The previous CEO had been forced to leave following a scandal involving a number of the homes where residents' money had gone missing and their families had called in the police. The finance director and the operations director had also resigned, leaving the company without any experienced senior management.

The board has tasked the new CEO with ascertaining the current position of the business and identifying a strategy to address the issues that arise. The CEO wants to address the strategy, deciding whether to divest or retain elements of the business.

The CEO has come to you, as the most senior member of finance staff, for assistance with this task. The first area that she wants help on is the problem that the business is having with its landlords. The company struggled to meet its most recent rental payment, which the bank eventually agreed to cover through an increase to the overdraft, as CCNH had no ready cash. She is upset that the chosen strategic measures of performance (earnings per share growth and operating profit margin) did not identify the difficulties that the firm is now facing. One of the other directors had mentioned gearing problems but the CEO did not follow what this meant.

Also, the CEO has heard of qualitative models for predicting corporate failure and wants to apply one at CCNH. Obviously, she wants to know if CCNH exhibits any symptoms of failure.

You have been given the outline financial statements to help with this task (Appendix 1).

Required

(a) Discuss why indicators of liquidity and gearing need to be considered in conjunction with profitability at CCNH. Illustrate your answer with suitable calculations. **(11 marks)**

(b) Explain one qualitative model for predicting corporate failure (such as Argenti) and comment on CCNH's position utilising this model. You are not expected to give scores, only to comment on the areas of weakness at CCNH. **(9 marks)**

(c) Advise the CEO why it is important to consider product portfolios when she determines her strategy for the business. **(5 marks)**

(Total = 25 marks)

APPENDIX 1

Outline financial statements for CCNH for the year just ended

Summary income statements

	General care $m	Special care $m	Total $m
Revenue	685	253	938
Operating costs			
Homes: payroll	397	139	536
running	86	24	110
Rents	193	64	257
Central costs	27	3	30
Operating profit	(18)	23	5
Interest			5
Profit before tax			0
Tax			0
Profit for the period			0

STATEMENT OF FINANCIAL POSITION

	General care $m	Special care $m	Total $m
Assets			
Non-current assets	244	87	331
Current assets	17	47	64
Total assets	261	134	395
Equity and liabilities			
Share capital			165
Retained earnings reserve			24
Long-term borrowing			102
Current liabilities	76	28	104
Total equity and liabilities			395

(Note. A breakdown of the long-term financing into two divisions has not been possible.)

52 Freeze (Sept 18)   49 mins

Assume it is 'now' September 20X8.

Freeze: Company information

Freeze is listed on the small Kayland stock exchange and supplies construction services to the oil exploration industry in Kayland. Demand for Freeze's services broadly relates directly to the world oil price. A recent fall in the world oil price has led to several corporate failures in the oil exploration industry as the exploration of new oil fields becomes unprofitable. In April 20X8, a major oil spill led to widespread environmental damage in Kayland. An initial investigation has indicated that the cause of the oil spill may be due to the incorrect installation of machinery by Freeze.

Quantitative failure model: the K Score

The K Score is a quantitative model used for predicting whether Freeze is at risk of corporate failure. The K Score model was developed by correlating recent historic data on financial ratios of all companies listed on the Kayland stock exchange with the incidence of subsequent corporate failure. The method of calculation of the K Score is shown in Appendix 1.

Corporate failure indicators and comparator information

A colleague of yours, who is an academic working in a Kayland university, has suggested that operational gearing and financial gearing[1] are the two most important indicators of corporate failure in the industry in which Freeze operates. To demonstrate this, she has introduced you to Thor, which is a privately-owned company based in Jayland. Thor provides similar services to Freeze in both the Kayland and Jayland oil exploration industries. Thor reports its financial results in Jayland dollars (J\$). An economic recession has recently begun in Jayland.

Extracts from the publicly available accounts of Freeze and Thor for the year ended 31 December 20X7 are both shown in Appendix 2. For comparison purposes, both extracts are in K\$.

[1] Financial gearing is defined as (preference share capital + long-term debt)/total equity.

Required

(a)   Evaluate the usefulness of the quantitative K Score model in predicting the corporate failure of Freeze and Thor.   **(11 marks)**

(b)   Using only Freeze's K Score for the year ended 31 December 20X7, assess whether Freeze is at risk of corporate failure.   **(5 marks)**

(c)   Evaluate your colleague's comments on the most important indicators of corporate failure in Freeze's industry, and using these indicators, assess whether Freeze is more or less likely to suffer corporate failure than Thor.   **(9 marks)**

                                                                          (Total = 25 marks)

APPENDIX 1

Calculation of the K Score[1]

K Score = $2.5K_1 + 5.0K_2 + 0.1K_3 + 1.9K_4$

Score	Definition
K_1	Net current assests/total assets
K_2	Profit before interest and tax/total assets
K_3	Market value of ordinary shares[2]/book value of non-current liabilities
K_4	Retained earnings/total assests

Notes

1   A K Score of 2 or less indicates that corporate failure is highly likely, whereas a score of 5 or above indicates that corporate failure is unlikely. Scores of between 2 and 5 are in the 'grey area', where futher analysis is required to determine the likelihood of corporate failure.

2   The average price of Freeze ordinary shares on the Kayland stock exchange during the year ended 31 December 20X7 was $10.60.

APPENDIX 2

Extracts from the management accounts of Freeze and Thor

EXTRACTS FROM THE STATEMENT OF PROFIT OR LOSS FOR THE YEAR ENDED 31 DECEMBER 20X7

	Freeze K$'000	Thor K$'000
Sales revenue	5,995	7,395
Variable costs	(4,150)	(2,435)
Contribution	1,845	4,960
Fixed costs	(1,100)	(4,055)
Profit before interest and tax (PBIT)	745	905

STATEMENT OF FINANCIAL POSITION AT 31 DECEMBER 20X7*

	Freeze K$'000	Freeze K$'000	Thor K$'000	Thor K$'000
Assets				
Non-current assets		1,971		2,147
Current assets				
Inventory	234		102	
Receivables	1,930	2,164	1,720	1,822
Total assets		4,135		3,969
Equity and liabilities				
Equity				
Ordinary shares ($1)		500		600
Other components of equity (share premium)		335		93
Retained earnings		2,300		2,250
		3,135		2,943
Liabilities				
Non-current liabilities				
Bank loan	75		25	
Debentures	190		120	
5% preference shares	90		237	
		355		382
Current liabilities				
Trade payables	500		505	
Bank overdraft	145		139	
		645		644
Total equity and liabilities		4,135		3,969

*The statement of financial position was approved by the board on 31 March 20X8.

53 Laurel and Parsley (APM Mar/Jun 18) 49 mins

Assume it is 'now' July 20X8.

Laurel and Parsley (LP) is an architectural consultancy firm, specialising in the design of large commercial buildings.

Workforce planning

Due to an economic recession, which began in late 20X7, demand for LP's services fell dramatically, and there was insufficient work for all of the firm's consultants. LP's chief executive officer (CEO) believes that the recession will be short and that LP should do all it can to retain its highly skilled and experienced workforce ready for when demand increases after the end of the recession. The rest of the board believe that the firm should cut the size of the workforce until that time, as LP already has an operational gearing ratio 50% higher than its main rival.

New projects

Despite the board's objections, the CEO asked for LP to prepare bids for work on non-commercial building projects, which have so far been unaffected by the recession. Though LP had little track record in designing non-commercial residential buildings, it successfully tendered a fixed fee for the design work on a large housing development. As the finance director had been absent due to illness for a year, the CEO prepared and submitted the bid himself. To meet the tight deadlines for submission of the bid, this was done at a time when most of the board were taking their annual holidays.

It quickly became apparent that the staff resources required for the housing development project were much greater than the CEO had anticipated in the bid. In the rush to submit the bid and start work, staff were not given clear milestones for completion of the project, or individual performance targets. This has led to staff working long hours, morale has fallen, and several experienced employees have since left the firm. The project is well behind schedule, and LP's client has said it will take legal action against the firm to recover any financial losses caused by the delay.

Argenti's A score

It has been suggested to the board that LP may be at risk of corporate failure, as it has score of 47 using the Argenti A Score model, which is shown in Appendix 1.

Required

(a)   Using Argenti's A Score model, evaluate whether LP is at risk of corporate failure.

(12 marks)

(b)   Advise LP what performance management systems are needed in order to improve performance in respect of each of the mistakes and symptoms you have identified in part (a). (7 marks)

(c)   Evaluate the usefulness of using qualitative models such as the Argenti A Score in predicting corporate failure. (6 marks)

(Total = 25 marks)

APPENDIX 1

Argenti A-Score model

Defects

↓

Mistakes

↓

Symptoms

54 Lopten (12/13, amended) 98 mins

Company information

Lopten Industries (Lopten) is one of the largest listed consumer durables manufacturers in the world, making washing machines, tumble dryers and dishwashers. It has recently expanded into Beeland which is a developing country where incomes have risen to the point where demand is increasing for Lopten's goods among the growing middle-class population.

Lopten believes in the economies of scale of large manufacturing sites with dispersed selling branches in the markets in which it operates. Therefore, it has entered the Beeland market by setting up a local sales force and supporting them with a national marketing campaign. The company is currently selling only two products in Beeland (both are types of washing machines):

- A basic product (called Cheerful) with functions which are comparable with the existing local competitors' output

- A premium product (called Posh) which has functions and features similar to Lopten's products in other developed countries

Both products are manufactured and imported from its regional manufacturing hub, which is in the neighbouring country of Kayland.

Competitive environment

The competitive environment in Beeland is changing rapidly. The washing machine market used to be dominated by two large local manufacturers which make simple, cheap and reliable machines. There are two other major international manufacturers apart from Lopten. One of these has already opened a factory in Beeland and is producing machines similar to Cheerful to compete directly with the existing local producers. The Government of Beeland has supported this new entrant with grants, as it is keen to encourage inward investment by foreign companies and the resulting expertise and employment which they provide. The other international competitor is now considering entering the Beeland market with more highly specified machines similar to Lopten's Posh brand.

Mission, critical success factors and performance metrics

Lopten's stated mission is to be the 'most successful manufacturer of its type of products in the world'. The board has set the following critical success factors (CSFs) for Lopten's Beeland operations:

(1)   To obtain a dominant market presence
(2)   To maximise profits within acceptable risk
(3)   To maintain the brand image of Lopten for above average quality products

The board is considering using the following key performance indicators (KPIs) for each product: total profit, average sales price per unit, contribution per unit, market share, margin of safety, return on capital employed (ROCE), total quality costs and consumer awards won.

(Note. Margin of safety has been defined as [actual sales units – breakeven sales units]/actual sales units.)

The board has asked you as a consultant to assess its current performance measurement systems, and the first thing they want you to do is to calculate the various indicators it is considering using.

The board is also interested in how well the KPIs address issues in the external environment. Therefore, the second thing they want you to do is to use PEST analysis to identify issues in the

Lopten's external environment, and then evaluate the effectiveness of the suggested KPIs in addressing these issues.

A third issue the board is interested in is the relationship between the KPIs and Lopten's CSFs. In relation to this, the board have requested that you take each CSF in turn and evaluate how the KPIs which they are considering fit to the CSF which has been selected.

Next, the board wants your thoughts about the balance between planning and controlling represented by the KPIs, as they want to ensure that these match what they should be doing at the strategic level in Lopten. Specifically, the board wants you to assess the extent to which the suggested KPIs would be suitable for using in planning rather than controlling.

The data given in Appendix 1 has been collated for your use.

Marketing strategies

As well as its work on Lopten's performance measurement systems, the board is also considering two new marketing strategies going forward:

Plan A is to continue operations as at present allowing for 4% growth p.a. in volumes of both Cheerful and Posh.

Plan B is to dramatically reduce the marketing spend on Cheerful and to reallocate resources to focus the marketing on Posh. This is expected to lead to an anticipated growth in volume of 15% p.a. for Posh and flat sales for Cheerful.

The target operating profit for the Beeland operation in two years' time is set at $135m and the board wants an evaluation of these strategies in meeting that target.

The Board would like an evaluation of whether the two proposed marketing strategies will enable Lopten to achieve its operating profit target.

Required

Write a report to the board of Lopten which responds to their instructions for work on the following areas:

(a) Calculation of the KPIs suggested by the board for the assessment of performance of the Beeland operations   **(11 marks)**

(b) Use of a PEST analysis to identify issues in the external environment and then evaluation of the suggested KPIs in addressing these issues   **(11 marks)**

(c) The fit between KPIs and CSFs   **(10 marks)**

(d) The use of the KPIs for planning rather than controlling   **(5 marks)**

(e) Evaluation of two marketing strategies   **(9 marks)**

Professional marks will be awarded for the format, style and structure of the discussion of your answer.   **(4 marks)**

Note. All figures are real for the purpose of this scenario so that inflation can be ignored. Also, round to the nearest $m as appropriate.

                                                                                                (Total = 50 marks)

APPENDIX 1

Beeland operation's information for the most recent financial year

	Cheerful	Posh	Total
Variable costs	*$ per unit*	*$ per unit*	
Materials	90	120	
Labour	60	80	
Overheads	40	50	
Distribution costs	45	45	
Quality costs	20	30	

	Cheerful	Posh	Total
Variable costs	$ per unit	$ per unit	
Fixed costs	$m	$m	$m
Administration costs	18	18	36
Distribution costs	16	16	32
Quality costs	6	6	12
Marketing costs	80	80	160
Other data	$m	$m	$m
Revenue	448	308	756
Capital employed	326	250	576
	Units	Units	Units
Total market size (millions)	9.33	1.33	10.66
Beeland operation's sales (millions)	1.12	0.44	1.56

Notes

1   Cheerful has won one best buy award from the Beeland Consumer Association.

2   Posh has won four best buy awards from the Beeland Consumer Association.

3   The allocations of fixed costs are based on a recent activity-based costing exercise and are considered to be valid.

55 Chiven (Mar/Jun 18)   98 mins

Company information and aim

Chiven Stores (Chiven) is a listed clothing retailer in Beeland. Its overall aim is 'to become the largest clothing retailer in Beeland and deliver exceptional value to its shareholders'. It has recently dropped down the clothing retailer rankings from fourth to fifth largest. Shareholders have expressed concern at the lack of dividend growth at a time when spending in the Beeland clothing market has been growing.

Performance reporting

There has been a recent change of chief executive officer (CEO) and the new CEO has identified that the performance reporting at Chiven is not fit for the needs of the business. She has asked you to prepare a report to the board to address the performance measurement and management issues which she sees as most important. Her plan is to achieve the overall aim by 'maximising our opportunities from new technology and increasing our currently small web presence'. She wants a detailed evaluation of the current performance report which is used by the board for its annual review of the business (Appendix 1). However, she wants this overall task split into two separate parts in your report, with the first being an evaluation of the existing set of measures and their presentation. In relation to this, the CEO has stated that the current performance report does not need a commentary though, as she and the finance director talk through the report in detail with the board.

For the second part of the task, the CEO wants you – using the data in Appendix 1 – to recommend, and justify, three new measures which you believe address key issues for the business but are not currently on the report. The CEO also wants you to include appropriate calculations for each of the measures you recommend.

Business integration and supply chain

In an additional effort to drive improvement and gain competitive advantage for Chiven, the board has decided to use the value chain as a business integration tool. The CEO has provided a copy of the value chain diagram which was discussed at the last board meeting (Appendix 2). She believes that further improvements in Chiven's performance can be achieved through simplification of the supply chain. The CEO believes that this has implications for the performance measurement and information systems at Chiven and wants your report to address this as well. She has asked you to advise on appropriate performance measures and systems for Chiven when using the value chain approach to simplify the supply chain.

Big data

Finally, the CEO has already identified one important reason for Chiven's poor performance and that is its failure to make use of 'Big Data' in relation to Chiven's web sales. She believes that the board does not understand the implications of the volume, velocity and variety of this data for the business and wants you to write a guide for them. She is aware that this is a new and rapidly developing area for most businesses, so she considers that the board should also be briefed about its risks and challenges.

The CEO needs you to include a section in your report for the board which discusses the development of Big Data and its potential impact on Chiven's information systems, including the risks and challenges it presents.

Required

Write a report to the board of Chiven to respond to the CEO's instructions for work on the following areas:

(a)   Evaluation of the existing measures and presentation in the current performance report

(20 marks)

(b)   The new performance measures you recommend **(8 marks)**

(c)   The implications on performance measures and systems of simplifying the supply chain

(7 marks)

(d)   Big Data, and its potential impact on Chiven's information systems **(11 marks)**

Professional marks will be awarded for the format, style and structure of the discussion of your answer. **(4 marks)**

(Total = 50 marks)

APPENDIX 1

Chiven Stores

Annual performance report for year ended March 20X8

Revenue ($m)			Region	A	B	C	Total	20X8 Total	20X7 Total
	Clothing								
		Men's		178	356	178	712		
		Women's		297	593	297	1,187		
		Children's		119	237	119	475		
			Total	594	1,186	594		2,374	2,351
	Other								
		Men's		19	39	19	77		
		Women's		32	65	32	129		
		Children's		13	26	13	52		
			Total	64	130	64		258	255
							Total	2,632	2,606

Operating profit margin ($m)			Region	A	B	C	Total	20X8 Total	20X7 Total
	Clothing								
		Men's		15.5	15.7	15.2			
		Women's		16.2	16.3	15.9			
		Children's		18.1	18.3	18.0			
	Other								
		Men's		15.5	15.8	15.2			
		Women's		16.2	16.4	15.8			
		Children's		18.1	18.2	17.8			
							Overall	16.5	16.5

	20X8	20X7
Number of stores	542	540
EPS ($)	0.56	0.56
Dividend per share ($)	0.28	0.28
EVA™ ($m)	21	24
Inventory turnover rate (days)	32	32
Average number of product line bought per supplier	66	64
Floor space (square meters)	850,000	828,00
Market share (%)	9.8	10.1
Number of employees	40,500	39,400
Number of suppliers	161	161
ROCE (%)	8.3	8.5
Number of accidents in stores	256	255
Average queuing time for customers (seconds)	125	128
WACC (%)	5.8	5.7
Average time between customer entry and employee greeting (seconds)	248	232
Inventory obsolescence/loss write-downs ($m)	25	25

APPENDIX 2

Value chain diagram

56 Folt (3/19)   98 mins

Folt Manufacturing: Company information

Folt Manufacturing (Folt) is a company, which is majority owned by its management team. A number of years ago, it was bought out of a larger multinational business by the management team. The management were supported by a venture capital firm, who provided the remaining equity and now supply all the debt required by the business at market rates. The business manufactures and sells digital imaging devices for use in a variety of industrial situations. A key component in its products is the image processing software which is included. Folt has a small team of software developers who are beginning to gain a reputation for innovative solutions.

Folt has faced increasing pressure in its home market of Beeland, from manufacturers in countries with lower cost bases. As a result, it has decided to invest in developing its image processing software rather than compete on the manufacturing of the hardware (the imaging devices). It will continue to sell the imaging devices but the manufacturing will be outsourced.

Folt's overall objective is unchanged and it is 'to provide an adequate return to its capital providers while growing the business into a world-class supplier in its areas of expertise'. The chief executive officer (CEO) has identified three factors which are critical success factors (CSFs) to achieving this objective. These are:

(1)   Keep capital providers satisfied;
(2)   Build a world-class software development team; and
(3)   Ensure that quality of the imaging devices meets market standards.

Performance measurement system

The CEO requires assistance from a performance management expert to create an appropriate performance measurement system for Folt. First, he needs recommendations of suitably justified key performance indicators (KPIs) for each CSF. The CEO has indicated that there should be a maximum of two KPIs per CSF in order to avoid information overload. Then, he wants an assessment of the use of this group of KPIs to measure the strategic performance of Folt.

Outsourced manufacturing: Initial plans

The company has selected a suitable manufacturer for the outsourced work. Xela Manufacturing (Xela) is based in Ceeland, which is a much lower cost environment than Beeland. Folt is preparing to enter into detailed contract negotiations with Xela.

The manufacturing will be done under licence from Folt. This means that Folt supplies the product designs but retains the intellectual rights to them and Xela manufactures to agreed standards of quality. Xela then despatches the devices back to Folt who add the software, package the product and send it to their customers. The quality standards will be set by the service level agreements (SLAs), which will be agreed in the contract.

In preparation for these negotiations, the CEO needs advice on the following three critical areas (target costing, responsibility for quality areas and sources of information) for the negotiation of the agreement.

Target costing

The CEO realises that he needs to understand the cost structure of the products in order to have a firm basis for price negotiation with Xela. He has heard that target costing could be helpful. Therefore, he needs to know how target costing works and how it might be used in this situation. In order to clarify the explanation, he has gathered information (Appendix 1) on one product (Product 123) which requires a redesign before being relaunched into the market. He wants an example calculation of the target cost gap and an explanation of how the result of this would impact on negotiations with Xela.

Responsibility for quality areas

The maintenance of existing quality is a critical concern for Folt, since it will focus on software as the key selling point, but this will not be sufficient for market success if the hardware does not meet market standards. The CEO wants to understand, in terms of the four areas of quality costs, how responsibility for each area should be attributed between Folt and Xela.

Sources of information

Folt has appropriate information systems in place for its existing manufacturing operation. The CEO and board are happy with their operation at present. However, Xela has indicated that its current information systems are purely financial, aiming to collect the required information for its financial reporting duties. The CEO is worried about this and wants an assessment of the impact of this on the management of quality within the contract.

It is now 1 September 20X5.

Required

Write a report to the CEO of Folt Manufacturing (Folt) to respond to the instructions for work on the following areas:

(a)	Key performance indicators	(16 marks)
(b)	Target costing	(10 marks)
(c)	Quality costs	(11 marks)
(d)	Information systems	(9 marks)

Professional marks will be awarded for the format, style and structure of the discussion of your answer. **(4 marks)**

(Total = 50 marks)

APPENDIX 1

Information on Product 123

The company aims for a profit margin of 20% on Product 123. Target price is $175 per unit, based on sales and marketing department research.

Cost details:

(1) The remaining commercial life of the product is two years.

(2) It is estimated that 250,000 units will be sold over the remaining life of the product.

(3) Materials cost $37 per unit.

(4) Each unit will take 0.5 hours of labour at an average cost of $25 per hour.

(5) Each unit will use 1.1 hours of machine time at an average cost (including overheads) of $32 per hour.

(6) Packaging and delivery will cost $8 per unit.

(7) The design costs of the unit are expected to total $2m.

(8) Inspections cost $100,000 per annum – the redesign will not affect this.

(9) The rate of failed products, either spotted by customers or by the inspection team, is expected to remain at 2.5%.

(10) Failed products will be reworked at an average cost of $20 per unit.

(11) The software package supplied by Folt costs $40 per unit.

57 Flack (Mar/Jun 16, amended) 98 mins

Company information and mission

Flack Supermarkets (Flack) is a multinational listed business operating in several developing countries. The business is divided into two divisions: Metro, which runs smaller stores in the densely populated centres of cities, and Hyper, which runs the large supermarkets situated on the edges of cities. Flack sells food, clothing and some other household goods.

Competition between supermarkets is intense in all of Flack's markets and so there is a constant need to review and improve their management and operations.

Flack mission is to be: 'the first choice for customers by providing the right balance of quality and service at a competitive price. We will achieve this through acting in the long-term interests of our stakeholders: earning customer loyalty, utilising all our resources and serving our shareholders' interests.'

Performance report

You are a performance management expert working for Flack, and the chief executive officer (CEO) wants your views on the company's performance report and whether it is fit for the

BPP LEARNING MEDIA

purpose of achieving the company's mission. The CEO has provided you with a copy of the company's most recent report as an example (Appendix 1).

This report is used at Flack's board level for the annual review of the company's performance. The divisional boards have their own reports.

The CEO has mentioned to you that there has been criticism of the board of Flack in the financial press, saying that the board is 'short-termist'.

Therefore, the CEO has asked you to evaluate the performance report to see if it is fit for the purpose of achieving the company's mission. However, the CEO also wants your evaluation of the performance report to include comments in relation to the criticism that the board is short-termist.

Performance measures

The board is considering introducing two new performance measures to address the objective of 'utilising all our resources'. These are revenue per square metre, and operating profit per square metre.

The CEO wants an evaluation of these two measures, explaining: how they might address the objective, what those ratios currently are, and how they could be used to manage business performance. The CEO told you that the information in the board report (Appendix 1) will assist in this work.

There have been disagreements between Flack's divisional management about capital allocation. The divisions have had capital made available to them. Both sets of divisional managers always seem to want more capital in order to open more stores but historically have been reluctant to invest in refurbishing existing stores. The board is unsure of capital spending priorities given that the press comments about Flack included criticism of the 'run-down' look of a number of its stores.

The CEO has asked you to assess the effectiveness of the current divisional performance measure of divisional operating profit and the possibility of replacing this with residual income, in the light of these problems. The CEO has told you that you are not required to calculate the current values.

New stores

As the company is opening many new stores, the board also wants an assessment of the use of expected return on capital employed (ROCE) as a tool for deciding on new store openings.

You have been given data for a new store proposal (Appendix 2), as an example to use when making your assessment.

The CEO has told you that the board wants the focus of your comments to be on the use of an expected value, not on the use of ROCE, as this is widely used and understood in the retail industry.

With this in mind, the CEO asked you to calculate the expected ROCE for the new store, and assess its use as a tool for decision making at Flack.

Information system

The CEO has proposed to the board that a new information system be introduced. She wishes to spend $100m on creating a loyalty card programme with a data warehouse collecting information from customers' cards regarding their purchases. Her plan is to use this information to target advertising, product range choices and price offers more efficiently than at present.

The CEO has asked you to include in your report an explanation of how the proposed new information system can help to improve business performance at Flack.

Required

Write a report to the board of Flack, in response to the CEO's instructions for work on the following areas:

(a)	Evaluation of Flack's performance report	**(14 marks)**
(b)	Evaluation of the new performance measures (revenue and operating profit per square metre)	**(8 marks)**
(c)	Changing the divisional performance measure	**(8 marks)**
(d)	The use of expected ROCE	**(8 marks)**
(e)	The proposed new information system	**(8 marks)**

Professional marks will be awarded for the format, style and structure of the discussion of your answer.
(4 marks)

(Total = 50 marks)

APPENDIX 1

Board's performance report

FLACK YEAR TO 31 MARCH

	Metro budget 20X6 $'000	Metro actual 20X6 $'000	Hyper budget 20X6 $'000	Hyper actual 20X6 $'000	Flack budget 20X6 $'000	Flack actual 20X6 $'000	Flack actual 20X5 $'000	Change on PY
Revenue								
Food	1,093,521	1,104,567	5,431,277	5,542,119	6,524,798	6,646,686	6,513,752	2.04%
Clothes	765,465	773,197	3,801,894	3,879,483	4,567,359	4,652,680	4,536,363	2.56%
Other goods	328,056	331,370	1,629,383	1,662,636	1,957,439	1,994,006	1,964,096	1.52%
Total	2,187,042	2,209,134	10,862,554	11,084,238	13,049,596	13,293,372	13,014,211	2.15%
Cost of sales	1,994,583	2,014,730	10,199,937	10,408,099	12,194,520	12,422,829	12,186,796	1.94%
Gross profit	192,459	194,404	662,617	676,139	855,076	870,543	827,415	5.21%
Gross margins		8.80%		6.10%		6.55%		
Other operating costs	34,993	35,346	173,801	177,348	208,794	212,694	208,227	
Operating profit	157,466	159,058	488,816	498,791	646,282	657,849	619,188	6.24%
Operating margins		7.20%		4.50%		4.95%		
Finance costs					76,993	79,760	75,482	
Group profit before tax					**569,289**	**578,089**	**543,706**	6.32%
Tax					142,322	144,522	135,926	
Group profit after tax					**426,967**	**433,567**	**407,780**	6.32%
Total shareholder return						3.10%	2.70%	
Return on capital employed	13.2%	13.3%	13.2%	13.5%	13.2%	13.4%	13.2%	
Number of stores		533		208				
Total square metres		161,227		841,967				

APPENDIX 2

New store

The following data has been forecast by the Marketing Department for the new store based on Flack's existing experience. There are three possible scenarios:

Demand scenarios	Low	Medium	High
Revenue ($m)	12.5	13.0	13.5
Probability (%)	20	50	30
Forecast operating margin (%)	4.1	4.3	4.4

The new store is expected to cost $4.2m to buy, fit out and stock. The target ROCE for Flack has been set at 13%.

58 Cantor (6/14, amended) 98 mins

Company information and mission

Cantor Group (Cantor) is a listed company with two subsidiaries, both involved in food and drink retailing in the small country of Deeland. Its mission is 'to maximise shareholder value through supplying good value food and drink in appealing environments for our customers'.

Cantor Cafés (Cafés) is the original operating company for the group and is a chain of 115 cafés specialising in different coffee drinks but also serving some simple food dishes. Cafés has been running successfully for 15 years and has reached the limit of its expansion as the café market is now considered to be saturated with competition. Further growth will occur only as the opportunity to obtain profitable, new sites is presented, although such opportunities are not expected to be significant over the next few years.

Cantor Juicey (Juicey) was started by the Cantor Group two years ago. Now, it is made up of 15 juice bars which serve a variety of blended fruit juice drinks and health snacks. The products served by Juicey have benefited from an increased awareness in Deeland of the need to eat and drink healthily. Cantor Group expects to increase the rate of property acquisition in order to feed the rapid growth of this business, intending to open 25 outlets per year for the next four years.

Cantor Group organises its two subsidiaries in a similar way, as they are involved in similar areas of business. There is one exception to this, namely in the arrangements over the properties from which the subsidiaries operate. Cafés rent their properties on the open market on standard commercial terms with a five-year lease at a fixed rental payable quarterly in advance. Juicey, on the other hand, has made a single arrangement with a large commercial landlord for all of its properties. Juicey has agreed that the rent for its sites is a percentage of the revenue generated at each site. Juicey believes that it can continue its expansion by obtaining more sites from this landlord under the same terms.

Performance reporting systems

The board of Cantor is reviewing the company's performance reporting systems, and in relation to this the chief executive officer (CEO) has asked for your thoughts on the current report, which you have been given a copy of (Appendix 1). This report contains information for both the subsidiaries and the group and is used by all three boards.

The CEO has asked you to evaluate the current report. However, the CEO has advised you that the board does not require an evaluation of Cantor's performance.

Cost structures

A second area the CEO wants you to consider is the cost structures at Cantor, and the implications of the mix of fixed and variable elements in the key cost areas of staff and property for performance management.

The CEO has asked you to provide an assessment of the fixed and variable elements of these two key costs in each of the subsidiaries, and the impact which this may have on performance management of these costs. However, the CEO told you that detailed calculations are not required.

Value based management (VBM) and Economic value added (EVA™)

At a recent shareholder meeting of Cantor, one of the large shareholders expressed concern that the group lacks focus and suggested the introduction of value-based management (VBM) using economic value added (EVA™) as the measure of value. Cantor's CEO has asked you, the group's strategic management accountant, to give the board more information on the implications of this suggestion. She has asked you to produce an example calculation of the EVA™ for the Group using the current data (Appendices 1 and 2), justifying any assumptions made, and commenting briefly on how the shareholders might view the result.

The board also needs to have the VBM system explained and evaluated, to be able to make a decision about its use at Cantor. To this end, the CEO has asked you explain how VBM could be implemented at Cantor, and to evaluate its potential impact on the group.

Potential changes to mission statement

Finally, the board is considering amending the mission statement to include more information on the ethical values of the company. The area being considered for inclusion in the overall mission is the treatment of employees as it is felt that they should share in the progress and profitability of Cantor since a happy working environment will help them to better serve the customers.

The proposed new mission statement would read:

'To maximise shareholder value and to provide a fair deal to our employees by supplying good value food and drink in appealing environments for our customers.'

The CEO has asked you to consider how the Group's performance in the area regarding employees could be measured using the current management information at Cantor. You have been given additional information from the management information system to assist with this task (Appendix 3).

The CEO would like you to use this additional information, and the current performance report where appropriate, to provide justified recommendations for suitable performance measures to reflect the proposed change in the company's mission statement.

Required

Write a report to the CEO of Cantor to respond to her instructions for work on the following areas:

(a)	The current performance report	**(15 marks)**
(b)	Fixed and variable elements in the key cost areas	**(6 marks)**
(c)	The example calculation of economic value added (EVA™) for the Group	**(9 marks)**
(d)	Implementing VBM at Cantor	**(10 marks)**
(e)	Performance measures for the revised mission statement	**(6 marks)**

Professional marks will be awarded for the format, style and structure of the discussion of your answer.   **(4 marks)**

(Total = 50 marks)

APPENDIX 1

Cantor Group   Year to 31 March

	Cafés Budget 20X4 $	Cafés Actual 20X4 $	Juicey Budget 20X4 $	Juicey Actual 20X4 $	Group Budget 20X4 $	Group Actual 20X4 $	Group	Industry average
Revenue								
Drink	47,437,500	46,521,000	5,130,000	5,398,000	52,567,500	51,919,000		
Food	15,812,500	15,913,000	570,000	582,000	16,382,500	16,495,000		
Total	**63,250,000**	**62,434,000**	**5,700,000**	**5,980,000**	**68,950,000**	**68,414,000**		
Cost of sales								
Drink	12,808,125	12,560,670	1,385,100	1,457,460	14,193,225	14,018,130		
Food	3,478,750	3,500,860	125,400	128,040	3,604,150	3,628,900		
Total	**16,286,875**	**16,061,530**	**1,510,500**	**1,585,500**	**17,797,375**	**17,647,030**	25.8%	
Gross profit	**46,963,125**	**46,372,470**	**4,189,500**	**4,394,500**	**51,152,625**	**50,766,970**	74.2%	72.8%
Staff costs	16,128,750	15,920,670	1,453,500	1,524,900	20,082,250	21,345,000	31.2%	30.9%
Other operating costs								
Rent	2,875,000	2,875,000	342,000	358,800	3,929,000	3,945,800		
Local property tax	920,000	920,000	60,000	60,000	980,000	980,000		
Insurance	276,000	282,000	18,000	18,400	294,000	300,400		
Utilities	874,000	861,000	61,500	62,900	935,500	923,900		
Marketing	6,957,500	6,888,000	627,000	750,000	7,584,500	7,638,000	11.2%	10.0%
Depreciation	4,427,500	4,427,500	353,400	353,400	4,780,900	4,780,900		
Total	**16,330,000**	**16,253,500**	**1,461,900**	**1,603,500**	**18,503,900**	**18,569,000**	27.1%	
Operating profit	**14,504,375**	**14,198,300**	**1,274,100**	**1,266,100**	**12,566,475**	**10,852,970**	15.9%	15.3%
Finance costs					798,000	801,000		
Group profit before tax					**11,768,475**	**10,051,970**	14.7%	
Tax					2,942,119	2,512,993		
Group profit after tax					**8,826,356**	**7,538,977**	11.0%	

Costs and profit as a % of revenue

APPENDIX 2

Data about the group for the financial year:

1 Debt/Equity   30.0%

2 Cost of equity   15.7%

3 Tax rate   25.0%

4 Group ROCE   19.0%

5 Group capital employed: $53,400,000 at period start and $58,500,000 at period end.

6 Pre-tax cost of debt   6.5%

7 There has been $2.1m of tax paid in the year.

8 It is estimated that half of the marketing spend of $7.638m is on building the Cantor brand long term.

9 It is further estimated that there has been the same level of annual spending on long-term brand building in the years leading up to 20X4.

APPENDIX 3

Additional management information for 20X4

	Cafés	Juicey	Group
No. of employees			
At year start	1,495	96	1,611
Leavers	146	15	161
Joiners	152	35	187
At year end	1,501	116	1,637

Note. Group numbers include Cafés, Juicey and head office numbers.

59 Boltzman Machines (12/14, amended)   98 mins

Company information and mission

Boltzman Machines (Boltzman) is a listed, multinational engineering business. Its mission is 'to maximise shareholder value through engineering excellence'.

Boltzman has two divisions, one manufacturing aerospace parts and the other automotive parts. The company is known for innovation and it allows its managers much autonomy to run their own divisions and projects. However, there has been recent criticism at a shareholders' meeting of the executive management for not listening to shareholders' concerns and allowing this autonomy to run out of control.

Therefore, the board at Boltzman has been reviewing a number of aspects of the way performance is controlled and managed in the business. However, there are a number of initiatives already running within the company, which the board feels may help to address the shareholders' concerns.

The initiatives which are running at present are:

(1)   An analysis of stakeholder influence at Boltzman leading to suitable strategic performance measures

(2)   A benchmarking exercise of the performance measures from Initiative 1 with Boltzman's main competitor, General Machines

(3)   The introduction of quality initiatives bringing lean production methods to Boltzman

(4)   The introduction of a balanced scorecard performance measurement system

The chief executive officer (CEO) has asked for your views on the impact these initiatives could have on performance management within the company.

Analysis of stakeholder influence

A stakeholder analysis has been completed by one of Boltzman's managers (Appendix 1) but she has gone on holiday and has not written up a commentary of her results. Therefore, the CEO wants you to take the information in Appendix 1 and explain the results.

The CEO wants you to do two things in particular: to briefly justify appropriate management approaches to each of the stakeholders, and, based on this, to evaluate the appropriateness of the suggested performance measures in Appendix 1. However, the CEO has stressed that you should not, at this stage, suggest long lists of additional indicators.

Benchmarking exercise

The CEO wants you to use the suggested performance measures from the stakeholder analysis to benchmark the performance of Boltzman against General Machines. The CEO stated:

> Make sure that you calculate the measures given in Appendix 1. You should also add two justified measures of your own using the data provided. However, restrict yourself to these seven measures and don't drown us with detail about individual business units. As well as benchmarking Boltzman's performance, please can you also evaluate the approach to benchmarking used.

A junior analyst has already gathered the data for you to use in the benchmarking exercise (Appendix 2).

Quality initiatives

Boltzman has stated that one of its strategic aims is to be the highest quality supplier in the marketplace. In order to achieve this, the Head of the Aerospace Division has already started a project to implement just-in-time (JIT) manufacturing. The CEO has sent you an extract of the email proposing this change (Appendix 3). The CEO feels that there are some important elements hinted at but not developed in this email. In particular, the CEO wants you to explain the problems of moving to JIT manufacturing at Boltzman.

Balanced scorecard

Finally, the CEO feels it is important that the company's performance is measured across a range of non-financial areas as well as financial ones. He believes that the balanced scorecard would provide a good choice, but has asked you to evaluate its suitability as a performance measurement system in the light of the shareholders' recent criticism, and the other initiatives currently in progress at Boltzman.

Required

Prepare a report to the board of Boltzman to respond to the CEO's instructions for work on the following areas:

(a)   Managing stakeholders, and the appropriateness of the suggested performance measures

(14 marks)

(b)   Benchmarking Boltzman against General Machines   (16 marks)

(c)   Just-in-time manufacturing   (7 marks)

(d)   Using the balanced scorecard as a performance measurement system   (9 marks)

Professional marks will be awarded for the format, style and structure of the discussion of your answer.

(4 marks)

(Total = 50 marks)

APPENDIX 1

Key stakeholders	Level of interest	Level of power
Shareholders	Low – institutions have delegated management to the board and are only interested in financial returns	High – ability to vote out existing management
Employees	Medium – in a high skill industry employees are interested in the new opportunities which the market can present	Low – although there is a group of key employees in product development whose skills must not be lost
Customers	Medium – some of the parts supplied by Boltzman are unique and specifically designed for the customer	High – as there are few major players in the aerospace and automotive businesses, the loss of a customer would have a significant impact on Boltzman
Suppliers	Medium – Boltzman is one of the large customers to many of the company's suppliers	Low – the suppliers are generally bulk component producers and there is significant competition for Boltzman's business

Suggested performance measures:

- Return on capital employed
- Economic value added
- Revenue growth
- Average pay per employee
- Net profit margin

APPENDIX 2

The figures are drawn from the financial statements for the year to September 20X4.

	Boltzman 20X4 $m	General Machines 20X4 $m
Revenue	23,943	25,695
Cost of sales	18,078	20,605
Other costs	2,958	3,208
Operating profit	2,907	1,882
Financing costs	291	316
Tax	663	718
Net income	1,953	848

	Boltzman 20X3 $m	Boltzman 20X4 $m	General Machines 20X3 $m	General Machines 20X4 $m
Non-current assets	16,335	16,988	17,716	17,893
Current assets	10,618	11,043	11,515	11,630
	26,953	28,031	29,231	29,523
Equity	8,984	9,961	9,744	10,083
Non-current liabilities	9,801	9,739	10,629	10,405
Current liabilities	8,168	8,331	8,858	9,035
	26,953	28,031	29,231	29,523

		Boltzman 20X4	General Machines 20X4
Notes:			
No. of employees		86,620	93,940
Staff costs	($m)	4,731	4,913
Revenue for 20X3	($m)	22,506	25,438
Product development costs	($m)	2,684	2,630
No. of top 10 biggest potential customers where the business has top tier supplier status:			
Aerospace		6	6
Automotive		7	8

A suitable cost of capital for both companies is 11%.

The tax rate is 28%.

APPENDIX 3

Extract of Head of Aerospace's email on his quality initiative:

In order to improve the quality and profitability of our products, we intend to begin by introducing a lean approach to manufacturing.

The first step in our move to lean manufacturing will be the introduction of JIT manufacturing. Although this will be a difficult process, the financial rewards in reduced working capital required and a decluttering of the workplace should be significant. We will have to consider how this change impacts up and down our supply chain with customers and suppliers.

60 Merkland Sportswear (6/15, amended)　　98 mins

Company information, mission and business aims

Merkland Sportswear (MS) is the market leader in sportswear in Ceeland, selling a variety of sportswear products under its own well-known brand. It is primarily a product development and marketing business as it contracts out all of its manufacturing to third parties around the world and it mostly sells its products through third-party retailers. It has only one store which is located in the capital city of Ceeland. The purpose of this store is to act as a centre for its marketing activities and to be a tangible representation of the MS brand. However, the main marketing activity for MS is the recruitment and promotion of star sportsmen and women as MS brand ambassadors. MS tries to have the most well-known sports star in each of the ten most popular sports in Ceeland as an ambassador.

You are a performance management adviser to MS, brought into the company by the chief executive officer (CEO) to help the board with a number of issues.

Performance dashboard

The first area in which the board of MS requires your input is in a review of the existing performance dashboard for MS, and you have been given a copy of the dashboard (Appendix 1). The dashboard is deliberately kept focused as it is for board use and the CEO has indicated that the three performance headings of 'financial, design and brand' will be kept at this time. The board has accepted that there may need to be up to two metrics for each of 'brand' and 'design' but they want to keep the number of financial metrics at three.

The mission statement of the business is designed to be broadly appealing. It is 'to inspire Ceelanders to compete'. From a business perspective, the aims are more focused; MS aims to grow as a business and to maximise shareholder wealth. The CEO further clarified the broad strategy to achieve these aims saying, 'We want to inspire competition not just in our customers but also within the company, to seek our greatest competitive advantage. We will achieve this by creating innovative products which provide reduced risk of injury and enhanced sporting performance supported by the best marketing operation in Ceeland.'

Review of competitive position

In order to assist in providing more detailed strategies to achieve the company's aims, the board has instituted a review of the competitive position of MS by commissioning a SWOT analysis, and you have also been given a copy of this (Appendix 2).

The CEO wants to you assess the existing dashboard metrics (Appendix 1) and then use the SWOT analysis to suggest improvements to the dashboard metrics within the constraints the CEO has outlined.

Child labour scandal

You have been given details on a recent new development in the market.

Nush Sportswear, one of the major competitors of MS, has recently suffered a scandal which has been widely reported. An investigative reporter discovered that one of the suppliers who manufactured sports shoes for Nush had been using child labour. The country in which the manufacturer worked had rules prohibiting child labour, but enforcement of these rules was very weak. This story has been widely covered in the media and has led to consumer boycotts and a review by the Ceeland business regulator into Nush's sourcing policies. It has been discovered that this is common practice in the sports footwear business where manufacturing is outsourced to such countries.

Potential responses to the child labour scandal

MS's shareholders have reacted with alarm to the potential damage that this could do to MS's brand. They have asked the board to consider changing their policy of outsourcing footwear manufacture.

The board is considering two alternative responses:

(1) Review and ensure that all outsourced footwear manufacture complies with appropriate employment terms and conditions (where necessary manufacturing would move to third-party companies in countries with appropriate regulation and enforcement); or

(2) Create a manufacturing operation for MS in order to have full control of operations.

In Response 1, the review of existing third-party manufacturers is being performed by a team from the Procurement Department. They have also considered the impact of moving all footwear sourcing to more strictly regulated environments. The results of this investigation are given in Appendix 3.

The CEO has asked you to assess the qualitative and quantitative impact of this response on performance management at MS, using the data in Appendix 3.

In Response 2, the board is considering setting up a factory for the manufacture of all MS footwear, but it wants to understand the impact of this on MS's existing performance metrics.

This has prompted the CEO to give you some further tasks.

Operating profit of the factory

The board needs a forecast of the profit from the factory as there are three distinct economic scenarios under which it might operate (see Appendix 4 for details). In relation to this, the CEO has asked you to calculate the expected operating profit of the new factory, and to evaluate the use of this method of decision making under risk.

Impact of the new factory on dashboard metrics

The board also wants to know how the new factory will impact on the existing performance dashboard. However, since the probabilities of these economic scenarios are under debate, the CEO has said that they want this work to be independent of the results of the profit calculation from Appendix 4. Therefore, the CEO wants you to use an estimate of $103m profit before interest and tax from the new factory to evaluate the impact of the new factory on the dashboard. (This estimate is before product development and marketing costs as it only represents the manufacturing operation at the factory.)

The CEO wants you, using 20X5 figures as a base, to evaluate the impact of the new factory on the values and choice of metrics in the existing dashboard.

Value chain

The consultant who prepared the SWOT analysis has mentioned to the board that if it is thinking of reviewing its existing strategies, then it should consider using the value chain to secure competitive advantage.

The CEO would like an explanation of the implications of using the value chain for performance management at MS. (An outline of the value chain is given in Appendix 5.)

Required

Write a report to the board of MS to respond to the CEO's instructions for work on the following areas:

(a) Assessment of the existing dashboard metrics, your suggested improvements to them

(Note. You should ignore the impact of the Nush scandal in this part of the question.)

(16 marks)

(b) The impact of Response 1 on performance management at MS (8 marks)

(c) The expected operating profit of the new factory (6 marks)

(d) The impact of the new factory on the values and choice of metrics in the existing dashboard (10 marks)

(e)   The implications of using the value chain for performance management   (6 marks)

Professional marks will be awarded for the format, style and structure of the discussion of your answer.   (4 marks)

(Total = 50 marks)

APPENDIX 1

MS performance dashboard

REPORT FOR THE YEAR TO MARCH 20X5

	20X5	20X4	20X3	Change 20X5/20X4 %
Financial				
Revenue ($m)	273	238	209	14.7
Operating profit ($m)	71	60	54	18.3
ROCE (%)	41.7	37.5	36.0	11.2
Design				
Design awards won	2	2	1	0.0
Brand				
Awareness (%)	64	63	59	1.6

Note. Design awards are national clothing design awards which address both the look of and technology in a product. Brand awareness is the percentage of those sampled who could identify the company's logo and can name at least one of its products.

APPENDIX 2

SWOT (completed before the Nush scandal was reported)

S:	W:
• High market share • Excellent brand awareness • Strong revenue growth (compared to industry average of 11%) • Supply chain management	• Loss of a key brand ambassador (who was injured when he tripped over the laces of his MS boots) • Weak IT expertise
O:	T:
• New products in the market for new sports (such as those being introduced at each World Championships)	• Growth of social media as main marketing channel

APPENDIX 3

Procurement review of new outsourced footwear manufacturers

Currently, MS buys two million pairs of shoes at an average of $21 per unit (a pair of shoes) and we assume an average selling price of $75. Cost per unit will increase by 10%. Additionally, there will be a need to perform annual audits of these suppliers which will cost $0.5m.

The change of policy will be marketed as sustaining the values of MS. The MS ethics code states 'we will play fair and source our goods responsibly'. This marketing will cost $0.8m p.a. but it is hoped that this will produce a gain in market share. However, the increase in sales cannot be estimated at this time as competitors are making similar moves. The reviewer commented, 'It would be helpful to know how many units we would need to sell in order to cover these increased costs so this can be used as a marketing target.'

APPENDIX 4

New factory

The data collected on the new factory depends on three possible economic scenarios in response to MS's change in sourcing policy:

	Bad	Medium	Good
Probability	30%	60%	10%
Units manufactured ('000)	1,800	2,000	2,200
Variable costs per unit ($)	21	22	23
Fixed costs ($'000)	2,500		

	$'000
Capital required	
Building and equipping	36,000
Working capital	11,000

Notes

1 One unit is one pair of shoes.
2 Assume all units made are sold.
3 Assume an average selling price of $75.
4 The total Ceeland market for this type of shoe is estimated as 6.25m p.a.

APPENDIX 5

Value chain analysis

61 Monza Pharma (Sept/Dec 16, amended)   98 mins

Company information and objectives

Monza Pharma (Monza) is a developer and manufacturer of medical drugs, based in Beeland but selling its products all over the world. As a listed company, the overall objective of the company is to maximise the return to shareholders and it has used return on capital employed (ROCE) as its performance measure for this objective. There has often been comment at board meetings that it is good to have one easily understood measure for consideration.

The company has three divisions:

- The Drug Development Division develops new drug compounds, taking these through the regulatory systems of different countries until they are approved for sale;

- The Manufacturing Division then makes these compounds; and

- The Sales Division then sells them.

Balanced scorecard

Monza's share price has underperformed compared to the market and the health sector in the last two years. The chief executive officer (CEO) has identified that its current performance measures are too narrow and is implementing a balanced scorecard (BSC) approach to address this problem. The current performance measures are:

- ROCE
- Average cost to develop a new drug
- Revenue growth

The CEO engaged a well-known consulting firm which recommended the use of a BSC. The consultants began by agreeing with the board of Monza that the objective for the organisation's medium-term strategy was as follows:

- Create shareholder value by:

    - Innovating in drug development
    - Efficiency in drug manufacturing
    - Success in selling their products

The consulting firm has presented an interim report with the following proposed performance measures:

- Financial: ROCE
- Customer: Revenue growth
- Internal business process: Average cost to develop a new drug
- Learning and growth: Training days provided for employees each year

The CEO and the lead consultant have had a disagreement about the quality and cost of this work and as a result the consultants have been dismissed. The CEO has commented that the proposed measures lack insight into the business and do not appear to tackle issues at strategic, tactical and operational levels.

The CEO has decided to take this work in-house and has asked you as the performance management expert in the Finance Department to assist him by writing a report to the board to cover a number of areas.

Balanced scorecard and performance measures

Following the disagreement with the consultants, the CEO is worried that the consultants may not have been clear about the problems of using the BSC in their rush to persuade Monza to use their services.

Therefore, the CEO would like you to assess the problems of using a balanced scorecard at Monza.

The CEO also wants you to evaluate the choice of performance measures currently used by Monza, and those proposed by the consulting firm.

ROCE calculations

There has been a debate at board level about how ROCE should be calculated. The marketing director stated that she was not sure what profit figure (of which at least four were available) should be used and why, especially given the large variation in results which this gives. She also wondered what the effect would be of using equity rather than all capital to calculate a return on investment.

You have been provided with some basic data (Appendix 1) to assist you in quantifying and evaluating these possibilities.

The CEO has asked you to evaluate the effect of choosing different profit and capital measurements for different measures of return on investment, and to recommend a suitable approach for Monza.

Total quality management

In addition to these concerns about performance measurement, the board is considering introducing a total quality management approach within Monza. Quality of output is critical in such a heavily regulated industry where the products can be a matter of life and death. There has been discussion about testing this idea within the Manufacturing Division. However, first, the CEO wants to understand, the costs associated with quality issues within that division. To help you with the work required, he has supplied some detailed information in Appendix 2.

The board also requires an outline evaluation of how a total quality management (TQM) approach would fit within the Manufacturing Division.

The CEO has summarised the work you are required to do here: 'Analyse the current quality costs in the Manufacturing Division, and then briefly discuss how implementing TQM would affect the division.'

New information system

Finally, the drug development divisional managers have been lobbying for a new information system which will assist their research chemists in identifying new drug compounds for testing. The new system will need to be capable of performing calculations and simulations which require high computational power and memory but will also need to have access to external data sources so that these scientists can keep up with developments in the field and identify new opportunities. The CEO is worried about the cost of such a new system and wants to know how it would fit within the existing lean management approach within that division. As such, the CEO has asked you to advise, briefly, on how the Drug Development Division can aim to make the new information system 'lean'.

Required

Write a report to the board of Monza to respond to the CEO's instructions for work on the following areas:

(a)	The problems of using a balanced scorecard	**(8 marks)**
(b)	The performance measures currently used, and those proposed by the consulting firm	**(12 marks)**
(c)	The different measures of return on investment	**(11 marks)**
(d)	The quality costs in the Manufacturing Division and the impact of implementing TQM	**(10 marks)**
(e)	The new information system in the Drug Development Division	**(5 marks)**

Professional marks will be awarded for the format, style and structure of the discussion of your answer.

(4 marks)

(Total = 50 marks)

APPENDIX 1

Financial data for Monza for the most recent accounting period

	$m
Revenue	8,001
Costs	2,460
Gross profit	5,541
Other costs	3,248
Restructuring costs	482
Operating profit	1,811
Finance costs	266
Profit before tax	1,545
Tax	419
Profit after tax	1,126

Capital structure from the statement of financial position

Shareholders' equity	1,161
Long-term debt	8,739

Note. Restructuring costs relate to a major project which completed during the period.

APPENDIX 2

Cost information for the Manufacturing Division for the most recent accounting period

(1) Batches rejected at factory valued at $17m which have a scrap value of $4m.

(2) Training of factory staff which cost $8m.

(3) Regulatory fines costing $5m (due to drug compounds being outside the specified range of mix of chemical ingredients).

(4) Discounts given following customer complaints due to late delivery costing $22m.

(5) Factory product testing department cost $12m.

(6) Cost of raw materials was $1,008m.

62 Dargeboard Services (Mar/Jun 17)　　　98 mins

Company information and mission

Dargeboard Services (DS), a listed company, provides facilities management (FM) services where it manages such activities as cleaning, security, catering and building services on behalf of its clients. Clients can outsource to DS a single activity or often outsource all of these aspects in a full service contract.

The mission of DS is 'to give the shareholders maintainable, profitable growth by developing the best talent to provide world-class services with maximum efficiency'.

Systems review

The board have asked the chief executive officer (CEO) to review the effectiveness of Dargeboard's systems for performance measurement and management. She has turned to you to begin this process by considering the strategic performance dashboard of DS. She has supplied the most recent example in Appendix 1.

She has tasked you with aiding her in writing a report to the board which will cover some key aspects of strategic performance reporting at DS.

The first thing the CEO wants you to do is to evaluate the links between the current key performance indicators (KPIs) at DS (as shown in Appendix 1) and its mission, and therefore how well the KPIs measure the achievement of the mission. The CEO has asked you to do this by showing how each KPI links to all or part of the mission. However, she has told you that she does not want suggestions of new indicators.

Next, the CEO has asked you to look at each of the current set of indicators in turn, and to examine the assumptions underlying the calculation of those indicators, as shown in Appendix 1. There has been a suggestion made in the press that DS is producing a biased set of results aimed to mislead the markets. This would then artificially boost the share price and so boost the value of the senior management's share holdings. As a result, the CEO wants you to assess the assumptions and definitions used in the calculation of the indicators.

Third, the CEO has asked you to evaluate the other presentational aspects of Dargeboard's strategic performance dashboard against best practice.

Reward and remuneration schemes

The idea of employee share ownership has always been at the heart of DS's remuneration schemes. Its aim is to support an entrepreneurial culture and is a key differentiator in the market for new employees. The current reward system grants shares based on the appraisal of the individual by the line manager against vague categories such as leadership and entrepreneurship. The results of this scheme have been that only about 5% of staff received their maximum possible bonus in previous years and half of them received no bonus at all. Increasingly, this has led to the staff ignoring the reward scheme and describing it as 'only for the bosses' favourite people'.

In response to this, the board have been discussing methods of analysing and improving the rewards system at DS. One non-executive director suggested using Fitzgerald and Moon's building block model. The CEO was asked to consider this as a project separate from the issues of performance measurement mentioned above.

The CEO will select suitable indicators from the dimensions but has asked you to explain to the board what is meant by results and determinants in this context, and how the dimensions link to standards and targets.

Finally, the CEO believes that there are two types of reward scheme which might suit DS, and she has provided you with details of the schemes (Appendix 2). The CEO would like an assessment of the relative strengths and weaknesses of the two reward schemes.

Required

Write a report to the board of Dargeboard Services (DS) in response to the CEO's instructions in for work on the following areas:

(a)	The links between the key performance indicators (KPIs) at DS and its mission	**(8 marks)**
(b)	The assumptions and definitions used in the calculation of the KPIs	**(12 marks)**
(c)	DS's performance dashboard compared to best practice	**(8 marks)**
(d)	The building block model	**(6 marks)**
(e)	Assessment of the two reward schemes	**(12 marks)**

Professional marks will be awarded for the format, style and structure of the discussion of your answer. **(4 marks)**

(Total = 50 marks)

APPENDIX 1

Dargeboard Services: Strategic performance dashboard

Year to 31 December 20X6

	Cleaning	Security	Catering	Building services	Full service	Total	Total 20X5
Operating profit margin	6.5%	6.4%	6.5%	4.9%	5.9%	5.9%	5.8%
Secured revenue	76%	85%	92%	88%	93%	88%	87%
Management retention	86%	74%	87%	82%	89%	85%	87%
Order book ($m)	1,160	875	357	1,553	3,359	7,304	6,807
Organic revenue growth	7.1%	4.3%	5.0%	8.1%	7.9%	7.2%	4.6%
ROCE						17.2%	16%

KPI definitions and notes

(1)   Cleaning, security, catering and building services headings are for single service contracts.

(2)   No commentary is provided as the CEO talks the board through the dashboard at each board meeting.

(3)   Secured revenue is long-term recurring revenue. This is the percentage of budgeted revenue which is already contracted. The budget is often not completed until well into the year as it is a complex process. In 20X6, the original budget showed revenue of $1,565m with the final budget signed off at the end of Q1 showing $1,460m. The secured (contracted) revenue for the period was $1,285m. The accounts show a year end revenue of $1,542m.

(4)   Management retention is the percentage of managers who were still employed throughout the whole year. The figure only includes those employees on full-time contracts (about 65% of all managers).

(5)   Order book is the total cash value of future contracted revenue. DS has contracts which run up to 10 years into the future.

(6)   Operating profit margin. This excludes exceptional items such as the reorganisation of the catering business which cost $55m in 20X6, where revenue was $245m.

(7)   Organic revenue growth is calculated by using the total revenue figure as reported in the accounts. It includes net acquisitions which brought in revenue of $48m in 20X6.

(8)   Return on capital employed (ROCE). Capital employed is total assets less current liabilities from the statement of financial position.

APPENDIX 2

The CEO is considering two schemes, one based on the current scheme and a new scheme.

Scheme 1 (based on the current scheme)

The reward system grants shares in DS based on the appraisal of the individual by the line manager against vague categories (leadership and entrepreneurship). The line managers have been informed that their bonus will in turn be partly dependent on how well they perform this appraisal. The expectation will be that as a result, 20% of staff will receive their maximum possible bonus and 20% will receive no bonus.

Scheme 2 (the new one)

Under scheme 2, employee targets are to be derived from the strategic indicators depending on the employee's area of responsibility. The senior management (with help from line management where appropriate) will cascade down the strategic indicators to the relevant operational or tactical level for that employee.

There will be five targets set by senior and line management in consultation and the employee will then get up to 50% on top of their basic salary as a bonus (10 percentage points for each of the targets achieved).

63 Thyme Engine Products (Sept/Dec 17)   98 mins

Company information and objectives

Thyme Engine Products (Thyme) manufactures jet aircraft engines for the commercial aircraft market. This is a worldwide business although Thyme's production and development are all based in the country of Beeland. Thyme is a listed company and its stated overall objective is to be 'a world-class jet engine manufacturer trusted by our customers to deliver excellent products'. Its promise to its shareholders is that it will maximise their returns. The strategy to achieve this is to use world-class engineering to design engines and high quality production and customer service in order to drive profitable growth.

Thyme's share price has recently suffered as a result of the failure of a new engine design which led to large cash losses and a difficulty in obtaining new financing. There has also been a bribery scandal involving a senior manager and one of its key customers. As a result, a new chief executive officer (CEO) has been employed and she has begun a major review of systems at Thyme.

Performance reporting – dashboard

The first area which the CEO wants to examine is the information given to the board for strategic decision making in both the planning and controlling of the business. The Government of Beeland has been encouraging information sharing between businesses and has recently sponsored awards for management accounting. The winner of the engineering sector has produced a sample dashboard template (with dummy figures) for an annual review and this is given in Appendix 1. The CEO realised that the winner had a very similar overall objective and strategies to Thyme and wants to know what it is about this dashboard that helped it win the award. To this end, she has asked you to evaluate why the dashboard in Appendix 1 was award winning. The CEO does not want a new dashboard for Thyme at this stage, although she thinks there may be some useful, specific comments to make about the contents of the dashboard given Thyme's recent problems.

Integrated reporting

The CEO has also recently been reading about integrated reporting and in the light of this review of the dashboard, the CEO has also asked for you to include a section in your report explaining your views on how integrated reporting might have an impact on the type of information prepared by the company's management accountants.

Total quality management

As high quality engineering products lie at the heart of Thyme's competitive advantage, there has been a total quality management (TQM) approach to the management of all resources and relationships throughout the business. Thyme currently has a project under consideration to develop a new simple jet engine which would compete in the crowded market for small corporate jets. In order to compete in this market, it is believed that a target costing approach to this new engine would be beneficial. You have been given some data about the price and cost of the new engine (Appendix 2).

The CEO wants you to calculate the target cost gap for the new engine using the data you have been given, and then she wants you to assess how the use of target costing would fit within the existing TQM approach for this new engine.

Quality costs

The new engine project has further raised the profile of quality as a broad issue at Thyme and the CEO wants your advice on the costs associated with quality. She needs to know the cost of each of the four categories of quality costs. She has gathered data in Appendix 3 for this exercise. She is happy that she has identified that prevention costs are complete, but is worried that some of the possible costs for the other three categories are missing and needs suggestions of cost areas to be examined to identify these missing items. In addition, she wants advice on the relative importance to Thyme of each of the four categories. She has summarised the work she requires from you as follows: 'I would like you to categorise and calculate the costs of quality, using the data I have given you. I would then like you to suggest cost areas to be examined, and to evaluate the relative importance of each category to Thyme.'

BPP
LEARNING
MEDIA

Required

Write a report to the CEO of Thyme to respond to her instructions for work on the following areas:

(a)   The award winning dashboard **(15 marks)**

(b)   The impact of integrated reporting on the type of information prepared by the company's management accountant **(6 marks)**

(c)   The target cost gap for the new engine, and how target costing would fit with the existing TQM approach **(12 marks)**

(d)   The costs of quality **(13 marks)**

Professional marks will be awarded for the format, style and structure of the discussion of your answer. **(4 marks)**

(Total = 50 marks)

APPENDIX 1

Award winning performance dashboard

Report for the year to June 20X7

	20X5	20X6	20X7	Budget variance 20X7	Growth 20X6 to 20X7	Budget 20X8
Financial						
Revenue ($m)	10,652	11,213	11,500	234(F)	2.6%	11,776
Operating profit margin	16.2%	16.8%	17.2%	0.2 percentage points (F)	0.4 percentage points	17.2%
EVA™	746	774	815	48(F)	5.3%	803
Total shareholder return	6.5%	6.8%	11.1%	4.5 percentage points (F)	4.3 percentage points	7.5%
Design						
Class leading products in:						
Fuel efficiency	3	3	3	0		3
Noise levels	2	2	3	1(F)		3
Chemical emissions	1	2	3	1(F)		3
Manufacturing						
Percentage of orders right first time	92.0%	92.4%	93.7%	0.7 percentage points (F)		93.0%
Delivery						
Deliveries on time	88.0%	89.9%	88.2%	0.2 percentage points (F)		88.0%
Market share (as percentage of market leader)	33.0%	35.2%	38.1%	1.1 percentage points (F)		39.0%

Commentary:

The revenue growth of the business remains strong above the average growth for the sector of 1.5%.

EVA™ is positive and growing indicating increased shareholder wealth.

Healthy and continuing growth in market share reflects an increased number of class-leading products and improvements in 'right on time' service to customers.

There have been no major new business risks arising during the period while market volume growth continues as expected.

APPENDIX 2

New jet engine

	$'000/engine
Competitor price	2,500
Raw materials	200
Subcomponents bought in	600
Skilled labour	625
General labour	125
Production overheads	275
Planned profit margin	15%

Notes

1   Design and development has cost $120m and the engine is expected to sell approximately 1,200 units over its lifetime.

2   Sales and marketing costs are expected to be approximately 20% of the selling price.

3   The planned selling price is expected to match the competitor's price with the brand reputation of Thyme providing the competitive edge.

APPENDIX 3

Quality costs identified in current year

	$m
Repairs and replacements under customer warranties	223
Customer relationship management – complaint handling	56
Performance testing of final assembly	110
Performance testing of subcomponents from suppliers	28
Costs of re-inspection after repairs arising from final assembly testing	95
Training in quality control	11
Maintenance of inspection equipment	36

Notes

1   The company spent $92m in the year buying higher quality raw materials to use in manufacture.

2   The company's revenue was $11,500m in the current year.

64 Fearties (Sept 18)   98 mins

Company background

Fearties Security (Fearties) is a business, owned and run by the Feartie family, which provides security personnel for other businesses (eg factory guards and security staff at large public events, for example, music concerts). The business has grown along with the market for outsourcing of security personnel roles, and Fearties is one of the largest of such service providers in Beeland.

The Feartie family has always managed the business to increase profits without excessive risk-taking. Most of the family are financially dependent on the business through their pay and dividends. The founder of the business was an accountant and it has become a family tradition that the chief executive officer (CEO) would always have an accounting background. As a result, the performance reporting has always focused on financial results.

Recent events

A new generation of the family has risen to power with a goal of increasing growth by expanding Fearties' operations into different countries, using its existing reputation for reliability. The newly appointed CEO has recognised that the choice of key performance indicators (KPIs) may not be suited to the current business environment, where the company is facing various issues:

- Changing government regulation with most customer-facing Fearties staff now required to hold a certificate showing they are aware of the relevant laws and health and safety procedures regarding their duties. Indeed, this factor is a reason for the growth of outsourcing to Fearties;

- Difficulty in recruitment and retention as the pay for customer-facing staff is low by Beeland's standards (even though Fearties provides full training for them); and

- Legal difficulties arising from claims of Fearties staff being too aggressive in the pursuit of their duties.

The CEO has asked you to prepare a report to the board on the following performance management matters for Fearties and has provided you with information in Appendix 1 and Appendix 2 which may help you with the first two tasks:

Existing KPIs and introduction of the balanced scorecard

The CEO is considering the introduction of a balanced scorecard approach and wants an evaluation of whether the existing key performance indicators cover the financial perspective for the board. She has provided you with a draft copy of the most recent board report to illustrate current reporting (Appendix 1). This draft has been prepared quickly by a junior accountant and the CEO believes that there is an error in the return on capital employed calculation which you should correct. She then requires reasoned recommendations for two indicators within each of the remaining three perspectives (customer, internal business process and innovation and learning). These indicators should address the issues facing the business.

Use of customer surveys

In the past, the board has resisted the introduction of customer surveys due to worries about the ability to measure performance using this method. The CEO is aware that many of the new indicators from the introduction of the balanced scorecard are likely to be non-financial. Therefore, she has asked that you evaluate, for the board, the problems associated with measuring and managing performance using non-financial performance indicators (NFPIs) at Fearties, using customer surveys as an illustration.

Management style

Given these changes, there may have to be changes to the management style at Fearties. Therefore, the CEO also wants your assessment of the existing management style at Fearties and a justified recommendation for an appropriate approach. She has been taught about Hopwood's styles of using budget information (budget-constrained, profit-conscious, non-accounting) and so wants a brief definition of these prior to your assessment and recommendation.

Human resources management: targets and appraisals

Finally, given the issues facing Fearties noted above, the board will need advice on how to align human resource management with the organisation's strategy. The current appraisal system consists of an annual appraisal meeting between the individual and their line manager and then, a discussion of the targets for that individual (which are all financial, based on the projections for the next financial year), followed by an explanation of their bonus payment based on the previously agreed targets.

For this part of your report, the CEO wants you to provide advice on the management setting of targets in the light of the move to using a balanced scorecard. This should be followed by a discussion of how these targets should be used within the appraisal system. The CEO has told you that, at this stage, no changes to the reward system (basic pay plus an annual bonus) at Fearties are desired.

Assume it is now 1 September 20X8.

Required

Write a report to the board of Fearties to respond to the CEO's instructions for work on the following areas:

(a) Evaluation of the existing key performance indicators (KPIs), and recommendations for additional indicators for the balanced scorecard **(20 marks)**

(b) The problems associated with using non-financial performance indicators **(8 marks)**

(c) Management styles **(10 marks)**

(d) Advice on setting targets and then discussion about using the targets in appraisals **(8 marks)**

Professional marks will be awarded for the format, style and structure of the discussion of your answer. **(4 marks)**

(Total = 50 marks)

APPENDIX 1

Key performance indicators

	20X8 $m	20X7 $m
Revenue	686	659
Operating profit	36	34
Cash flow from operating activities	64	64
Dividends paid	14	13
Return on capital employed	21.1%	20.4%

APPENDIX 2

Other information:

Fearties Security

Year ended 30 June 20X8

Profit information

	20X8 $m	20X7 $m
Revenue	686	659
Operating profit	36	34
Profit after tax	20	19

Assets and liabilities

	20X8	20X7
Non-current assets	54	51
Current assets	213	211
Current liabilities	151	148
Non-current liabilities	21	21
Net assets	95	93
Equity	95	93

Dividend history

	$m
20X8	14
20X7	13
20X6	13
20X5	13
20X4	11
20X3	10

BPP LEARNING MEDIA

65 Rezillos (Dec 18)   98 mins

Rezillos: Company information

Rezillos Engineering (Rezillos) is a listed company, manufacturing pumps and valves for use in the chemical industries. These highly engineered components must be integrated into Rezillos' customers' own plant and equipment. The company has grown significantly via acquisition in the last 20 years to become a worldwide business.

The overall objective of the company is 'to deliver sustainable growth in value to the shareholders by working in partnership with customers to deliver innovative and value-for-money solutions utilising the skills of the highly-trained workforce'.

The chief executive officer (CEO) has recognised that the company has been so focused on making acquisitions that it has not improved other aspects of management. He has asked you to produce a report for the board of Rezillos to cover a number of areas.

Performance reporting system

The CEO would like an evaluation of the performance reporting system used at the strategic board level by Rezillos. The current performance report used for the annual review at board meetings is given as an example (Appendix 1).

Customer survey

At the most recent round of meetings with stock market analysts, the board has been criticised about a customer survey whose results were announced at these meetings. The criticisms centred on the method of calculation, sampling and the disclosures in the press release. The board of Rezillos is concerned by the impact of this on their reputation in the market and needs to understand whether the criticism is justified. The press release and some further internal details about the method and the results of the customer survey are given in Appendix 2. The CEO wants you to assess the analysts' criticism of the customer survey results.

Benchmarking proposal

Rezillos has three divisions based in its three countries of operation (Beeland, Teeland and Veeland). In order to drive forward the integration of the divisions, the CEO has decided that they should be benchmarked against each other. However, he is aware that this is not the only method of benchmarking. Therefore, initially, he wants you to explain the different types of benchmarking and provide an evaluation of the usefulness of the proposed type of benchmarking for the divisions.

Finally, the CEO has supplied the data in Appendix 3 and has asked you to complete the benchmarking exercise and to comment on the metrics used and the results.

It is now 1 December 20X8.

Required

Write a report to the board of Rezillos to respond to the CEO's instructions for work on the following areas:

(a)   Evaluation of the performance reporting system used at board level   (13 marks)

(b)   Assessment of the analysts' criticisms of the customer survey results   (9 marks)

(c)   (i)   Explanation of the different types of benchmarking, and evaluation of the type
                proposed   (9 marks)

        (ii)   Completing the benchmarking exercise, and commenting on it   (15 marks)

Professional marks will be awarded for the format, style and structure of the discussion of your answer.   (4 marks)

                                                                        (Total = 50 marks)

APPENDIX 1

Rezillos							Year to 30 September			Profit as a % of revenue	
	Beeland	Teeland	Veeland	Total	Total	Growth				Company	Industry average
	20X8	20X8	20X8	20X8	20X7						
	$m	$m	$m	$m	$m						
Revenue	738	2,030	923	3,691	3,504	5.34%					
Cost of sales	497	1,391	601	2,489	2,363						
Gross profit	241	639	322	1,202	1,141					32.6%	29.8%
Other operating costs											
Selling and distribution costs	89	208	101	398	380						
Administration costs (note 1)	74	171	83	328	321						
Total	163	379	184	726	701						
Operating profit	78	260	138	476	440	8.18%				12.9%	9.7%
Finance costs				88	88						
Group profit before tax				388	352					10.5%	
Tax				78	71						
Group profit after tax				310	281					8.4%	
Return on capital employed (ROCE)				8.64%							

Note. Administration costs contain an allocation of product development costs to each division.

APPENDIX 2

Press release from Rezillos: Customer survey results

Rezillos has performed an extensive survey of its customer base and is proud to announce an average customer rating of 7.0 (out of 10). This bears positive comparison with a leading competitor of Rezillos who performed a survey last year scoring an average rating of 6.0.

The survey asked for a customer rating on a scale of 0 to 10, where 10 was exceptional, 5 was good and 0 was unacceptable.

End of press release

Extract from Rezillos internal document on calculation of customer rating

The survey was carried out by the staff at head office who sampled customers from all three divisions.

Raw data

Customer number	Rating	Account size ($m)	Division
1	10	1.5	Beeland
2	9	3.3	Beeland
3	9	2.1	Beeland
4	6	6.4	Beeland
5	6	152.0	Teeland
6	6	11.2	Beeland
7	6	10.5	Beeland
8	6	74.0	Veeland
9	5	21.0	Veeland

Other notes

1   The company has 180 customers in total.

2   The customer number is an identification number for administrative purposes.

3   Each division has its own marketing and customer support function although product development is a head office function.

APPENDIX 3

(All data is for 20X8 unless otherwise stated)

The benchmarking exercise is partly complete with the metrics needing to be calculated identified by question marks.

	Beeland	Teeland	Veeland
Benchmarking metrics			
Growth of market	8.5%	3.2%	5.0%
Revenue growth	12.5%	3.2%	4.8%
Operating margin	10.6%	12.8%	15.0%
Inventory days	162	162	?
Order book growth	5.2%	5.3%	?
Number of face-to-face interactions with division's top 10 key customers	260	120	40
Percentage of revenue from new products introduced in the last three years	24.9%	29.0%	?
Reduction in incident rate	3.4%	0.0%	?
Utilisation of learning and development programme	1.20	1.26	?

Notes

1   The industry standard method of calculating incident rate is:

Incident rate = number of incidents per year × 200,000/number of employee labour hours paid

2   The company's employees work on average 40 hours per week for 50 weeks per year.

3   Utilisation of learning and development programme is measured by the number of training days per employee.

4   Key customers are designated by the divisional management.

5   A single inventory management system has been implemented across the whole company.

The following data has been collected to assist in the completion of the benchmarking exercise:

	Veeland
Revenue from new products introduced in the last three years ($m)	163
Cost of sales ($m)	601
Inventory ($m)	267
Number of incidents (20X8)	68
Number of incidents (20X7)	74
Number of employees (20X8)	6,600
Number of employees (20X7)	6,250
Order book ($m) 20X8	932
Order book ($m) 20X7	885
Number of training days	6,450

Answers

1 ENT Entertainments

(a)

Division	Market growth (%)			Average of annual growth rates (20X0–X3)
	20X1	20X2	20X3	
Restaurants	1.0	1.0	–	0.67
Cafés	9.0	11.0	9.0	9.66
Bars	(2.0)	(3.0)	(3.0)	(2.67)
Dance clubs	6.0	5.9	9.0	7.01

	Market share (%)		
	ENT market share	Market leader	Relative market share
Restaurants	0.50	3.00	0.17
Cafés	1.01	3.00	0.34
Bars	3.50	3.00	1.17
Dance clubs	10.99	15.00	0.73

BCG analysis and evaluation of performance

Restaurants Division – This division has a low market share of a market sector with low growth, making it a **dog** in the BCG classification. The Restaurant Division therefore looks a likely candidate for **divestment**, unless it has any links with any of the other divisions in ENT's business.

BPP
LEARNING
MEDIA

Cafés Division – The Cafés Division also has a relatively low market share, but it is operating in a market sector with high growth. It should therefore be classified as a **question mark**.

The market sector is already showing good growth, but it currently seems quite fragmented. There could be additional opportunities for ENT to grow by acquiring some rival businesses. Alternatively, if ENT does not want to invest in this way, it might consider selling its Café Division to another business looking to consolidate in the sector.

Bars Division – The Bars Division is the market leader (high market share) in a market which has low (actually, negative) growth. This should be classified as a **cash cow**.

The Bars Division is currently ENT's largest division, and it contributed about 55% of the group's total revenue in 20X0. The current decline in the bars market should therefore be a concern for ENT, given the Bars Division's role as a cash cow in the group. ENT is likely to want to use the Bars Division to generate cash for the other businesses in its portfolio, but if the bars market starts declining in time this may limit the division's ability to generate cash for the rest of the group.

The fact that the bars sector seems to be in the mature stage of its life cycle also highlights the importance of controlling costs. The degree of profit growth ENT will be able to generate through increasing revenues seems limited, so instead it could look at reducing costs as a means of increasing profitability.

Dance clubs – The Dance Clubs Division has a moderately high market share (although still less than 1) in a market with reasonably high growth. This should currently be classified as a **question mark** as ENT is not yet the market leader in the sector, but it has the potential to become a star if it can achieve market leadership.

Its market share is already relatively close to the market leader's share, so with continued investment the division could grow to become the leader. The performance of this division is likely to be crucial to ENT's longer-term success, particularly if the performance of some of ENT's more mature businesses continues to decline.

(b)   **Context for performance** – The BCG provides a useful context in which to assess the performance of the different divisions. For example, it illustrates to management that they shouldn't expect the Bars Division to grow at the same rate as the Clubs Division, due to the underlying differences in the growth rates of the two sectors.

Management approach – Equally, identifying the differences in the growth potential of the different divisions identifies that different styles of management will be appropriate for the different divisions. For example, the Clubs Division may require capital investments to enable it to sustain its rate of growth, but the focus in the Bars Division (in a more mature business sector) should be on cost control.

Help set performance metrics – By helping to set expectations and approach in this way, managers can then also tailor their performance management systems and metrics to reflect the different contexts of each of the divisions. So, the metrics for the high growth divisions (cafés and clubs) should be based on profit or return on investment, while the metrics for the low growth divisions (bars and restaurants) should be focused on maintaining margins, cash control and cash generation.

Limitations of BCG approach

Problems of definition – Although we have identified that the BCG matrix can be useful for providing a context for performance management, its usefulness is limited by its simplicity. For example, a business unit is only considered to have a high market share if its relative market share is greater than 1. By definition, however, this means that only the market leader can have a high market share, and therefore also there can only be one star or cash cow in each market sector.

Overlooks possible synergies – Another issue which arises from the simplicity of the model is that it treats business units in isolation, and in doing so can overlook possible synergies between them. For example, some of ENT's bars and restaurants may be linked to its clubs, such that customers may go for a drink or a meal and then go on to a club afterwards. However, if in time the restaurants and later some of the bars are divested then this link between the business units will be lost.

Defining the market sector – Another potential issue with using the BCG matrix comes from defining market sectors themselves. For example, the Bars Division has launched a new wine bar format which appears to have been successful. This suggests it has been growing, although the rest of the Bars Division has actually had negative growth. However, this raises an issue of whether the wine bar format should be treated as a separate sub-section (and as a 'question mark' which is given the support and investment needed to grow) or whether it should be subject to cost control in the same way that the rest of the Bars Division is.

Portfolio analysis, not performance management – It is also important to remember that the BCG matrix was designed for analysing a product portfolio, not as a performance management system. Therefore, while it can help to determine the appropriate performance management approach for a business, it is not in itself a performance management system.

(c)   (i)   **Focus on cost budgets** – The bonus element (50%) of the remuneration package is based on divisional performance against cost budget. As a result, divisional managers are likely to focus on controlling costs. Such an approach may be appropriate in the Bars and Restaurants Divisions, but is unlikely to be suitable for the faster-growing divisions (cafés and clubs).

In the Cafés and Clubs Divisions, ENT should be looking to encourage growth, but the current remuneration package is unlikely to do this. As a result, there is likely to be a lack of **goal congruence** between the divisional managers and the ENT overall.

Short-term performance – In a similar way, the focus on controlling costs may also lead to divisional managers taking a short-term view of performance. Again, it may actually be more beneficial for some of the divisions to spend now (for example, on marketing) in order to increase revenues and profits in the future.

Use of EVA™ – There also appears to be an inconsistency between this focus on cost budgets and the use of EVA™ as the measure of divisional performance. The underlying logic behind EVA™ will be to try to **maximise the wealth of ENT's shareholder** – which is the company's objective – but this is not necessarily the same as controlling costs.

Importantly, EVA™ specifically identifies that some costs which are treated as expenses in the financial statements (for example, advertising costs) should actually be considered as investments for the future.

Therefore, rather than basing the bonus element of the managers' reward package on achieving cost budgets, ENT may be better advised to base the bonus element on achieving target EVA™ figures. In this way, the reward system at divisional level will reflect the **company's overall objective**.

(ii)   **Context** – The fact that some of ENT's divisions should be focusing on growth (cafés, clubs) while others (bars, restaurants) need to focus on cost control suggests that different management styles may be appropriate for the different divisions.

Budget-constrained style – Under a budget-constrained style, a manager's performance is primarily assessed by their ability to meet the budget on a short-term basis, particularly in relation to ensuring that actual costs do not exceed budgeted costs. 50% of the bonus elements at ENT are based on achieving the cost budget numbers set by the board, which suggests that ENT may be using a budget-constrained style.

A budget-constrained style can be appropriate in a business where it is important to keep costs under control, which suggests that it may be appropriate to use this style in the Bars or Restaurants Divisions. However, it is less likely to be appropriate for the Cafés or Clubs Divisions.

Moreover, the budget-constrained style often leads to poor relationships between managers and subordinates, and also encourages the manipulation and misreporting of information, so ENT needs to be aware of these potential problems.

BPP
LEARNING
MEDIA

Profit-conscious style – Under a profit-conscious style, a manager's performance is evaluated more in terms of long-term performance, and the ability to generate future growth, rather than short-term performance and cost control.

This style is likely to be appropriate for the Cafés or Clubs Divisions at ENT. However, the current bonus structure suggests that this style is not being used, which could suggest that not only do ENT's remuneration packages need revising but also that the management styles need reviewing too.

2 BPC

Workbook reference. Chapter 1 of the Workbook considers Porter's five forces model and how it can be applied in the performance management process. Chapter 15 discusses corporate failure.

Top tips. In **part (a)** BPC is assessing **its option to enter the cardboard tube market** so remember this when you use the five competitive forces to comment on the information in the question. If you have time, it is a good idea to write a little introduction explaining a model and your understanding of how a scenario can be appraised using that model. We have done this in two sentences.

Part (b). In APM, you should be prepared to explain the advantages and disadvantages of using different models, as well as being able to apply them to different scenarios. In this part of the requirement, there is no need to apply your answer to the scenario, but simply to demonstrate you are aware of the potential limitations of Porter's model.

Part (c) draws on your knowledge of predicting corporate failure though there is very little in the scenario to comment on. However, note that JOL Co has already been mentioned in note (3) in the scenario.

Rather than labouring to apply your answer to the scenario, you may have to make general comments. Although you don't need to use a model to answer this requirement, Argenti's A score could also be a useful guide here, as the factors included within defects, mistakes and symptoms are a good mix of financial and non-financial indicators.

Marking scheme

			Marks		
(a)	Comments (on merit):				
	Each of the five forces	5 × 2	10		
	Conclusion		1	Max	10
(b)	Limitations – up to 2 marks for each limitation discussed	Up to 5			5
(c)	Comments (on merit)				
	Fall in market share significant (with percentage 18%)		1		
			1		
	Indicators	6 × 1.5	9	Max	10
				Total =	25

(a) **Porter's five forces and the option to enter the cardboard tube market**

Porter's five forces model assesses **five competitive forces** that affect a firm's positioning in its market and ultimately its profitability.

BPC is considering whether it wants to enter the cardboard tube market. So using the model to assess the option to enter this market:

(i) **Threat of new entrants**. A new entrant such as BPC will bring **more competition** and **extra capacity**. The strength of this threat depends on the barriers to entry to the market such as high fixed costs or expertise in technology. It also depends on the response of the existing competition in the market. New machinery to make the tubes costs from $30,000 per machine, it only needs one operator and the expertise needed to operate it is fairly low as an operator only needs one day's training. This appears to be a high threat. Another threat would be the foreign multinational company which has the machinery to manufacture cardboard tubes.

(ii) **Threat of substitutes**. A substitute product is a good or service produced by another industry which satisfies the same customer needs. PTC has a range of plastic tubes that can be used to **house** small products. This use appears to be different from that of the manufacturers who use the tubing to **wind products around**. It is possible that the uses could be extended to satisfy some of the uses made of cardboard tubes. However, the plastic tubes are at present an average of 30% more expensive than the cardboard tubes on offer.

(iii) **The bargaining power of customers**. Customers, who appear to be manufacturers, use the tubing for a variety of purposes and buy very large quantities. The customers seem to have some bargaining power in their purchasing as they buy in bulk, and may also be price sensitive as the tubing costs a tiny part of the total cost and they may wish it to remain so. The product is not likely to be specialised and so customers could switch suppliers readily. There are four main suppliers with similar ranges, so customers have some choice. This also appears to be a high threat.

(iv) **The bargaining power of suppliers**. Suppliers can drive up prices for goods and services supplied to the industry. Obviously a monopoly supplier with a **differentiated product** will have more influence than a range of small suppliers with a simple product. The tubes are made from a specialist paper that can be in short supply. So suppliers do have some influence. Again this is another high threat.

(v) **Rivalry amongst current industry competitors**. The intensity of competition within an industry will affect overall profitability. The industry has four main manufacturers with 80% share in total and between 18% and 26% share each. So the industry is fairly concentrated. There has been little market growth recently at 2% p.a. and the product is undifferentiated. Therefore the competition is likely to be quite strong for a shrinking market and a homogenous product. This therefore poses yet another high threat.

In summary, there are some good reasons for entering the market, which include **low entry barriers,** as the manufacture of the product is unspecialised (though this could be a threat once BPC has established itself in the market and wishes to keep out other competition). There is also a **small likelihood of substitution.** However, the market is likely to be **very competitive** with a **high concentration of entrenched competitors and customers who have considerable buying power.**

On balance, the option to enter the market for cardboard tubes appears to be unattractive and BPC should consider alternative strategies for improving performance.

(b) **Limitations of the five forces model as a technique for assessing the attractiveness of an industry**

Problem of market definition – The aim of Porter's model is to identify the level of profits which can be sustained in an industry or market. However, it can sometimes be difficult to define exactly what the industry or market in question is – particularly for a large organisation, or one operating in a complex environment. Even in the BPC example, are cardboard tubes and plastic tubes in the same 'tube' market, or should they be distinguished on the basis of the different materials used?

This issue around market definition identifies a potential problem with Porter's model. The model is best used for analysing **simple market structures**, but analysis of the different forces can get very difficult in more complex industries with lots of interrelated segments or product groups.

Environmental change – Moreover, the model **assumes relatively static market structures**. However, this is often not the case in today's markets. For example, technological breakthroughs can change business models in relatively short timescales. Yet while the model can provide some useful analysis of the new market structure once it has emerged, it can only offer limited advice for any preventative measures.

The need for careful analysis is, perhaps, most important in the area of substitute products or services. It takes a particular alertness to discern potential substitutes in the early stages of their development.

Equally, while there may currently be strong barriers to entry into an industry, new technological developments could remove or severely reduce those barriers to entry.

Competition or co-operation? – It is also important to recognise that Porter's model is based on the idea of competition between firms. It assumes that companies try to achieve competitive advantages over other players in the markets as well as over suppliers or customers. With this focus, it does not really reflect the dynamic of approaches such as strategic alliances, electronic linking of information systems of all companies along a value chain, or in a virtual organisation, in which the focus is primarily on collaboration rather than competition.

(c)   **JOL Co and corporate failure**

JOL Co had a market-leading share of 30% just 3 years ago. The current market share is 18% (see Working) so there has been a decline of 12% in 3 years. There are several performance indicators that could be used to flag up corporate failure. These are both financial and non-financial indicators and could include:

(i)   **Declining profitability.** JOL is losing market share in a slow growing market. It is very likely that profitability will be affected. If JOL starts to make losses it will become unviable to continue operating.

(ii)   **Decreasing sales volume.** JOL has lost market share in a near static market and therefore it has lost sales.

(iii)   **An increase in gearing.** JOL may well need to borrow if it is not earning sufficient revenue to fund operations and future growth. This is usually achieved through increasing its overdraft limit or long-term debt which can eventually lead to lenders refusing further borrowing. High levels of debt or financial gearing create financial risk affecting the company and its stakeholders.

(iv)   **Poor financial controls.** Organisations that lose control over costs and operations can fail spectacularly. Audit committees that do not exercise proper controls can fail to spot fraud or mismanagement.

(v)   **Lack of planning.** The remark by the MD suggests that JOL has not done anything to date to stem the decline in market share. This shows a lack of planning by the board having let things drift for three years.

(vi)   **Frequent changes in senior executives.** Mobility can be a sign of dissatisfaction with how the company is performing. The challenge of turning around a troubled company is outweighed by whether the company can be saved and the risk of being associated with a failed company.

Working: Market share

From Note (3) in the scenario: The four leading manufacturers have a market share of 80%. The market leader has a market share of 26%, so the other three (including JOL) together have a share of 54%. The three are equal in size, so each company has a share of 54/3 = 18%.

3 CRC

Marking scheme

			Marks
(a)	1 mark per point		
	Advantages and disadvantages of current system	8	
	Advantages and disadvantages of ABB	8	
	Conclusion	2	
			Max 13
(b)	Calculations		
	RFID tagging	2	
	Warehouse staff wages	2	
	Heating & lighting	1	
	Cost per receipt	1	
	Total variance	2	
	Variance per receipt	2	
	Commentary on the variances	4	
			Max 12
			Total = 25

(a)   **Advantages of the current budgeting system**

CRC managers use the previous year's results as a starting point when drafting their budgets, and increase the variable costs according to any anticipated growth in volumes. This is an example of incremental budgeting.

An advantage of incremental budgeting is that it is quick and easy to prepare. The budgeting system at CRC has remained unchanged for a long time and it is unlikely managers will have experience in any other method of budget setting. While CRC was growing steadily, and relatively slowly at approximately one new store every two years (approximately 18 years/10 stores), the use of incremental budgeting may have been appropriate. But as CRC is now entering new locations, such as out of town shopping centres and possibly food retailing, incremental budgeting is unlikely to be appropriate.

Incremental budgets can also be flexed according to anticipated activity levels. The manager of the central warehouse has done this, rather simplistically, by increasing costs of running the warehouse to reflect the anticipated increase in volumes in 20X6.

Disadvantages of current budgeting system

The use of incremental budgets can encourage slack. This includes incorporating extra costs into the budget to make it more achievable, or spending up to the budgeted amount to ensure that a larger budget is set next year. This may be the case particularly at CRC, as managers are appraised based on achieving their budget. The manager of the central warehouse appears to be building in slack by increasing the budget for heating and lighting when the general rate of inflation is zero. This will make it more likely that the manager will receive a positive appraisal next year, as it will be easier to achieve the budget.

Incremental budgeting does not encourage CRC to look for new and innovative ways of doing things. The level of automation in the warehouse is lower than in competitors and CRC appears to have just increased the budget for more staff to manually handle items in response to increased volumes. The introduction of the RFID system is, though, an example of the use of technology to increase efficiency in the warehouse.

Incremental budgeting is only appropriate where costs are already well controlled and operations are efficient. Otherwise, poorly controlled costs and inefficiencies are just incorporated into the next period's budget. Staff resistance to the introduction of the RFID system, and their difficulties in using it, suggest that this might not be the case.

Advantages of activity-based budgeting (ABB)

The principle of ABB is that it is activities, such as the goods inwards and goods outwards in the central warehouse, which drive costs. By understanding what drives the cost, such as the number of receipts from suppliers and the number of despatches to stores, CRC can take action to control the drivers of the costs and eliminate activities which are not value adding. ABB is particularly useful where overhead costs form a large part of total costs.

ABB can help identify critical success factors which CRC must do well, such as being able to put items away in the warehouse quickly and accurately and to retrieve them efficiently. This is more likely to be done right first time as ABB focuses on the whole of an activity.

ABB is useful, as CRC is changing the nature of its operations. It is undergoing rapid expansion by opening four new stores a year. There is also likely to be a change in the nature of its business, with the opening of its first out of town store and possible acquisition of a food retailing business. The incremental approach to budgeting may no longer be appropriate given the scale and nature of these changes. ABB may be more suitable as the business becomes more complex.

Disadvantages of activity-based budgeting (ABB)

One of the main disadvantages of ABB is the time and resources which are needed to implement it, for example, by identifying activities and their costs drivers. In the short term, overheads may not be controllable, which will reduce the benefits of implementing ABB.

CRC has used all its financial resources to fund its expansion and has only old and basic IT systems compared to its competitors. Its current systems are not enterprise resource planning systems (ERPS), unified databases or networked systems. Significant investment in CRC's IT systems will be needed to collect and process large volumes of data on cost drivers and activities which would be required to implement ABB. There may also be resistance to the change from staff, who may also require extensive training, as they will be unfamiliar with the ABB approach.

Conclusion

CRC should adopt ABB, mainly as a response to the significant changes in the business and its increasing complexity.

The out of town store and the food retailing business will both be supplied from CRC's existing central warehouse. The nature of these businesses may be different from the existing business. For example, out of town stores may require despatches that each contain a larger number of items from the goods outwards section. Food retailers may require smaller, more frequent despatches to prevent spoilage. The current approach of incremental budgeting, in the central warehouse at least, is unlikely to be appropriate. The benefits of implementing ABB do, however, need to be compared to the financial cost and disruption of doing so.

(b) **Activity-based budget for the central warehouse for YE 30 June 20X6**

	Total $	Goods inwards $	Good outwards $	Other $
Warehouse manager's salary*	55,000	–	–	55,000
Lease of RFID system*	75,000	45,000	30,000	–
RFID tagging (W1)	72,000	72,000	–	–
Warehouse staff wages (W2)	315,000	157,500	157,500	–
Heating and lighting (W3)	10,000	–	–	10,000
Total	527,000	274,500	187,500	65,000

Annual number of receipts into goods inwards expected	9,000
Cost ($) per receipt into goods inwards	30.50
	(274,500/9,000)

*As already calculated by the analyst

Comments on variance analysis

The total expected cost for receipts into goods inwards for July 20X5 was $19,825 ($30.50 budgeted cost per receipt × 650 receipts). The actual cost was $18,000, giving a favourable variance of $1,825. It cannot be identified, on the basis of the information available, the cause of the $1,825 variance, as the breakdown of the $18,000 actual cost would be required.

100,000 items were processed in July 20X5 which is the same as the budgeted amount. However, the number of receipts budgeted was 750 (9,000/12), whereas the actual number of receipts was only 650, equivalent to $27.69 ($18,000/650) per receipt. This is a favourable variance of $2.81 per receipt.

It appears that the favourable variance may be due to the receipt of larger quantities of items from suppliers in each delivery. If some of the goods inwards costs are variable with the number of items this would result in a cost saving. This could be because of the reduction in the number of suppliers, with fewer suppliers individually supplying more items.

Workings

1 *RFID tagging*

Expected volume of items received in the month = 100,000

Each member of staff can tag 35,000 items per month, so 2.86 (100/30) staff are required – say three annual wages cost is 3 × $24,000 = $72,000

2 *Warehouse staff wages*

Number of staff required in budget year = 14 (12 + 2) Total warehouse staff wages = 14 × $22,500 = $315,000

Of which $157,500 (50% of $315,000) relate to each of goods inwards and goods outwards

3 *Heating and lighting*

As inflation is zero the cost included in the budget should be $10,000.

4 Drinks Group

Workbook reference. Different approaches to budgeting are discussed in Chapter 3 of the Workbook.

Top tips.

Part (a). A sensible approach to this question might be to think about the benefits and drawbacks of incremental budgeting in general terms, and then think how these would affect its suitability for each of the different divisions. For example, the scenario identifies that F is growing quite rapidly, so how would this affect the suitability of incremental budgeting in F?

The question specifically asks about its suitability at 'each division' so it is important that you deal with the different divisions in turn, although the similarities between S and H mean you could look at them together.

Part (b). Up to six out of the eight marks available here were for calculations, so this part of the question should have offered you some easy marks. However, it is important you apply the information given in the scenario correctly; for example, noting that administrative costs are fixed, although cost of sales and distribution costs are variable.

Also, remember that because you now have actual figures for Quarter 1 of the current year, the rolling budget should include budgeted figures for Quarter 1 of the next year.

Finally, note that not all the marks in this part of the question are available for calculations; so you still need to comment on the potential benefits (or drawbacks) of using rolling budgets for F.

Part (c). One of the key issues highlighted in the scenario is that the managers of the manufacturing divisions are very doubtful about the value which M adds. Therefore, to try to remove these doubts, the approach to budgeting in M needs to be one which challenges and justifies any proposed expenditure before it is approved. On this basis, zero-based budgeting would seem to be appropriate.

Part (d). The context of this question is the contrast between top-down budgeting (with little participation) and bottom-up budgeting (which involves much greater participation).

However, a useful way to approach this part of the question could be to think how the degree of participation changes in the different types of budget you have considered in parts (a), (b) and (c).

DG's current (incremental) approach appears to be essentially a top-down process with little participation from the divisions. This could provide your analysis of the current level of participation (and if DG decides to retain incremental budgeting in the S and H Divisions, a top-down approach could remain appropriate there).

But could DG successfully introduce rolling budgets or zero-based budgeting (in F and M respectively) without having a greater degree of involvement from divisional managers? Consequently, what level of participation will be appropriate at DG in the future?

Examining team's comments. Candidates are reminded that budgeting is a core topic, and candidates will be expected to know the relative merits of different methods of budgeting, and how to apply them in a scenario.

In part (a), some candidates seemed to assume that because incremental budgeting was being questioned it must be flawed for all the divisions, and they then sought reasons to justify this well. This is a poor approach to any question, however, because it pre-judges the outcome without any consideration of the evidence given in the scenario. In this case, incremental budgeting would actually be appropriate at the stable H and S Divisions.

Candidates generally performed well in part (b) although many did not bother to prepare the new quarter's figures which keep the budget rolling forward. As a result they missed out on some easy marks.

In general, part (c) was answered poorly, and candidates were unable to identify the relevant circumstances at M (such as the project-based nature of marketing activity) which suggest possible budgeting methods.

For part (d) most candidates identified the current level of participation in the budgeting process, although some candidates assumed that the current process was all top-down – ignoring the fact that division managers have input into growth estimates. The best candidates realised that, as different budget methods would be appropriate for the different divisions, the level of participation in each division would also vary, depending on the budget method.

Marking scheme

			Marks
(a)	Evaluation of the advantages and disadvantages of incremental budgeting in general – 1 mark per relevant point	Up to 5	
	Recommendations about the suitability of incremental budgeting in S and H Division – 1 mark per relevant point	Up to 3	
	Discussion about the suitability of incremental budgeting for F – 1 mark per relevant point	Up to 3	
	Discussion about the suitability of incremental budgeting for M – 1 mark per relevant point	Up to 3	
			8
(b)	Explanation of the rolling budget process – 1 mark per relevant point	Up to 2	
	Calculations (up to 6 marks in total for calculations):		
	Actual figures in Q1	1	
	Revenue; Cost of sales; Distribution costs; Administration costs; Operating profit – 1 mark for correct figures for each line in the budget	Up to 4	
	Budgeted figures for Q1 in the next year	1	
	Comments on the use of rolling budgets at F – 1 mark per relevant point	Up to 3	
			8
(c)	Recommendation of an appropriate method (1 mark), plus 1 mark per valid point justifying the choice of method	3	3
(d)	Explanation of top-down vs bottom-up budgeting – 1 mark per relevant point	Up to 2	
	Evaluation of use of bottom-up control at DG, and its impact on current processes	Up to 6	
			6
		Total =	25

(a) Incremental budgeting

Advantages

Not too time consuming – DG currently uses incremental budgets. One of the main advantages of incremental budgets is that they are relatively quick and easy to prepare. This is a general advantage at DG given the time constraints which the Finance Department is currently experiencing in relation to the information systems implementation.

Stable environment – Incremental budgets are also appropriate for stable environments, where current or historic figures can provide a reliable basis for projecting future figures, and where only small changes are required to those figures.

Disadvantages

Accepts inefficiencies – A major problem with incremental budgets is that, by their nature, they reinforce existing practices. The fact that the FD has identified that the most promising area for performance improvement lies in better internal control practices suggests that there are inefficiencies in DG's current processes, which are likely to be reflected in its current figures. However, by basing future years' budgets on the current figures, these inefficiencies will be perpetuated rather than challenged. Consequently, for example, DG may miss opportunities to make cost savings.

Can encourage spending – Similarly, managers may feel they have to spend the full amount of their current year's budget in order to preserve the same level of budget next year, even though the expenditure may not actually be required at the moment. Once again, such an approach could lead to DG's costs being unnecessarily high.

H and S Divisions

Stable markets – Both H and S Divisions are in stable markets. The fact that sales growth is unlikely suggests that incremental budgeting could be appropriate for them.

Moreover, such an approach would fit with the managers' preference for maintaining existing practices rather than changing them.

Margin improvements – Because H and S have limited opportunities to increase revenues, in order to increase their profitability they will need to improve their margins. However, incremental budgeting will not be suitable to help them do this.

In order to improve their margins, the divisions will need to challenge and reduce their costs. However, by basing future budgets on current figures, an incremental approach will not provide the stimulus for continuous improvement which is required.

F division

Rapid growth – F's rate of growth means an incremental approach is unlikely to be suitable for it. Its rapid growth means that budgets based on current results will quickly become out of date.

The customer complaints and the managers' complaints could both be symptoms of the constraints which incremental budgets have placed on the business. For example, the complaints about late deliveries and poor quality could result from F trying to satisfy rapidly increasing demand whilst also facing budget constraints – which mean it either doesn't have sufficient capacity to keep pace with demand or it has to use poorer quality materials in order to reduce material costs.

The managers' complaints pick up on this point further. If the cost budgets have been set in line with current levels of demand, they are unlikely to be sufficient to cope with the higher levels of demand.

M Division

Justifying costs – The managers of the manufacturing divisions are sceptical of the need for a marketing department and using an incremental budget will not do anything to change their opinion of this.

The current budgetary approach at M (simply adding a percentage to the current year's expenditure) doesn't require M to justify its spending. Until it does this, however, it seems unlikely that M will be able to change the other division's perceptions of it.

Perhaps more importantly, though, simply adding a percentage to the current year's spend could lead to unjustified expenditure. For example, if the Marketing Division commits some expenditure this year on the basis that it is currently within budget (rather than because the expenditure is necessary and will add value for DG) next year's budget will be uplifted from the higher figure. Under such circumstances, the budget will continuously be higher than it needs to be. Again, this would justify the other managers' scepticism about the amount of value that M adds to the company.

(b) Under a rolling budget, another accounting period is added to the budget when the most recent one finishes. The budget is then recalculated using the actual data from the most recent period as a basis.

Because F Division's budget is based on a quarterly basis, the rolling budget will include actual figures for Quarter 1 of the current year, and then forecasts for Quarters 2–4 of the current year, along with Quarter 1 of the following year.

Based on the assumption that cost of sales and distribution costs increase in line with sales, and that administration costs remain fixed as in the original budget, F's rolling budget would be as follows:

	Q1	Q2	Q3	Q4	*Total*	Q1
	Actual	*Forecast*	*Forecast*	*Forecast*	*Forecast*	*Forecast*
	$'000	$'000	$'000	$'000	**$'000**	$'000
Revenue	17,932	18,470	19,024	19,595	**75,021**	20,183
Cost of sales	(9,863)	(10,159)	(10,464)	(10,778)	**(41,264)**	(11,101)
Gross profit	8,069	8,311	8,560	8,817	**33,757**	9,082
Distribution costs	(1,614)	(1,662)	(1,712)	(1,764)	**(6,752)**	(1,817)
Administration costs	(4,214)	(4,214)	(4,214)	(4,214)	**(16,856)**	(4,214)
Operating profit	2,241	2,435	2,634	2,840	**10,149**	3,051

As we noted in part (a), F is growing rapidly, and the rolling budget gives F's managers the scope to increase their variable costs to reflect that growth, rather than being constrained by the original budget.

As a result, F should be better able to sustain its growth, and the level of complaints about late deliveries and poor quality (which could otherwise jeopardise its growth) should be reduced.

Moreover, the rolling budget should provide managers with more realistic targets against which to compare actual performance. In this way, the rolling budget provides a more effective control mechanism than an annual budget, which could potentially be disregarded as being out of date.

It is likely that additional resources in the Finance Department will be required to prepare rolling budgets, because updated budgets will need to be prepared each quarter rather than on an annual basis as they currently are. However, the benefits which F's managers would derive from having rolling budgets should outweigh the additional costs incurred to prepare them.

(c) **Justifying expenditure** – The scepticism from the managers of the manufacturing divisions about the need for a marketing department (M), in conjunction with the board's requirement that M's costs should be carefully controlled, suggests that an incremental budget may not provide a robust enough framework for M.

Zero-based budgeting – By contrast, a zero-based budgeting approach may be appropriate, and this is the approach recommended for M.

As each marketing campaign is run as an individual project, it seems more appropriate for M to budget for the campaigns on a project by project basis. A zero-based budget approach would provide a suitable framework for doing this, with the cost of each campaign having to be justified at the start before the campaign is approved.

Under a zero-based budget, M would need to justify every cost which is required for a specific marketing campaign. If a cost element cannot be justified, then no resources will be allocated to it in the budget.

Tighter control – Such an approach should also appease the managers of the manufacturing divisions because it will mean that marketing expenditure is being much more tightly controlled.

(d) **Top-down budgeting**

In a top-down budgeting environment, budget figures are essentially imposed on operational managers and other budget holders by senior management. Operational managers have very little participation in the budgeting process.

Limited participation – The divisional managers at DG do appear to have some input into the budget process because they discuss the market growth estimates with the head office finance managers before the budgets are prepared.

However, the budgeting process still appears essentially top-down, and this appears to be causing resentment about the divisional managers – particularly the F managers who want to be less controlled by constraints 'imposed' by the board.

Bottom-up control

In contrast to top-down budgeting, a bottom-up approach would allow divisional managers **much greater participation** in preparing and setting their own budgets.

This would appear to be the approach which the F managers want, because their greater participation in setting the budgets should mean they feel 'less controlled' by the board.

Improved motivation – If the divisional managers have a greater sense of ownership of the budgets, this should also increase their motivation to achieve the budget targets.

Accountability – Equally, if managers are going to be held accountable for their performance against budget targets, it seems fair that they should have some input into setting those targets; for example, so that they think they are realistic.

Improved decision making – Moreover, the divisional managers at DG should have a more detailed knowledge of their markets than the board. Therefore, by allowing the managers to participate in the budgeting process, the quality of decision making and budgeting may also be improved. In this respect, a bottom-up approach would benefit DG as a whole, not just the divisional managers.

Similarly, if the divisional managers do more of the work to prepare the budgets, this means the budgeting process is less onerous for the senior management team, which allows them more time to spend on other matters.

Levels of participation

Overall control – At DG, the budget system in each business is the main method of central control. Therefore the board needs to ensure that the budgets remain in line with overall corporate objectives, and are not too easily achieved.

Consequently, it appears that an approach which combines aspects of both top-down and bottom-up budgeting would appear to be most appropriate for DG.

It is important that the managers are involved in the budget-setting process, because their own personal targets are set around achieving the relevant budget numbers.

Equally, however, it is important that head office should also be involved, to ensure that the budgets fit with DG's overall strategic objectives and that budget targets remain challenging.

Also, it is debatable how far the managers of H and S Division will voluntarily drive down costs without close monitoring from the head office. In this respect, the board may decide that the control which is imposed by a top-down approach is still required in relation to these two divisions, and therefore the level of participation for these two divisions will be lower than for the other two divisions.

Rolling budgets – If DG introduces rolling budgets for F, the process of preparing these budgets should be delegated to the divisional managers. On the one hand this is due to the resource constraints within the Finance Department, but on the other it is because the divisional managers should be more aware of changes in the market which need to be reflected in the updated figures. However, senior finance staff should still review the budgets, and the underlying assumptions behind them, to ensure they seem reasonable.

Zero-based budgeting – If M adopts zero-based budgeting, divisional managers will have a crucial role to play in the budgeting process, because they will need to assess what activities and expenditure are required to support each campaign.

5 Godel

Workbook reference. Different approaches to budgeting and different types of budget variance are discussed in Chapter 3 of the Workbook.

Top tips.

Part (a). It is important that you focus specifically on the planning and operational variances here rather than discussing the variances shown in the operating statement more generally. As such, the figures you need to be looking at are those shown in the 'Detailed variances' at the bottom of the operating statement.

Part (b). The requirement here is to 'evaluate' the budgeting system. An 'evaluation' should include both the advantages and the disadvantages of the system. As the examining team's comments (below) indicate, if you are asked to evaluate something, it is important that you give a balanced argument – and don't focus only on the advantages or the disadvantages.

One possible way of approaching this requirement would be to use 'PRIME' as a framework for your answer, and to evaluate how well the budget reflects the elements of 'PRIME' – planning, responsibility, motivating, evaluating performance. (This is the approach we have used in our suggested solution.)

Part (c). Note the verb here is also 'evaluate' – so you need to consider what the potential benefits from moving to a bottom-up approach might be, but also what factors may limit those benefits or make it an unsuitable approach.

Importantly, you need to think about not only the context of the scenario here (for example, Godel's command and control management style), but also your evaluation of the current approach to budgeting – in part (b). If Godel is going to change its approach to budgeting, it will only be worth doing so if the new approach helps to address the problems with its current system. But does it?

There is an important general point to note here. Just because the FD has proposed a change in the approach, this doesn't necessarily mean the change is appropriate.

Examining team's comments. In part (a), most candidates appeared not to know the definitions of operating and planning variances, and so those who attempted this question talked about all the other variances in the appendix rather than answering the question.

Part (b) of this question was also inadequately attempted. Too many candidates saw only the negatives of the existing system, and few identified its positives for a traditional company like Godel in a mature market. This meant students failed to grasp that the current budgeting system at Godel was actually well suited to its needs; and therefore (part (c)) that a change in the budgeting process was neither required nor likely to be beneficial for Godel.

Marks

(a)   Definitions of planning and operational variances – 1 mark

Advice about planning and operational elements of total
variable cost variances – up to 3 marks

Advice about planning and operational elements of sales price
variance – up to 3 marks

Total for part (a): up to 6   6

(b)   Benefits of budgeting for Godel – 1 mark per relevant point –
up to a maximum of 6

Points could include:

- Planning and co-ordination – meeting overall strategy
- Responsibility
- Integration
- Motivation
- Evaluation of performance

Problems with budgeting at Godel – 1 mark per relevant point –
up to a maximum of 6

Points could include:

- Time consuming and unnecessary
- Lack of recognition of planning failures
- Insufficient planning and operational analysis
- Impedes continuous improvement

Total for part (b): up to 12   12

(c)   Description of bottom-up budgeting – up to 2 marks

Evaluation of appropriateness of bottom-up budgeting for
Godel – up to 6 marks

Total for part (c): up to 7   7

Total = 25

(a)   **Planning variances** result from the assumptions or standards used in the original
budget-setting process not being accurate. For example, if the original budget assumed
that sales prices would be increased by 2%, but market conditions have meant that sales
prices could only be increased by 1%, the resulting sales price variance should be treated
as a planning variance.

In effect, a planning variance is the difference between the original budget and the budget
as it would have been revised with the benefit of hindsight.

Operational variances, in effect, are the differences between this 'revised' budget, and
actual performance. Operational variances result from the decisions of operational
managers, rather than issues with the original budget-setting process.

Variable cost variance

The total variable cost variance considers a number of costs together, and so it is unlikely
that any gains or problems highlighted by it can be attributed to one individual. As such,
the variable cost variance has little use for Godel, although highlighting the total variance
could, in turn, identify the need for more detailed analysis to identify the specific causes of
the variance.

The $20,680 favourable planning variance suggests that the standard costs have been set too high, and therefore most of the apparent cost improvements are due to this. Compared to the planning variance, the operational variance is very low ($580) which suggests that the operational managers have had little impact in driving down costs in the month.

Sales price variance

The sales price variance indicates the extent to which sales prices were incorrectly estimated in the budget (planning variances) and how effective the sales managers have been in negotiating higher prices with customers (operational variances).

The adverse planning variance ($15,600) suggests that the original budget was too optimistic in the initial price it set for Godel's sweets. However, the favourable operational variance ($6,640) suggests that the sales managers have been quite successful in their price negotiations with customers, although not successful enough to overcome the adverse planning variance.

The initial price-setting process should be examined, to identify why prices were budgeted too high. For example, Godel's market intelligence about the prices being set by competitors, or the commercial situation of its customers (the supermarkets) may have been faulty.

(b)   **Cost control** – Godel's competitive strategy is based on it being a cost leader, and therefore it will be very important for the company to control its costs effectively.

The budgeting system provides a mechanism for monitoring costs, and overall it seems that Godel is being successful in controlling its costs – as its total costs show a favourable variance.

Planning – More generally, budgets can be used to help communicate and co-ordinate all the management activities within Godel towards its overall strategic plan – minimising costs, and winning supermarkets' business.

Responsibility – The budget can also help to attribute responsibility for performance, and to identify which managers are responsible for which costs. For example, the favourable material usage variance indicates that fewer raw materials were required than planned, which suggests the Production Manager has been able to reduce waste and/or improve the efficiency of the production process.

Motivation – Although the managers do not appreciate the time taken by the budgeting process, the standard costs and assumptions being used in the budget are nonetheless discussed with them before being included in the budgets. The fact that the managers have the chance to participate in the budget process should help to motivate them to achieve the budget figures set.

In particular, it is important that managers are given the chance to identify any areas of the budget which they think are not realistic or achievable – otherwise the budget will become demotivating to the managers and their teams.

The CEO's feeling that there is no dysfunctional behaviour at Godel, and that all the managers are working in the best interests of the company, suggests that the budgeting system is not damaging motivation, even if it is not necessarily doing anything to enhance it.

Evaluation – Budgets assist performance evaluation by identifying variances which can then be analysed and investigated. This is particularly important for areas where actual performance is adverse to budget, to enable corrective action to be taken to improve future performance.

At Godel, sales are underperforming the budget both in terms of volume and price. However, more favourably, labour costs are considerably under budget – with the favourable labour 'efficiency' variance suggesting that staff are working efficiently.

Problems with Godel's budgeting system

Although the top-down nature of Godel's budgeting system fits with the organisation's strategy and management style, there are nonetheless still several problems with it.

Time consuming – The nature of Godel's business – in a mature market, and with little scope for innovation or new product development – mean that budget setting should not be a complex process. However, the managers' complaints suggest that the current process is very time-consuming.

The managers may be exaggerating here, and their complaints may be more of an indication of the fact that the budgets ultimately have limited value to them (because the operational variances are relatively small), and therefore they do not want to spend much time preparing them.

Nonetheless, there appears to be a danger that Godel's current budgeting system may have become more complicated than it needs to be.

Planning variances – The bulk of the variances at Godel relate to planning variances, rather than operational variances. This reinforces the suggestion that there is little point spending lots of time on the operational aspects of the budget but, instead, more time could be spent analysing the external factors with a view to reducing the level of planning variances.

Responsibility – The fact that the operational managers are frequently asked to explain variances which are not their fault suggests that the distinction between operational and planning variances needs to be more extensive.

Currently, the analysis between operational and planning variance is quite limited in scope. However, for example, instead of only analysing the total cost variance into operational and planning variances, some of the main cost headings in the operating statement could also be analysed in this way, so that managers are only held responsible for the operational variances.

No incentive to reduce cost – Although the CEO does not believe the managers build slack into their budgets, the use of standard costing nevertheless does not provide any incentives for them to try to reduce costs further. Given Godel's strategy as a cost leader, it would be beneficial to it if the budget system encouraged a system of continuous improvements in relation to efficiency gains and cost reductions.

However, given the mature nature of the business, Godel's senior management may feel that it is unlikely there will be a need to update budgeted costs on a regular basis and that a review of them once a year is sufficient.

(c)   **Bottom-up budgeting**

The FD's suggestion is a response to managers' complaints that the current variances are not their fault, and so it appears that the FD's intention is to make the managers more accountable for variances, and more motivated to achieve their budgets.

Typically, the arguments in favour of bottom-up budgeting are: that managers should be motivated to achieve their budgets if they have been involved in setting them; and that operational managers should have better knowledge than senior management of the conditions their business units face, meaning that the resulting budgets should be more realistic and achievable.

However, the nature of Godel's business and culture means that bottom-up budgeting may not be appropriate or beneficial.

Fit with culture – The operational managers already discuss the budget assumptions and standard costs, but do so without having the responsibility of producing the budget. Managers are therefore already involved in the budget-setting process, but in a way which fits with the 'command and control' management style at Godel. Moving to a bottom-up approach does not appear to fit with this style.

Resistance to change – The fact that many of Godel's employees have worked for the company for many years could mean that they will be uncomfortable with the change. Equally, if the managers – like most of Godel's employees – like the straightforward nature of their work, they may resent the additional burden of having to prepare their own budgets. Conversely, however, some managers may welcome the change if they feel it will give them more control over their budgets.

Time consuming – If the managers have to produce the budgets themselves, this is likely to increase their complaints about the budget process being time consuming. Similarly, the managers could complain that the increased amounts of time they have to spend preparing budgets is reducing the time they have available for other aspects of their roles.

Dysfunctional behaviour – As the CEO has noted, the current, top-down approach to budgeting means there is no dysfunctional behaviour, as represented by budget slack or excessive spending. However, bottom-up budgeting could increase the risk of dysfunctional behaviour as operational managers will focus on the individual concerns of their business area rather than Godel's overall corporate objectives. Equally, managers may create budgetary slack, and set targets which are too easy to achieve – although any targets which are obviously too easy should be challenged when the draft budgets are reviewed centrally.

Controllability – Most importantly, perhaps, even though the managers have set the budgets, they are still likely to argue, justifiably, that some of the variances they have to explain are not their fault. The proposed changes do not address the weakness in the lack of distinction between operational and planning variances (which we highlighted in part (b)).

Godel's sales are dependent on the state of the general economy and competitive forces – factors which are outside the control of operational managers. Therefore, operational managers cannot be held responsible for variances resulting from unforeseen changes in the level of sales.

Therefore, reiterating the point made in part (b), rather than changing the way the budgets are prepared, a more useful improvement to Godel's performance management systems would be to distinguish the main cost variances into operational and planning variances.

6 Perkin

> **Workbook reference.** Budgeting and budgeting systems are discussed in Chapter 3 of the Workbook.
>
> **Top tips.** Although good exam technique is important in all APM questions, it is particularly useful in this one – especially reading all three requirements and identifying how the different parts of the question fit together. The issues being discussed in part (c) highlight one of the weaknesses in Perkin's current budgeting system (the lack of planning and operational variances). However, while it will be important to mention this weakness in part (a), you should not discuss it in detail there – in order to avoid duplicating your answer between parts (a) and (c). Similarly, although perhaps less immediately obviously, the extent to which internal factors have compounded external factors – part (b) – can also be seen as a result of the weaknesses in Perkin's current budgeting system.
>
> **Part (a).** The scenario highlights a number of problems which Perkin has experienced, so one approach to this requirement could be just to work through the scenario and identify which of these are due to weaknesses in the current budgeting system, or its lack of suitability for the environment in which Perkin operates.
>
> However, a more structured approach for trying to identify the weaknesses might be to use 'PRIME' as a framework for your answer.
>
> **P**lan – Does the budget process encourage budget holders to plan how to achieve targets which support the company's overall strategic objectives?
>
> **R**esponsibility – Do the budgets help to allocate responsibility, and specify which managers control which costs?
>
> **I**ntegration – Does the budget structure help to ensure that the activities of one area support another?
>
> **M**otivation – Do the budgets help to motivate managers?
>
> **E**valuation – Do the budgets allow trends in performance to be identified and investigated?
>
> The scenario identifies a number of issues where Perkin's budgeting system does not help to achieve these 'PRIME' characteristics; and so you can then highlight these as weaknesses of the system.

However, note that you are asked to evaluate the system's suitability for Perkin's environment, as well as the weaknesses in the system. A key point to realise here is that Perkin is operating in a dynamic, fast-moving environment. Therefore, to what extent are incremental budgets, which are produced annually and enforced rigidly, likely to be suitable?

Although the requirement does not ask you to recommend an alternative budgeting system, it could be helpful to think whether the characteristics of alternative budgeting models (eg rolling budgets) would make them more appropriate than Perkin's current system. If another model seems more suitable, briefly mentioning this could help support your evaluation of the suitability (or unsuitability) of the current system.

Part (b). The scenario clearly identifies a number of external factors which have affected Perkin's performance during the year (eg rising silver prices; the fire at the customer), and these factors in themselves are outside Perkin's control.

In effect, however, this requirement is looking at the extent to which factors can fully be classified as controllable or uncontrollable. The key question in Perkin's case is: Although the initial factors were external (uncontrollable), has Perkin's internal response (controllable) also had an impact on its performance?

Part (c). As we noted at the start of these 'Top tips', the link between part (c) and part (a) in this question is important, because the change being suggested in part (c) addresses one of the weaknesses you could have identified in part (a) – the current lack of any analysis between planning and operational variances.

The third paragraph of the scenario is also important here. We are told that the main board significantly revises the budgets, but then divisional managers are appraised on the financial performance of their divisions. Does this seem a fair way of appraising the manager's performance?

Note, however, that the verb in part (c) is 'discuss' rather than evaluate. Therefore you need to focus specifically on the potential benefits of the change – not, for example, the extent to which those benefits could be limited by any difficulties associated with trying to analyse the variances.

Marking scheme

		Marks
(a)	Evaluation of current budgeting system	
	Weaknesses in current system – 1 mark per relevant point – up to 12 marks	
	Suitability of the system for Perkin's environment – 1 mark per point – up to 5 marks	
	Conclusion – 1 mark	
	Total for part (a): up to 14	14
(b)	Discussion of controllable and non-controllable aspects – up to 2 marks	
	Identifying external factors which contributed to Perkin's poor performance – 1 mark	
	Evaluating the extent to which the external factors as opposed to internal weaknesses were responsible for Perkin's poor performance – 1 mark per relevant point; up to a maximum of 4	
	Total for part (b): up to 6	6
(c)	Definition of planning and operational variances – 1 mark	
	Discussing the benefits of distinguishing between planning and operational variances – 1 mark per relevant point; up to a maximum of 4	
	Total for part (c): up to 5	5
		Total = 25

(a)   Perkin uses a traditional approach to budgeting, which has a number of weaknesses.

First of all, the budgeting system does not seem aligned with Perkin's **corporate objective** which focuses on innovation and continuous product improvement. Innovation is a key competitive advantage to both component and device manufacturers in this industry and the products which incorporate Perkin's components are subject to rapid technological change as well as changes in consumer trends. The markets in which the two divisions operate appear to be evolving, as seen by the high popularity of the smartphone model which was designed for playing games. This may mean the distinction between smartphone and gaming devices could be becoming less clear cut. Management time would probably be better spent considering these rapid changes and currently the budgeting process does not facilitate that.

In reality, the budget process at Perkin is **time consuming** and probably therefore a costly exercise. Divisional budgets go through a lengthy process of drafting and then revision by the main board before they are approved. The approval often happens after the start of the period to which they relate, at which point the budgets are already **out of date**. This also means divisional managers are trying to plan activities for the next financial year without a set of finalised targets agreed, which could impact the effectiveness of decisions made.

Another weakness is that the budgets are **only prepared annually,** which is clearly too infrequent for a business such as Perkin. The process is also rigid and inflexible as deviations from the planned targets are not tolerated. Sticking to rigid, annual budgets can lead to problems such as P Division not being able to cope with increasing popularity of a particular product and even other short-term changes in demand like those driven by seasonal factors, or one-off events such as the factory fire. Linked to this problem of budgetary constraints is that to cut costs to achieve the budgeted net profit, managers closed one of the three research and development facilities in G Division. As identified at the outset, a successful research and development function is a key source of long-term competitive advantage to Perkin.

It also appears that Perkin fails to **flex the budgets** and consequently the fixed budgets had discouraged divisional managers from deviating from the original plan. P Division did not make technical modifications to its components due to the cost of doing so, which meant they were unable to supply components for use in the new model of smartphone and had to discount the inventories of the old version. It is unclear why G Division did not take on additional staff to cope with increased demand following the reopening of their customer's factory, but it may be because managers felt constrained by the budget. This then caused long-term detriment to Perkin as it lost the preferred supplier status with its main customer.

Another problem created by annual budgeting is the **management of short-term changes in costs and prices.** A key component of Perkin's products is silver, which fluctuates in price, and though it is not clear how much effect this has on Perkin's costs, any problems in supply could disrupt production even if only a small amount of silver were required. Also Perkin exports goods worldwide and probably also purchases materials, including silver, from overseas. The business is therefore exposed to short-term movements in foreign currency exchange rates which may affect costs and selling prices.

Similarly, there also seems to be **considerable uncertainty** in sales volumes and prices which creates problems in the forecasting process for the two divisions. P Division did not anticipate the high demand for the new component which meant it had to discount products it had already manufactured in order to achieve its forecast sales volumes. G Division did correctly forecast the demand, but based on past growth in the market which may be too simplistic in a rapidly changing industry. Lack of up to date information will hinder decision making and overall performance at Perkin. Perkin would perhaps be better adopting a rolling basis for forecasting.

The two divisions share manufacturing facilities and are likely to compete for other resources during the budgeting process. The current budgeting system does not encourage resource, information or knowledge sharing, for example, expertise in forecasting silver requirements. Divisional managers are **appraised on the financial performance of their own division** and hence are likely to prioritise the interests of their own division above those of Perkin as a whole. P Division would not reallocate its manufacturing facilities to G

Division, even though G Division needed this to cope with extra demand following reopening of the customer's factory. The current system is therefore not encouraging goal congruence between the divisions and Perkin as a whole and a budgeting system, if done effectively, should encourage co-ordination and co-operation.

Managers may find the budgeting process **demotivating** because it is **time consuming** for them and then the directors override the forecast which they had made. It is also unfair and demotivating to staff to appraise them on factors which are outside their control. This also identifies another weakness in Perkin's budgeting system related to control, as there does not seem to be any planning and operating variance analysis performed to assess exactly where performance is lacking, and so no appropriate management information is provided. In fact it is not even clear just how often divisional managers receive reports on performance throughout the year. Any budgeting system without regular feedback would be ineffective. It should even be noted that for the industry in which Perkin operates the use of only budgetary targets as a measure of performance is narrow and internal. It should be utilising information from external sources as well to assess performance in a more relevant and contextual way.

Given the rapidly changing external environment and the emphasis on innovation and continuous product development, the current budgeting method does not seem appropriate for Perkin.

(b)   As the shareholder representative noted, external factors have adversely affected Perkin's performance over the last year. However, the way Perkin has responded to the external events has also contributed to the problems it has faced. As such, it is important that Perkin doesn't simply use the external factors as an excuse for its poor performance, thereby failing to acknowledge the internal factors and behaviours which have also contributed to it.

The current lack of any detailed analysis into the reasons why Perkin's actual performance varies from budget means it is difficult to hold managers to account for their performance. However, as the three examples we evaluate below demonstrate, the factors that affect performance cannot be categorised entirely as controllable (internal) or as uncontrollable (external). Instead, Perkin's performance reflects a combination of both types of factors.

The **unexpectedly high popularity of the new smartphone** with the large screen was an external factor. However, P Division's inability – or unwillingness – to make the necessary technical modifications to its own components to support the new screen was an internal factor, resulting – as we noted in part (a) – from the fact that Perkin does not flex its budgets.

Similarly, the **global shortage of silver** during the year (and the corresponding increase in silver prices) was an external factor. However, the lack of communication between G Division and P Division which led to G buying silver when P already held large inventories reflected an internal weakness. If the two divisions had liaised more effectively, the impact of the short-term increase in silver prices could have been reduced (or perhaps even avoided) if Perkin was able to wait until prices fell again to top up its inventories.

Again, the **fire which affected G's main customer** was an external factor. However, G's refusal to recruit extra staff to fulfil increased demand when the customer's factory reopened, and P's refusal to allow some of its manufacturing facilities to be used to meet this demand, are both internal decisions. However, it was these responses – rather than the fire itself – which led to Perkin losing its preferred supplier status with the customer.

As we noted in part (a), the response to the silver price increase and the fire both reflect the lack of goal congruence between the divisions and Perkin as a whole. Again, though, this is an internal weakness, reflecting dysfunctional behaviour which has resulted from the way divisional performance is rigidly assessed against budget. Therefore, although external factors have contributed to G's poor performances, internal weaknesses have also played a significant part in G's poor performance.

(c) **Planning variances** result from actual events and circumstances differing from the assumptions used in the original budget. For example, the fire at its main customer meant that the annual growth of 5% anticipated in G's sales forecast was too high (because the budget had not anticipated the fire). The lost sales resulting from the fire should be treated as a planning variance.

In effect, a planning variance is the difference between the original budget and the budget as it would have been revised with the benefit of hindsight.

Operational variances then reflect the differences between this 'revised' budget and actual performance. Operational variances result from the ongoing decisions of divisional managers, rather than issues with the original budget-setting process.

We have already noted – in part (a) – that the lack of planning and operating variance analysis is a weakness, because it means Perkin cannot accurately identify the reasons why actual performance is below budget. Given the dynamic nature of Perkin's markets (and the fact that budgets are only produced annually) it seems likely that there could be significant planning variances.

By isolating these planning variances, Perkin could then get a fairer reflection (through the operational variances) of how well the **divisional managers** are performing. This will also increase the effectiveness of the budgeting system as a **control mechanism** – comparing the manager's actual controllable performance against budgeted targets.

Currently, the divisional managers are appraised on the financial performance of their divisions, so they are being held responsible for planning variances as well as operational variances. However, as the budgets are determined by the main board, the managers should not be held responsible for planning variances over which they have little (or no) control.

Equally, however, by isolating the planning variances, Perkin can get a better insight into the degree to which the original budget was inaccurate. If it becomes clear that the majority of the variances result from changes in circumstance, which couldn't have been known when the annual budget was originally set, this could reinforce the argument for moving away from the current budgeting system – for example, to rolling budgets.

7 Jolt

Workbook reference. Business process re-engineering is discussed in Chapter 4 of the Workbook, as are ethical issues and their impact on business performance. Information systems are discussed in Chapter 6.

Top tips.

Part (a) – Although the requirement has been set within the overall context of business process re-engineering (BPR), the key issue for Jolt here is how the proposal could improve its performance specifically in relation to its retail customers' key demands:

- Lower prices
- Meeting performance targets in relation to lead times and quality

Therefore, a useful way to structure your answer would to look at each of the demands in turn, and to evaluate the impact the proposal could have on them.

Also, as you have been given cost information in Appendix 1, it is important that you use that. As Jolt is under pressure to lower prices, a key question in relation to the outsourcing plan should be: what impact will it have on Jolt's costs? BPR aims to achieve 'dramatic' improvements in performance – but will outsourcing provide any significant reductions in costs?

As with all APM questions, it is also important to think about the context of the scenario in practical terms. For example:

- What impact might outsourcing the manufacture of swimwear to a supplier 17,000 km away be expected to have on lead times?

- Similarly, will outsourcing affet Jolt's ability to control the quality of its products?

Part (b) – The scenario has highlighted what appears to be a significant difference in the quality of Jolt's information systems compared with that of its competitors. The second paragraph of the scenario tells us: Jolt uses 'unreliable spreadsheet-based systems for planning and reporting' and 'often fails to produce, accurate, timely and consistent data'. By contrast, we're told (in the fourth paragraph): Jolt's competitors 'have invested in sophisticated software to consolidate orders' so that each shipping container is full before being dispatched, and they also have an automated purchase invoice processing system, integrated with their suppliers' systems.

This contrast between Jolt's systems and those of its competitors should give some clues about the sorts of improvements Jolt needs to make to its systems – particulalry if it is relying on an outsourced supplier.

Also, think about the more general context of the BPR proposal – for example, how will teams working in different locations be able to access performance information?

Part (c) – Although the requirement just asks you to assess the 'potential impact of Jolt's ethical standards', did you notice that the opening pargraph told you 'Jolt is known for its high ethical standards towards its workers, suppliers, and the environment'?

Having identified this, a useful way to structure your answer could be to use each of the aspects – workers; suppliers; the environment – as headings, and then assess how they could be affected by the proposals, or how the desire to behave ethically in relation to them might affect the acceptability of the proposal. For example, in relation to suppliers: will the new outsourced manufacturer have the same high standards the Jolt has? (And if it doesn't, what implications might this have for Jolt?) Or, in relaton to the environment: what impact might shipping goods from a supplier 17,000 km away have on Jolt's environmental credentials?

Marking scheme

		Marks
(a)	Explanation of BPR – 1 mark	
	Evaluate impact of proposal in relation to lower prices – 1 mark per relevant point – up to 6 marks	
	Evaluate impact of the proposal in relation to meeting performance targets – 1 mark per relevant point – up to 6 marks	
	Total for part (a): up to 11	11
(b)	1 mark per relevant point	
	Development of information systems required for BPR – up to 6 marks	
	Total for part (b): up to 6	6
(c)	For assessing the impact of ethical standards relating to workers – 1 mark per relevant point point – up to 4 marks	
	For assessing the impact of ethical standards relating to suppliers – 1 mark per relevant point – up to 3 marks	
	For assessing the impact of ethical standards relating to the environment – 1 mark per relevant point – up to 3 marks	
	Total for part (c): up to 8	8
		Total = 25

(a) **BPR**

BPR is the fundamental rethinking and radical redesign of business processes to achieve dramatic improvements in in key areas of performance, such as cost, quality, service and speed. For Jolt, the BPR proposal aims to meet the retailers' demands for lower prices, and the requirement to meet performance targets relating to lead time and quality.

Lower prices

To be able to sell swimwear at lower prices, Jolt proposes reducing costs by outsourcing production to an overseas supplier. The current average production cost of manufacturing is $5.00 per unit. The cost of purchasing from an external supplier is $4.00, which is $3.50 purchase cost, plus $0.50 ($5,000/10,000) shipping costs. This 20% ($1.00/$5.00) saving is a significant improvement in financial performance, but not a dramatic one, and may not fit the definition of BPR. Exchange rate movements could reduce the cost saving significantly. In the near future, expected changes to international trade tariffs will increase the unit cost to $4.35 ($4.00 + 10% of $3.50), and reduce the cost saving to just 13% ($0.65/$5.00).

Unless Jolt decides to outsource the remaining 50% of production and close its factory completely, factory overheads of $0.95 per unit may still be incurred and just be re-allocated to Jolt's other sportswear products, possibly totally eliminating the cost saving.

Combining several jobs into one is a characteristic of a re-engineered process. As such, reorganising staff into multidisciplinary teams may create overhead savings, such as by reducing the number of staff employed by the automation of purchase invoice processing. These savings will be offset by additional costs, such as investment in new information systems, retraining staff to work in unfamiliar roles, or incentivising them to work overseas.

Re-engineered processes often allow workers more autonomy to make decisions. Giving teams more autonomy to set prices may allow Jolt to set prices reflecting the customers they serve and to prevailing market conditions.

Meeting performance targets

Lead times

Current lead times for customer orders are unknown. As the proposed supplier is 17,000 km away, goods will take several weeks to be transported by sea. This may increase lead times significantly, though may be offset by faster production times in larger factories. As Jolt's sales are seasonal, retailers may pre-order in advance, reducing the importance of long lead times. To minimise shipping costs, shipping containers must be full, which may mean deliveries will be in larger quantities and which may increase the lead times.

Quality

Jolt is already known for producing high quality products. The quality of the new supplier's products is unknown. Any deterioration in the quality of Jolt products would undermine its reputation and reduce long-term business performance as fewer consumers would buy them. Monitoring of quality standards is more difficult when using external suppliers, especially at long distances, than when manufacturing in Jolt's own factory. In re-engineered processes, work is performed where it makes most sense to do so. In this respect, having staff responsible for quality and supplier audits working close to the manufacturing site will help Jolt maintain performance in supplier relationship management.

(b) **Development of information systems**

Functional departments currently have their own spreadsheet-based systems for planning and reporting. The data from these is unreliable and inconsistent. They are inadequate to provide the timely and accurate performance data, which Jolt needs to meet retailers' performance targets.

Jolt must establish a shared database accessible by all parts of the multidisciplinary teams. This should be updated in real time, so workers in different time zones are using current data. The database should include financial data, such as cost information, and non-financial data relating to lead times and quality. Information systems must be able to provide teams with reports of performance data, and budgets, specifically for the accounts which they manage.

Fast and reliable internet services will be required, for example, so that team members can participate in online meetings, as they will be unable to meet in person.

Jolt may need to invest in specialised systems, such as the sophisticated software used by its competitors to minimise shipping costs by ensuring shipping containers are shipped fully loaded. Systems development may be required to integrate with suppliers' bespoke systems so as to automate purchase invoice processing. Jolt must evaluate whether the benefits arising from all of these changes to its information systems are worth the cost and disruption of implementing them.

(c) **Impact of high ethical standards**

Impact on workers

Jolt is known for its high ethical standards towards workers. Following the BPR, at least 500 (50% of 1,000) manufacturing workers are likely to be left without jobs. As Jolt's competitors have already closed their factories, these workers may be unable to find new jobs doing similar work, though jobs may be created in the new supplier's factory.

Staff who remain in work may become demotivated if they think that BPR will be extended to all of Jolt's products. This may reduce financial performance by reduced productivity, increased staff turnover or difficulties recruiting new staff.

Staff may also be demotivated if they are placed in unfamiliar roles, or may be unwilling to learn new skills. Other staff may welcome, and be motivated by, the opportunity to perform new types of work, learn new skills or work overseas. This will probably increase their individual performance.

Suppliers

Any association with unethical practices, for example, if the new supplier were found to be using unacceptable working practices, could seriously harm Jolt's reputation for high ethical standards. This could reduce financial performance, as consumers may not buy Jolt's products, or potential investors could be discouraged from providing capital. Part of the team located close to the manufacturing site is responsible for supplier audits, which may help to reduce this risk.

Environment

Jolt should consider the environmental impact of shipping goods long distances. The environmental credentials of the new supplier are unknown. As Jolt voluntarily publishes a corporate sustainability report, any deterioration in its performance on environmental issues will become widely known. This could lead to reduced financial performance if consumers switch to competing products.

8 Booxe

Workbook reference. Business process re-engineering is discussed in Chapter 4 of the Workbook. Appraisals and human resource management more generally are discussed in Chapter 12.

Top tips.

Part (a) – Although the requirement here was to 'Assess the financial impact' of the project, the majority of the six marks available were for calculations, and should have proved relatively easy marks to score.

Perhaps the most obvious way to assess the impact of the project is through a cost benefit analysis – and this is the approach we have used in the suggested solution below. However, the marking guide indicated that using other methods – such as payback period or accounting rate of return – would have been equally acceptable.

The crucial point to identify from the calculations is that the benefits significantly outweigh the costs over the life of the project (eight years), but you only need to write a couple of sentences after the calculations to explain this. There are only six marks in total for this part of the question – so there isn't time for a lengthy assessment of the project here.

Part (b) – Whereas part (a) of the question looked at the financial impact of the project, part (b) now looks at two non-financial impacts of it – on culture, and on Booxe's management information systems. And, note, to score well in this part of the question you have to discuss the impact of BPR on both of the areas required by the question: (i) culture and (ii) management information systems.

The scenario is also important in this question because it highlights that Booxe currently operates within a traditional, functional structure. However, BPR focuses on processes and process team rather than functional departments. This change will be central to the impact BPR has on culture at Booxe.

And it will also have important implications for the company's management information systems – for example, will performance reports structured around departments still be relevant in a process-oriented structure? And how might performance measures need to be redesigned to reflect the new approach?

Part (c) – A sensible approach to this part of the question would be to consider the purpose of an appraisal system, and then consider the issues in Booxe's appraisal system in the light of this, before suggesting possible solutions to them.

The reference in the last paragraph of the scenario to 'the appropriate balance between control and staff development' should have given you an indication of the points which needed to be considered here. Obtaining the right balance between control and development is one of the key issues in any appraisal process – but Booxe's current process appears to place very little emphasis on the 'control' aspect of appraisal.

Marking scheme

Marks

(a) Calculations: Up to 5 marks
   Costs: Depreciation – 1 mark; Total cost – 1 mark
   Savings: Warehousing – 1 mark; Purchasing – 1 mark
   Net benefit: 1 mark
   Comments: 1 mark for suitable comments on the calculations
   Total for part (a): up to 6   6

(b) Definition of BPR – 1 mark per relevant point – up to a maximum of 2
   Analysis of the impact of BPR on culture at Booxe – 1 mark per relevant
      point – up to a maximum of 5
   Analysis of the impact of BPR on management information systems/
      accounting systems at Booxe – 1 mark per relevant point, up to a
      maximum of 5
   Total for part (b): up to 11   11

(c) Definition of appraisal and the appraisal process – 1 mark per relevant
      point – up to a maximum of 2
   For advice on the purpose of appraisal at Booxe – 1 mark per relevant
      point – up to a maximum of 4
   For advice on the balance of control and development in the appraisal
      process – 1 mark per relevant point – up to a maximum of 4
   Total for part (c): up to 8   8

                                                                   Total = 25

(a)   **Annual cost benefit of the new system**

$

Benefits of new system (cost savings)

Warehouse staff	10 × 25,000 × 50%	125,000
Purchasing staff	32,000 × 8.5/5	54,400

Annual costs of new system

Depreciation – hardware	220,000/8 years	(27,500)
Depreciation – software	275,000/8 years	(34,375)
Ongoing servicing cost		(22,500)

Net benefit   95,025

Tutorial note

Alternative methods – eg payback period, or accounting rate of return – are equally acceptable. Payback period (as shown below) is 3 years, 2 months; ie well within the 8-year expected life of the new system.

Payback period

	Year 0 $	Year 1 $	Year 2 $	Year 3 $	Year 4 $	
Hardware	(220,000)					
Software	(275,000)					
Annual savings						
Warehouse staff		125,000	125,000	125,000	125,000	
Purchasing staff		54,400	54,400	54,400	54,400	
Annual costs						
Servicing costs		(22,500)	(22,500)	(22,500)	(22,500)	
	(495,000)	156,900	156,900	156,900	156,900	132,600

Payback:	**3 years, 2 months**	(24,300/156,900) × 12 = 2 months

---

The pilot BPR project will yield a benefit of $95,025 per year, meaning it is financially successful.

There are likely to be some other costs which are not included in this analysis, such as redundancy or retraining of the staff whose workload has been reduced, and the training costs for staff on the new system. However, given the figures involved, the project should still be beneficial even when these have been accounted for.

(b)   BPR is the fundamental rethinking and radical redesign of business processes to achieve dramatic improvements in critical contemporary measures of performance, such as cost, quality, service and speed.

Culture

Process teams – One of the key consequences of BPR for organisations is a shift from a functional structure to process teams, in order to achieve a more efficient delivery of products and services.

This will have a significant impact on Booxe, since the company has historically been divided into functional departments. The pilot project has shown the effect that BPR could have on the warehousing and purchasing departments.

Skills – The change to a process approach may require employees to retrain in order to gain additional skills. One of the characteristics of BPR is that it leads to multi-skilling; but given Booxe's current (bureaucratic, traditional) culture, it is likely that staff will have specific roles, rather than developing multiple skills.

Organisational hierarchy – BPR also leads to a flattening of organisational structures (from hierarchical to flat). Since processes become the work of the whole team, then similarly the team becomes responsible for managing the process.

Interdepartmental issues become matters the team resolves itself, rather than requiring managerial intervention. As a result, BPR means companies require less managerial input, and managers have less to do.

Although it is not clear which aspect of the cultural change required by the BPR project the warehouse manager was uncomfortable with, the risk that BPR would diminish their role could have played a part in the decision to take early retirement.

Change management – Nonetheless, the change required at Booxe – to shift from a well-established functional structure to a process-based structure – is likely to be a major change. Therefore, for it to be implemented successfully will require effective communication and leadership from senior management – for example, explaining the benefits of BPR to the staff, and overcoming any resistance they may have to it.

Management information systems

Performance measures – Performance measures under BPR must be built around processes rather than departments. This again is likely to require a significant change to Booxe's management information systems (assuming that Booxe's current accounting system reflects the functional structure of the organisation).

Focus on value adding – The aim of management information under BPR is to identify where value is being added in processes, so that activities where resources are employed without producing a valuable outcome can be eliminated.

Activity-based costing – As the CEO has suggested, activity-based costing (ABC) is often used to model the business processes as part of BPR. Again, however, the change to ABC from Booxe's traditional overhead absorption based on labour hours could be quite significant for the company's management information.

ABC will provide a more detailed method for allocating overheads and, in turn, should allow Booxe to calculate more accurate product costs, and determine the profitability of each product more accurately.

However, ABC will be more time consuming to administer than Booxe's current basis of overhead absorption.

Performance reports – The change from functional departments to process teams will mean that financial reports also have to be redesigned around process teams.

Also, the variances to budget, used as control indicators, may need to be revised following the introduction of the activity-based approach to overhead allocation.

(c) **Purpose of appraisal**

The overall purpose of appraisal is usually seen as the improvement of employees' performance, but appraisals can also be useful for assessing current performance; determining rewards; selecting people for promotion; and for identifying employees' training and development needs.

Control and staff development

The issue of finding an appropriate balance between control and staff development (which the CEO has identified) highlights one of the inherent problems with appraisals.

Judgement and control – One of the key purposes of appraisals is to assess how well employees have performed (against targets and objectives), with a view to determining pay increases and promotion. This reflects the judgement and control aspect of appraisal.

Development – On the other hand, the development aspect of appraisals focuses on assessing employees' training and development needs; to support them, and to help them perform better in the future.

Booxe's appraisal system

Despite the issue of resolving the balance between control and development aspects, organisations need some kind of performance assessment for their staff.

However, appraisal systems are often criticised as being irrelevant to the organisation's work. And this may well be the case at Booxe.

The current system has become very informal, possibly due to the fact it is not taken very seriously by either the appraiser or the appraisee.

Control aspects – In order for the appraisal process to become relevant to Booxe's work, the control aspects need to be linked to the organisation's overall goals – such as driving down costs, to support the overall strategy of cost leadership.

Development – However, the appraisal system also needs to be linked to the development of appropriate skills and greater motivation among the staff. (This could be particularly important if employees' jobs are redesigned following BPR.)

It is not clear whether Booxe's current appraisal system is linked to the employee rewards, but if the 'control' elements of appraisals are linked to a suitable reward system, this should help to increase performance in the company as staff strive to meet the performance targets set in their appraisals.

However, it is important that the appraisal process still reflects the culture and strategy of the company. Although Booxe has a strategy of cost leadership, there is also an appreciation of craft skills among the workforce. As such, the 'development' aspects of the appraisal process may be important for enabling staff to highlight new skills they want to learn. But equally the 'control' element of the appraisal process may be important for improving efficiency and controlling costs.

It seems likely that the general discussions about how to improve employees' efforts – which currently constitute Booxe's appraisal process – may be focusing more on the 'development' aspects of appraisal, rather than the 'control' elements. However, it seems that the CEO may be looking to change this, by evaluating the balance between control and development in the process.

9 PLX Refinery

Workbook reference. Environmental management accounting is covered in Chapter 4 of the Workbook.

Top tips. Although **part (a)** is only worth six marks there are still effectively two parts to the requirement. What cost categories could aid transparency in internal reporting? And what cost categories could aid transparency in external reporting? Make sure you address both in your answer, and make sure you give examples, as you are instructed to do.

There are also two stages to answering **part (b)**: 'explain' then 'evaluate'. However, don't just explain the techniques in general terms; make sure you link them back to PLX's environmental and strategic performance.

Similarly, in your evaluation, make sure you look specifically at how the techniques could be useful in managing performance at PLX. And because you are 'evaluating' them, try to include some limitations in using them as well as the advantages of using them.

Also, note that requirement (b) asks you how the techniques can assist in managing environmental **and** strategic performance. So, for example, how might a better understanding of environmental costs affect strategic decision making (as well as the more obvious issues of how might an understanding of environmental costs affect environmental performance)?

Part (c). The scenario tells us that PLX's existing information systems focus on financial performance. So how will they have to change in order for PLX to implement input/output analysis?

Part (d). The figures given in the scenario indicate that there are some significant environmental costs associated with the project. Consequently, whether they are included in a project appraisal or not will have a significant impact on the perceived profitability of the project. In effect, then, you could approach by asking: What are the potential problems with Kayplas's current costing approach? And then, how could a life cycle costing approach help address these problems?

Marking scheme

		Marks
(a)	Up to 2 marks for each cost area discussed – Up to a maximum of 6 marks	
	To score 2 marks, the discussion of each cost must include relevant examples, linked to the scenario.	
	Total: up to 6	6
(b)	Up to 2 marks for explaining each technique, and explaining its link to environmental performance – Up to a maximum of 6 marks	
	Up to 3 marks for an evaluation of the techniques.	
	Total: up to 9	9
(c)	Identifying the need for non-financial information – 1 mark	
	Up to 2 marks for comments on sources and difficulties of collecting physical information	
	Total: up to 3	3
(d)	Up to 2 marks for calculation of life cycle costs	
	Up to 2 marks for calculating the product profits of the two approaches	
	Up to 4 marks for discussing the potential improvements and issues identified by life cycle costing.	
	Total: up to 7	7
		Total = 25

(a) PLX will need to identify existing and new cost information which is relevant to understanding the environmental impact its operations have.

Operating costs – PLX's current management accounting system is already likely to record conventional costs such as raw material costs and energy costs. However, the costs of waste through inefficiency will not be recorded. If they were, however, this should encourage PLX's management to reduce the amount of waste generated by the company's processes.

Additionally, a number of environment-related costs (such as waste filtration) are currently classified within overheads, meaning that they are not very transparent to management. Similarly, the regulatory fines are also likely to be included within overheads. However, if all these environment-related costs were classified separately they would immediately be more visible to management.

Decommissioning costs – The profit forecast for Kayplas highlights that PLX incurs a number of significant costs at the end of a project, for example the costs of decommissioning equipment, or cleaning industrial sites once they stop being used.

These costs (because they are large) can have a significant impact on the shareholder value generated by a project, and can also make significant demands on PLX's cash resources. However, because they occur at the end of a project there is a danger that they will be given a lower priority if management focuses on short-term financial measures, such as annual profit.

Reporting on costs – As well as making the costs more visible to management, increasing the focus on environmental costs could also be beneficial to PLX from a public relations perspective. If PLX highlights these costs in its financial reports, and also highlights the actions it is taking to reduce to reduce its environmental impact, it can demonstrate to pressure groups and the regulator that it is taking its environmental responsibilities seriously.

Reputational costs – By contrast, if PLX is deemed not be taking its environmental responsibilities seriously, this could result in adverse publicity for the group, and ultimately could lead to consumer boycotts and lost revenues.

(b)   **Input/output analysis**

Input/output analysis compares the physical inflows into a process with the outflows, with the assumption being that the difference between inflows and outflows must have either been stored in the process or lost as waste. In this way, the physical quantities lost as waste could be quantified and costed, highlighting that inefficient processes have a financial impact on a business.

By adopting input/output analysis, PLX would be forced to focus on how efficiently it uses its resources and the environmental costs of its processes, as well as the level of waste and externalities generated by them.

ABC

Traditional ABC allocates costs to cost centres or cost drivers on the basis of the activities that caused the costs.

Environmental ABC looks to distinguish between environment-related costs and environment-driven costs.

Environment-related costs are attributed specifically to an environmental cost centre, for example, waste filtration at PLX.

Environment-driven costs are not allocated to a specific environmental cost centre, but still relate to environmental drivers. For example, PLX may reduce the working life of some of the machinery in its refinery to reduce pollution levels in the later years of its working life. The increased annual depreciation charges that will result from this are environment-driven costs.

Applying ABC in this way will help PLX identify and control environmental costs.

Life cycle view

Life cycle costing looks to record a product's costs and revenues across the whole of its life, rather than for a single year, or for a specific phase of its life (such as the production phase).

This is important because it highlights the importance of costs incurred **prior** to production and those incurred **after** production ceases (for example, in PLX's case, the costs of decommissioning plant and equipment). These costs can often be very large, and so could have a significant impact on the shareholder value generated by a project. As a result they may potentially influence the decision about whether or not to undertake a project.

Given the nature of PLX's business, it is very important that any investment appraisals capture all the costs generated over the whole life cycle of a project – including decommissioning costs, which for the Kayplas project are estimated at $18m.

Evaluation

Costs – One of the major issues PLX would face if it chooses to introduce input/output analysis or environmental ABC is that it will need to collect significant additional amounts of information from the management accounting system, and there are likely to be costs involved in upgrading the system to be able to provide this.

Benefits – At the same time, while the techniques can help improve PLX's economic and environmental efficiency, it may be difficult to quantify the benefits which will accrue from using the techniques. Therefore, it may be difficult to justify introducing the techniques on the basis of a financial cost/benefit analysis.

Strategic benefits – However, perhaps the stronger case for using the new techniques is a non-financial one. PLX believes it will be strategically important to be at the forefront of environmental developments, and using the new techniques will demonstrate its commitment to this.

By demonstrating its commitment to environmental issues, PLX could improve its **public image**, appease the **pressure group** (Green Kayland) and reassure the **Government** it is helping to improve its treatment of the environment.

(c) **Physical measurements** – In order to implement input/output analysis PLX will need to measure the physical amounts of materials being processes through the refinery. Therefore, its information systems will need to record physical measurements as well as financial data. PLX may need to modify its existing database structure or add additional records in order to do achieve this, and such alterations could be costly themselves.

PLX will also have to introduce systems for monitoring the physical volumes of raw materials, waste and recycled materials within the refinery's processes.

The focus of PLX's current information systems, suggests that financial performance measures are currently seen as the most important, so the change to collecting and using data about physical measurements could seem a significant change for PLX's culture.

However, there could ultimately be financial benefits from recording this non-financial information. For example, if the information which is collected helps to identify efficiency improvements, in turn these could help improve PLX's operating profits and its earnings.

(d) PLX's traditional performance measure of product profit for Kayplas suggests it will generate a profit of \$41.5m over five years. However, this ignores the environmental costs (of waste filtration, and carbon dioxide exhaust extraction) as well as the cost of decommissioning at the end of the project.

By contrast, a life cycle analysis would include all of these costs:

Kayplas product profit	\$m
Traditional view:	
Revenue:	149.4
Production, marketing & development costs	107.9
Product profit (over 5 years)	41.5
Profit margin	27.8%
Kayplas product profit	\$m
Adjusted for environmental costs:	
Revenue	149.4
Production, marketing & development costs	107.9
Waste filtration	8.1
Carbon dioxide exhaust extraction	5.3
Decommissioning costs	18.0
	139.3
Revised product profit	10.1
Profit margin	6.8%

When the environmental costs are all included, the forecast profit margin on the Kayplas project is reduced from 27.8% to 6.8%, which makes it a much less attractive investment. Moreover, if the actual costs of decommissioning in five years' time are higher than the forecast (\$18.0m) – for example, due to changes in environmental legislation in the next five years – then the profit margin will be reduced even further.

BPP LEARNING MEDIA

Importantly, also, life cycle costing makes the post-production costs visible at the start of the project and in the design stage of the product. This should help PLX appreciate early in the project the need to minimise the costs of decommissioning. So, for example, it could investigate whether it could design any of the equipment to be used to produce Kayplas in such a way that it could also be used to produce Kayplas2.

10 Alflonnso

Workbook reference. You should already be familiar with activity-based costing from your earlier studies (in *Performance Management*), but it is revisited, in the context of activity-based management, in Chapter 13 of the Workbook. Environmental management accounting is discussed in Chapter 4.

Top tips.

Part (a) (i). A useful starting point here would be to think what activity-based costing (ABC) is, and how it differs from traditional overhead allocation. Then think about the way Alflonnso currently allocates overheads to products – ie on the basis of revenue (for waste treatment overheads) or not at all (for R&D costs). How does this compare to the way overheads would be allocated using ABC? Which is likely to provide a more accurate indication of the profitability of the different products?

The calculations you need to do in part (a) (ii) highlight the importance of waste treatment overheads and R&D costs on product profitability. So, in effect, the requirements for (a) (ii) could have acted as a pointer towards some of the key issues to consider in (a) (i) – which highlights the importance of exam technique in terms of reading all the requirements for a question before starting to answer it.

Part (a) (ii). The calculations themselves should be relatively straightforward. However, note that the overheads are not allocated only to these three products. For example, the $300m of waste treatment costs relates to the total of 55 million litres, not just to the quantities of waste by-product generated by ALF7, Red and Green.

Part (b). The figures shown in Appendix 1 should have provided some context for this requirement. Appendix 1 suggests that Red is the most profitable of the three products. However, will this still be the case using ABC, and considering the products' entire life cycles?

The calculations themselves for this question are not difficult, but there are a number of elements to them, so it is important to follow a structured approach:

- Appendix 1 shows profits for a single period, and the waste treatment costs calculated in (a) (ii) are also for a single period (year). So, first you need to calculate a revised annual profit for each product.

- Next you need to multiply the revised annual profit by the product's life cycle, to find life cycle profit.

- The life cycle profit then has to be adjusted for any pre-production or post-production costs (for example, decommissioning costs).

- Finally, the total life cycle cost has to be divided by the number of litres produced over the product's life cycle to identify the average profit per litre over the life cycle.

Once you have done the calculations, don't forget you also need to comment on the results. How does the relative profitability of each of the products compare to that in Appendix 1, and what are the main reasons for any differences?

Part (c). In the scenario, the CFO talks about a presentation she watched which showed how EMA can help to reduce three categories of cost – conventional, contingent and reputation – and improve performance as a result.

As such, a sensible approach would be to use each of these categories as headings in your answer, and to consider how EMA could affect them. For example, how might EMA affect decision making, which in turn could affect the division's performance in relation to each of the categories?

The scenario highlights some potential reputation issues quite clearly – for example, about Green's unsuitability for use in climates where crop production is already difficult. The sequence of the requirements in the question should also help you here. For example, one of the main life cycle costs in your calculations in part (b) should have been decommissioning costs, which would be a good illustration of contingent costs.

The scenario might seem to give you less information about 'conventional costs' – but might this be revealing in itself? In traditional accounting systems, environmental costs are not apportioned to products, and are simply included as general overheads. If managers don't have any information about these costs, how can they manage them? How could EMA help managers in this respect (and consequently, how could it improve the performance of the division)?

Examining team's comments.

Part (a) (i) was generally poorly done, as candidates did not answer the question set. Most candidates gave definitions or descriptions of activity-based costing, but – while these were technically correct in almost every case – they did not address the specific issue of how ABC could help the Agrochemicals Division assess the profitability of its products. It is vital that candidates recognise that only around 25% of the marks in APM will be awarded to definitions and rote learned knowledge. By contrast, in this requirement, candidates could have obtained full marks without giving a definition at all, and purely applying their knowledge to the scenario.

In **part (b)**, many candidates showed a fundamental lack of technical competence by failing to distinguish between costs that occurred on an annual basis and those that related to the product's overall life.

Candidates must also appreciate that if they are asked to comment on the results, then what is required is more than simply saying 'this figure is larger than that one' – which can be seen from the figures themselves. Instead, in a question like this, the commentary should consider the implications of the figures: will they change a decision? Does the use of one technique fundamentally change the cost or product, and what are the implications of this?

In **part (c),** as in part (a) (i), the majority of the marks available were for applying EMA to the practices of the Agrochemicals Division. Would practice change? How? What might be involved? However, a number of candidates' answers largely only defined and/or explained EMA, without considering its potential benefits to the division. Unfortunately, answers based on theory alone can only score around 25% of the marks available, meaning they fall well short of the number of marks required to pass.

Marking scheme

			Marks
(a)	(i)	Generic explanation of purpose of ABC – 1 mark Application to scenario – 1 mark per point Total for part (a) (i): up to 5	5
	(ii)	Waste treatment costs – 2 marks R&D costs – 1 mark Total for part (a) (ii): up to 3	3
(b)		Revenue, direct costs, overheads (given in scenario) – 1 mark	
		Waste treatment costs – 1 mark	
		Total net profit over life cycle (before other life cycle costs) – 1 mark Scientific study – 1 mark	
		Decommissioning cost – 1 mark	
		R&D costs – 1 mark	
		Total litres – 1 mark	
		Average profit per litre over life cycle – 1 mark	
		Comments on calculations – up to 3 marks	
		Total for part (b): up to 9	9

(c)   Description of EMA – up to 2 marks

Impact of EMA on each cost category: conventional, contingent, reputation – up to 3 marks per category

Total for part (c): up to 8   8

Total = 25

(a)   (i)   **ABC**

ABC allocates costs to products based on the activities which actually drive the cost. This helps to allocate the costs more accurately.

At Alflonnso, the group accounting policy is to allocate waste treatment overhead costs on the basis of revenue, which is arbitrary and does not reflect the cost drivers (for example, the amount of waste created by each product). From the analyst's calculations, R&D costs do not seem to be allocated to specific product costs at all. This may be appropriate elsewhere in the group, where different products may consume similar levels of overheads, but the three new products being evaluated consume quite different amounts of R&D and waste treatment overheads.

It is therefore inappropriate to charge these costs to the products on the basis of revenue. Charging these costs on the basis of the activities which drive them – which are research hours and volume of waste by-products, for R&D costs and waste treatment costs respectively – will give a more accurate costing. This will provide a better basis on which to evaluate the new products and set appropriate prices.

(ii)   **Calculation of waste treatment cost**

	ALF7	Red	Green
Quantity of waste by-product (m litres)	8.0	34.0	0.75
[m litres produced/no. of m litres to make 1 litre of waste]	[100/12.5]	[85/2.5]	[75/100]
Allocated total $300m according to quantity of waste as proportion of total 55m litres:			
Annual waste treatment allocated ($m):	43.6	185.5	4.1
	[8 × 300/55]	[34 × 300/55]	[0.75 × 300/55]

R&D cost

	ALF7	Red	Green
Allocated total $60m according to required hours of research as proportion of total 30,400 hours:			
R&D treatment allocated ($m):	1.6	16.8	7.9
	[800 × 60/30,400]	[8,500 × 60/30,400]	[4,000 × 60/30,400]

(b) **Average unit cost of each product over total life cycle**

$m	ALF7	Red	Green
Revenue (given)	800.0	1,105.0	825.0
Direct material, labour and energy (given)	(524.0)	(724.0)	(565.0)
Factory overheads (given)	(80.0)	(122.0)	(74.0)
Waste treatment (from part (a) (ii))	(43.6)	(185.5)	(4.1)
Total annual net profit	152.4	73.5	181.9
Life cycle duration (years)	3	15	8
Total net profit over life cycle (before other life cycle costs)	457.2	1,102.5	1,455.2
Scientific study ($4m × 20 years)	–	(80.0)	–
Decommissioning cost	–	(45.0)	–
R&D cost (from part (a) (ii))	(1.6)	(16.8)	(7.9)
Total net profit over life cycle	455.6	960.7	1,447.3
No. of litres produced over the life cycle (m)	300	1,275	600
Average profit per litre over life cycle	$1.52	$0.75	$2.41

From the analyst's calculations in Appendix 1, Red has the highest profitability per litre of the three products at $2.26, but this only covers a single period. As such, it does not consider costs which occur before production commences or after it ceases. When the costs of the products over their entire life cycles are taken into account, Red has the lowest average unit profit, the highest being Green at $2.41. This change has occurred as the R&D costs, the cost of the study which will span 20 years and the decommissioning costs have now been recognised. Knowing the costs over the entire life cycle of a product will help the Agrochemicals Division to better evaluate its investment decisions, determine appropriate prices and generate an acceptable margin.

(c) **EMA**

EMA involves the production of non-financial and financial information to support internal environmental management processes. This could involve measuring the physical movements of inputs to a production process, such as materials and energy, and outputs such as waste.

The Agrochemicals Division could also record financial data on costs and savings related to the environment. It appears that, in common with most other businesses, these costs are not currently identified by Alflonnso's accounting system and they lie hidden within overheads.

Managers have no incentive to reduce these environment-related costs as they are not even aware of them, or the costs of poor environmental practices. EMA allows an organisation to identify environment-related costs and take steps to control them. Such costs are often categorised into conventional costs, contingent costs and reputation costs.

Conventional costs

These costs include the cost of energy and raw materials, and may remain hidden within overheads. The energy costs of the three new products in the analyst's income statement are simply combined with raw material and direct labour costs. This does not, for example, highlight the relatively high energy cost to produce Green. Being unaware of this cost, managers are unable to take steps to redesign the specification or production process for the product in order to reduce the cost.

Contingent costs

These are costs which are incurred in the future, for example, the decommissioning costs of the plant used to manufacture Red. This cost is significant, at an estimated $45m, but occurs 15 years in the future and so the estimation is unlikely to be accurate.

Identification of these contingent costs will at least allow the Agrochemicals Division to more accurately estimate the cost of each of the three new products. Also, by identifying these costs at an early stage, this may allow managers to redesign the specification or production process for the product in order to reduce the cost and help prevent managers from focusing only on short-term performance.

Reputation costs

Reputation costs are incurred where an organisation acts in a way which may cause harm to the environment, and include sales lost as a result of loss of reputation. These costs are hard to quantify. For example, the accumulation of the existing product, ALF6, in the soil is said to have a potential effect on crop yields which may lead to future claims from users of the product or to loss of sales due to its potential harm to the environment.

Similarly, Alflonnso's failure, by producing Green, to improve crop yields in countries where food production is already scarce is likely to arouse disapproval by public and governments in the 25 countries where it operates. This again may result in lost sales or refusal by governments to grant licences for Alflonnso to operate.

Making managers aware of these reputation costs should focus their attention on the need to manage the risks of them occurring.

11 Sberry

Workbook reference. Risk analysis techniques, and the impact that different risk appetites can have on decision making are discussed in Chapter 5. Analysing the external environment (including PEST analysis) is discussed in Chapter 1.

Top tips.

Part (a). A substantial part of this requirement involves the calculation of the profit Sberry from the three products under the different exchange rates. Make sure you think carefully about the details in Appendix 1 when doing this: for example, Sberry is based in Deeland, so all the figures need to be reported in D$. Also, note that only half of the cost for each product is for materials imported from Kayland (so only half of the unit cost needs to be adjusted for changes in exchange rate).

However, the question does not simply require you to do a calculation, you also need to 'advise' which product each of the three stakeholder groups would choose to export. So make sure you clearly state which product each group will choose, and briefly explain your rationale for this.

In this context, a key part of this question is identifying which risk analysis technique (eg maximax; maximin; expected value) each stakeholder group will use as the basis for making their decision.

The scenario tells us 'the employees have a cautious approach to the proposal' while the directors 'are keen to earn the large bonus' based on the profit made by the product. The shareholders 'neither avoid nor seek risk'. Which analysis technique do these factors suggest each group will use?

Part (b). Having applied the different techniques in part (a), you now need to think about the potential problems with the techniques themselves.

For example, is there any guarantee the best possible outcome selected under a maximax approach will actually be achieved. Similarly, Appendix 1 tells us the probabilities for the movements in exchange rate have been 'estimated' by the finance director. But if these estimates prove incorrect, what impact could this have on the expected values?

Part (c). The opening paragraph of the scenario tells us that levels of income are rising in Kayland, and that Kayland has a slower rate of technological obsolescence than Deeland. Later on, the scenario tell us that a previous product launch had been unsuccessful, because the product breached safety regulations which Sberry had a poor understanding of.

These are all factors which could be included in a PEST analysis. Importantly though, the requirement is not asking you to produce a PEST analysis, but to advise how it could help Sberry maximise its performance in Kayland. A key issue here is to remember that environmental factors are potential opportunities and threats, but in order to respond effectively to these opportunities and threats Sberry will first have to identify them. How will PEST analysis help it do that? Equally, how could identifying key environmental factors be useful for Sberry in deciding which aspects of performance are most important to measure and monitor?

Finally, to score well in this requirement, make sure you relate your answer specifically to the scenario, rather than – for example – talking, in general terms about the benefits of a PEST analysis. As such, try to make use of the pointers in the scenario – for example, about technological obsolescence, safety regulations.

Marking scheme

		Marks
(a)	Calculations – up to 8 marks	
	Exchange rates – 1 mark	
	Revenue – 1 mark	
	Revenues converted to D$ – 2 marks	
	Total costs (in D$) – 3 marks	
	Expected values – 1 mark	
	Justification of the approach selected for each stakeholder group – up to 3 marks (1 per stakeholder group)	
	Selection of correct product based on the approach selected – up to 3 marks (1 per stakeholder group)	
	Total for part (a): up to 14	14
(b)	1 mark per point	
	Problems in using the risk and uncertainty analysis techniques	
	Total for part (b): up to 5	5
(c)	1 mark per point	
	Advising how PEST analysis can improve performance in Kayland	
	Total for part (c): up to 6	6
		Total = 25

(a) **Employees**

Employees are cautious about the proposal to export to Kayland, and are risk averse. They would use the maximin rule, which is the choice of product with the best of the lowest outcomes. In this case, this is Blue.

Directors

Directors are paid a high bonus dependent on profitability of the product chosen. As they have served on the board for many years, there appears to be little chance that they would be removed by making a poor choice. They are risk seekers, and will use the maximax rule, that is, the choice of product with the best possible outcome. In this case, this is Green.

Shareholders

Shareholders are risk neutral. They will choose the product with the highest expected value; in this case this is also Blue, which has an expected value of D$82,728.

Total profit

Probability	Exchange rate (W1)	Red D$	Blue D$	Green D$
0.75	2.20	67,273 (W2)	73,637	54,546
0.25	1.80	95,555 (W3)	110,000	111,111
Expected value (W4)		74,344	82,728	68,688

Workings

1   *Exchange rate*

$D strengthens by 10% against $K: 2.00 + 10% = 2.20

$D weakens by 10% against $K: 2.00 – 10% = 1.80

2   *Total profit at exchange rate of $D1.00 = $K2.20*

	Red	Blue	Green
Revenue in K$	400,000	540,000	960,000
	(50,000 × K$8.00)	(60,000 × K$9.00)	(160,000 × K$6.00)
Revenue in D$	181,818	245,455	436,364
	(400,000/2.20)	(540,000/2.20)	(960,000/2.20)

Cost of imported materials (D$)			
Red (50,000 × 1.20 × 2.00/2.20)	54,545		
Blue (60,000 × 1.50 × 2.00/2.20)		81,818	
Green (160,000 × 1.25 × 2.00/2.20)			181,818
Cost of other materials (D$)	60,000	90,000	200,000
	(50,000 × D$1.20)	(60,000 × D$1.50)	(160,000 × D$1.25)

Total profit (D$)			
Red (181,818 – 54,545 – 60,000)	67,273		
Blue (245,455 – 81,818 – 90,000)		73,637	
Green (436,364 – 181,818 – 200,000)			54,546

3   *Total profit at exchange rate of $D1.00 = $K1.80*

	Red	Blue	Green
Revenue in K$ (W2)	400,000	540,000	960,000
Revenue in D$	222,222	300,000	533,333
	(400,000/1.80)	(540,000/1.80)	(960,000/1.80)

Cost of imported materials (D$)			
Red (50,000 × 1.20 × 2.00/1.80)	66,667		
Blue (60,000 × 1.50 × 2.00/1.80)		100,000	
Green (160,000 × 1.25 × 2.00/1.80)			222,222
Cost of other materials (D$) (W2)	60,000	90,000	200,000

Total profit (D$)			
Red (222,222 – 66,667 – 60,000)	95,555		
Blue (300,000 – 100,000 – 90,000)		110,000	
Green (533,333 – 222,222 – 200,000)			111,111

4   Expected value

	Red D$	Blue D$	Green D$
Red (0.75 × 67,273) + (0.25 × 95,555)	74,344 (50,455 + 23,889)		
Blue (0.75 × 73,637) + (0.25 × 110,000)		82,728 (55,228 + 27,500)	
Green (0.75 × 54,546) + (0.25 × 111,111)			68,688 (40,910 + 27,778)

(b)   Sberry's three key stakeholder groups will use different criteria to make decisions on the Kayland opportunity according to their attitude to risk and reward. The maximin and maximax rules and the expected value can be used to determine the decisions which each group will make.

Maximin and maximax rules

The maximin rule, the choice with the best of the lowest outcomes, which would be preferred by the employees, can be an excessively risk averse approach. As Sberry's products have short product lives, it must constantly develop new products, so some commercial risks will have to be taken.

The maximax rule, which the risk-seeking directors prefer, has the problem that it may be overly optimistic. Product choices with the maximum reward or profits may also be riskier, and could mean that directors take risks which exceed the shareholders' risk appetite so as to earn high bonuses.

A problem with both of the maximin and maximax rules is that they both ignore the probability of the outcome actually occurring.

Expected value

The expected value approach is a long run average which can be applied to decisions which are repeated many times. The actual expected value is not a possible outcome and will never occur in practice. Though Sberry may have developed many products, it has no experience of forecasting exchange rates and so the expected value approach may be inappropriate.

The expected value approach relies on estimates of probabilities, such as for average exchange rates. These may be subjective or difficult to make, which limits the value of this approach.

(c)   ### Identifies opportunities or threats

Analysing the external environment in Kayland will allow Sberry to identify opportunities and threats. It can maximise performance by taking actions to exploit opportunities, such as developing the new products to take advantage of growing income levels and the slower rate of technological obsolescence in Kayland.

A draft PEST analysis has indicated that the exchange rate between D$ and K$ is a key economic factor affecting performance. By identifying this, Sberry can act to maximise performance, such as by analysing the effect of exchange rates on profits of the new products or hedging against adverse exchange rate movements. A thorough analysis of safety regulations in Kayland may prevent the problems which occurred with the failure of the previous product launch.

Identifies CSFs, KPIs and helps set targets

PEST analysis can help identify critical success factors (CSFs) and key performance indicators (KPIs). Having identified product safety as a legal factor affecting performance, a CSF may be to abide by safety regulations in Kayland. The number of breaches of safety regulations would be a suitable KPI.

The PEST analysis can be used to set targets appropriate for the environment in Kayland. A CSF for Sberry is that it produces products for long enough to recover their development costs and make an acceptable profit. A target for the KPI of length of time in production could be 24 months in Kayland, where technical obsolescence is slower, rather than the target of 18 months in Deeland.

BPP
LEARNING
MEDIA

12 Sweet Cicely

Workbook reference. The impact of external factors on performance management, and the impact of risk and uncertainty – including risk analysis techniques – are covered in Chapter 5 of the Workbook.

Top tips. Although **Part (a)** is presented as a single requirement, there are actually two elements (Advise...; Evaluate...) so make sure you address both of these in your answer.

The second paragraph of the paragraph tells us 'SC must choose a size [of factory] most suited to the expected demand for its products'. It then tells us 'demand for SC chocolate bars will be influenced by external factors' before identifying a number of factors which could affect demand. These external factors are all potential sources of risk and uncertainty, so you should use them to illustrate the advice you are giving.

Note also the requirement refers to both 'risk' and 'uncertainty' so think about the distinction between the two. A useful way to structure your answer could be to consider each issue – risk, and uncertainty – separately; for example, beginning with a brief description of what each is, and then using relevant examples from the scenario to illustrate why it will be important for SC to consider each of them in the decision-making process.

For the second part of the requirement ('Evaluate the use of PEST'), one approach could be to think how an awareness of the political, economic, social and technical factors in the environment could help SC manage the risk and uncertainty surrounding the project. A useful way to do this could be to use each of the four factors (P,E,S,T) as a heading in your answer, and then think about the issues in the scenario which relate to that factor. This is the approach taken in ACCA's official solution.

Importantly, though, note that you are not asked to use PEST analysis to **identify** the potential risks and uncertainties; but rather how SC could use it to help **manage** these risks and uncertainties. For example, political instability in cocoa growing regions is a political risk, but can SC manage that risk, or – if it can't – what are the implications of this risk for the project?

An alternative approach to this requirement would be to 'evaluate the use of PEST' in terms of assessing the potential advantages and drawbacks of using PEST analysis as a basis for managing the potential risks and uncertainties surrounding the project. If you took this approach, you would still get credit for relevant points you make. Again though, note that the requirement asks about managing risks and uncertainties, not simply identifying them.

Parts (b) and (c) look the use of at different risk analysis techniques for evaluating projects. In part (b) you need to take account of the different risk appetites of the board and the shareholders, whilst in part (c) the requirement refers to a risk neutral investor. So, in part (b) the potential techniques to consider could be maximax; maximin and minimax regret, while part (c) requires you to use expected values.

Part (b). A key step in answering this question is identifying the risk appetites of the two different stakeholder groups. The scenario tells us, in the penultimate paragraph, that the board wants 'to minimise the opportunity cost of making the wrong decision about the size of the new chocolate factory'. So which of the potential techniques will they use to evaluate the three options? Similarly, in the first paragraph of the scenario, we were told, the new shareholders 'are prepared to accept a high level of risk' in order to increase SC's performance. So which technique will they use?

Part (c). As noted above, risk neutral investors will use expected values in order to evaluate potential options, so you need to use the data in Appendix 2 to calculate the expected values of the three options, and then recommend the option with the highest EV.

Note, however, that this requirement doesn't only involve the calculation. There is also a second element: to explain any problems with using expected values to make the choice about which factory to set up.

Marks

(a) Consideration of risk and uncertainty – 1 mark per valid point, up to 8 marks

Discussion of use of PEST analysis – 1 mark per point, up to 8 marks
Total for part (a): up to 14

14

(b) Calculation and comments on the board's preference – up to 4 marks

Comments on new shareholders' preference – up to 2 marks
Total for part (b): up to 6

6

(c) Calculation of expected value – 1 mark

Recommendation, and drawbacks of expected value approach – 1 mark per point

Total for part (c): up to 5

$\underline{5}$

Total = $\underline{\underline{25}}$

(a) **Importance of incorporating risk and uncertainty in making long-term decisions**

Risk relates to the variability of outcomes, the probabilities of which are known, or can be estimated. Uncertainty occurs where the outcomes and their probabilities are unknown. The variability of demand for SC's chocolate bars is a risk, and the probabilities of different levels of demand can be estimated. The outbreak of conflict in a cocoa growing region affecting cocoa prices cannot be assigned a probability, and so is an uncertainty.

The market price of cocoa and the demand for chocolate bars are examples of exogenous variables which significantly affect the performance of SC. Exogenous variables arise from outside the business, and the business doesn't have any control over them. Climatic conditions, soil erosion, for example, all affect the price of cocoa, and therefore the performance of SC.

When investors evaluate businesses, they take into account prospective returns and the level of risk involved. Therefore, managers should consider risk and return when evaluating projects on their behalf. Long-term strategic planning requires forecasts to be made about future events, such as the price of cocoa. These future events are by definition unknown, and subject to risk and uncertainty. Risk and uncertainty must, therefore, be considered when making long-term plans, such as opening the new factory. The further forward plans are projected, the riskier, and more uncertain, events are likely to be, as it is harder to predict what conditions will be. This means that consideration of risk and uncertainty is even more important when making long-term decisions than when making short-term decisions.

Use of PEST analysis

To incorporate risk and uncertainty into long-term strategic planning, SC must identify and monitor the most important exogenous variables, taking action to manage the risks they present. As a traded commodity, the risks of rising cocoa prices could be managed (hedged), for example, by using cocoa futures. The board member's comments suggest planning for the cake business was poor, and did not adequately consider the importance of exogenous variables. Risks in the macro environment could be identified using a PEST analysis.

Political factors

The market price of cocoa is affected by conflicts and political uncertainty, so consideration of these external factors is needed to incorporate risk and uncertainty into long-term planning. By identifying factors such as political instability or conflict, SC can improve its long-term performance by sourcing cocoa from more stable regions. The

BPP
LEARNING
MEDIA

political situation in a region can change rapidly, which might make it difficult to incorporate these risks into long-term planning, as there is a high degree of uncertainty.

The introduction of increased taxes on products containing sugar is a political factor affecting the long-term demand for SC's products. Once introduced, this factor is likely to operate in the long term and be more predictable. Identifying this, SC could develop products containing less sugar and so reduce the amount of these additional taxes on its products.

Economic factors

Economic factors such as the variation in long-term interest rates can influence SC's performance by affecting exchange rates or overall consumer demand. By identifying these factors, SC could hedge against currency exchange rates. In the longer term, SC could locate its operations in a country where the risks from exchange rate fluctuations are lower, or diversify geographically to spread the risk.

Social factors

Overall demand for chocolate products will be influenced by social factors such as consumer tastes or increased awareness of healthy eating. SC can improve its long-term performance by not investing in a chocolate factory at all, if it believes demand for its products will fall sufficiently to make the venture unprofitable.

Technological factors

The increased cocoa yields from genetically modified crops may reduce long-term cocoa prices and SC could incorporate this into the net present value calculations for the factory. There may be unpredictable consequences which are harder to plan for, such as the acceptance by consumers of genetically modified foods.

(b) **Board**

The board wants to minimise the opportunity cost of making the wrong decision about the size of the new chocolate factory, which means to minimise the regret of making the wrong decision. The minimax regret rule would be the appropriate method to use so they would choose the project with the lowest maximum regret.

The regret table is as follows:

	Option 1	Option 2	Option 3
Annual demand			
50 million	0.0	(12.0)	(36.0)
60 million	(10.0)	0.0	(40.0)
70 million	(11.0)	(1.0)	0.0
Maximum regret	**(11.0)**	**(12.0)**	**(40.0)**

Option 1 is the option with the lowest maximum regret ($11m), and that would be the option preferred by the board according to their risk appetite. A drawback of using the minimax regret rule is that the probabilities of the outcomes are not considered.

New shareholders

The new shareholders are keen to increase the long-term performance of the business and are prepared to accept a high level of risk to achieve this. They will choose the option with the maximum possible outcome, which is option 3, with a maximum possible net present value of $17m. This is known as the **maximax rule**. This also takes no account of the probabilities of the outcomes, and also tends to be over-optimistic. It also ignores the fact that even risk seekers have a risk–return trade off.

(c) **Expected value of each option**

Option 1 – (0.3 × 3.0) + (0.4 × 0.5) + (0.3 × –2.0) = $0.5m
Option 2 – (0.3 × 5.0) + (0.4 × 2.0) + (0.3 × –1.0) = $2.0m
Option 3 – (0.3 × 7.0) + (0.4 × 1.5) + (0.5 × –2.0) = $2.1m

The risk neutral investor's choice, for year 1 only, would be option 3, with an expected value of $2.1m.

Problems of using an expected value approach

A risk neutral investor would use the expected value approach to choose between the three options. The expected value is a long run average, and is only appropriate where a decision is repeated many times. This does not appear to be the case at SC which has made only one attempt at strategic expansion in the last several years. For the same reason, the expected value will not equal the actual outcome.

Determining the probabilities, of the market price of cocoa for example, is subjective. Even analysis of historical market prices is not necessarily a guide to what will happen in the future. The expected value approach is suitable for a risk neutral investor. This does not apply to the key stakeholders at SC, and hence this approach is inappropriate for use in the decision on the three options. Determining the payoffs is also difficult when demand is subject to uncertainty. SC should not make a decision on the factory based only on the first year's operating profits, and should take a longer term view, for example, based on discounted cash flows.

13 Turing

Workbook reference. Risk appetite and the different methods which can be used for decision making under uncertainty are covered in Chapter 5 of the Workbook. The issues involved in managing performance in JVs are discussed in Chapter 14.

Top tips.

Part (a). For each of the firms, you need to assess the risk appetite and then recommend a method of decision making under uncertainty which is appropriate for that risk appetite.

The reference to 'uncertainty' was very important here, because it indicated that you should use techniques such as maximax and maximin, rather than expected values.

Note also that the requirement is to recommend an appropriate method for each firm. Therefore, you must make a clear recommendation, rather than evaluating the advantages and disadvantages of possible different methods for each firm. You will need to evaluate the appropriateness of different methods in order to decide which method is most suitable for each firm, but the final answer itself needs to be a recommendation.

When evaluating the method more appropriate for Riemann, a key point to note is the business's need to achieve a guaranteed minimum level of return, in order to aid the survival of the business. As such, this means that maximin should be chosen as the appropriate method, rather than minimax regret. However, the examining team indicated that students would be given some credit for suggesting minimax regret, because it is a risk averse solution (and therefore fits Riemann's risk appetite). However, minimax regret is not as clearly focused on obtaining a minimum level of return.

Part (b). Having identified in part (a) which method each firm would use, you now have to apply the methods in order to determine which turbine each one would choose to build.

The calculations in this part of the question should have been relatively straightforward, and the marking guide indicates that you could have scored marks in part (b) for correct calculations of minimax regret, even though it was not one of the methods which should have been recommended in part (a) – which were maximax and maximin.

Part (c). Parts (a) and (b) should have clearly identified one of the major problems facing the joint venture: that the different circumstances and risk appetites of the two venture partners are going to make it difficult for them to agree on strategic decisions. In this case, how do they decide which turbines to build, since Turing will want to build the 8 MW design, and Riemann will want to build the 3 MW design?

More generally, answering part (a) should also have helped you identify that the two firms are likely to have different cultures and management styles – which again could make it difficult for them to work together to manage the JV.

Marking scheme

Marks

(a)   Turing

Assessment of risk appetite – 1 mark per relevant point up to a maximum of 3 marks

Method of decision making – 1 mark for selecting an appropriate method (maximax); 1 mark for describing the method

Riemann

Assessment of risk appetite – 1 mark per relevant point up to a maximum of 3 marks

Method of decision making – 1 mark for selecting an appropriate method (maximin); 1 mark for describing the method

Total for part (a): up to 9

9

(b)   Calculations:

Variable costs – 2 marks

Total costs – 1 mark

Revenue – 2 marks

Profit – 1 mark

Maximax result – 1 mark

Maximin result – 1 mark

Conclusion – 1 mark

Total for part (b): up to 8

8

(c)   For each relevant point (linked to the scenario) about potential problems in managing the JV – 1 mark

Potential points include: differences in goals and choice of performance measures between the venture partners; different risk appetites; differing time horizons for achieving results; deadlock in decision making; different management styles, and cultural differences between the venture partners; information sharing; intellectual property.

Total for part (c): up to 8

8

Total = 25

(a) **Turing**

Risk appetite

The appetite for risk at Turing will be determined by the three VCs, which collectively own 90% of the company.

Each of the VCs hold a large portfolio of investments, and are prepared for some of these to fail provided that others show large gains. As such, the VCs are **risk seekers**.

The other key stakeholders at Turing are the management team, who own the remaining 10% of the company. The fact the management have been given an equity stake in the business, coupled with their ambition and their enjoyment of the challenges of introducing new products, suggests that they will be comfortable with the high-risk approach taken by the VCs.

Turing's management are also likely to be attracted to projects which are innovative, such as the 8 MW unit. They enjoy the challenges of introducing new products, and are likely to be motivated by the prospect of developing a world-leading unit.

Method of decision making

Maximax – The fact that both of Turing's key stakeholder groups (the VCs and management) are prepared to accept high-risk approaches suggests that Turing will be a risk seeker. As such, the appropriate method of decision making under certainty for it will be maximax.

Using the maximax approach, the design choice selected will be the one which offers the highest maximum profit possible, across any of the three demand scenarios.

Riemann

Risk appetite

The risk appetite at Riemann is likely to be determined largely by its investors – particularly as it has recently had to seek emergency refinancing.

Riemann's shareholders are concerned about the survival of the business, and its debt providers will also be concerned about its survival – and therefore its ability to repay any loans.

Riemann's management are also primarily concerned with the survival of the business. Although they do not own any shares in the company, they will lose their jobs if the company collapses.

The fact that Riemann's shareholders and management both view TandR as a way to generate additional cash flow reinforces the fact that their primary concern is with identifying initiatives which can help secure the survival of the business.

The precarious nature of Riemann's current position suggests that all of its key stakeholders will be **risk averse**.

Equally, they are likely to favour projects which will start generating income soon. As such, the 8 MW unit – which takes two years longer to develop than the others – may be less attractive to Riemann than the two units which can be developed more quickly.

Method of decision making

Maximin – Riemann's focus on the survival of the business means that a maximin approach to decision making under uncertainty will be appropriate for it.

Using the maximin approach, the design selected will be the one which maximises the lowest profit which could be achieved across the three demand scenarios.

(b)   **Turbine design types**

Demand		1,000	1,500	2,000
		$m	$m	$m
Revenue				
8 MW	$20.8 per unit	20,800	31,200	41,600
3 MW	$9.6 per unit	9,600	14,400	19,200
1 MW	$4.6 per unit	4,600	6,900	9,200
Variable cost				
8 MW	$10.4 per unit	10,400	15,600	20,800
3 MW	$4.8 per unit	4,800	7,200	9,600
1 MW	$1.15 per unit	1,150	1,725	2,300
Fixed cost				
8 MW		7,500	7,500	7,500
3 MW		820	820	820
1 MW		360	360	360

Profit	1,000	1,500	2,000	Max payoff $m	Min payoff $m
8 MW	2,900	8,100	13,300	**13,300**	2,900
3 MW	3,980	6,380	8,780	8,780	**3,980**
1 MW	3,090	4,815	6,540	6,540	3,090

Maximax = $13,300 earned by the 8 MW units

Maximin = $3,980 earned by the 3 MW units

Due to the differences in their preferred methods of decision making under uncertainty, Turing and Riemann would choose to build different turbine design types. Riemann would choose to build the 8 MW units, while Riemann would choose to build the 3 MW units.

(c)   **Problems of managing performance in a JV**

Decision making – As we have seen in part (b), one of the main problems in a JV will be that of reaching a consensus between the venture partners when making strategic decisions.

This could be a particular problem for TandR, given that both partners own 50% of the venture, and so it is difficult to prioritise the interests of one partner over those of the other.

Goals and objectives – As well as their differences in attitude to risk, it appears that the venture partners have different goals and objectives for the venture. In this case, Riemann's primary goal from the venture is to generate additional cash flow in the short term. However, Turing appears to be more interested in the potential long-term returns which can be earned from designing and manufacturing the turbines. As such, it could be difficult for the venture partners to agree what TandR's goals and objectives should be.

Similarly, the venture partners could have different interests in relation to the performance measures they consider to be most important. Although TandR could measure a variety of different indicators – including profit, growth and cash flows – Riemann is likely to prioritise cash flow measures and short-term performance indicators, while Turing is more likely to be interested in the growth and the longer-term prospects of the business, for example.

Management styles – In the same way that Turing and Riemann have different attitudes to risk, it is also likely that they will have different management styles and organisational cultures. This could cause problems at an operational level at TandR, since it is run by a group of managers from each of the JV partners – and therefore who may adopt different management styles.

Sharing capabilities and information – One of the problems, in general, with JVs is that they require the venture partners to share information, capabilities and intellectual property with each other. However, many of these elements may be commercially sensitive, and so the venture partners will be reluctant to share too much information about their own business with each other.

In this respect, establishing a climate of trust between the venture partners is likely to be important for the success of the JV. However, if the venture partners have very different cultures and management styles – as Turing and Riemann seem likely to – this trust could be harder to achieve.

Valuing the contribution of the venture partners – Another issue which arises from sharing information and capabilities relates to how the value of the different partners can be valued. It is likely that Turing's blade design skills will be a significant advantage for the venture, for example. However, it is likely to be difficult to measure the contribution that intangible assets (such as skills and competences) make to the venture in their own right.

Nonetheless, given that both partners hold a 50% stake in the venture, if one of them thinks they are contributing significantly more value to the venture than the other, this could quickly become a source of disagreement between the partners.

14 Luvij

Workbook reference. The characteristics which affect the usefulness of information are discussed in Chapter 6 of the Workbook, as are unified corporate databases. Performance management issues in relation to joint ventures are discussed in Chapter 14.

Top tips.

Part (a). The final paragraph in the scenario provides some useful clues for this requirement: for example, by highlighting the managers have difficulty understanding the large volume of data; and that they often receive it too late for it to be useful. They are clearly issues which reduce the value of the information to them.

A useful way to approach this requirement could be to think of the characteristics of good information, and then whether Luvij's information demonstrates those characteristics. As the requirement asks you about 'factors which might limit the usefulness' of the information, you need to focus specifically on problems, or potential problems, with the information.

However, as well as explaining the potential limitations of the current information, you are also asked to evaluate how the use of a unified corporate database could help to overcome these limitations.

We have structured our answer so that after each 'limitation' in the current information we evaluate how using a unified corporate database could help to overcome the limitation. However, you could equally look at all the potential issues with the current information first, and then evaluate how a unified database could help to overcome them.

Crucially though, to score well, it is important that you address both parts of the requirement, and assess them specifically in the context of Luvij, rather than making generic points about the characteristics of good information, or the benefits of using a unified corporate database. For example, the second paragraph highlights that design trends in the market change frequently – so it is important of receiving information quickly. The current spreadsheet is only circulated at the end of each quarter. So will that limit its usefulness, and could the unified corporate database help to ensure information is available more quickly?

Part (b). The requirement here also has two elements: advising the board about problems, first, with measuring the performance of the joint venture; and second, managing the performance of the joint venture.

Again, though, the final paragraph provides a useful clue to some of the issues here, by highlighting that the businesses have different objectives. These objectives have been explained in more detail earlier in the scenario: with Luvij wanting to expand its capacity in order to become the market leader, but Shirville simply wanting to use up spare capacity in its factory until the lease expires in three years' time.

A key question to ask yourself here is: what are the implications of these differences in objectives, and how could they create problems for the joint venture?

Similarly, the scenario tells us that Luvij aims to sell high quality children's footwear to independent footwear retailers, while Shirville produces high volumes for supermarkets and chain stores. So this should also prompt you to think about the different strategies each company is pursuing (differentiation vs cost leadership?) and therefore the aspects of performance which will be most important for them to measure and manage. If the two partners are prioritising different aspects of performance, what implications could this have for the joint venture and its chances of success?

Examining team's comments. Part (a) was generally well answered. Candidates identified the missing areas of information needed by the company and then connected these to the benefits which could achieved by using a unified corporate database.

Candidates also generally performed well in part (b) with many answers describing the differences between the two organisations and how this would affect the joint venture.

Marking scheme

Marks

(a) 1 mark per relevant point

    Limitations of the usefulness of the external information currently used –
      up to 8 marks

    Evaluation of the use of a unified corporate database to overcome those
      limitations – up to 8 marks

    Maximum for part (a): 15 marks   15

(b) 1 mark per relevant point

    Problems of performance measurement – up to 6 marks

    Problems of performance management – up to 6 marks

    Maximum for part (b): 10 marks $\underline{10}$

                                              Total = $\underline{\underline{25}}$

(a) **Usefulness of information**

> **Tutorial note.** This suggested solution uses the characteristics of good information as a framework for assessing the external information Luvij currently uses. However, there are a variety of ways to structure this answer, and you would receive credit for relevant points you make, even if the structure of your answer is different from the suggested solution.

Relevant

For the external information to be useful, it should be relevant to the needs of the users. The information in the quarterly spreadsheet contains sales data as well as information on market trends in designs. All of this information may not be relevant for all of the departments to which it is circulated. For example, data on design trends may not be relevant to the production department using it to plan production capacity.

A unified database, integrating data from different sources, would make data more relevant to users by giving users only information and reports which are relevant to them and sharing data from all relevant departments. Users would not waste time interpreting data which is irrelevant to them.

Timely

For external information to be useful, it must be available when needed. This is particularly so in the fashion industry where designs change quickly and where competitors may offer short-term discounts. The external information at Luvij is only sent at the end of each quarter, which is likely to be too infrequent in the fast moving industry in which Luvij operates. Additionally, as the information is prepared by one staff member, there could be delays in producing it if they were on sick leave, for example.

A unified database would ensure that data was available instantly, especially if linked to retailers' own systems' real-time sales data. This should improve the speed of decision making.

Accurate

To be useful, information must be accurate. Entering large volumes of data into a complex spreadsheet is prone to error, as well as being time-consuming. Inaccurate data may lead to poor decision making.

A unified database would process all data automatically with minimal human intervention, and would thus be less prone to inaccuracies. All departments would share identical data.

Communication

Although the spreadsheet of external information at least ensures that all departments have access to the same data, the large volume of data may be difficult to understand. Managers may be overloaded with data, much of which they do not need.

A unified database would allow users access only to information which they need. This would be in an easy to use format, perhaps with the ability to drill down to more detailed information held in the database.

Emailing data to a large number of staff may mean that confidential or commercially sensitive information, such as on design trends, is shared with staff who do not require it. A unified database would restrict access to information, using passwords, only to staff who are authorised to receive it.

Cost effective

The cost of producing the external information should not exceed the benefits of doing so. Costs of the current system include not only the costs of employing the team to compile the information but also time spent collecting, processing or interpreting data which may be inaccurate, irrelevant or out of date.

Using a unified database would incur costs of buying, maintaining and developing the system, as well as staff training. An evaluation must be made whether these costs are justified by the benefits. Some adaptation of the existing system, such as increasing the frequency of reporting the information, or sending different sets of information to different departments, may be more cost effective.

(b) **Problems of performance measurement in the joint venture**

Measuring the performance of the joint venture may require Luvij and Shirville to share confidential information, which they may be unwilling to do. Luvij's innovative designs for children's footwear and Shirville's knowledge of advanced production techniques are both likely to be commercially sensitive.

It is unclear exactly what each of the parties contributes to the joint venture. Luvij is providing innovative designs, and Shirville is providing advanced manufacturing machinery and production techniques. As each party is providing different things to the joint venture, it may be hard to measure the contribution, to profit for example, from each party.

Luvij and Shirville will have their own information systems. These may be incompatible, or it may be difficult or costly to integrate them. Each party may measure or collect information in a different way, which will mean information used to measure the performance of the joint venture is not prepared on a consistent basis.

Problems of performance management

Luvij's objective for the venture is to become the market leader in high-quality children's footwear. Shirville's objective is to utilise spare production capacity in a factory where the lease is due to expire in three years. As the parties have different objectives, it may be hard to develop performance metrics for the joint venture. The share of the chosen market may be a key performance metric for Luvij, and return on capital employed may be appropriate for Shirville. The metrics chosen may conflict, and their relative importance may be unclear. This will make it difficult for managers to manage the joint venture according to each of the venture partner's objectives.

Luvij's objectives for the joint venture are long term, whereas Shirville may choose to end the joint venture upon expiry of the factory lease in just three years. Establishing timescales for performance objectives may be difficult as each party has different time horizons for the venture.

Luvij is entering a new market and has already invested heavily in market research and product design. Shirville seems to have a much lower risk appetite, as it only wants to utilise spare capacity. Managing performance may be difficult because Luvij may wish to make decisions which involve a higher level of risk than Shirville may wish to accept.

The parties have may have different expectations of the level of quality of products arising from the joint venture. Luvij manufactures high-quality footwear and will want its range of children's footwear to be of a quality consistent with its women's footwear range. Shirville supplies supermarkets and high street stores, probably with lower quality products. Disagreement about acceptable levels of quality may damage performance of the joint venture.

15 TREN engine components

> **Workbook reference.** Lean manufacturing and lean information systems are covered in Chapter 6 of the Workbook.
>
> **Top tips.** This question focuses on one specific part of the APM syllabus: 'Evaluate whether the management information systems are lean and the value of the information that they provide...'
>
> To answer the question, it is necessary to identify the requirements of a lean information system (part (a)) and then to discuss why the existing 'traditional' management accounting system at TREN may fail to do this (part (b)).
>
> Having established the difference between the two types of system, you then need (part (c)) to identify the changes which are needed to convert TREN's 'traditional' systems into 'lean' systems.
>
> Note that there is no requirement to link your answer to part (a) directly to the scenario. However, your answers to parts (b) and (c) do need to be linked directly to the scenario.

(a)   A lean information system should provide value to the users of the system. Key principles are the **elimination of waste, speed of information flow,** and **clarity**.

Elimination of waste – A lean system seeks to eliminate all waste. In an information system, waste is created by errors in the information, which means that incorrect information is used and wrong decisions may be taken. Alternatively the information has to be corrected when the error is identified, and this results in a cost of correction. Correcting errors does not add value, because the error should not have occurred, and correcting errors is wasted effort.

Efficiency in the flow of information – A lean manufacturing system is one in which there is an efficient flow of items through the manufacturing process. In a lean information system, there should be an efficient flow of information. Information should be available to individuals when they need it, and there should not be unnecessary delays in providing it or making it available.

While efficiency in the flow of information means that information should be available when it is needed, it should not be provided before it is needed. Information should be available 'just in time' (JIT). This is the concept of **pulling items** through the system rather than pushing them through. If information is provided before individuals are ready to use it, it does not have value.

Clarity is also an element of lean information. Information must be clear to the people who use it and should therefore be presented in a form that they can understand and use. If information is presented in a form that is difficult to understand, it will be difficult to use. Unless it is used for its intended purposes, information has no value.

Together, the elimination of waste, efficiency of information flow, and clarity of information are qualities of an information system that give value to the information that the system produces.

Reasons why lean principles may not lead to improvements in productivity and profitability

In many situations, an organisation supposedly using lean principles has not experienced the improvements in productivity and profitability expected. It is difficult to know whether this is due to shortcomings in the lean philosophy or whether the techniques involved are being **interpreted and applied correctly**.

Change in approach – To be successful, lean techniques should be seen and treated as outward signs of a more **fundamental approach** to operations and quality. However, many organisations seem to treat the techniques as the end itself – they have a mistaken belief that simply putting structures and mechanisms (eg quality circles) in place will improve efficiency and quality. Sustainable differences require a change in thinking and in culture – which are difficult to achieve.

Cost-cutting exercise – Lean production is often viewed as a simple cost-cutting exercise rather than a fundamental commitment to eliminating waste and adding value. Many companies use lean manufacturing to improve quality and reduce costs. But the benefits most businesses realise are only a fraction of what could be achieved if these strategies were applied in conjunction with the aim of creating a workplace with real organisation and order, and with an engaged workforce who take pride in their work.

(b) There are several reasons why TREN's current management accounting system does not fulfil the requirements of a lean information system.

Errors – There are many errors in data capture for the cost accounting system. Errors represent waste in the system, by providing incorrect information about costs, or requiring correction when the errors are found. Errors also reduce the confidence of users in the information that the system provides.

'Push' system – Monthly variance reports are provided but not until two months after the end of the month. There are two weaknesses in this reporting system. The first is the delay in making information available if required. The information about performance is being held by accountants and is not made available to the managers who can use it.

The second problem is that the information is pushed out to management in the form of monthly variance reports, when it would be more appropriate to make the information available when management want to use it for monitoring and control purposes. The information system is dictating how and when the information should be used, whereas management should be doing this.

Not encouraging lean manufacturing – More fundamentally, it can be argued that traditional cost and management accounting methods provide managers with inappropriate information that encourages the wrong sorts of management for an organisation that uses lean manufacturing methods. A key feature of lean manufacturing is the elimination of inventory, because holding inventory is wasteful. Absorption costing, however, encourages manufacturing at full capacity, even if this means manufacturing items that are not yet needed by customers, so that inventory will build up. This is because high volumes of production reduce the unit costs of manufacture by spreading overhead costs over a larger volume of output.

Variance reporting of efficiency also encourages greater volumes of output, because greater efficiency means faster production. When the workforce is paid a fixed wage or salary, attempts to improve efficiency will result in greater production quantities and a build-up of inventory.

The current reporting systems therefore encourage managers to control operations in a way that is inconsistent with lean manufacturing.

(c)   **Error reduction** – To create a lean management accounting system, waste must be eliminated and information flow improved. The causes of the data errors in data capture are not known. The problem may be the use of manual documentation for recording costs, or errors in input by inadequately trained staff. Methods of recording costs should be investigated, and the target should be to eliminate input errors entirely.

Flows of information – The flow of information must be improved, so that up to date information is available to management when they want it. The speed of entering data into the accounting system should be reviewed, and the aim should be to minimise the delay between recording data and inputting it into the accounting system. Automated methods of monitoring inventory movement or recording labour times may be considered.

User access to information – The accounting system should also allow managers online access to information about costs, so that they can obtain and use the information they need at a time that they need it. This should apply to senior management as well as to management at the operational level.

Cost allocation – The information provided by the accounting system should be reviewed, and absorption costing should be abandoned. There may be some value in using activity-based management to monitor and control overhead costs, but the most important requirement should be to value inventory at direct materials' cost. This means that there will be no incentive to produce at high capacity volumes or operate at unnecessary levels of efficiency. Favourable capacity and efficiency variances will not affect inventory costs and so will not improve management performance.

Performance measures – Different items of information should be provided for performance measurement purposes. Traditional performance measurement methods for materials – price and usage variances – should be used to control materials costs. For labour, however, non-financial measures of performance may be appropriate, such as production cycle times of throughput times and the ratio of idle time to active time for the workforce. The company is considering JIT purchasing for its main suppliers: if so, a suitable measure of performance may be the order to delivery cycle time for purchase orders.

In a lean information system, information should have a practical use and support the aims of management. The management accounting system should be changed so that it provides value – a practical purpose, with no waste, rapid information flow and clarity of meaning.

16 Forion Electronics

Workbook reference. ERPSs are discussed in Chapter 6 of the Workbook. Sources of data are also discussed in Chapter 6, while non-financial performance indicators are discussed in Chapter 10.

Top tips.

Part (a). As is the case with a number of APM questions, note that there are two elements to this requirement: first, you need to discuss the integration of information systems in an ERPS; then, second, you need to discuss how the ERPS at Forion may affect performance management issues there.

The first element doesn't specifically require any application to Forion. However, you could use the issues which Forion is facing, and the different departments mentioned in the scenario, to illustrate the way an ERPS could integrate information from different systems.

The marking guide indicates that six out of the ten marks for this requirement are available for the second element – discussing how the ERPS can affect the performance management issues at Forion.

Even if you didn't know much about an ERPS, you should have been able to identify how deficiencies in the information sharing between departments could lead to the problems identified in the scenario. There are six marks available for three problems; so two marks per problem. If, for each problem, you provide a brief discussion of the likely causes of each problem, and then indicate how better information sharing could help to avoid that problem, this should help you earn the majority of the marks available for this part of the requirement.

Part (b). An important factor to consider here is the relationship between Forion and BAS. BAS is a supplier to Forion, and Forion has chosen BAS because of its reputation for quality and new product development. This suggests Forion considers these aspects of performance to be important (and Forion has previously identified it needs to have high-visibility, durable screens in order to be competitive – so visibility and durability could be considered as aspects of 'quality').

A useful way to answer the question would be to consider how well the performance measures chosen allow Forion to assess BAS's performance in the areas which it has identified as important.

In this respect, don't just think about the aspects of performance selected, but also think about the practicalities of measuring the performance. How easy will it be to measure whether or not BAS achieves the desired levels of performance?

Part (c). Note that the question requires you to make two separate comparisons: financial vs non-financial data; and internal vs external data. Also, it is important that you discuss the issues specifically in the context of the SLA between Forion and BAS. For example, will BAS be happy to use internal performance data prepared by Forion given that it (BAS) could be liable for a financial penalty if it fails to achieve the target performance levels?

Examining team's comments (for part (c)) – Evaluating the reliability of data has been a common topic in past exams, yet candidates' answers to this question were unexpectedly poor. Many candidates seemed unaware of what constitutes internal and external sources, and – surprisingly – many considered audited, financial data to be amongst the least reliable sources. In addition, many candidates discussed the type of information that both parties to the alliance would need, without discussing its reliability (which is what the requirement actually asked for).

Marking scheme

		Marks
(a)	For general description of an ERPS and how it integrates information: 1 mark per relevant point – up to 5 marks	
	For specific discussion of the impact an ERPS could have on the problems at Forion: 1 mark per relevant point – up to 6 marks:	
	Total for part (a): up to 10	10
(b)	For relevant points about the usefulness of the three areas for measuring performance – 1 mark per point	
	Note. In order to score a clear pass, all three issues must be addressed.	
	Total for part (b): up to 8	8

(c)   For relevant points about the relative reliability about the different types of
        data – 1 mark per point

   Note. In order to score a clear pass, both issues (financial/non-financial; and
        internal/external must be addressed.

   Total for part (c): up to 7   7

                                                                        Total = 25

(a)   An ERPS is a software system which supports and automates the business processes in
        an organisation. An ERPS can assist in identifying and planning the resources needed to
        perform many different activities in different departments across the whole organisation –
        including inventory management, manufacturing, distribution, invoicing and accounting.
        An ERPS can incorporate support functions such as human resource management and
        marketing.

        As such, an ERPS enables the performance information from all departments that are
        involved in operations or production to be integrated into one system, thereby assisting the
        flow of information between the departments and across the organisation as a whole.
        Integrating performance information in this way would seem very useful to Forion, given
        the problems it has encountered to date.

        As well as improving the flow of information between the department in an organisation,
        ERPSs can help to improve linkages with outside stakeholders – for example, by
        incorporating customer relationship management (CRM) and supply chain management
        (SCM) software.

        Again, this would seem very useful to Forion, given the high number of customer and
        supplier relationships it has to manage.

The impact of an ERPS on performance management issues at Forion

Information sharing – The board has suggested that a number of the performance
management problems at Forion arise from poor communication and information sharing
between departments; not least because each of the departments has its own information
system rather than having an integrated system across the organisation as a whole.

As such, by providing an integrated system which assists the flow of information between
departments, an ERPS could help to solve the three problems identified.

Amount of subcomponents ordered – This reflects a problem with the information being
shared between the Purchasing Department (which orders the subcomponents) and the
Manufacturing Department (which uses them). If the Purchasing Department has incorrect
or out of date information, this will lead to it ordering the wrong amount of subcomponents,
which in turn means that Forion's inventory handling and storing costs will be higher than
they need to be.

However, if Forion had an ERPS, information from the Manufacturing Department would
automatically be shared with the Purchasing Department, meaning the Purchasing
Department should be able to identify the quantities of subcomponents to order more
accurately.

Stock-outs or obsolescence – Both of these problems arise from the amount of goods
being manufactured not reflecting the expected level of orders. Although the Marketing
Department may produce good sales forecasts, if these forecasts are not shared with the
Manufacturing Department, it will not know what quantities of different goods it needs to
make. If it produces too few, this will lead to stock-outs (and a loss of potential revenue);
while obsolescence results from producing too many units of a good which cannot then be
sold. (The risk of obsolescence could be a particular concern for Forion as a manufacturer
of electronic goods.)

If the Marketing Department's forecasts were captured in an ERPS, they would be available to the Manufacturing Department when it was setting its production plans.

Lack of delivery vehicles – The delivery schedule needs to incorporate sales information (customers' orders) and manufacturing information (when goods will be available).

If the Warehouse Department only becomes aware of a customer order after it has scheduled all its delivery vehicles this would help to explain why there seem to be insufficient vehicles to meet customer deadlines. Similarly, if there are delays in manufacturing which the Warehouse Department isn't aware of, this could mean that goods can't be included in their scheduled delivery, and will require an additional delivery and an extra vehicle to fulfil the customer order.

By linking the manufacturing schedule, customer orders, and the delivery schedule, Forion should be able to schedule its deliveries as efficiently as possible, to make best use of its delivery fleet.

Equally, though, by having greater visibility over orders and the manufacturing schedule, the Delivery Department should be able to identify in advance any times when it will not have sufficient vehicles of its own to fulfil all the orders required. Knowing this, it can then make arrangements for a third-party logistics company to deliver the order in time to meet the customer's deadline.

(b) **Usefulness of performance areas**

The three performance areas selected (quality of manufacturing; timeliness of delivery; technical upgrades) all seem appropriate. The 'quality' area derives from underlying logic behind the alliance – Forion's need for high-visibility, durable screens; timeliness of delivery will be important for the smooth operation of the production process; and the ability to make technical upgrades is likely to be critical in a rapidly changing market – such as the market for smartphones.

Quality of manufacturing – BAS's strong reputation suggests the number of faults should be low. Nonetheless, as screen manufacturing is a key part of the assembly process, and having high quality screens is likely to be a critical success factor for the phone overall, it will be important to measure performance in this area.

There could also be significant costs involved in remedying any faults with the screens. If the faults are identified during internal inspection, the time taken to fix them will delay delivery. If the faults are identified by customers, Forion will incur the cost of repairing – or replacing – the faulty phone. Customers' dissatisfaction with faulty items may also mean they are less likely to buy a Forion smartphone again in the future.

Time of delivery – The screen is a key component of the phone so delays to shipments could cause significant disruption to the production process if Forion is trying to use a just-in-time (JIT) production process. Conversely, if Forion holds inventory 'just in case', then concerns about delayed shipments could lead to it holding higher levels of inventory than it might wish to.

If Forion wants to use a JIT production process, then implementing the ERPS and giving BAS access to the system could be very useful. For example, this would give BAS greater visibility around when screens are needed and in what quantity.

Technical upgrades – Whilst upgrades are likely to be important in keeping Forion's phone competitive, it will be difficult to measure BAS's performance against the metric as it is currently defined. For example, there is no timescale in which BAS needs to provide the upgrade, and deciding when the market demands an upgrade could be subjective.

If performance in this area cannot be measured effectively, BAS could pay less attention to it. Although, in theory, building financial penalties into the agreement is appropriate, Forion may not be able to apply them if it cannot measure whether or not BAS has achieved the target levels of performance.

Moreover, as Forion selected BAS as its strategic partner due to its strong reputation for quality of manufacturing and new product development, it is surprising that both of these acknowledged strengths are being measured, rather than any areas of potential weakness.

BPP LEARNING MEDIA

(c)   **Reliability of financial vs non-financial data**

The requirement to produce annual accounts, and to have them audited, means that there should be robust controls in place around the production of financial data. Although non-financial data will be useful to management in controlling the business, it may not be subject to the same scrutiny and controls as financial data.

Similarly, financial data will be quantitative and objective, whereas non-financial data can sometimes be subjective; for example, an issue with a phone screen which some customers may report as a fault, other customers may not report.

Although the subjectivity of non-financial data can sometimes make it difficult to measure, this does not appear to be a problem in this context. The fault rates and the number of shipments overdue should be relatively easy to measure.

Internal vs external sources

Forion is likely to place greater reliance on its own data rather than external data (for example, as provided by BAS in relation to shipments supplied). As such, Forion is likely to use its own warehouse records to determine the number of shipments which are overdue, although this means that Forion will need to have sufficient controls in place to ensure that expected and actual delivery times are recorded accurately.

However, if both parties place greater reliance on their own data than the other party's data, this could be a source of problems for the alliance; for example, if the number of shipments BAS believes to be late differs from the number Forion believes to be late. This could be a particular issue here, given the financial penalties relating to performance.

In this case, it may be useful for both parties to have the right to inspect (audit) each other's data to confirm the reliability of that data.

17 Quark Healthcare

Workbook reference. Developments in IT systems (such as the introduction of RFID tags) are discussed in Chapter 6 of the Workbook. Lean systems are also discussed in Chapter 6.

Top tips.

For **part (a)**, it is very important that you think about the impact of the RFID system specifically in the context of the areas highlighted by the CFO: (i) the costs and benefits associated with producing information from the system; (ii) the impact of the system on the nature of the information supplied; (iii) changes to performance management reporting; and (iv) how the new information could be used to improve control at the hospitals.

To this end, it would be sensible to use each of the CFO's suggestions as headings in your answer, to make sure you cover all of them.

The 'control' issues and their impact on performance should be relatively easy to identify from the scenario – for example, staff are unable to find equipment because it hasn't been replaced after being used, and as a result patient care is delayed while staff waste time trying to find the equipment.

However, the marking guide indicates that only 6 out of the 12 marks for this requirement are available for internal control issues. So don't spend too long on this one area at the expense of the other areas.

Nonetheless, the problems staff face in finding equipment and drugs provide a link between parts (a) and (b) of the question. One of the key principles of 'lean' systems is the removal of waste and non value adding activities. Time spent looking for equipment or drugs clearly doesn't provide any value to hospital patients. Similarly, 'lean' systems aim to promote efficiency.

So a sensible way to approach **part (b)** will be to evaluate how far the RFID system can reduce waste and improve efficiency at the hospital.

Part (c). The scenario highlights that an earlier system which the hospital had tried to introduce has not been fully implemented due to complaints from the medical staff. The medical staff are clearly key stakeholders at the hospital and so if they oppose a new system it is unlikely to be successful.

This provides the context to the first part of the requirement: how the medical staff's attitudes will influence the design and implementation of the system.

However, note that there are effectively two parts to the requirement, with the second looking at issues around responsibility and accountability.

One of the key issues here, though, is how the system can promote accountability given the 'strict social order' among the staff. For example, can a nurse be responsible for a piece of equipment being in the wrong place if it has been moved by a doctor?

Marking scheme

Marks

(a)   Costs and benefits associated with producing the information from the
        RFID system – 1 mark per relevant point up to a maximum of 3 marks

Impact of the RFID system on the nature of the information supplied –
        1 mark per relevant point up to a maximum of 3 marks

Changes to performance reporting resulting from the implementation of
        the new system – 1 mark per relevant point up to a maximum of 3 marks

Use of information from the new RFID system to improve control at the
        hospitals – 1 mark per relevant point up to a maximum of 6 marks

Total for part (a): up to 12   12

(b)   Definition of lean systems – up to a maximum of 2

Analysis of the impact of the RFID system on the management of the
        hospital – 1 mark per relevant point, up to a maximum of 7

(Within this 7 marks, up to 2 marks are available for definition of the
        5 Ss of lean)

Total for part (b): up to 7   7

(c)   Evaluation of how the attitude of medical staff will influence the design of
        the new system – 1 mark per relevant point, up to a maximum of 4

Evaluation of how the system might be used to promote responsibility and
        accountability – 1 mark per relevant point, up to a maximum of 4

Total for part (c): up to 6   6
                                                                                            Total = 25

(a)   **Costs and benefits of the system**

Cost – There is likely to be considerable cost associated with the hardware and software needed to establish the RFID system. A significant amount of time may also be required to tag the equipment and drugs which are to be included in the system.

However, the costs should be compared to the benefits which will accrue from the system:

Efficiency savings – Hospital staff will save time because they will no longer have to search for items once those items have been tagged.

Patient care – Improvements in patient care as a result of hospital staff being able to find equipment or drugs immediately rather than having to search for them.

Impact of the nature of the information supplied

Non-financial information – Although the information being supplied about Quark's equipment and inventory is non-financial (relating to the location and quantity of equipment and drugs in Quark's hospitals), it should already be included in the hospital's information systems.

Timeliness and accuracy – However, the major impact of the new system should come from the improvements it can provide to the timeliness and accuracy of the information being recorded. The RFID tags will update information on a **real-time basis**. Moreover, because movements are **recorded automatically** the problem of the register not correctly reflecting the physical location of an asset will be overcome.

Batches of drugs – However, the quality of the information provided by the RFID tags may be less reliable for the drugs which are delivered in a single packaged batch. If a tag is applied to a batch as a whole when it is delivered to the hospital, then the information provided by the tag will no longer be reliable once the batch is opened and drugs are used from it. Instead, there will still be a need for the hospital to physically count the quantities of these drugs actually held in inventory, rather than relying on the RFID information alone.

Performance management reporting

Weekly physical checks – Under its existing systems, Quark has to make weekly physical checks of the drugs held in inventory in order to update its records on the basis of those checks. However, the information provided by the RFID tags should mean that inventory records can be updated on a real-time basis, rather than being dependent on these weekly checks.

Access to information – The fact that the RFID information will be available on terminals throughout the hospitals should also help the speed with which staff can locate items of inventory or equipment. The ease and speed with which staff can search the information will depend on the number of terminals which are installed. It would also be useful for relevant staff to receive training on how to search for information on the terminals.

Improved control

Control over drugs – Quark's existing accounting systems aim to avoid theft and obsolescence of equipment and drugs. RFID tags should improve controls over security by providing greater transparency about the location of assets. For example, the tags will make it easy for staff to check that all the high-value drugs are stored in secure locations, thereby reducing the risk of them being stolen.

Reduced obsolescence – Additionally, the information available about the date drugs were delivered should help staff identify the order in which different batches of a drug should be used to prevent obsolescence and wastage.

Tagging equipment – We have already noted that tagging items of equipment will allow staff to find them more quickly and thereby provide faster service to patients. However, the RFID tags will also enable the hospitals' management teams to ensure that pieces of equipment are replaced and locked away in secure areas once they have been used. This again should help reduce the risk of theft, but perhaps equally importantly staff should be reminded of the importance of replacing items after they have been used, and of storing them in useful locations. This also links to the ideas of 'lean' systems which the CFO is interested in.

(b)   **Lean systems**

Removal of waste – The aim of 'lean' systems is to minimise the amount of resources (including time) which are consumed by the activities of an organisation. A key element of this comes from identifying and eliminating all non value adding activities. In this context, 'lean' also involves the systematic elimination of waste.

In relation to information systems, waste arises from difficulties in accessing and retrieving information, or from having to correct inaccurate information. This kind of 'waste' has clearly been an issue for Quark – for example, where staff have had to waste time looking for equipment or drugs which have not been not stored in the correct place. Such activity is clearly not value adding; rather it detracts from the value (care) which Quark can offer to its patients.

Improved efficiency – In contrast to this, the goal of a 'lean' operating system is to get the right things to the right place at the right time. In the context of Quark, this could mean enabling staff to know where equipment is so that it can be made available in the right place when it is needed by patients. Consequently, introducing the RFID system should help the operations management at the hospitals become leaner.

'Lean' systems can also have wider cultural implications which could be beneficial at the hospitals, in particular in relation to changing attitudes towards 'waste' and 'inefficiency'. The instances of equipment lying unused in one area of the hospital while being searched for in another area (to the detriment of patient care) would seem to be symptomatic of waste and inefficiency in the hospitals.

5 Ss – Lean principles are often characterised through 5 Ss, which could usefully be introduced at Quark:

Structurise – Identify the things which are most important and introduce order where possible. At Quark this could mean identifying the optimal locations for storing equipment, on the basis of where it is used most frequently.

Systemise – Arrange essential items in order so that they can be quickly and easily accessed. The RFID system will make it easier for staff to locate the equipment and drugs they need.

Sanitise – Keep the working environment clean. Be tidy, and avoid clutter. Although the RFID system should help staff to find drugs and equipment more easily, there is a danger that staff may think that this reduces the need for them to replace them after use, or to keep stocks of drugs tidy and in order.

Standardise – Make cleaning and checking a routine. For example, the RFID information could be used by management to check that equipment is replaced after use; and staff could even be monitored on the extent to which they keep their sections of the hospitals tidy.

Self-discipline – Sustain via motivation; for example, by reporting on performance. The system could produce exception reports highlighting pieces of equipment which had not been returned to a secure store once they were no longer being used. Corrective action can then be taken to return the equipment to an appropriate store area.

Impact of the RFID system

In some organisations, 5Ss has become a cleaning and housekeeping exercise only, and the underlying philosophy behind the concept has been lost. If this happens, then RFID's ability to make the management system leaner will be reduced. However, if the RFID information system is seen as an important part of quality management at the hospitals, then its impact should be more beneficial.

(c) **Key stakeholders** – The **medical staff** are likely to be key stakeholders in the hospitals, so their attitude to the new system is likely to be very important. If they resist the system, then its implementation is unlikely to be successful, as appears to have been the case with the new method for recording drugs administered to patients.

In this respect, it will be important to consult the medical staff over the design and implementation of the RFID system. Not only does consulting them recognise their position as key stakeholders, but also it gives them the opportunity to ensure the system is designed in a way which provides them with the information they need.

Improvements to patient care – Crucially, consulting the medical staff about the design of the system should help encourage them to accept it rather than resist it. Equally, it will be important that medical staff realise that the primary purpose of the system is to enable equipment and drugs to be found more easily – thereby improving patient care – rather than as a piece of bureaucracy. If the medical staff realise the benefits of the system, they should be more willing to accept it.

Usability – The user-friendliness and ease of use of the new system will also influence how successfully it will be implemented.

Again, this highlights the importance of consulting the medical staff, to ensure that the system is designed in a way which makes it easy for them to use. Some of the complaints from the nurses and specialist doctors about the new method of drug administration may have been caused by the system proving difficult or time consuming to use.

Responsibility and accountability

The RFID system will provide much greater transparency as to where equipment or drugs are actually being stored, and can provide management with the information to control how well staff are looking after the hospitals' assets. However, in itself, the system cannot promote responsibility or accountability.

Quark will also need to identify who is responsible for ensuring assets are held in the right place at the right time. For example, responsibility schedules could be introduced for each department or ward identifying which assets the nurses are responsible for and which the doctors are responsible for.

Quark's management should only hold people accountable for assets being in the right place if those people have control over how and where those assets are used. For example, can a nurse be held accountable for equipment being in the wrong place if a doctor has moved it? Crucially, if nurses start being criticised for items not being stored in the correct place when those items have been moved by a specialist doctor, this is likely to demotivate the nurses, and could also create resentment between the nurses and the doctors.

18 Nelson, Jody & Nigel

Workbook reference. Performance management information systems, and lean principles, are discussed in Chapter 6 of the Workbook.

Top tips.

Part (a). There are two aspects of the information system you need to assess here: whether it is effective in reducing waste; and whether it adds value to NJN's workflow.

A sensible approach to this requirement is to work through the scenario and identify features in the current system which relate to waste or adding value. Do these features reduce waste? Or are they actually creating waste?

For example, (in paragraph 2) we are told 'Packing lists are manually input...' and in the third paragraph we are told that in 8% of packing lists, at least one item is not available in the location or the quantity specified by the WIS, and these discrepancies have to be investigated. Do features like these suggest the system is effective in reducing waste?

Similarly, in the second paragraph of the scenario we are told the retail stores 'do not currently have access to real-time inventory levels'. As such, is the system adding any value – compared, for example, to a system in which the retail stores could see the inventory levels, and therefore didn't try to order an item which was unavailable?

The scenario provides a number of hints towards points to include in your answer, so if you use these efficiently you should be able to score well on this part of the question.

Part (b). Before we can identify whether the three proposals will help to eliminate the different types of waste we first need to identify what these types of waste are. The sixth paragraph of the scenario suggests one: activities which do not add value to the customer; but waste can also result from over-production or holding excess inventory.

Having identified the causes of waste, we then need to ask will the proposals help to address then (or, are there problems with the proposals which will limit their effectiveness. One way to consider this might be to ask what changes NJN will have to make as a result of the proposals (and whether these will be beneficial)? For example, shutting down the additional means NJN will be able to hold less inventory (which is one of the types of waste).

Part (c). Since the question asks whether 'each of the 5Ss' is adequately measured by the performance metrics a sensible way to structure your answer would be to use each 'S' as a sub-heading, and then to ask:

- What does that 'S' involve?
- Do any of the measures (in Appendix 1) relate to those aspects of performance?

For example, 'Sanitise' involves being tidy and avoiding clutter, so assessing the tidiness of the warehouse would help to measure this.

Note the verb is 'evaluate' so – where possible – you should try to present a balanced argument: identifying areas where 'S's are adequately measured, as well as areas where they are not.

Examining team's comments

Part (a). This was generally well done, with candidates able to identify and discuss the problems from the scenario. The better candidates then tied these problems to the operation of the information system and often made good suggestions for improvements.

Part (b). Although candidates were asked to view the reduction of waste as an application or lean principles, few structured their answers using lean ideas about waste. Nonetheless, by keeping their answers focused on the specifics of the scenario and the proposals, candidates still scored well in this requirement.

Part (c). Candidates' performance on this part of the question was mixed, as many did not appear to know the meaning of the lean principles (5Ss) given. However, candidates did offer some useful evaluation of the indicators from first principles (about reducing waste or increasing efficiency).

Marking scheme

		Marks
(a)	Assessing whether the existing WIS is effective in reducing waste and adding value – 1 mark per relevant, valid point	
	Total for part (a): up to 10	10
(b)	Advising whether the three proposals will help to eliminate waste – 1 mark per relevant, valid point	
	Total for part (b): up to 6	6
(c)	Evaluating whether performance metrics adequately measure the 5Ss. 1 mark per relevant point, up to a maximum of 3 for each 'S'	
	Total for part (c): up to 9	9
		Total = 25

(a) Manual input

At NJN, at least some of the inputs to the WIS are manual, and that means they are prone to error. This is time consuming and costly.

The packing lists which are received in the shipping containers are input manually. If incorrectly input, the quantities of items in the locations in the WIS will also be incorrect. Incorrect information in the WIS wastes time by needing teams to investigate the discrepancies, reconcile inventory records with those held by the manufacturer, and correct the information held on the WIS.

Furthermore, customers will not receive the items they have ordered, as in 8% of picking notes, items are not in the location they should be, or are in insufficient quantities. This is a high proportion of errors. Staff will waste time looking for items stored in the wrong locations. This will cause customer dissatisfaction and mean that larger quantities of inventory will need to be held, which is a wasteful use of storage space. Fewer complete orders can be fulfilled per unit of warehouse space, than would otherwise be the case. Both of these are sources of waste.

In the longer term, this means NJN staff must undertake a series of cyclical inventory counts in order to correct the information held in the WIS. This is wasteful activity which does not add value to customers, and should be eliminated.

The provision of accurate inventory information will also be of value to the retailers who can place orders only for items which are available, rather than only finding out about unavailable items by receiving an email from NJN. This would lead to increased customer satisfaction by avoiding having stock outs of particular items by ordering alternatives.

NJN should consider the use of barcodes or radio frequency identifiers (RFIDs) on products, to ensure that accurate data is input into the WIS. Using these devices, the product numbers and quantities of goods entering and leaving the warehouse could be automatically read into the WIS, without any intervention from warehouse staff. This would reduce the time taken to manually input the data and improve its accuracy.

An effective information system may interface directly with the manufacturers' and retail customers' information systems through electronic data interchange (EDI). This would increase service levels by ensuring that all parts of the value chain had access to accurate and timely information.

Time delays

The packing list batches are not available until up to 48 hours after receipt of the goods. The information held in the WIS will therefore be out of date. Items which are required for sales orders may be unavailable for picking. The use of automated input, where possible, will increase the timeliness of the information input into the WIS. This will reduce the labour cost of correcting the system and improve the number, accuracy, and completeness of orders despatched to customers.

Currently, all picking notes are printed in the warehouse office, which may be some distance from the area where items are picked. This also implies the existence of a bottleneck in the provision of information to the staff picking the items and wastes staff time moving to and from the warehouse office to pick up the reports. An improvement would be to ensure that information is available when and where it is needed, using terminals in the warehouse, or portable devices such as tablets. This would reduce time spent collecting picking information.

Similarly, in order to investigate discrepancies, staff have to obtain special reports which the warehouse manager extracts from the WIS. Again, this is a bottleneck which could delay staff getting the correct information, and may mean that the reports are inconsistent depending on the parameters set to run them. An effective system would eliminate these problems by providing standardised reports when requested, and in an optimal location.

Complex presentation of information

Effective systems add value to information when they organise and present the information in a clear way, without excessive detail. This allows the users to easily and quickly identify the information they need. It prevents wasting time obtaining the information in the first place, and correcting errors caused by interpreting it incorrectly.

The picking sheets show the 12-digit product codes which can easily be misread, increasing the likelihood of errors. A better system would present the information in a more accessible way and prevent information overload; for example, showing product descriptions or product codes only for the items to be picked.

(b)   **Eliminating waste**

There are two main types of waste at NJN which can be identified using lean principles: waste which does not add value to the customer, and waste which occurs due to variations in demand and demands on staff.

Reorganising the warehouse to place high volume items near to the despatch area will help reduce the type of waste where the movement of staff to pick goods is more than should be required. Less movement, which means less staff time and cost, will be required by staff to pick these items and bring them to where they are to be despatched. It may be, however, that large and bulky items should be placed nearer to the despatch area instead, to save on the time spent transporting them to the despatch area. This may also address the increased seasonal demand for certain types of product, as products which are popular for that specific period could be stored more closely to the despatch area.

The cost of absenteeism is a waste caused by demanding too much of staff at busy times to compensate for inefficient organisation in the warehouse and errors in the WIS. The cost of searching for items which have been put in the wrong physical location at busy times is a waste due to variation in activity levels.

Another type of waste which does not add value to the customer is holding excessive inventory, for example, the additional warehouse space which NJN has rented. By not making efficient use of the warehouse space it has, NJN is reducing its level of output, and revenue, relative to the resources available to it. In addition, the extra warehouse space means more time spent by staff moving through the warehouses trying to locate goods.

The cyclical inventory counts which the Management Consultant has suggested do not add value to the customer and are also more demanding for staff. This is a wasteful activity, correcting the errors which have occurred in the WIS. NJN should instead concentrate on ensuring that errors do not occur in the first place, which will cost less than correcting them.

(c)   **Lean principles (5Ss)**

The 5Ss in the adoption of lean principles during the warehouse reorganisation are Structurise, Systemise, Sanitise, Standardise and Self-discipline.

Structurise

This involves introducing order where possible, for example, by ensuring that items in the warehouse are arranged so that they are easy to find. This would also include segregating damaged or obsolete inventory, or discarding it from the warehouse.

The management consultant has suggested the measure of the proportion of inventory not stored in order of its alphabetical description, with 'A' nearest the despatch area and 'Z' furthest away. This may measure how easy to find each product is, but would not necessarily make best use of all available space or make the picking process more efficient. It may also be subjective and prone to errors caused by the interpretation of the product description, for example, in deciding if cricket balls should be measured under 'C' or 'B'.

Systemise

This principle involves organising items so that they are easy to use. At NJN, this means being able to accurately pick the correct items in the shortest possible time. It could also cover access to other resources, such as having computer terminals close to where they are needed.

The measure relating to the storing of goods alphabetically seems to conflict with the Consultant's recommendation to place the high volume lines close to the despatch area. Whereas storing goods alphabetically may make items easy to find, it does not necessarily make them easy to use (pick). By storing the high volume items near to the despatch area, the average time taken to pick orders would be reduced.

Sanitise

This principle means to be tidy and avoid clutter. This helps make things easy to find, allows easy access of staff around the warehouse, and helps make a safe working environment. The warehouse manager's daily assessment of tidiness is a suitable measure of this principle, which is a subjective assessment.

There is the possibility that the assessment will be biased, especially if the warehouse manager who is undertaking the assessment is also having his performance evaluated on the tidiness of the warehouse. The characteristics of what constitutes a tidy warehouse, compared to an untidy one, will need to be defined. There is the possibility of inconsistent measurement if someone other the warehouse manager does the assessment, or the assessment is done at different times of the day.

Standardise

This principle involves finding the best way of undertaking a process or task, and applying it consistently. The suggestion of the number of accidents caused by goods which have not been stored or picked in the correct way would measure this. As NJN should aim to have no accidents, this should be a performance measure with a target level of zero.

Self-discipline

This principle relates to sustaining the other Ss by motivating employees. Motivation is subjective, and hard to measure. None of the performance measures the management consultant has suggested directly measure this principle. The consistency in which specific tasks or processes are performed could be a measure of how well they are being sustained.

19 Great National Trains

Workbook reference. Performance management in not for profit organisations is discussed in Chapter 9 of the Workbook. Integrated reporting, and the management accountant's role in providing information for integrated reports, are discussed in Chapter 6.

Top tips.

Part (a). Although the context of this question is the issues faced when setting and measuring objectives in a public sector organisation as opposed to a commercial organisation, the requirement is to discuss the difficulties faced specifically by GNT, rather than the difficulties faced by public sector organisations in general.

The difficulties GNT faces may be the same as those faced by public sector organisations in general (for example, multiple stakeholders, with conflicting objectives; the prevalence of qualitative objectives); to score well in this question you need to relate the difficulties specifically to the problem of setting and measuring objectives in GNT.

Also, note that you have to consider the difficulties in two different contexts: the difficulties of **setting** objectives; and then the difficulties of **measuring** performance against those objectives.

The reference to measuring performance against objectives could have highlighted the idea of 'SMART' objectives. For example, are GNT's (qualitative) objectives specific enough to measure; are they time-bound ... and consequently, how effectively can they be measured?

Part (b). In effect, this requirement is asking you about the elements which should be included in an integrated report. The scenario tells you that GNT's current report focuses largely on financial and operational performance for the last year only, meaning that there is little information about GNT's wider strategy or future outlook. However, these are key elements of an integrated report.

Part (c). The focus of this question isn't the integrated report as such, but the role of the management accountant in producing information for the report. What additional information (if any) would be required to produce an integrated report, and what potential difficulties could the management accountant face in providing that information?

Tutorial note. The suggested solutions provided here are designed to show the range of points you could have made in answer to this question, and are consequently much more comprehensive than an answer you would be expected to produce under exam conditions.

(a) **Setting objectives**

Range of stakeholders – As a public sector organisation, GNT has a wide range of stakeholders, including: government, passengers, freight companies, the rail regulator, and society as a whole (for example in relation to carbon emissions). The three subsidiary companies (Passenger, Freight, Track) could also be viewed as stakeholders of GNT.

However, the different stakeholder groups have different expectations of GNT, which in turn means that GNT has multiple objectives to achieve.

Prioritising objectives – Unlike commercial organisations, which have an underlying objective to be profitable and to deliver value for their shareholders, as a public sector organisation, GNT does not have a single defining objective of this kind.

The number of elements in GNT's current strategic objectives highlights the potential difficulties of identifying which elements of performance are most important: reliability, punctuality, safety, cost effectiveness, or environmental impact.

Conflicting interests – Moreover, the nature of these objectives means that GNT may inevitably not be able to achieve all of them, because some of them could be mutually exclusive. For example, GNT might be able to improve reliability and safety, and possibly also to reduce its environmental impact, by investing in new trains, but such a major investment would have significant cost implications, and therefore may not be viewed as being cost effective.

This again highlights the difficulty GNT faces in trying to satisfy the needs of different stakeholder groups. For example, the decision to reduce the number of passenger services on (less profitable) rural routes appears to be driven by a need for cost effectiveness, but reducing the level of services has a detrimental impact on local residents for whom the rail service provided a vital means of transport.

To complicate matters further for GNT, in some cases single stakeholder groups may have multiple interests in the railway. This increases the difficulty GNT has in prioritising its objectives. For example, while supermarkets are clearly concerned by the environmental impact of their supply chains, the reliability and punctuality of freight deliveries are likely to be equally, if not more, important to them. If GNT's key stakeholders have different interests in this way, then its own goals and objectives have to address these different aspects of performance.

Subsidiary company objectives – The interests of the different groups of external stakeholders also create difficulties for GNT in managing the performance of its subsidiary companies. Reliability and punctuality are clearly issues for both passenger and freight trains and so need to be reflected in the objectives and KPIs for both subsidiaries.

However, as passenger services generate more revenue than freight services (50% vs 40% of total revenue) this suggests that greater focus will be given to ensuring passenger services run on time than freight services. Equally, though, the suitability of a KPI measuring punctuality of freight services could be reduced if freight trains are delayed as a result of having to wait for passenger trains to use a section of track in preference to them.

Tutorial note. *Additional point about conflicting interests and objectives*

If GNT focuses primarily on its passenger services, and ensuring that these are on time, there is a danger that freight services get overlooked within its portfolio. However, given that demand for freight services has been increasing in recent years – due to congestion on the roads – freight services could be a source of growth for GNT. Therefore, it could face a dilemma around how to achieve growth in its freight services alongside maintaining punctuality levels for its passenger services.

Measuring objectives

SMART objectives – Effective objectives should be 'SMART' – specific, measurable, attainable, relevant and time-bound.

GNT's overall strategic objective does not exhibit a number of these characteristics. For example, instead of 'continuing to reduce' its level of carbon emissions, GNT's objective would be more specific and measurable if it sought to 'reduce carbon emissions by 5% each year'.

Selecting performance measures – For GNT's performance measurement system to be effective, the aspects of performance which are measured (the KPIs) should be linked directly to GNT's critical success factors and, in turn, to its overall strategic and financial objectives.

However, the difficulties we have identified in relation to setting objectives could also create difficulties in terms of performance measurement.

In particular, if GNT is struggling to decide what its performance priorities are, it may end up measuring performance in too many areas (rather than concentrating only on the **key** performance indicators). If GNT's managers and the board become overloaded with information, this could actually reduce their ability to assess GNT's performance and make strategic decisions effectively.

Objectives and controllability – It appears that there is only a single strategic objective for GNT as a whole, rather than there being strategic objectives for the three subsidiary companies as well. However, each of the individual companies has its own KPIs.

This situation could create problems in relation to controllability. For example, one of Freight's KPIs is the proportion of trains arriving at their destination on time. However, if there is a signal failure (Track's responsibility), Freight's punctuality performance will suffer, even though the cause of any delays is outside its control. Equally, as we have already mentioned, freight trains could be delayed by passenger trains, if they are given priority on the rail network.

Stakeholder influence – There could also be a danger that the aspects of its performance which GNT chooses to prioritise will be influenced disproportionately by interests of the stakeholders which hold the greatest power. For example, if GNT considers the government to be its most important stakeholder, it could focus on the objectives and performance measures which are most important to the government, potentially at the expense of the interests of other stakeholders such as customers, or its staff.

This kind of prioritisation of objectives could create problems for GNT, though. For example, a focus on cost effectiveness (to please the government) may lead to under-investment in new trains. But as GNT's trains (particularly its diesel engines) become increasingly old and unreliable, customers may feel their objectives are not being met. In turn this could lead to them seeking alternative modes of transport and GNT losing customers as a result.

This situation again reflects the problems associated with identifying GNT's key strategic objectives. GNT's performance measures need to be selected to help ensure it meets its key performance objectives. However, if GNT has a number of (potentially conflicting) performance objectives, then the process of selecting performance measures also becomes much more difficult.

Measurement vs management – Whilst GNT can measure factors such as punctuality or safety, these measures by themselves provide relatively little insight into the factors determining performance levels. For example, Freight's punctuality figures could be affected by a number of different factors. Similarly, assessing the safety of the rail network in GNT is likely to be far more complex than simply measuring the number of signals passed at danger.

Therefore, while individual aspects of performance can be measured, a range of factors all need to be considered before any actions are taken to improve individual aspects of performance.

(b) **Context of performance reporting** – In an integrated report, GNT will still report on its financial and operational performance, as it currently does, but the report should make clear to readers the extent to which GNT has achieved its strategic objectives. For example, as well as reporting its KPIs for punctuality, the report should highlight the extent to which GNT has achieved its objectives in relation to the reliability and punctuality of its services.

Importantly, in an integrated report, GNT will also report on social and environmental aspects of its performance. Currently, there appears to be little emphasis in GNT's performance management and reporting on the way it manages and develops its 'human capital' (staff). However, as human capital is one of the six categories of capital identified within the integrated reporting framework, this should encourage GNT to evaluate the contribution of its people to its performance.

Impacts on different categories of capital – More generally, performance reporting within an integrated report should explain the outcomes of an organisation's performance in terms of six categories of capital: financial; manufactured; intellectual; human; social and relationship; and natural. Using these six categories could provide GNT with a framework for analysing its performance; for example, 'manufactured' capital could relate to track work and station upgrades, while 'social and relationship' capital could relate to improving customer satisfaction or customer loyalty.

However, the 'integrated' nature of the reporting also means that in its report GNT should highlight the interrelatedness and dependencies between different factors which affect its ability to create value over time. For example, investing in new engines (manufactured capital) should help to improve performance reliability and reduce pollution (natural capital), but these benefits will come at the financial cost of acquiring the new engines.

Importantly though, one of the key aims of integrated reporting is to reflect the longer-term consequences of the decisions organisations make, in order that they make more sustainable decisions. So, in its integrated report, GNT would be able to highlight the longer-term benefits of investing in the new engines.

Future strategy and outlook – The current annual report appears to focus on GNT's financial and operational performance in the last year. In this respect, it is a backward-looking report. However, an integrated report would provide greater focus on future strategy and outlook.

In an integrated report, GNT would provide not only a summary of past performance but also a summary of how the organisation's strategy, governance and performance can lead to the creation of value in the future – in both the short and the long term; for example, how the investment in new trains or new tracks can help GNT provide an improved service to its customers.

Opportunities and risk – By focusing on its own financial and operational performance, there is a danger that GNT's current report may become inward-looking. However, in an integrated report it would also highlight the opportunities and risks which affect its ability to create value, and how it is dealing with them. Although GNT has a monopoly over rail services in Pecoland, it competes directly against road transport for both passenger and freight services. So, for example, GNT should use its integrated report to explain how it plans to use increasing road congestion as an opportunity to promote rail travel as a substitute for road travel.

Equally, however, GNT needs to consider the risks and threats to its business model. Even though the current Minister of Transport and the Rail Regulator oppose privatisation, this could change if a new government was elected in Pecoland. However, one way to increase GNT's resilience to any threat of privatisation is to demonstrate the value it currently creates, and thereby to highlight to any future governments that keeping the rail network under national control remains the best way to create value from it.

(c) **Amount of information** – The board's scepticism towards integrated reporting appears, at least in part, to come from its concerns about the extra cost and effort involved in producing an integrated report.

However, integrated reporting does not necessarily entail producing **more** information, and one of the potential benefits of integrated reporting is that it encourages organisations to produce shorter, more streamlined communications, rather than longer reports.

Instead of focusing on the quantity of information provided, the focus in integrated reporting is more about changing the way information is presented.

For example, instead of presenting information about GNT's commercial, social and environmental performance in distinct 'siloes', integrated reporting would seek to highlight the connections between these different elements. In this way integrated reporting aims to provide stakeholders with a more holistic understanding of an organisation and its performance.

Therefore, rather than requiring the management accountant to prepare lots more information, the change to integrated reporting may be more likely to require the management accountant (and members of GNT's senior management) to consider how different performance measures and indicators relate to each other.

Stakeholder interests – However, integrated reporting also seeks to respond to stakeholder interests by providing them with the information they want about the performance and direction of an organisation. As we have seen in part (a), there are a number of stakeholders with an interest in GNT and, if each of them want information about different aspects of performance, there is a danger that this could end up creating information overload in the report.

As part of its preparations for producing an integrated report, GNT could introduce a stakeholder engagement process with key stakeholders to identify what they want to know about the performance and direction of the organisation.

Additionally, the management accountant (in conjunction with the management team at GNT) will need to decide what data is most appropriate to collect, as well as what data it is possible to collect given the management information systems currently in operation at GNT.

Type of information

Reporting or focusing on strategy – An important theme in successfully applying integrated reporting is that it is not simply about reporting for its own sake, but that the information being reported needs to focus on an organisation's core strategy.

From the examples given in the scenario, it seems that the KPIs which GNT already monitors are linked to its key objectives. If this is the case, then again integrated reporting should not require the group management accountant to produce additional performance measures. However, rather than simply preparing the figures the management accountant would be expected to highlight the significance of the figures, and how they are affecting GNT's ability to create value.

Non-financial KPIs – Another important benefit of integrated reporting is that it helps organisations to make clearer links between financial and non-financial performance.

By focusing on value generation in its broadest sense (rather than, for example, narrower goals of revenue generation) integrated reporting will also encourage organisations to review the set of performance measures they use. One of the main consequences of integrated reporting is likely to be the increased use of non-financial data to gain a clearer picture of an organisation and its performance.

In this case, however, it seems that a number of GNT's KPIs are already non-financial, suggesting that GNT already appreciates the link between non-financial and financial performance. This again suggests that introducing integrated reporting may not require the introduction of many additional KPIs, although some may be required in relation to 'human capital' if this is not already covered by any of the existing KPIs.

Issues

Nonetheless, the increased importance on non-financial information could produce a number of issues for the group management accountant:

- Can GNT's current management information systems supply the full range of non-financial data which stakeholders would wish to see in an integrated report?

- If the data cannot be obtained from GNT's current systems, how can the management accountant obtain the information?

- More generally, can non-financial information be gathered and verified within financial reporting timelines?

- How can the accountant ensure the information is reliable and, more generally, what assurance is there over non-financial data in the report? (Non-financial data is typically not audited in the same way that financial data is; but if stakeholders are going to rely on this data, then GNT should consider obtaining some kind of 'assurance' over the data.)

Tutorial note. *Additional potential issues facing the management accountant*

Integrated reporting is not yet mandatory, and there are currently no standard formats for producing integrated reports. Therefore a significant practical issue the accountant will face when producing GNT's first integrated report will be to decide what information to include in the report and how to present it.

If the management accountant has to develop and produce the integrated report in addition to their existing work, this means the accountant will have less time available for that existing work. As a result, there is a danger management reports could be delayed, or the quality of them could be reduced – particularly in the short term, following the introduction of integrated reporting.

---

20 Amal

Workbook reference. Big Data is discussed in Chapter 6 of the Workbook.

Top tips.

Part (a). Note that there are effectively two parts to this requirement: (i) choosing and calculating appropriate performance indicators, and then (ii) commenting on the indicators you have calculated.

The context of the scenario could also be important here. Amal and Kayland Air both appear to be pursuing differentiation strategies, whereas Cheapo Air is a budget airline.

The requirement doesn't specify how many performance indicators you should analyse. The key point here is perhaps not the quantity of indicators you calculate, but making sure they are relevant.

We have chosen four in our answer below. However, this is not an exhaustive selection. If you have made other relevant calculations, and then commented on them, you would have got credit for this.

A sensible approach here is to select indicators which relate to Amal's key business issues (eg fuel costs), identify the key drivers behind them (eg fuel cost per seat kilometre) and then provide a short commentary showing how the indicator links to the companies' strategies and the issues mentioned in the scenario.

Part (b). There are four areas for you to explain here, and eight marks available, so two marks per area. This means you are not expected to write in depth about any of the areas. However, make sure you explain how the areas could be used to help Amal's performance, rather than explaining what the benefits of Big Data are.

In effect, the key areas from the conference already identify the benefits of Big Data, so you need to think practically here, and assess how Amal could use them.

Part (c). Although the question doesn't ask you to discuss the characteristics of Big Data – and so you can't pass the requirement just by doing this – thinking about the characteristics should nonetheless help you identify the potential implications Big Data could have for an organisation's information systems. For example, what implication could the 'volume' characteristic have for the capacity of an organisation's information systems?

Examining team's comments for part (a). The overall quality of the commentary which candidates provide in relation to numerical results they have calculated remains a concern. Simply putting the numbers which have been calculated into a sentence isn't an analysis of the figures. For example, saying 'Amal has a higher profit margin than either Kayland or Cheapo' doesn't add any value to a reader (who has already seen the calculations which show this). Consequently, such a statement will not score any marks.

However, good answers used the numerical work as an opportunity to show they have understood the scenario; for example, by commenting that Amal's higher profit was not surprising given that Amal is a 'premium airline'.

Marks

(a) Calculations – up to 6 marks
1 mark for each meaningful indicator selected
2 marks for load factor or similar measure of capacity utilisation
Commentary – 1 mark per relevant point, up to 7 marks
Total – up to 12 marks   12

(b) For explaining how Big Data could improve performance in each of the
four key areas identified – up to 2 marks per area
Total – up to 8 marks   8

(c) For identifying potential implications of Big Data on Amal's management
information systems – 1 mark per relevant point
Total – up to 5 marks   5

Total = 25

(a) The following performance indicators could be used to analyse the three airlines:

	Amal	Kayland	Cheapo
Operating profit margin	630/5,430	54/7,350	127/2,170
	11.6%	0.7%	5.9%
Capacity utilisation (load factor)	79,619/100,654	82,554/105,974	40,973/46,934
	79.1%	77.9%	87.3%
Revenue/staff member ($'000)	5,430m/32,501	7,350m/56,065	2,170m/5,372
	167	131	404
Fuel cost/seat kilometre ($)	1,480m/100,654m	1,823m/105,974m	535m/46,934m
	0.015	0.017	0.011

Operating margin – Amal has the highest operating margin of the three airlines (11.6%), which suggests it is being run efficiently overall.

We might expect Amal to achieve a relatively high margin because it appears to be pursuing a **differentiation strategy**. However, Kayland, which appears to be pursuing a similar strategy, generates an operating profit margin of less than 1%.

Capacity utilisation – By showing, on average, how full each airline's aircraft are this indicator shows how well the airlines are using their asset base (ie their aircraft).

Amal and Kayland's performance is similar in this respect, but Cheapo's is significantly better. This is likely to be because Cheapo (a low cost airline) is pursuing a **cost leadership** strategy. Amal might consider reducing its prices to try to improve capacity utilisation, but it needs to do so in the context of its overall strategy. If it reduces prices too much, it may end up compromising the quality and service it offers to passengers, but these elements are crucial to its strategy as a differentiator.

Revenue per staff member – This is an important measure in the context of the recent disputes over working conditions and pay. Amal's staff appear to be performing better than Kayland's, which in turn might strengthen their claims for a pay rise.

The comparison between Amal and Cheapo's performance for this measure may be less meaningful. Cheapo **outsources** many of its activities, meaning its staff numbers will be significantly lower than Amal which carries out the corresponding activities **in house**.

Fuel costs – The board's interest in new fuel-efficient aircraft indicates that reducing fuel costs is an important concern for Amal.

Again, Cheapo appears to be controlling its fuel costs better than Amal or Kayland. This might be because it has more **fuel-efficient planes**, which would support the board's argument for Amal investing in new aircraft. However, Cheapo may have negotiated more favourable fuel contracts with its suppliers, or be using lower grade fuel.

> **Tutorial note.** It is important to use fuel cost per **seat** kilometre as the performance indicator here rather than fuel cost per **passenger** kilometre, because we are looking to monitor the fuel efficiency of the aircraft, rather than the airline's ability to fill their aircraft with passengers.

(b) Amal's business strategy as a premium airline, coupled with the difficult trading conditions, mean that it is increasingly important for the company to provide its customers with the best services and experiences possible, so that they choose to fly with Amal in preference to another carrier. Increasing the data it holds about customers, and potential customers, should help Amal's management make better decisions, and thereby should help the company achieve this.

Detecting key trends – Analysing conversations on social media could help Amal identify potential trends in customer demand; for example, if there are major events taking place in a particular place, or if certain resorts are increasing (or decreasing) in popularity as holiday destinations. Being able to forecast demand more accurately – and almost in 'real time' – could help Amal boost revenue, through applying **dynamic pricing**. For example, Amal could keep prices high on flights which are going to be popular, but could reduce prices on flights which look like they are going to have a lower capacity utilisation in order to try to boost demand for those flights.

Customer selection process – One of the key issues here is for airlines to understand the reason why potential customers have not completed their transaction – for example, this could be due to price, seat availability, difficulties in the booking process itself. In this respect, if Amal was able to capture data about the stage in the booking process which causes potential customers to abandon their booking, it could then look at ways to tackle the problem – for example, if there was a confusing user interface on the Amal website this could be amended to make booking easier. Equally, applying the 'velocity' aspect of Big Data, if a customer abandons a transaction, and Amal already has their contact details, the customer could immediately be sent an incentive to try to encourage them to complete the purchase.

In-flight sales – Amal currently offers a standard selection of in-flight products across all its flights. However, the amount of products Amal sells (and therefore the amount of in-flight revenue ancillary revenue Amal generates) is likely to depend on how well the products offered meet customer needs. By analysing the purchasing patterns of different passengers (or different types of passengers) on different routes, Amal could customise the range of products it offers on different flights, to focus on the products which are most likely to appeal to the passengers on a particular flight.

Customer satisfaction – In the same way that conversations on social media could help to identify trends in demand, they could also help to indicate how satisfied customers are (or aren't) with their flights and the service they receive from Amal. However, although knowing whether customers are satisfied or not is useful, perhaps the greater value will come from identifying any factors which are reducing satisfaction levels so that Amal can then address the causes of any problems and take steps to improve its performance in those areas.

(c)   Big Data is typically characterised by a range of 'V' characteristics – volume, variety, velocity and veracity.

Capacity – The potential benefits to Amal of Big Data will come from the useful information it can extract from large amounts of data. However, the 'volume' and the 'variety' of the data could also require increased information systems capacity in order to capture and store the data correctly. If the data is not stored correctly, this will undermine its veracity – its integrity and reliability as a basis for making decisions.

The fact that a number of IT staff are already working on the website upgrade project could be a problem here, if it means that there aren't sufficient staff available to increase the information system capacity to the degree required for Big Data.

Analytical tools – As well as having the capacity to store Big Data, Amal will need the right analytical tools and technologies to be able to analyse it, because it is too large and unstructured to be analysed through traditional means. Again, the lack of available IT staff could present problems here.

Data overload – A more general concern to beware of is the difference between data and information. Management decisions need to be based on relevant information, not raw data. Therefore, by itself, increasing the volume of data available to Amal would not necessarily provide managers with better information for decision making. Here again, Amal would need analysts with the experience and expertise to be able to extract meaning from the captured data, but it seems unlikely that Amal has any such staff currently available.

Similarly, if the volume and variety of the data means that Amal's current information systems are not able to process it, the 'velocity' aspect of Big Data will be undermined. If IT teams or business analysts become burdened with increasing requests for ad hoc analysis and one-off reports (because the systems cannot process the data automatically), the information and analysis from Big Data will not be available for decision makers as quickly as they might want.

21 Chicory

Workbook reference. Financial performance measures, including ROCE and EBITDA, are discussed in Chapter 7 of the Workbook. Benchmarking is covered in Chapter 1.

Top tips.

Part (a). The marking guide for part (a) of this question is very instructive here:

For part (a) (i), up to 3 marks (out of the total of 6) are available for evaluating how useful ROCE is as a performance measure in this situation.

For part (a) (ii), up to 6 marks (out of the total of 10) are available for evaluating how useful EBITDA is as a performance measure.

As such, more marks are available in part (a) as a whole for the evaluation of the **measures**, than for evaluating the **performance** of the two organisations. The examining team have said many times that, at Strategic Professional level, candidates will not simply be asked to perform calculations, and this question provides a good illustration of that point. Although it is important you calculate the ROCE and EBITDA for both companies correctly, you then need to comment on the figures you have calculated ('Evaluate the relative financial performance...') before moving on to think about the advantages and disadvantages of the measures themselves.

Another point that the examining team make regularly is that theoretical knowledge alone is not sufficient to pass the APM exam. This is also pertinent here, because, to score well in this question, you mustn't just evaluate the usefulness of ROCE and EBITDA in general terms, but specifically in the context of the scenario. For example, in the first paragraph you are told: 'Chicory's objective is to maximise shareholder wealth' – but will using ROCE as a performance measure encourage that?

Part (b). The same point about making use of the scenario also applies to part (b). To score well here, you mustn't simply talk about the problems of benchmarking in general terms, but instead you should focus specifically on the problems of benchmarking Chicory's performance against Fennel's, using the data which Fennel has agreed to share.

The scenario should provide you with a number of clues you could use here. For example, Fennel is based in Veeland (whose economy is growing rapidly), while Chicory operates in Deeland (which is experiencing an economic slowdown) so how might this affect the comparability of the two companies' performance?

Also, don't concentrate purely on the written scenario, and forget about Appendix 1. For example – look at the dates for the data being proposed for the potential comparison. Fennel's data (31 December 20X5) is 18 months older than Chicory's (30 June 20X7). What implications does that have on its usefulness in the benchmarking exercise?

Examining team's comments.

Part (a). Many candidates scored poorly on the calculations, with few being able to calculate these correctly for both ration. This is disappointing, because ROCE and EBITDA are ratios which a professional accountant should be fully able to calculate. The evaluation of the methods was generally performed well though.

Part (b). Candidates generally scored well here and demonstrated good knowledge. However, as we have said before, it will be unusual for a question at APM level to ask for purely generic theory. Instead, questions will require theories or models to be applied to a particular situation. Unfortunately, some candidates lost the opportunity to score more marks here by not relating their knowledge to the companies described in the scenario. Also, some candidates wasted time discussing how benchmarking can be used to evaluate performance, or explaining the benchmarking process itself, despite the requirement asking specifically about the **problems** of the benchmarking exercise proposed in the scenario.

Marking scheme

			Marks
(a)	(i)	Calculation of Chicory's and Fennel's average capital employed – up to 2 marks	
		Calculation of both companies' ROCE – 1 mark	
		Comment on the results of the ROCE calculation – 1 mark	
		Evaluation of ROCE as a performance measure – up to 3 marks	
		Total for (a) (i) – up to 6 marks	6
	(ii)	Adjustments to operating profit to get EBITDA – up to 2 marks	
		Calculation of both companies' EBITDA – 1 mark	
		Comment on the results of the EBITDA calculation – 1 mark	
		Evaluation of EBITDA as a performance measure – up to 6 marks	
		Total – up to 10 marks	10
(b)		Advising on relevant problems of the benchmarking exercise – up to 2 marks per point	
		Total – up to 9 marks	9
		Total =	25

(a) (i) **ROCE**

As can be seen in the Working, Chicory's ROCE is 13.6% and Fennel's ROCE is 14.9%. Fennel has apparently performed better than Chicory. One benefit of using ROCE as a performance measure in this benchmarking exercise is that it gives a percentage figure and can compare businesses of different sizes. ROCE does not, however, give the absolute level of return. In this case, Fennel has both a higher capital employed and a higher percentage return.

BPP
LEARNING
MEDIA

ROCE is easy to calculate and will be familiar to Chicory's management as it is currently one of Chicory's main financial performance indicators. The figures required to calculate ROCE are readily available from published data, which makes this a good financial performance measure for benchmarking.

ROCE shows a weak correlation with Chicory's objective to maximise shareholder wealth, which may limit ROCE's usefulness as a performance measure in this benchmarking exercise. ROCE may be distorted by accounting policies or where different businesses have different levels of intangible assets. This may lead to drawing incorrect conclusions from the exercise. A big disadvantage of using ROCE in this benchmarking exercise is that it may encourage managers not to invest in new non-current assets, which contradicts Chicory's strategy of investing in charging points.

Working: ROCE calculations

Chicory:

Opening capital employed (Total assets – current liabilities)	$78.0m	(138.0 – 60.0)
Closing capital employed	$59.0m	(140.0 – 81.0)
Average capital employed	$68.5m	((78.0 + 59.0)/2)
ROCE (Operating profit / average capital employed)	13.6%	(9.3/68.5)

Fennel:

Average capital employed: (170 × 0.25) + (176 × 0.75)	$174.5	
ROCE	14.9%	(26.0/174.5)

(ii) **EBITDA**

Using Chicory's main financial performance indicators of ROCE, Fennel has performed better than Chicory. When depreciation of non-current assets and the write-off of goodwill in Chicory are added back to operating profit to calculate EBITDA, Chicory's performance, with an EBITDA of $52.0m, is slightly better than that of Fennel, which has an EBITDA of $51.0m.

EBITDA as a proxy for cash flow

EBITDA is easy to calculate from published data, and easy to understand. It is a measure of underlying performance, as it is a proxy for cash flow generated from operating profit. As Chicory is having cash flow difficulties following the unsuccessful acquisition, EBITDA would be a relevant measure for this benchmarking exercise. EBITDA does not, however, take into account the cash flow effect of working capital changes, for example, by Chicory negotiating longer payment terms with its suppliers.

Excludes items which are not relevant to underlying performance of the business

Tax and interest are distributions from profits, unrelated to the underlying performance of the business. Excluding them from measures of performance, therefore, gives a better understanding of the underlying performance of Chicory and Fennel. This is important for the benchmarking exercise since Fennel appears to suffer much lower rates of tax, probably due to the tax incentives given by the Veeland government. Loans underwritten by the Veeland government may be at artificially reduced rates of interest and should also be excluded when measuring performance.

Similarly, depreciation, amortisation and write-offs such as goodwill are not relevant to the current year's underlying performance and may relate to previous years. For example, adding back the write-off of goodwill in Chicory means the two businesses have identical EBITDAs, albeit that Fennel has much greater capital employed.

EBITDA affects comparability of the benchmarking data

Using EBITDA as a performance measure in the benchmarking exercise makes the data for the two businesses more comparable and removes one element of subjectivity, such as in determining useful economic lives of non-current assets. EBITDA does, however, ignore the replacement costs of these assets. This might limit the usefulness of comparisons between Chicory and Fennel if one were to lease non-current assets and the other to purchase them. The introduction of a new accounting standard on the treatment of leases may, however, remove this limitation.

Unlike Chicory's existing measure of ROCE, which is a percentage measure, EBITDA is an absolute measure and so makes it difficult to compare businesses of different sizes. As a profit based measure, its usefulness is also limited by subjective assumptions made in the calculation of profit, or by inconsistent accounting policies. Development costs may be capitalised in Veeland, but not in Deeland, which may make a comparison against the benchmark difficult.

Working: EDITDA calculations

	Chicory $m	Fennel $m
EBITDA		
Operating profit	9.3	26.0
Add back:		
Depreciation on non-current assets	18.0	25.0
Write off of goodwill	24.7	–
EBITDA	52.0	51.0

(b) **Benchmarking**

Benchmarking the performance of Chicory against a similar business implies that there is a best way to operate. Though Fennel may be similar to Chicory, there is no indication that it is best in class and benchmarking against it may be inappropriate.

For example, Fennel has taken advantages of tax incentives and loan guarantees to finance new investments. These do not exist in Deeland, so Chicory may be unable to fund investment in this way. It may have to consider leasing assets instead, or accept a slower rate of growth if it wishes to set up charging points in Deeland.

Benchmarking is essentially a catching up exercise. The financial data for Fennel is 18 months older than that for Chicory and may already be out of date. In 20X5, Fennel improved operational performance by investment in IT. The effect of this is not reflected in the financial data given. Benchmarking performance against historical data may not be relevant for current or future performance. The electric car market in Veeland has grown rapidly in the last two years. This growth is not reflected in the financial performance data given for Fennel, nor is the falling price of components for the charging points.

Although Fennel has agreed to share data, this data may be inaccurate or misleading. Though initially the benchmarking exercise is only against Fennel, it may be difficult to find other comparable businesses to benchmark against in the future. The data required for calculation of the three financial performance indicators used in the benchmarking exercise is likely to be readily available and audited, however, which means it is reliable.

A large part of Fennel's business relates to providing charging points for charging electric cars. Though this is a business model Chicory intends to follow in the future, it is very different to its existing business, and so benchmarking against Fennel may be misleading unless more detailed data relating to the two activities can be obtained.

Similarly, Fennel operates in a different country, where the economy is much stronger. Performance targets set following the benchmarking exercise may be unachievable for Chicory. Fennel's financial data has been converted into $ from its home currency. Movements in exchange rates may make the benchmarking data less comparable, especially if the economies in Deeland and Veeland are growing at different rates.

22 Landual Lamps

Workbook reference. Transfer pricing is covered in Chapter 8 of the Workbook.

Top tips.

Part (a). As the requirement asks you to 'evaluate' the current system of transfer pricing, it might be useful to start by considering what the aims of transfer pricing are. Then, having identified the aims, you can then evaluate how well Landual's current transfer pricing system fits with those aims.

Does the current system promote goal congruence between the individual divisions and the company as a whole?

Does the current system enable the performance of the individual divisions to be measured fairly?

The distinction between the markets available for the two types of component is important: there is a readily available external market for electrical components, while there is no external market for housing components. Therefore a market-based transfer price could be appropriate for the electrical components and a cost-based transfer price could be appropriate for the housing components.

But is it fair to include transport, marketing and bad debt cost in the transfer price for electrical components?

And is it fair that the price of housing components should be at cost only, with no mark-up? On the other hand, should the transfer price for housing components be based on actual production costs or budgeted production costs?

An important part of your 'evaluation' should be what impact these possible changes to the current transfer pricing systems could have on divisional performance. You should demonstrate this through the 'illustrative calculations' the requirement asks for.

Part (b). The change being proposed is to include variable production costs only (rather than total production costs) in the transfer price for housing components. The illustrative calculations here should be relatively simple, but a key issue is what impact the changes have on the profitability of the two divisions. Does the revised position accurately reflect the value added to Landual as a company by the different divisions?

Part (c). The requirement here asks you to evaluate the impact of the changes on the profit in the divisions as well as on the company as a whole. So you need to look at the impact of the changes on four different elements: the new Housing Components Division; the new Electrical Components Division, the Assembly Division, and Landual overall.

Again, you need to calculate the divisional profits under the new structure, and then consider what benefits (or drawbacks) the changes might yield for the divisions, and for Landual overall.

The biggest change will see the Housing Components Division change from a profit centre to a cost centre. Although the 'profit' in the Housing Division will fall significantly because it no longer has any revenue, what might be the benefits of making this change? Remember, the housing components are only sold internally anyway.

Examining team's comments. This question was generally poorly answered with weak (often no) efforts at handling the quantification issues – recalculating the current transfer price; and calculating the impact of the two proposed changes on the various entities in the scenario. As a result, this meant candidates often had very little to say in evaluating or giving advice in the narrative parts of their answers.

For example, in part (b) if the (simple) quantification work was not done, candidates could not see that the proposed change will lead to lower profits in the division which provides the key competitive advantage of the company.

As a general point, during their revision candidates would be advised to consider the impacts that strategic changes – such as designation of cost, profit and investment centres – would have on the performance management of divisions or departments within a company.

Marks

(a) *Electrical components*

Evaluation of the basic policy to use market-based transfer price – Up to 2 marks

For comments on adjusting market price to exclude additional costs (of transport, marketing and bad debts) – 1 mark

For calculating the impact on divisional profits of adjusting market price – 1 mark

Housing components

Evaluation of the basic policy to use cost-based transfer price – Up to 2 marks

For comments about including a mark-up on cost in the transfer price – Up to 2 marks

For comments about the merit of using actual or budgeted costs as the basis of the transfer price – Up to 2 marks

For calculating the impact on divisional profits of including a mark-up, and of using budgeted costs – Up to 2 marks

Total: Up to 10

10

(b) For calculating the new revenue figure for the Components Division – 1 mark

For calculating the revised profit figures for each entity – 1 mark each

For comments on the impact of the changes – 1 mark per valid point; Up to 4 marks

Total: up to 6

6

(c) For calculating new profit figures for each entity (Housing, Electrical, Assembly, Landual) – 1 mark per entity – Up to 4 marks

For evaluating the impact of the changes on the profit in the divisions and for Landual overall – 1 mark per valid point – Up to 7 marks

Total: up to 9

9

Total = 25

(a) **Aim of transfer pricing** – The aim of transfer pricing is to ensure goal congruence between the divisions of an organisation and the organisation as a whole, by ensuring that the performance of the divisions is measured fairly and is not distorted by any internal transfers.

A good transfer pricing system will also maintain a level of managerial autonomy for the managers of the different divisions in an organisation.

Electrical components

Market-based transfer price – As there is already an external market for electrical components, it seems appropriate to use a market-based transfer price for electrical components. The Assembly Division can choose either to buy components from an external supplier or to source them internally from the Components Division, depending on the respective prices charged by the two sources.

Under the current system, the Components Division generates a contribution of $383,000 to head office costs from the sale of electrical components: $1,557,000 – $804,000 – $370,000. Given the generic nature of the components, we would not expect the contribution to profit to be very high, so this figure seems reasonable.

Adjustments to market price – However, the Assembly Division could legitimately argue that the transfer price charged by the Electrical Components Division should be lower than the open market price, because transferring the components internally doesn't incur transport or marketing costs in the way that an external sale would. Also, there is no risk of bad debt. Therefore, the $269,000 in respect of these costs should be deducted in order to get an adjusted market price.

If these adjustments are made, then the contribution to head office costs from electrical components within the Components Division falls to $114k ($383,000 – $269,000).

Housing components

Actual production costs – The transfer prices for housing components are based on actual production costs. Again, this seems appropriate because these components are designed specifically for Landual's products, so there is no external market for them.

However, because the price set for the housing components only covers the actual **production** costs, the proceeds from the sales of the housing components will not make any contribution towards the allocated head office costs.

As a result, since the housing components account for 84% of the division's total sales by revenue ($8,204/$9,761) it will be very difficult for the Components Division ever to earn a significant profit.

Since the housing components make a significant contribution to Landual's competitive advantage, it would seem fair if they are rewarded with greater divisional profit than they currently get. Therefore, rather than selling the components at cost, Landual could consider a transfer price which includes a mark-up on actual production costs. This would also redistribute the divisional profit between the Assembly and Components Divisions.

If a mark-up of 25% (for example) were applied to the total actual production costs of the housing components ($8,204,000) this would generate additional profit of $2,051,000 for the Components Division. If this mark-up were applied, the Components Division would then show a profit of $1,973,000, while the Assembly Division would only show a profit of $668,000.

Actual vs budget costs – Because the Components Division uses actual production costs rather than budgeted costs as the basis for its transfer price, there is no incentive for the Components Division to control or reduce its costs, because it knows it will recover any additional costs through the price charged to the Assembly Division. By contrast, if budgeted productions were used as the basis for the transfer price, the cost of any adverse variance would continue to be borne by the Components Division.

The current system, based on actual production costs, may be part of the reason behind the $575,000 adverse cost of sales variance in the Components Division for the last year.

Revised divisional reports

The divisional reports could be adjusted to reflect these points:

- Costs relating to transport, marketing and bad debts are no longer included in the transfer price of electrical components: $1,557,000 – $269,000 = $1,288,000

- Transfer price for housing is now based on budgeted cost, with a mark-up for 25%: ($6,902,000 – $575,000) + $1,302,000 = 7,629,000 + 25% mark-up = $9,536,000

		Components	Assembly
Sales	Electrical	1,288	
	Housing	9,536	
	Sub-total	10,824	15,794
Cost of sales	Electrical	804	1,288
	Housing	6,902	9,536
	Sub-total	7,706	10,824
Fixed production costs			
	Electrical	370	
	Housing	1,302	
	Sub-total	1,672	1,268
Allocated head office costs		461	2,046
Profit		985	1,656

(b) **Variable costs basis**

The proposal will reduce the revenue of the Components Division (and correspondingly the cost of sales of the Assembly Division) by the fixed production costs relating to housing components: $1,302,000. There will be no change to the company's overall profit as a result of the change.

This change further tilts the balance in the relative profitability of the two divisions towards the Assembly Division.

Given that the housing components are specifically designed for Landual's products, and therefore could be a source of significant competitive advantage, the proposed change doesn't seem particularly appropriate. The Components Division adds significant value to Landual's overall product, but the change seems to be emphasising the importance of the Assembly Division to the company.

If the results are balanced too heavily in favour of the Assembly Division, this will understate the importance of the work done by the Components Division, and could demotivate its staff. This would be a mistake given the intricate nature of the work.

Despite these concerns, the decision to use variable costs as a basis for transfer pricing (rather than total costs) is not necessarily a bad one. The clarity gained by using only variable costs may help Landual to set the optimal prices and profits for its products.

Tutorial note. The following solution shows the full data for the two divisions under the revised basis. However, you did not need to show these figures in full to earn the marks available here (for the new revenue figure for the Components Division, and for the revised profits figures for both divisions).

		Components	Assembly
Sales	Electrical	1,557	
	Housing	6,902	
	Sub-total	8,459	15,794
Cost of sales	Electrical	804	1,557
	Housing	6,902	6,902
	Sub-total	7,706	8,459
Fixed production costs			
	(No changes)	1,672	1,268
Allocated head office costs		461	2,046
Profit/(loss)		**(1,380)**	**4,021**

(c) **Housing Division**

Cost centre – Under the proposed changes, the Housing Division will be a cost centre only.

Given that the Housing Division only sells its (bespoke) products to the Assembly Division, and therefore the difficulty of determining a fair revenue figure for its work, it seems more appropriate to treat the Housing Division as a cost centre rather than a profit centre. Treating the division as a cost centre is better aligned with the ideas of responsibility accounting.

Moreover, because the focus of the division will now be on cost control, this should help avoid adverse cost of sales variances like the one incurred in the last year. The performance measures and reward packages in the division will also need to be redesigned to reinforce the focus on costs.

In addition, the change in status could enable a greater focus on the quality of the division's output, which will be important given the key role which the housing components play in Landual's overall manufacturing process.

In this respect, it is important that the change from being a profit centre to becoming a cost centre is not seen as downgrading the status of the division. If it is, such a perception will demotivate the divisional managers, and any fall in morale is also likely to filter through the staff.

Electrical Division

Under the proposed new divisional structure, the Electrical Division will make a profit of $335k (see Working at the end of the answer).

As the electrical components are generic and could easily be obtained externally, it is appropriate to continue treating the Electrical Division as a profit centre. Under this basis, Landual has the information it needs to decide whether to 'make or buy' the electrical components for its lamps.

The current figures, showing that the Electrical Division is making a contribution to head office costs, suggest that the Electrical Division should continue to supply components to the Assembly Division.

Assembly Division

The changes do not directly affect the Assembly Division. However, being able to see the Electrical Division's results more clearly will allow the managers of the Assembly Division to ensure that the Electrical Division remains competitive (compared to any external suppliers which could provide the components instead).

Landual

The changes have no direct effect on the company's reported profit. However, if the changes help to improve cost control (in the Housing Division) and reinforce the need for competitiveness (in the Electrical Division), they should help to improve the company's profits in the future.

Working: Revised profits for each of the divisions, and for the company as a whole

Allocated head office costs for the Components Division have been reallocated between the Housing and Electrical Components Divisions in proportion to their cost of sales.

	Housing $'000	Electrical $'000	Assembly $'000	Landual $'000
Sales			15,794	15,794
Electrical		1,557		
Housing				
Cost of sales				
Electrical		804	1,557	804
Housing	6,902		8,204	6,902
Fixed production costs			1,268	1,268
Electrical		370		370
Housing	1,302			1,302
Allocated head office costs (apportioned in line with cost of sales)	413	48	2,046	2,507
Profit/(Loss)	(8,617)	335	2,719	2,641

23 Laudan Advertising Agency

Workbook reference. Objectives, critical success factors (CSFs) and key performance indicators (KPIs) – and the relationship between them – are discussed in Chapter 2 of the Workbook. Transfer pricing is discussed in Chapter 8.

Top tips.

Part (a)

(i) The scenario identifies that LAA has published four objectives on its website:

- To delight our clients by the quality of our work
- Provide excellent value for money to our clients
- Give our clients access to specialist and local knowledge
- Ensure our clients return to us time after time

As the requirement asks how identifying the CSF will help LAA to manage performance 'in order to achieve its stated objectives' it is important to consider how the CSF could relate to each of the objectives in turn. The question verb is 'evaluate' – so if the CSF is more relevant to some objectives than others, highlighting this would be a relevant part of your evaluation.

Similarly, for **part (ii)**, you need to evaluate how the KPI helps (or doesn't help) to achieve each of the four objectives. The comments in Appendix 1 of the scenario relate to the KPI in question, so these comments should have provided you with some useful clues to help answer this part of the requirement.

Importantly, note that the question is asking about the extent to which the CSF and the KPI might help LAA achieve its objectives. It is not asking whether the CSF or the KPI are appropriate measures, so you shouldn't waste time evaluating the measures themselves.

Part (b). A sensible approach to a requirement like this – to assess the need for a transfer pricing policy – is to start by thinking what the main aims of the transfer pricing policy would be: for example, to enable performance evaluation of divisions; to maintain divisional autonomy; and to promote goal congruence.

Then think how well – or not – these aims are achieved under LAA's current arrangements (in the absence of a transfer pricing policy). The scenario provides a lot of information about how the current practices for transferring goods between the different divisions are causing problems, in terms of performance management, autonomy and goal congruence. These are the same areas which the transfer pricing policy would address. So, what does this suggest about the need for a transfer pricing policy at LAA?

Although ACCA's suggested solution (below) isn't specifically structured around the aims of a transfer pricing system, the examining team have stated that such an approach would have been acceptable for this question.

Part (c). In order to advise whether an organisation should use a particular approach to something, you need to consider what the potential advantages or disadvantages of that approach are. And, to score well in this requirement, that is what you need to do here.

The scenario tells us that LAA's current transfer pricing arrangements appear 'to be based on full cost' plus a substantial mark-up. So, in effect, you need to consider what the potential benefits, or problems, with using a market value transfer price would be, compared to the current 'cost plus' approach.

Marking scheme

		Marks
(a)	Discussion of the CSF in relation to achieving the stated objectives – up to 6 marks	
	Discussion of the KPI in relation to achieving the stated objectives – up to 6 marks	
	Total for part (a): up to 8	8
(b)	For each relevant point about the need for a formal transfer policy – 1 mark each	
	Total for part (b): up to 9	9
(c)	Benefits of a market value approach – up to 6 marks	
	Problems with a market value approach – up to 6 marks	
	Total for part (c): up to 8	8
	Total =	25

(a) (i) **CSF of high quality design**

Delight clients with quality of work – The directors of LAA have identified the importance of producing high quality creative designs as a CSF to ensure successful advertising campaigns, and therefore client satisfaction. It is likely that having this as a CSF will help LAA achieve its objective to 'delight clients with the quality of work', as creative design is an important part of the service which LAA provides.

Value for money – It is not clear, however, whether this CSF will help achieve the second of LAA's objectives to provide excellent value for money. It may be that other agencies produce a similar quality of work, but charge a lower price. Alternatively, the quality of LAA's design work may exceed that required by the client, who will be unlikely, therefore, to perceive it as good value for money.

Specialist and local knowledge – Identifying this CSF will not directly help achieve the stated objective of providing clients with access to local and specialist knowledge. External suppliers may have more specialist knowledge than LAA can realistically replicate in its own design department.

Client retention – The relationship between the quality of the creative design and the clients' perception of its value for money will determine whether the fourth objective, to have returning clients, will be achieved or not. All other things being equal, high quality design work will probably make clients more likely to return. Other aspects of LAA's service, though, such as designing effective advertising campaigns and negotiating competitive rates for media buying, may be at least as important to the client.

(ii)   **KPI to buy 90% internally**

Setting a KPI should lead managers to try to achieve this target, as they are appraised (and presumably rewarded) according to their performance against the target.

Delight clients with quality of work – Having this target will only help achieve the objective of delighting clients if the quality of the design done internally exceeds that done by third-party external designers. Though LAA has set up the 'centre for design excellence', this does not automatically mean the quality of work is any better than external agencies.

Value for money – Encouraging managers to buy creative services internally does not necessarily help achieve the objective of giving value for money for clients. Managers at both B and C have indicated that the prices charged by the in-house design department are significantly higher than other agencies in the market. The use of the internal design department may not be best value for the client.

Specialist and local knowledge – Encouraging the use of internal services may not help achieve LAA's third objective to offer specialist and local knowledge to clients. The design department is based entirely in Geeland and may not meet the needs of clients in other countries. The manager of B has already commented that the department did not understand the requirements of consumers in Veeland. This is also inconsistent with the objectives to delight clients and to have them return to LAA.

Client retention – Similarly, managers in A have also commented that the internal department did not have specialist knowledge to meet the needs of a new client. Again, encouraging managers to use the internal department seems contrary to the objectives of providing clients with specialist knowledge in order to delight them and to have them as return customers.

(b)   **Transfer pricing policy**

Autonomy of the subsidiaries

The purposes of a transfer pricing policy are to encourage subsidiaries' autonomy, facilitate performance evaluation and promote overall goal congruence with the aim of LAA to maximise shareholder wealth.

As the three subsidiaries are profit centres, they will tend to make decisions which maximise their own profit. This may be at the expense of the other subsidiaries. By charging a higher transfer price to B and C for design services, A will increase its own revenue and also the costs for B and C. This may also be at the expense of LAA as a whole, for example, as C's client was unhappy with the high charges levied by A.

A transfer pricing policy helps to prevent subsidiaries from acting in an entirely self-interested way where this may not be in the best interests of LAA as a whole. Though a transfer pricing policy should promote autonomy of the subsidiaries, LAA's head office should have the power to impose a transfer price to maintain goal congruence across the organisation. This is not currently happening, and the high transfer prices charged for design services are causing dissatisfaction.

Both B and C have commented that they have spent large amounts of time trying to negotiate transfer prices with A. This is a waste of managers' time. The ability of head office to impose a transfer price, or the existence of a clear transfer pricing policy, would allow managers more time to deal with other key aspects of the business, such as ensuring client satisfaction.

Performance measurement in the three subsidiaries

A transfer pricing policy will enable the performance of the individual subsidiaries to be fairly measured. If the policy is unfair, for example, the gross margin at subsidiary C was reduced by the seemingly excessive transfer prices charged by A, managers' motivation will be reduced, especially if this reduces the subsidiaries' managers' rewards.

Setting clear, transparent and understandable transfer prices

Managers at B have complained that the basis for setting the transfer price from A is unclear. A transfer pricing policy should ensure that the basis for setting the prices is transparent, straightforward and well understood by managers so that they do not see prices as being set unfairly and thus become demotivated.

The basis for the prices set between subsidiaries in different countries should also be clear about how exchange rate movements are reflected in the transfer price, so that managers' performance is not appraised on factors which are outside their control.

Also, the transfer pricing policy for transfers between different countries should ensure that the prices are likely to be acceptable to the local tax authorities. The tax authorities in Veeland, where B is located, are already investigating the transfer prices charged by A. This is presumably because the authorities suspect that the transfer price may be set at an artificially high level in order to reduce tax paid on profits earned in Veeland. Having a clear transfer pricing policy may help to demonstrate that B is operating within relevant taxation laws and is acting ethically in setting a fair transfer price. As the internal design department has no external customers, then it may be preferable to operate it as a separate cost centre and make all transfers at marginal cost.

(c) **Market value transfer prices**

Advantages of setting transfer prices on the basis of market value

Transfer prices on the basis of market value reflect the prices of purchasing creative design services on the open market. Both buying and selling subsidiaries will know what the market price is and be able to compare this to the price they are paying or charging internally.

Where subsidiaries have autonomy to negotiate their own transfer prices, in order to maximise the performance of the individual subsidiaries, the transfer price agreed is likely to reflect market price. The buyer will be unwilling to pay more than the price it can pay on the open market. The seller will be unwilling to charge less to sell internally than can be obtained on the open market. This encourages efficiency in A, which has to compete with external suppliers of creative design services.

Where a market value transfer price is used, it will usually be beneficial for buyer and seller, as well as for LAA as a whole, to transfer internally. This is because selling and administration costs overall for both parties are reduced, and the buyer should get better customer service and reliability of supply by buying internally.

The transfer price charged by A currently includes an allowance for marketing costs and bad debts. These are unlikely to be incurred where internal transfers are made. The cost savings may be shared by both parties and the transfer price reduced to a level below the market value. This lower transfer price is known as the adjusted market price.

If the transfer price charged by A is calculated on a different basis from market value, which appears to be the case as A's prices are higher than the market rates, the subsidiaries will waste time arguing over the transfer price. This current approach may improve the subsidiaries' own performance, but this is not in the best interests of LAA overall.

Disadvantages of using market price

The use of external market price will only be the optimal transfer price when a perfectly competitive external market exists. For example, though creative services can be purchased on the open market, those services may not be identical with those provided internally. Subsidiary A had to use a third-party design agency for its new client as it did not have the industry knowledge to do the work itself. In this case, there may not be an equivalent service available internally to those available externally, and vice versa. There may therefore be no realistic option to buy on the open market in this situation and the use of an external market price as a transfer price would be inappropriate.

The market price may be temporary, changing according to capacity of the service providers or changes in economic circumstances or, in the case of LAA, short-term variations in the exchange rate. In this case, the transfer price would need to be frequently changed if it were to continue to reflect market conditions. This would be time consuming and probably confusing to the subsidiaries' managers.

Where allowance is made in the transfer price for the reduced costs, for example, of marketing and bad debts, it may be difficult to agree an adjusted market price which is acceptable to both A and the subsidiary purchasing design services from A.

24 Jenson, Lewis & Webb

Workbook reference. The concepts of controllability and accountability are discussed in Chapter 8 of the Workbook. EVA™ is also discussed in Chapter 8.

Top tips.

Part (a). The context for this question is the issue of controllability, and the fact a manager's performance is not necessarily the same as a division's performance. This is the point which the export division manager appears to be making when she suggests it is not appropriate to use the division's net profit margin to appraise here performance.

To score well in this question it is important that you relate your answer specifically to the scenario and the context, rather than talking about controllability and accountability in general terms. For example, Appendix 1 shows that the division's net profit is shown after deducting apportioned head office costs – but is it appropriate to include them in an assessment of the divisional manager's performance?

Part (b). The importance of looking, in part (a), at specific issues from the scenario is reinforced in part (b).

In effect, part (b) involves recalculating controllable profit – but the evaluation in part (a) should have helped to identify the items which need to be excluded from the original net profit figure in order to generate the controllable profit.

As so often in Advanced Performance Management questions, it is important to pick out all the clues from the scenario. For example:

- In the first paragraph, you are told the Export Division is a profit centre (whereas the Domestic Division is an investment centre). In terms of controllable profit, what is the significance of the Export Division being a profit centre rather than an investment centre?

- Similarly, in the second paragraph you are told that the $KL weakened by 15% against the £SL half way through the year. What is the significance of this?

Note, that although the majority of the marks in part (b) are for 'appropriate calculations', you also need to make a recommendation (based on your calculations) as to whether or not the manager should receive her bonus.

Part (c). A useful way of approaching this requirement could have been to consider the advantages and disadvantages of using EVA™ as a measure of performance compared to net profit margin, and weighing up the relative advantages and disadvantages to advise whether or not EVA™ is appropriate.

For example, JLW's objective is 'to maximise shareholder wealth'; so is EVA™ more appropriate than net profit margin for measuring how well an organisation is generating wealth for its shareholders?

Importantly, as always in Advanced Performance Management, make sure you consider the appropriateness of EVA™ specifically in the context of the scenario, rather than giving a generic discussion of its potential advantages and disadvantages. For example, since the EVA™ calculation is influenced by WACC, is it appropriate for a profit centre (like the Export Division)? Or, since Appendix 1 suggests that the Domestic Division is significantly larger than the Export Division, how useful will EVA™ be in comparing the relative performance of the divisions (since it generates an absolute value, rather than a percentage)?

Examining team's comments.

Part (a). To score well in this part of the question, it was important to pick up on the issues mentioned in the scenario and examine their impact on the question. Those candidates who did this, scored well in this part.

Part (b), which required a calculation of the relevant profit to judge the manager's performance in order to assess their suitability for a bonus payment, was generally done well.

Part (c), which required an evaluation of the suitability of economic value added as a divisional performance measured was answered surprisingly poorly. This was often due to candidates believing that the question required a lengthy description of the method of calculation of the indicator, rather than focusing on its suitability for use in the scenario.

Marking scheme

		Marks
(a)	Evaluation of manager's comments – 1 mark per relevant point Traceable net profit calculation – 2 marks Total for part (a): up to 7	7
(b)	Depreciation and allocated head office costs – 2 marks Currency gain – 2 marks Controllable revenue – 2 marks Controllable profit margin – 1 mark Conclusion/recommendation – 1 mark Total for part (b): up to 8	8
(c)	Evaluation of EVA™ – 1 mark per relevant point Total for part (c): up to 10	10
	Total =	25

(a) **Assessing managerial vs divisional performance**

A key characteristic of divisional performance measurement is that divisional managers, and the divisions themselves, should only be appraised on performance that they control. For example, costs which are not controlled by divisional managers, such as JLW's apportioned head office costs, should be added back to profit when appraising manager's performance.

Similarly, as Export Division is a profit centre, divisional managers are not able to make capital investment decisions and so depreciation is out of their control and should be added back to profit for their appraisals. Domestic Division is an investment centre, so managers there can make investment decisions, and depreciation is a cost which they can control.

On 30 June 20X6, the $KL weakened by 15% against the £SL. This meant Export Division benefited from an increase in revenue which was not under the control of the divisional manager. This amount must be deducted from revenue when calculating the controllable net profit for Export Division.

The net profit arrived at after items which are not under managers' control are added back is known as the 'controllable profit'. This is what divisional managers should be appraised on. This is because it is unfair to appraise them on factors outside their control, and may mean they become demotivated or give up trying to improve performance, which is not in the interests of JLW as a whole.

Divisional performance should be evaluated on all the items which relate directly to the division which is its 'traceable profit'. Allocated head office costs do not directly reflect the activity of the division and should be excluded when calculating the traceable profit.

The traceable net profit for Export Division, after adjusting for allocated head office costs, was $KL905,000 (Working), and the traceable net profit margin was 11%.

A difficulty with calculating controllable and traceable profits in this way may be that it is difficult to determine which items are controllable or not. For example, though the new machine purchased for Export Division by head office did lead to improvements in productivity, the extent of this increase must be attributed to good management, or otherwise, by the divisional managers. This increase in productivity is therefore due partly to controllable factors, and partly to uncontrollable.

Working: Traceable net profit

	$KL'000
Reported net profit	545
Add back: Allocated head office costs	360
Traceable net profit	905
Traceable net profit margin (905/8,000)	11.3%

(b) **Export division manager's bonus**

The controllable net profit is arrived at after items which are not under the manager's control are added back. The net profit margin controllable by the manager of Export Division is 10%. Given that it is difficult to assess the effect of the increased productivity on controllable net profit, the manager should be awarded her bonus for the year. This is because the controllable net profit margin of 10% exceeds the target of 8%.

Workings

1 *Controllable net profit margin for Export Division; year ended 31 December 20X6*

Controllable net profit	$KL'000
Reported net profit	545
Non-controllable items	
Add back:	
Depreciation	395
Allocated head office costs	360
Deduct:	
Currency gain	(522)
Controllable net profit	778

Controllable revenue	
Reported revenue	8,000
Deduct currency gain	(522)
Controllable revenue	7,478

Controllable net profit margin (778/7,478)	10.4%

2 *Currency gain*

Six months revenue from 1 July 20X6 was increased by 15% due to currency gain.
Six months revenue before currency gain 4,000/1.15 = 3,478
Therefore non-controllable currency gain is 4,000 – 3,478 = 522

As the exact increase in productivity resulting for the new machinery on Export Division is unclear, it is difficult to accurately adjust the controllable net profit margin to reflect this. It would seem the divisional manager is benefitting from productivity improvements which are not entirely under her control. To reduce the controllable net profit margin to 8%, the threshold at which the manager is awarded her bonus, the net profit would have to fall by approximately $KL179,760 (778,000 − (7,478,000 × 8%)). This is equivalent to 3.7% of cost of sales (179,760k/4,800,000). It is difficult to conclude, therefore, whether the 'significant' improvement in productivity would make the difference between the manager of Export Division receiving her bonus or not.

(c) **EVA™ as a performance measure for Export and Domestic Divisions**

EVA™ makes adjustments to the financial profit to calculate the economic value generated by each division, and then makes a deduction for the cost of the capital invested in the division. A positive EVA™ indicates a division is creating value above that required by those who finance the business. It is therefore consistent with JLW's objective to maximise shareholder wealth. Appraisal of divisional performance on this basis would therefore align the interests of managers with those of JLW's shareholders.

EVA™ involves making many adjustments to operating profit and capital employed. These may be time consuming, and be poorly understood by managers. The manager of Export Division has already commented that she finds the bonus calculations difficult to understand. Failure of managers to understand the EVA™ calculations would make it difficult for them to work towards targets set for the division.

EVA™ avoids distortion from estimates and financial policies

EVA™ avoids the financial results from being distorted by accounting policies and estimates made by divisional managers, for example, the $KL75,000 bad debt provision made in Domestic Division, as increases in provisions are added back to operating profit in the EVA™ calculation. Whilst this provides a consistent basis to evaluate performance of divisions within JLW, EVA™ is not suitable for comparing divisional performance as it is an absolute measure and does not make allowance for their relative sizes.

EVA™ encourages managers to take a long-term view

The advertising costs for the new range of paints would be capitalised as these generate future value. The use of EVA™ would encourage managers to incur costs, such as these, which will benefit the business in the long term.

However, the calculation of EVA™ is backwards looking, and based on historical financial information, whereas shareholders need information about future performance on which to base their decisions.

EVA™ takes into account the cost of capital

The current performance measure of net profit margin is a poor measure as it takes into account neither the absolute net profit achieved, the capital employed in the division, nor the cost of capital. By making a deduction for the cost of capital employed in the division, the EVA™ calculation makes managers consider both the capital employed and the cost of capital in their divisions.

Export division is a profit centre and managers do not have control of investment decisions. Therefore, it is not a suitable measure for the evaluation of the performance on Export Division because there is no controllable capital employed. Domestic Division is able to control investment decisions, and does have controllable capital employed, so EVA™ would be a suitable measure for evaluating Domestic Division's performance.

However, to use the weighted average cost of capital (WACC) in the EVA™ calculation requires a number of assumptions and estimates to be made, for example, in calculating the cost of equity or market value of debt. The WACC is normally based on historic data, which may not reflect circumstances in the future, and may not be accurate.

25 Stillwater Services

Workbook reference. EVA™ is discussed in Chapter 8 of the Workbook. Stakeholder management and the potential impact of stakeholders on performance are discussed in Chapter 4.

Top tips.

Part (a). Up to ten of the marks available in part (a) are for calculations. There should be some relatively easy marks here (for example, for identifying the adjustments to operating profit), even if you don't get all of the figures correct.

A few months before the exam which included this question, a technical article was published on ACCA's website – 'Economic value added versus profit-based measures of performance'. This article explained the adjustments to operation profit which are required in EVA™, as well as the logic behind them. Candidates who had read (and understood) this article should have been well placed to tackle this question. This highlights the importance of reading relevant technical articles on ACCA's website as part of your preparation for your exams.

One particular point to note in relation to the EVA™ calculation itself: Remember that your calculations for the capital employed figure need to be based on the published accounts figure at the start of 20X2, not at the end of it.

However, also note that the question requirement isn't simply to calculate EVA™; you should also have used the EVA™ figure you have calculated to evaluate SS's performance. In other words, how well is it creating value for its shareholders?

Part (b). The reference in the requirement to 'analysing the potential influence' of different stakeholder groups should have suggested that Mendelow's ideas of power and interest could be relevant here. However, perhaps more importantly, the reference to 'managing different stakeholder groups' should have also alerted you to the potential conflict of interests between different groups. In particular, how are the regulator's interests likely to differ from shareholders' interests, and how do these differences affect SS's directors?

Part (c). As in part (a), this part of the question combines calculations with a discussion related to the figures you have calculated. Crucially, though, you must make sure your ROCE calculations relate solely to the regulated parts of SS's business.

Also it is vitally important that you recognised that the ROCE target of 6% is the **upper** limit that SS can achieve on its regulated business, not a minimum target it is trying to achieve.

This is very important because the presence of this target means that SS has very little scope to increase its profits from regulated business. So, in terms of performance management for SS as a whole, what implications does this have for the role of unregulated business in increasing the company's profits?

Examining team's comments. The calculation of EVA™ was discussed in a technical article on ACCA's website, and had clearly been well prepared for by many candidates who scored most of the calculation marks available in part (a). The calculations of net operating profit after tax (NOPAT) could be done by starting from PAT, or from Operating Profit, and both approaches gained credit. The weakest area of the calculations was the adjustments to capital employed.

Most candidates realised the need to comment on the figures they had calculated and gave a summary sentence. However, many candidates did not offer any broader comment on the key assumptions in the EVA™ method, or the limitations of the method. This could be seen as a failure to appreciate the need to 'evaluate' performance using EVA™, rather than simply to 'calculate' performance.

Part (c) was generally poorly answered, with many candidates not appearing to realise that the ROCE target was an upper limit on the company. Few candidates spotted that the constraints on the regulated side of the business would mean that the unregulated side would be the engine of growth for SS, while the regulated side could act as a cash cow.

Marks

(a) Adjustments to operating profit:

Non-cash items	0.5
Accounting depreciation	1
Doubtful debts	1
Research and development	1
Interest	0.5
Tax (cash amount paid; tax on interest)	Up to 2

Capital employed figure:

Capital employed (per accounts) at start of year	0.5
Provision for doubtful debts	1
Other non-cash items	1
WACC	1
EVA™	1

Note. Maximum 10 marks available for calculations   10
Comments about SS's performance, consistent with EVA™
calculation – 1 mark per relevant point   Up to 3

13

(b) Analysis of different interest and power of each stakeholder
group – up to 2 marks each   Up to 6
Identifying potential conflicts between interests of regulator
and shareholders   1

5

(c) *Calculations:*

ROCE (on regulated business only)	1
Maximum regulated operating profit allowed	1
Operating margins (regulated vs non-regulated business)	1
Other relevant calculations	1

Commentary:

On calculations – 1 mark per relevant point	Up to 2
On performance management of regulated areas of SS – 1 mark per relevant point	Up to 2
On performance management of unregulated areas of SS – 1 mark per relevant point	Up to 2

7

Total = 25

(a)

	$m	$m	Comments
Operating profit		68.00	
Add back: Depreciation	59.00		
Doubtful debts	2.00		
Research and development	12.00		
Other non-cash items	7.00		
		80.00	
Less: Economic depreciation		−83.00	
Tax		−9.00	Cash amount only
Tax adjustment on finance charges		−5.75	$23m × 25%
NOPAT		**50.25**	

		$m	Notes
			Based on figure b/f at
Capital employed		637.00	start of 20X2
Add back: Provision for doubtful debts	2.50		(see Working)
Other non-cash items	6.00		Non-cash items in 20X1
		8.50	
		645.50	

		$m	Notes
WACC:			
Equity: 40% × 16%		6.4%	
Debt: 60% × 5% × (1 − 25%)		2.3%	
		8.7%	

EVA™:
NOPAT − (Capital employed × WACC)
50.25 − (645.5 × 0.087)   **−5.91**

No adjustment for depreciation required at the start of 20X2.

Working	$m
Provision for doubtful debts at end of 20X2	4.5
Movement in year	−2.0
	2.5
Provision at start of year	

Negative EVA™ – SS's negative EVA™ figure for 20X2 suggests that, instead of creating wealth for its shareholders, it is actually destroying value. More specifically, the value which SS is generating (NOPAT) is not sufficient to cover the economic cost of the capital it has employed to generate that value.

Such a position is not sustainable in the long run, and will lead to dissatisfaction amongst SS's shareholders. SS could look to address this issue either by increasing its net operating profit or by reducing its cost of capital; or through a combination of both.

NOPAT – SS's current NOPAT of $50.25m leaves it with a negative EVA™ of $5.91m. At the current cost of capital, SS would need to increase its NOPAT to $56.16m to break even on EVA™.

Cost of capital – Alternatively, SS would break even on EVA™, with its current level of NOPAT, if its WACC was 7.8% ($645.5m × 7.8% = $50.3m). In this respect, SS's current cost of equity (16%) appears high, particularly given the highly regulated nature of the industry. Moreover, given that 80% of SS's sales (for water and sewage services) are for services which are necessities for everyday life, there is relatively little risk that demand will fall. Again, this suggests that SS's cost of equity should be lower than it currently is.

Asset base – SS could also look to reduce its asset base by selling under-utilised assets. If it could reduce the amount of capital employed without any significant reduction in its NOPAT, this could help its EVA™ break even or become positive.

(b)   **Regulator**

Interest – The regulator is likely to have a high interest in SS. Although the regulator will only be interested in SS's regulated services, these still constitute 80% of its total revenue. The regulator's interest is in controlling the prices SS charges, and the returns it generates.

Power – The regulator also has a high level of power to influence SS's performance. Not only does the regulator set the level of pre-tax ROCE which SS is allowed to generate, but it also has the power to impose significant fines if SS exceeds this figure.

Shareholders

Interest – Although the shareholders will be interested in the wealth which SS creates for them, they will be less interested in the day to day business of the company and the operational decisions taken within it. (They have delegated authority for these to SS's management.) Therefore, shareholders' interest in performance management at SS is likely to be lower than that of both the regulator and SS's management.

However, shareholders' interests are likely to differ from those of the regulator. Whereas the regulator is interested in controlling profits, the shareholders are likely to want SS to maximise the profits and earnings it generates.

Power – It is not clear how SS's shares are distributed, but this could determine the level of power the shareholders have. If SS's shares are owned primarily by institutional investors they are likely to have more power than if the shares are held by a large number of private investors. For example, institutional investors will have more voting power than individuals, and so could look to replace SS's management if they felt the company was underperforming.

It seems that SS's shareholders have at least a moderate level of power since the board is trying to drive performance for the shareholders' benefit.

Management

Interest – SS's management have a high level of interest in the company's performance, because if the company is unsuccessful their jobs will come under threat. However, SS's management also have to ensure that the conflicting interests of the regulator and the company's shareholders are managed successfully.

Power – The management team also have a relatively high level of power because they dictate the strategies which the company will pursue. However, the presence of a strong regulator means that the management team's power is less than it would be in an unregulated market because, for example, performance levels in SS's regulated services have to comply with the parameters imposed by the regulator.

(c)   Target ROCE: 6%

Operating profit from regulated business: $46.0m

Average capital employed: (779.0m + 761.0m)/2 = $770.0m

ROCE: 5.97%

Alternative calculation:

The examining team's answer uses capital employed at the end of 20X2, rather than average capital employed during the year.

Under this basis ROCE is: 46.0m/779.0m = 5.90%.

Return within prescribed limit – The return which SS generates from its regulated business (5.97%) is within the limit set by the regulator (6.0%).

However, because SS's current return is so close to the limit there is very little scope for it to increase the profitability of the regulated aspect of the business. The maximum operating profit that SS could generate in its regulated business is $46.2m ($770m × 6%).

Non-regulated activities – The constraints on the regulated business increase the importance of the non-regulated activities as a potential source of profit growth for the business.

Additionally, the operating profit margins which SS earns from non-regulated business are significantly higher than those from regulated business.

Regulated services: $46m/$276m = 16.7%

Non-regulated services: $22m/$69m = 31.9%

Consequently, SS should be looking to expand its non-regulated business, as a source of profitable growth.

In effect, SS's regulated business could be seen as a 'cash cow'. SS should look to invest cash generated by its regulated business to help support the expansion of its non-regulated business (either through organic growth or through acquisition).

Cost control – The regulator's primary concern appears to be that SS doesn't increase its prices unjustifiably. If SS has little scope to increase prices, then in order to maintain its profits it needs to ensure that its costs do not increase significantly either.

Therefore, controlling costs will be a key element of performance management within the regulated part of the business. On the one hand this highlights the importance of variance analysis (comparing actual costs to budget), but on the other hand it also suggests the importance of identifying potential cost savings (for example, through efficiency improvements).

Lack of investment – The target level of 6% is lower than SS's WACC (of 8.47%; see part (a)). If SS uses WACC as a discount rate for decision making, then it would be reluctant to invest in the regulated part of the business at all.

The infrastructure in the regulated side of the business is likely to suffer as a result. This could have an adverse effect on other aspects of SS's performance. For example, if SS has increasing problems with burst water mains due to lack of investment in its infrastructure, this could lead to an increase in repair costs, and also a decline in customer service if customers' water supplies are disrupted.

Growth – By contrast, the focus of performance measures for the non-regulated services should be on revenue and profit growth. For example, SS should look to set targets for revenue growth or market share growth. However, it is equally important for SS to set targets for profit margins, to ensure that it doesn't sacrifice profitability in search of revenue growth.

26 Essland Police Forces

Workbook reference. The use of league tables in relation to measuring public sector performance is discussed in Chapter 9 of the Workbook.

Top tips.

Part (a). It is vital that you read the requirement very carefully before starting to answer this requirement.

In particular, note the following:

- You are asked to evaluate the **method** of calculating and measuring the force scores, not to evaluate the performance of the different forces based on their force scores.

- You need to evaluate how useful the league tables are in improving the performance of the police forces in the context of achieving the Department of the Interior's aims and goals.

The scenario reiterates this first point, with the reference to the CEO's comment: 'I'm not interested in the performance ... I'm interested in the method of assessment.'

Nonetheless, the statistics provided in Appendix 1 are very important to the question; for example, for indicating other measures which could potentially be included eg number of police force employees per head of population.

In relation to this second point (about the usefulness of the tables) a key question is: how well do the variables included in the tables relate to the Department's overall aim (achieving value for money) rather than being linked to the Department's goals?

Part (b). Although the majority of requirements in APM require you to apply your knowledge specifically to a scenario, the first part of this requirement asks you to discuss the merits of league tables in general terms.

However, the second part of the requirement then links directly back to the scenario. The CEO has raised concerns about how staff will respond to the introduction of the league tables, and has also raised concerns about how appropriate it will be to transfer league tables from the schools sector into the police forces. Are these concerns valid? For example, will the league tables lead to police forces focusing only on the measures of performance included in the league tables at the expense of other aspects of performance?

In terms of structuring your answer, it could be useful to use the main points of the CEO's concerns as headings for your answer and then address them in turn.

Marking scheme

Marks

(a)   Evaluating the appropriateness of variables used in the context of achieving the overall aim of the Department of the Interior – 1 mark per relevant point – up to a maximum of 3 marks

       Evaluating the appropriateness of variables used in the context of achieving the detailed goals of the Department of the Interior – 1 mark per relevant point – up to a maximum of 5 marks

       For relevant comments on other indicators which could be included in the tables – up to a maximum of 2 marks

       Evaluating the allocation of the weightings across the different forces – 1 mark per relevant point – up to a maximum of 4 marks

       Up to 2 marks for other relevant points

       Total for part (a): up to 14   14

(b)   General evaluation of league tables – 1 mark per relevant point – up to a maximum of 4 marks

       Comments on employees' attitude to the introduction of the system – up to a maximum of 2 marks

       Impact of the league tables on employee behaviour and their sense of accountability – 1 mark per relevant point – up to a maximum of 5 marks

       Appropriateness of using league tables from schools in relation to the police forces – 1 mark per relevant point – up to a maximum of 2 marks

       Total for part (b): up to 11   <u>11</u>

                                                                   Total = <u>25</u>

(a)   **Choice of variables selected**

       The variables used to measure the force score should be aligned to the aims and goals of the police forces. At the highest level, the two main aims of the police forces are: to provide a **value for money** service, and to ensure the **security** of the community.

Detailed goals – However, the detailed goals of the Department focus primarily on crime, justice and community support without providing any more detail about the economy, efficiency or effectiveness (value for money) of the policing service.

Choice of 'ranks' – In turn, the four 'ranks' used to calculate the force score appear to be derived from the detailed goals, rather than the overall aims.

Goal	'Rank' indicator used
Tackling the underlying causes of crime	Rank 1 – number of reported crimes
Bringing perpetrators to justice	Rank 2 – proportion of reported crimes solved
Providing protection and support for individuals and communities	Rank 3 – user satisfaction score (for service offered by police forces)
Responsiveness, accessibility and community engagement	Rank 4 – responsiveness (to calls) Rank 3 – user satisfaction will also reflect responsiveness, accessibility and engagement more generally

The indicators selected don't measure all aspects of the goals exactly, but they provide a reasonable coverage of them. For example, one way to reduce the number of reported crimes would be to tackle the underlying causes of crime so that fewer crimes are committed.

Nonetheless, the 'ranks' could still be improved. For example, the number of public meetings between the police and the local community could be used to measure the level of community engagement.

Value for money

More importantly, however, because the goals focus on tackling crime and promoting community safety, the ranks also focus on these aspects of performance rather than the degree of value for money achieved by the police services. For example, whereas the current Rank 2 is based on the solution rate for crimes, it might also be useful to measure the number of crimes solved per police force employee in order to assess the efficiency of the police service.

The data which the police forces already keep (Appendix 1 in the scenario) would be suitable for calculating some value for money performance measures. For example, using the data already available, the following additional 'rank' scores could be calculated:

	C	D	E	F
Number of police per 10,000 population	49.6	48.9	50.0	52.7
Cost of police force per head of population ($)	323.2	331.1	336.5	340.0
Number of crimes solved per police force employee	5.0	5.2	5.4	4.2

Weightings used

Another potential issue with the current system is that it assigns the same weighting to each of the four ranks. This approach has the benefit of simplicity, but it also presumes that each aspect of performance is equally important to the performance of the force. In practice, this may not be the case, but no explanation is given to justify the weightings used.

Importantly, however, the weightings used could affect the overall ranking of the forces in the league table. Currently, Force F is top ranked, while Force C is bottom ranked. However, if, for example, user satisfaction was given greater weighting than the other factors, this would be likely to mean that Force E became top ranked.

Equally, as we noted earlier, if value for money measures were included, the rankings would also change – particularly because Force F performs worst in relation to this area.

Therefore, the Department faces a trade-off between preserving the simplicity of the calculations and including additional factors and prescribing different weightings to different factors.

Additional point:

Impact of using ranks – The difference between the best and worst performing forces in relation to call handling is only 3 percentage points (94% vs 91%), whereas the equivalent difference for user satisfaction is 12 percentage points (80% vs 68%). However, both of these performance spreads generate a difference of 0.75 in the forces' scores. In this way, the ranking system currently being applied doesn't take into account the degree of variation in performance between the different forces for any of the measures.

(b)   **Merits of league tables in performance management**

Benchmarks – By providing a single performance summary, league tables can provide a useful way of benchmarking performance between not for profit organisations. Moreover, because they are not directly competing with each other, not for profit organisations should be more willing to exchange data than commercial organisations, thereby making it easier to carry out a benchmarking exercise.

Benchmarking performance in this way could help identify areas of best practice among the police forces, and could help to motivate poorer performers to improve their performance levels to bring them closer to the best performers.

Limited comparisons – In effect, benchmarking and league tables are both relative measures of performance – comparing the performance of an organisation against other similar organisations. However, there could still be other organisations (not included in the benchmarking exercise) which are performing better.

In this case, although Force F performs best at call handling (with 94% of calls answered within 10 seconds) this figure may still be relatively low compared to the performance of the other emergency services (fire, ambulance) in Essland or compared to police forces in other countries.

To overcome this issue, the league tables could try to include figures for comparable organisations (in particular, foreign police forces). However, it could be difficult to find the comparable data necessary to calculate a force score for a foreign police force (as opposed to benchmarking individual elements of performance).

Factors affecting performance – One of the main issues with league tables is that while they can highlight variations in performance, they do not take account of any factors leading to those variations in performance. For example, the number of reported crimes per 10,000 of population could reflect the social and economic conditions of a region.

Controllability and motivation – Perhaps even more importantly, the police forces do not have the power to affect the external environment, such as economic conditions. Therefore, if the police forces feel their performance is being judged on factors they cannot control, introducing the league tables could serve to demotivate, rather than motivate, the forces.

As the CEO has pointed out, the police forces have strong union representation. Therefore if the forces resist or resent the introduction of the league tables, with the backing of their unions, the forces could potentially discredit the league tables, and possibly even the way the Department of the Interior manages the forces.

Measure fixation – Another potential issue with league tables is that they could lead to the police forces concentrating on those aspects of performance which are included in the tables at the expense of others. The notion that 'what gets measured, gets done' would seem to be appropriate here.

In particular, the league tables do not currently include any measures linked to the value for money provided by the forces. Therefore, the league tables could lead the police forces to overlook this aspect of the Department's aims, because they are focusing solely on the aspects of safety and security being measured in the league tables. So, for example, the police forces could recruit additional staff to answer phone calls (and improve their call handling score) but it is debatable how much value for money this would provide overall.

Use of league tables from the schools sector – Although the introduction of school league tables may have been successfully applied in Essland's schools, there are some significant differences between schools and police forces which may make the use of league tables less appropriate for the police forces.

Users of the league tables – In particular, parents in Essland have a choice about which school their children attend, so they can use information about the relative performance of different schools to help them make that choice. However, residents cannot choose which police force is responsible for their safety and security – unless they relocate to a different area of the country. Therefore, whereas the school league tables can help users (parents) in their decision making, the police force league tables do not have an equivalent benefit for the residents of their regions.

Number of measures included – Additionally, the school league tables are entirely based on a single measure of performance (exam results) whereas the force score tries to include a wider range of factors. However, as we have already noted, this then raises questions about which factors should be included in the tables, and whether all the factors being considered are equally important.

27 Beeshire Local Authority

Workbook reference. The issues surrounding performance measurement in public sector organisations are discussed in Chapter 9 of the Workbook. The importance of non-financial performance indicators, and the difficulties around measuring qualitative aspects of performance are discussed in Chapter 10.

Top tips.

Part (a). A useful starting point for understanding the importance of non-financial indicators in public sector organisations will be to think about the goals and objectives of those organisations, and how they differ from commercial organisations.

The first paragraph of the scenario provides some very useful pointers here. We are told the goal for BLA's Waste Management Department is 'to maintain Beeshire as a safe, clean and environmentally friendly place', and also that the department does not charge residents or businesses for most of its services.

If it doesn't charge for its services it can't possibly make a profit, which therefore rules out any profit-based performance measures. Nonetheless, the scenario tells us, BLA has so far 'focused on financial measures of performance' rather than, for example, quality of service. Does such an approach seem consistent with the department's goals, or might looking at non-financial performance indicators be more constructive?

Part (b). There are several different elements in the requirement, so it is important that you cover all of them to score the marks available in this part of the question.

In effect, the requirement can be broken down into three parts: (i) explain how value for money provision should be assessed; (ii) by suggesting (and justifying) suitable performance indicators; and then (iii) calculating performance in relation to those indicators.

Value for money is typically measured in terms of the three Es: economy, efficiency and effectiveness. So a useful approach to this requirement would be to explain the Es first, and look at each one in turn to suggest suitable performance indicators for it. The requirement to 'calculate justified performance indicators using the information in the scenario' should have been a reminder that the indicators you suggest need to be specifically relevant to the scenario, rather than being generic measures of economy, efficiency or effectiveness.

Part (c). In the same way that a useful approach to part (a) was to think how public sector organisations differ from commercial ones, a useful starting point for this requirement would be to think how qualitative factors of performance differ from quantitative ones. What are the key characteristics of qualitative data?

The key characteristic of qualitative data is that it is subjective (based on people's opinions). Once you identify this point, the difficulties of measuring it should become easier to identify.

However, note you aren't only asked to discuss the difficulties of measuring qualitative performance; you also need to suggest appropriate solutions to help BLA overcome the difficulties associated with measuring qualitative performance.

Marks

(a)   General discussion of the usefulness of non-financial indicators in public sector organisations – up to 4 marks

For identifying examples relevant to BLA – up to 4 marks:

Total for part (a): up to 6   6

(b)   General description of VFM (economy, efficiency, effectiveness) – up to 3 marks

For discussing each heading (economy, efficiency, effectiveness) in relation to BLA – 1 mark per relevant point – up to 12 marks

Total for part (b): up to 12   12

(c)   For identifying difficulties of measuring qualitative factors of performance – 1 mark per valid difficulty identified

For suggesting appropriate solutions for BLA – 1 mark per relevant point

Total for part (c): up to 7   <u>7</u>

Total = <u><u>25</u></u>

(a)   Unlike commercial organisations which have an underlying objective to maximise the profits they generate for their shareholders, it is often much harder to define the objectives of public sector organisations.

Multiple objectives – The Waste Department's goal identifies three potential objectives: cleanliness, safety, and environmental friendliness. As such, its performance indicators will need to measure how well it is performing in these three areas. However, as none of the areas are financial, non-financial performance indicators – such as survey scores for how clean residents or tourists feel the area is – are likely to be more relevant than financial ones.

Lack of profit measure – The goal also highlights that generating a profit is not a priority for the department in the way it is for commercial organisations. The chief executive's desire to keep costs under control suggests that financial performance measures (focusing on costs) will still be important. However, if BLA focuses too much on cutting costs (for example, by reducing the frequency of waste collections), this could be detrimental to the primary goal of maintaining cleanliness and safety. As such, BLA needs a range of performance indicators, linked to how clean, safe and environmentally friendly the area is.

Difficulty in selecting financial measures – As with many public sector organisations, the results (output) from the Waste Department's services are non-financial: for example, clean streets, a safe environment. Therefore it will be difficult to find any financial indicators which measure the outputs of the department's services in any meaningful way.

Consequently, in any assessment of the department's services it will be difficult to introduce any direct comparison between cost (financial) and benefits (non-financial). In addition, it could be difficult to define the cost unit against which to measure the department's performance. For example, should BLA be measuring the cost per tonne of waste collected, or the cost per household?

(b)   **Value for money**

The extent to which BLA provides value for money services should be assessed in relation to:

Economy – the extent to which services of an acceptable quality are provided at the cheapest cost possible

Efficiency – the way BLA's services are organised, to ensure that the department maximises the benefits and outputs it obtains from its resources

Effectiveness – the extent to which the Waste Services Department's activities achieve its goals

Possible performance indicators at BLA

Economy

BLA's staff costs account for 44% of its total costs, and so the extent to which BLA controls its staff costs will have a significant impact on the economy of its services.

The average salary for BLA's waste collection staff is $31,429 compared to the national average of $29,825. The fact that BLA's average salary exceeds the national average suggests its services are not being provided as economically as they could be. However, this may reflect the fact that Beeshire is a wealthy area, so wage levels in general may be higher there than in other parts of the country. Equally, though, by paying above the national average for staff, BLA may be able to recruit more experienced or higher quality staff. As a result, this could improve its efficiency.

Another significant cost driver for BLA is likely to be its fleet of vehicles. Therefore, it could also measure economy in relation to the costs it pays for its vehicles, their fuel and their maintenance.

Efficiency

Benchmarking the performance of BLA's waste collections against the national figures indicates that BLA is relatively efficient:

	BLA	Nationally
Tonnes of waste collected per member of staff	629	583
Cost per tonne of waste collected ($)	114	123
Staff cost per tonne of waste collected ($)	50	51

This supports the point we made earlier: that although BLA's average salary is above the national average, BLA benefits from the greater efficiency of its staff.

Effectiveness

Effectiveness needs to be measured against a variety of aspects, linked to the need for waste collection:

Public health concerns – The fact that waste is only collected every 14 days (compared to the national average of 12 days) could suggest that BLA is less effective in maintaining public health. However, the level of public health concerns could also be measured by the number of complaints about vermin or other problems related to waste. If the level of complaints BLA receives is in line with national average (or below it) there would seem to be little reason to increase the frequency of the collections it carries out.

Clean and attractive streets – Finding a way to measure the cleanliness of BLA's streets could be difficult, because 'cleanliness' is inherently subjective, and therefore difficult to quantify. However, BLA could use the number of complaints it receives from residents or businesses as an indirect measure. If the number of complaints is relatively low, this would suggest that the cleanliness of the streets is being maintained at an acceptable level.

Increased recycling – The Government has set a target of 40% of all waste to be recycled, therefore BLA needs to measure the percentage of its total waste it recycles. It currently recycles 43% of all waste collected (950,000/2.2m). As such, BLA has already achieved the target level, and the proportion of waste it recycles is above the national average (41%).

Nonetheless, as the Government is planning to increase the levy charged on landfill, it will be important for BLA to ensure the proportion of waste that it recycles is as high as possible. As such, this remains an important indicator to monitor.

(c) **Difficulties of measuring qualitative performance**

Subjectivity – One of the main problems in measuring qualitative performance is that it is based on people's opinions and judgements and therefore is subjective. For example, people's assessment about what constitutes an acceptable level of cleanliness in BLA's streets may differ, and this in turn could affect the degree to which the area's streets are perceived to be 'clean'.

Equally, as Seeland is currently in a long recession, some people may prefer that waste be collected less frequently to allow the local government to save money, instead of, for example, increasing local taxes to pay for more frequent collections. In this case, people's priorities could dictate their willingness to complain about uncollected waste or the frequency of collections.

The fact that the underlying data is qualitative rather than quantitative can, in itself, create problems for measurement. For example, if the Waste Management Department receives a phone call from a resident complaining that some uncollected waste is 'disgusting', it will be difficult for the department to gauge whether this is a more serious or less serious problem than the uncollected waste described by another resident as 'foul'.

Currently, BLA records the number of complaints it receives, but there is no indication of the seriousness of these complaints – possibly due to the subjective nature of the data involved.

Scoring – One way of addressing the problem of subjectivity could be to try to make the data quantitative. For example, the Waste Management Department could introduce a scoring system to judge how satisfied residents are with the cleanliness of their streets. The scoring system could ask residents to rate cleanliness on a scale from 1 to 5, with '1' signifying 'Very satisfied' and '5' signifying 'Very dissatisfied'.

However, scoring systems are still subjective, because the level of cleanliness which one person grades as 'Very satisfactory' may only be deemed 'Satisfactory' by another person. In general, there is also a tendency to score towards the middle in this type of scoring system: people feel more comfortable selecting scores in the range '2' to '4', rather than using the extreme scores of '1' or '5'.

Trends – One way to reduce the subjectivity in non-financial performance measures is by looking at trends over time rather than one-off metrics – for example, monitoring trends in the average scores for cleanliness.

Although individual scores will still be subjective, looking at average scores over time can help to overcome this subjectivity and highlight changes in quality or satisfaction. For example, if the residents are surveyed about the cleanliness of BLA annually, and the average score declines from one year to the next, this should provide a good indication that the quality of the waste collection services is declining.

28 Teeland Universities

Chapter references. Not for profit organisations and the concept of 'value for money' are discussed in Chapter 9 of the Workbook.

Top tips.

Part (a). Teeland's Government wants to assess the value for money provided by universities in the country, and a senior politician has asked for advice on how to do this. The reference to 'value for money' should have prompted you to think about the three Es – economy, efficiency and effectiveness – and these would have provided a useful framework for structuring your answer. (ACCA's marking guide also indicates that there were up to three marks available for a general description of the three Es approach in the context of assessing value for money in public sector organisations.)

Since the requirement refers specifically to the performance data in Appendix 1, a sensible way to approach this question would be to think what the data in the appendix can tell us about the universities' performance – in relation to economy, efficiency and effectiveness.

Remember that 'effectiveness' relates to the extent to which an organisation is achieving its objectives. The three objectives for universities in Teeland are clearly identified at the start of the scenario, so the universities' effectiveness should be judged in relation to these three points.

In this respect, as well as thinking about the relative performance of the four universities described in the scenario, it would be relevant to consider how useful the data in Appendix 1 is for assessing value for money. For example, one of the universities' objectives is 'to engage in high quality research' but would the data in Appendix 1 help the Government to assess the quality of the universities' research?

More generally, when thinking about value for money and the three Es, it is important to think about the linkages between the different Es. This point is relevant here as well. For example, if a university looks to reduce its costs (to improve economy) what impact might this have on the standard of education or the quality of its research (effectiveness)?

Part (b). Although the requirement asks candidates for benefits and problems, it is important to note that it asks about the problems of 'implementing the proposal to introduce league tables', and not simply 'the problems of league tables'. So think about the practical implications of implementing the tables, not just the potential disadvantages of league tables more generally.

As is often the case, the scenario provides some useful clues here – in particular by highlighting the level of resources which will be needed to compile the league tables. (In Veeland, there is a special government department of 150 staff who administer a similar system of performance measurement.)

To score well in this question, you need to address both the benefits and the problems associated with the league tables, although on balance there are actually more problems than benefits (and the relative marks available in the marking guide reflect this).

The short descriptions in the scenario of each of the four universities should also have been useful for identifying some of the problems with the proposal – for example, by raising concerns about how comparable the universities actually are. However, the more general problems of league tables (for example, in terms of motivation or behaviour – what gets measured, gets done) would also be relevant here.

Note that the solution below is, deliberately, longer than an answer that a student would be expected to write under exam conditions, in order to show the range of valid points that could have been made in response to this question.

Examining team's comments. In part (a), many candidates made good use of the three Es to structure their answers. Good answers also used the data in the scenario to illustrate the points being made.

Part (b) was answered fairly well in general, with candidates splitting their answers into two sections (benefits and problems) and illustrating their answers with specific issues relating to the universities in the scenario.

| Marking scheme |

Marks

(a) General description of three Es approach (economy, efficiency, effectiveness) in public sector organisations – up to 3 marks

   Applications of the three Es to assess the performance of the three universities – 1 mark per relevant point – up to 12 marks

   Total for part (a): up to 12   12

(b) Potential benefits from the league tables (linked to improving the universities' performance) – 1 mark per relevant point – up to 6 marks

   Potential problems associated with the league tables – 1 mark per relevant point – up to 10 marks

   Total for part (b): up to 13   13
                                                          Total = 25

(a) Public sector organisations such as the Teeland universities receive all their funding from central government and do not have the generation of profit as an objective. Furthermore, their objectives such as 'improving the standard of education of the citizens of Teeland' cannot be measured in financial terms. The value for money of the universities can be assessed using the three Es framework of economy, efficiency and effectiveness.

Economy

This involves obtaining the inputs to the service at the lowest possible cost, while still maintaining the quality of the inputs. In practice, this may be difficult to do, and a reduction in cost may lead to a reduction in quality.

From the performance data given, the average annual payroll cost per member of academic staff is highest in Northcity University at $62,286 ($109m/1,750). This is 51% higher than Eastcity University, which has the lowest cost at $41,237 of the four universities given. The high costs in Northcity University may reflect the fact that staff there may be more highly qualified or that highly skilled, trained staff are attracted to work there because of the high standards of teaching and academic research.

A higher payroll cost per member of academic staff may not necessarily mean a particular university is not giving good value for money. The relatively high salary costs in Southcity University of $62,083 may simply reflect the higher costs of living in the capital city and so comparison between the regions may be inappropriate.

As such, there may be a conflict between this performance measure and the ability of the universities to achieve their objectives, such as to improve educational standards in Teeland. The politician's proposal to reduce salary levels for new recruits may reduce the number of appropriately qualified and skilled staff who wish to work there. This may reduce the standard of teaching and academic research and, as a result, the universities' performance against their stated objectives.

This means that focusing solely on economy would not ensure the universities achieve value for money.

Efficiency

Efficiency measures the amount of outputs relative to the amount of inputs. The number of academic staff per student may be a suitable measure, but there may be differences between universities which would make it hard to compare results.

For example, there are 10.1 (17,600/1,750) students per member of academic staff in Northcity University, which is ranked number one in the Teeland Government's provisional league table. There are 17.9 in Westcity University which is ranked much lower at 21. It would seem, therefore, that increasing the number of students relative to the number of academic staff as per the politician's proposal may reduce the performance of the universities against their stated objectives and as such will not increase value for money.

The politician's comparison with the number of students per academic staff in neighbouring Veeland may not be appropriate. Whilst the politician's assertion that educational standards are higher in Veeland may be correct, the undertaking of high quality academic research may not be a key objective of the universities there, or the quality of research may be lower than in Teeland.

Effectiveness

Effectiveness measures whether the objectives of the organisation are being met. The stated objectives of the Teeland universities are to improve the overall standard of education of citizens in Teeland, to engage in high quality academic research and to produce well-qualified university graduates to meet the needs of the graduate jobs market in Teeland.

Objective to improve the overall standard of education in Teeland

Currently, there is no direct measure of the performance of the universities' stated objectives to increase the level of education of the citizens of Teeland. The number of graduates entering graduate jobs and the results of the TSOR survey may indirectly measure the effectiveness of the universities in achieving this aim. More direct measures such as the number of students completing their studies or obtaining good results in university exams may be more appropriate.

The effectiveness of the universities in improving the standard of education should really be related to the entry requirements of each university. Westcity University is the lowest ranking of the four universities in the provisional league table and has the lowest proportion of graduates entering graduate jobs at 50% (1,750/(11,200/3.2)). It also receives the lowest amount of research funding per student at around $1,250 ($14m/11,200), but it has the lowest entry requirements, which have been relaxed to encourage students from a more diverse range of backgrounds to study there. Therefore, the improvement in educational standards relative to students' attainment on entry may be higher than the position in the league table may suggest.

Objective to engage in high quality academic research

The stated aim of the universities to engage in high quality academic research is also not currently measured. The amount of research funding received from government and other organisations by each university may indirectly reflect the quality of the research there as providers of funds for research would probably look to fund high quality research.

This measure may, however, equally reflect that some types of research are more expensive than others. Southcity University, which is successful in science and technology subjects, receives $15,592 per student compared to $5,000 in Eastcity, which specialises in arts and humanities subjects. The funding received may be more indicative of the past quality of academic research rather than future quality, or may not even reflect the quality of the research and may be high due to wastage or inefficiency. The definition of 'quality' of research is unclear.

Objective to meet the needs of the graduate jobs market

The number of graduates from each university obtaining graduate jobs each year is an indirect measure of how well each university is achieving this objective. However, the number of graduate jobs filled may simply reflect the number of students at each university and demand for graduate jobs in the economy.

Many graduates, including the most talented of them, may take graduate jobs overseas, in which case the measure of graduate jobs filled may not be a clear measure of the objective to meet the needs of the graduate jobs market in Teeland. A more precise measure of graduates entering graduate jobs in Teeland may be more appropriate. Even this may be misleading, if graduates later return from overseas to enter graduate jobs in Teeland.

The definition of what is a 'graduate' job is subjective and likely to change over time, for example, as a result of changes in the economy. This again limits the usefulness of this measure in determining whether universities have met this objective.

The TSOR survey is a measure of effectiveness reflecting a basket of measures, one of which is students' own perceptions of their future job prospects. The measures in the TSOR survey are, however, highly subjective according to individuals' personal perceptions, for example, about students' job prospects and the quality of teaching at the university. Furthermore, the survey covers a wider range of factors such as their overall satisfaction with university life. As such, this may not reflect the stated aims of the universities in Teeland. The TSOR score for Westcity University is considerably higher than for all the other universities, despite it having the lowest overall ranking.

(b)   **Effect of league tables on the quality of the Teeland universities**

League tables encourage competition between universities

The publishing of league tables of the performance of the universities in Teeland should stimulate competition for high ranking between them. This should encourage them to find better ways to improve the quality of the service, achieve their performance objectives, and deliver greater value for money.

BPP
LEARNING
MEDIA

Sharing of resources may be discouraged

However, this may discourage knowledge or even resource sharing between the universities if they see themselves in competition for the best students and limited research funding. This could particularly be a problem if the university leaders were given performance targets and rewards based on their university's position in the league table. They may be encouraged to undertake 'gaming' and focus solely on their position within the league table to the detriment of other aspects of performance. This may mean the objectives for the universities overall in Teeland may not be achieved.

University leaders may focus on a narrow range of objectives

Students' overall experience of university life may be influenced by access to social, pastoral and sporting facilities.

Management time and resources may be diverted away from these important areas by focusing on a narrow range of performance objectives such as improving educational standards and high quality research in order to boost the position in the league table.

Use of league table to ensure accountability of the universities

If the performance league tables are made publicly available, for example, on the internet as they are in Veeland, this should ensure the performance of the universities is transparent. This will mean that they are held accountable by the public for the quality of service and value for money which they provide.

League tables give choices to students and staff

To be really effective, league tables should provide users of the performance data, such as the public, with the ability to make choices based on the data given. Prospective students and staff will be able to make choices about which university to study or work at according to their position in the league tables. In addition, providers of funding such as the Government will be able to identify where corrective action or additional funding may be required.

This could also be a disadvantage of using league tables, as the best students are likely to be attracted to the best universities, which are in turn likely to attract the most funding for academic research. This may cause a reduction in the overall performance of lower ranking universities, and therefore a failure of the universities as a whole to achieve the stated aim of improving educational standards in Teeland.

League tables may not reflect variation of standards at each university

There may also be considerable variation of the standards within one university, which a ranking in a league table will not address. For example, Southcity University offers courses in a variety of subjects and is particularly successful at science and technology subjects. This may mean that it achieves a high overall ranking in a league table, whereas its performance in other subjects may be weaker. For all of these reasons, the provision of league tables or performance data at a lower level, such as by subject area, may therefore be a better way to make the universities accountable to the public.

Regions may not be directly comparable

There may be inherent differences between universities which make comparison using league tables misleading or of limited value. For example, Eastcity University specialises in teaching arts and humanities. It may be inappropriate to compare it to universities offering a wide range of courses or specialising in science and technology subjects. Similarly, it may be misleading to compare universities of different sizes or in locations in different parts of Teeland. Universities which also attract students from outside Teeland, for example, those in capital or major cities, are likely to have more access to the most able students.

Due to its capital city location, Southcity University may incur additional costs of providing facilities and have to pay staff more to reflect the higher cost of living there. It may be more appropriate to produce league tables at a lower level, like within individual cities, to make the comparisons more meaningful and eliminate the effect of regional variations such as this.

There may be differences in the way different universities collect and report performance data. These problems can be reduced by the use of consistent and enforced policies for compiling performance data.

Resources required to produce league tables

Other problems relate to the targets chosen, external influences on results and cost of collating and measuring performance for the league table.

In Veeland, there is a sizeable government department dedicated to measuring performance. The cost of collecting performance data and compiling the league tables may therefore outweigh the benefits to be gained from doing so. It will use up resources which could be used, for example, in providing additional funding to the universities themselves.

Performance measures used to create league tables may be confusing and conflicting

By having a large number of targets such as in Veeland, this may cause confusion to managers, who may not know which to focus on. Similarly, it may be difficult to decide which performance measures are the most important.

Many performance measures chosen are likely to conflict. Reducing the salaries paid to academic staff may make it harder to recruit and retain experienced and well-qualified staff, which may lead to failing to meet the universities' key objectives.

Similarly, increasing the number of students per member of academic staff is unlikely to help achieve any of the universities' objectives as staff will have less time available for teaching and for engaging in high quality research.

League tables may demotivate staff and students

The Teeland politician's proposed target of a 5% annual increase in the number of students entering graduate jobs sounds very challenging and may be unrealistic. This will be especially so if accompanied by a reduction in the number of academic staff and a reduction of the salaries of new recruits. If the targets are felt to be unachievable by the university leaders, they may become demotivated, and give up on trying to achieve them altogether. This will especially be the case if this is an 'all or nothing' target. A more realistic target may at least ensure that some progress is made.

Students may also become demotivated if their university ranks poorly in league tables, even if the students themselves are satisfied with the standard of education they are receiving.

Similarly some performance measures, such as the number of students entering graduate jobs, which may be highly dependent on the economic conditions in Teeland, are not entirely under the control of the university leaders. The economic conditions in Teeland will be a key factor in determining the number of graduate jobs available there. University leaders may become demotivated by this measure as well and stop trying to improve.

The relative importance of different performance measures is subjective

The weighting of the different performance measures used by the Teeland Government in arriving at the provisional ranking of the universities is subjective. It is difficult to determine which measures are the most important, and hence how each should be weighted. The opinions of different stakeholders on which are the most important measures will also vary. Academic staff and students may view different measures as important compared to the providers of finance (the Teeland Government) and organisations which recruit university graduates.

Determining the relative importance of different performance measures in order to publish a league table is therefore difficult. Furthermore, the measures chosen, and their relative weightings, could differ from those in other countries. This would make it difficult to benchmark performance against universities in other countries, such as Veeland.

29 Tosemary and Rhyme Hospital

Workbook reference. Issues surrounding performance measurement in not-for-profit organisations are discussed in Chapter 9 of the Workbook. Management styles are discussed in Chapter 12.

Top tips.

Part (a). A useful starting point for this requirement might be to think about the objectives of not-for-profit organisations, and how these differ from the objectives of commercial organisations. Then think how the nature of these objectives will influence the aspects of performance which are important to measure.

A key point to remember in relation to performance management in any organisation is that performance indicators should measure how well an organisation is performing against its objectives. The scenario clearly states TRH's objectives – eg to give prompt access to high quality medical treatment for patients. The key aspects of this objective (promptness; high quality) are non-financial; so what implications does this have for the type of performance indicator which are important for TRH to measure?

Part (b). The second of TRH's objectives tells you the three elements of the value for money framework – economy, efficiency and effectiveness – and you should use these to structure your answer.

For each of the three Es you need to do two things: (i) select – and **justify** – an appropriate performance measure, using the data provided in Appendix 1; (ii) compare TRH's performance for that measure against the national average, in order to **evaluate** whether TRH is delivering value for money.

Note, however, that for the first element you aren't simply asked to identify a performance measure, but to justify it. To score well here you need to explain how the measure you have selected will help TRH assess the economy, efficiency or effectiveness of its performance as appropriate.

For the second element, you need to calculate the relevant performance indicators for TRH, and for the national average. However, remember the verb here is 'evaluate', and not just 'calculate'. So, for example, if TRH's performance for a given metric is worse than the national average, what does this suggest about how well TRH is delivering value for money?

Part (c). The model underlying this requirement was Hopwood's management styles – budget-constrained; profit-conscious and non-accounting, and, the question you need to ask yourself is: what are the characteristics of a budget constrained style?

Even if you couldn't remember much about the model, the penultimate paragraph of the scenario gave you some clues which you might have been able to use. For example, there is a focus on achieving financial budgets; and most of the performance data relates to financial targets.

In effect, these are of the key characteristics of budget-constrained management – and identifying this should have helped you realise that the management style at TRH is budget-constrained.

Note, however, that the question doesn't only ask about the style, but also asks to advice on the implications of this for managing TRH's performance. Again, the penultimate paragraph of the scenario could be very useful here. For example, if doctors at TRH have to work longer hours than their colleagues, often without being paid overtime, what could the consequences of this be – in terms of quality of medical treatment, or in terms of staff retention?

As we noted in relation to part (a), it is important that an organisation's performance management systems enable it to measure how well it is performing against its objectives. This point is also relevant here: if TRH's managers are focusing primarily on short-term financial performance, what implications could this have on TRH's ability to achieve its objectives?

Marks

(a) Importance of non-financial performance indicators – 1 mark per
    relevant point

Maximum for part (a): up to 5 marks   5

(b) Definition of value for money (3 Es) – 1 mark

For each 'E' (economy, efficiency, effectiveness):

Selecting, and justifying, an appropriate performance measure, and
    using this to evaluate whether TRH is delivering value for money –
    up to 4 marks each

Maximum for part (b): up to 10 marks   10

(c) Evaluating the extent to which TRH's management style is budget
    constrained – 1 mark per relevant point

Advising on the implications of a budget-constrained approach at TRH –
    1 mark per relevant point

Up to a maximum for part (c) of 10 marks   10

Total = 25

(a) **Lack of profit-making objective**

Not-for-profit organisations do not, by definition, have profit as an overriding motive.
Patients are not charged for receiving treatment, so TRH does not have a revenue stream. It
may also be difficult to define a cost unit as this could be cost per patient arriving at
hospital or cost per patient successfully treated.

Not-for-profit public sector organisations, such as TRH, have strict constraints on the
amount of funding they receive, such as a fixed amount of funding received entirely from
the government. They cannot obtain funding from elsewhere, so financial measures cannot
be ignored completely. TRH must exist within its financial means, and the use of budgets to
control costs is critical.

TRH provides an essential public service. Political, legal and social influences would prevent
it from closing down a service just because it became more expensive or uneconomic to
provide it. For all of these reasons, financial objectives are less relevant than for most
commercial organisations, and its objectives are mainly non-financial in nature.

Not-for-profit organisations also undergo more public scrutiny and have multiple
stakeholders, so non-financial indicators will be necessary to manage expectations. For
example, patients are stakeholders who will have relatively little interest in how TRH exists
within its financial constraints. They will have much more interest in non-financial
performance, such as how quickly and successfully they are treated.

Multiple objectives

Not-for-profit organisations have multiple objectives, and it may be unclear which are the
most important. Except for some aspects of giving value for money to the taxpayer, TRH's
objectives are all non-financial.

The outputs or benefits of the services provided are non-financial in nature, for example,
giving prompt and high-quality treatment to patients. Therefore non-financial performance
indicators are required to measure performance.

(b) Value for money in public sector organisations can be measured using the 'three Es': economy, efficiency and effectiveness.

Economy

Economy means obtaining resources at the lowest cost. Doctors' salaries will be a significant expense for TRH, and salary per doctor is a suitable measure of economy. Doctors at TRH have an average salary of $150,000 ($3.75m/25), compared to the national average of $175,000 ($4.20m/24).

The relatively lower salaries of doctors may be due to differences in levels of experience or that they work unpaid overtime. It may also be one of the reasons why the staff satisfaction is so much lower at 9% compared to the national level of 89%.

Efficiency

Efficiency relates to obtaining the greatest possible outputs from the resources available. Treating patients is a key objective of TRH, and the number of doctors is an important resource. The number of patients treated per year by each doctor is a good measure of efficiency. In TRH, each doctor treats an average of 975 (24,375/25) patients per year, 17% more (975 vs 833) than the national average 833 (20,000/24). This may be because they work longer hours than their colleagues in other hospitals.

Effectiveness

Effectiveness means how well TRH achieves its objectives. TRH has multiple objectives, one of which is to provide high quality medical treatment for patients. Where patients are re-admitted to TRH because their treatment had failed, this represents a failure to provide high-quality medical care, so the rate of re-admission of patients is a measure of effectiveness. The rate of re-admission at TRH is 7.5% (1,830/24,375), much higher than the national average of 1.5% (300/20,000). TRH seems to have performed relatively very poorly in this respect.

Summary

Overall, the results from the measurement of the 3Es are consistent with the doctor's comments that they are working without being paid overtime and treating more patients than their colleagues in other hospitals. TRH appears to deliver better economy and efficiency than the national average. This seems to be reducing performance, however, in respect of providing high-quality medical treatment for patients, where TRH is less effective than the national average.

(c) **Extent to which the management style is budget constrained**

A budget-constrained management style emphasises the need to achieve short-term performance measures, for example, the annual financial budgets.

The doctor said that TRH has always achieved its total financial budgets, and this is supported by the fact that the doctors' salaries for the year to 31 August 20X7 equalled the budget set for the period. Though it is unclear what NFPIs are measured at TRH as a whole, doctors receive only a limited set of financial and non-financial performance data. The discussion about this data, however, is mainly related to financial targets. This implies greater emphasis is given to performance against financial targets, rather than non-financial ones.

All of this suggests that TRH has a budget-constrained management style. An advantage of this is that it ensures TRH operates with the financial constraints of the fixed amount of funding received from the government.

Implications of a budget-constrained approach at TRH

This management style encourages short-termism, by encouraging doctors to work long hours without being paid overtime, or not making funding available to recruit new doctors to alleviate the situation. An implication of this is that TRH may reduce its performance against its objectives, and this is already seen by the relatively high rates of re-admission as an indicator of a reduced quality of medical treatment. Job-related tension is a consequence of a budget-constrained management style, and the low staff satisfaction score could have resulted from this.

This management style encourages manipulation of results, or the way they are measured, to show better performance. At busy times, more patients are referred to the nearby larger hospital. There is apparently no medical need for this, which is inconsistent with the objective to deliver high-quality treatment. It appears to be a way to distort waiting times to demonstrate improved performance in treating patients promptly. From patients' perspective, though, this will mean they are treated less promptly than if treated at TRH.

Being unable to recruit new doctors reduces TRH's flexibility in reducing waiting times at busy periods, as the steps already taken seem to have had minimal effect. This management style does not encourage innovation, probably because doctors have insufficient time for this. Though this may have long-term benefits, it seems to be taken as less important than the other key objectives, to provide prompt, high-quality treatment.

30 Coruisk

Workbook reference. Quality management and JIT are discussed in Chapter 11 of the Workbook.

Top tips. Candidates that structured their answers with a brief description of JIT followed by **more lengthy, detailed advice about how this system impacted on the existing purchasing and production systems** would score well. In APM you should always try to apply your knowledge to the scenario, and excellent scores were achieved by candidates **who used the details of the current systems:**

- Poor-quality raw materials purchased
- An untailored approach to deliveries by the company's suppliers
- The existing quality review process
- The remuneration scheme

Examining team's comments. In part (b) 'a significant minority of candidates could not identify the difference between the easily distinguished, broad categories of conformance and non-conformance costs'. It was also noted that, in part (b), markers had latitude to allow for different but justified allocations of quality costs.

Marking scheme

		Marks
(a)	Definition of JIT – up to 2 marks	
	Purchasing and production – 1 mark per point up to 13 marks	
	Maximum	13
(b)	Calculations:	
	Prevention costs – 1 mark	
	Appraisal costs – 1 mark	
	Internal failure costs – 1 mark	
	External failure costs – 1 mark	
	% of sales – 1 mark (OFR)	
	Comments – up to 7 marks	
	Maximum	12
	Total =	25

(a) Just-in-time (JIT) is defined as a system which has the objective of producing or procuring products as they are required and not for inventory purposes. Coruisk is being asked to produce to JIT principles, the basis of which is where production is driven by demand for the finished product. Each part of the production process is therefore determined only by what is required for the next stage of production.

Currently, it is clear that Coruisk is not ready to produce to the JIT principles which Ericht is requesting and that Coruisk needs to make fundamental changes to its operations to be able to do so. These changes address the following areas:

Purchasing

Coruisk has too many suppliers at present. Adhering to JIT production principles involves reducing suppliers to a minimum and establishing strong relationships with them, based on flexibility and understanding of each other's needs. Coruisk's four main suppliers are too many to develop this type of close relationship with, especially since these suppliers operate to different working practices. The effect of this, from a JIT production perspective, would be that Coruisk would require to undertake discussions with each supplier about the fundamental changes which would be required for the supply of goods in a JIT production environment. Coruisk would not have the time to do this with all four suppliers nor would the supply of goods from four companies be desirable. Coruisk should choose two of the companies it feels it has the strongest relationship with and initiate discussions with them around its needs when producing to JIT principles.

When producing to JIT principles, suppliers will effectively be an extension of Coruisk's own business. As such, Coruisk must be aware of and must understand how changes in suppliers' operations will affect Coruisk's own operations. It is clear that Coruisk does not currently have this level of relationship. The supplier who is seeking to optimise the cost of its delivery vehicles, for example, is undertaking practices which are very much opposed to the type of practices which Coruisk will need when it is producing to JIT principles. JIT only produces goods when needed by the next stage in the process (the 'kanban' principle) and Coruisk would need its supplier to understand this and be willing to supply it with goods accordingly. This would clearly be impossible for a supplying company which is insistent on supplying full-load quantities only.

Coruisk must also ensure that the raw material it receives is defect free, unlike the goods which are received currently from one supplier. Having the wrong quantity of material or material which is sub-standard, is unacceptable if Coruisk is producing to JIT principles as such problems will mean an inevitable delay in supplying goods to Ericht. Coruisk will therefore need to spend time in defining and agreeing requirements with suppliers to clarify requirements in terms of both quality and quantity and may need to also develop improvement teams with their suppliers to ensure that the raw material it receives is reliable.

Coruisk will most likely need to undertake official supplier assessments as part of this as such assessments and on-going reviews are a vital part of ensuring the quality of the raw material in a JIT production system.

Production

The manner in which Coruisk produces its goods will need to change significantly. Efficiency can no longer be measured by volume of output. Ericht will seek supply of goods as and when required in order to avoid obsolete inventory and Coruisk must adapt to this. The concept of producing as much as possible is one which Coruisk may struggle to abolish. It is clearly embedded in the culture of the organisation with its importance confirmed by the awarding of a bonus based on the quantity of goods produced. Presumably this bonus has been awarded without taking account of any goods which have been rejected and it is possible that the current system is encouraging production to be undertaken quickly with rejected goods seen as an acceptable part of the production process.

Producing to JIT principles would demand a fundamental rethink at Coruisk in terms of the way production runs are determined. Of most significance, initially, is that such runs would be shorter as all parts of the production process should match the rate at which Ericht is demanding the final product. For example, Coruisk can no longer focus on producing large runs of one dress. Necessary changes here may involve the development of machine cells. Such cells are composed of groups of team members to facilitate operations by eliminating setup and unneeded costs between operations. Cells might be designed for a specific process or part of a product. In Coruisk's case, this may mean workers being grouped together by the dress they are producing at that time rather than as part of a long production run. Enhancing worker flexibility, and developing their skillset in several areas of the operation, may be the best way to react to this new environment where demand is much more unpredictable. This may also involve changing the layout of the factory to try to ensure production is as flexible as possible.

Coruisk cannot supply faulty goods to Ericht and the previous belief that a 5% rejection rate was acceptable practice must be replaced by an understanding of the zero defects philosophy. This will require more fundamental change as quality of the finished good will need to be assured throughout the production process and not simply inspected at the end. This will most likely involve an initial discussion with Ericht as to the quality level it is seeking and, potentially, a redesign of the current processes and systems to which Coruisk is operating. For example, prevention and appraisal costs would be expected to increase as Coruisk would have to establish both goods inwards testing procedures and testing procedures for work in progress. There would also be a need for Coruisk to develop a culture where workers are flexible in terms of their capabilities and trained much more in identifying defective products (and ensuring they do not progress further on the production line) than in ensuring the maximum quantity of output is produced.

(b)   **Cost of quality report**

	$'000	$'000	% of revenue ($4.5m)
Costs of conformance:			
Prevention costs:			
Preventative maintenance	8		
Total		8	0.18%
Appraisal costs:			
Quality control supervisor	35		
Quality audit	2		
Total		37	0.82%
Costs of non-conformance:			
Internal failure costs:			
Rework cost	72		
Machine downtime	38		
Scrap	58		
Total		168	3.73%
External failure costs:			
Cost of complaints from Ericht	135		
Foregone contribution from lost sales	85		
Product recalls and cost of good returned	180		
Total		400	8.89%
Overall total	613		13.62%

The results of the cost of quality report are representative of a company which undertakes quality control as opposed to quality assurance in that the majority of the costs relate to failure, either of an internal or external nature. Additionally, since the costs have been amassed for the first time for this task, it is possible that they are inaccurate and probably understated as some costs are likely to have been omitted.

Costs of conformance

Coruisk will need to invest more in quality audits and, possibly, in testing equipment to ensure that the product is being produced to the right standard as it progresses through the production process. Whereas there may still be a requirement for final inspection, it should not be someone's full-time occupation and the supervisor may be more meaningfully deployed elsewhere for at least part of his/her role. These practices should reduce both the internal and external failure costs, particularly those of scrap and rework, which both appear very high currently. Machine downtime is perhaps due to the very little amount currently spent on preventative maintenance and the cost of internal failure should also fall with enhanced maintenance.

Costs of non-conformance

The significant external failure cost is of most concern. To operate to the JIT principles which Ericht is seeking, Coruisk has to ensure that these costs are as close to zero as possible. It is concerning, for example, that 3% ($135,000) of the revenue figure is taken up by dealing with complaints from Ericht. Some of this may be due to misunderstandings between the companies which could be rectified by the closer working relationship that JIT production principles demand. Nevertheless, it is clear that Coruisk must ensure that it addresses these costs as it is completely reliant upon Ericht for its business.

The amount of money attributed to product recalls and cost of goods returned (4% of the revenue figure) is concerning as this suggests that defective products have not been detected in Coruisk's current quality control system. This may be due to the bonus system currently in place and the desire to produce quantity, quickly, and not quality. A change to the production process should address this but it could be met with hostility if the workers' bonus is under threat and Coruisk may need to introduce an alternative bonus scheme based on a quality-related metric which specifies, for example, the percentage of defects detected.

The forgone contribution from lost sales is also concerning as it indicates that Ericht has alternative supplier(s). It is possible, given the cost detailed of dealing with complaints from Ericht, that this figure is considerably higher than Coruisk is estimating.

The balance of the costs must change so that the majority of Coruisk's costs are prevention and appraisal (costs of conformance) and not costs of internal/external failure (costs of non-conformance). Coruisk must ensure that it is producing to the standard which Ericht requests at the first time of asking and therefore Coruisk must ensure that it provides more training for staff, more preventative machine maintenance, more supplier appraisal and vetting as mentioned previously and moves to encourage a culture of zero defects with no faulty goods moving forward in the production process.

31 Navier Aerials

Workbook reference. You should already be familiar with activity-based costing from your *Performance Management* studies at Applied Skills level. Activity-based costing in relation to cost reduction (in the context of Activity-based management) is covered in Chapter 13 of the Workbook. Quality management is covered in Chapter 11.

Top tips.

Part (a). In order to evaluate the impact of using activity-based costing (ABC), compared to the existing costing system, we need to know what difference there is between the cost allocations under the two systems. Accordingly, you need to do the calculations before you can begin to evaluate the impact of any change.

Note the cost allocations should be 'per dish', not 'per order'.

Once you have done the calculations, you then need to compare the allocations under the two systems. For example, are the cost allocations similar under the two systems, or are there any significant differences? How accurate is the FD's assumption that the cost of the additional CC for specialised dishes is $100 per dish?

Remember that ABC is likely to be more time consuming than the current method. So are the cost allocations sufficiently different under the two methods to justify the extra work involved in applying the ABC method?

Part (b). Make sure you read the requirement for part (b) very carefully. Although the issues of cost reduction and quality management in the CC Department are important, the key element in the requirement relates to how **information** about the activities can be used and improved.

So, for example, whilst reducing the number of customer complaints could reduce complaint handling costs, Navier needs to know what the main reasons for customer complaints are in order for it to tackle the causes of those complaints. If Navier doesn't have any information about why customers are complaining, how can it decide what changes need to be made to its current processes?

Examining team's comments. This question was generally answered poorly, with weak efforts at handling the quantification of the two costing systems, compounded by lack of knowledge about quality issues.

Part (a) required candidates to use the partially completed calculations in the question to work out cost per dish (using the two methods for allocating overheads), and then to consider the implications of the results. Many candidates seemed perplexed that the calculations were not more difficult; and yet commonly failed to do them accurately.

In an APM question, candidates could easily be presented with data which has already been prepared (by a more junior accountant) and then be asked to complete or to assess/interpret the work done. However, candidates seemed ill-prepared for this kind of task, and for evaluating the impact of ABC on overhead absorption systems.

The scenario presented a situation which candidates could easily come across in real life. The FD has estimated the impact of different product types, and candidates were then required to do the work more accurately and comment on the results. A key question posed here – which few candidates identified – was: is the effort required to generate a more accurate overhead allocation worth the effort?

Candidates should be wary of simply **assuming** that the newer, more complex method (in this case, ABC) is the best solution in practice.

Part (b) moved from the performance measurement aspect of the scenario into the performance management implications. The question required an assessment of the information available about each of the activities, and how that information can be used – or improved – in order to help reduce cost and improve quality.

Unfortunately, most candidates displayed a weak grasp of quality cost issues, and also failed to prioritise their work towards the major cost areas of 'handling enquiries and prepared quotes' and 'complaints handling'.

Marking scheme

Marks

(a)   Calculating the number of dishes – 1 mark

Calculating the standard absorption cost per dish – 1 mark

Calculating costs to be allocated to each dish using ABC; 1 mark per
type of dish – up to 2 marks

For comments on the consequences of using the current costing system –
1 mark per valid point, up to 4 marks

For comment on the impact of using ABC – 1 mark per valid point, up to
7 marks

Total: up to 13   13

(b)   For general comments on costs for each activity – 1 mark per point;
         up to 2 marks

         For comments on pre-sales work and related information required –
           1 mark per point; up to 2 marks

         Complaints handling: for comments about complaints handling as a
           non value adding activity, and information required in relation to
           complaints handling – 1 mark per point; up to 4 marks

         For potential benefits of quality management in the CC Department,
           and information required in relation to quality management – 1 mark
           per point; up to 4 marks

         For other relevant points: 1 mark per point, up to a maximum of 2 marks

         Total: up to 12

                                                                                    12
                                                                    Total = 25

(a)   **Current absorption costing** – Under the current costing system, the total costs of the CC
         Department are allocated to each dish by dividing total departmental costs by the total
         number of dishes. Under this basis, the cost of CC per dish is $8.03. This cost is then added
         to the other costs incurred in the production of the dishes (such as material and labour) to
         obtain a total cost per dish.

         Specialised dishes – The FD adds an additional $100 per specialised dish to cover the cost
         of CC in relation to these dishes. However, because the total costs of the CC Department
         have already been absorbed in the $8.03 charge, this additional charge means that CC
         costs will be over-absorbed. (Assuming that Navier manufactures 1,600 specialised dishes
         per year, the CC cost over-absorbed will be $160,000.)

ABC costing

As Navier produces two different types of product, which use different amounts of the CC
Department's resources, applying ABC will enable overhead costs to be allocated to the
different products more accurately.

The activity-based analysis (see Working: Costs per dish) shows that the costs of CC per
standard dish should be $6.22, instead of $8.03. As a result, the profit per dish will be
higher under the ABC system than under the current system.

Under the activity-based system, the CC costs attributed to each specialised dish are
$106.05. It should not be a surprise that the costs attributed to the specialised dishes are so
much higher than for the standard dishes because of the disproportionate amount of time
spent handling enquiries, preparing quotes and dealing with complaints in relation to
specialised dish orders.

Working: Costs per dish

Standard absorption cost per dish

		$
Total cost of CC Department		707,000
Number of dishes (16,000 × 5.5)	88,000	
Standard absorption cost per dish		8.03
FD's adjusted cost per specialised dish		108.03

Activity-based costs

	All orders	Standard	Specialised
Total costs ($)	707,000	537,320	169,680
Average dishes per order		6	1
Number of orders	16,000	14,400	1,600
Total number of dishes ($)		86,400	1,600
ABC absorption cost per dish ($)		**6.22**	**106.05**

The difference between the allocated CC costs of specialised and standard dishes under the activity-based system is $99.83 ($106.05 – $6.22). This appears to justify the FD's estimate, under the current system, of adding $100 to the CC costs of a standard dish in order to find the costs of a specialised dish.

However, the fact that the absorption costs of both standard and specialised dishes are lower under the ABC system than under the current system again suggests that costs are being over-absorbed under the current system. (No adjustment is being made to the basic figure of $8.03 to reflect the additional $100 costs being allocated to the specialised dishes.)

Evaluation of ABC analysis

Value-adding activities – ABC analysis enables Navier to identify the activities which are driving the higher costs of the specialised dishes.

Given the CEO's wish to be able to identify non value added activities, further analysis could then be undertaken to determine whether customers value the additional CC work associated with their bespoke dishes (and therefore whether the additional costs of almost $100 per dish add value or not). If there are any processes which do not add value for the customers, these should be removed or redesigned.

Cost benefit analysis – Although the ABC exercise has enabled costs to be allocated to the two types of product more accurately, it is debatable whether the extra effort involved in calculating the activity-based costs is worthwhile. The FD appears to have been able to estimate the costs to be allocated to the products reasonably accurately before any ABC analysis was undertaken.

If the current absorption calculations are adjusted to correct the over-absorption in relation to the specialised dishes, then the costs to be allocated per dish (see Working below) would be very similar to those proposed under the ABC system.

		$
Total cost of CC Department		707,000
Costs attributable to specialised dishes		(160,000)
General costs to apportion		547,000
Number of dishes (16,000 × 5.5)	88,000	
Standard absorption cost per dish		**6.22**
FD's adjusted cost per specialised dish		**106.22**

(b) Cost activities

The main cost activities in the CC Department are pre-sales (handling enquiries and preparing quotes: $282,800) and post-sale (handling customer complaints: $176,750). Together, these activities account for 65% of the total cost of the department.

Sales enquiries – The pre-sale work is vital for converting customer enquiries into firm orders. Currently just under 46% of all enquiries are converted into actual orders (16,000/35,000). Given the importance of pre-sale activities for the CC Department, it would be useful to know how effectively the department converts enquiries into orders compared to other similar departments.

In this respect, some kind of benchmarking exercise could be very useful. Navier could try to benchmark its enquiries to orders ratio against its competitors (competitor benchmarking), although its competitors may not publish this information as they may consider it to be commercially sensitive. Alternatively, Navier could monitor the number of enquiries and its own conversion rate of enquiries to orders over time (historical benchmarking).

Complaints handling – Complaints handling should be seen as a non value adding activity. Whilst dealing effectively with customer complaints is important from a relationship management perspective, it doesn't in itself add any value to the product which customers buy from Navier. Instead, complaint handling is only required where the products or services customers receive do not meet the standard they expect.

Quality management – In this respect, reducing complaint handling costs could be linked to quality management. If the quality of Navier's products is improved, this should reduce the number of customer complaints, and in turn the level of customer handling costs.

Currently there are 3,200 complaints per year in respect of 16,000 orders. Although there could be more than one complaint in relation to a single dish, this level of complaints suggests that there is a complaint in relation to approximately 20% of Navier's total orders, which seems quite a high proportion. Moreover, the level of customer complaints (**external failure costs**) suggests that there is scope for Navier to improve its internal controls so that problems can either be prevented or else detected before they reach the customer.

In order to reduce the number of complaints, Navier needs to identify what is causing them. There could be a number of different issues which lead to complaints. Some of the complaints may relate to the CC Department, while others are likely to result from the manufacturing process.

If the CC doesn't understand a customer's order correctly, the instructions it passes on to the manufacturing and installation teams are also likely to be incorrect.

Equally, although the instructions were correct, there could be problems with the work undertaken by the manufacturing and installation teams. It is not clear what level of supervision and inspection is in place, but it is possible that this needs to be increased in order to prevent and detect quality issues. In this respect, it may be beneficial for Navier to increase the level of inspection and detection costs, in order to reduce the level of non-conformance costs which would otherwise result if a dish does not meet the customers' expected standards.

Financial information – The other activities in the CC Department (such as credit checks and order processing) are administrative, and the financial information systems can provide some measures of their quality. The quality of order processing can be measured by reference to the number of invoice disputes or the value of credit notes issued. Equally, the effectiveness of Navier's credit checks can be assessed by measuring the level of bad debts incurred.

32 Tench

> **Workbook reference.** Quality issues and Japanese business practices and management accounting techniques such as Kaizen costing and JIT are discussed in Chapter 11 of the Workbook.
>
> **Top tips.**
>
> **Part (a).** A common theme across a number of areas of performance management is: 'What gets measured, gets done'. And this theme is relevant here too. If Tench starts focusing on quality and quality costs, this should help it increase the quality of its cars.
>
> However, before you start discussing the impact of quality costs in this way, it would be sensible to explain what quality costs are. The analysis of costs into 'prevention', 'appraisal', 'internal failure' and 'external failure' costs could be a useful way of thinking about the range of quality costs which could affect Tench.
>
> Whereas part (a) asks you to discuss aspects of Tench's current costing system, parts (b) and (c) focus on its planned new systems. In effect, then, this question as a whole is highlighting the contrast between traditional views of quality costs (part (a)) and the Japanese approaches based around the ideas of continuous improvement (Kaizen) and JIT.

Part (b) picks up on this point specifically, and a key point to note here is the distinction between cost reduction (in Kaizen costing) and cost control (in traditional approaches). However, note that there are two sub-requirements to this part of the question: the impact of Kaizen costing on: (i) Tench's costing systems, and (ii) employee management.

Part (c) then considers the related issue of moving to a JIT system. Note that you are asked to 'evaluate' the effect, so you need to consider the advantages and disadvantages of doing so. In this respect, it is important you appreciate the context in which Tench currently operates. It is based on a former communist state and still seems to have a very bureaucratic culture; how suitable is such a context for introducing JIT systems?

Part (d) then considers the related issue of TQM. This should have been a straightforward part of the question. However, time management is important here to make sure you get time to gain these easy marks.

Importantly, to score well in all four parts of this question, you need to answer the question set. Answers which simply **describe** quality costs, Kaizen costing, TQM and JIT systems in general terms will earn very few marks.

Marking scheme

		Marks
(a)	Impact of quality costs – 1 mark for each relevant point made, up to 4 marks	
	Use of quality costs and explanation of traditional view of quality costs – 1 mark for each relevant point made, up to 3 marks	
	Maximum of 6 marks	6
(b)	Description of Kaizen costing – up to 4 marks	
	Comparison of standard costing with Kaizen costing – 1 mark for each relevant point, up to 3 marks	
	Effect of Kaizen costing on employee management – 1 mark for each relevant point, up to 3 marks	
	Maximum of 8 marks	8
(c)	Description of JIT purchasing and production – up to 2 marks	
	Benefits of JIT for Tench – 1 mark for each relevant point, up to 2 marks	
	Problems of introducing JIT at Tench – 1 mark for each relevant point, up to 3 marks	
	Maximum of 6 marks	6
(d)	Explanation of importance of TQM – up to 2 marks for each relevant and fully explained point, up to 5 marks	5
		Total = 25

(a) **Quality costs hidden** – It is likely that Tench's quality costs are currently hidden within overheads and the standard costing system. Tench's quality costs are likely to relate to: designing and developing quality control equipment; inspection and performance testing; and repairs and reworking. The current costing system will need to be modified to allow Tench to view its quality costs separately.

The quality costs can be categorised into two groups:

Costs of conformance – These are the costs of achieving the desired quality standards.

They will include **prevention costs** (such as staff training and building quality into the design of the cars and Tench's business processes) aimed at preventing cars being rejected on the grounds of poor quality.

They will also include **appraisal costs** such as the costs of inspecting components coming in from suppliers and inspecting the cars while they are being built and once they are completed.

Costs of non-conformance – These are the costs which arise if Tench's cars do not meet the required quality standards. They will include internal failure costs and external failure costs.

Internal failure costs arise if a fault is identified before a car leaves the factory and has to be rectified. **External failure costs** arise if the fault is identified by the customer once they have bought the car. External failure costs could include both the cost of repairing cars returned from customers and the administration costs of maintaining a customer complaints department.

Opportunity costs

There could also be opportunity costs related to quality which are not currently recognised by Tench; for example, the loss of possible future sales resulting from dissatisfied customers, or the impact on the manufacturing process of having to repair faults rather than working on new cars.

Impact of quality on Tench's costing systems

Tench's management appear to have already recognised the need to focus more on the quality of their cars in order to compete with the new (foreign) entrants into the market.

However, identifying and collecting quality costs will reinforce the importance of quality, and will sustain management's focus on quality. In addition, applying the logic that 'What gets measured, gets done', the focus on quality should allow Tench to make the quality improvements it needs to compete more effectively with the new imports.

Traditional view of quality

The discussion of costs of conformance and non-conformance represents the traditional view of quality which suggests that there is an optimal effort that minimises quality faults, although it never entirely eliminates them. This approach recognises that there is a trade-off between the costs of conformance and non-conformance, up to a point where the cost of reducing the error rate any further is greater than the benefit from preventing that additional fault.

(b)   **Kaizen costing** – In contrast to traditional costing systems which focus on **cost control**, Kaizen costing systems focus on **cost reduction**.

Kaizen costing involves a process of **continuous improvement** in which the costs of producing a product are constantly reduced over the product's life.

Functional analysis is applied at the design stage of a new product, and a **target cost for each function** is set. The functional target costs are added together and the total becomes the **product target cost**.

Once the product has been in production for a year, the actual cost of the first year becomes the starting point for further cost reduction in the second year, and so on into subsequent years.

Impact of Kaizen approach at Tench

Kaizen costing vs standard costing – Tench currently applies the standard costing system, where the focus is on **cost control** rather than **cost reduction**.

However, because Kaizen focuses on continuous improvement and cost reduction, standard costs have much less value for monitoring performance as they are fixed over the relevant period. However, the nature of Kaizen costing means that the 'standard' costs themselves should be reduced over time.

Therefore, the impact of introducing Kaizen costing at Tench is likely to be significant. Whereas standard costing doesn't provide any motivation to improve performance levels, the whole focus of Kaizen costing is on cost reduction and performance improvement.

Employee management

Attitude to employees – Kaizen costing will also have a significant impact on employee management at Tench, because the **management attitude to employees** will be different under Kaizen compared to a standard costing approach.

In standard costing systems, employees are often viewed as the **cause of problems** in an organisation. Under Kaizen, employees are viewed as the **source of solutions**, and they are **empowered** to find, and implement, these solutions.

Culture change – This idea of employee empowerment indicates the way that changing the costing system will also lead to a major **cultural change** at Tench. Tench appears to have a history of bureaucratic control, but now employee teams will be empowered to make changes themselves rather than having to have them approved by a management hierarchy first.

Implementing Kaizen – In time, the Kaizen system should increase staff motivation through empowerment. However, in the shorter term there could be difficulties in encouraging workers who are used to a command and control structure to change their behaviour and suggest possible improvements themselves.

(c) **Demand–pull system** – The essence of JIT systems is that they are demand–pull systems, rather than supply–push ones. Materials are only purchased (JIT purchasing), and finished products are only produced (JIT production) as needed to meet actual customer demand.

This is in contrast to traditional manufacturing systems in which manufacturers forecast demand for their products in the future and then try to smooth out production to meet that forecast demand.

Effect on Tench

Benefits of JIT systems – However, one of the main characteristics of traditional manufacturing systems is that they lead to high levels of inventory being held. By contrast, by only producing goods as they are needed, JIT systems significantly reduce **inventory levels, factory floor space required** and **reduce working capital requirements**, all of which could be beneficial to Tench.

Moving to a JIT system should also make Tench's **production processes more flexible** and should **reduce** throughput times, leading to faster response times to changes in product specification or customer demands.

Potential drawbacks of JIT systems

Supplier reliability – In order to implement JIT successfully, Tench will need to be able to rely on its supplier. With no inventories to fall back on, any disruption in supplies (in relation to either the quality or timeliness of deliveries) could force production to cease, which is likely to be costly for Tench.

If there is not already a **JIT culture** in Essland, it may be difficult for Tench to find **suppliers** who are capable of meeting the required **quality and delivery standards** needed to run a JIT system.

Performance measures

Quality measures/supplier performance – The increased importance of quality and reliability which are necessary in JIT systems means that Tench's performance measures will need to include quality measures, and will need to monitor supplier performance in delivering the quality required.

Multi-skilled teams – Another feature of JIT production is that teams are multi-skilled. Teams need to be formed to work by component or product rather than by the type of work performed. This means that **functional divisions of cost** become less appropriate. By contrast, performance measures focusing on **spare capacity** or **bottlenecks** in production are likely to become more important. Also, as staff will need training to work in the new teams, measures surrounding the **amount and effectiveness of training** will be required.

(d) **JIT systems incorporate:**

   (i) **JIT production**, which is a system driven by demand for finished products so that work in progress is only processed through a stage of production when it is needed by the next stage. The result is **minimal** (or in some cases non-existent) **inventories of work in progress and finished goods.**

   (ii) **JIT purchasing**, which seeks to match the usage of materials with the delivery of materials from external suppliers. This means that **material inventories** can be kept at **near-zero levels.**

   Production management within a JIT environment therefore needs to **eliminate scrap and defective units** during production and **avoid the need for reworking of units. Defects stop** the **production line**, creating **rework** and possibly resulting in a **failure to meet delivery dates** (as **buffer inventories** of work in progress and finished goods are **not held**). TQM should ensure that the **correct product** is made to the **appropriate level of quality** on the **first pass through production.**

   For JIT purchasing to be successful, the organisation must have confidence that the **supplier** will **deliver on time** and will deliver **materials of 100% quality**, and that there will be no rejects, returns and hence **no consequent production delays**. This confidence can be achieved by **adopting supplier quality assurance schemes** and stringent **procedures for acceptance and inspection of goods inwards**, which are integral parts of TQM.

33 Pitlane

Workbook reference. Target costing and Kaizen costing are discussed in Chapter 11 of the Workbook.

Top tips.

Part (a). Although we often tell you that the majority of the marks in Advanced Performance Management relate to analysis and evaluation, calculations are still an important part of performance management – and therefore you should still expect there to be some calculations in the exam. All 6 of the marks for part (a) of this question relate to calculation.

The calculations themselves should not be difficult, but you need to work carefully through the scenario and the Appendices to gather relevant information; for example, a 15% net profit margin is required (fourth paragraph of the scenario); and there is a 10% uplift on the basic price (Appendix 1).

Note that you are asked to calculate the gap for each of the three years, so it would be sensible to lay out your answer in a three column format, with one column for each year.

You should then be able to slot in the relevant figures, in a format something like this:

Price	x
Margin required	(x)
Target cost	x
Expected cost	(x)
Cost gap	**x**

Part (b). The process of calculating the cost gap in part (a) should have reminded you how the process of target costing works:

- Set an acceptable price
- Determine the required margin
- Derive the cost

Thinking about these general principles could be a useful starting point for tackling this requirement. But note the requirement asks you to 'Advise on the extent to which target costing could help...' so, as well as the potential benefits of target costing, you also need to identify factors which could reduce the extent to which it could help.

For example, identifying a target cost up front will allow management to Pitlane's managers to assess whether Booster can be produced for that price. If it can't, are there any ways to reduce cost?

However, the target cost ultimately depends on the price set. How does the uncertainty over price (for example, Pitlane's ability to charge 10% more than its competitors) affect the extent to which target costing could help Pitlane achieve the 15% net profit margin required by the shareholders?

Part (c). A useful starting point here might be to think about key features of Kaizen costing – continuous improvement – and then identify how this could be important for the Booster project. For example, Appendix 1 shows that average price is expected to fall over the three years, so Pitlane will also need to reduce costs to maintain the 15% profit margin.

The penultimate paragraph in the scenario also identifies that 'staff have never been encouraged to suggest any ways to improve the manufacturing process.' How would this situation be different under a Kaizen costing approach?

Examining team's comments. Part (a) required a basic calculation of the cost gap. Many candidates scored well on this part. However, a significant number chose to present their answers using absolute figures rather than 'per unit'. This is not only a failure to answer the question requirement, but it also illustrates a lack of understanding about the application of the method, where per unit calculations are most helpful.

Part (b). Candidates scored reasonably well on this part but often failed to score as many marks as they could because they did not analyse all the problems areas mentioned in the scenario. The scenario will often provide hints of areas to consider in an answer, and good candidates use these to efficiently compile high marks in the longer parts of questions.

Tutorial note. The Examining team's comment about using the hints in the scenarios is a very important piece of advice which applies to many, if not all, of the scenario questions in Advanced Performance Management.

Marking scheme

		Marks
(a)	Calculations:	
	Estimated unit selling price – 1 mark	
	Less: 15% net profit – 1 mark	
	Target total cost per unit – 1 mark	
	Less: Fixed cost per unit – 1 mark	
	Target direct cost per unit – 1 mark	
	Cost gap – 1 mark	
	Total for part (a): up to 6	6
(b)	General description of target costing – up to 2 marks	
	Advice on target costing for Pitlane – 1 mark per relevant point	
	Comments about additional revenue generated from features – up to 2 marks	
	Total for part (b): up to 12	12
(c)	General description of Kaizen costing – up to 2 marks	
	Advice on using Kaizen costing at Pitlane – 1 mark per relevant point	
	Total for part (c): up to 7	7
		Total = 25

(a) Calculate cost gap for each of the three years of the Booster's life

	20X8	20X9	20Y0
	$	$	$
Basic selling price	180.0	170.0	160.0
10% uplift for features/packaging	18.0	17.0	16.0
Estimated selling price	198.0	187.0	176.0
Less: 15% net profit	(29.7)	(28.1)	(26.4)
Target cost per unit	168.3	159.0	149.6
Current expected cost			
Estimated total direct cost per unit	134.0	134.0	134.0
Estimated fixed cost per unit (see Working)	44.1	44.1	44.1
Estimated total cost per unit	178.1	178.1	178.1
Cost gap	**9.8**	**19.2**	**28.5**

Working: Fixed cost per unit

Fixed overhead cost per unit   = Total fixed overheads/Number of units sold
= $10,000,000/227,000
= $44.05

(b)

> **Tutorial note.** The solution for part (b) is a detailed solution showing the range of relevant points which could have been included, for tutorial purposes. Candidates were not expected to produce a solution as detailed as this.

Target costing

Pitlane currently operates a traditional cost plus pricing method, where customers pay a fixed mark up on Pitlane's standard cost. This has been appropriate because the components currently produced have been manufactured in the same way for some time and their cost structure is well understood. Actual costs of production are very close to the standard costs. There is little competition in the market for Pitlane's current products, as a long-term contract was recently renewed with its biggest customer.

In contrast, for the proposed Booster product, the market price is only estimated. To compete with similar products, the Booster will need to sell at a price reflecting that of competitors' products, taking into account the different benefits and quality which each product has.

Target costing begins with taking the price which the market will pay for the product for a given market share. From that, the required profit margin is deducted to arrive at a target cost. The difference between the estimated cost for the product and the target cost is the cost gap. Where the estimated costs exceed the target cost, steps are taken to reduce the cost gap. The product can then be sold at a price which the market will accept, and which generates an acceptable profit margin.

Determining the market price

Pitlane's marketing department has estimated the average market price of competitors' products and the likely market share over the three years of the scheme. The estimates are based on the success of a similar scheme in Veeland, and the assumptions used could be incorrect. Electricity prices may already be higher in Veeland than in Deeland, meaning consumers there would reduce their energy costs more by installing solar panels. Similarly, consumers in Veeland could save more on energy costs if there is more sunshine there than in Deeland, enabling solar panels to generate more energy. Both factors would, in this case, reduce the take up of subsidies by consumers in Deeland and the amount they would be willing to pay for solar panels.

The domestic solar energy market is new in Deeland, and Pitlane has no experience in estimating market share or price for this type of product. Pitlane's belief that consumers would be willing to pay a 10% premium for highest quality packaging, or for the Booster to communicate with consumers' mobile phones, may be incorrect.

Calculating the target cost using the required profit margin

Pitlane charges a 15% profit margin on its existing projects. The shareholders' financial objective indicates that they require the same profit margin to be earned on Booster.

For its existing products, Pitlane can set a selling price based on its own costs, whereas the Booster's price must reflect external market conditions more closely. Target costing will focus Pitlane on the external environment by considering prices and relative benefits of competitors' products.

Estimating the total costs of Booster

The total direct costs of Booster have been estimated at $134.00. The fixed overhead per unit relating to Booster for the three years of the scheme is $44.05, making total estimated costs per unit of $178.05. The cost estimates may be incorrect, especially as Booster is new, and different from Pitlane's existing products. As Booster includes costs which are fixed, estimating sales volumes is also crucial in determining costs per unit.

Pitlane has no recent experience of developing new products or of estimating costs and sales volumes for them. This makes it more likely that the cost estimates for the Booster will be incorrect. Estimating the total costs is needed for the next stage in the target costing process, to identify the cost gap.

Reducing the cost gap

A big advantage for Pitlane of using target costing is that it is often easier to reduce costs of a product at the design stage rather than after it has entered production.

As Boosters are not sold directly to consumers, the buyers of the product, who are professional installers, may not see value in the highest quality packaging. This could be a significant yet unnecessary cost, to be eliminated at the design stage. In deciding what costs to eliminate, Pitlane will have to take into account the effect of these on the quality and perception of the final product.

The features where the Booster can communicate with consumers' smartphones, and the use of highest quality packaging, are believed to enable Pitlane to charge 10% more than competitors' products. The $3.8m (see Working below) of estimated additional total revenue from the packaging and smartphone features may not justify the $2.8m upfront development costs for the smartphone feature alone, especially if the time value of money were to be taken into account. Consumers may not value these two features or be prepared to pay more for them. Eliminating them would therefore have little effect on sales volumes and would enable Pitlane to charge a more competitive price, or obtain higher gross profit margins.

Due to damage of sub-components when assembling the prototype, the estimated assembly labour cost assumes highly skilled labour will be used. This is 30% more expensive than other labour. By providing additional training, lower paid labour could be used to produce the Booster, and hence reduce the cost gap.

Pitlane plans to purchase the four main sub-components in bulk from six different suppliers. Consolidating suppliers, or using suppliers in lower cost countries, could help reduce the cost gap by reducing purchase costs. Moving to a just-in-time (JIT) production system, rather than buying supplies in bulk, would help reduce costs of holding inventory as suppliers would only deliver sub-components when needed. This may increase other costs such as by requiring investment in information technology. It would also take time to develop the close relationship required with suppliers.

Another source of waste is due to internal transport and handling, which forms over 5% of the total direct cost of the Booster. This will also increase production cycle times, and is an unnecessary process which does not add value. It could be eliminated by changing the layout of the factory, or reorganising production into teams and ensuring all production was done at a single factory, rather than in both of Pitlane's factories.

Working: Additional revenue from smartphone feature and highest quality packaging

20X8: 60,000 units × $198 = $11,880,000
20X9: 75,000 units × $187 = $14,025,000
20Y8: 92,000 units × $176 = $16,192,000

Total revenue (over 3 years) = $42,097,000

10% premium = $42,097,000 × 10/110 = $3,827,000

(c) **Kaizen costing**

Unlike target costing, which occurs at the beginning of a product's life, Kaizen costing is a process of long-term continuous improvement by cost reduction throughout the life of the product.

The Booster will be produced only for the three years during which the Deeland Government offers subsidies and tax incentives. Generally, Kaizen costing is used over longer periods, and it is likely the full benefits of this approach will not be achieved in such a short timescale. The target cost is the starting point for Kaizen costing. After production begins, each period's target is based on the previous period's reduced costs.

Target costing can achieve large cost reductions at the design stage of the product, eg by choosing not to develop the smartphone feature. Kaizen costing, however, reduces costs in much smaller, incremental steps.

The need for continuous improvement

Even though Booster's share of the market rises over the three years of the project, the market price falls, as does the size of the market. This means that in order to achieve the shareholders' financial targets, the direct costs of the Booster must fall over the three years. Continual incremental improvements using Kaizen costing, and measuring these improvements against targets from the previous period rather than the original estimated cost, could help to achieve this.

Ways to reduce waste using Kaizen costing

Traditional costing methods often see employees as the cause of high costs, whereas Kaizen costing sees the employees as a source of ideas on how to reduce costs. The Manufacturing Director's comments, that the damage caused by employees to delicate sub-components may mean it may not be possible to produce the Booster, indicates that Pitlane is currently following the traditional approach. Employees are seen as the source of the waste.

To benefit from Kaizen costing, Pitlane must undergo a culture change to encourage employees to suggest ideas, perhaps using quality circles, to reduce costs. That way, improvements could be made in the way sub-components are assembled during production, which would shorten the production cycle and lead to a reduced cost of scrapped items.

34 Thebe

> **Workbook reference.** Quality issues and Six Sigma are considered in Chapter 11 of the Workbook.
>
> **Top tips.**
>
> **Part (a).** The scenario highlighted that customer service is likely to be key to helping the business grow. However, the absence of any non-financial information in the performance report presented to the board suggests that the board isn't monitoring customer service levels.
>
> You should have identified that this seems odd, given the importance of customer service to the business's success. But, if the non-financial performance information was included in the performance report alongside financial information, this would help redress the balance.
>
> **Parts (b) and (c)** of this question provide a good illustration of why it is important to read all the requirements before starting to answer a question.
>
> In **part (b)** of the question you are asked to discuss the general ways in which Six Sigma could help improve quality. You shouldn't spend time discussing **how** Six Sigma is implemented in this part of the question, but rather how the process of implementing Six Sigma (in general terms) improves the quality of performance in an organisation.

The reason why you shouldn't discuss how Six Sigma is implemented in part (b) becomes clear when you look at part (c) of the requirement: to explain and illustrate how the DMAIC method could be applied at Thebe.

Part (c). A sensible approach to this question would be to use 'DMAIC' as the framework of your answer, and then to work through each of the elements (Define, Measure etc) in turn.

However, note that you aren't asked simply to explain DMAIC in general terms, but to illustrate how it could be applied specifically at Thebe, so make sure you include examples of issues from the scenario.

Examining team's comments. Part (b) was poorly answered, with much evidence of candidates trying to use DMAIC as a template for their answer, although the question asked about the Six Sigma method in general rather than a specific implementation method. This was possibly caused by candidates not reading the whole question before starting to plan their answer, and not identifying the links between parts (b) and (c).

Marking scheme

		Marks
(a)	1 mark per relevant point up to 2 marks for each benefit of non-financial performance measures evaluated	
	Up to 8 marks	8
(b)	1 mark per relevant point up to 2 marks for each way Six Sigma can improve performance	
	Up to 8 marks	8
(c)	Up to 3 marks for each stage of the DMAIC process; being 1 mark for a general description and 2 marks for application to the scenario	
	Up to 9 marks	9
		Total = 25

(a) **Importance of non-financial measures** – The CEO has identified that customer service is crucial in growing the business and differentiating it from competitors (such as FayTel) which suggests that providing excellent customer service is a critical success factor for Thebe.

By performing well in this area of the business, Thebe should be better placed to perform well financially than if it offers poor customer service.

In this case, there would seem to be a clear link between non-financial performance and financial performance. However, if the board is not aware of how well Thebe is performing in key operational (non-financial) areas of the business they may not notice performance issues which could subsequently have an impact on Thebe's financial performance.

What gets measured gets done – Thebe's employees and line managers are likely to pay more attention to those areas of the business in which performance is being measured, compared to those areas which are not being measured.

Similarly, there is a danger that what doesn't get measured, might not get done. The focus of the board meetings, on financial performance, suggests that this might be prioritised over non-financial aspects of performance.

However, the fact that the CEO has championed the project to improve billing accuracy suggests that he believes it is important. In turn, however, this suggests Thebe should be measuring its performance in relation to billing accuracy – for example, through measuring the number of complaints it receives from customers who are complaining that they have been billed incorrectly.

Information for decision making and control – The current position suggests that it could be difficult for the board to know how to improve Thebe's performance, if it does not have adequate information about its current performance. Although the CEO is aware that all telephone businesses (including Thebe) have problems in relation to applying incorrect tariffs, it seems unlikely that he will have any actual information about how Thebe is performing in this area of the business.

Again, having this information would have been useful before deciding to undertake the project to improve the quality and accuracy of billing – both to decide whether the project was necessary and to see how much impact the project has on the quality of Thebe's billing.

Linkages – However, directors will need to be careful which non-financial measures they choose to monitor, and in particular how the non-financial measures link to Thebe's financial performance. For example, there will be little value in monitoring aspects of operational performance which add little value to Thebe's financial performance. Indeed, the CEO may find that, ultimately, customers choose their telephone provider based on price rather than the quality of customer service they receive.

In this respect, it is also important that the directors continue to monitor financial performance as well as non-financial performance, because there is no guarantee that favourable performance in customer service or other non-financial areas will necessarily translate into favourable financial performance. For example, even though Thebe may provide its customers with accurate bills, and may provide a very high level of customer service, its revenues may still fall if FayTel introduces new tariffs so that customers can get a cheaper phone service by switching to them.

Despite the increased importance of non-financial performance measures, the ultimate measure of Thebe's performance will be how well it generates financial value for its owners.

(b)   **Focus on the customer** – One of the key aspects of Six Sigma methodology is that it requires organisations to have a genuine focus on the customer. Thebe's CEO has clearly identified that customer service is crucial to the success of the business, and so the project to improve customers' bills is an important element of this.

Importance of facts and data – Another important element of Six Sigma is that it highlights that decisions should be taken on the basis of facts and data, rather than intuition, and this in turn highlights the importance of performance measurement.

This is evident at Thebe in the way that data has been sourced from customer feedback. This data could relate, for example, to the number of customer complaints, or to customer satisfaction ratings.

Business process improvement – One of the key themes in Six Sigma is that processes are the key to success. Therefore implementing Six Sigma will encourage Thebe to identify which processes (and which activities within a process) are critical to its success, so that it can then focus on understanding those processes and improving them where necessary.

Involvement of management – When an organisation commits to Six Sigma, it will normally appoint an implementation leader and a steering committee at a senior level, to oversee the implementation. By involving management in this way it highlights a business's commitment to improving quality; as appears to be the case at Thebe where the CEO is championing the project to improve service quality.

Increased profile of quality issues – Six Sigma project teams are made up of staff experienced in the process under review. By involving team members in the project, they will realise the importance of quality issues, and improve their knowledge of quality management.

The nature of Six Sigma **project leadership** means that managers should learn from working with layers of trained experts. For example, line managers who are 'Green Belts' helping to lead a Six Sigma project can learn from 'Master Black Belts'.

Collaboration – Another key theme in Six Sigma projects is the need for collaboration between staff from across different departments or divisions within an organisation. In this way, Six Sigma implementation highlights the importance of the whole organisation focusing on quality, not just individual departments. For example, the project team at

Thebe brings together line managers from all three business units, as well as from the billing department.

(c) **Define customer requirements/Define the problem**

Customers' underlying requirement is that they are billed accurately, and if they aren't this could lead either to delayed revenue (while the customers dispute their bills) or lost revenue (if customers switch to an alternative provider).

However, the organisational structure at Thebe highlights that this project also needs to focus on complaint handling as well as billing itself, and in this respect customer requirements may need to be defined further. It is likely that there will be a minimum acceptable level of service (for example, that billing errors are corrected), but Thebe should identify ways which its customers feel would improve its service above that minimum level: for example, in relation to how quickly any complaints are responded to; or by offering some form of compensation as a goodwill gesture.

Measure existing performance

The CEO's customer service project has highlighted two key areas of focus: the accuracy of customers' bills, and the handling of complaints.

Accordingly, Thebe needs information to assess how well it is performing in both of these areas; so it needs to measure its performance in both areas. For example, Thebe could measure the number of customer complaints per million bills issued, or the average time it takes to resolve a customer complaint fully. (Measures such as looking at the number of complaints links directly to Six Sigma methodology which identified that there should be less than six defects per million.)

However, when selecting the aspects of performance to measure, it is important that Thebe focuses on those areas where improvement will be valued by the customer, rather than, for example, areas which are easy to measure.

Analyse the existing process

In part (a) we identified that the Six Sigma methodology highlights the importance of facts and data, rather than intuition. This stage of the DMAIC process focuses on collecting the data, which can then be analysed to identify the root causes of problems in Thebe's existing processes.

Thebe can then focus its improvements towards those issues which lead to the most problems (complaints). If a relatively small number of problems give rise to the majority of complaints, then this will highlight the importance of tackling the causes of those problems as the most urgent priority. For example, if a large proportion of customer complaints relate to the length of time it takes Thebe to issue revised bills, then it will be important to analyse what factors are slowing down the process.

Improve the process

Once the causes of problems have been analysed, Thebe should then be able to identify potential changes which could be made to improve performance in these areas of its business. For example, in relation to the time taken to reissue corrected bills, Thebe may need to consider whether it needs more staff to be authorised to make changes to bills.

However, before any specific improvements are recommended it will be important for Thebe to check that they are feasible; for example, that they will not be prohibitively expensive to implement, and that Thebe has the resources necessary to implement them.

Control the process

Once the improvements have been implemented, the line managers (and the board) need to continue to monitor performance to ensure that the benefits from reduced complaints and improved customer satisfaction are maintained.

At an operational level, Thebe can do this by continuing to monitor complaint numbers – perhaps by means of exception reporting, so that managers are only alerted of a potential issue if the number of complaints increases above a specified threshold level.

However, Thebe can also measure its success in relation to customer service levels more generally in relation to customer retention rates or the churn rate (the percentage of existing customers lost each year).

If the company has successfully improved its performance in those areas which customers value as important, then the number of customers who switch to another service provider should be reduced. This in turn will mean that a greater proportion of the new customers which Thebe acquires will contribute to growing the business rather than replacing lapsed existing customers.

35 Posie

Workbook reference. Quality management and Six Sigma are discussed in Chapter 11 of the Workbook. Responsibility centres are covered in Chapter 8, while information systems and performance reports are discussed in Chapter 6.

Top tips.

Part (a). Arguably the most important words in the requirement are 'could be implemented'. This is because they indicate that the advice you need to give the board is about how the project could be implemented; not how Six Sigma could help Posie to reduce the level of returns from customers.

The specific reference in the requirement to the 'DMAIC' methodology should help you structure your answer. If you use each of the five elements of 'DMAIC' as headings to provide a framework for your answer, you can then assess the activities which Posie needs to undertake at each phase of the project.

Note, however, that the marking scheme indicates that there were more marks available for advice given in relation to the 'define' and 'measure' phases of DMAIC than for the other three. The CEO's concerns about the quality of Posie's data should have alerted you to the fact that 'measurement' of performance is currently an issue at Posie. This, in turn, is reflected in the marking scheme – where up to six marks are available for advising on the 'measure' phase of DMAIC.

Part (b) (i). The last paragraph of the scenario sets up the context for this requirement – identifying that the data generated by Posie's current IT systems isn't sufficient to identify which responsibility centres are the root cause of the problem of customer returns. This reference should highlight the need to produce performance information at a responsibility centre level.

However, the requirement is not only about responsibility centres; you should also think more generally about the qualities of good performance reports (eg level of detailed provided, timeliness) and whether the current returns data enables Posie's management team to manage returns effectively.

Part (b) (ii). It should be obvious that re-designating the overseas subsidiaries as revenue centres means that their managers will only be held accountable for their revenue (rather than for revenues and costs, as they currently are). Hence, performance data will need to focus on revenues. However, simply stating this one point is only likely to earn you one mark (and there are up to four marks available here). So, you also need to think more widely here: for example, even though the divisional managers' focus will be on revenue, there will still be costs associated with operating the subsidiaries. How will these be recorded and controlled?

Examining team's comments. The standard of candidates' responses to part (a) was mixed, but responses to part (b) were, generally speaking, quite poor.

Part (a) asked how a Six Sigma project could be implemented using DMAIC methodology. The use of DMAIC methodology was central to this requirement but some candidates demonstrated little knowledge about how it worked. These candidates scored very few, if any, marks.

Candidates who explained the DMAIC methodology scored a few marks, but the majority of the marks in this question were earned by applying the methodology to the scenario. One of the main shortcomings in many answers was a failure to recognise properly how to relate the data given to each part of the methodology (ie define, measure, analyse, improve, control) and how this all connected to customer requirements and expectations.

Part (b) (i) was answered poorly overall, as many candidates did not read the requirement properly and offered responses which considered the impact that identifying and improving the level of customer returns could have on the organisation's performance. Such responses scored few marks, because the question asked specifically about the impact on the organisation's information requirements.

The impact of Six Sigma projects and a DMAIC methodology on information requirements can be fundamental – in particular, in relation to the 'measure' and 'analyse' aspects of DMAIC.

More generally, candidates sitting APM need to be aware of the impact that new initiatives or developments could have on the information requirements in an organisation. For example, if a project is introduced, what information will be required to measure its performance? Can the organisation's systems provide the information required? How will the information be captured?

Part (b) (ii) was also answered very poorly. Few candidates attempted this question in a meaningful way, and many failed to differentiate between the two types of responsibility centre.

Marking scheme

			Marks
(a)		Use of DMAIC	
		Define – 1 mark per point – up to 4 marks	
		Measure – 1 mark per point – up to 6 marks	
		Analyse; Improve; Control – 1 mark per point – up to 3 marks for each heading	
		Total for part (a): up to 15	15
(b)	(i)	Definition of responsibility centres – 1 mark	
		Impact on information requirements of the need for greater detail about customer returns – 1 mark per relevant point; up to a maximum of 6	
		Total for part (b) (i): up to 6	6
	(ii)	Impact on information requirements due to the re-designating overseas subsidiaries as revenue centres – 1 mark per relevant point; up to a maximum of 4	
		Total for part (b) (ii): up to 4	4
		Total =	25

(a)   The DMAIC process is a technique used to implement Six Sigma to improve existing processes. It is split into five phases as described below.

Define the problem

The CEO is concerned that the increase in returns from customers is increasing costs and threatens to affect the Posie brand.

Six Sigma focuses closely on the requirements of the customer, and it is important for Posie to be clear exactly what customers' requirements are, and specifically why products are returned.

The objective of the project needs to be clear – in this case to reduce the number of customer returns.

Customers will expect certain minimum requirements from the manufacturing and packaging process, for example, that they can assemble the furniture properly and all the necessary components for them to be able to do this are included in the box. Customers will also expect the goods to be delivered undamaged within a reasonable time, and at the time and date promised when the order was placed. Customers' perceptions of quality should correspond to the price paid, though different customers will have different expectations of this.

Beyond this basic requirement, there may be aspects of the manufacturing product which further enhance the customers' experience of the product, and presumably of the Posie brand. Customers may be particularly pleased with furniture which is delivered early or at a time especially convenient to them, or which is robust, durable and 'well made'. These perceptions are subjective, and may equally relate to design or the quality of raw materials as to the manufacturing process. By identifying where the products exceed customers' expectations, it may be possible to focus more on these aspects in the future. While products which significantly exceed customers' expectations will enhance the Posie brand, it may also indicate a quality of manufacture which is too high and allow Posie to reduce manufacturing costs in accordance with its cost leadership strategy whilst still having mainly satisfied customers.

Measure the existing process

The current returns figures do give some data to as to why products are returned, but their usefulness is limited as it is unclear which of the categories relate to defective manufacture, and which relate to activities of other divisions. The ambiguity of the data and category definitions will need addressing to enable the process to be measured effectively.

Returns in Category 1 could be because the goods were not manufactured or packed properly in the Manufacturing Division, but could also be due to poor design, or customers losing components or simply being unable to assemble furniture.

Damaged goods in Category 2 probably do not arise because of defective manufacturing either, though customers may wrongly categorise defective goods as damaged. For the other categories it is less clear. Though goods may become damaged by the distribution company, it seems that only a small number of returns relate directly to them.

Returns in Categories 3 and 4 could be due to defective manufacture or if the customer had simply changed their minds and no longer wanted the product. In Category 3, the identification of 'defective' items is too broad.

Returns in Category 5 which arrived late are clearly not due to manufacturing defects and, as this causes only 2% of returns, is relatively insignificant.

Currently 10% of Posie's sales are of products from other manufacturers. There is no indication from the data given how many of the returns relate to these products, nor of the total number of returns relative to the number of items sold.

Therefore the existing data are insufficient to reliably measure existing performance and take no account of inputs such as raw materials. Only items which customers value should be measured. The CEO has suggested more detailed data are required, for example, on overall customer satisfaction with the manufacturing, but this is at 93% which already seems high and there is little point in incurring costs to measure what customers are already satisfied with. In the context of the Six Sigma project at Posie, there is little that can be done to improve this particular area and such items should not be measured.

Analyse the process

This stage is where the root causes of the problems are identified. Additional information may be needed, for example, to analyse customer returns by type of product, by country of sale or with a clearer definition of what is meant by 'defective'. By doing so, Posie may identify areas of the business where customer returns are particularly high and so be able to focus on these.

Improve the process

At this stage the proposals for improving the process are implemented and availability of resources and likely costs of making the improvements need to be carefully considered. Posie may need to consider which aspects of the production or packaging process could be improved, for example, by better maintenance or calibration of machinery. Additional training of staff may also be required.

Control

This is the ongoing monitoring that the reduction in customer returns due to defective manufacturing is being maintained. Reporting on the number of returns may be done by exception if they reach a particular level. In Posie, it seems likely that the data on customer returns used to manage this process will need to be redesigned to make it clearer in which responsibility centre the problems arise. The ongoing monitoring may indicate that some of the earlier stages in the DMAIC process need to be revisited.

(b) (i) The CEO wants to identify which responsibility centres are the root causes of the problem of customer returns. A responsibility centre is a part of the business where a manager has specific authority and accountability for its performance and so Posie will need information relating to aspects of performance specific to the centre. For example, performance data relating to the reasons for customer returns need to be clearly segregated between responsibility centres. Currently, the information compiled on customer returns does not do this and some categories of return may result from manufacturing defects but some will be from problems outside the Manufacturing Division, or even outside Posie itself, for example, from poor quality raw materials purchased externally, or because of late deliveries or damaged goods caused by the distribution company.

Once information has been analysed and responsibility has been identified, then the managers of those areas will need the information drilled down into even further, as in order to improve they need to know which specific areas they can control. It would be unfair to make managers responsible for aspects of performance which they are unable to control, and the board member responsible for manufacturing quality has recently resigned because of this.

Posie needs to ensure it produces performance data to an appropriate level of detail so as not to overload the users with too much data. For board level reporting, the information in the current board reporting pack may be too detailed and it would be sufficient just to produce summary data on the overall level of returns relative to sales. Responsibility centres would need much more detailed information, perhaps even down to product or production line level.

However, Posie should also consider the costs and resources required to provide more detailed performance data. Given Posie's cost leadership strategy, the costs of data collection may outweigh the benefits of doing so.

Performance data should be provided at an appropriate frequency. For the Posie main board, monthly reporting may be sufficient to alert them to any problems. Responsibility centres will need much more frequent, even daily or weekly, details of the levels of customer returns so that they can react quickly to any problems identified. At the moment, the returns data are compiled every six months, possibly due to the difficulties in obtaining data from the IT systems in the overseas businesses. Even for a board level report, this seems much too infrequent.

(ii) At the moment, the overseas subsidiaries are being designated as profit centres and managers will be held accountable for both revenues and costs. As they do not manufacture, it seems reasonable to designate them as revenue centres. As such, managers would be held accountable for just revenues as they have little or no control over costs as most goods for resale are purchased from the Manufacturing Division.

The performance data produced by Posie's subsidiaries' IT systems will therefore switch to focus more on revenues rather than costs. As revenue centres they may well have some freedom to change selling prices. Posie will need to ensure the subsidiaries have information to monitor the impact of different pricing strategies and will need to provide the management of these subsidiaries with information gleaned from the external environment. It will be important to evaluate competitors' pricing strategies when making pricing decisions.

A potential problem with providing only performance data relating to revenue is that managers could focus too much on achieving revenue targets rather than maintaining or improving profitability. As they are autonomous subsidiaries, there will be aspects of their own costs, such as staffing costs and other overheads, which they will be able to have some control over. It is important that Posie ensures the management still has sight of this information to ensure that such costs are still controlled effectively.

Furthermore, if the overseas managers are only held responsible for sales, this may mean they do not focus sufficiently on addressing reasons why goods are returned, and so levels of returns may increase. This means that once Posie undertakes the exercise to identify the root causes of the returns from customers, this information is shared and monitored.

Posie needs to be aware of these issues when determining information requirements if the reclassification of the subsidiaries goes ahead. It will not be as simple as assuming that they will now only need information on revenues.

36 Albacore

Workbook reference. Controllability and accountability are discussed in Chapters 3 and 8 of the Workbook. Performance management styles are discussed in Chapter 12.

Top tips.

Part (a). The scenario identifies that the budget in Albacore is imposed by the corporate centre and a number of costs are also controlled centrally. However, in terms of assessing a shop manager's performance, is it fair to assess them on factors they cannot control?

The current branch information measures the shop's performance, rather than the manager's performance. How would the branch information for the Tunny branch be different if it only included factors the manager could control? This should suggest the improvements you could make to the report in relation to the second part of the requirement – drafting an improved report.

Importantly, though, note that part (a) is **not** asking you to assess the performance of the branch manager; it is asking you to assess the **suitability of the information** as a means of appraising the shop manager's performance.

Part (b). In effect, there are three component parts to this requirement: (i) analyse the performance management style; (ii) evaluate the current performance appraisal system; and (iii) suggest suitable improvements to the reward system for the shop managers. To score well here, you need to address all the different parts of the requirement.

Marking scheme

Marks

(a)   Calculation and discussion of operation and planning variances – 1 mark
      per point, up to a maximum of 4

      Discussion of other variances – 1 mark per point, up to 2

      For highlighting the importance of measuring controllable costs – 1 mark

      Revised performance report distinguishing controllable and
      non-controllable costs – 1 mark

      For highlighting the importance of controllable profit as a measure of the
      manager's performance – 1 mark

      Total: up to 8 for suitability of existing report

      Alternative report – highlighting controllable costs, controllable profit –
      Up to 3

      Comments on report – including controllability, realistic budgets – 1 mark
      per point, up to 3

      Total: up to 5 for alternative report and justifications for changes
      Total: up to 13   13

(b) Analysis of performance management styles – 1 mark per relevant point, up to a maximum of 6

Evaluation of performance appraisal system – 1 mark per relevant point, up to a maximum of 6

Total: up to 12

12

Total = 25

(a) **Accountability** – The managers should only be held responsible for those aspects of performance they can control. However, the branch information does not appear to distinguish between the factors that the shop managers can control and those they can't, which suggests the information is unsuitable for assessing the managers' performance.

Budgets – If one measure of the manager's performance is comparing actual performance against budget, then it is important that the budgets are realistic and achievable.

The fall of 12% in sales across the industry as a whole suggests that the original shop budget (showing the same figures as the previous year) was unrealistic.

Although the shop shows an overall gross margin variance of $17,340 (adverse) based on the original budget, this can more usefully be split into **planning** and **operational** variances as follows:

Planning variance		$	
Original sales	(1)	266,000	
Revenue variance due to economic conditions (12%)	(2)	31,920	(A)
Gross profit variance (gross margin 60%)		**19,152**	(A)
Operational variance			
Actual sales		237,100	
Revised budgeted sales	(1)–(2)	234,080	
		3,020	(F)
Operational variance (gross margin 60%)		**1,812**	(F)

The operational variance more accurately reflects the shop manager's work in promoting sales, and here we can see that the manager's efforts have actually reduced the fall in gross profit by $1,812. The overall gross profit variance (of $17,340 adverse) comprises an adverse planning variance of $19,152 partially offset by a favourable operational variance of $1,812.

Discounting – One area where the managers have a degree of autonomy is in setting prices; for example, it is possible they could reduce the sales price of particular titles to boost sales of those titles. This is therefore an aspect of the manager's performance which could be measured, for example, by looking at the sales price and volume for individual product lines, and then looking at the impact of any promotions on gross profit.

The figures for the Tunny branch suggest that the manager has not made use of the discounting authority, though. The actual gross margin achieved for the year has remained constant with the budget (60%) but discounting would have led to a reduction in the margin percentage.

Controllable and non-controllable costs – A number of non-controllable costs are currently included in the manager's performance assessment. In particular, the shop manager will have very little scope to control **property costs**, as the shop heating, lighting and rental contracts will all be managed by the Central Purchasing Department. The shop managers may have some control over the amount of heat and light that are used in their shops, but the managers don't have any control over the unit prices paid for them.

Similarly the managers can't control their own wages. However, it is reasonable to classify the **part-time staff costs as controllable**. The managers manage the staffing for their shops, and so they could save on part-time staff costs by working longer hours themselves.

Consequently, a fairer way of assessing the shop managers' performance would be to distinguish costs into two groups: controllable (marketing; part-time staff) and non-controllable (managers' wages; property costs).

Controllable profit – Following on from this, a controllable profit could then be shown as well as the overall shop profit. The shop manager's performance should then be assessed on the controllable profit performance of their shop only.

If we apply this logic to Tunny branch, then instead of the shop manager facing an adverse variance of $12,840, she would have achieved a positive variance of $6,312, and would therefore have been entitled to a bonus, because she has actually been performing well in difficult economic circumstances.

Improved report

The revised report should split costs into two groups as we have suggested above (controllable, and non-controllable) to show the controllable profit as well as the shop's overall profit. In addition, it would be useful to analyse variances into operational (controllable) and planning (non-controllable) variances, because this enables a greater understanding of the causes of the variances.

Revised performance report

TUNNY BRANCH: YEAR TO SEPTEMBER 20X1

		Budget $	Actual $	Variance $	Planning variance $	Operational variance $
Sales		266,000	237,100	(28,900)		
Cost of sales		106,400	94,840	11,560		
Gross profit		159,600	142,260	(17,340)	(19,152)	1,812
Controllable costs						
Marketing		12,000	11,500	500		
Staff costs	Part-time staff	38,000	34,000	4,000		
Controllable profit		109,600	96,760	(12,840)	(19,152)	6,312
Non-controllable costs						
Staff costs	Manager	27,000	27,000	–		
Property costs		26,600	26,600	–		
Shop profit		56,000	43,160	(12,840)		

The report now highlights that if the gross profit planning variance ($19,152) is added back to the controllable profit (of −$12,840), the manager would have achieved a positive variance in her controllable profit of $6,312.

(b) **Budget-constrained style**

The performance management style at Albacore seems to be **budget-constrained style**, in which the predominant focus is a short-term one, centred around achieving the budget set.

This style can be seen in the way the shop managers' performance is primarily evaluated on their ability to meet the budgets set, even though the general economic conditions mean that the budgets are no longer realistic or achievable.

Job-related tension – One of the characteristics of the budget-constrained style is that it leads to job-related tensions and poor relations between staff and the managers. This appears to be the case at Albacore, where the shop managers have complained about the way they are managed and their remuneration.

Performance manipulation – The budget-constrained style can often motivate staff to manipulate performance reports to try to make it look as if they have achieved their budget targets. However, given the centralised nature of control at Albacore, it seems unlikely that any such performance manipulation would be possible at shop level.

Alternative performance management styles

Profit-conscious style – In contrast to the short-termist nature of a budget-constrained style, under a profit-conscious style, a manager's performance is evaluated in relation to their ability to increase the general **effectiveness of their business unit** in relation to the organisation's **long-term purposes**.

It is possible that such a style could be suitable for Albacore, given the management team's aim of running the business in order to maximise profits. However, the long-term perspective may be at odds with the venture capitalist's likely requirements.

Non-accounting style – Budget information is relatively unimportant in performance evaluation, and other non-financial factors are deemed to be more important.

Performance appraisal system

Reflects budget-constrained style – The performance appraisal system at Albacore reflects the budget-constrained management style in the business.

Lack of discussion and negotiation – The shop managers appear to have little or no opportunity to influence their shops' budgets; they are simply presented to the managers at their annual appraisals.

Despite this, the bonus criteria appear to be rigidly enforced. If the Tunny branch manager's experience is representative of the other managers, it appears that the failure to achieve budget has led to no bonus being paid at all.

This is despite the shop still being profitable (making an operating profit of $43,160), and the manager's **controllable profits actually being higher than budget** (see part (a)).

This total lack of discussion and flexibility in the appraisal system, along with the apparent lack of appreciation of the managers' efforts in difficult economic conditions, is likely to **demotivate them**, and this appears to be the case, with the managers (justifiably) calling the current system unfair.

Improvements to the reward system

Focus on controllable aspects of performance – As we have noted in part (a), the reward system should distinguish between the **manager's performance** and the **shop's performance**.

If the managers feel that they are being judged on aspects of performance they can control, this should help to **motivate them**, and hopefully as a result also improve their performance.

However, given that Albacore's aim is to maximise profits, it is still important to monitor the shop's performance overall as well as the manager's profits. One possible solution might be to base part of the manager's bonus on their own performance (controllable profit) while another part of it could be determined by the shop's performance overall.

Stepped bonuses – Although the current bonus is 'up to 30% of basic salary', it is not clear how this is calculated. The current system seems to have an 'all or nothing' approach under which managers get a bonus if their shop achieves budget, and they don't if it doesn't.

One way this system could be improved is by introducing a graded system. For example, the amount of bonus the managers get will be determined by actual profit as a percentage of budget, with the bonus amount increasing above certain trigger levels. For example, above 90% of budget = 3% bonus; above 95% of budget = 6% bonus; above 100% = 9% etc.

Budgets agreed – Rather than the annual budget being determined centrally and then imposed on the shop managers, the managers should be involved in setting the budgets. The managers could be aware of factors that will affect the performance of their shops that central management are not aware of. Such a process may lead to more realistic budget targets being set for the shop, and in doing so increase the managers' motivation.

Nonetheless, it may still be necessary for the senior management team to adjust the budgets overall, to bring them in line with Albacore's overall financial objectives or any performance expectations the venture capitalist may have.

Non-financial factors – Finally, the reward system could recognise longer-term and non-financial factors in the manager's performance. For example, they could be rewarded for innovative marketing ideas and staff development (eg part-time staff from their branch who progress to become managers in other branches).

37 Cuthbert

Workbook reference. BPR is discussed in Chapter 4 of the Workbook. Reward systems are discussed in Chapter 12.

Top tips.

Part (a). The scenario highlights that the cancellation of the army's order for jackets was 'the latest in a series of problems in production at Cuthbert' which has prompted the directors to look at using BPR 'to radically change the production process'.

The scenario also specifically identifies the three main elements of the proposed BPR project at Cuthbert:

(1) Reorganising production lines into teams
(2) Making machinists responsible for quality (changing job roles)
(3) Tracking batches with RFID tags (instead of the paper batch cards currently being used)

As such, it is vital to look at how each of these three specific elements could influence performance at Cuthbert, rather than simply considering the potential influence of BPR in general terms. A useful way to structure your answer would be to use each 'element' as a heading, and then assess how the changes arising from that element could affect operational processes at Cuthbert. For example, what are the potential implications of reorganising the production lines into teams?

Note. The 'operational' element is important here. Your answer needs to focus on how the BPR project could influence day to day activities and performance, not the wider impact it could have on Cuthbert's financial performance or its reputation.

Part (b) looks at Cuthbert's reward systems, but there are two distinct parts to the requirement, so make sure you address both of them in your answer:

(1) Evaluating the effectiveness of the current reward system

(2) Recommend – and justify – how the reward systems will need to change if the BPR project goes ahead

One of the key issues when evaluating any reward system is the extent to which it influences staff behaviour, and in turn how this affects their performance. This is an important consideration in evaluating Cuthbert's reward system. For example, the fact that the machinists are rewarded for the **number** of items they sew is likely to encourage the machinists to work quickly, but a focus on speed alone could have a negative impact on quality – and quality problems were a major factor in the army cancelling its order from Cuthbert.

Another important point to note from the scenario is that each machinist's weekly bonus is determined by the number of items that they, individually, sew each week. However, the proposed BPR process will lead to production lines being reorganised into teams. Moreover, machinists will now be responsible for quality (as well as quantity).

These points from the scenario should have helped you answer the second part of the requirement; for example, if machinists are now working in teams, bonuses based on team performance may be more appropriate than ones based on individual performance. Similarly, if machinists are responsible for quality, will bonuses based purely on the number of items produced be appropriate?

The requirement isn't only about the machinists, though, so it is important to consider the reward systems in relation to the different grades of staff identified in the scenario – machinists, supervisor, and factory manager.

Marking scheme

	Marks
(a) Up to 2 marks for an explanation of BPR	
For advising how each of the three elements of the BPR proposal could affect operational performance at Cuthbert – up to 4 marks for each of the three elements (up to 12 marks in total)	
For other practical advice about how BPR could affect operational performance at Cuthbert – 1 mark per relevant point, up to 4 marks	14
(b) Evaluation of Cuthbert's current reward system – 1 mark per relevant point; up to 8 marks	
Recommendations for changes to the reward system if the BPR project goes ahead – 1 mark per relevant point; up to 6 marks	11
	Total = 25

(a) **BPR** involves radical and fundamental changes in the way processes in organisations are designed. A focus on the needs of the customer, and customer satisfaction, are key to BPR. BPR aims to improve key performance measures such as reducing costs, improving quality, service delivery and customer satisfaction.

The proposal is to move away from the existing functional structure where staff are attached to only one stage of the production process, or even to one type of machine within each function, to team working. This is a radical change for Cuthbert and, as such, is an example of BPR.

Reorganising into teams

Currently, there is very little multi-skilling of production staff at Cuthbert. This was seen where there were insufficiently trained zip machinists available for the emergency order for the Ceeland army, even though there were enough machinists to sew buttons. This led to the emergency order failing to meet the customer's requirements as it was not delivered on time.

Furthermore, it seems that machinists also prefer to work on one particular type of machine. This is probably because they are currently rewarded according to the speed of production, rather than the quality of production, and can work faster when using just one machine.

A change to team working would imply job enlargement for machinists, who would need to be trained so that they were multi-skilled in different parts of the production process. They could then perform the roles of other members of their team, to ensure that there were no bottlenecks in production.

The cost of reorganisation and the costs of training the machinists should be outweighed by the resulting improved efficiency and flexibility of production. In this way, there is more focus on the outcome (goods of the correct quality produced on time) and less focus on the individual tasks within the process, which is a key principle of BPR.

Production teams are responsible for quality

Cuthbert's brand has a strong reputation, and the use of its products for protection in harsh environments and by the armed forces means that quality is a key element of customer satisfaction. Cuthbert must be able to manufacture goods which are free of defects, unlike the emergency order for the Ceeland army.

Reorganising the production into teams of machinists, sometimes known as production 'cells', would make machinists responsible for decisions about quality of a particular product type. This should lead to improvements in quality and therefore to meeting the needs of the customer.

Reducing the number of processes for checking is typical of a re-engineered process, and the quality checking currently performed by the supervisors would no longer be necessary. The production teams will be managing themselves in this respect, and the distinction between supervisors and machinists will be removed, which is again typical of organisations which have undergone BPR.

Encouraging machinists in each team to suggest improvements in the production process should bring about improvements in both quality and efficiency, and hence a reduction in costs. It is the machinists who are closest to the production process and may be able to see how it can be improved. Cuthbert could also consider a more formal system of incremental continuous improvements such as Kaizen costing.

Tracking with RFIDs

Typically, organisations with re-engineered processes end up having a flatter hierarchy. It seems that the supervisors' current roles will no longer be required if the proposal is adopted. Quality checks will no longer be undertaken by them, nor will recording of batches, which will become automated using RFID tags. This should save salary costs and improve lines of communication in the business.

The use of RFID tags would capture the information required to manage the production process at source, and there would be no distinction between the gathering of information and processing it. This is in contrast to the current system of inputting batch data into a spreadsheet, and is a feature in organisations which have undergone BPR.

Practical and cultural aspects of the proposal

New performance measures related to quality rather than just quantity produced will have to be developed and processes and systems developed in order to record and report these. New rewards systems will also have to be developed and introduced as a result of the changes proposed.

The proposal, by definition, represents a significant cultural change for Cuthbert, and may meet resistance by staff who may perceive it as a threat and a one-off cost-cutting measure rather than a fundamental long-term change in the business. It will also affect the organisational hierarchy, relationships between employees and the roles within Cuthbert. There will be significant costs with training staff and with the disruption the transition may cause.

(b) **The current reward system**

The machinists are currently paid a basic hourly wage plus an amount depending on how many items they sew. This will encourage them to work quickly, which will reduce product costs. However, as they are not directly rewarded for the quality of the work which they produce, they may not be motivated to produce high quality work. Furthermore, in order to work quickly, machinists prefer to work on only one type of machine. This reduces Cuthbert's overall flexibility to respond to customer needs, as illustrated by the failure to deliver the emergency order for the Ceeland army.

The production supervisors also receive a bonus according to how many items machinists in their team are able to sew. This too does not reward the production of high quality work, and supervisors may also neglect quality in order to increase the speed of production. The machinists in their teams could also see it as unfair that the supervisors obtain a bonus based on what they see as their efforts.

The Production Manager does not receive a bonus for production or quality. It seems that he has currently no direct motivation to improve on either of these two aspects of the process.

At 5% of salary, the bonus related to Cuthbert's overall profits is relatively small and it is unclear whether it is a significant motivator to any of the employees. Furthermore, machinists in particular may perceive their own efforts as too remote from the company's overall profit for them to bother to achieve it. Even if they were to be motivated by this, it is unclear what proportion of the total costs are related to direct labour as Cuthbert incurs many other costs such as advertising to maintain the brand. If the costs of direct labour were relatively low, even a large improvement in production efficiency by the machinists may have little effect on overall profit.

Changes to reward systems under the new proposal

The existing reward systems would likely need to change if the move to team-based production were to be adopted.

It may still be appropriate to reward machinists with volume-related bonuses but, as they worked in teams, a team-based performance bonus would be more appropriate. In that way the rest of the team would ensure that any underperforming machinists would improve their performance.

Rewards based on other factors such as quality, innovation, on-time delivery and the ability to work as part of a team would also be appropriate and consistent with the machinists' enlarged job role. This would be a significant change for Cuthbert, where machinists are now being encouraged for the first time to bring about improvements in the production process. Rewards based on direct costs of production, or for the number of suggestions made by each machinist may be appropriate here.

New performance measures would need to be developed against which to align rewards to ensure that employees work towards the overall objectives of the organisation. New reporting systems will need to be put in place to feed back information regarding quality to each cell. This may incur additional costs in the development of existing or new information technology systems.

The commitment of senior management to these changes would be required, as well as communication and training of employees at all levels. This may again incur additional costs and divert management time away from existing activities.

38 Beach Foods

Workbook reference. Financial performance measures including EVA™, ROI and RI are discussed in Chapters 7 and 8 of the Workbook. Control and management styles are discussed in Chapter 12.

Top tips.

Part (a). Note the requirement here is to 'Assess the use of ...' so you should focus on the potential advantages and disadvantages of using EVA™ as a performance measure, rather than, for example, describing how EVA™ would be calculated, or detailing the different adjustments which might be required to calculate it. In this respect, it is important to note (from the second paragraph of the scenario) that Beach already uses EVA™, so we can assume that Beach's management accountants already know how to calculate it.

Part (b). The need to evaluate management's performance as well as the division's performance should have prompted you to think about issues of controllability. For example, if Baby's managers cannot control the R&D costs which are recharged to the department, is it fair to include them in an assessment of the manager's performance?

The reference to 'the assumptions made' also relates to the profit figure being used to assess performance – again, recognising the difference between divisional and managerial performance. Crucially, though, your 'assumptions' should relate to the level of profit to include, not the cost of capital figure to use. The cost of capital figures used must be that for the division (11%), not the one for Beach as a whole (7.5%).

Part (c). Note the requirement here is that you recommend suitable styles, rather than discussing or evaluating different styles. Also, note that you need to recommend a suitable way to control each division (cost/profit/ investment centre) as well as recommending a suitable management style (budget-constrained, profit-conscious and non-accounting). In both cases, the options to choose from were identified in the scenario – control styles in the third paragraph, and management styles in the fourth.

Importantly, the requirement asks for recommendations for **each** division, so you need to cover all three divisions – Baby, Chocolate and R&D – not just the two operating divisions (Baby and Chocolate).

Examining team's comments on part (c). This part was poorly answered as many candidates clearly did not know the criteria for the choice of responsibility centre, even though the centre headings to choose from were given in the scenario. Such a lack of knowledge continues to surprise the examining team.

Lengthy descriptions of the three management styles were not helpful here either, as candidates were expected, instead, to demonstrate their understanding of the styles by applying it to the scenario.

Marking scheme

		Marks
		Marks

(a) For relevant points assessing the use of EVA™ as a divisional performance measure – 1 mark per point

Total for part (a): up to 8   **8**

(b) Calculations:

For applying the correct method to calculate RI – 1 mark

For applying the correct method to calculate ROI – 1 mark

For correct calculation of both RI and ROI based on different profit figures (controllable profit, profit after R&D, divisional profit) – 1 mark per profit figure used; up to a maximum of 4 marks

Comments: 1 mark per relevant comment up to a maximum of 4 marks

Total for part (b): up to 7   **7**

(c) Up to 4 marks for valid recommendations for any one division

All recommendations must be justified within the answer to gain credit

High marks within the answer for any divisions can only be scored by discussing both the type of centre and the management style which would be appropriate

Total for part (c): up to 10 $\underline{10}$

Total = $\underline{\underline{25}}$

(a)   **EVA™ as a divisional performance measure**

Advantages

Maximising wealth – Beach's overall objective is to maximise the family's wealth through their shareholding – in effect, to maximise shareholder wealth.

One of the main benefits of EVA™ as a performance measure (rather than profit-based measures such as ROI) is that it is a value-based approach, and therefore it will be aligned to the overall objective of maximising shareholder wealth.

Goal congruence – Moreover, using EVA™ as a divisional measure will help to ensure that decisions taken at divisional level support the best interests of Beach as a whole, rather than just the individual division.

The **other advantages of EVA™** are:

(i)   It gives an absolute measure of performance, and so shows the overall contribution the divisions make to the company.

(ii)   The basic test of performance is simple. If a division has a positive EVA™, then it is generating a return above that required by the providers of finance. (ROI requires a target level to be set, usually based on benchmarking to the industry sector.)

(iii)   The adjustments required when calculating net operating profit after tax mean that it is closer to cash flows than traditional accounting profits are, and also mean that EVA™ is less subject to choices in accounting policies.

(iv)   EVA™ encourages investment in the future (for example, in advertising and development) by adding back these costs to profit in the performance period and treating them like capital expenditure. This will reduce the temptation for dysfunctional, short-termist decision making, which could otherwise be a problem where the capital employed figure from the financial statements is used in ROI and RI. This is likely to be particularly appropriate at Beach where R&D is significant.

Disadvantages

However, EVA™ does also have some disadvantages. Some of these are also disadvantages of ROI and RI, and some are specific to EVA™.

All three measures are dependent on historical data and so have limited use in forecasting future performance.

The directors' complaint that EVA™ is complicated to understand appears reasonable, because of the number of adjustments which need to be made to the information from Beach's financial statements. By contrast, ROI and RI are derived from headline information in the financial statements which would be more familiar to the board. A related issue here would be the time and cost involved for Beach's management accountant in calculating the division's EVA™.

EVA™ (like RI) uses a charge for the capital employed in the division. EVA™ uses the weighted average cost of capital (WACC) for the company as a whole, which may not reflect the risks of the manufacturing divisions. Also, as an unlisted business, WACC may be difficult to estimate. By contrast, RI uses a notional cost of capital based on the risk of the divisions – although this will also be subject to an element of judgement and estimate.

Unlike ROI (which gives a percentage measure, rather than an absolute measure) EVA™ will not help to assess relative divisional managerial performance at Beach if the divisions are of different sizes.

(b)   **ROI and RI**

A key consideration when calculating either ROI or RI for Baby is what profit figure to use for the calculations.

The data in Appendix 1 suggests three potential profit figures, which could be used for assessing the performance of Baby as a division, and its manager:

Controllable profit – The only costs included in controllable profit are those under the direct control of the divisional manager (ie the divisional operating costs of $121m).

R&D costs recharged – Although the divisional manager cannot influence the costs of the R&D Division, Baby's divisional revenue includes the profit which results from new products and ideas generated by the R&D Division. Therefore, in order to match costs with revenues more fairly, a proportion of the R&D Division's costs should be included in Baby's profit figure.

Divisional profit – The division's performance (as distinct from the manager's performance) should take account of all relevant costs, including Baby's share of the head office management fees. As such the divisional profit ($60m) would be an appropriate figure to use in this respect.

Performance analysis

Regardless of which profit figure is chosen, Baby seems to be performing relatively well. Baby's EVA™ is positive ($35m) and its RI is also positive.

In terms of ROI, the return based on divisional profit (14.2%) is lower than the ROI for similar entities (20%), but the return based on controllable profit, or profit after R&D, is higher than the benchmark figure. However, we do not know which profit figures were used in the benchmark figure, which means we cannot tell whether Baby's ROI figure is above or below the average achieved by similar entities.

	Controllable profit	Profit after R&D	Divisional profit
ROI			
Profit ($m)	99	88	60
Capital employed ($m)	424	424	424
ROI	**23.3%**	**20.8%**	**14.2%**
RI			
Profit ($m)	99	88	60
Cost of capital ($m)			
(424 × 11%)	46.6	46.6	46.6
RI ($m)	**52.4**	**41.4**	**13.4**

(c) **Management styles for the divisions**

Baby Division

Responsibility centre – Baby's position as the star in Beach's portfolio, coupled with the fact it is developing and introducing new products, means that the division's focus should be on growth rather than cost control.

As such, it might seem appropriate for Baby to be treated as an investment centre, giving its managers autonomy to develop their business as they see fit.

However, it is not clear whether the divisional managers have the authority to make capital investment decisions or whether these are taken by head office. (Chocolate had to get approval from head office to upgrade its production line.)

If the authority for investment decisions remains with head office, then Baby should be treated as a **profit centre**, and managed according to its ability to generate profit.

Management style – A profit-conscious style focuses on longer-term performance and objectives (such as growth) whereas a budget-constrained style focuses on short-term performance and cost control.

Therefore, given the nature of Baby's market – and the market's rapid growth – the profit-conscious style would seem more appropriate for Baby.

However, elements of a non-accounting style (such as new product development) may also be appropriate.

Given the costs associated with new products and rapid growth (such as the publicity campaign Baby ran to support its new product launch), we recommend that a **non-accounting style** is applied initially.

However, once the market sector begins to mature, then given Baby's strong market share its focus should shift to optimising its profits – at which point, a profit-conscious management style should be adopted.

Chocolate Division

Responsibility centre – As the Chocolate Division is the cash cow in the portfolio, Beach needs it to generate the profits and cash necessary to support Baby's growth.

However, as a cash cow, and operating in a market with limited growth opportunities, Chocolate is unlikely to receive much investment. As such, it would seem appropriate to treat Chocolate as a profit centre.

Nonetheless, it appears that Chocolate does still makes some capital expenditure (for example, the upgrade to its main production line). As such, it could be appropriate to treat Chocolate as an **investment centre**, so that its managers have the autonomy to take these decisions, rather than having to wait for head office to approve them.

Management style – Because it is operating in a mature market with limited growth opportunities, cost control is likely to be crucial in maintaining Chocolate's profitability. As such, a **budget-constrained style** will be the most appropriate management style for Chocolate.

R&D Division

Responsibility centre – The R&D Division does not generate any revenue in its own right, and therefore should be treated as a cost centre.

Nonetheless, it is important that the contribution the division makes to the group (through the overall profit generated by the products it develops) is not overlooked. The complaints which Baby's managers make about the recharge suggests they are only thinking about the costs rather than the revenue which the new products have generated for them.

As such, whilst Beach should continue to treat the R&D Division as a cost centre for control purposes, it would also be useful to **monitor the profit generated by each new product** over its life cycle, to demonstrate the division's value to the group as a whole.

Management style – As the R&D Division is a cost centre, it might seem appropriate to apply a budget-constrained management style.

However, it is important that potentially profitable developments are not rejected simply to keep the division's costs within a fixed budget – and there is a danger this could be the case under a budget-constrained management style.

Therefore, elements of a non-accounting style might also be appropriate – with a focus on the number of new product ideas being generated, and the market reaction to new products being developed.

As such, it may be necessary to adopt a management style which combines some elements of the **budget-constrained style** with others from the **non-accounting style**.

39 Pharmaceutical Technologies

Workbook reference. The balanced scorecard is discussed in Chapter 13 of the Workbook.

Top tips.

For part (a), you should be asking 'how well will the proposed measures help PT deliver its objectives and, in turn, its corporate strategy?' The scenario provided you with considerable detail about objectives and measures, and you should have used it to help answer this requirement.

Part (b). Note there are two distinct parts to this requirement. The first is a pure test of knowledge: describing a method for analysing stakeholder influence. Mendelow's matrix seems the obvious choice here.

However, don't spend too long on this part of the requirement (**briefly** describe ...), because the second part of the requirement is more substantial: analyse the influence of four different external stakeholders on the regulator. Note that the question refers to stakeholders who could influence the regulator (not PT). Although some of the stakeholder groups identified by the working group (eg doctors, patients) could also be stakeholders of the regulator, it is important that you analyse their influence in relation to the regulator.

However, as there are only eight marks available for part (b) in total you should only give a relatively brief analysis of each stakeholder's influence on the regulator – highlighting what power they have, and how interested they will be in exerting that power.

In part (c), you need to establish how BDR differs from PT, because this will affect how the scorecard is applied in both organisations. In effect, the requirement is asking how the application of the scorecard would vary in a private sector organisation (PT) compared to a public sector one. To score well here, you need to make a comparison between the two, rather than simply talking about the application of the scorecard at one or other of them.

Marking scheme

		Marks

(a)   1 mark per relevant point – up to a maximum of 10

Relevant points include:

Evaluation of whether each of the measures suggested cover the
    perspective intended

Consideration of whether there are other suitable measures

Discussion of linkages between the measures and the company objectives

Discussion of the difficulty of collection of appropriate data, and ranking
    the measures

Total: up to 10   10

(b)   Description of suitable method of stakeholder analysis – 1 mark per point –
    up to a maximum of 2

Analysis of the power and interest of each stakeholder – 1 mark for power,
    and 1 mark for influence of each stakeholder – up to a maximum of 8

Total: up to 8   8

(c)   1 mark per relevant difference between the application of the scorecard at
    BDR and PT.

Differences must be clearly linked to the scenario to score the marks
    available.

Total: up to 7   7

Total = **25**

(a)   Financial measures

The financial perspective has not been altered from the existing measures of strategic performance. These are appropriate to address the objectives of enhancing shareholder wealth, although it has been argued that measures such as economic value added (EVA™) or shareholder value added are better long-term measures of this topic. Also, it is more common to use share price and dividend per share to reflect total shareholder return.

Although it is important to look at earnings and profits, PT's financial measures overlook the importance of cash flow and liquidity, which will be essential to its survival, especially given the long lead-times for introducing new products. Therefore it should also include a measure relating to its cash flows in its scorecard.

Customer perspective

PT has two different types of customer: users (healthcare providers and patients) and the people who fund the drug use (insurance companies or government). The measure currently proposed seems to focus mainly on the end users. However, their concerns may not always be same as those who are paying for a course of treatment. For example, the healthcare providers and patients are likely to focus primarily on how effective the product is as a cure. However, the funding bodies will also be interested in the cost of the treatment in comparison to the cost of treatments from PT's competitors.

Therefore, PT should consider a measure looking at the cost of its drugs; for example, comparing the cost of its drugs against similar alternative drugs offered by rival manufacturers.

Internal business processes

One of the objectives from the medium-term strategy is to improve the efficiency of drug development. Performance measures designed to improve the standard of design and testing, and to reduce the time to gain regulatory approval, should help achieve this objective.

These measures also help support the financial objectives. If PT can reduce the time it takes to get new drugs approved by the regulator, it will also be able to be start selling those drugs more quickly, thereby increasing sales and earnings.

Learning and growth

The third of the objectives from the medium-term strategy highlights the importance of innovation in the drug approval process. The measures in the learning and growth perspective of the scorecard should therefore directly help PT to achieve this objective.

We are not told anything about the relative importance or ranking of any of the measures in the scorecard, but it is debatable whether the number of training days attended is the main measure of learning and growth. Reducing the time to market of new products, and increasing the percentage of drugs that gain final approval, are likely to be more directly strategically important.

Measurement issues

Although the measures suggested seem largely appropriate in relation to PT's objectives, the management will also need to consider how practical it will be to collect data for some of the non-financial measures. For example, an assessment of whether PT has exceeded industry standard on design and testing is likely to be subjective, unless there are industry-wide quality audits which formally assess companies against a common set of criteria.

Conversely, measures should not be chosen because they are easy to measure. The number of training days undertaken by staff will be easy to measure by staff. However, there may be a danger that staff will simply end up going on training days simply to achieve a target number of days. Training will only be valuable to PT and its staff if it is relevant and appropriate for the people attending.

(b) **Stakeholder influence**

A stakeholder's influence over an organisation can be analysed in relation to the stakeholder's power and interest, using Mendelow's matrix.

Power identifies the extent to which a stakeholder (or group of stakeholders) has the power to influence a decision or situation. The level of **interest** reflects the likelihood that a stakeholder will exercise their power in relation to any given decision or situation.

This approach can be used to analyse the four key external stakeholders of BDR: the drug companies, the Government, healthcare providers, and patients.

BPP
LEARNING
MEDIA

Drug companies

Interest – likely to have a **high interest** in BDR, because it makes the final judgement about whether a product can be sold in the country. Without approval from BDR, the drug companies will not have any products to sell.

Power – **little power** to influence BDR. BDR's responsibility is to the public and to public health, rather than to the drug companies. Therefore, BDR needs to be (and be seen to be) independent from the drug companies.

Government

Power – **high power** because it appoints the board of trustees and also directly funds BDR.

Interest – will have a keen interest in public health overall, but their direct interest in BDR is likely to be **relatively low.** The Government has appointed the trustees to manage BDR on its behalf so it is unlikely to intervene in decision making at BDR (unless there is a specific financial or medical scandal which requires it to do so).

Doctors and healthcare providers

Interest – will have a **high level of interest** in the approval process, because they will want to be confident that any new drugs approved are safe for use. They will also have an interest in BDR's role in encouraging the development of beneficial new drugs. These new drugs could help them treat patients and diseases that they would not otherwise be able to treat as effectively.

Power – likely to have **low power** over the approval process because BDR is an independent regulator (although they may be able to exert some power by lobbying the Government).

Patients

Interest – will have a **high level of interest** in the drug approval process because they will want to be reassured that any drugs approved are safe. However, they will also have an interest in potential new cures being available on the market quickly.

Power – in the same way that healthcare providers only have low power, so patients also only have **low power** over any decisions made at BDR.

(c)   **Differences in objectives** – BDR's objectives are less explicitly financial than PT's, not least because it does not have any shareholders. Therefore the emphasis the balanced scorecard places on non-financial performance will be relevant for BDR.

Stakeholder structure – BDR is a public sector organisation, while PT is a commercial organisation, which means that the Government is a much more important stakeholder for BDR than for PT. It is likely that this will need to be reflected in BDR's scorecard, with there being a political dimension to measuring performance.

Complexity of the scorecards – BDR's scorecard is likely to be quite complex, because it needs to reflect the diverse nature of its stakeholders and their interests. For example, on the one hand, drug companies will be keen for new drugs to be approved as quickly as possible, while healthcare providers and patients will be most interested in the risk-benefit profile of any potential new drugs. Equally, the Government will want effective drugs and treatments to be available for patients, but in terms of paying healthcare providers the Government may not be willing to pay for drugs it considers to be too expensive.

In this respect, the **customer perspective** of BDR's scorecard is likely to be crucial because, in effect, the drug companies, healthcare providers and patients are all BDR's customers. In PT's scorecard the relative significance of the four perspectives is likely to be more equal. The financial perspective will be very important for satisfying shareholders, while the internal business processes and learning and growth perspectives will be crucial in developing and manufacturing the new drugs effectively. Process and innovation are likely to be less directly important in BDR because it doesn't develop 'products' of its own.

Selecting performance measures – However, the nature of BDR's work means that it will be quite hard to measure how well it is performing against its objectives. For example, determining whether a medicine has an 'acceptable balance of benefit and risk' will involve a degree of judgement and selectivity, and it is likely to be difficult to set a quantifiable performance measure to determine whether this objective is being achieved.

Potential conflicts – Of BDR's three objectives, the easiest to set quantifiable measures for is likely to be 'encouraging new beneficial product development' because a performance measure could be set around the number of new products developed. However, there is a danger that imposing quantifiable measures in this way may have unintended consequences. For example, it may lead to new drugs being introduced even if the new product is not a significant improvement on an existing drug.

40 Victoria-Yeeland Logistics

Workbook reference. The balanced scorecard (BSC) is discussed in Chapter 13 of the Workbook. Reward systems and reward management are discussed in Chapter 12.

Top tips.

Part (a). One of the key arguments in favour of multi-dimensional performance measurement systems (such as the BSC) is that an organisation's financial performance ultimately reflects its performance in key non-financial areas.

This is the broad context of part (a) of this question, but read the requirement very carefully: it does not ask about the impact that success in the customer perspective will have on Victoria's financial position in general terms. Rather it asks specifically about the impact that success in the customer perspective will have on the three financial metrics identified in Appendix 1. Therefore, your answer must also focus specifically on the impact that achieving the success factors in the customer perspective is likely to have on Victoria's return on capital employed (ROCE), profit margin and revenue growth.

Part (b). As the marking guide indicates, there are two marks available for each metric you recommend: one for calculating a suitable metric; and one for justifying why you have chosen it. Therefore, as is so often the case in APM, the requirement is not simply about calculation. Justifying the metric you have chosen is equally as important as the calculation.

Note, also, that there is a second part to the requirement – a discussion about the problems of using customer complaints as a performance measure. For example, can Victoria be sure that all customer complaints are valid?

Part (c). The requirement asks you to advise on 'the reward management issues outlined by the CFO'. The context for this requirement is provided by the last paragraph in the scenario, but crucially you need to recognise that there are two sets of issues here: one relating to the senior management bonus scheme, and one relating to the operational managers' bonus scheme.

As the marking guide indicates, you can only score up to five marks for advising on the issues with either scheme, so it is vital to analyse both schemes in order to score well on this requirement.

The fact that the shareholders have been complaining about the senior management's bonus should be a clue that agency theory is an issue here – is the scheme designed with shareholders' best interests in mind, or management's?

Similarly, in relation to the operational managers' scheme, the fact that the scenario identifies a change to the way that bonus targets are set should prompt you to question whether these changes are appropriate.

Examining team's comments. Many candidates used the building block model as a template for their answer but failed to go further than a generic response – around the need for standards to be fair, achievable and owned, and for rewards to be clear, motivational and controllable. In order for answers based around the model to score well, candidates needed to show how each aspect could be applied to the specific scenarios at Victoria.

Candidates seemed unwilling to say that employees (either senior management or operational managers) may be unhappy but this need not be an issue for Victoria, as there will usually be a conflict of interest between employees and the company/shareholders. Good answers identified and discussed how to address this issue fairly. However, simply stating that employees should set their own targets is not a practical solution, nor one which is commercially valuable to Victoria.

Marks

(a) For relevant points discussing the linkage between customer perspective and the financial perspective – 1 mark each

Note. Answers must discuss all three financial metrics in order to score the full 5 marks.

Total for part (a): up to 5   5

(b) Each suitable performance measurement recommended – up to 2 marks (for each of four perspectives; so up to 8 marks in total)

(1 mark for calculating a suitable metric; 1 mark for justifying the choice of metric)

For discussing the problems of using customer complaints as a performance measure – up to 4 marks

Total for part (b): up to 11   11

(c) For relevant points relating to issues in the senior management reward system – 1 mark each, up to a maximum of 5

For relevant points relating to the operational managers' bonus scheme – 1 mark per relevant point, up to a maximum of 5

Total for part (c): up to 9   9

Total = 25

(a) **Links between customer perspective and financial perspective**

The success factors identified for the customer perspective should help Victoria to increase customer satisfaction. Since the delivery business in Yeeland appears to be very competitive, increasing (or, at least, maintaining) customer satisfaction levels is likely to be crucial to Victoria's financial success.

Revenue growth – Since the market is saturated, in order to increase its revenues Victoria will need to win new customers (from its competitors) whilst retaining its existing customers. Victoria's reputation for delivering packages quickly, safely and on time is likely to be crucial in helping it attract business from competitors.

In addition to increasing its customer numbers, Victoria could consider increasing its selling prices as a means of increasing revenue. In effect, Victoria could look to differentiate itself from its competitors, by virtue of its service quality, and could then charge premium prices for its service. The success factors linked to the customer perspective are ones in which Victoria will need to outperform its competitors in order to pursue a differentiation strategy successfully.

Profit margin – Charging premium prices should provide a direct way of increasing profit margins.

Alternatively, increasing customer numbers should enable Victoria to benefit from economies of scale, which in turn could improve profit margins by reducing unit costs. For example, if Victoria can increase its capacity utilisation (the number of packages on each delivery lorry) the amount of fixed costs apportioned to each package on that lorry will be lower.

Return on capital employed – As the ways of increasing revenue and profit margins will not require any additional capital expenditure, then any increases in operating profit should also increase Victoria's ROCE.

(b)   **Ability to meet customers' transport needs**

This success factor can be measured by the proportion of customer requests which Victoria is able to undertake.

$$\frac{\text{Total number of packages transported}}{\text{Total number of customer transport requests}}$$

$$\frac{548,000}{610,000} = 89.8\%$$

Ability to deliver packages quickly

This measure needs to take account of how far packages have to travel as well as how long it takes them to get to their destinations. Therefore, a suitable measure will be one which measures **time taken per kilometre** (rather than one which measures time taken per journey).

$$\frac{\text{Total package minutes}}{\text{Total package kilometres}}$$

$$\frac{131,520,000}{65,760,000} = 2.0$$

Ability to deliver packages on time

This measure needs to reflect the proportion of packages which are delivered within the time window given to the customer.

$$\frac{\text{Deliveries within agreed window}}{\text{Total number of packages transported}}$$

$$\frac{(548,000 - 21,920)}{548,000} = 96\%$$

Ability to deliver packages safely

This measure needs to reflect the number of packages delivered undamaged as a proportion of the total number of packages transported.

$$\frac{\text{Deliveries with no reported damage}}{\text{Total number of packages transported}}$$

$$\frac{(548,000 - 8,220)}{548,000} = 98.5\%$$

Problems of using customer complaints as a basis for performance measurement

Victoria delivers packages to a large number of different customers, and it could respond to problems with their delivery in different ways. This means it will be difficult for Victoria to get an accurate picture of the number of deliveries which were damaged or late.

Problems understated – Some customers may not bother to report that a package has been delivered late or was damaged. However, due to the inconvenience caused by the lateness or damage they will use one of Victoria's competitors to deliver their packages in future.

In such cases, the performance measure gives a misleading impression that Victoria is performing better than it is. And, given the importance of customer retention in Yeeland's competitive market, this could have very significant consequences on Victoria's revenue performance in the longer term.

If Victoria recorded its own delivery performance it could take direct action to try to retain customers who have suffered from late or damaged packages. For example, acknowledging the problem at the point of delivery, it could offer to discount the next order for a customer whose package is delivered late.

Problems overstated – In contrast to customers who do not report valid complaints, others may report unjustified complaints in the hope of obtaining a refund or a credit against future orders. Currently, the measures simply record the number of complaints received, even though some of these may not be valid.

In this respect, it would be better to measure the number of refunds or discounts given (as an indicator of the number of valid complaints) rather than simply recording the total number of complaints.

(c) **Senior managers' reward system**

Assuming that the members of the senior management team are all on the board, the potential problem here is that senior management could be deciding their own bonuses.

Agency issues – As such, there is a danger that the reward system will favour the managers' interests, rather than those of Victoria's shareholders. For example, if the targets used to determine managers' bonuses are easy to achieve, this will maximise the chances of managers receiving bonuses. This would justify the shareholders' complaints that the bonuses are not suitable – because they are not supporting Victoria's objective of maximising shareholder wealth.

The introduction of the BSC should help to align the senior management's objectives with those of the shareholders, particularly in relation to the financial perspective. However, the financial measures suggested for the BSC do not directly address shareholder wealth, because they are essentially still based around profitability rather than value-based management.

Controllability – The fact that the market is saturated, and dominated by two international companies, will constrain management's ability to grow revenue. Similarly, fuel prices – which management cannot control – will be a significant influence on profit margin. This again suggests these may not be the most appropriate measures to use when assessing management's performance.

Operational managers' reward system

Choice of measures – Although the senior managers assess the operational managers' performance, it is not clear what measures are used as the basis of this assessment. The measures of performance against which operational managers are assessed should be aligned to Victoria's overall objectives.

However, the measures should also relate to the aspects of performance that the operational managers can influence (and therefore will typically come from the 'customer' and 'business' perspectives in the scorecard).

Setting own bonus targets – However, the suggestion that the operational managers should be involved in setting their own bonus targets does not seem appropriate. In the same way that senior management shouldn't set their own performance targets, neither should operational managers.

Although it could be beneficial to explain the **target setting process** to the manager, this should not be confused with the idea of letting managers set their own targets. Targets should still be set by a higher level of management, and should be set at a level which is stretching but achievable.

The target set should then be explained to the managers so that they understand what they have to do in order to earn their bonus.

41 Soup

Workbook reference. The balanced scorecard is discussed in Chapter 13 of the Workbook.

Top tips.

Part (a). The number of times the word 'passenger' is mentioned in the scenario should have been an inherent clue that managing passenger (or 'customer') satisfaction should be a key part of Soup's performance management process.

The last paragraph highlights this point even more clearly, with the reference to the need for performance measures which 'balance the need of passengers with the requirements of the shareholders'. The reason why the scorecard is called the 'balanced scorecard' is because it encourages organisations to develop performance measures which ensure a 'balance' between the four perspectives. As such, it is also important to try to think how performance information in each of the four areas could be useful for Soup – don't just focus, for example, on the benefits of having passenger-focused performance measures.

Also, make sure you take note of the instructions the CEO has given in the last paragraph. She has said, specifically, that she doesn't want a list of suggested performance measures; instead she wants to know **why** those performance measures will help to improve Soup's performance.

Similarly, note that the CEO has specifically said that she doesn't want to know about how to improve Soup's performance, but instead how to improve Soup's performance management systems. Recognising the distinction between 'performance' and 'performance reporting' is absolutely crucial in APM. In a question like this – where the focus is on Soup's performance management system – you will score no marks for suggestions about how to improve the company's underlying performance.

Part (b). Whereas your focus in part (a) should have been on Soup's performance management systems, the focus here is on the underlying performance – in particular, the occupancy rates on Soup's trains.

The third paragraph of the scenario provides details of the capacity of Soup's trains, so you need to use these details in conjunction with the data at the end of the scenario to work out how many seats are available per day compared to the number of passengers.

However, note that you aren't asked simply to calculate occupancy rates, but rather to evaluate the comment that Soup's trains are overcrowded. So, how far do the figures you have calculated support the comment?

Part (c). The focus in this third part of the question returns to the balanced scorecard as a performance management system. However, whereas part (a) looked at the ways the scorecard could improve the performance management system at Soup, part (c) now looks at the problems which Soup could encounter when applying it.

There are two key points to note here, though. First, the requirement is looking specifically at the problems which could be encountered in 'selecting and interpreting performance measures' – not, more generally, about the problems which could be encountered in introducing the balanced scorecard. Second, you are asked to assess the problems 'Soup may encounter ...' rather than to discuss the problems in general terms. To score well in this part of the question, it is vital that you link your answer directly back to Soup.

Examining team's comments. In **part (a)** the majority of candidates clearly knew the structure of the balanced scorecard, but the question did not simply ask for an explanation of the four perspectives of the scorecard. It asked how the scorecard could improve the performance management system at Soup – therefore candidates needed to explain how using the scorecard could be beneficial to Soup.

The calculations for **part (b)** were generally done well. However, few candidates then attempted to discuss the claim of overcrowding in any detail, other than to say whether or not capacity was exceeded. The scenarios in APM are intended to reflect real world examples, and – in this scenario – discussing practical considerations could have been beneficial.

Part (c) was answered well by many candidates, who understood the advantages and disadvantages of the model, and then demonstrated how they related to the scenario.

However, one of the main weaknesses in many responses to this question was a failure to specifically answer the question which focused on 'selecting and interpreting' – so, for example, issues arising from conflicting metrics. Several candidates simply discussed the difficulties in implementing a balanced scorecard approach (such as commitment from management) and a general discussion of target setting (such as measure fixation). We have said this many times before, but candidates must ensure that they specifically answer the question that has been set.

BPP
LEARNING
MEDIA

Marks

(a) For relevant points about how using the balanced scorecard could improve. Soup's performance management system – 1 mark per point, up to a maximum of 10 marks

No marks are to be awarded for a list of new measures without justifying why they would benefit Soup

A maximum of 1 mark is to be given for a generic description of the balanced scorecard without clear references to the scenario

Total for part (a): up to 10   10

(b) For relevant calculations – 1 mark each, up to 4 marks
- Seats available per train
- Seats available per day by region/time
- Seat occupancy by region/time
- Total seat occupancy

Comment on whether the figures are consistent with government's claims about overcrowding – 1 mark

Other comments – up to 2 marks

Up to 2 additional marks for identifying journey time is an important factor and for attempting to quantify journey times from the data given

Total for part (b): up to 7   7

(c) For each problem Soup may encounter – 1 mark per relevant point, up to 2 marks per problem

Problems include:
- Selection of appropriate measures
- Prioritisation of measures
- Difficulties of making measurements
- Conflicting measures
- Overload of measures

A maximum of 3 marks to be given, in total, for general problems of applying the balanced scorecard, but not applied to Soup

Total for part (c): up to 8 $\underline{8}$

Total = $\underline{\underline{25}}$

(a) The balanced scorecard consists of four perspectives: customer, internal, innovation and learning and financial. It requires an organisation to have a number of goals supported by performance measures in each perspective. The customer perspective measures what it is that customers value from the business; internal looks at what processes the organisation needs to be successful; innovation and learning considers how future value can be created; and the financial perspective measures whether performance is acceptable to investors.

It is useful because it uses both internal and external information to assess performance and measures **financial and non-financial aspects** of a business to ensure long-term future success, rather than just focusing on historic results. It can also be used as a mechanism to link key performance indicators (KPIs) into the critical success factors which are vital to deliver strategy.

Financial perspective

Soup currently uses return on capital employed (ROCE) as its key financial performance measure, but this does not correlate directly with the **objective to maximise shareholder wealth** and could encourage short-term decisions to be taken at the expense of long-term success. This is the case at Soup which purchased old trains and subsequently failed to reinvest, meaning that Soup's ROCE is probably higher than its rivals. However, the trains are becoming unreliable and their condition is deteriorating. In the long term this will reduce customer satisfaction and financial performance.

Using the scorecard, Soup should have a **broader range of financial measures** which encourage managers to take decisions, such as investment decisions, consistent with the objective to maximise shareholder wealth in the long term. Economic value added would be a suitable measure to help achieve this, and would be preferable to the current focus on ROCE.

Customer perspective

Soup does measure growth in passenger numbers which could be a measure of customer satisfaction. However, it is a limited, quantitative measure. Though Soup does have rivals and is likely to be required to operate a specified level of service under the terms of the licence from the Government, some passengers may be forced to travel on Soup trains, rather than those of another operator because of where they live or the times they need to travel. The number of operators (competitors) is limited by the capacity of the railway infrastructure as well as by passenger demand. This means that the level of repeat customers may not be appropriate for Soup.

Passenger numbers are also externally focused but again this fails to fully consider the environment in which Soup operates. Within the customer perspective Soup could use a range of performance measures. This will be beneficial as where passengers are able, they are likely to choose to use Soup if they provide a good service. This can be easily measured by surveying or asking passengers' opinions. This will give Soup more qualitative information about their customers and their expectations, which will vary; for example, passengers will have different perceptions of overcrowding, or what is an acceptable delay. Certain groups may be more affected by overcrowding like frequent travellers and the elderly. Passengers who are unable to find a seat will probably be the most dissatisfied, though this will depend on how long their journey is. Other aspects of Soup's service may be less valued than reliability and occupancy, like wireless access and the on-board café, but will be important to certain groups.

Another key element of customer satisfaction will relate to the amount of fare paid. Fares are regulated in Deeland so the interaction between fares and other aspects of the service is unknown. Many customers, while valuing a particular aspect of the service, may be unwilling to pay more for it; some may accept a reduction in the level of service if fares were reduced.

This detailed information about customers will allow Soup to focus performance improvements on key areas using more external data to make decisions.

Internal processes

Measures of the internal processes are likely to be closely linked to customer satisfaction. Soup apparently neglects this area in its performance management system. The scorecard could be used to help to address reliability, overcrowding and environmental factors.

Reliability will be highly valued by customers, especially those who travel frequently and who rely on rail travel to get to work. The number of trains arriving late would be a suitable measure of reliability, as would the number of train services cancelled, though the length of the delay is also critical and should be carefully defined. The scorecard would allow more detailed measures as some of the factors affecting reliability will be within Soup's direct control but others such as failures in the railway infrastructure are controlled by the Government. This is useful information for Soup to effectively assess its controllable performance and feed back as necessary to external parties.

Seat occupancy, the number of passengers on a train compared to the number of available seats on different routes and at different times, is a suitable measure of train overcrowding and is important for passenger safety. To fully utilise its trains and achieve its objective of maximising shareholder wealth, Soup must try to maximise both the seat occupancy and the amount of time its trains are actually running. These internal measures would then help to support financial targets.

Soup's licence to operate rail services in Regions A and B expires in three years' time and, as with the operator from whom Soup purchased the trains, it may not be renewed. Soup must balance the needs of shareholders for short-term increases in dividends and share price with the long-term need to renew to its operator's licence.

Innovation and learning perspective

The creation of long-term future value can be addressed by the innovation and learning perspective. The immediate scope to innovate the service experienced by the passenger is limited, but there are some quick wins available in the choice in the on-board café and improving the reliability of the internet access. Also time spent training staff may improve customer satisfaction and reduce maintenance time. Fundamental innovation like the use of faster or environmentally less harmful trains requires long-term planning and large capital investment. The scorecard will encourage Soup to be forward looking, unlike the present system which is limited to historic performance.

(b) To measure the extent of overcrowding, some measure of occupancy is needed. The number of passengers per available seat can be used as a measure of occupancy.

		Region A		Region B	Total
Seats available					
Per service (70 per carriage)		490		420	
Seats available per day					
Peak times	4 services	1,960	4 services	1,680	
Other times	6 services	2,940	8 services	3,360	
Total		4,900		5,040	9,940
Passenger demand per day					
Peak times		2,500		1,400	
Other times		2,450		1,850	
Total		4,950		3,250	8,200
Occupancy (demand/availability)					
Peak times		127.6%		83.3%	
Other times		83.3%		55.1%	
Total		101.0%		64.5%	82.5%

Overall occupancy (82.5%) is significantly below 100%, which means on average there are more seats available than passengers. This is not consistent with the Government's claims that the trains are overcrowded. However, these averages may be misleading as trains running on certain days or at certain times may be relatively overcrowded. This may generate customer dissatisfaction even on services which are on average not fully occupied. The total number of passengers without seats would be a better measure.

There are **significant variations between regions and times travelled,** with only the trains in Region A travelling at peak times being over-occupied. This affects only 18% (4/22) of all services.

The people most affected by this will be the 28% of the passengers travelling at peak times in Region A who are unable to obtain a seat. This represents only 9% (28% × 2,500/8,200) of total passengers per day. There is some overcrowding, but the claim that Soup's trains are overcrowded seems exaggerated given the data provided. However, certain routes or specific times or sections of the trains may be more affected and more analysis is needed.

The impact of overcrowding on passengers also depends on the length of journeys passengers are making, with the lack of seating typically causing a greater inconvenience to passengers on long journeys compared to passengers only making a shorter journey. Equally, some passengers may board a service at intermediate stations, rather than travelling the full length of a route. These passengers are relatively more likely to have to stand, but will have to stand for a shorter length of time than passengers who are travelling the full length of the route.

(c)   When applying the balanced scorecard in Soup, the measures need to be chosen carefully. A balance needs to be struck, and only measures which help Soup to **achieve its objectives** should be chosen. Currently Soup focuses on short-term financial measures such as ROCE, whereas the balanced scorecard considers more **long-term measures**.

Some measures are more important than others, so **prioritising measures** will be difficult. Customers may value some aspects of the service more than others; for example, the choice available in the on-board café is probably unimportant to most passengers provided they can obtain some food and drink. The punctuality of Soup's trains or whether they even run at all is fundamental to achieving customer satisfaction and needs careful measurement. Soup must have measures for regulatory or safety reasons too.

Some aspects of the business may be **harder to measure** than others. For example, it may be relatively easy to measure seat occupancy as a measure of overcrowding, but passengers' perceptions of overcrowding may differ. Non-financial aspects such as customer satisfaction may be subjective and any surveys done may not reflect the experience of the majority of passengers. Performing and analysing surveys would also be time consuming and resource intensive.

Measures chosen may conflict. Overcrowding may be unwelcome by passengers but making them less crowded conflicts with Soup's presumed objective of fully occupied trains. Time spent maintaining trains to reduce their impact on the environment or ensure reliability will mean they are not operational for periods of time, though safety will be a key factor here.

Care must be taken to **avoid overloading** with too many performance measures. The current objective to maximise shareholder wealth is very broad. Having a clearer strategy would enable Soup to determine suitable performance measures so it is not overloaded with KPIs which do not contribute towards achieving this strategy.

42 Graviton

Workbook reference. The performance pyramid is discussed in Chapter 13 of the Workbook. Problems of performance measurement are discussed in Chapter 12.

Top tips.

Part (a). The scenario identifies that the CEO is 'unhappy with the current performance measurement system', and that there are 'major gaps in the current list of key metrics used'. Equally, the evidence from the press reports suggests that Graviton is being successful in some areas, whilst performing less well in other areas.

A sensible approach to this question might be to think how far these variations in Graviton's current performance reflect the areas which are monitored by Graviton's current performance measures; and then to think how far the weaknesses in the current system could be addressed by using the performance pyramid.

Crucially, however, note that the requirement asks you to evaluate Graviton's performance measurement **system**, not its current performance. You will not earn any marks for discussing Graviton's performance as such.

Part (b). The issues listed by the board (myopia, gaming, ossification) are three of the problems listed by Berry, Broadbent and Ottley in relation to the use of performance measures.

If you were aware of Berry, Broadbent and Ottley's list, then identifying the problems at Graviton should have been relatively straightforward, because evidence of them is fairly clearly illustrated by the scenario.

A sensible way to approach this part of the requirement would be to take each of the three problems in turn; provide a short definition of the problem; assess whether they apply to Graviton; and then suggest possible solutions for the problem.

There are ten marks available for this part of the question, so if you describe each problem (one mark each) and then make a couple of relevant points applying each problem to Graviton (two marks per problem) this would enable you to score almost all the marks available.

If you weren't familiar with Berry, Broadbent and Ottley's terminologies, you are likely to have struggled with this part of the question. Nonetheless, you should have realised that the issues at Factories 1 and 2 had been included in the scenario for a reason. Therefore, even if you didn't know what myopia, gaming and ossification were, the scenario should have given you a clue that these issues were linked to problems with the company's performance measures, and so you should have been able to suggest appropriate performance management solutions to them.

Marking scheme

Marks

(a) General description of performance pyramid (including diagram of
        (the model) – up to 3 marks

All the remaining marks must have specific relevance to Graviton:

Current issues at Graviton where current performance measurement system
     leads to tunnel vision and focus on selected aspects of performance only –
     1 mark per relevant point, up to maximum of 5 marks

Linking performance metrics to the company's vision – 1 mark per relevant
     point, up to a maximum of 4 marks

Using performance pyramid to identify ways Graviton's current performance
     measures could be improved: Market satisfaction; financial performance;
     customer satisfaction; flexibility; productivity; quality; delivery; cycle time;
     waste – 1 mark per relevant point, up to a maximum of 6 marks

Total for part (a): up to 15   15

(b) Clear definition of each term – 1 mark per term, up to a maximum of 3

For assessing whether the problems apply at Graviton, and for suggesting
     appropriate solutions – 1 mark per relevant point, up to a maximum of
     3 for each problem

Total for part (b): up to 10   10

Total = 25

(a) **Performance pyramid** – The logic of the performance pyramid is that although
       organisations operate at different levels (for example, strategic and operational) those
       levels need to support each other in achieving business objectives. The structure of the
       pyramid seeks to highlight the links between the day to day operational performance and
       overall strategic performance.

Graviton's current performance measurement system

The aim of Graviton's current performance measurement system (to provide a list of
measures at strategic, tactical and operational levels of management) seems to be
consistent with the logic of the performance pyramid (to link strategic and operational
performance drivers).

However, the CEO's concern that there are gaps in the current list of metrics could also be
linked to a concern that the current performance measurement system at Graviton is
concentrating attention on certain aspects of performance to the detriment of other
aspects of performance.

Tunnel vision – Although this is not one of the problems listed by the board executives, the focus on selected measurements, at the expense of others, characterises the problem of tunnel vision in performance measurement systems.

For example, Graviton's recent results might suggest that the focus of the company's attention has been on revenue growth rather than profitability, which could help to explain why revenue has risen considerably more rapidly than operating profit in the last year. In such a case, the problem could be addressed by including performance metrics relating to operating costs or profit margins.

More generally, one way to prevent tunnel vision being a problem for an organisation is to ensure that the dimensions of performance being measured are comprehensive, and include metrics relating to all the critical success factors in the organisation. Importantly also, this means that performance measures shouldn't focus narrowly on financial indicators, but should also address the range of processes and driving forces which guide an organisation's ability to achieve its strategic objectives.

This recognition of the importance of focusing on the range of processes and activities which shape an organisation's ability to achieve its strategic objectives is one of the key characteristics of the performance pyramid.

Moreover, the pyramid does not focus purely on financial objectives, but includes a range of objectives of **external effectiveness and internal efficiency**. Lynch and Cross propose that these elements of effectiveness and efficiency are the key driving forces on which company objectives are based.

The pyramid diagram highlights the way the performance of operational and business processes underpins an organisation's financial performance:

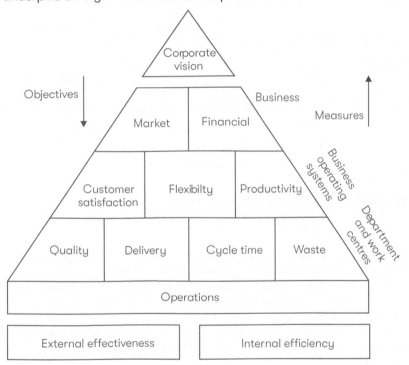

Corporate vision

Shareholder wealth – Graviton's overall objective is to maximise shareholder wealth; and therefore it seems surprising that the performance measures do not include **total shareholder return** (thereby recognising the importance of dividends and share price growth).

It is possible that Graviton is using return on capital employed (ROCE) as an overall measure of productivity and performance, but given the company's objective refers specifically to maximising 'shareholder wealth' then a performance measure focusing specifically on shareholder return would be more appropriate.

Moreover, the absence of any measures linked to the level of dividends may also explain why Graviton's dividend growth has not been strong – leading to criticism from the institutional investors.

Focus on changing market trends – Graviton's business aim is to satisfy changing market trends, and it seeks to do this by maintaining flexibility in production and close control across the supply chain. The elements of 'flexibility' and 'productivity' are included at the business operating system level in the performance pyramid, but it seems that they are higher level objectives at Graviton.

Flexibility – The measure of the average time for bringing new designs to market in Graviton's performance measurement system supports the importance of flexibility in its operations.

However, the current performance system does not measure the company's ability to replenish successful product lines, and therefore to take advantage of consumer demand. Whilst it is important for Graviton to introduce new designs quickly, it is equally important for the product availability of different clothes to reflect levels of demand.

Production control – Equally, however, it is important to maintain the quality of the production process. The criticisms from customers about the durability of Graviton's clothes may suggest there are issues relating to the controls in place in the production process.

The current performance measures do not include any measures around production quality or durability.

The apparent lack of focus on the production process could also help to explain why operating profits are increasingly significantly less than revenue. If Graviton's cost controls in the production process are weak, this would lead to falling operating profit margins.

Market and financial performance

The pyramid suggests that the two key drivers for obtaining overall corporate vision are **satisfying the market** and **performing well financially**.

Financial performance measures – Although Graviton's performance dashboard includes figures for revenues and profits, it doesn't show figures for profit margins. And despite profit increasing slightly from 20X1 to 20X3, the operating profit margin has fallen from 21.8% to 18.6% over this period. This again suggests that there could be issues with rising costs or weak cost control, but the current performance measurement system doesn't draw attention to this.

Alternatively, there could be a danger that Graviton has sacrificed profitability in order to achieve revenue growth.

Productivity – The pyramid also suggests that productivity is a key driver in obtaining financial objectives, and the nature of Graviton's market means that production efficiency is likely to be very important.

The measure of 'deliveries on time' could be seen as linked to this; but it seems unlikely to be the most important indicator to measure productivity. Given the nature of the clothing industry, a measure of waste or obsolescence (such as inventory write-offs) would seem to be more instructive. One of the keys to Graviton's success will be getting the right clothes to the right place at the right time. If it is too slow in producing clothes, and its designs become obsolete before it has had a chance to sell them, this could have a significant impact on Graviton's operating profit margins.

Market satisfaction – The performance pyramid suggests that customer satisfaction and flexibility are crucial in achieving market satisfaction.

We have already noted that Graviton uses 'time to market' as a measure for its ability to introduce new products in response to changing market trends, suggesting that it already considers this aspect of flexibility is important in achieving its corporate objectives.

Customer satisfaction – Although the current performance measures do not directly measure customer satisfaction, revenue growth could be seen, indirectly, as an indicator of customer satisfaction levels. If customers are not satisfied with the products they have bought from Graviton in the past, they are unlikely to make any repeat purchases.

Quality – In this respect, customer criticism over the durability of Graviton's clothes should be seen as a concern, because if these concerns remain they could hinder the company's sales and revenue in the future.

Alternatively, though, we could question how much customers value durability in a fast-changing industry. If customers are regularly buying new clothes to keep up with the changes in fashion, how important will durability actually be in their decision about which clothes to buy?

In this respect, it would be useful for Graviton to estabish how important the issue of durability is in customers' decision-making process. If it is significant, then it would be useful for Graviton to include a related metric (such as the number of customer complaints) in its performance measures.

Design awards – Although the current performance measures don't specifically refer to product quality, the number of design awards could also be seen, indirectly, as an indicator of quality – and possibly also of customer satisfaction. Graviton's clothes would be unlikely to be nominated for awards if they are felt to be of poor quality or if customers are critical of them.

Again, however, measuring the number of design awards is not the most obvious way of measuring quality or customer satisfaction (both of which are highlighted in the performance pyramid as drivers of external effectiveness).

(b) **Myopia**

Myopia relates to the problems caused by short-termist decisions leading to the neglect of longer-term objectives.

This currently appears to be an issue at Factory Site 2, where the factory appears reluctant to invest in any new machinery in order to preserve its excellent return on capital employed.

However, the failure to invest in the new machinery has led to a significant adverse variance in the cost of repairs and maintenance. It also seems likely that Site 2's production is less efficient than it would otherwise be if it had invested in some new machinery.

The use of ROCE as one of the metrics in the performance measurement systems (and in particular annual ROCE figures) could be one of the main reasons for myopia within Graviton; and specifically at Factory Site 2. One solution for this specific issue would be to include a performance measure for production efficiency (eg number of breakdowns or repairs required) at each of the factory sites.

More generally, Graviton could address the issue of myopia by measuring performance over a longer time period than a single accounting period.

Gaming

The problem of 'gaming' relates to the deliberate distortion of a performance measure in order to secure some kind of strategic advantage.

There is clear evidence of gaming at Factory Site 1, where the manager is manipulating revenue and profit figures (by delaying invoicing) in order to achieve profit targets.

It is not clear whether Graviton has an internal audit department, but if it does one specific action which could be taken is a review of the invoicing procedures, or a review of period-end cut-offs, to try to prevent such manipulation recurring.

More generally, the problem of gaming also appears to have been driven by the desire to achieve short-term (annual) performance targets. So, as with the proposed solution to myopia, one solution would be to reward performance over a longer time period than a single accounting period. For example, the factory manager's profit targets could be set as an average figure over a number of periods, rather than having single targets for individual periods.

Additionally, behaviour such as the factory manager's could be addressed by promoting a culture of honesty within the organisation. It is not clear whether Graviton currently has a corporate Code of Ethics, but a Code of this sort could be useful for highlighting the standards of behaviour which are expected in the company.

Ossification

The problem of 'ossification' relates to an unwillingness to change a performance measurement system once it has been set up. Ossification is likely to be a particular problem when the current system appears to be showing adequate results – because this situation could be hiding issues which could be highlighted if different measures were being monitored.

Ossification appears to be a problem at Graviton, where the board is sceptical of change and has argued that the business's good performance means there is no justification for changing the performance measurement system.

The CEO will have to convince the board that Graviton's current good performance has been achieved despite the current performance measurement system rather than because of it. More specifically, the CEO will need to highlight how the gaps in the current list of key metrics will lead to longer-term difficulties in achieving Graviton's overall objective to maximise shareholder wealth.

Once again, recognising the importance of longer-term performance is likely to address this problem. For example, the remuneration and incentive plans for Graviton's executives and board members could be linked to the longer-term, sustainable performance of the company, rather than to its historical results, or to its results in the short term.

43 Totaig

> **Workbook reference.** EVA is covered in Chapter 8 and value based management is covered in Chapter 14.
>
> **Top tips.** In part (a), the question presented a four part structure for this advice, which included: selection of measures and targets, timescales, appropriate management levels and difficulties in managing performance using VBM. A good answer required practical comments on these areas, not in generic terms but in a way that was applied to the scenario; 1 mark was available per point.
>
> In part (b), the discussion element of the question required a discussion of the difficulties of using EVA AT THIS COMPANY was required. Again, 1 mark was available per point and could have reflected the background of the management team, the increasing challenges facing the company and the issues created by changing depreciation policy (for example).

Marking scheme

		Marks
(a)	1 mark per point (under the four headings):	
	– Selection of measures and targets	
	– Timescales	
	– Management levels	
	– Difficulties	
	Maximum for part (a)	15
(b)	Calculation of NOPAT:	
	Advertising cost – 1 mark	
	Decrease in allowance – 1 mark	
	Interest – 1 mark	
	Calculation of adjusted capital employed – 1 mark	
	Calculation of EVA™ – 1 mark	
	Conclusion – 1 mark	
	Difficulties of EVA™ – 1 mark per point, up to 5 marks	
	Maximum 10 marks	
	Maximum for part (b)	10
	Total =	25

(a)   **Selection of appropriate measures and targets**

Value drivers create long-term value. Totaig is facing competition from overseas businesses which will soon be able to produce at a similar unit cost to Totaig and produce items of comparable quality. The unit cost of production and product quality would be value drivers for Totaig and targets should be set for these two measures.

Targets should be both financial and non-financial. This will ensure that there is not too much emphasis on financial targets, which tend to be backwards looking, rather than relating to the present value of future cash flows, which is the focus of value‐based management (VBM).

The existing targets of return on investment (ROI) and operating margin are backwards looking. They will also discourage managers to make investments, for example, in product development, which might be detrimental to Totaig's long-term performance. This is because investments in new products will reduce both of these measures in the short term.

Having targets related to product quality would ensure that the business does not focus too much on cutting the unit cost of production, for example, by using cheaper, lower quality materials. It appears that to create long-term value, Totaig must be competitive on both unit cost of production and product quality.

Timescales to which the targets should relate

Totaig must set short-term and long-term targets, which should be linked together, for key value drivers. Competitors will be able to produce at a similar unit cost to Totaig within a year. A suitable short-term target would therefore be to reduce unit production costs within that timescale. As VBM is concerned with long-term value, Totaig should set longer-term targets relating to quality in anticipation of the new competitors' ability to improve on this aspect within three to five years.

The possible need to invest heavily in product development and make acquisitions will probably require longer-term targets to be set.

Levels in the business to which the targets should relate

Value can be created at all levels in the company, and targets should be set according to the different layers of management. Targets relating to unit cost of production and product quality are under the control of operational managers, and these would be suitable for this level of management.

Targets relating to possible future acquisitions are under the control of the directors, who are the strategic decision makers.

Difficulties in measuring and managing performance using VBM

Totaig will require good information to implement VBM. It may be difficult to identify value drivers and reporting systems need to be able to provide the information which is required. Currently, IT systems are basic and outdated for a business of its complexity. This may mean that it is difficult to identify value drivers for the setting of targets. The implementation of VBM may require significant investment in IT systems to measure performance against targets and take up management time. The costs of implementing VBM may exceed the benefits.

The operational managers are unlikely to have any experience of VBM since most of them joined Totaig, which itself has never used VBM, when the business first started. They will require training on VBM if they are to understand the targets set. For example, new value-based performance measures, such as EVA™, will be needed, which will be unfamiliar to directors and managers in the business.

Using VBM to manage performance at Totaig will require a culture change amongst all employees, who will need to work towards creating shareholder value. The directors will need to demonstrate commitment to the use of VBM in order to motivate operational managers to accept the change. Currently, some directors at Totaig seem not to be convinced of the usefulness of the approach.

It may be difficult to measure economic depreciation, for example, or to determine whether, and for when, the anticipated heavy investment in product development will create value. These difficulties will affect the reliability of performance measures for value, such as EVA™, in managing performance.

(b) Calculation of EVA™

	$'000
Profit after tax	6,630
Advertising costs expenses	450
Decrease in allowance for doubtful debts	(200)
Interest net of tax (1,500 × 78%)	1,170
NOPAT	8,050

	$'000
Opening capital employed	88,944
Opening allowance for doubtful debt	500
Adjusted opening capital employed	89,444

	$'000
NOPAT	8,050
After-tax WACC × adjusted capital employed (9% × 89,444)	(8,050)
EVA™	0

As EVA™ is zero, Totaig has neither created nor destroyed value.

Difficulties of using EVA™ as a performance indicator

The cost of capital can be difficult to measure reliably and can change over time. Totaig's current WACC is 9%, but due to the existence of floating rate loans and changes in the market value of debt, the WACC will not remain constant. The cost of equity may also change over time if shareholders require different levels of return to reflect changing business or financial risks, for example.

It is assumed that, at Totaig, economic depreciation and accounting depreciation are the same. A difficulty in using EVA™ is that it is hard to estimate economic depreciation. Also, as the directors are considering changing the depreciation policy for the year ended 30 June 20X6, this may distort comparisons of EVA™ between different years.

The calculation of EVA™ can be complex and poorly understood by managers. If managers do not understand the measure, they are less likely to be able to achieve targets for EVA™ as they will not know how. There may be a large number of adjustments to make in calculating EVA™. Currently at Totaig, only a few adjustments are required. If the business starts to make acquisitions and invest heavily in product development, there may be more adjustments to be made in future calculations.

As EVA™ is an absolute figure rather than a percentage, it is difficult to compare with businesses of different sizes – for example, if Totaig was to undertake financial benchmarking against its competitors.

EVA™ uses historical data which may not be relevant to future performance. It may be hard to determine if and when advertising expenditure is value adding, for example.

44 APX Accountancy

Workbook reference. The building block model is discussed in Chapter 12 of the Workbook.

Top tips.

Part (a) is a pure test of knowledge. You are simply asked to describe Fitzgerald and Moon's model; you do not need to apply it to the scenario.

However, in parts (b) and (c) you do need to apply your knowledge of the model to the scenario.

It is vital that you read the requirement for **part (b)** carefully and answer the question set. You are asked to evaluate APX's performance **management system**, not APX's performance.

Notice also the link between parts (b) and (c). In part (b) you need to evaluate the existing system, and then in **part (c)** you need to explain and suggest improvements. Therefore, you should not have suggested any improvements while you were answering part (b); but should have saved these for part (c) instead.

Part (d) – At one level, the marketing manager seems to be highlighting the importance of non-financial performance measures, which seems reasonable. However, he also seems to have overlooked the environmental factors which have contributed to the relative financial performance of the different service areas. Has the Business Advisory Division really performed best financially because it has the highest customer service score, or because the business advisory sector had a growth year across the industry as a whole?

Examining team's comments. It was sad to note how many candidates did not even know the names of the three building blocks. This demonstrated inadequate preparation for the examination.

Better candidates had read the full requirement to the question before beginning their answers, and so held back from offering improvements to the faults recognised in part (b) until their answers to part (c) of the question.

(a) **Performance measurement in service businesses** – Fitzgerald and Moon's building block model aims to provide a framework to improve performance measurement in service businesses.

The model suggests that performance systems should be based on three concepts: dimensions, standards and rewards.

Dimensions – The model identifies six dimensions (competitive performance, financial performance, quality of service, flexibility and resource utilisation and innovation) and suggests that the performance measures companies choose should focus on these six areas.

The model also suggests that the dimensions can be divided into two sets: **results** (competitive performance and financial performance) and **determinants** (the other four). The logic here is that controlling and improving performance in respect of the determinants will then lead to improved results.

Standards – This aspect of the model relates to the targets which are chosen to be measured. Here, the model highlights three key properties which performance measures (standards or targets) should possess: **ownership, achievability** and **fairness**.

Rewards – Finally, the model also highlights the properties which reward schemes need to possess in order to encourage staff to work towards the performance standards set. Again, there are three key properties: **clarity, controllability** and **motivation**. The reward system needs to help motivate staff and, in order to achieve this, staff need to be clear about the goals they are working towards, and feel that the rewards are related to areas of responsibility that they can control.

(b) The current performance management system appears to be based primarily on financial performance, and so does not focus on a number of the determinants highlighted by the building block model.

Dimensions

Results – The current system does allow **financial** and **competitive performance** to be measured. The figures for **revenue growth** and **profit margin** can be used to measure APX's financial performance, while the data on accounting industry revenue can be used to calculate **market share**.

Determinants – However, the management information collected provides less opportunity to measure the determinants of performance. The customer service score could be used as an indicator of the quality of service offered, but there appears to be no information on which to measure flexibility and resource utilisation and innovation.

Standards

Measuring competitive performance – The industry figures will allow APX to monitor its market share, and its revenue growth relative to the industry as a whole, but they only look at revenue rather than profit. Therefore, it does not look as if APX can measure its profit margin against the industry as a whole.

Consequently, any standards for profitability will have to be **set internally**; for example APX could measure the profitability of each of its business streams. However, this could raise issues in relation to **achievability** and **fairness**. Given that Emland is currently in a recession, it is perhaps to be expected that the growth and margins in the audit businesses will be lower than those in the Business Advisory Division, so the fact that this is the case does not necessarily tell us anything about the relative performance of the divisions.

The scenario does not tell us anything about the target scores for customer service or how these are set, so we cannot comment on this aspect of the standards.

Reward system

Clarity – Non-partners receive a bonus based on their line managers' annual review, but the scenario does not indicate what aspects of their performance staff are judged on in this review. If they are not clear what their performance is being judged on, or if the judgement is perceived to be too subjective, this may serve to demotivate staff.

Controllability – APX's performance management system appears to focus predominantly on financial indicators, which may suggest that financial measures are used as the basis for the annual review. Again, though, this could be a cause for concern, because non-partners have relatively limited scope to influence revenue or profit margins.

Divisional or group-wide performance – There may be similar issues of controllability in relation to the partners' reward system. The partners currently receive a share of profit, but it is not clear if this profit share is based on APX's profit as a whole or the profit for their area of the business. If the partners feel their rewards are being based on measures they cannot control, this is likely to adversely affect their motivation. For example, if partners' rewards are based on group profits, then partners in the Audit Division may not maximise their own performance if they know that they will benefit (regardless of their own division's performance) from the favourable performance of the Business Advisory Services Division.

(c) **Cover all dimensions of performance** – One of the key improvements a building block system can make to performance management is ensuring that all the key dimensions of successful performance are measured.

At APX, this will mean considering the importance of flexibility, resource utilisation and innovation to the firm's success and then developing performance measures for these dimensions.

Flexibility – Flexibility is likely to be important for APX in terms of the scheduling of its work (to meet client deadlines) and, in this respect, flexibility is also likely to have an impact on customer satisfaction. Accordingly, APX could introduce a performance measure looking at the percentage of jobs delivered on time.

Resource utilisation – APX's key resource is its staff, so it would seem very important to measure staff utilisation rates. One way of doing this would be to measure the percentage of chargeable hours worked as a percentage of total working hours, and such a measure would provide APX with information about the productivity of its staff. Moreover, if this measure were recorded on a monthly basis it would highlight periods when the business is busy and when it is less busy. The partners could then try to win new clients who need work done in APX's less busy periods.

Innovation – Innovation could be useful for improving APX's internal systems and working practices, but its impact is likely to be greater in relation to the new services APX can develop for its clients. In this case, it may be useful to have a performance measure which looks at the percentage of revenue earned from new customer initiatives.

Standards and rewards

Although the introduction of additional measures which cover the non-financial dimensions of successful performance is perhaps the biggest improvement the building block approach could make to APX, there are also **issues with the way standards are currently set**.

To address this, APX needs to ensure that the measures chosen (and performance targets set) are **achievable** and **fair**. In turn, this should encourage the staff to try to achieve the performance targets.

Similarly, the current rewards system should also be reviewed to ensure that it serves to **motivate partners and staff**. For example, if this is not already the case, an element of the partners' profit share should be based on the profitability of the work from their divisions, rather than it all being based on APX's profitability overall.

Equally, it may also be beneficial to give the non-partners their own targets or objectives for the year, because then the line managers have some more clearly defined objectives to assess their staff against in the annual review process.

(d)

> **Top tip.** The measure being commented on is customer service, not customer satisfaction. You may have been tempted to discuss the potential trade-off between financial and non-financial performance measures – by suggesting that APX might be able to increase customer satisfaction by reducing its prices, and thereby also reducing its profit margins.
>
> However, we have focused specifically on the customer service score, rather than customer satisfaction more generally, and so we have not included this more general argument in our suggested solution below.

Importance of customer service – Customer service is undoubtedly important for a service firm like APX, because if the service it offers its customers is poor it may look for other advisers.

It is not clear what factors contribute to the customer service scores which customers give, but the quality of the advice which APX gives its clients is likely to be an important factor in its ongoing success, so this aspect of customer service is important to measure.

Reasons for scores – However, the inherent nature of the services provided could also contribute to the customer service scores, and so, in this respect, the marketing manager's statement could be misleading.

APX's clients have to have an audit, and they may almost resent this if they perceive the audit brings them little value. So the fact that the audit gets the lowest customer service score may reflect this rather than the quality of APX's audit staff.

External environment – However, perhaps more importantly, the marketing manager seems to be attributing the Business Advisory Division's favourable performance to its customer service score alone, without considering the environmental factors which have also affected its performance. The current recession in Emland has led to an increase in demand for business advisory services across the industry as a whole. It seems likely that APX's performance reflects this more than its customer service scores.

Equally, the marketing manager's implication that the customer service score is a more important performance metric than financial measures is also misguided. Whilst it is important that APX considers non-financial aspects of performance, it should not do so at the expense of financial performance measures. Instead, APX's performance evaluation needs to consider both financial and non-financial performance measures.

45 Vunderg

Top tips. This was based on a windows manufacturer considering the implementation of ABM.

Part (a). This required advice on how ABM could improve strategic performance.

To score well this required a brief definition of ABM and then an extraction of relevant practical information from the scenario to support the introduction of ABM (high overheads, complexity of products and customers etc).

Part (b). This required an assessment of the limitations of ABM (eg of the impact of closure of a product line) and potential implementation issues (eg staff opposition).

Again, to score well this required an extraction of relevant practical information from the scenario to argue against the introduction of ABM (main product is standardised, ignores life cycle etc).

Examining team's comments. This was the most poorly answered question of the three in this exam, with many candidates generally aware of activity-based costing, but much vaguer on ABM.

Part (a) of the question asked how ABM could help improve the strategic performance of the company. Some candidates took the productive path of discussing the general benefits of the method and then illustrating each of these for the relevant products. Many candidates though took the approach of treating each product type individually, which lead to answers that repeated the same general point several times (wasting time) and not discussing the impact of their advice on the business overall.

Part (b) of the question required candidates to assess the limitations of using ABM in context and the problems with its implementation. Candidates provided fair answers on the general problems of identifying cost drivers and issues in resourcing the implementation of ABM. However, their lack of knowledge of ABM lead to generally weak answers, lacking in detail relevant to the company.

There were a number of candidates who provided the benefits of ABM again in this part, so not answering the question.

Marking scheme

		Marks
(a)	1 mark per relevant point	
	Defining ABM	2
	Choosing which products to manufacture	4
	Review of costs, prices and designs	4
	Customer profitability analysis	4
		Max 13
(b)	1 mark per relevant point	
	Limitations of the ABM method	9
	Implementation	5
		Max 12
		Total = 25

(a) **Activity based management**

Activity based management (ABM) applies activity based costing (ABC) principles in order to satisfy customer needs using the least amount of resources. Activity based costing groups overheads into cost pools for an activity and identifies the cost driver for each activity. This gives a more accurate calculation of product costs.

ABM makes it possible to better control costs by controlling the activities which drive the costs. ABM would also help Vunderg to identify value added activities and non-value added activities. Activities which do not add value should be reduced, which would allow cost reduction without affecting the quality of service or product for Vunderg's customers.

Choosing which products to manufacture

ABM can help to improve Vunderg's performance in terms of deciding which products to manufacture. This is particularly important where a large proportion of a company's costs are overheads. This is the case in Vunderg, where overheads relating primarily to procurement, customer administration and product design are high. By understanding the cost of a product, and therefore its profitability, Vunderg can decide whether to discontinue an unprofitable product or whether to produce a new one. This will be relevant for the proposed large windows for commercial buildings. These are bespoke items and the cost will include a large amount of overheads, such as design.

Loss making products identified using ABM are often those which are highly customised and produced in low volumes, such as the conservatories. By using ABC principles, Vunderg could identify the high overhead costs of the sourcing of special materials and finishes for these by the procurement department. Using ABM, Vunderg could take action to reduce these costs, for example, by standardising the range of materials and finishes used so that the procurement department spends less time sourcing them. The conservatories earn 8% of Vunderg's total contribution in 20% of the factory space. This implies that conservatories account for a disproportionate level of factory overheads.

Review of costs, prices and designs

By understanding what drives the costs of a product, Vunderg can take actions to make an unprofitable product profitable – for example, in response to the initial quality problems when the glasshouses were first manufactured, but which now command premium prices. The use of ABM may have led to a faster resolution of these initial quality problems by identifying the causes, or drivers, of the product cost and taking action to manage these.

ABM will also help identify products which may need to be re-priced. For example, customers may be prepared to pay more for the use of special materials and finishes in the conservatories. Vunderg could charge customers more for the use of special materials and finishes to cover the high overhead cost associated with procuring them.

ABM may identify possible improvements to the design of a product by focusing on activities which add value for the customer and eliminating those which do not. Selling leaking conservatories does not add value to the customer and incurs rectification costs. The improvement in design to prevent the leaks occurring in the first place is an example of how ABM can be used to make the conservatories business more profitable.

Customer profitability analysis

Customer profitability analysis (CPA) involves apportioning overhead costs to different types of customers, or categories of customers, using ABM principles. This enables a better understanding of the profitability of selling to different customers and can help Vunderg to decide whether to stop selling to certain customers or take other actions to improve their profitability.

At Vunderg, CPA would be most useful for the glasshouses which are sold through 40 different retailers. Some of the costs of selling to these customers, such as trade discounts, should be relatively easy to identify. Other overhead costs, such as those driven by the number of customer orders processed, may only be identified using ABM principles and may differ considerably between customers as the size of orders they place varies greatly.

The profitability of selling to the 40 retailers will therefore also vary considerably. Vunderg could act to improve the profitability of the least profitable ones. This could include insisting on minimum order sizes to reduce the costs driven by the number of orders processed. They could also offer more product training or contribution towards advertising costs to increase sales volumes.

(b) **Limitations of using the ABM method identifying key activities and drivers**

It may be difficult to separately identify all of the key activities and what drives them, which makes the application of ABC principles difficult. It may also be hard to assign responsibilities for individual cost pools which may cut across departmental boundaries.

Limited use

ABM is most useful where products are customised and contain high overhead costs such as design, procurement and customer administration. While the use of ABM may be worthwhile for the conservatories business, which is highly customised, and for the bespoke windows for commercial buildings, 84% (9,800/11,679) of Vunderg's contribution is from windows used in residential housing. These are highly standardised and are likely to include few overhead costs; for example, relating to design and after sales service. The manufacturing process after many years will already be efficient. The costs may already be well understood and controlled, in which case the implementation of ABM may not be worthwhile. Vunderg does, however, need a good understanding of the overhead costs, as the residential windows market is competitive.

As windows are highly standardised, Vunderg may be unable to pick and choose which items to produce. Design, specification and size will be dictated by the large construction companies who buy them and who will expect Vunderg to supply a complete range of windows. These companies would just buy from a competitor if Vunderg stopped producing the items they needed. As this market is very competitive, there may be little Vunderg could do to improve profitability, for example, by increasing prices, so the use of ABM to choose which products to sell could therefore be of little use. Similarly, as there are only a few large construction companies, the use of ABM may also not be worthwhile as Vunderg could not realistically stop trading with any one of them, nor could it raise prices because of the competitive market.

Incorrect decisions

Despite the difficulties in using ABC, for example, in identifying cost drivers, the use of cost drivers to charge overhead costs to conservatories should give a clearer indication of their profitability than under the current system. Vunderg can then take action to increase the profitability of these products, for example, by increasing the prices or reducing the costs.

The decision on whether these products should be discontinued should, however, take into account the effect on glasshouse sales as customers like to buy glasshouses which match the materials used in the conservatories. Discontinuing conservatories could reduce contribution from glasshouses by up to 17.1% (650/3,800), a total loss of contribution of approximately $166,000 (17.1% of $969,000), which is significant. As conservatories are at the start of their life cycle, expecting them to be profitable immediately could be unrealistic.

Just because a large proportion of factory space is dedicated to manufacturing conservatories, this does not mean that these costs will be saved in the short term if the products are discontinued. The depreciation or lease costs of the factory are fixed. Vunderg's main business is saturated and there is no prospect that the factory space could be better used in making other products. The factory may already not be fully utilised.

Problems of implementing ABM resource and cost impact

As Vunderg does not have an ABM system, considerable resources and management time will be needed to set this up. There may be resistance from staff, for example, because they do not want to change from the current costing system, which has been in use for a long time. Staff may not understand the benefits of ABM, or how it works. They would need training, which is expensive, and it may take a considerable time before ABM is working effectively.

As Vunderg has only basic information systems, it may need to invest in these in order to collect large volumes of data on costs. Vunderg will have to consider whether the benefits of implementing ABM are greater than the costs of doing so.

46 LOL cards

Marking scheme

		Marks
(a)	Up to 2 marks on the explanation of VBM and then up to 2 marks on how it aids focus in the management process	
	Maximum for part (a)	4
(b)	Workings:	
	NOPAT 1	
	Capital employed 1	
	Cost of capital 1	
	EVA™ 1	
	Assumptions 0.5 each up to a maximum of 1.5	
	EPS 1	
	Share price 3 × 0.5	
	Comments: 1 mark per reasonable point up to 2 on EPS and share price and 2 on EVA™.	
	Maximum for part (b)	12
(c)	1 mark for each relevant point made up to a maximum of 3	3
(d)	1 mark for each relevant point made up to a maximum of 6	6
		Total = 25

(a) What VBM involves and how it can focus the company on shareholder interests

The VBM approach starts with the primary objective of the business as shareholder wealth maximisation and develops a performance approach based on this. At the strategic level the primary measure of performance is EVA™ because this EVA™ is equivalent to discounted cash flow in the long term which is a widely used method of valuing shares by equity analysts.

EVA™ is used as the sole measure of performance by management and even throughout the organisation (at strategic, tactical and operational levels) thereby avoiding the conflict between multiple objectives and resulting measures. The variables within EVA™ that drive performance such as PBIT can be used by management to achieve value-based targets set down from the strategic value-based goal.

(b)   **An assessment of the financial performance of LOL using EVA™. Evaluate this against EPS and share price performance**

EPS has fallen by 23.4% (21.88 in 20X9 ($35m/$160m) compared with 16.75% in 20Y0 ($26.8m/$160m)) which suggests the company is not favoured by investors but the average share price has only fallen from $12.20 to $10.70 over the same period which doesn't suggest the company is out of favour as much. Indeed this is against a sector fall of 26% (907.1/1,225.6) over the same period and a main market index decline of 34.9% (1,448.90/2,225.40) thus inferring LOL has actually outperformed its sector and the main market.

The sector comparison is more relevant to LOL's performance as this includes only comparative companies. The view of the market that LOL is outperforming its sector is confirmed by the calculation of EVA™. This remains positive at $22.6m in 20Y0 compared with $29.6m in 20X9. Calculations are in Appendix 1. Thus LOL continues to create value for shareholders even in difficult conditions.

(c)   **Evaluate VBM against traditional profit-based measures of performance**

Value measures take into account capital employed and the cost of capital and are therefore considered superior to profit measures which capture these less clearly. They are adjusted to take out accounting adjustments so they arrive at cash flow measures which are less affected by accounting adjustments. In the case of LOL the accounting and economic depreciation are assumed to be the same but may differ if additional information becomes available.

However, EVA™ and other value-based measures are complex and unfamiliar to calculate and so may be off-putting to management used to profit measures. They also contain assumptions on the capital asset pricing model (used to calculate the cost of capital) and data is historic and so may change in the future. For instance, share values are calculated based on dividend flows in the future. However, provided users are aware of the assumptions and become familiar with the process of calculating EVA™ it could be a useful measure.

EVA™ can be manipulated by choosing projects with low set-up costs to massage the initial EVA™ figure which then falls in later years. It also fails to recognise the increase in shareholder wealth over the life of the project better captured by the use of net present value.

(d)   **Traditional cost allocation systems**

Traditional costing systems, notably **absorption costing**, assume that all products **consume resources in proportion to their production volumes**. While this may be true for overheads such as power costs, it does not necessarily hold for all overheads, especially those connected with support services.

The amount of **overhead allocated** to individual products by absorption costing therefore bears **very little resemblance** to the **amount of overhead actually incurred** by the products and hence gives management **minimal understanding of the behaviour of overhead costs**. Consequently management also only have a limited ability to control/reduce overhead costs.

ABC/ABM approach

Activity-based costing (ABC) attempts to overcome this problem by identifying the activities or transactions (**cost drivers**) which underlie an organisation's activities and which cause the incidence of the activity, and hence the cost of the activity (overheads) to increase. Costs can then be attributed to products according to the number of cost drivers they cause/consume using cost driver rates.

ABM is the term given to those **management processes that use the information provided by an activity-based cost analysis to improve organisational profitability**.

ABM and cost reduction

Because ABM analyses costs on the basis of what causes them, rather than on the basis of type of expense/cost centre, it provides management with vital information on why costs are being incurred. If management can **reduce the incidence of the cost driver, they can reduce the associated cost**.

ABM involves a variety of **cost reduction techniques**.

- Ensuring activities are performed as efficiently as possible
- Reducing or eliminating the need to perform activities that do not add value for customers
- Improving the design of products
- Developing better relationships with customers and suppliers

In short, it aims to ensure that customer needs are met while fewer demands are made on organisational resources.

APPENDIX 1

Workings: EVA™ calculation

EVA™ calculations for the periods given are:

	20X9 $m	20Y0 $m
Profit after interest and tax	35.0	26.8
Interest (net of tax at 25%)	3.0	5.9
Net operating profit after tax (NOPAT)	38.0	32.6
Capital employed (at year start)	99.2	104.1

Assumptions:
Economic and accounting depreciation are equivalent.
There are no non-cash expenses to adjust in the profit figure.
There are no additional adjustments to make regarding goodwill.

Cost of capital
$WACC = (\%e \times Ke) + (\%d \times Kd)$

20X9	$(50\% \times 12.7\%) + (50\% \times 4.2\%)$	=	8.45%
20Y0	$(50\% \times 15.3\%) + (50\% \times 3.9\%)$	=	9.60%

EVA™ = NOPAT − (Capital employed × WACC)

20X9	$38.0 - (99.2 \times 8.45\%)$	=	29.6
20Y0	$32.6 - (104.1 \times 9.6\%)$	=	22.6

47 Bazeele

Workbook reference. Value-based management is discussed in Chapter 13 of the Workbook. Economic Value Added (EVA™) is discussed in Chapter 8.

Top tips.

Part (a). A useful way to approach this requirement would be to begin by thinking what the key features of a VBM approach are. Having done this, you can then begin to assess how these differ from Bazeele's current approach, and therefore whether moving to a value-based management approach is appropriate to Bazeele.

Note that, in the scenario, the CEO has said 'The shareholders are unsure what VBM is' so it could be useful to begin your answer with a brief explanation of what VBM is.

However, the requirement doesn't actually ask you to describe the VBM approach, or how it might be implemented, but specifically whether the VBM approach is appropriate for Bazeele. So the main focus of your answer needs to be whether VBM would be appropriate in the context described in the scenario.

For example, the second paragraph of the scenario identifies Bazeele's current objective to maintain its level of ROCE, with business units having an objective to maintain net profit margins. In the fourth paragraph we're then told business unit managers have postponed staff training because it was expensive. But is this decision taken with a view to maintaining short-term profit, or generating value for shareholders in the longer-term? (And, if there are problems in Bazeele's current approach, could these be solved by moving to a value-based approach?)

Part (b). As with part (a), a useful way to approach this requirement would be to think about the aspects of performance which would be important in a VBM approach and compare them to the areas which currently seem to be important. Identifying the differences between the two should help to identify the changes Bazeele would need to make it if adopts a VBM approach.

The structure of the question should also help you to identify one of these changes. The CEO has raised the possibility of using EVA™ to measure whether or not Bazeele creates value for its shareholders (and you then need to calculate EVA™ in part (c)). This should be a clue that EVA™ might be a more suitable measurement system to use, rather than simply measuring ROCE and profit margins like Bazeele currently does.

Also, we're told that Bazeele currently has no information about customer satisfaction levels. But, if maintaining customer satisfaction is important in maintaining the company's success (and therefore its future value), is this something it will need to start measuring under a VBM approach?

More generally, might any changes to Bazeele's culture be required in order to adopt VBM successfully? In the scenario the CEO has said 'Personally, I dislike change, but would not object to the adoption of VBM if it was thought to be beneficial.' The fact that the CEO has made this comment, could be a clue that change **will** be required.

Part (c). Although the requirement asks you to advise whether Bazeele has generated economic value, this part of the question essentially requires you to calculate economic value added, using the information provided in Appendix 1. If EVA™ is positive this will mean Bazeele has generated value for its shareholders; if EVA™ is negative, this will suggest Bazeele has destroyed value.

Although you don't need to include this in your answer, it might be useful to write out the EVA™ formula at the beginning of your plan, to provide you with an overall structure for the calculation.

All of the points in Appendix provide you with figures, or adjustments, which are relevant to the EVA calculation, so you need to work methodically through them and assess how they fit into the calculations. For example, what adjustments need to be made to the stated net profit of $10m (Point 1) in order to determine the 'NOPAT' figure required. Similarly, what adjustments need to be made to the capital employed figure (Point 2) in order to calculate the figure for economic value of assets?

Then, how do you calculate the weighted average cost of capital, which you need to apply to the economic value of assets in order to determine the capital charge?

Examining team's comments. Parts (a) and (b) were both poorly answered and reflected a lack of understanding of the VBM approach. Many candidates provided lots of irrelevant information in an attempt to disguise their lack of knowledge.

Candidates' answers to part (c) were often good. However, a significant number of candidates made simple errors where they had correctly identified an adjustment to make to profit, or capital employed, but then added it when it should have been subtracted, or vice versa. This suggests candidates may have simply learned the adjustments, but then failed to do sufficient practice questions before the exam, so that they didn't know how to apply what they had learned.

Marks

(a)   1 mark per relevant point

General explanation/evaluation of VBM – up to 2 marks
Application to Bazeele – up to 4 marks
Recommendation of whether or not a VBM approach is appropriate for
Bazeele – 1 mark
Maximum for part (a)   7

(b)   1 mark per relevant point

Changes required on adoption of VBM – up to 7 marks
Maximum for part (b)   7

(c)   Calculation of EVA WACC – 1 mark

NOPAT adjustments:
Depreciation – 1 mark
Economic depreciation – 1 mark
Interest – 1 mark
Tax on interest – 1 mark
Reduction in bad debt provision – 1 mark
Advertising – 1 mark

Capital adjustments:
Difference in accumulated depreciation – 1 mark
Add back: increase in bad debt provision
Calculation of EVA™ – 1 mark

Conclusion: whether value is created or destroyed – 1 mark

Up to a maximum for part (c) of 11 marks   11
                                                                            Total = 25

(a)   **Appropriateness of VBM approach**

In the context of VBM, value of a business is measured by discounting cash flows at the business's cost of capital. When investment returns exceed the cost of capital, value will be created for shareholders. When returns are lower than the cost of capital, value will be destroyed.

The VBM approach is to ensure that all activities and decisions in a business are undertaken so as to create value for shareholders. Currently, Bazeele's overall objective is to maintain ROCE at historic levels, but this does not necessarily create value for shareholders.

This is particularly so now that Bazeele has diversified into hiring large items of plant for use in major infrastructure projects. These projects last up to 10 years, so the time value of money is likely to be significant, as is the initial capital expenditure for the plant. Long-term hire agreements may give an acceptable ROCE, but may have a negative net present value, and hence destroy value for shareholders. The prediction of large increases in bank interest rates will increase Bazeele's cost of capital, and further reduce the net present value of long-term agreements.

Similarly, business unit and branch managers are given the objective of maintaining net profit margins. Thus, managers may avoid activities which reduce profits in the short term, but which have future long-term benefits and create value for shareholders, such as investment in staff training.

With VBM, decisions are taken to create value for shareholders by considering value drivers, which are any factors which affect the value of the business. Value drivers may be non-financial, such as the customer satisfaction which may have been improved by the postponed staff training. A VBM approach is, therefore, suitable for Bazeele as it will encourage creation of value for shareholders.

(b) **Changes required**

To adopt a VBM approach, Bazeele would need to use a different set of performance indicators, as ROCE and net profit margin do not necessarily create value for shareholders. Economic value added (EVA™) is a performance measure for shareholder value. Though more complex to calculate and more difficult to understand than the existing measures, EVA™ does encourage managers to make decisions, such as undertaking staff training, which have future long-term benefits. By encouraging managers to make investments which give a positive EVA™, value will be created for shareholders.

With VBM, managers would be given targets according to their areas of responsibility. For example, the board may have objectives to maximise value by making acquisitions which create value. Branch managers' objectives may be focused on non-financial value drivers such as customer satisfaction.

To identify value drivers, Bazeele will need good information which is accurate, reliable and timely, for example. It is unclear whether the current management information system is able to provide good information, but the CEO has said that information on customer satisfaction is not available. Resources, such as financial investment, time and training, may be needed to improve Bazeele's management information. Managers may resist the change in culture which would be required to adopt VBM; not least the CEO would need to set the 'tone at top' for what would be a disruptive and major change to Bazeele. However, the benefits of adopting VBM seem to outweigh the costs of doing so.

(c) **Economic value**

As the economic value added (EVA™) is negative – ie ($13.1m) – Bazeele has destroyed value for shareholders.

Calculation of net operating profit after tax (NOPAT)

	$m	$m
Net profit after tax		10.0
Add: depreciation on non-current assets	6.0	
Deduct: economic depreciation	(14.0)	
		(8.0)
Add: interest (accounted for in the WACC)	15.0	
Less: tax on interest ($15.0m × 20%)	(3.0)	
		12.0
Deduct: reduction in bad debt provision		(4.8)
Add: advertising for long-term benefit		0.6
NOPAT		9.8

Calculation of economic value of assets

	$m
Capital employed at the start of the year	250.0
Deduct: difference in accumulated depreciation	(16.0)
Add back: increase in bad debt provision	4.8
Economic value of assets	238.8

Calculation of EVA™

	$m
NOPAT	9.8
Deduct: capital charge ($238.8 × 9.6%) (W1)	(22.9)
EVA™	(13.1)

Working
Weighted average cost of capital (WACC)
Cost of equity   12.0%
After tax cost of debt: 8.0%   (10% × (1 – 20%))
WACC: 9.6%   ((40% × 12%) + (60% × 8.0%))

48 Dibble

Workbook reference. ABC and ABM are discussed in Chapter 13 of the Workbook.

Top tips. The opening paragraph of the scenario tells us that 'Dibble has always absorbed production overheads to the cost of each product on the basis of machine hours'. In other words, Dibble currently uses a simple absorption method of cost allocation. In effect, the context for part (a) of this question is based around the differences between ABC and overhead allocation based on a simple absorption method.

Part (a) (i) asks how ABC could be implemented. Thinking about the contrast between ABC and Dibble's current method of overhead allocation could help you identify the additional information needed to implement ABC. Dibble currently allocates all of its overheads to the cost of each product on the basis of machine hours. But what would it have to do differently if it was using an ABC approach?

Note, however, that there were only four marks available for this part of the question, so you were only expected to provide a relatively brief overview of the key features of ABC.

Part (a) (ii) asks whether it may be more appropriate to use ABC in the Timber and Steel Divisions instead of the current absorption costing method. In effect, having identified the key features of ABC in part (a) (i), you now need to consider its potential advantages and disadvantages, and the contexts in which it is appropriate, in order to assess whether it would be appropriate for the two divisions in question.

To score well here, it is vital that you appreciate the main characteristics of the Timber and Steel Divisions – and the differences between them. The Timber Division produces a limited range of standardised products. By contrast, the Steel Division produces a wide range of bespoke products. (And, as the fourth paragraph of the scenario tells us, the board of the Steel Division feels the pricing structure may be too simplistic, and it is not sure of the profitability of some groups of products.)

The key point to note here is that it seems likely that the Steel Division will benefit from a more detailed (and accurate) method of allocating overhead costs, and therefore ABC would seem to be appropriate for that division. However, the existing basis seems perfectly adequate for the Timber Division.

Note that, in the scenario, the CEO tells you he doesn't want detailed calculations. So you shouldn't waste time trying to use the figures from the management accounts to assess the impact of introducing ABC.

Note also – as a general point in APM exams – just because a model (or approach) is new, this doesn't necessarily make it better than the existing one. It needs to be appropriate to the context. ABC is more time consuming than absorption costing so, in this case, would the benefits it might generate for the Timber Division justify this extra effort?

Part (b) asks how ABM could be used to improve business performance in the company as a whole.

A useful approach to this requirement could be to think about the key principles of ABM – for example, satisfying customer needs while using the fewest resources possible; eliminating activities which do not add value for customers in order to focus on value-adding activities; improving the design of products – and then assess how Dibble's performance might be improved if it applied these principles.

For example, the scenario tells us that protective coatings are added to Steel products, by subcontractors, at the end of the production process. These are then returned to the Steel Division for dispatch to the customer. But does returning the products to Dibble add any value? Or could they be sent directly from the subcontractors to the customer?

Think also about how part (b) of the question fits with part (a). One aspect of ABM is the way organisations can use ABC information to help manage costs, and to focus on those activities which add value. The scenario has identified that the Steel Division has concerns around the pricing and profitability of its products; but introducing ABC could help to address these concerns. In turn, if Dibble has a better understanding of pricing and product profitability, could this help to improve its (financial) performance?

Examining team's comments. Part (a) (i) required candidates to advise the CEO on how to implement ABC. This should have been a relatively simple question, but it was not answered very well.

Although candidates appeared to know the terminology of ABC, it was often not correctly used. A lack of understanding of the basics of ABC also meant that it was difficult for candidates to score well in the next part of the question.

Part (a) (ii) required candidates to assess the appropriateness of ABC compared to the current costing systems in the Timber and Steel Divisions. This part was answered reasonably well, although the weaknesses in candidates' basic understanding of ABC – shown in part (a) (i) – often led to vague answers. In particular, it was surprising to find that candidates often seem unaware that ABC is specifically an overhead allocation system.

Part (b) asked candidates to advise on the benefits ABM would bring to Dibble. This part of the question was not well answered. Many candidates provided lists of benefits that were not specifically related to an activity-based approach, and again reflected candidates' lack of understanding of the general principles of such an approach – in particular, analysing activities' cost drivers, and cost pooling.

Marking scheme

			Marks
(a)	(i)	Implementation of ABC – 1 mark per relevant point	
		Total for part (a) (i): up to 4	4
	(ii)	Appropriateness of ABC – 1 mark per relevant point – up to a maximum of 6	
		Problems with ABC – 1 mark per relevant point – up to a maximum of 6	
		Total for part (a) (ii): up to 8	8
(b)		Improving performance using ABM – 1 mark per relevant point	
		Differences must be clearly linked to the scenario to score the marks available.	
		Total for part (b): up to 13	13
		Total =	25

(a) (i) **Implementation of ABC**

ABC is an alternative to absorption costing, which is the method currently used by Dibble. ABC is a detailed fact gathering and data analysis technique.

In order to implement ABC production, overheads need to be grouped into cost pools as in the analysis of production overheads for Dibble in the management accounts extracts.

Then cost drivers for each cost pool must be identified. Cost drivers are the activities which bring about the costs; for example, the set-up of the CAM machinery in Steel Division will be driven by the number of batches of production.

Once the cost pools and their associated cost drivers have been established, the cost per unit of cost driver can be calculated for each individual activity. The overhead costs are absorbed into each unit based on how much of the activity the unit uses, therefore, for example, units which require more inspection and testing will be allocated more of those costs. The overhead costs are then added to the prime costs in order to calculate the full cost of production.

(ii) **Appropriateness of ABC**

ABC is especially useful where there is a wide range of complex products and where production overheads form a larger proportion of total production costs. In Steel Division, there is a large range of products, many of them bespoke or one-off designs. Production overheads form 28% (4,472/(20,605 − 4,533)) of total production costs, and the use of ABC will be appropriate in this division.

ABC enables a more accurate cost of production to be calculated, which is very useful in setting product prices. This could be especially useful in Steel Division which has a wide range of products subject to a number of manufacturing processes. It will help to ensure that each product is priced high enough in order to produce an acceptable margin, but not so high as to become uncompetitive. This is especially important as Steel Division's strategy is to produce bespoke products at prices comparable to competitors which produce simpler, more conventional products.

ABC enables managers to determine what activities drive the costs, and so focus on reducing those activities to control costs. Not all production overheads, for example, inspection costs of the coatings in Steel Division, are related to production volumes. It is equally possible to apply ABC techniques to overheads other than production overheads.

Problems with ABC

ABC is less useful in businesses such as Timber Division where there is a small range of relatively simple products and where production overheads only comprise around 1% of total production costs. Of the production overheads in Timber Division, storage is by far the biggest and is likely to be driven by production volumes.

It may be difficult to determine what the drivers of production costs are. Storage costs could also be related to the insolvency of a customer. It may be impossible to allocate all overheads to the specific activities which drive them and so management will have to apply judgement.

Calculation of ABC may be time consuming, complex and poorly understood by managers. As such, the time and expense of doing so may not be justified. This appears to be the case in Timber Division where there are only a few, relatively simple products and few production overheads. Whereas in Steel Division, where there is a wide range of more complex products and a high proportion of production overheads, ABC is more appropriate than the traditional absorption costing method currently used at Dibble.

(b) **ABM**

ABM is the use of ABC methods in order to improve organisational performance by meeting the needs of customers using the lowest possible amount of resources or costs. ABM can be applied at the operational level or to help develop strategy.

Product pricing

By accurately determining the cost of each product using ABC, Dibble would be able to ensure that prices are set so as to achieve an acceptable margin and also remain competitive with the prices currently charged in the rest of the market.

Steel Division charges customers a standard mark-up of 10% on top of the $650,000 subcontractor costs for the coating and painting of the steel. This means that customers are only being charged $65,000 whereas the costs of storage of goods awaiting subcontract work and of transporting the goods to the subcontractor total $695,000.

By identifying the cost pools relating to the subcontract work, Steel Division can determine that it is making a loss on the subcontract work as a whole. It could therefore adjust the price of painted and coated products to ensure that an acceptable contribution margin is achieved. This is an example of operational ABM. At the strategic level, this type of information could help Dibble decide which product types to develop or discontinue.

The same principle may also apply where ABC can be used to identify which types of customers are the most profitable. In that way, resources can be focused on retaining and managing these customer groups. Action can be taken by additional advertising or product development in order to focus on these particular markets. By analysing customer profitability, it may be possible to reduce costs or increase revenue to make certain customer groups or product lines more profitable, in both the short and long term.

By identifying lines of business with poor profitability, Dibble could discontinue selling to particular customers, or selling particular products, if appropriate action could not be taken to improve profitability.

Analysis of activities

By analysing the activities which drive the costs, Steel Division could determine which activities may not be required or could be done in a more efficient way. It may be possible to introduce improvements in the short term, for example, changes in the production process which may improve efficiency. In the longer term, strategic changes could be made to the way in which activities are undertaken, such as by outsourcing other activities in addition to the painting and coating which is currently outsourced.

Identifying the costs of transporting painted finished goods back from the subcontractors to Steel Division could lead them to evaluate ways to reduce this cost, for example, by despatching goods to customers directly from the subcontractors' premises. This is a non value added activity, ie one which consumes resources, such as time and cost to transport goods to and from the subcontractors, but which is of no additional value to the customer. In contrast, ABM may help identify value-adding activities, such as the coating and painting, which customers are prepared to pay for.

Of the five categories of production overheads, only machining time is a value-adding activity, sometimes categorised as a primary activity. Setting up the CAM machinery is a secondary activity, which does not itself add value, but is required in order to perform a value-adding activity (machining).

The other overheads, storage, transfer and inspection, are all non value adding activities which should be eliminated or reduced. By identifying the activities which drive these costs managers can attempt to do this.

However, given the nature of Dibble's products, it is likely that some inspection will still be required for safety or commercial reasons, as shown by the litigation case relating to the faulty product. The production manager's proposal to increase the costs of inspection is inappropriate as, having identified inspection as a non value adding activity, it would be better to focus attention on getting the product right first time.

Design improvements

Steel Division has a wide range of relatively complex or even bespoke products. ABM can help managers take decisions at the product design stage, where many of the product's costs are already committed. These can include using fewer or more standardised components, such as a more limited range of paints and coatings.

Where strategic decisions are being taken, for example, about new product lines or lines of business, such as with Steel Division's strategy to develop novel innovative products, ABM can help assess whether such developments are likely to be profitable at an early stage. This would help avoid development costs for products which could turn out to be unprofitable. This could also help allocate resources, such as capital investment, to the most profitable lines of business.

Performance measurement

For ABM to be successful, it will require the commitment of senior management and effective communication and training of employees at all levels in the organisation as to the benefits and methods of ABM. This will incur management time and cost, and divert attention from existing management activities.

New performance measurement systems will need to be developed. Employee rewards will need to be aligned to key performance measures, such as the reduction of non value adding processes like inspection. This will ensure that employees work towards the objectives of the organisation. Additional information gathering systems, or adaptations to existing information systems, will also be required, which will again incur additional cost and may disrupt existing activities.

49 Zones

Workbook reference. The Performance Pyramid (Lynch & Cross) is discussed in Chapter 13 of the Workbook. Six Sigma methodology is discussed in Chapter 11.

Top tips.

Part (a). Although you need to link your answer to the scenario, this requirement is essentially about the benefits of the performance pyramid as a performance measurement system.

Nonetheless, the scenario does include a number of points which you could refer to to illustrate how the pyramid could help Zones achieve its corporate vision (which requires it to provide quality, reliability and value for customers):

The opening paragraph of the scenario tells us that, historically, Zones has had 'an excessive focus on financial objectives' (whereas the pyramid encourages non-financial measures to be assessed alongside financial ones).

The third paragraph tells us that the CEO believes that 'reductions in customer satisfaction and flexibility, caused by a decline in operational performance' may have led to the deterioration in Zones' financial performance. ('Customer satisfaction' and 'Flexibility' are two of the factors identified at tactical level in the pyramid which influence 'market' and 'financial' performance at strategic level).

The performance pyramid model is provided for you in Appendix 1, which should also help you identify relevant points in the scenario that you can use to illustrate how the model will be useful to Zones. Equally, however, the fact that the model is provided for you in Appendix 1 means that you should not spend time describing the model in generic terms; but rather focus specifically on how Zones could use it to help improve its performance.

Part (b). The requirement refers specifically to 'operational performance' so it is important that you remember that the factors in the bottom row of the pyramid (quality; delivery; cycle time; waste) relate to 'operational' performance.

So, in effect, this requirement is asking you to evaluate how useful the three new measures identified in Appendix 2 (vehicle utilisation; fuel consumption; on-time stops) could be for measuring and managing these aspects of performance.

A useful way to structure your answer (and the approach taken in the solution below) would be to take each of the three new measures in turn and then assess how well it will enable Zones to measure and manage the aspects of performance. Note the verb here is 'evaluate' so you should try to include a balanced assessment, including aspects of the measure which make it suitable, as well as ones which make it unsuitable.

BPP LEARNING MEDIA

Instead of structuring your answer around the three measures, you could have structured your answer around the four operational factors identified in the pyramid. Again, though, to score well you need to 'evaluate' how well the measures will allow each aspect of performance to be managed.

Part (c). Although your answer here needs to focus on the suitability of the two measures in Appendix 3, it would be useful to think about the characteristics of the Six Sigma methodology (and DMAIC) before assessing the suitability of the measures.

In particular, two of the key principles when deciding which aspects to measure (the 'M' in 'DMAIC') are: focus on what the customer thinks is important; and only measure things that can be improved.

In Appendix 2, we are told that customers make complaints if deliveries are not made on time, but a tiny fraction of these relate to deliveries which are not made within 30 minutes of the delivery time. If customers are happy for deliveries to be made within 30 minutes of the booked time, are on-time stops (within 10 minutes of the booked time) something which is important for customers?

Equally, is deliveries fail because the customer is unavailable, how does this affect Zones' ability to improve performance against this measure?

Marking scheme

		Marks
(a)	1 mark per point	
	Advising how the performance pyramid helps Zones to achieve its corporate vision – up to 7 marks	
	Total for part (a): up to 7	7
(b)	1 mark per point	
	Evaluate the extent to which each measure can be used to measure and manage operational performance – up to 3 marks per measure	
	Total for part (b): up to 9	9
(c)	1 mark per point	
	Evaluating the suitability of the two measures – up to 4 marks each	
	Conclusion on the suitability of the two measures – up to 2 marks	
	Total for part (c): up to 9	9
		Total = 25

(a) The performance pyramid covers not only financial performance but also performance relating to a wide range of underlying processes which drive financial performance. As such, it helps to set financial and non-financial performance measures, such as on-time stops. Non-financial measures are leading indicators which can help to achieve long-term future financial performance. This would be useful to Zones, which has had excessive focus on financial objectives and inadequate systems to measure and manage performance of the underlying processes driving financial performance. It is unclear exactly what the current financial objectives are.

The elements of the pyramid are interrelated, and each level in the pyramid supports the one above it. For example, on-time stops will increase customer satisfaction, which will eventually lead to greater market share, one element of the corporate vision.

Objectives cascade down the pyramid from the strategic to the operational level. The vision to increase shareholder wealth can be supported by financial objectives such as EVA™ at the level below. Measures flow up the pyramid, so that measurement of on-time stops can help determine whether Zones is achieving customer satisfaction.

The pyramid ensures that all aspects, both internal and external, of performance are measured. The right hand side of the pyramid covers internal efficiency, such as flexibility and productivity, while the left hand side covers external effectiveness, such as customer satisfaction. Using on-time stops again as an example, which relates to the quality (external effectiveness) element of the pyramid, will lead to improved performance up the left hand side of the pyramid.

(b) Operational performance is represented by the four elements at the bottom level of the performance pyramid, which are quality, delivery, cycle time and waste. It is unclear what quality means in the context of the corporate vision, though the measure of on-time stops could be interpreted as a measure of quality, which is valued by customers. There is no direct measure of cycle time, for example, the time taken between collecting a parcel and delivering it. Also, there is no direct measure for delivery, which in this context would be the amount of time needed to arrange a collection or delivery.

Vehicle utilisation

This is a good way to measure waste. The greater the utilisation of vehicle capacity, the lower the waste, for example, of vehicle running costs. In the long run, higher vehicle utilisation would mean the number of vehicles operated could be reduced for the same level of activity. This would lead to increased productivity and financial performance, so helping to achieve the corporate vision.

Vehicle utilisation will vary, according to location, time of year and type of vehicle used, and is also measured inconsistently, according to the type of vehicle. Vehicle utilisation may be too broad a measure, making it difficult to manage performance. Areas of poor performance may mask other areas of good performance. Similarly, measuring utilisation as an average between that at the beginning and end of each day may not actually represent the average utilisation during the day.

Fuel consumption

Reducing fuel consumption would lead to a significant increase in financial performance at Zones. Measuring average fuel consumption per kilometre travelled does not, however, relate directly to activity, for example, to the number of parcels delivered.

Average fuel consumption will vary between type of vehicle and between rural and urban areas. A large vehicle may have high fuel consumption per kilometre travelled, but will also carry a large number of parcels. Average fuel consumption per kilometre is not a good measure of waste, or any other aspect of operational performance. To be useful in managing operational performance, this measure should be changed to average fuel consumed per parcel delivered. In this case, this would be a suitable measure for waste.

On-time stops

Customers are likely to value on-time stops very highly, and along with value for money, this will be one of the main reasons they will choose to use Zones. This is reflected in the corporate vision. The proportion of on-time stops is a measure of operational performance which relates to the quality element of the performance pyramid and is a key driver of customer satisfaction.

> **Tutorial note.** Answers structured on the basis of the four operational elements of the pyramid would also be acceptable.

(c) The DMAIC acronym stands for define, measure, analyse, improve and control. These are the five phases by which the Six Sigma methodology is implemented. To be suitable for use in the DMAIC method, measures defined must have certain characteristics.

Percentage of stops made within 10 minutes of the booked time

According to the Six Sigma method, only those measures which are valued by the customer should be measured. On-time stops will be valued by customers, and contribute to customer satisfaction.

Currently, however, of all complaints which Zones receives from customers relating to stops not made on time, less than around one per million of these relate to those made within 30 minutes of the booked time. This level of complaints is so low that this would already achieve the very low level of failures targeted by implementation of the Six Sigma methodology. (The goal of Six Sigma is to reduce failures to a rate of less than 3.4 in a million.)

It seems that customers will not value stops made within 10 minutes of the booked time, any more than they would value those within 30 minutes. Another principle of Six Sigma methodology is not to measure what customers are already satisfied with. They are already satisfied with stops made within 30 minutes of the booked time.

The percentage of stops made within 10 minutes of the booked time is not a suitable measure. The time and costs of making the measurements will exceed the benefits of doing so.

Failed deliveries

Failed deliveries will represent a considerable cost to Zones in terms of wasted fuel and driver time. It may also reduce flexibility by using up vehicle capacity which could be used to carry more parcels. Even though deliveries may fail due to traffic congestion, they will still reduce customer satisfaction.

The percentage of failed deliveries is currently 5%, well above the target rate for failures under the Six Sigma methodology (ie less than 3.4 in a million accuracy), and in this respect would be a suitable measure.

According to the Six Sigma method, only those measures which can be improved should be measured. Failed deliveries arising from customers being unavailable to take the delivery is completely out of Zones' control. Deliveries failing due to incorrectly addressed parcels could be reduced to some extent, for example, by the use of information technology to check the correct address, but most failures due to this are outside Zones' control. As failed deliveries cannot be significantly improved, this is not a suitable measure.

50 Callisto

Workbook reference. Performance management in complex business structures is discussed in Chapter 14 of the Workbook. Management reports and the problem of information overload are covered in Chapter 6.

Top tips.

Part (a). Note that the requirement distinguishes between performance **measurement** and performance **management** issues. Accordingly, you need to consider both in your answer.

Note also that the requirement highlights that Callisto deals with two different types of external partner: individual workers (employees working remotely) and strategic partners (which are multinational companies). The issues Callisto faces in managing the performance of a multinational company are likely to be very different to those involved in managing an individual worker.

Part (b). The key problem with George's report appears to be information overload, so in the first part of your answer you need to consider how this will affect the usefulness of the report.

In effect, in the second part you then need to suggest ways to reduce the amount of figures and data being presented on the report. However, note the requirement is asking about the output of the report – essentially its presentation – so make sure you focus on this, rather than suggesting amendments to the underlying aspects of performance being measured, or the frequency of the report. There may be problems with these too, but you are not asked to comment on them, so you should not spend time doing so.

Examining team's comments. Although part (a) was presented as a single requirement, candidates were correct to split it into areas such as the general impact of such a complex structure on the business as a whole, and then the impact on employee management and strategic partner management. However, the key to scoring well was making points which were relevant for Callisto – related to the difficulties of measuring and managing home-working employees and strategic outsourcing partners.

Marking scheme

		Marks
(a)	Up to 2 marks per relevant point relating to performance measurement	
	Relevant points include (but are not limited to): Geographical distance; reliance on IT; difference between employees and strategic partners; technology solutions; use of service level agreements	Up to 9
	1 mark per relevant point relating to performance management Employees – up to 4 marks Strategic partners – up to 6 marks	Up to 8
	Maximum marks relating to performance management	17
(b)	Evaluation of proposed report and issues of potential information overload – 1 mark per relevant point – Up to 5 Suggested ways of improving presentation – 1 mark per point – Up to 5 (Note. Improvements should only relate to the presentation of the report.)	
	Total for part (b): up to 8	8
		Total = 25

(a) **Performance measurement issues**

Data collection – The main difficulties in performance measurement at Callisto are likely to arise from the fact that its employees do not work 'on site', and also a number of key business functions have been outsourced. As a result, before it can begin to measure its performance, Callisto first has to collect the necessary performance data for its remote workers and outsource partners.

IT systems – Callisto needs to rely on information technology for collecting and handling data from its partners and remote workers. As far as possible, this data should be collected and monitored automatically, for example making use of electronic data interchange.

Given the likely number of remote workers and partners that Callisto uses, it is likely that it will need a large database for storing this performance information.

However, in order for the database to be automatically updated (with inputs from remote staff and suppliers), Callisto will need the systems which staff and suppliers use to be compatible with its system.

While Callisto can control the systems its employees use, it seems unlikely that it will be able to exert much, if any, influence over the systems its strategic partners (which are multinational companies) use.

Measuring employees' performance – Callisto's employees log in to its own systems via the internet. In this way, although the employees are not physically in the premises, Callisto is still able to monitor aspects of their performance. For example, monitoring the number of hours employees are logged into the system gives an indication of the number of hours they have worked.

However, it is harder for Callisto to monitor the work the remote employees have actually done; for example, the number of videos they have edited, or the number of customer complaints they have resolved satisfactorily.

In this respect, it is important for Callisto to define its outputs clearly: for example, it should define the various steps which need to be completed for a video edit to be complete. If outputs are not defined in this way, there is scope for disputes between staff and managers about the amount of work they have done; for example, with staff claiming to have completed the editing on more videos than they actually have.

Strategic partners – Whereas Callisto's employees log on to its own systems, the strategic partners, such as RLR, will have their own systems. Therefore they will continue to use their systems rather than using Callisto's systems.

System reconciliations – As a result, there can be **discrepancies** between Callisto's systems and RLR's systems. Therefore, an added complication in the performance measurement process is that, before RLR's performance can be measured against the key SLAs, Callisto will first have to reconcile its inventory records with RLR's.

Lack of control – Without having any agreement over the figures, Callisto will not be able to enforce the SLAs. The disagreements with RLR illustrate this. For example, if an item is despatched late, it will be difficult for Callisto to prove that RLR has broken the SLA, if RLR argues that the item was not actually in stock when an order was placed, so that it couldn't be expected to despatch that item within three working days from when the order was placed.

The difficulty which Callisto faces is establishing whether RLR is responsible for the delay, or whether the product suppliers are responsible.

SLAs as controls – This lack of control over the SLAs is likely to be a significant problem for Callisto, because the SLAs represent its key control over the relationship with its strategic partners.

A potential solution would be for the partners to agree a standard reporting format for all data relating to the SLAs. This would then remove the need for the reconciliations Callisto currently has to carry out.

Performance management issues

Employee management – Because Callisto's employees work from home rather than at company premises, the brothers cannot monitor what the employees are doing in the same way as they could if everyone was working in the same place. For example, Jeff and George cannot monitor what hours their staff are working, or how productive they are being.

Equally, because Jeff and George have no direct contact with their staff, it is difficult for them to judge how motivated the staff are.

Reward schemes – Because the brothers cannot directly monitor or control how productive their employees are being, they need to ensure Callisto's reward scheme is designed such that it encourages productivity and motivation. One way to do this would be to link the reward scheme directly to achieving agreed outputs and targets for each employee.

Managing strategic partners

Reliance on partners – A key issue Callisto faces is that it is reliant on external partners (such as RLR Logistics) for the successful day to day operation of its business. The nature of Callisto's business structure means that some of the functions which have been outsourced are business critical.

For example, if RLR decides not to renew its contract (when it is due for renewal in two months' time) this could create major problems for Callisto. Equally, the reliability of partners such as RLR is vital, because Callisto's customer service reputation will be damaged if products are delivered late.

However, there is a danger that Callisto's reliance on strategic partners in this way strengthens the strategic partners' bargaining power in any negotiations with Callisto (because it is unlikely that Callisto will be able to replace a strategic partner immediately if it stopped working for Callisto).

Relationship management – However, the success of the relationship between Callisto and its strategic partners is likely to depend on establishing an atmosphere of trust between the parties. Currently, it appears the trust between the partners is limited; meaning, for example, that Callisto feels it has to reconcile performance data between RLR's figures and its own. However, such reconciliations do not ultimately add any value for Callisto, so they are a wasteful activity. Therefore, if Callisto was able to trust RLR's figures, this would be beneficial because the detailed reconciliations would no longer be required.

Pricing – Another issue which will have to be managed is how the agreements between Callisto and its strategic partners can be arranged so that they are motivating and profitable for both parties. George has already acknowledged that Callisto operates on small profit margins, so it needs to secure sales growth and high volumes of business in order to be profitable.

However, Callisto is dependent on partners such as RLR to deliver a good quality service to its customers. If the customers don't receive this, then Callisto's reputation is likely to suffer, which in turn will reduce its ability to achieve the sales growth it needs (either by retaining existing customers or acquiring new ones).

So Callisto needs to negotiate contracts which motivate the strategic partners to deliver the high quality it needs, whilst at the same time not being prohibitively expensive for it. Therefore, Callisto needs to ensure that the contracts are motivating and profitable for both parties.

(b) **Content**

Information overload – Whilst having a daily report will mean that George has up to date and timely information, there is a danger that its frequency will actually lead to **information overload**. In practice, George may find he doesn't have time to look through a detailed report each day. We do not know how many employees work for Callisto, but its turnover ($120m per annum) suggests there are likely to be quite a large number of employees. Therefore, George's report is likely to contain a large amount of data for him to look at each day.

There is a also a danger that if George spends too much time looking at detailed, daily reports he may overlook more strategic issues in the business, or higher level trends in performance.

Control – It is not clear from the scenario whether the employees will be told that George is monitoring their productivity. However, if the employees know that George is monitoring their productivity on a daily basis, then this could prompt any who are not currently working as hard as they could to work harder. It seems likely that this is what George hopes will happen.

Usefulness of information – However, it is debatable how useful some of the measures George has chosen will be. For example, simply monitoring the number of complaints employees deal with doesn't reflect how long or complicated each complaint was. Equally, although an employee may have been logged on to the network this doesn't necessarily mean they have been working all the time they have been logged on.

The frequency of the reports could also be a problem in itself. If the reports looked at the average number of complaints employees dealt with in a month, this might be a fairer reflection of their activity than looking at a single day at a time.

Equally, it is not clear whether all the employees are expected to carry out all the tasks being monitored. For example, some may specialise in editing videos, while others concentrate on dealing with customer queries and complaints. However, this could mean that the report shows a large number of zeros in the columns for work the employees do not attend to.

Possible improvements

Sorting – If employees do have separate roles, George may find it more useful to produce separate reports for each role; for example, producing one report for video editors, and a separate one for customer service employees.

However, there are more fundamental ways in which George could improve the reports.

Exception reports – Instead of showing the performance of all employees, the report would only show results which are unusual or require attention; in other words, where an employee's figures are particularly high or particularly low.

Summaries and drill down reports – Alternatively, instead of showing performance for individual employees, the report could show totals in the first instance; for example, totals for the number of customer complaints dealt with, or the number of videos edited.

If George was concerned about any of the summary totals, he could then 'drill down' into the total figure, to find out why it was lower (or higher) than he expected.

Charts and graphs – However, perhaps the most significant change would be showing performance graphically, rather than as columns of figures.

In this way, George could see not only the actual daily figures, but could also place them in context – for example, by comparing them to a rolling average, or to a target.

By using charts or graphs, George would be able to see how performance is changing over time, which is something he would not be able to do from the proposed numerical report.

51 Coal Creek

Workbook reference. The importance of considering indicators of liquidity and gearing as well as profitability is discussed in Chapter 7 of the Workbook. Models for predicting corporate failure are discussed in Chapter 15.

Top tips.

Part (a). It is important you recognise that the main focus of this requirement is on the value of using different **indicators** rather than on CCNH's **performance** as such. In other words, you need to discuss why monitoring liquidity and gearing (in conjunction with profitability) is important rather than simply discussing CCNH's liquidity and gearing positions. For example, why would it be useful for CCNH to monitor its ability to pay its liabilities when they become due (rather than simply: What is CCNH's working capital position?)?

Also, although you are asked to 'illustrate your answer with suitable calculations' this does not mean that your answer should just become, in effect, a sequence of different ratios. The calculations should be used to **support** your answer, rather than **becoming** your answer in their own right.

In relation to gearing – remember that there are two aspects of gearing: financial gearing and operational gearing. The requirement doesn't limit you to dealing with one aspect or the other, and therefore you should have considered both in your answer. In CCNH's case, the question of monitoring the level of fixed costs compared to variable costs (operational gearing) seems to be particularly important.

Part (b). There are two aspects to this part of the requirement: (i) explain a qualitative model; and (ii) apply that model to the scenario in order to comment on CCNH's position.

However, note that 'explaining' the model doesn't simply mean listing the headings in the model; you need to explain why the different elements of the model could be useful for predicting corporate failure.

A sensible approach to part (b) of this question would be to illustrate each aspect of the model (in Argenti's case: defects, mistakes, and symptoms of failure) by referring to weaknesses at CCNH. In this way, you will ensure you address both aspects of the requirement: to explain the model, and to comment on CCNH's position.

The marking guide indicates that there are up to five marks available for describing the qualitative model, but up to six marks for using it to identify weaknesses in CCNH's position. Therefore, as so often in APM, there are potentially more marks available for applying a model to the scenario than for explaining the model itself.

Technical article. In the Technical Articles section of ACCA's website there is an article called 'Business Failure' which discusses different failure prediction models. If you haven't already done so, you are strongly advised to read this article to supplement your knowledge of this area of the syllabus.

Part (c). The scenario identifies that HC's revenue had grown significantly in the last two years. This could give you a clue that HC is in the growth phase of its life cycle. By contrast, GC is a mature business – with little scope for growth, and operating in a sector which is fully supplied. What implications does this have for the CEO's plans? Although the question requirement refers to 'product portfolios' rather than any specific model, the product life cycle model could be a useful framework to apply here, given that CCNH's two divisions appear to be at different stages of their life cycles. The BCG matrix could also be useful, although the scenario does not give any specific details about the relative market shares of SC and GC. (However, we do know that CCNH is one of the largest providers of residential care places in Geeland.)

Examining team's comments. Candidates still appear not to be reading question requirements carefully enough, with the result that they are not answering the requirements actually set. In part (a) of this question, instead of explaining why liquidity and gearing were important alongside profitability, many candidates chose to review the **performance of the company** in the scenario, leaving the reader to draw their own conclusions about the relative importance of liquidity, gearing and profitability.

Moreover, although many candidates successfully dealt with issues around financial gearing, only a few addressed the operational gearing in the business. It appeared that candidates failed to identify the cost structures (fixed/variable) within CCNH although this ought to be a basic point in the financial assessment of a business by a management accountant.

In part (b) few candidates demonstrated a clear understanding of the issues in using a qualitative model, and the Argenti model in particular. Only a minority could explain defects, mistakes made, and symptoms of failure. Although many students could quote the headings from the model, few could explain what they referred to. The wiser candidates tried to cover this shortcoming by illustrating each heading with an example from CCNH, and it was pleasing to see that candidates managed to score reasonably well in this part of the question by identifying the specific issues at CCNH.

Marking scheme

		Marks
(a)	Explaining liquidity, financial gearing and operational gearing – up to a maximum of 4 marks	
	For illustrating the importance of considering liquidity at CCNH – up to 4 marks	
	For illustrating the importance of considering financial gearing at CCNH – up to 2 marks	
	For illustrating the importance of considering operational gearing at CCNH – up to 4 marks	
	Total for part (a): up to 11	11

(b) For describing qualitative models (such as Argenti's A score model) and
    including examples of possible failure indicators – up to 5 marks

    For identifying weaknesses at CCNH – 1 mark per relevant weakness
    identified; up to a maximum of 6 marks

    Possible weaknesses include: culture of fraud in previous management;
    lack of senior management; poor cash flow planning; over-trading at SC;
    weak financial ratios; and inability to pay landlords.

    Total for part (b): up to 9   9

(c) For discussing life cycle stage and strategic position of SC and implications
    of this – up to 2

    For discussing life cycle stage and strategic position of GC and
    implications of this – up to 2

    For discussing the implications of CCNH's portfolio on any future strategy –
    up to 3 marks

    Total for part (c): up to 5   5

                                                                      Total = 25

(a) **Profit-based measures** – It appears that CCNH's current performance measures
(operating profit margin; earnings per share) are primarily focused on the amount of profit
the business is generating.

However, these measures have not identified the problems which CCNH is now facing, even
though these problems could potentially threaten the overall survival of the business.
Profit-based measures can often be insufficient to highlight issues relating to an
organisation's survival, either in the long term or the short term.

Liquidity

Liquidity – CCNH's liquidity relates to the level of funds it has readily available in order to
pay its liabilities as they become due; for example, having sufficient cash to pay its rents,
or to pay other suppliers.

CCNH struggled to meet its most recent rental payment, which suggests that it has
liquidity problems.

CCNH's liquidity – At the end of the year just ended, CCNH's current assets were $64m, but
its current liabilities were $104m. Therefore, its current ratio was 0.62. The fact that this
ratio is significantly less than 1 helps explains why CCNH is having trouble making
payments (such as its rental payments) when they are due. CCNH's current liabilities are
significantly greater than the funds it has available to pay them.

Furthermore, at the end of the year, CCNH has no ready cash.

As CCNH is a service company rather than a manufacturing company, it is unlikely to hold
a significant level of inventory. Therefore, given that CCNH has no ready cash, it seems
likely that the vast majority of CCNH's current assets are receivables.

Receivable days – The significance of receivables suggests that receivable days should be
a key performance measure for CCNH. If it can collect the amounts it is owed from
residents as quickly as possible, this should help increase the amount of funds it has
available to pay for its liabilities.

Currently, however, it appears that there may be problems collecting the amounts owed to
SC. SC's receivable days are 68 [(47/253) × 365], compared to only 9 for GC [(17/685) × 365].

Gearing – Whilst liquidity issues can often be a problem in the short term, looking at
gearing can highlight potential issues in the **longer term**. In this respect, monitoring
gearing helps an organisation **measure risk**.

Gearing indicates the level of an organisation's fixed regular liabilities compared to the
cash generators which will enable the organisation to cover its liabilities.

Financial gearing – Financial gearing is measured by the ratio of debt to equity. Debt is a fixed liability for an organisation (for example, the annual interest payments which are due on loans), and equity is the capital equivalent which needs to generate the funds necessary to cover the liability (for example, to pay the interest due).

If the gearing ratio is high, this indicates that an organisation has to cover large fixed liabilities from only a small equity investment. As a result, the business could be at financial risk.

As well as looking at the gearing ratio itself, a second indicator which could be useful in relation to financial gearing is **interest cover**. Interest cover compares an organisation's profit before interest to the level of interest payable; again indicating whether it is generating sufficient returns to cover its fixed liabilities.

Gearing ratio – CCNH's debt (long-term borrowings of $102m) is currently 54% of its equity (share capital + retained earnings: $189m). A gearing ratio of 54% by itself should not be a particular cause for concern because it is relatively low.

Interest cover – CCNH's interest cover appears to be more of a concern, though. Its operating profit was the same as the interest it had to pay for the year just ended, meaning that if its profit falls in future, CCNH may not be able to cover its interest payments.

CCNH appears still to have a relatively good relationship with its bank, since the bank agreed to increase CCNH's overdraft facility in order to enable it to make its most recent rental payments. However, if CCNH doesn't generate sufficient earnings to cover its interest payments this could be fatal for its relationship with its bank, and will also seriously damage its chances of receiving any further financing.

Operational gearing – Operational gearing (or leverage) compares the ratio of fixed costs to variable costs in an organisation, by comparing contribution to profit with operating profit (PBIT). Operational gearing helps to identify the level of **business risk** in an organisation.

If an organisation has high operational gearing this suggests it also faces a high level of business risk. High operational gearing means that an organisation's fixed costs as a proportion of its total costs are also high. This is risky because, although variable costs will fall if revenue falls, fixed costs will not. Therefore, an organisation with a high level of operational gearing may find itself unable to cover its fixed costs if its revenue falls.

This inability to cover fixed costs could have been the type of gearing problems which the director was talking about at CCNH; because it seems likely that CCNH has a **high level of fixed costs**.

CCNH's rent payments are a fixed cost, and they alone take up 27% ($257m/$938m) of its revenue. In addition, it seems likely that the central costs and the costs of permanent staff in the care homes will be relatively fixed.

The danger for CCNH of having a high level of operational gearing is that if its revenues drop then it will quickly become loss making, given that it was only just breaking even at the end of the last year. Again, this could have been the problem which the director was referring to.

Operational gearing ratio – If we treat rent costs, payroll costs and central costs as all being fixed (or relatively fixed), then the ratio between CCNH's fixed costs and variable costs (running costs) is 7.5:1 (536 + 257 + 30 = 823:110).

This ratio is very high, and so should also be viewed as a concern for CCNH.

In this respect, it is important for CCNH to see if it can change the nature of any of the costs within its business. In particular, it may be possible to use temporary or contract staff in its homes rather than permanent staff. Such a change would mean that staff costs effectively then become variable costs.

However, using temporary staff might also compromise the **quality of service** CCNH provides to its residents, which would not be acceptable.

(b) **Qualitative models of business failure** – Qualitative models of business failure look at a variety of qualitative and non-accounting factors to help identify the likelihood of corporate failure in organisations. These factors can include: the business environment (as exemplified by 'PEST' factors); the organisation's customer profile (for example, whether it is dependent on a small number of key customers); the level of management experience in the organisation; and whether the organisation has a history of qualified audit opinions.

Argenti's A score model – Argenti's A score model is a qualitative model which can be used to assess the risk of poor management causing corporate failure. The model looks at three different groups of indicators of poor management:

- Defects
- Management mistakes
- Symptoms of failure

These three groups are then further divided into a number of problem areas, and an 'A score' is obtained by assigning a score for each problem area. As such, Argenti's model attempts to quantify the causes of failure (defects, management mistakes) and the symptoms associated with failure.

'A scores' – The 'A score' model sets a maximum acceptable score of 25 overall. An 'A score' of greater than 25 indicates that an organisation is at risk of failing. However, the scores for each group of indicators are also important individually. In particular, if an organisation scores anything at all for 'symptoms' this immediately signifies that the organisation should be considered at risk of failing.

Defects

In Argenti's model, 'defects' are divided into 'management defects' and 'accounting defects'.

Management defects result from deficiencies in the senior management team: for example, a failure to separate the roles of chairman and CEO; having a passive board of directors; having a lack of experience and/or relevant skills among the senior management team; or having a management team with a poor record of responding to change in the business environment.

Lack of senior management – The fact that CCNH does not have any experienced senior management (following the recent departures of the CEO, finance director and the operations director) can be seen as a management defect for the company.

Accounting defects – Examples of accounting defects could be a lack of budgets or budgetary control, a lack of cash flow planning, and an absence of costing systems.

The fact that CCNH struggled to meet its most recent rent payments may suggest a lack of cash flow planning, particularly as CCNH had no cash available when the rent payments were due.

Management mistakes

If a company's management and accounting systems are weak, this could increase the chances of mistakes being made within the company. Argenti suggests that management mistakes should be analysed under three main headings: **high gearing; overtrading**; and **failure of major projects**.

As we saw in part (a), CCNH's financial gearing of 54% is actually relatively low, and so would not indicate a risk of failure. However, CCNH's high operational gearing should be viewed as more of a concern.

Moreover, SC's rapid growth, coupled with the apparent weaknesses in its credit control and receivables collection, may suggest that there has been some overtrading at SC. In turn, the weaknesses in SC's credit control (and the resulting high level of receivables) are straining the business's working capital.

Symptoms of failure

The logic of Argenti's model suggests that, over time, defects and/or management mistakes will lead to symptoms of failure emerging, at which point the prospect of corporate failure becomes more apparent.

These symptoms can be directly financial, such as poor ratios in the financial statements. However, evidence of creating accounting could also be a symptom of imminent corporate failure.

Equally, there can be non-financial symptoms of failure, such as high staff turnover, or declining market share.

CCNH's most recent financial statements show a number of symptoms of failure: CCNH made no profits in the last year, it has very low interest cover, and it has a very high operational gearing ratio. Moreover, the difficulty which CCNH faced in making its rental payments could be seen as an indication that failure is imminent.

In addition, the recent directors' resignations, coupled with the police investigation into the thefts of residents' money could be seen as symptoms of impending failure.

Overall position

Overall, it appears that CCNH's position is very weak, and it looks in serious danger of failing unless drastic action is taken to improve its performance.

(c)   **Portfolio mix** – An organisation needs to plan the range of products (or services) it offers so that it has a mix of products at different stages in their life cycles: for example, products at the growth stage alongside established (mature) products generating cash. Planning ahead in this respect is a vital element of organisational survival.

Special Care (SC) Division – SC appears to be growing rapidly, with revenue growth of 24% p.a. over the last two years. Therefore, it seems likely that SC is in the **growth stage** of its life cycle.

However, one of the characteristics of products in the growth stage of their life cycle is that capital investments are required in order to enable the business to expand in order to fulfil levels of demand. Consequently, the cash flows generated by products in the growth stage of their life cycle are lower than their profits.

This reiterates the importance of CCNH monitoring liquidity as well as profitability. However, in terms of the CEO's strategy, it also highlights the need to have a division within CCNH which generates sufficient cash to support SC's growth.

General Care (GC) Division – GC appears to be a mature business, operating in a mature sector.

The lack of opportunities for growth in the sector is characteristic of a mature sector. Usually, however, mature products are able to generate healthy profits. Equally, because they require relatively low levels of investment, mature products are usually cash generators for a business.

Given that CCNH is one of the largest providers of residential care places in Geeland, we could suggest that the GC Division be classified as a **cash cow** using the BCG matrix.

However, the CEO needs to assess how well GC displays the usual characteristics of a cash cow. Rather than being a cash generator and earning good profits, GC made an operating loss for the last year.

Given that GC is coming under increasing price pressure from its main customers (the public sector health organisations), it appears that **cost control** is likely to be very important for GC, in order to preserve its margins.

SBUs in portfolio – The combination of a growing business unit (SC) with a mature one (GC) should be a relatively beneficial one for CCNH, because the company should be able to use the cash generated by GC to support SC's growth.

However, the CEO will need to assess whether GC is actually able to fulfil this cash generating role. In particular, the CEO needs to consider whether GC is in danger of moving from a mature business to a declining business, and therefore whether divestment is an appropriate strategy. Equally, however, the CEO needs to consider what impact divesting of GC would have on CCNH's business portfolio.

52 Freeze

Workbook reference. Models for predicting corporate failure are discussed in Chapter 15 of the Workbook.

Top tips.

Part (a). Although the 'K Score' is a fictitious model, as explained in the scenario, you should have identified the similarities between it and Altman's 'Z Score' model. Therefore, thinking about the strengths and weaknesses of the Z Score model would have been a useful starting point for evaluating the usefulness of the K Score model in this scenario.

As with all APM questions, it is also important to identify the key points in the scenario which you can use to develop your answer. For example, in the opening paragraph, we're told there was an oil spill in April 20X8, which may be due to problems with Freeze's machinery. Given the timing of this, how useful is Freeze's financial information for 20X7 (approved by the board on 31 March 20X8) as a basis for evaluating its position now?

In the second paragraph, we're told the K Score developed by looking at the ratios of all the companies on the Kayland stock exchange. Why might this be significant?

- Do we know anything about the mix of companies listed on the stock exchange, (eg might the ratios vary for companies in different industries?

- We're told in the third paragraph that Thor is a privately-owned company, based in Jayland. (So how appropriate will it be to use the K score to predict the risk of Thor failing?)

Also, in the notes to Appendix 1, we're told there is a 'grey area' between 2 and 5 where further analysis is required to determine the likelihood of corporate failure. How might that affect the usefulness of the model?

Part (b). Although the requirement doesn't include the word 'calculate', the key thing you need to do here is to calculate Freeze's K score, using the formula in Appendix 1 and the financial results in Appendix 2. The calculations themselves should be relatively straightforward, but make sure you follow the formula exactly; eg K_3 is based on the market value of shares (not the book value).

Once you've calculated the score, you can then use it to assess whether Freeze is at risk of corporate failure – using the indicators given in Appendix 1: <2 means failure is highly likely: >5 menas failure is unlikely; with 2–5 being the 'grey area'.

Part (c). The paragraph about 'Corporate failure indicators' in the scenario tells you that a colleague has suggested that 'operational gearing and financial gearing' are the two most important indicators in Freeze's industry.

Note, however, the requirement requires you to do two different things:

- One evaluating the significance of the **measures** (ie evaluate the comments about the importance of operational and financial gearing)

- The ther looking at the relative risk of failure of the two **companies** (ie calculating the gearing ratios for both companies, in order to assess whether Freeze is more likely to fail than Thor).

In relation to the first of these elements, a useful starting point could be to think about the impact a company's operational and financial gearing could have on its risk of failure. However, even if these are important measures, is there any evidence to support the claim that they are 'the two most important indicators'?

For the second element, the calculations should again be relatively straightforward, provided you remember the formula for operational gearing. (The formula to use for financial gearing is given in the scenario, so make sure you use that.) However, you've been asked to 'assess' whether Freeze is more or less likely to fail than Thor. So don't simply do the calculations; you also need to comment on their implications for the two companies' risk of failure.

Marks

(a) 1 mark per relevant point

Usefulness of using quantitative models in predicting the corporate failure of
Freeze and Thor – up to 11 marks

Total for part (a): up to 11   11

(b) Calculating the K Scores (K_1 to K_4) – up to 4 marks

Conclusion on the likelihood of corporate failure – 1 mark

Total for part (b): up to 5   5

(c) 1 mark per relevant point

Usefulness of operational gearing ratio as an indicator of potential failure –
up to 4 marks

Usefulness of financial gearing ratio as an indicator of potential failure –
up to 3 marks

Conclusion on Freeze compared to Thor – up to 2 marks

Total for part (c): up to 9

$$\text{Total} = \underline{\underline{\frac{9}{25}}}$$

(a) **Objectivity**

The K Score can be calculated easily from readily available financial data. Both Freeze and
Thor will publish their financial results, so the financial data will be readily available. There
is no subjectivity required in calculating the score, which can be easily compared between
different companies, at different points in time, or against the likelihood of corporate
failure. However, the translation of Thor's results into K$ from its reporting currency of J$
may make it less appropriate to compare their K Scores.

Uses historical data

Historical financial data is used to calculate the K Score, which is therefore backwards
looking. This data may be out of date, and significant events or market changes may have
occurred since the period to which the data relates.

The data given to calculate Freeze's K Score is from the year ended 31 December 20X7 and
is already almost a year out of date. In April 20X8, an oil spill led to widespread
environmental damage in Kayland. The oil spill was thought to have been caused by the
incorrect installation of machinery by Freeze. This will probably have a major impact on
Freeze's performance during 20X8, for example, due to fines or loss of customer trust. This
is not reflected in the historical financial data given, which was approved by the board on
31 March 20X8.

Data may be unavailable or unreliable

Financial data needed to calculate the K Score may be unavailable. For example, as a
privately owned business, Thor will not have a market value for equity, which is required to
calculate the K Score.

The data may also be unreliable as a basis for calculating the score, though as a listed
business Freeze will be subject to audit and listing regulations, so its published data is
probably reliable.

Appropriateness of the K Score model

A quantitative model, such as the K Score, identifies financial ratios which significantly
differ in value between surviving and failing companies. Statistical analysis is then used to
choose the weightings for these ratios in a formula for the score, which can be used to

identify companies which exhibit the features of previously failing companies. The company being analysed must be similar to those being used to build the model for the results to be relevant.

The K Score model is based on recent data for all Kayland listed companies and Freeze is a construction company in the oil exploration industry. It may, therefore, be too dissimilar to other industries on the small Kayland stock exchange, for example, in the markets it serves. Also, as the Kayland stock exchange is small, there may be insufficient data from failing companies on which to base the model.

Thor is based in Jayland, so the K Score model, which is based on data from the Kayland stock exchange, is unlikely to applicable.

K Score may not give a clear indication of corporate failure

The K Score may not always give a clear indication of whether corporate failure is likely. K Scores of between 2 and 5 lie in the 'grey area', where further analysis is needed in order to reach a clear conclusion.

The K Score is only a measurement at a single point in time, in this case 31 December 20X7, and without undertaking measures at different times, it will not indicate whether a company is becoming more or less likely to fail. As the K Score is based on statistical correlations of financial ratios with subsequent failure, it does not give any suggestions on how to reduce the likelihood of corporate failure.

(b) **Freeze's K Score and risk of failure**

$$K \text{ Score} = 2.5K_1 + 5.0K_2 + 0.1K_3 + 1.9K_4$$

$$= (2.5 \times 0.367) + (5.0 \times 0.180) + (0.1 \times 14.930) + (1.9 \times 0.556)$$

$$= 0.918 + 0.900 + 1.493 + 1.056$$

$$= 4.367$$

Workings:

K_1: Net current assets/total assets = (2,164 − 645)/4,135 = 0.367

K_2: Profit before interest and tax/total assets = 745/4,135 = 0.180

K_3: Market value of ordinary shares/book value of non-current liabilities = (500 × 10.60)/355 = 14.930

K_4: Retained earnings/total assets = 2,300/4,135 = 0.556

Freeze's score of 4.367 is in the grey area, so further analysis will be required in order to determine if corporate failure is likely.

(c) **Operational gearing**

Operational gearing indicates the level of business risk which companies face, by measuring the relative amount of fixed costs. Companies with high operational gearing (ie high levels of fixed costs) have high business risk. They are less able to cover their fixed costs if contribution falls due to a reduction in revenue or if there is an increase in variable costs. Highly geared businesses are therefore more likely to fail than those with lower operational gearing.

The recent recession in Jayland may adversely affect Thor's contribution, as might movements in exchange rates between the Kayland dollar and Thor's home currency.

The demand for services in the oil exploration industry varies directly with the world oil price. The recent fall in world oil prices will result in a reduction in oil exploration activity. Companies with high fixed costs are therefore more likely to fail in these circumstances.

The operational gearing ratio is defined as contribution/PBIT. Freeze's operational gearing ratio is 2.48 (1,845/745), whilst Thor's is 5.48 (4,960/905). Thor is more highly geared and therefore more likely to suffer corporate failure.

Financial gearing

The financial gearing ratio measures financial risk and reflects the company's ability to service its long-term debt. Similarly to operational gearing, high financial gearing makes companies more likely to suffer corporate failure because they are less able to make interest payments if trading conditions deteriorate.

Both Freeze and Thor publish their financial results, so the data required to calculate financial gearing will be readily available.

The financial gearing ratio is defined as (preference share capital + long-term debt)/total equity. Freeze's financial gearing ratio is 0.11 (355/3,135), whilst Thor's is 0.13 (382/2,943). Thor is marginally more highly geared and therefore more likely to suffer corporate failure.

Conclusion

Both Thor's operational and financial gearing are higher than those of Freeze. In this respect, Thor is more likely to suffer corporate failure than Freeze.

It is unclear, however, whether the colleague's view that operational and financial gearing are the two most important indicators in predicting corporate failure in this industry is correct, as both Freeze and Thor have not yet failed. There may be many other important indicators of corporate failure, including non-financial ones.

53 Laurel and Parsley

Workbook reference. Corporate failure is discussed in Chapter 15 of the BPP Workbook.

Top tips.

Part (a). The Appendix to the scenario in this question is unusually short, so you may have been wondered why it had been included. However, one possible answer to this question is that you would been given the three main facets of the model in the Appendix so that you used them as headings to structure your answer, rather than – for example – spending a lot of time discussing the model in theoretical terms.

The scenario highlights a number of issues at LP which could be a cause for concern – eg the CEO over-ruling the board on strategy; high gearing; problems with the housing project; low staff morale; high staff turnover. To score well in this question you not only have to identify these issues, but you also have to assess whether they characterise any of the facets of Argenti's model (defects; mistakes; symptoms of failure). Remember, the requirement asks you to evaluate 'the risk of corporate failure', not simply to identify problems or weakness at LP.

Also, note the final paragraph tells you that LP has a score of 47 on the A score model. What does that tell you about its risk of failure?

Part (b). When planning your answer to this question overall, it is important to note the link between parts (a) and (b). In part (b) you are asked what systems are needed in order to improve performance in respect of 'each of the mistakes and symptoms you have identified in part (a)'. In order to do this, you first have to have identified some 'mistakes and symptoms' in part (a), which reinforces the importance of structuring your answer to part (a) according to the three elements of the model: defects; mistakes; symptoms.

For part (b) itself, the word 'systems' is a key word in the requirement. You aren't asked what LP could do, in general terms, to help overcome its mistakes and symptoms, and thereby improve performance. Instead, you are asked specifically 'what performance management **systems** are needed' to help achieve this. So your answer should focus on the systems, not simply actions or initiatives LP could take to improve performance. For example, if projects are falling behind schedule (as the house building project is) some kind of project management system (showing key dates and milestones) be useful to identify potential delays so that action can be taken to overcome them.

Part (c). Having used the A score model in part (a) to evaluate whether LP is at risk of failing, you are now asked to evaluate the usefulness of qualitative models (like the A score) as a basis for predicting corporate failure.

Note the verb here is to 'evaluate' the usefulness, so you should try to present a balanced assessment of potential benefits from using the models, as well as weaknesses or limitations.

Note also that the requirement asks about the usefulness of the models overall, not specifically in relation to their usefulness for predicting corporate failure at LP. Therefore, you don't have to link your points to LP, although you may find it useful to refer back to the context of the scenario to illustrate some of the points you are making about the benefits/limitations of the models.

Examining team's comments. Part (a) was generally answered well, with candidates demonstrating a good understanding of the model and how the three key facets – defects, mistakes, symptoms – relates to the specifics of the company's situation. However, some candidates appeared unsure about the differences between the three facets in the model, meaning they didn't categorise problem areas correctly. Some candidates didn't use the model at all, and just highlighted the main problem areas within the company. Such responses can never score well in a question like this. The skill being tested is candidates' ability to apply the model to the scenario, and in order to do this, candidates need to demonstrate they know how the model actually works.

Part (b) proved challenging for a number of candidates, due to them misreading the question. These candidates focused their answers on what the company might do now to get out of the situation it found itself in, rather than the performance management systems which might be needed. Such responses gained some credit, but did not address the main focus of the question.

In **part (c)**, candidates appeared to recognise the requirement behind the verb 'evaluate' and offered a discussion of the advantages and disadvantages of the models. Some candidates also brought in the use of quantitative models (to contrast with qualitative models) which was a good point to introduce in the light of the question ask. Candidates should be aware that the use of a verb such as 'evaluate' involves an informed discussion in which they are expected to present different points of view – provided these are relevant to the overall evaluation.

Marking scheme

Marks

(a) Explaining Argenti's A score model – up to 2 marks

Conclusion based on the overall score (47) – 1 mark

1 mark per point, which MUST be in the correct category:

Defects – up to 5 marks

Mistakes – up to 4 marks

Symptoms – up to 3 marks

Total for part (a): up to 12   12

(b) 1 mark per point:

Failure of big project (mistake) – up to 3 marks

Operational gearing (mistake) – up to 3 marks

Symptoms – up to 3 marks

Total for part (b): up to 7   7

(c) 1 mark per point:

Advantages of qualitative models in indicating corporate failure – up to 4 marks

Disadvantages of qualitative models in indicating corporate failure – up to 4 marks

Total for part (c): up to 6   6
                                          Total = 25

(a) **Risk of corporate failure in LP**

The Argenti A Score assigns scores to management defects and accounting defects, which are effectively weaknesses which can lead to failure, mistakes, and symptoms. Symptoms are indications that the business is actually failing. The resulting score indicates whether or not LP is or is not at risk of corporate failure. Firms with low scores (typically below 18) are not at risk of failure, whereas firms which are at risk usually score above 25. Between these two scores (18–25), there is a 'grey area' where further analysis is required to reach a conclusion about the risk of failure. However, LP's score is significantly higher than 25, indicating the firm is at high risk of failure.

Defects

The chief executive appears to be an autocrat, which is a management defect under the Argenti A Score model. LP decision's to prepare bids for work in areas it had little track record in was the strategy preferred by the chief executive, even though the rest of the board wanted to reduce the workforce to reduce operating gearing after the start of the recession. This suggests that the chief executive has a dominant influence over the rest of the board and that the board of directors is passive, which is another management defect.

The submission of the bid was done when most of the board members were on holiday, so in this respect too, the board was passive as it had no opportunity to discuss or review the bid. Similarly, the bid was made when the finance director was on long-term absence. An ineffective finance director is a management defect which increases the risk of corporate failure.

The fact that the amount of staff resources, and therefore cost, required to perform the work on the housing development was greater than anticipated was an accounting defect which increases the risk of failure.

Mistakes

LP undertook a large project in an area where it had little experience, and at a fixed fee. This was a high-risk venture, particularly as LP failed to set clear milestones for the project or put in place adequate performance management systems. This is a management mistake which, in the absence of suitable insurance cover, may mean LP is unable to meet any legal claims brought against it.

LP has an operational gearing ratio which is 50% higher than its nearest rival. Failing to address this high level of fixed cost, for example, by reducing the workforce for the duration of the recession, is also a management mistake which increases the risk of corporate failure.

Symptoms

Any symptoms of impending problems would indicate a high risk of corporate failure, even if LP's A Score were to be below the maximum acceptable score of 25. The low staff morale, and staff leaving the firm due to working long hours with unclear individual performance targets, is a symptom that the firm is at risk of failure.

(b) **Mistakes**

The failure of the big project for the design work for the housing development, and the high operational gearing, are management mistakes which increase the risk of corporate failure. To improve performance in these areas, LP needs effective performance management systems.

(1) **Failure of the big project for the design work for the housing development**

LP should identify critical success factors (CSFs) for improvement in performance. Big projects, especially those which are outside LP's usual activities should be fully scrutinised by the board, and the risks of the project thoroughly assessed. This would help prevent LP taking on projects for a fixed fee, where the costs of performing the work are poorly understood. The use of realistic budgets and clear project milestones would have helped identify that the major project was failing and allowed corrective action to be taken. Clear budgets and project milestones should be key performance measures to identify failure of the major project.

BPP
LEARNING
MEDIA

(2) **Operational gearing**

From the CSFs, LP must develop key performance indicators (KPIs). The operating gearing is an obvious KPI to help reduce the firm's high operating gearing. Cash forecasts would also help to identify and correct high operating gearing. Performance targets such as these should be clearly communicated and linked to employee rewards.

Symptoms

Clear milestones and performance targets were not set for the housing development project and the project has fallen behind schedule. This has led to low staff morale and to staff leaving the firm. All of these are symptoms of corporate failure.

Performance against the targets should be regularly monitored, for example, by using staff appraisals and surveys to monitor staff satisfaction. This could indicate where additional training or support is required.

Measuring staff turnover would help measure this symptom of corporate failure so that LP could try to identify why staff were leaving.

(c) **Advantages of using qualitative models in predicting corporate failure**

The subjectivity of the A Score can be an advantage over quantitative indicators of corporate failure, as it allows the person calculating the A Score to use their own professional judgement in considering individual circumstances.

It also recognises factors which have been observed in failing companies and which often can be seen in organisations before they reach a terminal state.

The A Score model incorporates financial (such as the operating gearing ratio), and non-financial factors, which give a more holistic assessment of whether failure is likely than just looking at either financial or non-financial factors alone.

Disadvantages of using qualitative models in predicting corporate failure

Calculating the A Score is subjective and requires experience and professional judgement, for example, in determining whether LP's board is passive. In reality, passive will be on a scale rather than just passive or not, which also makes it difficult to compare the score between organisations.

The A Score focuses on internal factors, which limits its usefulness. The economic recession has had a serious impact on LP, which calculating the A Score alone would not consider. Further analysis of the external environment, such as using a PEST analysis, or calculation of competitors' A Scores, would consider external factors in determining whether LP is at risk of corporate failure.

Another limitation of the A Score model is that it is only a snapshot at a particular time and does not indicate when corporate failure may occur. Defects and management mistakes may take a long time before they lead to corporate failure. In LP, corporate failure may occur if it is subject to legal action for the delay of the housing project. Conversely, the recession may end and LP may no longer be at risk.

The fact that the A Score does not give a definitive indication of whether failure will happen may mean inappropriate decisions are taken as a result of the analysis. It must be considered whether the time and cost in calculating the score are justified by the benefit of doing so. The results of the A Score may be inconclusive and indicate that the subject is in the 'grey area'. This will require yet further analysis before a conclusion can be reached. However, such a situation does not appear to apply to LP, which is currently clearly at risk of corporate failure using the A Score model.

[Answers to the 50-mark Section A questions begin on the next page.]

54 Lopten

BPP
LEARNING
MEDIA

Marks

(a) Calculation of variable costs – 2 marks
Fixed costs – 1 mark each
Calculation of profit for each product – 1 mark
Average sales price per unit – 1 mark
Calculation of contribution per unit – 1 mark
Calculation of market share – 1 mark
Calculation of breakeven point – 1 mark
Margin of safety – 1 mark
ROCE – 1 mark
Total quality costs – 1 mark
Total for part (a): up to 11 marks

11

(b) PEST factors

For identifying relevant issues (political, economic, social
and technological) in the scenario – up to 2 marks for each issue identified

For commenting on the relevance of the suggested KPIs to each issue –
up to 2 marks per issue

Total for part (b): up to 11 marks

11

(c) For evaluating how well the KPIs fit with the CSF to obtain a dominant
market presence – up to 4 marks

For evaluating how well the KPIs fit with the CSF to maximise profits
within acceptable risk – up to 4 marks

For evaluating how well the KPIs fit with the CSF to maintain brand
image for above average quality products – up to 4 marks

Total for part (c): up to 10 marks

10

(d) For each relevant point about the suitability of the KPIs for planning or
controlling – 1 mark per point

Total for part (d): up to 5 marks

5

(e) For calculating contribution (1 mark) and profit (1 mark) for Plan A – up
to 2 marks for calculations for Plan A

For calculating contribution (2 marks) and profit (1 mark) for Plan B –
up to 3 marks for calculations for Plan B

For calculating difference in actual profits vs target profits under the
two plans – 1 mark

For relevant points evaluating whether the strategies will enable the
business to achieve its target profits – up to 4 marks

Total for part (e): up to 9 marks

9

Professional marks – for style and structure of report – up to 4 marks

$\dfrac{4}{}$

Total = $\underline{\underline{50}}$

Report

To: Board of Lopten Industries

From: Consultant

Date: [today's date]

Subject: **Strategic performance and performance indicators**

Introduction

This report calculates the KPIs suggested by the board for measuring Lopten's performance, and then evaluates the effectiveness of those KPIs in addressing issues in the company's external environment. The report also evaluates how well the KPIs measure performance in relation to Lopten's CSFs. The report concludes by evaluating two marketing strategies which have been proposed, and their impact on Lopten's ability to achieve its target operating profit in two years' time.

(a) **KPIs**

The board has identified a number of KPIs which can be used to assess the performance of the Beeland operations.

These are shown below:

	Cheerful	Posh	
Total profit ($m)	42.4	45.0	See Appendix 1
Average sales price per unit ($)	400.0	700.0	
Contribution per unit ($)	145.0	375.0	
Market share (%)	12.0	33.1	
Margin of safety (%)	25.9	27.3	See Appendix 1
ROCE (%)	13.0	18.0	
Total quality costs ($m)	28.4	19.2	
Consumer awards won	1.0	4.0	

(b) **Issues in Lopten's external environment**

Political factors

Government grants – The Government has given grants to an international manufacturer (one of Lopten's competitors) which has opened a factory in Beeland. Lopten will not be eligible for any similar grants, however, because it manufactures its washing machines at its regional hub in Kayland and then imports them into Beeland – rather than manufacturing them in Beeland.

It will be difficult for the KPIs to measure the impact of the government grants directly. However, monitoring average sales price per unit of Lopten's machines (compared to the competitors' machines) could indicate whether the government grants have enabled the competitor to sell its machines more cheaply than Lopten can. Equally, if the Government imposes any import tariffs on Lopten's machines this could adversely affect their average price compared to the price of the competitors' products.

Similarly, the market share KPI could also help Lopten assess whether the Government's actions are influencing Lopten's market share (as a result of the competitor's washing machines becoming relatively cheaper than Lopten's products).

Economic factors

Market growth – The growth of the middle class, and rising incomes in Beeland, is leading to an increase in demand for Lopten's products.

The KPIs do not directly include any measure of sales growth rates (for example, by measuring annual sales increase compared to the prior year). However, measuring market share does provide an indicator of the rate at which sales of Lopten's washing machines are increasing relative to its competitors' sales.

Foreign exchange risk – Lopten's reported financial performance from its operations in Beeland could also be affected by movements in currency exchange rates between Beeland, Kayland and Lopten's own country. However, the KPIs do not reflect this foreign exchange risk.

Social factors

Customer tastes – As national income in Beeland continues to increase, it is likely that there will be increasing demand for premium products (such as Posh) relative to more basic products (such as Cheerful). This would justify the approach, taken in marketing Plan B, to focus Lopten's marketing resources onto Posh.

Again, a measure of the sales growth rates for the two products would be useful for identifying changes in demand, but the KPIs do not currently provide this. However, the market share KPI could be useful for identifying how successful Lopten is in selling products – particularly Posh.

Technological factors

Developments in technology could affect Lopten in two ways:

New features – Technological developments could mean that Lopten needs to develop new features for its washing machines (for example, if competitors introduce new features into their machines). However, this could be less of an issue in Beeland than developed countries, because Beeland's customers may not yet be as demanding as customers in more developed countries.

Moreover, as Lopten manufactures its products at a regional hub, and only sells them locally, it seems unlikely that the Beeland operation will have any impact on product development for the company as a whole. Therefore, although none of the KPIs address new product development, this seems to be reasonable.

Reduced costs – New technologies could also improve the efficiency of the manufacturing process for Lopten's existing products; for example, by increasing the levels of automation in the manufacturing process.

As such, this should help to reduce the cost of producing Lopten's washing machines. While any such cost reductions will be reflected in the contribution per unit KPI, the contribution figure is also affected by selling price.

Therefore, a more effective indicator to use in order to measure the impact which technological developments have had on the manufacturing process would be 'Manufacturing cost per unit'.

(c) **Links between CSFs and KPIs**

Dominant market presence

Market share – The market share KPI provides an indication of Lopten's presence in the market but, in order to gauge whether or not it dominates the market, Lopten's market share also needs to be measured relative to its competitors. In this respect, a KPI of 'relative market share' (comparing Lopten's market share to that of the market leader) could be more suitable.

Growth strategies – One way in which Lopten could seek to increase market share is by reducing the price of its products in order to increase demand for them. However, this will also affect KPIs for average price per product.

It is important that Lopten doesn't discount the price of its washing machines too aggressively, to the extent that they no longer generate a contribution to profit. In this respect, the contribution per unit KPI will be valuable in ensuring that a balance is maintained between profitability and increasing market share.

Maximise profits within acceptable risk

Profit for each product – The amount of profit earned for each product is one of Lopten's KPIs, so this should encourage a focus on profits. Although the KPI only shows profit for a single period, monitoring this profit figure over a number of periods will highlight trends in the level of profit being earned.

Contribution per unit – The contribution per unit KPI can also be used to monitor how effectively Lopten is controlling its variable costs relative to the price of its products. A focus on cost control in this way should also help to increase profits.

ROCE – ROCE indicates how efficiently Lopten is using its capital in order to generate profits. As such, this KPI should also encourage profit maximisation, although there could be concerns that using ROCE as a profit measure encourages short-termist behaviour (for example, not investing in new capital projects even though such investment would be beneficial in the future).

Risk – The margin of safety provides an indication of the extent to which sales would have to fall before Lopten reaches a breakeven profit situation. In this way, the margin of safety could provide an indication of the level of risk relating to the marketing and pricing strategies of both types of washing machine.

Maintaining brand image for above average quality

Consumer awards – The number of consumer awards won provides an indicator of the reputation of Lopten's products because consumers are unlikely to nominate a product for an award if they are unsatisfied with the quality of the product.

Quality costs – The 'quality cost' KPI gives an indication of how much Lopten has spent on quality management but, by itself, it doesn't give any insight into whether the quality of Lopten's products is 'above average'. For example, are there customer reviews which could be used to rate the quality of Lopten's products against rival products?

In this respect, the KPIs might be improved by including a more specifically customer-focused indicator (for example, customer satisfaction ratings, or numbers of complaints) which could potentially also be benchmarked against competitors' products.

Finally, the need to 'maintain brand image' suggests a need for marketing activity. However, there are no KPIs which monitor the level of effectiveness of Lopten's marketing activities in Beeland.

(d) **KPIs and planning**

Forward looking – KPIs which are to be used for planning (rather than control) need to be forward looking.

Control indicators – In general, financial performance measures tend to be backward looking rather than forward looking, in the sense that they are used to compare the actual performance achieved against some kind of budget or target. For example, KPIs for 'Contribution per unit' and 'ROCE' are more likely to be useful for controlling performance.

In order to monitor its control indicators effectively, though, Lopten should look to measure actual performance against budget or forecast. Currently, it appears to monitor actual performance only, with no reference to either a budget or prior years. However, having some kind of benchmark against which to measure actual performance will help the board to identify those areas where corrective action may be required to improve performance.

Planning indicators – By contrast to financial indicators, non-financial indicators can often be more appropriate as planning indicators.

Margin of safety – In Lopten's case, the margin of safety could be useful as a planning indicator. The margin of safety addresses the risk of making a loss going forward; although, at the moment, the size of the margin should reassure the board that it can afford to take a reasonable degree of strategic risk without jeopardising the survival of the Beeland operation. For example, even if sales of both types of washing machines fell by 25%, Lopten would still make a contribution to profit from its operations in Beeland.

Consumer awards – The number of consumer awards won could also be useful as a planning indicator. Customers' perceptions of Lopten's products will shape the company's ability to increase sales in the future. For example, if Lopten can continue to win awards for 'Posh', it could highlight this in any marketing material designed to boost sales of the product. Moreover, if Lopten can use its success in winning awards to illustrate the quality of its products, it could then use this as a factor which differentiates its washing machines from competitors' products. In turn this could be used to justify Lopten's washing machines being sold at a higher price than rival products.

Planning vs control – In general terms, planning activities tend to be high level, strategic activities, whereas control measures tend to be more appropriate at an operational level. In this respect, the mix of Lopten's KPIs seems rather unusual – because, although the KPIs are presented to the board, there appears to be a greater focus on control indicators rather than planning indicators.

However, this issue could be addressed by modifying the indicators to include market share growth, for example, rather than simply market share. In this way, the board could look to use growth trends to help establish financial projections, rather than solely looking at their market share percentage at a given point in time.

(e) **Impact of marketing strategies**

Plan A

	Most recent $m	Year 1 $m	Year 2 $m
Contribution			
Cheerful	162.4	168.9	175.7
Posh	165.0	171.6	178.5
Fixed costs	240.0	240.0	240.0
Profit	**87.4**	**100.5**	**114.2**

Plan B

	Most recent $m	Year 1 $m	Year 2 $m
Contribution			
Cheerful	162.4	162.4	162.4
Posh	165.0	189.8	218.2
Fixed costs	240.0	240.0	240.0
Profit	**87.4**	**112.2**	**140.6**

The target operating profit in two years' time is $135m. If the board pursues Plan A, Lopten's forecast operating profit will be approximately $21m below the target at this point.

By contrast, if the board adopts Plan B the target profit figure could be achieved.

However, it would seem likely that there is more uncertainty around the figures used in Plan B than those in Plan A. In particular, Plan B assumes an annual growth rate of 15% in demand for Posh.

It is possible that the level of growth in the economy in Beeland can support this level of growth, because demand for premium products could be sustained by the continuing growth of the middle-class population in the country.

However, the prospects of achieving a growth rate of 15% per year are also likely to depend on the effectiveness of Lopten's marketing expenditure. In this respect, it is important to question how much impact any additional marketing expenditure will have. Lopten already spends $80m on marketing of Posh, and so it is debatable whether the additional marketing expenditure will generate proportionately more sales, or instead whether the effectiveness of the expenditure will be reduced by decreasing marginal returns.

In addition, the board needs to consider whether it is realistic to assume that sales of 'Cheerful' will remain constant – even if marketing expenditure on the product is reduced, as proposed in Plan B.

Conclusion

Lopten's current KPIs focus primarily on internal aspects of performance, rather than including a balance of internal and external factors. In addition, the link between the KPIs and Lopten's CSFs – particularly the need to obtain a dominant market presence – appears relatively weak.

Currently, the focus of the KPIs appears to be on control, rather than planning, whereas the board's focus should ideally really be more forward looking. The board should consider revising the KPIs used, in order to address these concerns.

The current marketing plan (Plan A) will not enable Lopten to achieve its profit target of $135m in two years' time. Therefore the company could be advised to adopt Plan B, which has the potential to achieve this figure. However, Plan B assumes some fairly ambitious growth figures, so it will be important to assess how realistic these are before starting to implement the new marketing strategy.

APPENDIX 1

	Cheerful	Posh
Units sold (millions)	1.12	0.44
	$m	$m
Revenue	448.0	308.0
Variable costs		
Materials	100.8	52.8
Labour	67.2	35.2
Overheads	44.8	22.0
Distribution costs	50.4	19.8
Quality costs	22.4	13.2
Contribution	162.4	165.0
Fixed costs	18.0	18.0
Distribution costs	16.0	16.0
Quality costs	6.0	6.0
Marketing costs	80.0	80.0
Total fixed costs	120.0	120.0
Total profit	**42.4**	**45.0**
	$m	$m
Margin of safety		
Contribution per unit ($)	145.0	375.0
Units sold (millions)	1.12	0.44
Breakeven sales (millions)	0.83	0.32
Margin of safety	**25.9%**	**27.3%**

55 Chiven

Workbook references. Performance reports are discussed in Chapter 6 of the Workbook, as is Big Data. The value chain is discussed in Chapter 4.

Top tips.

Part (a). In the scenario you are told that the CEO wants your evaluation of the performance report split into two separate parts in your report; ie parts (a) and (b) of the question.

Your recommendations for the three new measures should be covered in part (b) of the requirement. Therefore, your focus in part (a) should have been:

- Evaluating the choice of existing measures used
- Evaluating the presentation in the report

In the Workbook we referred to the technical article on ACCA's website about 'Reports for Performance Management' which highlights four basis criteria which can be used to evaluate an organisation's performance reports:

- **Purpose** – What is the purpose of the report? Does the report provide information which is relevant to the organisation's performance against its mission or objectives?

- **Audience** – Who is the report produced for? Is it appropriate for its audience and their requirements?

- **Information** – What information is needed – financial and non-financial; quantitative and qualitative? Does the report provide the information which is needed to fulfil its purpose and satisfy its audience?

- **Layout** – Does the report make it clear for readers to identify the most important information?

Although you didn't have to use these criteria to answer the requirement, they could have given you a useful framework for answering this question. For example, how well do the performance measures included in the report help the board assess Chiven's performance against its aims?

Similarly, in terms of the audience – is the information provided in the report suitable for board members (or is some of it too detailed, and more appropriate for operational managers?)

The points about 'layout' are also directly relevant to your evaluation of the way the report is presented: does the report make it clear for readers to identify the most important information? Remember that having large amounts of information in a report isn't always beneficial, because there is a danger of information overload. Could that be a potential issue here? Also, does the way the information is presented help the board members understand performance? For example, instead of presenting simply presenting revenue figures for 20X8 and 20X7 might it be more useful to indicate % growth between the two years?

Overall, note that there are 20 marks available for this part of the question though, so you need to cover a sufficient large number of relevant points to score well here.

Part (b). The CEO's request (in the second paragraph of the scenario) asked you to identify 'three new measures which you believe address key issues for the business' but are not currently on the report.

However, note that you also need to carry out appropriate calculations for the performance measures you recommend. So, to score all the marks here, you need to recommend (and justify) measures which not only address key issues, but can also be calculated using the indicators already provided in Appendix 1.

Although the CEO has identified increasing Chiven's online presence (ie increasing online sales) as one of her aims, there is no information available to calculate any performance measures you might recommend in relation to it. So, for example, if you recommended a measure relating to online sales, you would receive a mark for identifying a measure which relates one of the key issues the business is facing, but you would not be able to earn any marks for calculations.

Part (c). The paragraph in the scenario about 'Business integration and supply chain' identifies that the CEO believes that simplifying Chiven's supply chain could help improve the company's performance, but doing this will have implications for Chiven's performance measurement and information systems.

The CEO has asked you to advise on appropriate performance measures and systems when using the value chain approach to simply the supply chain. Importantly, the main focus of your answer needs to be on the supply chain, not the value chain. So, for example, you shouldn't spend time describing all the activities in the value chain. The only areas of the value chain which are relevant here, are ones which relate to the supply chain.

Also, note that the requirement asks you to advise on two different things: (i) performance measures which would be affected by the simplification, and (ii) information systems which would be involved. It is important you address both parts of this requirement. Equally, when advising on relevant performance measures, you should identify existing measures from Appendix 1 which are relevant to the supply chain, rather than introducing additional new measures of your own.

Part (d). In the scenario, you are told that the CEO believes the board does not understand the implications the 'volume, velocity and variety' characteristics of Big Data could have for Chiven, so she wants you to write a guide for them.

Therefore when the CEO's instruction to you ask you to discuss 'the development of Big Data and its potential impact on Chiven's information systems', the three 'V's should provide you with a useful framework for your answer. In effect, you can provide a short discussion of each of the three V's and its impact on Chiven's information systems. Importantly though, don't simply discuss the 3 V's in general terms, but illustrate how they could be relevant to Chiven (because this is what the Board will be interested in).

Equally importantly, note that in additional to discussing the 'V' characteristics, the requirement also asks you to discuss the risks and challenges that Big Data presents to Chiven. This could include challenges in relation to storing large volumes of unstructured data, but you should also think more generally about the risks involved in storing data – particularly personal data (as illustrated by the numbers of stories in the 'real world' about companies being affected by data breaches).

Overall. Remember that you have been asked to write a report, so make sure the style and structure of your answer, as well as its tone, is appropriate for a report.

Examining team's comments

Part (a). Responses to this part were disappointing, and candidates could have scored much better had they related their answers to the aims and critical success factors of the company in the scenario. Some candidates **did** indicate that the company had two aims, and evaluate whether the report addressed these aims. However, the company also had four subsidiary critical success factors, and very few candidates addressed whether the report measured these factors.

The ability to evaluate whether the measures in a report are appropriate for a company to help it achieve its critical success factors and overall aims is one of the main learning outcomes of the APM exam.

Some candidates also offered quite lengthy general descriptions about what a report should contain. While this might earn a mark for recognising the purpose of the report, to score well in this question candidates must discuss the contents of a report in the context of the company in the scenario. Candidates have to offer analysis and justification as to whether the specific report in the question has the content and presentation of a high quality report. If it does, then candidates need to be able to justify why the content and presentation are appropriate and of high quality. Alternatively, if it does not, then candidates need to be able to justify why the report, in its current format, is not helping the company achieve its aims and its critical success factors.

Part (b). This question was generally poorly answered. Candidates often ignored the CEO's instruction to use the data in Appendix 1 and recommended other measures based on a broader consideration of the business. Justified suggestions are rewarded where possible, but this approach made calculation impossible and so meant candidates inevitably lost marks.

Candidates must also recognise that it is the justification for measures which is tested in a question like this, not simply the calculation. Candidates need to demonstrate that they understand the company and its situation, and therefore how the measure they are recommending will improve on those already being used. Any improvement should be justified in terms of helping the company to better achieve its aims.

Part (c). Although the value chain was given as an Appendix, many candidates still spent time explaining the value chain, and offering definitions of each of the nine components. Such responses clearly did not address the question asked, and so earned few – if any – marks.

Few candidates appeared to appreciate that the focus of this question was on the supply chain and so the value chain was only relevant insofar as it might help simplify the supply chain. Therefore, candidates should have focused on the specific parts of the value chain that related to supply. However, most candidates failed to appreciate this and offered generic measures for different components of the value chain that did not relate to the scenario.

Part (d). Many candidates scored well on this question, particularly in relation to the risks and challenges where they outlined, with some justification, the difficulties that the company might face in using Big Data.

However, some candidates demonstrated a lack of technical knowledge in relation to Big Data, as they outlined the challenges of collecting data in general, not specifically Big Data. Similarly, the 3Vs – velocity, variety and volume – were sometime explained in general terms, rather than in the context of Big Data.

Report. Candidates who had practised writing professional answers scored in the presentation area. Markers were looking for suitable report headings and sub-headings, an introduction, a logical structure, and a clear, concise style. Most candidates performed well in this area, scoring 3 or 4 marks.

Marking scheme

		Marks

(a)   Identifying the company's aims, and key aspects of performance relating
    to them – 1 mark per relevant point, up to 4 marks

Evaluating if the aims are measured – 1 mark per relevant point, up to 10 marks

General comments about the presentation of the report and the measures
    included – 1 mark per relevant point, up to 10 marks

- Eg repetition of measures, no grouping or structure, external
    information, focus on the strategic not operational, need for online
    measures as well as store-based measures.

Total for part (a): up to 20 marks   20

(b)   Justification of each performance measures – 1 mark each
    Calculations – up to 5 marks
    Other relevant points – up to 3 marks
    Total for part (b): up to 8 marks   8

(c)   Defining the value chain – 1 mark
    Identifying the activity types relevant to the supply chain – up to 2 marks
    Advising on appropriate performance measures – up to 3 marks
    Advising on information systems – up to 3 marks
    Maximum for part (c): up to 7 marks   7

(d)   Definition of Big Data – 1 mark
    Discussing impact of Big Data, using volume, velocity and variety to
        illustrate relevant examples for Chiven – up to 9 marks
    Risks and challenges of using Big Data – up to 6 marks
    Maximum for part (d): up to 11 marks   11
    Professional marks – up to 4 marks   4

                                                            Total = 50

Report

To: The Board of Chiven Stores (Chiven)

From: Accountant

Date: [today's date]

Subject: Performance reporting and management issues

Introduction

This report evaluates the current performance report used for the annual board review and suggests three additional important performance indicators. The performance measurement aspects of the use of the value chain to help to streamline the supply chain is considered. Finally, the impact, risks and challenges of Big Data for Chiven are discussed.

(a)   Performance report for annual board review

The basic role of the performance report is to allow the board to see if the mission is being achieved along with the subsidiary aims and strategically important initiatives set by the senior management.

Chiven's overall aim, or mission, breaks down into two parts:

- Becoming the largest clothing retailer in Beeland, which is measured by Chiven's market share, but without an indication of the market leader it is not possible to see if this is achieved; and

- Delivering exceptional value to its shareholders, which is measured through a number of measures (dividends, EPS, economic value added and ROCE). However, it is often the growth of these indicators year-on-year which would be more useful to assess performance rather than the absolute amounts. Additionally, market average information would be important for investors so they can compare their investment in Chiven with others in their portfolios.

The subsidiary aims and initiatives based on the CEO's comments are:

- Maximising opportunities from new technology
- Increasing web presence
- Making use of 'Big Data' in relation to Chiven's web sales
- Simplifying the supply chain

There are no measures of web sales or the impact of technology on the activities of Chiven which would allow measurement of the first three aims. The basic data does not appear to be collected as sales are reported in total and not for stores and for the website separately.

The final aim does appear to be measured by looking at the number of suppliers and also the number of product lines sold (number of suppliers × average number of product lines per supplier). Reduction of these numbers would indicate a more streamlined supply chain. This would also indirectly improve the probability of stock obsolescence and so reduce inventory write-downs.

General comments about the current report

The current report is likely to confuse the board as it presents too many indicators and so overloads the board with information. This could be improved by reducing the number of indicators. For example, it should be considered if there is a need for both economic value added and ROCE in the report as they perform similar functions.

The report does not appear to group or appropriately prioritise the indicators presented. Suggested headings for an improved report might be:

- Shareholder value performance
- Market leadership
- Impact of new technology
- Efficiency in the supply chain

For example, the main company aim relating to shareholder value should appear at the top of the report and include dividends, EPS, economic value added and/or ROCE. As already noted, the growth of these indicators year-on-year would be more useful rather than the absolute amounts.

There is a lack of external information (especially competitor information) such as the market leading market share.

There is a lack of forward looking information which given the aim of innovation through new technology would be important. Expected growth of web sales in the market generally would allow measurement of Chiven's performance in this area.

There is a lack of a summary of property costs which could be especially useful for comparison with web operations.

There are a number of indicators which are about the detailed operation of the stores (such as average time between customer entry and employee greeting or average queueing time for customers). These are of a more operational nature and may be distracting and unnecessary in the board report, as it ought to focus on the strategic indicators.

However, the board may take the view that such customer-experience centred indicators are strategically important as they are commonly used in retail. In this case, there ought to be equivalent indicators for the web-based sales, for example, relating to number clicks or pages needed in order to make a web sale.

(b) **Three new performance measures**

There are three performance measures, which currently do not appear on the report, which would improve presentation of Chiven's results. As noted above, the current report contains many absolute figures and some ratios would simplify the work of interpreting these results.

Key issues in the current report and from the perspectives of running the physical stores are the number of employees and the floor space of the stores. Therefore, it is suggested that the revenue and operating profit per unit for each of these variables would be helpful and these are also common indicators used in the retail trade.

	Total 20X8	Total 20X7
Revenue per employee ($)	64,988	66,142
Revenue per sq metre ($)	3,096.5	3,147.3
Operating profit ($m)	434.3	430.0
Operating profit per sq metre ($)	510.9	519.3

Operating profit per employee has not been calculated as the general body of employees are more concerned with sales rather than cost control and hence profits.

Tutorial note. Workings for new performance measures

		20X8	20X7
Revenue ($m)	From scenario	2,632	2,606
Employees	From scenario	40,500	39,400
Revenue per employee ($)		**64,988**	**66,142**
Floor space (square metres)	From scenario	850,000	828,000
Revenue per square metre ($)	Revenue/floor space	**3,096.5**	**3,147.3**
Operating profit margin (%)	From scenario	16.5	16.5
Operating profit ($m)	Revenue * margin	**434.3**	**430.0**
Operating profit per square metre	Operating profit/floor space	**510.9**	**519.3**

(c) **Streamlining the supply chain using the value chain**

The value chain divides the value activities of a business into different types and then examines the links between these in order to more efficiently build value within the business.

The supply chain simplification may involve reducing the number of suppliers and making the chain more efficient. The supply chain has an impact on three types of activity in the value chain: the main activity area is procurement (dealing with suppliers) but it could also include technology development (information systems) and inbound logistics. There may be other types of activity affected if these are outsourced.

The performance measures associated with this simplification are the number of suppliers and number of product lines supplied by each supplier (both areas are part of the existing reporting). They include the time taken to source new products and the revenue and profits obtained from these (new measures).

The information systems which would be involved would be those with contact to the suppliers obtaining product details and prices and also those liaising over delivery of these items. For example, these could be part of a just-in-time delivery system to reduce stock holding at Chiven.

(d) **The potential impact of Big Data for performance management at Chiven**

Big Data refers to the very large amounts of data which are now available through the increased use of technology and can be used to develop predictive information about human (customer and supplier) behaviour.

There are three characteristics of Big Data: volume, velocity and variety.

The large volume of data obtained. This is best understood by considering the relevant information gathering systems for Chiven. In stores, loyalty cards being swiped at checkouts allow the details of all products purchased, the time, amount and method of payment used. On the website and on Chiven's social media pages, in addition to the data which could be collected as for stores, every page visited and every product examined or commented upon would be recorded. This information would require system hardware to store and retrieve it.

The velocity of Big Data refers to the short timescales for information developed to affect decisions. The information could be gathered in nearly real time and this might be necessary in order to react quickly to information about customers who are considering a purchase. For example, it would be much less effective to text a customer with price-comparison information after they have left the store.

The software must be present to allow the kind of data mining and predictive analysis required to perform these tasks.

Big Data is 'big' due to the variety of types of information collected. Chiven could be looking at transaction data and browsing activities, as already mentioned, but also more unusual data types such as social media reactions (text and photographs) and geographical information from customer phones.

This data is both structured and unstructured and these require different responses from the information recording and processing systems.

Risks and challenges

Systems which can record and process the volumes of data being produced are expensive, both the hardware and software. The costs are falling but as already noted, the volumes of data available are rising and Chiven's competitors will be active in this area too. It will be a process which requires large spending in order to catch up with and pass those competitors and then, constant ongoing spending to maintain an advantageous position.

The storage of personal information (eg about customers) is an active area of new laws and regulation. Breaking these rules can be punished both in the legal sense but also in a reputational sense resulting in lost business. In particular, theft or loss of personal data can lead to civil legal action and bad publicity.

The data obtained from qualitative sources (such as social media) can be imprecise or inaccurate and lead to inaccurate conclusions. Some data collected may be incorrect. This is sometimes referred to as the veracity problem. Also, in large volumes of data, some data may become out-of-date quickly especially about a customer's precise location and so constant monitoring of the database will be required to avoid this.

56 Folt

Workbook references. CSFs and KPIs are covered in Chapter 2 of the Workbook, target costing and quality management are covered in Chapter 11.

Top tips. This was a relatively short question focusing on a range of classic APM issues including CSFs, KPIs and quality management – questions on these themes are common in the APM exam.

A report was requested, which included 4 professional marks, on the following areas.

Part (a). This asked for a justification of a maximum of two KPIs to fit three CSFs that were provided in the scenario, and then an evaluation of the collection of KPIs that had been chosen. There were many possible answers to this, but all should be along the theme of creating a logical performance hierarchy of KPIs which tie back to the overall strategy.

Part (b). This asked for an analysis of the application of target costing, including a definition and an explanation of how it could be used. The main requirement was to use data provided to illustrate the target cost gap.

Part (c). This required an explanation of the four categories of quality costs (4 marks) and then of who (of the company and an outsourced partner) had responsibility for each area. This required a close reading of the scenario to understand the split of responsibilities for quality management.

Part (d). This required an evaluation of the impact of an outsourced providers limited information systems on quality management. Even though the wording of the requirement was slightly confusing, the detailed instructions of what was required were contained within the relevant section of the scenario (this was also true for other requirements).

Examining team's comments.

Part (a). This part of the question was out of 16 and candidates generally scored about half the marks available. Part of the problem candidates encountered here appeared to be in not fully comprehending, for the first CSF, that it was two particular groups of capital providers who had to be satisfied. Many responses suggested KPIs that were clearly not relevant to the scenario in this regard. It is also clear that many candidates felt that justifying the measure they had offered could be undertaken by providing a definition of that term. Clearly, such comments are not appropriate when a justification is being sought. Candidates also found it challenging to offer KPIs for CSFs that were essentially non-financial in nature, and many responses offered financial KPIs which were not justified in the context of the CSF they were discussing.

Almost all candidates ignored the second part of the requirement of the question.

Part (c). Though this question was generally well done, there was a significant minority of candidates who did not understand what quality costs were and discussed costs in general. This is a fundamental lack of basic knowledge and such responses did not address any part of the question asked.

Some candidates also struggled to divide responsibilities accurately and did not refer to the specifics of the scenario to explain their response. With regard to external failure costs, for example, most candidates assumed that it would be the company who subcontracted the production that would be wholly responsible for these costs. It is clear, however, that if such errors and costs related to errors made by the company that was subcontracted to manufacture the product, the replacement cost would lie with them, even if the reputational damage with regard to the end-customer lay with the company that subcontracted the manufacture.

Part (d). Candidates found this very challenging and most candidates did not pass this part of the question. Responses here were either brief or not relevant to the scenario. Many candidates responded to a slightly different question, which was much more focused towards the qualities that information should have. Such responses did score some marks but did not address the main focus of the question, which was around the sources of the information.

Candidates also often offered unjustified, commercially unaware suggestions such as the companies purchasing an Enterprise Resource Planning (ERP) system. Such systems are very expensive and the overall profit on the venture would not justify further expenditure of this nature.

Marking scheme

<table>
<tr><td></td><td></td><td></td><td></td><td>**Marks**</td></tr>
<tr><td>(a)</td><td>Recommended KPIs – up to 4 marks for each CSF, must be justified</td><td></td><td>12</td><td></td></tr>
<tr><td></td><td>Staying within maximum of 2 KPIs per CSF</td><td></td><td>1</td><td></td></tr>
<tr><td></td><td>Evaluation as a complete system for Folt</td><td></td><td>6</td><td></td></tr>
<tr><td></td><td></td><td></td><td></td><td>Max 16</td></tr>
<tr><td>(b)</td><td>Target costing</td><td></td><td></td><td></td></tr>
<tr><td></td><td>Target cost</td><td></td><td>1</td><td></td></tr>
<tr><td></td><td>Design</td><td></td><td>1</td><td></td></tr>
<tr><td></td><td>Inspections</td><td></td><td>1</td><td></td></tr>
<tr><td></td><td>Reworking</td><td></td><td>1</td><td></td></tr>
<tr><td></td><td>Other costs</td><td></td><td>1</td><td></td></tr>
<tr><td></td><td>Cost gap</td><td></td><td>1</td><td></td></tr>
<tr><td></td><td>Definition of target cost</td><td></td><td>1</td><td></td></tr>
<tr><td></td><td>Conclusion</td><td></td><td>1</td><td></td></tr>
<tr><td></td><td>Impact on contract negotiations</td><td></td><td>4</td><td></td></tr>
<tr><td></td><td></td><td></td><td></td><td>Max 10</td></tr>
<tr><td>(c)</td><td>1 mark per relevant point</td><td></td><td></td><td></td></tr>
<tr><td></td><td>For each of the four quality cost areas: defining the cost areas with an illustration of how it applies to the scenario and giving a justified recommendation of its treatment under the contract</td><td></td><td></td><td></td></tr>
<tr><td></td><td></td><td></td><td></td><td>Max 11</td></tr>
<tr><td>(d)</td><td>1 mark per relevant point</td><td></td><td></td><td></td></tr>
<tr><td></td><td>Importance of quality information</td><td></td><td>2</td><td></td></tr>
<tr><td></td><td>Need for systems at Xela</td><td></td><td>2</td><td></td></tr>
<tr><td></td><td>Use Folt's systems</td><td></td><td>2</td><td></td></tr>
<tr><td></td><td>Need for monitoring</td><td></td><td>3</td><td></td></tr>
<tr><td></td><td>Impact on the contract (SLAs)</td><td></td><td>2</td><td></td></tr>
<tr><td></td><td>Other sources of information</td><td></td><td>2</td><td></td></tr>
<tr><td></td><td></td><td></td><td></td><td>Max 9</td></tr>
<tr><td></td><td>**Professional presentation**</td><td></td><td></td><td>4</td></tr>
<tr><td></td><td></td><td></td><td></td><td>Total = 50</td></tr>
</table>

Report

To:	The CEO of Folt Manufacturing (Folt)
From:	An accountant
Date:	[today's date]
Subject:	Performance measurement and outsourcing of manufacturing at Folt

This report recommends a set of key performance indicators (KPIs) for the identified critical success factors (CSFs) associated with the new strategy and evaluates these as a set of measures of the strategic performance of Folt. Further, in preparation for the negotiation of the outsourced manufacturing contract, advice is given on the use of target costing; the attribution of responsibility for areas of quality and the information required to monitor the quality of production.

(a) **Recommended KPIs for CSFs**

The chief executive officer (CEO) has identified three CSFs for the medium term. Performance towards these requires to be measured and so KPIs are recommended as follows:

Keep capital providers satisfied

There are two capital providers, the debt is all provided by the venture capitalist (VC) and the equity is provided by the management team and the VC combined with the management team taking the majority. A widely used and understood metric for performance would be return on capital employed (ROCE), which measures the returns to all capital providers as a group. It is defined as operating profit/capital employed. In order to properly understand performance, a target measure should be set for this, possibly by using an industry average as benchmark.

To break this down further would probably require return on equity and cost of debt measures and would, therefore, break the desire to keep the performance information brief. As there are only two capital providers and ROCE neatly summarises this, no other KPIs are suggested.

Build a world-class software development team

This is a difficult factor to measure with precision. Building a team could be measured by an increasing number of employees or number of projects undertaken. However, the important element in this CSF is the 'world-class' quality of the team. This could be measured by the input cost of the team, provided that they are recruited at competitive market rates, since higher wages would imply higher skills. Alternatively, it could be measured by the team's output in terms of commercial success (sales) or technical achievement (industry design awards).

Overall, therefore, being led by the output of the team, it is recommended that we use growth in number of projects undertaken and the number of industry design awards won as the KPIs for this CSF.

Ensure that quality of the imaging devices meets market standards

Again, this is a difficult factor to measure. Financial measures of quality are possible by looking at the effect on sales volume and profitability (both likely higher for higher quality). However, these are lagging indicators where quality effects can take some considerable time to trickle through to customer perceptions.

A more direct measure of the quality of current manufacturing would be through customer returns and product failure rates on factory testing. However, it can be difficult to obtain benchmarking information that will allow judgement of whether this is meeting market standards. Given that the company already does manufacture successfully, it should have historic data which, if products are selling at the required margins, would suggest that these data on failure rates and returns would be acceptable to the market. As the business is moving to outsourcing its manufacturing, it is the external failure rate data of the customer returns which will be more appropriate, as Folt will retain the key contact with the customer.

Overall, it is recommended that gross profit (a measure of both volume and profitability) of products and value of customer returns be used as KPIs. Both of these will need to be benchmarked to historic values in order to judge the maintenance of standards.

Performance measurement system

The KPIs suggested are:

- ROCE
- Growth in number of projects undertaken
- Growth in number of industry design awards won
- Gross profit
- Value of customer returns

The question of whether this is a suitable set of metrics to measure strategic performance really asks, does this measure the achievement of Folt's overall objective 'to provide an adequate return to its capital providers while growing the business into a world-class supplier in its areas of expertise'?

This objective can be broken down into:

- Providing an adequate return to its capital providers
- Growing the business
- Being a world-class supplier in its areas of expertise.

These KPIs do address the first part through ROCE and the second part partly through building the software team. However, the overall growth of the business is not measured financially through sales or profits and its target of being world-class is not measured through the number of markets which it has entered and is considered a leader. The final two KPIs have a more supporting role to play for the overall objective and these could be replaced by others measuring the concepts of growth and world-class supplier in order to provide a strategic view for the board of whether the company's mission is being achieved.

> **Tutorial note.** Credit is given for suitably justified metrics and then a consistent discussion of this in relation to the objectives of Folt.

(b) **Outsourced manufacturing: target costing**

Working (per unit):

	$	$
Target price		175.0
Target profit		35.0
Target cost		140.0
Costs:		
Software	40.0	
Materials	37.0	
Machine costs	35.2	
Labour	12.5	
Packaging and delivery	8.0	
Design	8.0	
Inspections	0.8	
Reworking costs	0.5	
Total costs		142.0
Cost gap		2.0

Note. It is assumed that it is the total design costs which are relevant to pricing the product, although it would also be possible to consider the original design costs as sunk and so only include the redesign element.

The target cost is calculated as the estimate of a competitive product price less the desired profit margin.

The illustrative calculation above shows that the current estimated cost is $2 per unit too high and so the product or the manufacturing process will need to be redesigned to cut these costs in order to meet the desired margin.

The costs will be split under the contract between the two parties. Therefore, Folt could press Xela to make cuts in its costs to meet the cost gap as the gap is not large (2.3% of the total costs for manufacturing [ie excluding software, design and packaging and delivery]) and it is stated that Ceeland is a lower cost environment than Beeland for manufacturing. However, it may be dangerous to Folt's strategy if these cuts adversely affect product quality.

(c) **Responsibility for quality areas within outsourced manufacturing**

This discussion relates to the quality of the manufactured device and should exclude issues with the software, packaging and delivery, which remain Folt's responsibility. Taking each of the four areas of quality costs in turn, the cost area is defined and the appropriate treatment under the contract discussed:

- Prevention costs are incurred to prevent the production of products which do not conform to specification (eg design of the product and manufacturing process). The product design costs will obviously lie with Folt and the costs for design of the manufacturing process will lie with Xela, although it would be sensible for Xela to replicate Folt's current process and indeed this may be required in order to maintain quality. However, Xela may want autonomy on this in order to make further gains from streamlining processes. There will need to be liaison between Folt and Xela to ensure that process designs are acceptable to both parties.

- Appraisal costs are costs to ensure that the products output by the manufacturer conform to standards. These costs will mostly lie with Xela as it will be the manufacturer. However, Folt will have to oversee this appraisal by checking on the quality data which Xela will supply under the contract.

- Internal failure costs arise when poor products are identified before despatch. These costs will remain the responsibility of the manufacturer (Xela) as they have control of the manufacturing facility and the appraisal operation there.

- External failure costs arise when poor products are identified after despatch to the customer. Where these costs relate to repair or replacement of faulty hardware products, they should lie with the manufacturer. It is worth noting in price negotiations that there are additional costs for Folt from these failures beyond immediate reworking costs, such as the impact on Folt's brand.

There may be reasonable argument from Xela that Folt should bear some of the non-conformance costs (internal and external failure) if the faults can be attributed to faulty product design work.

Obviously, all of these matters are subject to negotiation before the contract is finalised.

(d) **Impact of sources of quality information**

The maintenance of quality standards is a critical success factor for Folt. The ability to ensure this is based on the SLAs in the manufacturing contract with Xela. The monitoring of these SLAs will be done through information systems and so the quality and reliability of the information is critical to Folt's success.

The outsourcing contract must stipulate agreed quality metrics and also the targets for performance. These will have to be measured and reported by Xela to Folt. Xela does not at present have information systems capable of capturing the non-financial data which is likely to be required by the SLAs. It must therefore be a condition of the contract that suitable systems are put in place by Xela.

In fact, a simple solution would be for Xela to duplicate the existing systems at Folt. This would avoid the need for Folt to authorise (under the contract) any new system as it would then have a familiar one. It will also mean that the format of the reports is familiar and this too will ease the handover of operations.

However, this new system will be owned and operated by Xela, and so Folt will need to have access to it in order to verify that data is being input, processed and reported accurately. The detailed type of system audit work may be new to Folt. However, again by using the same system as currently exists, it should be possible to identify managers who monitor quality at Folt's existing manufacturing operation, to perform this task.

In summary, it will be important that any metrics and targets for these which are used under the contract are unambiguous. It will also be important to stipulate in the contract that Folt be given access to verify that this information is being produced accurately. This will help to avoid the possibility of gaming the contract by Xela.

Ultimately, customer complaints and returns will represent an external source of information on the quality of the products manufactured. However, it would be more effective to identify and address problems before they reach customers.

57 Flack

Workbook reference. Performance reports are discussed in Chapter 6 of the Workbook, as are management information systems. Performance measures (including ROCE, RI) are discussed in Chapter 7, while expected values are discussed in Chapter 5.

Top tips.

Part (a). A key point to note in this requirement is that you have been asked to evaluate the performance report, not Flack's underlying performance.

Also note that your evaluation needs to be in relation to the CEO's question of whether the performance report 'is fit for the purpose of achieving the company's mission'.

A key part of this requirement is identifying what information the performance report provides the board about the issues identified in the mission (eg earning customer loyalty; resource utilisation; serving shareholders' interests). A useful way to structure your answer could have been to use each of the issues identified in the mission as a sub-heading, and then consider what information – if any – the report provides the board in relation to that issue.

However, as well as evaluating the performance report in the context of Flack's mission, you also need to comment on whether the performance report is 'short-termist'. So to score well in part (a), you also need to address this issue: do the aspects of performance being included in the performance report encourage a short-term focus?

Part (b). The context for this requirement is that the CEO wants an evaluation of how the two new measures (revenue per square metre; operating profit per square metre) could help Flack assess the objective of 'utilising all our resources'.

Make sure you look at the CEO's request in the scenario very carefully, because it contains a number of elements:

- Explain how the new measures relate to the objective
- What the ratios are (ie **calculate** the ratios themselves, using the figures from Appendix 1)
- Explain how the ratios could be used to manage business performance

To score well here, you need to address all three of the elements. However, note that there are only eight marks available in total for this part of the question, so you only need to cover each element quite briefly.

Part (c). The board currently uses divisional operating profit as the measure for assessing divisional performance, but is considering replacing this with residual income. You are asked to assess this proposed change.

It is important to recognise the context of this proposed change. Flack has been criticised for its stores looking 'run down' and store managers have been reluctant to invest in refurbishing existing stores, preferring instead to use capital to open new stores. A key issue here is whether the change in performance measures will change managers' behaviour in this respect.

A useful approach to answering requirements like this which require a comparison between current and proposed measures is to identify what the potential problems are with the existing measure and then consider whether the proposed new measure will help to address them.

Importantly, note that in the scenario, the CEO has told you that you are not required to calculate the current values. In other words, you need to focus on the measures themselves, not on the performance of the divisions.

Part (d). There are two elements to this requirement: one a calculation (of the expected ROCE for the new store using the data in Appendix 2); the second an assessment of whether using ROCE based on expected values is an appropriate metric for evaluating new stores.

Once again, the information in the scenario provides very clear instructions for the focus of your answer. 'The board wants the focus of your comments to be on the use of an **expected value**, not on the use of ROCE, as this is widely used and understood in the retail industry.'

Similarly, it was crucial to use expected value operating profit as the basis of the ROCE calculation (ie expected value operating profit/capital cost) not operating profit from any of the individual demand scenarios.

Part (e). The 'proposed new information system' being referred to is a customer loyalty card scheme, supported by a data warehouse – as described in the penultimate paragraph of the scenario. The paragraph also describes three areas where the CEO thinks the scheme can help Flack become more efficient: target advertising, product range choices and price offers. These should provide some useful clues about how the scheme – which is essentially a marketing information system – could help improve Flack's performance.

More generally, it could also be useful to think back to Flack's overall mission, one of whose key elements is 'earning customer loyalty'. By definition, a customer loyalty card scheme should help to achieve that aim.

Overall. Remember that you have been asked to write a report, so make sure the style and structure of your answer, as a whole, is appropriate for a report. For example, a report should have a short introduction explaining the key issues to be discussed in it, and should have headings for each section or part.

Examining team's comments. Part (a) was generally well done. Candidates performed well when they used the signposts given in the scenario to identify specific issues to look for in Flack's performance report.

Part (b) again required candidates to address specific requirements identified in the scenario. However, this part of the question was not answered well, with many candidates failing to identify how the new measures fit with the specific strategy point they were intended to address. In addition, candidates often didn't pick up the simple calculation marks on offer by failing to recognise that they were working in $'000.

Part (c) was answered reasonably well, with candidates structuring their comments into criticism of the existing performance measure and then analysis of how the proposed new measure would address the issues with the existing measure. Unfortunately, a number of candidates decided to focus their answer on a different, new performance indicator of their own choice, which cost them a number of marks.

Part (d) was often well done, with many candidates scoring all the marks for the calculations. However, the commentary on the method often lacked an appreciation of the circumstances in which 'expected values' are appropriate. Also, many candidates ignored the advice to focus their answer on the concept of an 'expected' value for the indicator, rather than offering a general discussion of the indicator itself.

Part (e) was also generally well done, with most candidates showing an understanding of the information that a loyalty card system could provide and how that information could be used to improve the company's performance.

Report format. As we have seen in previous sittings, those candidates who had practised writing professional answers prior to the exam performed admirably in the presentation area (four marks). The markers were looking for:

- Suitable report headings;
- An introduction;
- A logical structure (signposted by good use of sub-headings); and
- A clear, concise style.

Marking scheme

Marks

(a) Performance report

Breaking down the mission – up to 3 marks

Two main aims, three CSFs/strategies, noting how these are
　logically connected

Comments on how report addresses mission and strategies –
　up to 6 marks

Missing information – up to 3 marks

Lack of external info; margins by product category

Report is 'short-termist' – up to 3 marks

Comments on presentation – up to 3 marks

Lack of narrative; data overload; rounding

Maximum for part (a)　　　　　　　　　　　　　　　　14

(b) New asset utilisation indicators

Addressing the mission – up to 3 marks

Calculations – 3 marks

Use in managing business performance – up to 5 marks

Maximum for part (b)　　　　　　　　　　　　　　　　8

(c) Divisional performance

Discussion of existing behaviour and measure – up to 5 marks

Discussion of new measure – up to 5 marks

Maximum for part (c)　　　　　　　　　　　　　　　　8

(d) Decision-making under risk

Calculations:

1 mark for method

1 mark for correct profit under each scenario

1 mark for expected operating profit

1 mark for expected ROCE

Comments – 1 mark per point; up to 4 marks

Maximum for part (d)　　　　　　　　　　　　　　　　8

ANSWERS

(e)   New information system

       Description and costs – up to 2 marks

       Benefits – 1 mark per point up to 8 marks

       Maximum for part (e)   8

       Professional 4 marks   4

                                               Total = 50

Report

To: Board of Flack

From: A. Accountant

Date: [today's date]

Subject: **Performance reporting and management issues at Flack**

Introduction

This report evaluates the current performance report for Flack and the introduction of two new performance measures. Then, the effect of a proposed change in the divisional performance measure is assessed. Next, the use of expected ROCE for new store proposals is evaluated. Finally, the report explains how the proposed new information system can help to improve business performance at Flack.

(a)   **Performance reporting at Flack**

The current report has a number of strengths and weaknesses. These will be discussed according to whether the report:

- Addresses the mission;
- Contains appropriate information for decision making;
- Shows signs of being short term; and
- Is well presented.

The current mission can be broken down into two parts:

- To be the first choice for customers; and
- To provide the right balance of quality, service and price.

There are three strategies for achieving this mission, reflecting stakeholder concerns:

- Earning customer loyalty;
- Utilising all resources; and
- Serving shareholders' interests.

Addressing the mission

Customer loyalty. The report does not address the first part of the mission (earning customer loyalty). This can only be measured using external data but the report is utilising only Flack's internal data. This part of the mission relates to the first strategy to gain customer loyalty. Customer loyalty could be gauged through repeat purchases or market share information but neither is supplied. This is clearly important to a retailer and may be more easily gathered once the data from the new information system are available for inclusion in this report.

The current report provides no measures of the balance of quality, service and price other than through the historic growth in revenue. It would only be through comparison with competitors or customer survey data that a picture of the mix of these qualities could be gained.

Utilising all resources. The second strategy of utilising resources requires that the key resources be identified. Clearly, the stores themselves (and thus the capital invested) are an important resource and the introduction of the revenue and profit per square metre and comparison with competitors will indicate the efficiency of their use. However, there are likely to be other important resources such as staff and no measure of their performance is offered. Staff costs are not shown in the trading account, although a more sophisticated measure such as revenue per employee is a commonly used metric and would address this.

Serving shareholders' interests. The report is much better on the third strategy of serving shareholder interests as it supplies two helpful measures: total shareholder return and return on capital employed. However, most shareholders will want comparison with benchmark returns within the retail sector and the market more widely, since these represent their alternatives.

Short-termism. The criticism of the company's management as being short term is reflected in the performance reporting. The only benchmarks in the report to compare actual performance against are the budget information and the previous year's figures. There are no longer-term forecasts or information on future capital investment. Also, there are few indicators which would be described as determinants of performance. These are often non-financial and focused on the external business environment (behaviour of customers and competitors).

As already noted, there is a significant gap in the information in the report as it contains no external information. Also, although revenue is broken down into broad product categories, no further information about growth within these categories nor the margins being earned is supplied. As a result, it could be questioned whether this breakdown is worthwhile.

Presentation. In terms of presentation, the data is clear and in a form which would be easily recognisable to those used to reading accounts. However, no narrative commentary is provided which would highlight the key features in the report such as major deviations from the budget or performance well outside industry norms. There should be a comment on each of the five areas within the mission and strategies as well as comments about specific, material issues arising in the period covered. The report could be made easier to read by reducing the volume of numbers present both by cutting out unnecessary measures (see earlier discussion of product categories) and also by rounding all figures to millions.

(b) **New asset utilisation indicators**

Revenue and operating profit per square metre reflect the utilisation of the key capital asset used in their generation (the store). Therefore, they are directly addressing a major part of the aim of utilising all resources; however, they do not address **all** resources which the business uses. There are likely to be significant staff costs and so similar measures of revenue and operating profit per employee could also be introduced in order to reflect these human resources.

	Metro	Hyper	Flack
Revenue per sq. metre ($)	13,702	13,165	13,251
Operating profit ($'000)	159,058	498,791	657,849
Operating profit per sq. metre ($)	987	592	656

These measures reflect the importance of the use of the store's space which is an area which the business does not give sufficient attention as is reflected in the problems with divisional performance measures. Focus on these measures will require addressing issues of volume of sales and the profitability of those sales. The two types of store at Flack will have different impacts on these measures. For example, the smaller Metro stores may be capable of earning higher margins as they are convenient to customers while selling lower volumes. The Hyper stores may concentrate on selling in volume to customers who come to buy in bulk. However, in terms of the overall performance of the business it is essential that Flack sells in high volumes as it is a low margin business but it must not sacrifice profitability, in effect buying customers' revenue by selling at or near a loss.

(c) **Divisional performance assessment**

The current measure of divisional operating profit reflects the trading in the period under consideration. Profit will link to the whole business's operating profit which is the correct level to reflect the efforts of the divisional managers. However, this measure only indirectly addresses the capital being used by the divisions (depreciation charged to operating profit). This is distorting the behaviour of the divisional managers.

The managers are not investing in refurbishing their stores which is causing the press (and presumably customers) to notice their run-down appearance. This may reduce the depreciation charge against operating profit. They are prioritising new store capital expenditure over the refurbishment since they are not being charged for the use of that capital (financing charges are deducted after operating profit is calculated). This may not be optimal since small spending on existing capital assets often yields higher returns than new spending (which may be subject to greater risks).

The proposal to change the divisional performance measure addresses the issue of not reflecting the capital used since residual income (RI) deducts an imputed interest charge. Divisions can then be set targets in terms of their RI. The difficulties in calculating RI lie in correctly setting the imputed interest rate and calculating the capital being employed by the division. However, since both divisions are types of stores they will have similar assets and so the same rules can be applied to each to fairly calculate the capital used.

An advantage of RI is that the imputed interest rate can be changed to reflect the different risks of the divisions. The two divisions here do not seem to have significant risk differences unless the geographical locations introduce these (city centres and city edges). However, it is worth noting that using RI can discourage investment. As net book values of assets fall over time, RI automatically increases and 'do not invest' could become an attractive option to the managers.

Overall, the proposed change addresses existing problems and would be considered a normal solution to measuring divisional performance in this industry.

(d) **Use of expected ROCE in new store appraisal**

The expected ROCE, based on the different demand scenarios, is as follows:

	Low	Medium	High	
Revenue ($m)	12.5	13.0	13.5	
Forecast operating margin (%)	4.1	4.3	4.4	
Forecasting operating profit ($m)	0.5125	0.559	0.594	
Probability (%)	20	50	30	
Expected operating profit ($m)	0.1025	0.2795	0.1782	**0.5602**

ROCE = Expected operating profit/Capital cost
     = $0.5602m/$4.2m = **13.34%**

The expected ROCE is greater than 13% which is Flack's required ROCE, so this should be an acceptable investment.

The use of expected values in the calculation of ROCE is appropriate if the probabilities used can be reasonably estimated and the decision is likely to be one which is made a number of times. Since Flack has opened many stores, it is likely to be able to predict volumes and margins with reasonable accuracy. Since Flack is going to continue to open stores, this decision will occur a number of times which makes using a probabilistic approach viable. In general, ROCE is considered neither as accurate nor as direct a measure of shareholder wealth as, for example, net present value (NPV).

(e) **Loyalty card system**

The proposed new information system will collect data from customers' purchases and store it for data mining purposes in a data warehouse. The capital required will be significant at $100m (the equivalent of about 24 new stores at $4.2m each). There will also be considerable annual running costs. However, the benefits could be significant, although quantifying them will be difficult as they depend on influencing customer behaviour and so are not simply cutting costs.

Improved customer loyalty. The new system will help to address the mission of Flack as it will help the board to understand customers better and so improve their loyalty to the business. By focusing offers on those things which customers enjoy Flack can enhance the brand and also take the opportunity to sell greater volumes alongside the offered products.

The data warehouse will allow data mining for relationships, for example, geographical preferences for products; links between price offers and volumes sold; products which are often bought together; and seasonality of product purchases. These relationships can then be used to address the CEO's three target areas of advertising, product range choices and price offers.

Advertising. Potentially, there will be cost savings by more efficient advertising. The data on each individual customer can be searched to profile customers and identify their individual preferences. Marketing can then be targeted to groups of customers using products which they commonly buy. Data mining will also identify associated products (those often bought together) so that offers can be grouped, for example, with a price reduction on buying a linked pair of products.

Product range. A problem in most retail businesses is the size of the product portfolio which they offer since more products (and potentially more suppliers) require more effort to manage. The new system may allow a Pareto-style analysis where the least profitable non-essential products are identified and can be cut from the product range.

58 Cantor

Workbook references. Performance reports are discussed in Chapter 6 of the Workbook. EVA™ is discussed in Chapter 8, and VBM is discussed in Chapter 13.

Top tips.

Part (a). A crucial point to note here is that the CEO has asked you to evaluate Cantor's performance **report**, not evaluate Cantor's **performance**.

There is a technical article on ACCA's website titled 'Reports for performance management' and this article suggests looking at four key aspects of a report to identify whether it is a good report or not: the purpose of the report; who the report is produced for; what information is needed; and the layout of the report.

A sensible approach to this question would have been to use each of these four aspects as headings in your answer, and then to evaluate how well the report deals with each of them.

Purpose – The examining team noted that candidates seemed reluctant to use the mission/strategy of the business to evaluate the report. A key issue in evaluating the report is whether it helps the board understand how well Cantor is achieving its mission/strategy.

Audience – Has the report addressed the needs of its readers? In this case, a key point is that the report has three groups of readers (the main group board, and the boards of each of the two subsidiaries). This should have prompted you to think whether a single report can satisfy the needs of these different groups. For example, how much detail will the different groups need about different aspects of the business?

Technical article. Part (a) of this question is the subject of a two-part technical article on ACCA's website: 'Improving your Advanced Performance Management Answers (Parts 1 and 2)'.

In the article, a member of the examining team highlights some of the errors which students made when answering the requirement to evaluate an organisation's current performance report. The article then goes on to demonstrate the sorts of points which candidates would have been expected to make in order to score well in this part of the question.

You are strongly advised to read this article as part of your preparation for your APM exam.

Part (b). The scenario has identified that the two key costs for review here are staff and property costs; and it also describes the rental arrangements of the two subsidiaries in detail.

Although this question is essentially about operating gearing, it is also important that you think about the different context of the two subsidiaries. Juicey's business appears more dynamic than Cafés', so what implications could this have for the appropriate balance of fixed and variable costs in each? Also, think about the nature of the costs involved. How can Cantor manage the balance between fixed and variable staff costs?

Part (c). In effect, the requirement here is to use relevant data from Appendices 1 and 2 in order calculation EVA. The scenario gives you a clue that there may be some areas where you need to make assumptions in the figures you use, but note you aren't simply asked to state any assumptions you made in your calculation, but to 'justify' them.

Although this question was generally well answered, with most candidates appearing to understand the adjustments to profit and capital employed that are required when calculating EVA™, the examining team highlighted three areas where candidates struggled:

- When calculating WACC, many did not seem to be able to work out the weighting coefficients from the debt/equity.

- Many did not appreciate that the cost of debt needed an adjustment for it to be post-tax.

- The capital employed figure used for working out the cost of capital employed should be based on capital employed at the start of the year, not at the end of the year.

There are two articles about EVA™ in the technical articles section of ACCA's website: 'Economic value added versus profit-based measures of performance – part 1 and part 2'. You are advised to read them as part of your exam preparation if you have not already done so.

Part (d). It is important to note that there are two parts to the CEO's request in the scenario: (i) explain how VBM could be implemented at Cantor and (ii) evaluate VBM's potential impact on the group.

One of the key elements of VBM is identifying the drivers which create value for an organisation, so that the organisation can then focus its performance management efforts on those drivers. This issue is also important in this requirement – because identifying Cantor's value drivers and performance targets linked to them will be a key part of implementing VBM at the organisation.

One follow-on question is then: how different are Cantor's performance metrics likely to be under VBM compared to its current performance measurement system? The degree of difference between them – and differences in the aspects of performance being measured – could be useful in evaluating the potential impact VBM could have.

Examining team's comments. The problem for the majority of candidates in part (d) was a lack of knowledge, with many talking vaguely about value without an understanding of it, or of VBM, in the context of the scenario. The fact that the question had just considered EVA™ ought to have provided a memory jog, but there is little indication that it did. Some candidates also incorrectly appeared to think that VBM and activity-based management (ABM) are the same thing.

Part (e). It is important that you think about the implications of the CEO's request in the scenario very carefully here.

Firstly, note that the performance measures suggested need to relate to the proposed change in the mission statement ('to provide a fair deal to our employees') rather than to the mission statement as a whole. As such, performance measures looking at shareholder value or customer satisfaction were not relevant here.

Secondly, note that you are asked to use the additional information (Appendix 3) and the current performance report (Appendix 1) as the sources for the performance measures you recommend. So, for example, although employee satisfaction surveys might, in other circumstances, be a good way of finding out about employee satisfaction levels, they are not appropriate here, because they do not relate to the information in the appendices.

Finally, you need to justify why the measures you have recommended are suitable, rather than simply listing the measures.

Overall – As is the case with all of the Section A questions in APM, remember that you have been asked to write a report, so make sure the style and structure of your answer, as a whole, is appropriate for a report. Markers are looking for an introduction, suitable report headings, a logical structure, signposted by the use of sub-headings, and a clear, concise style.

The post-examination report noted that a conclusion was not required for the four professional marks available in this question but, if candidates provided an appropriate one, they were given credit for doing so.

Marks

(a) Each relevant point about Cantor's performance report – 1 mark
Points must be based on the scenario information, and must focus on
   Cantor's performance report, rather than on its performance.

Possible relevant points include:
Assessment of whether the report supports Cantor's mission
Appropriateness of the level of detail provided for the three different boards
Use of budgets
Use of industry averages
Lack of historical/trend information

Total for part (a): up to 15 marks

15

(b) Each relevant point about the balance between fixed and variable costs
   in each of the subsidiaries, and the impact this may have on managing
   these costs – 1 mark

Total for part (b): up to 6 marks

6

(c) EVA™ calculation
Add back brand-building expenditure – 1 mark
Taxation and tax relief on interest – 2 marks
Capital employed – marketing – 1 mark
WACC – 1 mark
EVA™ result – 1 mark

Brief evaluation of the EVA™ result – 1 mark
Assumptions made – identified and justified – Up to 3 marks

Total for part (c): up to 9 marks

9

(d) For general description of VBM – up to 2 marks
Description of how VBM could be implemented at Cantor, and of what its
   potential impact could be – 10 marks

Total for part (d): up to 10 marks

10

(e) For calculations of suitable measures (eg average salaries; staff
   turnover rates) – up to 3 marks

For each relevant point in justifying performance measures – 1 mark
   per point
Total for part (e): up to 6 marks

6

Professional marks – for style and structure of report: introduction (1 mark);
   use of headings and suitable sub-headings (1 mark); clarity of report, and
   of language used – Up to 4 marks

4

Total = 50

BPP
LEARNING
MEDIA

ANSWERS

Report

To: CEO

From: Strategic management accountant

Date: [today's date]

Subject: **Performance reporting and VBM at Cantor**

Introduction

This report evaluates the current performance reports at Cantor, and the cost structures in the group.

It then calculates Cantor's EVA™ (as an alternative measure of performance to the profit-based measures currently used in the performance reports) before evaluating the potential impact that VBM could have at the group.

Finally, the report recommends some new performance measures to reflect the change in Cantor's mission statement.

(a) **Current performance report**

We can use four basic criteria to evaluate Cantor's current performance report:

Purpose – What the purpose of the report is, and whether it provides information which is relevant to Cantor's performance against its mission

Audience – Whether the report is appropriate for its audience and their requirements

Information – Whether the report provides information which is relevant for decision making and control

Layout – Whether the report's layout is clear for its readers, and identifies the most important information

Purpose

Performance against overall goals and objectives

One of the overall aims of Cantor's performance reports should be to enable the Board to identify how well the company is fulfilling its mission, and achieving its goals and objectives.

Cantor's mission statement identifies three key points:

- Maximising shareholder value
- Supplying good value food and drink
- Providing an appealing environment for customers

Shareholder value – The report currently only focuses on historic profits. It does not include any future cash flows, EVA™, share price or dividends – all of which could provide an indication of shareholder value.

As such, the report does not directly measure shareholder value. This point has also been highlighted by one of Cantor's large shareholders who has suggested the introduction of EVA™ as the company's main measure of value. (We will return to this point later in this report.)

One of the dangers of using annual profit as the main performance measure is that it can lead to a focus on short-term performance. However, shareholders are likely to be interested in longer-term value creation as well as short-term performance.

Nonetheless, the comparison between budget and actual performance in the report is useful – both as a means of control and for giving some insight as to whether Cantor is performing in line with strategic targets.

Good value food and drink – Comparing Cantor's gross profit against the gross profit for the industry as a whole can give some indication of whether Cantor provides good value or not.

Cantor's gross profit margin is slightly higher than the industry average (74.2% vs 72.8%) which might suggest that the prices Cantor charges its customers are slightly higher than the industry average. However, the gross profit margin by itself is not a good indicator of whether Cantor is offering good value, because it doesn't provide any insight into the reasons behind the relative margins (for example, Cantor's costs of sales might be lower than its competitors) or the quality of the food and drink it is offering might be higher, enabling it to charge higher prices.

Another limitation of the report is that it does not provide any historical comparisons, although these could potentially give some insight into how attractive Cantor is to its customers. If Cantor is consistently able to increase its revenues over time, this could be seen as an indicator that its customers feel it is providing them with good value.

Appealing environments for customers – It is difficult to measure the appeal of Cantor's cafés or juice bars from financial data alone (which is all the report provides). However, revenue growth gives some indication of customer satisfaction, because customers are unlikely to continue to use Cantor's premises if they are too unappealing.

Customer loyalty and price elasticity of demand could give a greater indication of the appeal Cantor's premises have for customers, but without surveying customers directly it will be difficult to assess the extent to which the environment has an impact on their purchasing decisions, compared, for example, to the price and quality of the food and drink provided in them.

Audience

The same performance report is used by Cantor's main group board, as well as the boards of the two subsidiaries. However, the information requirements of the subsidiary boards may be different to those of the group board.

Main board – The main board is less likely to be interested in detailed figures, and so a summary of key performance measures for each of the subsidiaries may be more useful to them than, for example, the detailed information about operating costs currently provided.

Subsidiaries' boards – The report seems to treat the subsidiaries in the same way as the group, using profit and comparison to industry average margins and budgets as the main assessment tools. However, the different nature of Cafés' and Juicey's business may make comparison to an overall industry average less meaningful.

Moreover, as the subsidiary boards are likely to be interested in more detailed performance issues than the main group board, it doesn't seem appropriate to only provide the subsidiary boards with the high-level overview which is produced for the group board.

For the subsidiaries, it would be useful to provide a more detailed breakdown of revenues and gross margins by product line, and by geographical region.

Similarly, it would be useful for the subsidiary boards to be provided with more detail about operating costs by geographical region so that they identify the profitability of different regions and, if necessary, they may then need to drill down further to look at the profitability of individual outlets if some appear to be underperforming.

It seems that the measure being used to assess subsidiary performance is operating profit, which is appropriate as it contains the elements of performance controllable by the subsidiaries' managers. However, if the performance reports are only produced annually this would not appear appropriate for the needs of the subsidiary boards. They need more frequent information, to allow them to control their operations effectively.

Appropriate information for decision making

The annual reporting period also reduces the report's usefulness as a basis of decision making for the subsidiaries' boards.

In relation to operational/tactical decision making, the report would be more useful if it provided greater detail for individual products or sites to assist the managers of the subsidiaries in their planning and control activities.

Conversely, at a strategic level, the report is likely to be more useful if it provided some external information – for example, competitor information – rather than focusing on internal financial information. Currently, the only external benchmarks provided are the industry average figures, but these may be less useful than figures for competitors which compete directly with Cantor in the same sectors of the market.

Also, for both boards, it would be useful to provide some historic information to help identify growth and trends. This is likely to be particularly important at Juicey, given the levels of growth it is currently enjoying.

Similarly, it would be useful, for both boards, if the report included some non-financial key performance indicators in relation to the three key areas of Cantor's mission: shareholder value, product value and customer satisfaction with Cantor's sites.

The current focus (on financial performance only) only provides the boards with 'lagging' information on how well Cantor has performed, rather than providing them with any 'leading' indicators – and some insight into how well it will perform in future.

Layout

In terms of presentation, the data is clear and in a form which would be easily recognisable to those used to reading accounts. However, it could be useful to provide a short narrative commentary in conjunction with the report in order to highlight the key points highlighted by the figures – such as major deviations from the budget, or areas where Cantor is performing significantly better or worse than industry norms.

The report could also be made easier to read by rounding all figures to thousands and thus removing unnecessary detail.

(b)   **Cost structures**

The costs in each of the two subsidiaries include a mixture of fixed and variable costs. In general terms, higher fixed costs will constitute a higher level of risk to Cantor than variable costs. If Cantor's revenues fall, but level of fixed costs remains unchanged, then its operating gearing will increase.

In practice, however, it may not be possible to analyse costs simply into 'fixed' and 'variable' costs. Some will be partly fixed and partly variable.

Staff costs

Staff costs are likely to be part-fixed and part-variable. As these represent a significant part of the cost base, it will be necessary to establish what element is fixed (how many staff are the minimum required to run a site?) and what element is variable (how many staff can be used as needed when the sites are busy?).

This cost area will be managed through decisions over the balance of the numbers of permanent and casual staff, with casual staff being used to manage fluctuations in business. As such, this suggests that Juicey may need to use proportionately more casual staff than Cafés.

Property costs

The nature of the property costs is also different in the two subsidiaries:

Cafés – Rent is a fixed cost for Cafés, with fixed rental charges being payable quarterly in advance.

Juicey – Rent is a variable cost, being a percentage of revenue.

This structure appears appropriate to the nature of the different businesses. Cafés is a mature business whose revenues are likely to be relatively stable and predictable – meaning that there should be little risk of it not being able to cover its rental costs each month.

By contrast, Juicey is a relatively new business, but it is also rapidly growing, and therefore agreeing negotiating variable rental costs is more appropriate for it.

However, the percentage demanded will reflect the risk which the landlord is taking on the success of Juicey and so is likely to be higher than a fixed rent, such as that negotiated by Cafés. As Juicey becomes established, it may be worth considering beginning to move to negotiating fixed rental deals for Juicey in order to cut this cost.

This last point illustrates the dilemma which many businesses face in thinking about the balance of fixed and variable costs. Variable costs are more desirable as they do not threaten the survival of the business but they are often higher than a fixed cost deal.

(c)   **Economic value added**

	$	Notes
Operating profit	10,852,970	
Add back: Brand building	3,819,000	50% of marketing expenditure
Less: Taxation	(2,100,000)	Tax paid in year
Lost tax relief on interest	(200,250)	Finance costs @ 25%
NOPAT	**12,371,720**	
Capital employed	53,400,000	At start of 20X4
Brand building expenditure capitalised	3,819,000	Spending in previous years
Adjusted capital employed	57,219,000	
Cost of capital employed (@ 13.2%)	**(7,552,908)**	See Working for WACC calculation
EVA™	**4,818,812**	NOPAT – Cost of capital employed

	$	Notes
Working		
Equity: 100/130 × 15.7%	12.1	
Debt: (30/130 × 6.5%) × (1-25%)	1.1	Adjusted for tax at 25%
WACC	13.2	

The EVA™ calculation suggests that the group's economic profits for the year (NOPAT) were significantly greater than its cost of capital – such that it was able to add $4.82m to shareholder value over the year.

However, the EVA™ which has been calculated is only an example, and it has made several simplifying assumptions which would need to be investigated in more detail if we started to use EVA™ as one of our main performance measures.

(1)   **Depreciation** – We have not made any adjustments to the depreciation charge, which assumes that economic depreciation is the same as accounting depreciation. However, this may not be the case, in which case the depreciation charge in NOPAT would need to be adjusted to reflect economic depreciation.

(2)   **Marketing and brand building** – We have estimated that half of the marketing spend relates to brand building, but this figure may need to be investigated more closely.

More importantly, perhaps, although we have added back the brand-building expenditure in 20X3 to adjust the figure for capital employed at the start of 20X4, we have not made any further adjustments for previous years. However, to calculate EVA™ properly, the total amount of the brand-building expenditure in the years leading up to 20X4 should all be added back to capital employed.

Subsidiaries – As with the current profit measures in the performance report, if Cantor decides to use EVA™, it may be useful to calculate EVA™ separately for the two subsidiaries as well as for the group. This will help to identify how much value each subsidiary is generating for the shareholders.

(d)   **VBM**

The premise behind VBM is that the value of a company is measured by its discounted cash flows, and value is only created when the capital which companies invest generates returns which are greater than the cost of that capital.

Therefore, in contrast to Cantor's current approach to performance measurement which focuses on profits, VBM will encourage a focus on future cash flows, and the creation of value.

Importantly, given Cantor's mission, management decision making under VBM focuses on what activities ('drivers') increase the value of a company – and create value for its shareholders.

The VBM approach also aligns strategic, operational and management processes so that they all work together to create value.

Understanding value drivers

Implementing VBM at Cantor will require that management understand the key value drivers which create value for the business.

Equally, VBM will also require management to establish processes which ensure that all business unit managers adopt value-based thinking when making decisions. For VBM to be effective, it will eventually have to involve every decision maker in the company.

Management processes and implementing VBM

There are four underlying management processes which govern the adoption of VBM (be it at group level, subsidiary level or operational level):

Step 1   A strategy is developed to maximise value

Step 2   Key value drivers are identified in relation to the strategy, and then performance targets (both short and long term) are defined for those value drivers

Step 3   Action plans are drawn up to define the steps to be taken to achieve the performance targets

Step 4   Performance measurement systems and incentive systems are set up to monitor performance against targets and to encourage employees to meet their goals

Strategy development

Corporate level – Using VBM, Cantor's management will need to devise a corporate strategy which focuses specifically on maximising the overall value of the company – including acquiring or disposing of business units if appropriate. Currently, Cantor appears to be growing organically – with the growth of Juicey – but the board should consider whether this growth needs to be reinforced with external growth.

Subsidiary level – Similarly, the subsidiary boards will need to evaluate whether there are any alternative strategies for their businesses which could enable them to achieve competitive advantage and to create value.

Target setting

Once Cantor has agreed its strategies for maximising value, this will need to be translated into specific targets which can be used to manage performance at both strategic and operational levels. The targets should be based on key value drivers, and should include both financial and non-financial aspects of performance – so, for example, customers' rating of the appeal of Cantor's sites could be used as a target if this is a key factor in maintaining customer satisfaction levels.

Impact of VBM at Cantor

Implementing VBM would require Cantor to introduce new performance measures based on the drivers, and the company's reward and incentive systems will need to focus on value creation and performance against value-driven targets.

Performance measures, targets and rewards will need to be developed at the group level, then at the subsidiary level and, finally, at the individual site level in order to ensure full co-ordination of the system across Cantor. In order to align the interests of employees and management with shareholder value – particularly in the longer term – the new reward system may include a share-based payment scheme.

The key benefits of VBM are the focus on value as opposed to profit, so reducing the tendency to make decisions which have positive short-term impact but may be detrimental in the long term. VBM thus will help to make Cantor more forward looking.

However, a danger of the VBM exercise is that it becomes an exercise in valuing everything but changing nothing. It is important that the detailed operational issues of the organisation are addressed through the new measures/targets.

A further difficulty in implementation is that the measurement of the key value drivers can often involve non-financial indicators and these can represent a significant change for accounting-based management information systems.

(e) **Performance measures – fair deal for employees**

The proposed change to the mission statement means that Cantor will need to find a way of measuring whether it provides a 'fair deal' to its employees. This will be inherently difficult to measure, due to the subjective nature of determining how Cantor treats its employees.

Staff turnover

However, the information about staff numbers and staff turnover given in Appendix 3 of Cantor's current performance report can provide some indication of employee satisfaction.

The figures indicate that the staff turnover rate for the group as a whole was 9.9% for the last year, with staff turnover being significantly higher in Juicey (14.2%) than in Cafés (9.7%). Some of this difference may be due to the fact that Juicey is a much newer and more dynamic operation, and that it may have been employing staff on short-term or temporary contracts. However, the variation in rates should still be investigated, and Cantor's staff turnover rates should also be compared against competitors if possible. If Cantor's staff turnover rates are higher than its competitors, this could be an indication that employee satisfaction at Cantor is lower.

Staff turnover rates

	Cafés	Juicey	Group
Average number of employees in 20X4	1,498	106	1,624
Number of leavers	146	15	161
Staff turnover rate (%)	9.7%	14.2%	9.9%

> **Tutorial note.** We have used the average number of employees across 20X4 to calculate staff turnover rates, but ACCA's marking guidance indicated that it was also acceptable to use year-end figures.

Average pay

The figures in Appendix 3 can also be used in conjunction with the staff from Appendix 1 to calculate the average wages Cantor pays to its staff:

	Cafés	Juicey	Head Office	Group
Average number of employees in 20X4	1,498	106	20	1,624
Staff costs ($'000)	15,921	1,525	3,899	21,345
Average pay per employee	10,628	14,387	194,950	13,143

These figures could again be compared to competitors to indicate whether Cantor is offering its staff fair – or competitive – rates of pay. Benchmark information is not currently provided in the performance reports, although the fact that Cantor's staff costs as a proportion of revenue are slightly higher than the industry average (31.2% vs 30.9%) suggests Cantor offers its employees a reasonably fair deal.

However, the overall Group figures appear to be distorted by the salaries paid to Cantor's head office staff, and the average wages earned by staff in the Cafés subsidiary are significantly lower than the group average of $13,143.

Conclusion

Cantor's current performance report has a number of weaknesses – in particular that it does not provide an indication of how well the group is performing against the three aspects of its current mission. The report focuses on Cantor's profitability rather than shareholder value, but moving to a VBM approach and introducing EVA™ as a performance measure could help to address this issue.

It would also be useful to produce separate reports for the main board and for the subsidiaries' boards, due to the differing information requirements.

59 Boltzman Machines

Workbook references. Stakeholder management is discussed in Chapter 4 of the Workbook; benchmarking in Chapter 1, JIT in Chapter 11, and the balanced scorecard in Chapter 13.

Top tips.

Part (a). Although the analysis of the different stakeholder groups in Appendix 1 indicates that Mendelow's matrix is the relevant framework for analysing the different stakeholder groups, you shouldn't spend time describing the matrix itself. Instead you need to use the aspects of the matrix (power; interest) as the basis for identifying how Boltzman should manage the different stakeholder groups; for example, by ensuring that any strategies it introduces are acceptable to key stakeholders.

In order to justify how Boltzman should manage the different stakeholder groups, you need to identify how important the different stakeholder groups are. However, you also need to consider the relative importance of the stakeholder groups in the second part of the CEO's request – evaluating the appropriateness of Boltzman's performance measures. In effect, the CEO is asking you to evaluate how far the measures relate to those aspects of performance which the stakeholders are most interested in.

Part (b). In APM, you need to be able to evaluate the approaches used to measure performance of an organisation, as well as being able to evaluate the performance of the organisation itself. In part (b) of this question you need to do both.

First you need to benchmark Boltzman's performance against General Machines (ie how well is Boltzman performing) and then you need to evaluate competitive benchmarking as a type of benchmarking (ie how useful is competitive benchmarking as a way of measuring/managing Boltzman's performance? Might other types of benchmarking be more useful?).

When tackling the first part of the CEO's instruction it is vital you do exactly what has been asked. The CEO has specifically told you to calculate the [suggested performance] measures given in Appendix 1, as well as two, justified measures of your own, using the data provided. There are five suggested performance measures in Appendix 1, so, in total, you need to include seven performance measures in the benchmarking exercise.

When choosing your two additional measures, it would be useful to think back to your stakeholder analysis and the assessment of Boltzman's current performance measures in part (a). For example, as far as possible Boltzman should try to benchmark the aspects of performance which are important for its competitive success.

Economic value added (EVA™) and development costs – When calculating EVA™, one of the potential adjustments needed to convert operating profit to net operating profit after tax (NOPAT) is adding back research and development costs which have been charged to the profit or loss account. In the notes for Appendix 2 there is a figure for 'Product development costs', but there is no specific indication whether these had been charged to the profit or loss account, or capitalised.

Given the level of product development costs ($2,684m) compared to the total of 'other costs' in the financial statements ($2,958m), and given the reference to 'development costs' only (rather than 'research and development'), the examining team's original assumption was that these development costs had been capitalised rather than charged to profit or loss. Therefore, no adjustment to operating profit would have been required when calculating NOPAT.

The suggested solution below has been produced on this basis. However, if candidates assumed development costs had been charged to profit and loss, and added it back when calculating NOPAT, they were given credit for doing so.

Part (c). Perhaps the most important word in the instruction for this part of the question is 'problems'. You are not being asked to explain what just in time (JIT) is, or what the advantages of a move towards JIT manufacturing might be, but what the problems which accompany that move will be. Appendix 3 gives you some pointers here by mentioning the impacts on the supply chain with customers and suppliers.

For example, under a JIT system, Boltzman will carry very little inventory. But what problems could this cause if Boltzman can't predict customer demand accurately, or if its suppliers don't deliver components when they are scheduled to?

Part (d). The final paragraph in the scenario provides important context for this requirement: the CEO has asked for you to evaluate the suitability of the scorecard in the light of the shareholders' criticism, and the other initiatives currently in progress.

The link between this requirement and Initiative 1 (part (a) of the question requirements) could be particularly important in this respect. In part (a) you were asked to evaluate the performance measures which have currently been suggested, so one way of assessing the suitability of the balanced scorecard would be to assess the extent to which using it would improve Boltzman's performance measures, compared to the ones currently suggested.

Importantly, though, this question requires an application of the scorecard to the scenario. You will score very few marks – if any – for simply describing the different perspectives of the scorecard.

Overall. Remember that you have been asked to write a report, so make sure the style and structure of your answer, as well as its tone, is appropriate for a report.

Marking scheme

Marks

(a) For analysing each of the four stakeholders, and identifying appropriate management approaches for each stakeholder – Up to 2 marks per stakeholder

For evaluating the appropriateness of the five performance indicators suggested – 1 mark per relevant point – Up to a maximum of 10 marks

Total for part (b): up to 14 marks   14

(b) For calculating ROCE; revenue growth; average pay per employee; net profit margin; and two other appropriate measures – 1 mark each – Up to 6 marks

For calculating EVA™ – Up to 3 marks
For justifying each of the two new indicators suggested – 1 mark per indicator

For evaluating the method of benchmarking – 1 mark per relevant point – Up to 6 marks

For a reasonable conclusion on Boltzman's performance compared to General Machines – Up to 3 marks

Total for part (c): up to 16 marks   16

(c) For each relevant difficulty of implementing JIT – 1 mark

Additional marks awarded for relating the difficulty to Boltzman

Total for part (d): up to 7 marks   7

BPP
LEARNING
MEDIA

(d)   For each relevant point relating to the suitability of the balanced scorecard
         as a performance measurement system at Boltzman – 1 mark

       (For answers structured around the four perspectives of the scorecard,
         no more than 2 marks are to be allocated to a single perspective.)

       Total for part (d): up to 9 marks   9
       Professional marks – for style and structure of report – Up to 4 marks   4
                                                                    Total = 50

Report

To: Board of Boltzman

From: Consultant

Date: [today's date]

Subject: **Performance management initiatives**

Introduction

This report looks at a number of performance management issues at Boltzman, in particular the way Boltzman measures and manages its performance in relation to its key stakeholders, and whether the aspects of performance being measured are ones which are important to the stakeholders. We then also benchmark Boltzman's performance against General Machines, and look at the problems which Boltzman could face in its move towards JIT manufacturing. We finish by assessing the suitability of the balanced scorecard as a potential performance measurement system for the company.

(a)   **Stakeholder management**

       The management approaches which are appropriate for different stakeholder groups depend on the **power** the groups have to influence strategic decisions at Boltzman and their **interest** in doing so.

       Shareholders – Shareholders have high power but have little interest in the strategic decisions being taken by Boltzman – provided those decisions lead to satisfactory financial results. As such, they should be kept satisfied, and this can be done by ensuring that their financial targets are met.

       Employees – Employees overall have little power, and only moderate interest; therefore the most appropriate way of managing them is to keep them informed of strategic decisions.

       However, the sub-group of key employees who work in product development have high power because Boltzman cannot afford for them to leave. As such, these key employees need to be kept satisfied, for example by continuing to provide them with training and opportunities to develop their skills through working with new technologies.

       Customers – Boltzman's customers appear to be its key stakeholder group, and they also appear to have a relatively high degree of bargaining power over it. The fact that Boltzman cannot afford to lose one of its major customers means that any strategic decisions need to be acceptable to them.

       Given that some of the parts are specifically designed for each customer, it would also seem appropriate to the key customers to be involved in product development, to ensure that the products meet their requirements. This level of co-operation should also help to strengthen the relationship between Boltzman and its customers.

       Suppliers – Their low power and relatively low level of interest mean that Boltzman's suppliers should require minimal effort.

The suppliers have low bargaining power in relation to Boltzman, which means that the company should be in a strong position to negotiate a favourable price for the goods it buys from them, and to ensure that the quality of them is maintained.

However, if Boltzman introduces JIT manufacturing it will need good relationships with its suppliers (as we will discuss in part (c) of this report), so this could increase the power of its suppliers.

Appropriateness of performance measures

Boltzman's performance measures should focus on the aspects of its performance which are important to its key stakeholders – which, in this case, are its customers and its shareholders.

Customers – None of the suggested performance measures relate to the interests of Boltzman's customers, which is a major drawback. For example, it would be useful to have some measures looking at customer satisfaction, in terms of both quality and value for money.

Shareholders – The shareholders are interested in financial returns, and four out of the five suggested measures (return on capital employed (ROCE), EVA™, revenue growth and net profit margin) relate to financial performance. This focus on financial performance is consistent with the shareholders' position as important stakeholders. Moreover, the use of EVA™ suggests that Boltzman is specifically aware of the need to maximise shareholder wealth, rather than simply to generate short-term profits.

Employees – The suggested measure – average pay per employee – makes no distinction between the key group of skilled employees and the other employees, which limits its usefulness. It would be more useful for Boltzman to compare the average of its product development staff (key staff) against a suitable industry benchmark, because retaining these staff is likely to be critical for the company's competitive success.

Suppliers – Given the relatively low power of Boltzman's suppliers, it is appropriate that none of the suggested measures relate to them. However, this will have to change if JIT is introduced – and, for example, the reliability of supplier deliveries becomes critical to Boltzman's internal processes.

(b) **Benchmarking**

Additional measures – The two additional indicators used in the benchmarking exercise have been chosen to provide some measures of Boltzman's performance in relation to its customers. As we have previously identified, customers are key stakeholders, but none of the performance measures previously suggested are customer focused. Therefore, including these additional indicators marks an improvement in the measures used.

Product development should help to maintain innovation in the business, which in turn should help to support ongoing growth. The number of customers who recognise Boltzman as a top tier supplier provides some insight into its bargaining power with its customers, and it gives some indication of the customers' perception of the quality of Boltzman's products.

Benchmarking results

	Boltzman	General Machines
Return on capital employed (see Working)	15.5%	9.2%
EVA™ (see Working)	$97m	$(1,165)m
Revenue growth (20X3–20X4)	6.4%	1.0%
Average pay per employee	$54,618	$52,299
Net profit margin	8.2%	3.3%
Additional indicators:		
Product development cost (percentage of revenue)	11.2%	10.2%
Top tier supplier status (out of 20)	13	14

Performance analysis

Financial performance – Boltzman appears to be performing better than General Machines in relation to all the financial indicators (ROCE, EVA™, and net profit margin).

Boltzman also appears to have better growth prospects than General Machines, and this may in part be a consequence of the greater attention it pays to product development.

Currently, General Machines is larger than Boltzman and has top tier status with marginally more large customers, but if Boltzman's growth rate (relative to General Machines) continues it may soon become larger than General Machines, and achieve top tier supplier status with more customers.

Benchmarking method

Competitive benchmarking – The benchmarking exercise is an example of competitive benchmarking, since Boltzman's performance has been compared against its main competitor, General Machines. This type of benchmarking can be useful for identifying areas where Boltzman needs to improve its performance to catch up with General Machines. However, it will not identify how Boltzman can gain any competitive advantage from it.

Also, it is unlikely that a competitor will share any detailed performance information with Boltzman, so the only aspects of performance which can be benchmarked are high level strategic ones, where the relative information is already publicly available (as is the case with the financial data currently being benchmarked). As a result, however, this kind of benchmarking will not provide Boltzman with any insights into how to improve its processes.

Functional benchmarking – As well as comparing its performance against direct competitors, it may also be useful for Boltzman to monitor its performance against 'best in class' performers from other business sectors. Since Boltzman is not competing with these companies, they may be willing to share operational data with it in a way that General Machines would not be. As such, Boltzman could identify ways of improving its processes and capabilities which in turn should help to improve its overall financial performance.

Functional benchmarking could be particularly useful in relation to Boltzman's quality initiatives, since it could compare its performance with other companies which are recognised for the quality of their products, and then hopefully find ways to improve the quality of its products, and to support its aim of becoming the highest quality supplier in the marketplace.

(c) **JIT manufacturing**

As the Head of Aerospace has suggested in this email, the move to JIT manufacturing could have a significant impact on Boltzman's supply chain – both upstream (with suppliers), and downstream (with customers).

Forecasting demand – Under a JIT system, Boltzman will manufacture parts in response to customer demand, rather than holding any significant volumes of parts as inventory. However, to do this effectively, Boltzman will need to be able to forecast customer demand accurately and plan its manufacturing activities accordingly. This demand planning will require close links between Boltzman and its customers.

Suppliers – As well as not holding stocks of finished parts, Boltzman will not hold any significant stocks of components under a JIT system. Therefore, Boltzman will be reliant on its suppliers to deliver orders on time, and without any defects, in order for the manufacturing process to run smoothly. Boltzman currently uses a large number of suppliers, and so it will need to review whether they are all sufficiently reliable to operate under a JIT system. Boltzman may find it more practical to reduce the number of suppliers it deals with, and to partner with a smaller number of suppliers whose reliability can be guaranteed (both in terms of the quality of the parts they supply and in terms of delivering on time).

Disruption to the supply chain – However, reducing the number of suppliers it uses and not holding any inventory makes Boltzman more vulnerable to any disruption in its upstream supply chain. One way of reducing the risk of disruption is to use local suppliers wherever possible. However, this would reduce the choice of suppliers available to Boltzman and also increases the suppliers' bargaining power over the company.

Factory design and factory processes – Introducing JIT will also have implications for the operational processes within Boltzman. For example, JIT organises production lines around the product or component being manufactured, rather than the type of work being done. Depending on how Boltzman's production lines are currently structured, they may need to be restructured to fit with the JIT approach.

Similarly, JIT requires staff to be multi-skilled and flexible. If Boltzman's operational staff currently have narrowly defined jobs, it is likely they will need to be retrained so that they have the variety of skills required to implement JIT successfully. However, this could cause problems in itself if the staff are resistant to changes in their working patterns.

(d)   **Balanced scorecard**

As we have identified in part (a) of this report, Boltzman's key stakeholders are its customers and its shareholders. However, none of the performance measures currently suggested relate to the interests of Boltzman's customers.

Customer perspective – The customer perspective of the balanced scorecard highlights the importance that successfully meeting customers' requirements will have on Boltzman's financial performance. Therefore, introducing the scorecard will reinforce the need for measures looking at customer satisfaction, which emerged from Initiative 1 (on stakeholder influence).

Financial perspective – The measures currently suggested concentrate mainly on financial aspects of performance. Again, as we noted in part (a), financial performance measures are important, especially given Boltzman's mission to maximise shareholder value.

The financial perspective of the balanced scorecard should ensure that financial indicators remain important performance measures at Boltzman.

However, the scorecard also highlights the importance that non-financial aspects of performance have in sustaining the company's financial performance. In particular, the scorecard suggests that a company's financial performance will be shaped by how well it meets its customers' needs, the quality of its internal business processes, and the degree of innovation and learning within it.

Innovation and learning – The innovation and learning perspective of the scorecard is again important for Boltzman considering the company's reputation for innovation, and for the pursuit of engineering excellence identified in its mission. If Boltzman doesn't maintain its innovativeness this could affect its competitive position which, in turn, could damage its performance in relation to the customer and financial perspectives of the scorecard.

Business processes – Boltzman's strategic aim to be the highest quality supplier in the marketplace suggests that it already needs efficient and effective business processes in order for it to achieve the levels of quality it wants to. However, the focus on business processes will become increasingly important as the company introduces lean production methods. As such, having some performance indicators focusing on process quality – as suggested by the business process perspective of the scorecard – would be suitable for Boltzman.

Shareholder concerns – Apart from their concerns about managerial autonomy, it is not clear what the shareholders' other concerns are, and therefore whether introducing the balanced scorecard will do anything to address them. Nonetheless, as the financial perspective of the scorecard addresses the question of how a company looks to its shareholders, by introducing the scorecard the board can demonstrate that it has recognised the importance of the shareholders and their concerns.

However, it is not clear how introducing the scorecard, by itself, will reduce the levels of autonomy managers will have. The shareholders' criticism in this respect appears to be about management styles and culture within Boltzman. Nonetheless, the 'balanced' nature of the scorecard means that managerial performance will be assessed under all four headings. Therefore, if the areas of performance against which managers' performance is measured are properly aligned to Boltzman's critical success factors (and, in turn, to its strategic aims and mission) this should reduce the scope for dysfunctional decision making, even if the managers still retain autonomy for their decisions.

Conclusion

Shareholders are a key stakeholder group, so the suggestion that Boltzman is not listening to shareholders' concerns needs to be addressed. The 'financial' perspective of the balanced scorecard reinforces the importance of measuring how well Boltzman is performing for its shareholders. However, the scorecard also highlights the importance of non-financial aspects of performance. Stakeholder analysis highlights that Boltzman's customers are a key stakeholder group, so the addition of customer-orientated indicators into the company's performance measures would be particularly beneficial.

The benchmarking exercise against General Machines indicates that Boltzman is currently performing well, relative to General Machines. However, it would also be useful to carry out a functional benchmarking exercise to compare some key operating processes against best in class performers.

APPENDIX

Tutorial note. ROCE figures are based on year opening capital employed figures, because this is also the starting point for working out capital employed in EVA™. However, it would have been acceptable to use closing capital employed figures when calculating ROCE (although not EVA™).

Treatment of development costs – ACCA's suggested solution for this question assumed that the development costs had been capitalised, rather than charged to profit and loss. As such they have not been added back to profit when calculating EVA™. Again, however, marks were given if an adjustment was made for product development costs.

Working: Calculation of ROCE and EVA™

	Boltzman $m	General Machines $m
Return on capital employed		
Profit before interest and tax	2,907	1,882
Capital employed:		
Equity	8,984	9,744
Non-current liabilities	9,801	10,629
	18,785	20,373
ROCE	**15.5%**	**9.2%**
EVA™		
Profit before interest and tax	2,907	1,882
Less: Tax charge	(663)	(718)
Tax benefit of interest (28% of financing costs)	(81)	(88)
NOPAT	**2,163**	**1,076**
Capital employed	18,785	20,373
WACC: 11%		
EVA™: NOPAT – (Capital employed × 11%)	**97**	**(1,165)**

60 Merkland Sportswear

Workbook references. SWOT analysis is discussed in Chapter 1 of the Workbook. The performance hierarchy linking strategic objectives and performance metrics is discussed in Chapter 2. Expected values are discussed in Chapter 5, and the value chain in Chapter 4.

Top tips.

Part (a). There are two distinct parts to this requirement: assess the current metrics; and then make suggestions for improving them. As the marking guide illustrates, the marks available were distributed roughly equally between the two parts, so to score well you needed to give due weight to both parts of the requirement.

The first part of the CEO instruction is to 'assess' the existing dashboard metrics. A useful way to approach this requirement might be to ask yourself what the characteristics of effective performance metrics are, and then to consider how well MS's metrics demonstrate these characteristics. Importantly, performance metrics enable management to identify how well an organisation is performing against its critical success factors (CSFs), and how well it is achieving its strategy. In turn, this means that the aspects of performance which are being measured should be ones which are linked to key elements of an organisation's strategy.

Therefore, before you can assess MS's performance metrics, you also need to identify its strategy. The third paragraph in the question scenario – which identifies MS's aims and then its broad strategy for achieving them – is crucial here. In effect, your assessment of the metrics should be an assessment of whether or not they will enable MS's management to determine if the company is achieving its aims and strategy.

Having assessed the current metrics, you are then asked to make suggestions for improvements. However, crucially, are asked to do so within the constraints outlined by the CEO in the scenario – ie that the existing performance headings (financial, design and brand) are retained, and that there are no more than three financial metrics, and no more than two for each of 'design' and 'brand'. The post-exam review comments (see below) indicated many candidates in the real exam failed to adhere to these constraints.

Also, note that the CEO has specifically asked you to use the SWOT analysis as the basis for your suggestions. Therefore a useful approach to this part of the requirement would be to ask if the current performance metrics will allow management to assess how the issues identified in the SWOT are affecting MS's performance. If factors in the SWOT are not being covered by the performance metrics, then these can provide the basis for your suggested improvements. However, remember, your suggestions must be within the constraints outlined by the CEO.

Examining team's comments for part (a). Although part (a) was often answered reasonably well, there were still a number of weaknesses in candidates' answers. A 'significant minority' of candidates chose to assess MS's performance, rather than assessing the performance metrics.

Also, candidates need to remember that, when making suggestions, justifying the suggestion is crucial. Candidates will not score enough marks to pass the requirement by listing alternative performance metrics – to score the marks available candidates must explain why the metrics they are proposing would be beneficial to MS.

Most worryingly, however, the majority of candidates ignored the instructions from the CEO to limit the number of metrics suggested. Many answers contained long lists of new metrics, which was not what was asked for at all.

Part (b). The CEO request is for you to assess the qualitative and quantitative impact of a change of outsourcing partners for footwear manufacture. The qualitative issues (around the ethical implications of using child labour) should have been relatively easy to identify from the scenario.

The information needed to calculate the quantitative impact is provided in Appendix 3, and the comment 'It would be helpful to know how many units we would need to sell in order to cover these increased costs' should have been a clear instruction that a breakeven calculation was required here.

As the marking guide indicates, four out of the eight marks available for this requirement related to the breakeven calculation. However, when this question was examined, the post-exam report suggested that a number of candidates appeared unable to perform the calculations, and the examining team reported that this was very worrying at Strategic Professional level (which is the level of the APM exam).

Part (c). You should have been able to score some relatively easy marks in the expected value calculation here – using the information you are given in Appendix 4 of the scenario. However, note that the CEO hasn't only asked you to calculate the operating profit, but also to evaluate the use of expected values as a method of decision making under risk.

Part (d). Here again there are two parts to the CEO's request: (i) evaluate the impact of the new factory on the figures in the dashboard (ie the results) and (ii) evaluate the impact of the new factory on the choice of metrics in the dashboard.

To identify the relevant issues here, it is crucial to think about the new factory in the context of MS's current business model. Currently, MS outsources all of its manufacturing. However, once the new factory is set up, MS will have its own manufacturing operation. This is particularly significant when thinking about the impact the factory will have on the metrics needed to assess performance.

The examining team's comments for this part of the question are also helpful here:

Examining team's comments. Many candidates attempted to recalculate the dashboard metrics but ignored the fact that the new factory was bringing in-house an existing process and so the change in operating profit was the difference between the new factory's profit and that which was made from existing outsourced sales. However, even if no calculations were attempted a number of candidates earned enough marks to pass this requirement by simply going through the metrics and discussing how the new factory affected them and what changes should be made now that MS has a manufacturing operation – something which it did not have prior to this change.

Part (e). Note that the CEO's instruction here does not ask you to describe the value chain, or to explain the implications of the value chain for performance management in general terms. Instead the CEO has asked specifically for an 'explanation of the implications of using the value chain for performance management at MS'. Linking your answer to the scenario was important to score well here.

A useful way of approaching this requirement could be to think how MS generates value through the different activities in its value chain, and then to consider what implications this has for the choice of performance measures or the way performance is measured at MS.

Report format. Finally, note that you were asked to write a report, and remember that there are four 'professional marks' available for the quality of your report. In this respect, markers are looking for suitable report headings, a brief introduction, and a logical structure to your report – signposted by the use of headings. They are also looking for your report to be written in a clear, concise style.

Marking scheme

Marks

(a) For identifying MS's aims and broad strategies – up to 2 marks

For evaluating how well the metrics support each aim and strategy:

Growth – 1 mark

Shareholder wealth – up to 2 marks

Innovation – up to 3 marks

Marketing – up to 3 marks

For other comments/suggestions linked to SWOT analysis:

Comments about supply chain management – up to 2 marks

Comments about social media and IT expertise – up to 3 marks

Comments about brand ambassadors – up to 3 marks

For adhering to the constraint on the number of metrics on the dashboard –
1 mark

Total for part (a): up to 16 marks   16

(b)   For calculations:

Increased cost of sales – 1 mark

Lost operating profit – 1 mark

New contribution per unit – 1 mark

Required sales – 1 mark

Comments (on qualitative and quantitative issues) – up to 4 marks

Total for part (b): up to 8 marks   8

(c)   For calculations:

Variable costs – 1 mark

Revenue – 1 mark

Profit – 1 mark

Expected profit – 1 mark

For comments (on expected value method) – up to 2 marks

Total for part (c): up to 6 marks   6

(d)   For calculations:

Operating profit under third-party manufacturing – 1 mark

Loss of operating profit – 1 mark

New capital employed – 1 mark

New ROCE – 1 mark

No change to other metrics – 1 mark

For comments (about the impact of the new factory on the values in the
dashboard, and/or on the choice of measures in the dashboard) – up to
2 marks

Total for part (d): up to 10 marks   10

(e)   For relevant points about the implications of the value chain on performance
management at MS – 1 mark per point

Total for part (e): up to 6 marks   6

Professional marks – for style and structure of report – up to 4 marks   4

Total = 50

ANSWERS

Report

To:	Board of MS
From:	Consultant
Date:	[today's date]
Subject:	Performance management at Merkland Sportswear (MS)

Introduction

This report looks at a number of performance management issues at MS, particularly in relation to the range of performance measures included in the dashboard. We begin by evaluating the existing measures used, before looking at the way the company's response to the child labour scandal in the sportswear manufacturing industry could affect its performance and its performance measurement system.

We finish by looking at how value chain analysis could influence performance management at MS.

(a) **Evaluation of current metrics**

MS's overall commercial aims are to grow as a business and to maximise shareholder wealth.

As these aims are essentially financial, it seems appropriate for the dashboard to include three financial measures, but only up to one each for 'design' and 'brand'.

Financial performance measures

Growth – Comparing the revenue figures to prior years can give an indication of the growth being achieved by the business. Including percentage change figure (for 20X5 compared to 20X4) on the dashboard also highlights the amount of growth achieved year on year. Similarly, the operating figures show whether this growth is profitable for MS.

However, because the dashboard doesn't give any revenue figures for the sportswear market as a whole, we cannot gauge how fast it is growing relative to its competitors, and whether its market share is growing or not.

Shareholder wealth – Return on capital employed (ROCE) shows how profitably MS is using its assets and, as such, could provide some indication of how well MS is generating wealth for its shareholders. However, ROCE is ultimately not a good metric in this respect.

One of ROCE's weaknesses is that it could encourage strategic decisions designed to increase short-term profit, potentially at the expense of investment for the future. More fundamentally, though, ROCE is a profit-based measure, and shareholder wealth would be better assessed through a **value-based measure**, which provides some insight into MS's ability to generate future cash flows. In this respect, MS should consider using **economic value added** (EVA™) as a metric instead of ROCE.

Non-financial performance

MS's broad strategy also identifies the need to create innovative products and to have an effective marketing operation – the best in Ceeland.

The current dashboard headings ('Design' and 'Brand') reflect the importance of these elements of performance. However, there are still some potential problems with the metrics used in each heading.

Design awards won – The design awards acknowledge the look and technology in a finished product; they do not directly measure the level of innovation in MS. (For example, the number of new features added to our products, or the number of new products developed would provide a more direct measure for innovation.)

MS's strategy also identifies that its products should help reduce the risk of injury and enhance sporting performance by their customers. The current dashboard does not measure how effectively the products are doing this. However, it could be difficult to provide metrics which cover all of these areas, given the constraints on the number of performance indicators to be included in the dashboard. As such, MS will have to decide whether reducing the risk of injury or enhancing sporting performance is likely to be the more critical success factor for its products.

Brand awareness – The level of brand awareness is likely to be influenced by the effectiveness of MS's marketing operations. The fact that brand awareness is increasing might suggest that MS's marketing operations have been effective. However, without any comparison showing brand awareness for rival brands it is difficult to tell how effective they are, and therefore whether MS has 'the best marketing operation in Ceeland'.

In this respect, market share might be a more appropriate measure – not least because it also links back to MS's aim to grow as a business.

Moreover, just because people can identify MS's logo or name one of its products does not mean they have a positive impression of the company or any desire to buy its products. By contrast, market share statistics can provide a measure of how well MS is identifying and satisfying customer requirements, and how effectively its marketing activities are influencing their purchasing decisions.

Potential improvements

Although the SWOT analysis suggests that supply chain management is a CSF for MS, the CEO's insistence that no new headings be added to the dashboard means that performance in this area cannot be reported directly.

However, MS's ability to manage its supply chain effectively will, indirectly, affect its revenue and operating profit margins. As such, it may be preferable to replace the absolute operating profit figures in the dashboard with percentage margin figures.

The following improvements could also be made to the non-financial performance metrics:

Design – We have already suggested that the number of new features added to our products might be a better performance measure than design awards won. The SWOT analysis suggests that, rather than just looking at new features, we could monitor innovation in relation to the number of new products introduced.

Brand – We have already suggested that market share would be a better metric than brand awareness.

However, the SWOT analysis also suggests that social media is going to become an increasingly important aspect of marketing activities – although MS's weak IT expertise may limit its ability to take advantage of this.

Linked to the overall performance metric of market share, MS could also monitor the number of followers it has on social media (eg on Twitter, or the number of 'likes' it has on Facebook) as an indicator of how effectively it is using these marketing channels.

Brand ambassadors – Despite the growth of social media, brand ambassadors still play an important role in promoting MS's brand, and the SWOT analysis highlights this by acknowledging the loss of a key brand ambassador as a strategic weakness. As such, it could be useful to include a metric for 'Number of ambassadors' under the 'brand' heading on the dashboard. However, as we have already suggested metrics for market share and social media followers – and can only have two in total for 'brand' – the board will have to decide whether including a metric for the number of ambassadors is more important than either of these.

(b) **Impact of Response 1**

Qualitative impact

Although there is not currently any evidence that MS's suppliers are using illegal labour, the fact that MS does not appear to have any assurance over the labour practices used by its suppliers (and is having to review them now) means there is a risk that this could be the case.

This means that the review proposed under Response 1 should be carried out as soon as possible. If MS does find that the appropriate employment terms and conditions have been breached (and, in turn, MS's own ethical code has been breached) it should be transparent and own up to these failings. However, at the same time, MS should also explain the actions it has taken (through either Response 1 or 2) to redress the problems and to prevent them from recurring. Taking action in this way should help to restrict the level of negative stakeholder reaction to any findings.

In particular, MS will have to manage the reactions of customers and the regulator if it finds evidence of any unethical practices in its supply chain.

Customers – Such findings will damage MS's reputation for ethical sourcing, and there is a danger that customers could boycott MS's products, threatening revenue and profit growth.

Regulator – The regulator will review MS's sourcing policies (as it did with Nush), and is likely to punish MS in some way for using suppliers who have acted illegally.

Employees – Any such breach would mean that MS has failed to follow the requirements of its own ethics code (to source goods responsibly) and this could damage employees' trust in the company as a responsible employer.

Assurance procedures – More generally, the review required by Response 1 also suggests that MS could benefit from regular assurance processes over its supply chain – to ensure that its suppliers comply with relevant employment legislation on an ongoing basis. Although the constraints on the performance headings in MS's existing performance dashboard mean there isn't scope to monitor performance there, it could perhaps be monitored at departmental level within the Procurement Department.

Quantitative impact

Impact on shareholders – The increased manufacturing costs, coupled with increased compliance and marketing costs, mean that MS's operating profit will fall by $5.5m if the number of shoes MS sells remains the same. MS will need to increase sales by 106,000 pairs of shoes to make good this shortfall.

However, since the problem of child labour appears to be a common problem among suppliers to sports footwear companies, if MS is able to demonstrate that it has responded rapidly and decisively to any potential problems in its supply chain, this action could help to differentiate it from its competitors, and in doing so could help generate these extra sales.

Annual cost:

		$m
Increase in cost of shoes purchased	$2.1 × 2 million pairs	4.2
Supplier audits		0.5
Marketing cost		0.8
Total (per year)		**5.5**

Contribution per unit	$
Price	75.0
Direct cost ($21 + $2.1)	(23.1)
	51.9

Number of units required to cover lost operating profit:	105,973

(c)   Expected operating profit of the new factory

	Bad	Medium	Good	
Unit manufactured ('000)	1,800	2,000	2,200	
Revenue ($'000)	135,000	150,000	165,000	
Variable costs ($'000)	37,800	44,000	50,600	
Fixed costs	2,500	2,500	2,500	
	94,700	103,500	111,900	
Probability	0.3	0.6	0.1	
Expected operating profit ($'000)	28,410	62,100	11,190	**101,700**

The expected operating profit from the new factory (before interest and tax) is $101.7m.

In practice, however, this is not the level of operating profit which the factory will generate in any of the three economic scenarios. Instead, the actual profit (depending on which scenario applies) will be either: $94.7m, $103.5m or $111.9m.

This highlights the underlying problem of expected value calculations: they only make sense if a scenario is played out a number of times, and therefore the expected value (as an average of the individual results achieved) is a meaningful figure. However, in this case, the decision to bring all of MS's footwear in-house is a one-off event, and therefore an average figure has little relevance in the decision making.

Moreover, the expected value is dependent on the probabilities assigned to each scenario. It is not clear how these have been determined, but it inevitably involves some degree of subjectivity.

(d)   **Impact of the new factory on the dashboard**

Financial metrics (20X5)

	Existing factory	New factory	Change (%)
Revenue ($m)	273	273	–
Operating profit ($m) (see Working 1)	71	66	–7.0%
ROCE (see Working 2)	41.7%	30.4%	–27.1%

The new factory will not affect the number of design awards won or brand awareness levels.

Impact on financial performance

Operating profit – The decline in operating profit indicates that manufacturing all of its footwear in-house will lead to an increase in MS's costs of approximately $5m per year.

Although the variable cost of manufacturing footwear in-house ($21–$23 per unit) is expected to be similar to that of buying footwear from an external supplier ($21 per unit), there will also be additional fixed costs associated with the new factory.

The increase in fixed costs will also lead to an increase in MS's **operational gearing**.

Non-current assets – As MS is primarily a product development and marketing operation – with no manufacturing operations of its own – it will have a relatively low level of fixed capital (buildings, equipment etc). As a result, it also has a relatively high ROCE.

However, establishing the factory will increase capital employed (as well as reducing operating profit), which explains the significant reduction in ROCE.

However, although establishing the factory (and taking full control of operations) may have a negative impact on ROCE in the short term, it could benefit MS in the longer term – for example, by helping it to avoid lost sales due to damaged reputation, or to avoid costs such as fines imposed by the regulator.

Impact on choice of metrics

Quality – If MS starts manufacturing footwear itself, then quality control will become an important aspect of performance management. Currently, product quality is not measured directly in the dashboard, but it would seem sensible to add an extra heading to reflect this new dimension – manufacturing – which has been added to MS's activities. (Alternatively, the 'design' heading could be expanded to allow additional metrics to be associated with it. But it would seem preferable to keep 'design' and 'manufacturing' as distinct activities.)

However, we must remember that MS has no experience of manufacturing. As such, it may be sensible to wait until the company has gained some operational knowledge of the factory operations before introducing a detailed metric for this area – for example, to avoid setting performance targets which are not realistic.

Gearing – The factory will cost $36m to build and equip, as well as increasing working capital by $11m. It is not clear how this additional capital will be funded, but if it involves debt then this will increase the company's financial gearing, and therefore the level of financial risk. There is not currently any measure of such risk on the dashboard, but again it may be necessary to add one.

Workings

1 *Impact of new factory on Operating Profit*

Average selling price ($)	$75
Cost of shoes ($)	$21
Operating profit per shoe	$54
Operating profit on 2 million shoes bought/sold	$108m
Operating profit from the new factory (per board's estimate given in the question scenario)	$103m
Reduction in operating profit	$5m

2 *Impact of new factory on ROCE*

Current capital employed (where operating profit (PBIT) is $71m and ROCE is 41.7%)	170.3
Additional capital employed: $36m + $11m	47
New capital employed	217.3
Revised ROCE: ($66m/$217.3m)	30.4%

(e) Value chain

A value chain provides an overview of the different activities within an organisation which combine to create value for customers. By identifying the activities which create value, the organisation can then focus on improving its performance in those areas – with the result that it also improves its performance overall.

Equally, however, the value chain can help an organisation to identify which aspects of performance are most important to measure – that is, those which relate to the key value-adding activities. In this respect, we might expect the metrics included in MS's dashboard to provide the board with information about how well the company is performing in these key activities. However, the current dashboard provides very little information about MS's performance in these activities.

Marketing and sales – To a degree, the dashboard heading for 'brand' could relate to the 'marketing and sales' activities in the value chain; but, as we have already suggested, simply monitoring brand awareness can only provide limited insight into the effectiveness of MS's marketing and sales activities.

Technology – In this respect, the linkage between technology (as a supporting activity) and marketing (as a primary activity) could also become increasingly important with the growth of social media as a marketing channel.

Logistics and operations – MS's current business model (with outsourced manufacturing and third-party retailers) means that a number of the primary activities (inbound/outbound logistics; operations; sales) are performed by third parties. Currently, MS does not appear to monitor the performance of its supply chain partners, but this is perhaps something it should consider doing, since these partners are responsible for generating a significant proportion of the value in MS's products.

Procurement – Although procurement is normally classified as a supporting activity on the value chain, MS's business model means that effective procurement (coupled with effective supply chain management, particularly with its upstream manufacturers) is likely to be crucial to the company's commercial success.

Moreover, the importance of outsourced manufacturers means that MS's performance management should not focus solely on its internal value chain, but also its value network (value system) more generally. (The Nush scandal provides an important reminder of this.)

Here again, the value chain also highlights the important supporting role that technology is likely to play – for example, in ensuring that the quantities of goods produced by different third-party suppliers responds effectively to the requirements of MS's third-party retailers (for example, to avoid either over- or under-production of different product lines).

Product design – Technology could also be important at MS in relation to creating innovative products; either through the way technology is used in the design process, or the way that technological developments make new materials available for use in MS's products.

'Design' has already been identified as one of the three performance headings in the dashboard, but technology development is likely to be a key supporting activity in relation to product design.

Although we have already suggested this point (in part (d) of this report) value chain analysis reiterates the idea that MS may need to include a wider range of metrics in its dashboard – to provide management with performance information about the range of activities which are critical in sustaining the company's commercial success.

61 Monza Pharma

Workbook references. The balanced scorecard (BSC) is discussed in Chapter 13 of the Workbook. The importance of the link between performance measures and objectives is discussed in Chapter 2. Financial performance measures (including ROCE) are discussed in Chapter 7. Costs of quality, and TQM, are discussed in Chapter 11. Lean information systems are discussed in Chapter 6.

Top tips.

Part (a). The BSC is one of the key performance measurement frameworks covered in the APM syllabus, so you should have a good understanding of it. However, the requirement here doesn't ask for you to describe the scorecard, or to explain how Monza could use the scorecard. Instead, the CEO asks specifically about the problems of using a scorecard at Monza. In other words, you need to think what the potential problems an organisation could face with using the scorecard, and then assess if these are likely to apply at Monza.

For example, one of the major problems with using the scorecard relate to choosing the measures to use – agreeing how many measures are required, and what the appropriate measures might be. Could this be a problem at Monza? The first paragraph of the scenario tells us that the board members frequently comment that 'it is good to have one easily understood measure for consideration' – but this would no longer be the case if the scorecard is introduced.

Part (b) requires you to evaluate two different sets of measures:

- The **current** performance measures (ROCE, average cost to develop a new drug, and revenue growth)

- The **proposed** measures presented by the consulting firm (ROCE, revenue growth, average cost to develop a new drug, training days provided)

As such, it is important that you address both sets of measures – but hopefully you noticed how similar the two sets of measures actually are in the scenario. So, are the measures the consultants have suggested really the most appropriate to use for the scorecard perspectives, or have the consultants simply rolled forward Monza's existing measures as far as possible?

One of the key issues when evaluating performance measures is the extent to which they enable managers to assess how an organisation is performing against its objectives. The opening paragraph of the scenario identifies that Monza's overall objective is to maximise its return to shareholders. Later on, the scenario also identifies that Monza aims to create shareholder value through innovation in drug development, efficiency in drug manufacturing, and success in selling its products. So the question is: how effectively do the performance measures enable Monza to assess how well it is achieving these aims?

Note that the CEO has asked you to 'evaluate' the choices of measures, so if there are some positive aspects to them you should include these in your answer as well as highlighting any problems or limitations with them.

Part (c). In order to 'evaluate the effect' of using the different measurements (as the CEO has asked you to do), you first need to calculate the returns using the different figures possible (as provided in Appendix 1).

At face value, Appendix 1 identifies four profit figures: gross profit, operating profit, profit before tax and profit after tax. However, the figures for the most recent accounting period also include restructuring costs of $482m. So, an additional consideration is the impact this could have on ROCE. Should the profit figures be adjusted to exclude these 'one-off' costs?

The marketing director's reference to 'using equity rather than all capital' should also have been a clue to calculate return on equity (ROE) as well as ROCE.

Remember, however, that the CEO has asked you to 'evaluate the effect' of using the different measures, not simply to calculate different measures. So you also need to consider what each of the measures shows. Think about the differences in the figures used to calculate the measures: for example, ROCE (operating profit/total capital employed) compared to ROE (profit after tax/equity capital).

Comparing the measures in this way is also necessary in order to 'recommend a suitable approach for Monza' – which is the final element of the CEO's request. In order to make a sensible recommendation, you first need to consider the usefulness of the different measures Monza could potentially use (and then recommend the one which is most useful).

As the marking guide indicates, only 4 (out of 11) marks in this requirement are available for calculating ROCE and ROE (with a further 1 mark for calculating gearing). Therefore, in order to pass the requirement, it is essential to make some relevant comments about the different metrics.

Here again, it is also important to think about Monza's underlying objective (to maximise its returns to shareholders). Which of the two measures (ROCE or ROE) is more suitable – and why?

Part (d). A useful starting point here would have been to categorise the information given in Appendix 2 into the different 'costs of quality' (prevention, appraisal, internal failure and external failure) and then to comment on the relative size of the costs in each category.

Even if you couldn't remember the individual 'costs of quality', you should still have been able to distinguish between 'costs' incurred in trying to prevent failure, as opposed to the costs incurred as a result of failure (or problems occurring).

The figures in Appendix 2 themselves should have given you a clue about the balance between prevention and failure, with the costs incurred on batches rejected and customer complaints being clearly the largest figures mentioned (thereby also suggesting that quality problems are having a significant adverse effect on the division's financial performance).

In this context, it should have been clear that the division's current approach to quality is substantially different to a TQM approach – where the focus is on preventing defects, and the ultimate goal is to achieve zero defects. Recognising this contrast should then help you answer the second part of the requirement: how implementing TQM would affect the division (and the way its staff think about quality).

Part (e). Although the CEO has asked you to advise how the division can make its new information system 'lean', a sensible approach to this requirement will be to consider what the characteristics of a lean system are. In effect, the way the division can make its system lean is by ensuring that it has demonstrates these 'lean' characteristics.

(Note, however, that the issue here is about making an information system 'lean'; not, for example, making the drug manufacturing process 'lean'.)

Overall. Remember that you have been asked to write a report, so make sure the style and structure of your answer, as well as its tone, is appropriate for a report.

Examining team's comments.

Part (a) asked for an assessment of the problems of using the balanced scorecard. In questions like this, candidates should focus on the theoretical areas where they believe the problems lie, and then to illustrate these by reference to the entity in the scenario. Unfortunately, what many candidates do is address the question by discussing another performance measurement system (which they believe may be more suitable). Making a suggestion as to an alternative may be worth merit, but it does not address the fundamental question asked. It is very important that candidates should know about the challenges arising from different management and control techniques, as well as the potential benefits from using them.

Part (b) asked for an evaluation of the current measurements and alternatives which had been suggested. Most candidates addressed the question asked, but they must appreciate the need to ensure that suggestions are justified and supported. For example, many suggested that 'more non-financial indicators are needed'. However, such comments are not worth merit unless they are supported by reference to points such as achievement of some of the company's specific objectives. When making comments like this, candidates should ask themselves: why is that relevant? Or, how/why would it benefit the company?

Part (c) was answered very poorly, as candidates did not demonstrate the technical knowledge that is expected at this level with regard to the composition of the measures of performance. At APM, candidates have to be able to interpret and discuss the results that measures are producing. Too many candidates described the measurements rather than evaluating their impact or usefulness. Candidates need to consider why some measures may be more appropriate than others. For example, which costs might one measure include that another doesn't? And why might this be significant in terms of performance measurement and management?

In **part (d)**, some basic technical knowledge was lacking in the analysis of costs. However, the part of the question relating to the implementation of a new technique was generally well answered as candidates focused on specific areas around implementation and tried to relate these to the entity in the scenario.

Part (e) was generally answered poorly. Most answers mentioned and explained either lean systems only or the department's production methods only, but the question required that both be considered together to assess the effect that one had on the other.

Marking scheme

		Marks
(a)	Problems with using the BSC Up to 2 marks per relevant point, specifically related to using the scorecard at Monza Maximum for part (a): up to 8 marks	8
(b)	Evaluating choice of current and proposed performance measures Evaluating current measures – 1 mark per relevant point, up to 6 marks Evaluating proposed measures – 1 mark per relevant point, up to 9 marks Maximum for part (b): up to 12 marks	12

(c) Variation in calculating return on investment
For calculating appropriate ROCE figures (including ROCE adjusted for
   restructuring costs) – up to 3 marks
ROE calculation – 1 mark
Gearing – 1 mark
Maximum for calculations – up to 5 marks

For discussion of ROCE – 1 mark per point, up to 5 marks
For discussion of ROE – 1 mark per point, up to 3 marks

For justified recommendation of a suitable measure – 1 mark
Maximum for part (c): up to 11 marks

11

(d) Quality costs and TQM in the Manufacturing Division
Discussion of categories of quality cost – up to 2 marks
Calculation/identification of quality costs – up to 3 marks
Discussion of results – up to 3 marks
Discussing how implementing TQM would affect the division – up to 5 marks
Maximum for part (d): up to 10 marks

10

(e) New information system
Aims of lean approach – up to 2 marks
Ways of achieving a lean system – up to 5 marks
Maximum for part (e): up to 10 marks

5

Professional marks – up to 4 marks

4
Total = 50

Report

To: The board of Monza

From: Performance management expert

Date: [today's date]

Subject: **Performance measurement and management issues at Monza**

Introduction

This report addresses the problems of using the BSC within Monza. The current and proposed
performance measures are evaluated and the main current measure is discussed in detail.
Quality costs and the new quality programme at the Manufacturing Division are analysed.
Finally, the lean philosophy is applied to the new information system for the Drug Development
Division.

(a) Problems with using the BSC

The BSC provides no aggregate or single summary measure of performance (in the way
that cash flow is used in a value-based approach, or in the way that ROCE is currently
used at Monza). Also, there is no simple, direct link between the BSC measures and
shareholder value, the main objective of Monza.

The measures in the scorecard can conflict; for example, cost controls (financial
perspective) can obstruct the investment needed in order to speed up manufacturing
processes (internal business perspective). Overall, the measures should seek to align with
the fundamental need to create shareholder value.

It can be difficult to select measures. In particular, there is the danger of losing sight of key
information in a plethora of indicators. This may be an issue for Monza as it has only had
three indicators in the past and this will now increase significantly – a potential of 12, if
there is one for each level of management (strategic, tactical, operational) for each of the
four perspectives of the BSC.

There must be management commitment to the change to the scorecard. In particular, there must not be a return to a focus on the financial measures which have been used in the past at Monza. Management should acquire the expertise for understanding non-financial measures through training.

There are potentially significant costs in collecting the additional information which will be needed for the new performance measures. Many of the measures will be non-financial and so new information systems will be required to collect and record the data.

(b)   **Choice of current and proposed performance measures**

Current measures

The current measures are all historic, financial ones and so the BSC approach will bring a longer-term view by using non-financial measures which consider those factors which might drive future growth, for example, those in the learning and growth perspective.

The current measures do not directly link to shareholder value which appears to be the overall aim of the company. A measure such as economic value added would do this more effectively.

The three measures do give a broad view of financial performance, though. ROCE is a widely used measure which it should be possible to benchmark against competitors.

As far as the divisions are concerned, there is a measure of success in selling through revenue growth, though this may be due to not only the Sales Division but also the drugs brought to market by the Development Division.

Average cost to develop a new drug is a financial measure of the Development Division's performance but this does not measure its aim of innovation in development. Indeed, this measure may conflict with that aim, as cost control of development may hinder innovative thinking. It would appear more appropriate to have a cost control measure associated with manufacturing, as its goal is to be more efficient. The performance of the Manufacturing Division is only measured indirectly through its effect on the financial performance of the company as a whole.

Consultants' proposed measures

The suggested measures do not seem to deviate much from the existing measures, though there may be an advantage in this as the new system would use existing information systems and known measures in that case. However, this advantage is secondary to the need to find measures which will drive useful performance in the four perspectives.

The proposed measures from the consultants' interim report mostly fit within the standard four perspectives of the BSC, although revenue growth is more appropriate as a measure from the financial perspective. Customer perspective measures should focus on the strategies which will achieve success in the eyes of the customers rather than just measuring the results of those strategies. Examples of this would be measuring the efficacy of the drugs which are developed by Monza or the reputation of Monza's medicines among the medical community.

Taking the others in turn, ROCE does not seem to be directly linked to shareholder value as, for example, economic value added or net present value would be. ROCE considers the performance over the whole capital base while the shareholders will be more directly concerned with returns on their equity investment. As a profit-based measure, ROCE may also be failing to target cash generation which is ultimately driving dividend payments and value creation for shareholders.

As already indicated, cost control in business processes is important but other measures of success such as time to market for the development of new products and quality initiatives should also be considered.

The fourth perspective (learning) is particularly relevant to a high-technology firm such as Monza. There will be considerable competitive advantage in having a highly skilled workforce. However, the measure proposed is imprecise as it values all training days, whether for knowledge workers or unskilled labourers, as equally valuable. Measures of the number of innovations within each division may be appropriate as these will be qualitatively different (new compounds developed, manufacturing quality improvements and sales techniques/initiatives developed).

BPP
LEARNING
MEDIA

Overall, the initial proposed set of measures does appear limited and does not address the overall aim of Monza or the problem of the narrowness of the existing set of measures.

(c) **Variations in calculating return on capital**

	ROCE	Return on equity
Using:		
Operating profit (W1)	18%	
Operating profit before restructuring (W2)	23%	
Profit after tax (W3)		97%

Tutorial notes

Workings for calculations

1. Operating profit ($m): 1,811
   Capital employed ($m): 1,161 + 8,739 = 9,900
   ROCE: 1,811/9,900 = 18.3%

2. Operating profit ($m): 1,811
   Add back restructuring ($m): 482
   Operating profit before restructuring ($m): 2,293
   Capital employed ($m): 9,900
   ROCE: 2,293/9,900 = 23.2%

3. Profit after tax ($m): 1,126
   Shareholders' equity ($m): 1,161
   Return on equity: 1,126/1,161 = 97.0%

ROCE is normally calculated by dividing operating profit by capital employed (debt and equity). The calculations above illustrate the possibilities of using the different return (profit) and capital figures available.

The ROCE figure should not use gross profit, as this ignores the operating costs not directly attached to sales, and at Monza these will include significant overheads from the Drug Development and Manufacturing Divisions which are relevant to overall performance. The return figure should match with the capital used to generate that return. As ROCE is calculated based on the return on total capital, it should not include financing costs, and so profit before and after tax are not consistent with this view.

The one area that could be discussed is whether to include the one-off costs of restructuring in performance. It would probably be best to disclose both figures to the company's stakeholders and to identify how any competitor would perform such a calculation for benchmarking.

A suitable approach for Monza

ROE may be a more suitable measure given Monza's focus on shareholder (not debt provider) performance.

In this case, the relevant return figure is the profit after tax as this is the return available to shareholders after the debt providers have been paid. The figure here (97%) is very large. This is due partly to the fact that the capital figures used in these calculations are from the financial statements and are not market values. (Market values of equity and debt would give a more accurate measure of performance both for ROCE and ROE.)

Another reason why the ROE is large compared to ROCE is that Monza is highly geared (88%). ROE, therefore, demonstrates the benefit of the chosen capital structure of Monza.

Overall, therefore, ROE is a better measure than ROCE as it fits with the prioritisation of shareholders as opposed to all capital providers.

> **Tutorial note.** Although we have recommended ROE, using ROE could have the effect of encouraging the continued heavy use of debt finance. (If a company's gearing ratio becomes too high, this can be a problem, not a benefit.)
>
> By contrast, ROCE does not reward the excessive use of debt finance, so you could have added this point as a word of caution alongside the recommendation.

(d) **Quality costs and TQM in the Manufacturing Division**

Quality costs are usually broken into four categories:

- Prevention costs, which relate to avoiding producing defective items in the first place;

- Appraisal costs, which relate to ensuring that the products produced meet an acceptable standard;

- Costs of internal failure, which relate to products that fail appraisal and how these are handled; and

- Costs of external failure, which relate to products that fail the standard but are still shipped to customers.

At Monza, for the most recent period, the following quality costs have been identified:

Prevention costs: $8m (training)

Appraisal costs: $12m (product testing)

Costs of internal failure: $13m (batches rejected)

Costs of external failure: $27m = $5m (fines) + $22m (discounts for late delivery)

Total raw material costs might hide relevant quality costs if the company is buying higher quality material to prevent problems of quality; however, this cannot be quantified in this scenario.

It can be seen that there were $40m of failure costs (internal and external) in the period but only $8m was spent on prevention (training). A 10% improvement in the failures could generate $4m in cost savings. In the light of this, the budget for improvements to production which prevent such failures could be significantly expanded. The analysis of quality costs should help to emphasise the importance of prevention by showing its financial value and this could be an important argument in favour of a TQM approach.

Impact of TQM on Manufacturing Division

TQM focuses on the customer perspective and the need for each part of the organisation to avoid defects in the chain of production.

Prevention is the key to improvement and so management should focus on avoiding defects through training and improved process design rather than appraisal. All employees must accept personal responsibility for their work and act to remove defects from production. Quality certification programmes are often instituted in order to encourage the focus on 'zero defects'. Quality circles may be formed as small, autonomous groups aimed at devising solutions to quality problems.

(e) **Making the new information system 'lean'**

Lean systems aim to get the right thing to the right place at the right time, first time. They aim to reduce waste while being flexible. The need for flexibility will be important for the Drug Development Division as it is constantly working in a changing environment.

The information in the system should be organised so that it can be retrieved with minimum difficulty – for example, if scientists need to access the results of past simulations.

The information will also have to be accurate so that time is not wasted in making errors.

The information should be presented clearly and, in particular, should not be excessive given the needs of the users. For example, if there are calculations and simulations which are obsolete or no longer required, these should be removed from the system.

The information should be able to be exchanged easily. This will be important in a collaborative environment such as a research group in the Development Division.

> **Tutorial note.** The 5Ss – structurise, systemise, sanitise, standardise, and self-discipline – could also be used here as a framework for your answer.

62 Dargeboard Services

Workbook references. The performance hierarchy linking mission statements and performance indicators is discussed in Chapter 2 of the Workbook. Reward schemes are discussed in Chapter 12, as is the building block model.

Top tips.

Part (a). A mission statement identifies an organisation's key purpose. By doing so, it can help to identify – at a high level – the aspects of performance which are important for an organisation, and therefore those aspects according to which its performance needs to be measured.

This question looks at this link between mission and performance measures, and specifically – as identified in the fifth paragraph of the scenario – whether the current set of KPIs measure the achievement of DS's mission.

The fifth paragraph of the scenario also provides a clear instruction pointer for how to structure your answer: 'by showing how each [KPI] links to all or part of the mission'. In other words, you should use each KPI as a sub-heading, and then evaluate the extent to which it links to the mission, and therefore whether monitoring it will help DS's management assess if the company is achieving its mission.

Note the CEO has asked you to 'evaluate' the links, so you should try to consider both the strengths of the KPIs (where they are clearly linked to the mission) as well as their weaknesses (where they are not linked to the mission). One important question here could also be: are all the elements of the mission (given in the second paragraph of the scenario) covered by the current KPIs?

Importantly, though, note the instruction in the fifth paragraph of the scenario, that the CEO 'does not want suggestions of new indicators'. Therefore, if you identify limitation or problems with the current measures, you need to highlight these, but you shouldn't then suggest alternative measures which could replace them, because there would be no marks available for doing so.

Examining team's comments for part (a). This part of the question required a common task (in a performance management exam) of identifying the mission from the scenario. Candidates were good at repeating the mission from the question, but few appeared to appreciate the structure of the mission, and how certain goals were subsidiary to an overall aim. However, most scored reasonably well, as they linked the indicators given to the parts of the mission.

Part (b). As with part (b), your approach to part (b) should also be to work through each of the indicators in turn, assessing the assumptions and definitions used in calculating them.

The sixth paragraph of the scenario provides some important context for your assessment. There has been a suggestion that DS is producing biased results, designed to mislead the markets, and in turn to boost the share price and the value of senior management's shares. As such, a key part of your answer needs to be an assessment of whether the indicators are being manipulated to make DS's performance appear better than it is, in the way the press report is suggesting.

Note the number of marks available for this part of the question. There are 12 marks available, and there are 6 KPIs to assess. This should be a clue that, to score well in this part of the question, you can't just say there are problems with the assumptions or definitions; you need to go on and explain why this is the case, particularly, in relation to them making the results misleading.

Examining team's comments for part (b). This part of the question required a detailed consideration of how performance measures are put together. However, candidates' responses tended to be very limited, with many candidates only scoring a single mark per indicator because they failed to develop their answers sufficiently. For example, it was often clear that a candidate had correctly identified that there was a problem with the calculation of a particular indicator, but very few candidates then attempted to quantify the impact of this problem.

Part (c). A key issue when answering this part of the question is that you need to evaluate the dashboard in the specific context of DS, rather than evaluating performance reports in general terms.

For example, DS's mission says the company aims to provide 'world-class services' but does the information in the dashboard provide any indication about how well DS is performing against its competitors, or against best-in-class service providers?

Similarly, we know DS offers a range of different activities to its clients (cleaning, security, etc), but does the report provide any indication of how each of the different areas is performing?

Once again, note the CEO has asked you to 'evaluate', so you should try to give a balanced assessment of the dashboard – highlighting areas where it helps managers assess performance effectively, as well as its potential problems or limitations.

Part (d). Although the requirement refers only to 'the building block model, you are not required to give an explanation of the whole model here. In the scenario, you are told the CEO specifically wants you to explain what is meant by results and determinants (in the model), and how the dimensions link to standards and targets. As these are the issues which the CEO has asked you to explain, these are the only issues which you should focus on in your answer.

Examining team's comments for part (d). Responses to this question were generally poor, as many candidates ignored the detailed requirement of the CEO and provided a generic answer that irrelevantly described the whole model.

Part (e). The sequence of requirements (d) and (e) and the context described in the final paragraph of the scenario should help provide you with some pointers for how to assess the two reward schemes.

The CEO is considering the Building Block model as a way of improving performance measurement at DS. So a good way of assessing the schemes could be to assess how well they display the characteristics of effective standards or rewards (as identified in the Building Block model).

For example, the Building Block model identifies that effective standards should be fair and achievable; and, in order for performance measure systems to operate successfully, rewards should be clear, motivating and controllable. How well do the two proposed schemes illustrate these characteristics?

The examining team's comments confirm that this was the expected approach here:

Examining team's comments for part (e). This part of the question was generally well answered, with many candidates using the Building Block model concepts to good effect by illustrating how the two reward schemes demonstrated the ideal features from the model.

Report format. Finally, note that you were asked to write a report, and remember that there are four 'professional marks' available for the quality of your report. As is the case in all report questions, markers are looking for suitable report headings, a brief introduction, a logical structure to the report – signposted by the use of headings – and a clear, concise style.

Marks

(a) For breaking down the mission statement and identifying the key elements of DS's mission – Up to 2 marks

For evaluating the links between the KPIs and the mission statement – 1 mark per relevant point

Total for part (a): up to 8 marks   8

(b) Up to 3 marks for relevant comments on each indicator:
Operating profit margin
Secured revenue
Management retention
Order book
Organic revenue growth
ROCE

Total for part (b): up to 12 marks   12

(c) 1 mark per relevant point about DS's performance dashboard

Total for part (c): up to 8 marks   8

(d) For explanation of results and determinants – 1 mark per relevant point – Up to 2 marks

For explanation of standards and targets, and key characteristics (ownership; achievable targets; fair): – 1 mark per relevant point – Up to 4 marks

Total for part (d): up to 6 marks   6

(e) Up to 2 marks for general discussion of assessment or reward schemes

For assessment of Scheme 1; 1 mark per relevant point – Up to 6 marks

For assessment of Scheme 2; 1 mark per relevant point – Up to 6 marks

Total for part (e): up to 12 marks   12

Professional marks – for style and structure of report – Up to 4 marks   4

Total = 50

Report

To: Board of DS

From: Accountant

Date: [today's date]

Subject: Strategic performance reporting and reward systems at DS

Introduction

This report assesses the coherence of the choice of key performance indicators (KPIs) with the mission of DS, followed by the assumptions used to calculate them. Other aspects of the presentation of the dashboard report are then evaluated. Finally, an overview of the operation of the building block model and an assessment of two proposed reward schemes are provided.

(a)   **Linking the mission to the current KPIs**

The mission statement can be broken into several parts. The principal aim is maintainable, profitable growth, and this is supported by three further goals: developing the best talent; providing world-class services; and being efficient.

The KPIs are linked to elements of this statement as follows:

- **Operating profit margin** shows that the organisation is profitable and also as a margin, it indicates efficiency in cost control.

- **Secured revenue** indicates the amount of revenue which is contracted and so has greater likelihood of being earned. Contracts give an indication of maintainability here only in the short term, however.

- **Management retention** links to the need for best talent though it does not measure developing that talent.

- **Order book** shows the maintainability into the future of the business though it does not show the average length of the contracts.

- **Organic revenue growth** shows historic growth and may indicate what the management are capable of achieving in the future.

- **ROCE** demonstrates the efficiency of profit-generation from the capital base of DS.

None of the measures are external (looking at the competitive environment) and so it is not possible to indicate if DS has 'world-class services'.

(b)   **Assumptions underlying the current KPI calculations**

Every KPI will involve some assumptions in its calculations. The aim of this section is to highlight how each indicator could be manipulated to show a better picture so that the business can avoid this in the future and the subsequent bad image portrayed in the investing community.

Operating profit margin is a standard performance measure and the only area which can be questioned is the categorisation of costs below this line; for example, the movement of operating costs into 'exceptional costs' below this line in order to artificially inflate this indicator. If the $55m reorganisation cost was included in overall operating profit, which was $91m (= 5.9% of $1,542m), then the business would show an operating margin of 2.3%. The catering business would show a loss of $39m.

Secured revenue represents long-term recurring revenue streams. A good picture will show a high percentage of secured revenue but will be below 100% so that management can indicate that budget targets are being exceeded. It is worrying that the budget is completed well after the year start as this may indicate such manipulation. If the original budgeted revenue figure is used then the secured revenue for 20X6 was 82%.

Management retention only includes retention of employees on full-time contracts which at 65% of all managers excludes a material number. Poor treatment (and thus retention) of part-time managers is therefore ignored. This may be a particular issue for managers with young children who often take advantage of such contracts.

Order book is a total 'value' figure, but is this the cash or present value figure? By choosing cash value of the contract, this will give a much larger figure than the discounted present value, especially where some revenues will not be received for ten years.

Organic revenue growth is calculated by using the total revenue figure as reported in the accounts. The main purpose of stating organic is that it is growth from within the organisation as it stands and so acquisitions should be ignored. Currently organic revenue growth is 7.2% (this is given), so the 20X6 revenue is $1,542m / 1.072 = $1,438m. Excluding the impact of the $48m from acquisitions (Note 7) means that organic revenue in 20X6 is $1,542m − $48m = $1,494m. This means that organic revenue growth would fall to ($1,494m / $1,438m) −1 = 0.039, ie from 7.2% overall to a less impressive 3.9%.

ROCE. Capital employed is being calculated using the statement of financial position figures which may exclude many intangible assets. As such it may overemphasise the tangible capital base which is not as important in a service business such as DS. The focus on this measure can lead to sub-optimal decisions.

(c) **Evaluation of the strategic performance dashboard**

The current information used by the board is both financial and non-financial allowing different elements of the mission to be measured. However, none of the measures are external, looking at the competitive environment, and so it is not possible to indicate if DS has 'world-class services'. Also, the measures do not focus on shareholder concerns, although the mission statement indicates that they are the principal stakeholders. Other measures beyond ROCE might have been expected given that priority, such as EPS or dividend per share. No breakdown of ROCE is provided for each business unit, this may be due to the lack of availability of capital employed figures for the units but it does seem an odd inconsistency since ROCE is the best KPI provided for shareholder use.

No revenue figures are given and as most figures are ratios it is not possible to gauge the absolute scale of the business. It is particularly surprising that an absolute profit measure is not included on the dashboard given the importance of profitable growth to shareholders.

Generally, there is a lack of external figures to allow benchmarking or the assessment of the competitive position of DS.

The breakdown of results into business sectors will help to judge the performance of the managers of those units but they may not be comparable; for example, comparing building services and security, it seems that building services is growing more rapidly but with weaker margins. Also, it may be that the employment market is different between each sector and so no comparison of management retention figures is sensible. Again, it may be helpful to provide either an external benchmark through industry averages or an internal one through a historic trend for these sector specific indicators.

The report does have good qualities as it is brief and clearly presented. The use of ratios makes for easy understanding.

(d) **The Building Block model**

The model takes the important step of distinguishing within the dimensions of performance between what is the desired outcome (results) and what are the drivers of those results (determinants). It then highlights the need to measure both of these within the performance reporting systems of an organisation.

The standards are the target level for the specific measures chosen for each dimension appropriate to an employee's performance. Employees must take ownership, so they need to be persuaded to accept the target and be motivated by the targets. Targets must be achievable and so challenge the employee without being viewed as impossible to achieve and therefore demotivating. For example, they must take account of external market conditions beyond the control of the employee, but this can be managed by benchmarking against an industry average. Targets must be fair; for example, different businesses within DS must be measured against their respective sector (catering, security, etc.).

(e) **Assessment of the proposed reward schemes**

As the board is already considering using the Building Block model, it is appropriate to outline the main criteria in the model for reward schemes.

Rewards must be:

- Clear, that is, understood by the managers;
- Motivating, that is, of value to the employee; and
- Controllable, that is, related to their area of responsibility.

Scheme 1

The scheme has the benefit of continuing with the successful policy of offering an equity share in DS. It continues to utilise the knowledge of the line manager in performing the appraisal. It attempts to address a problem of the current scheme – that the breadth of the categories gives the line manager scope to continue to show favouritism to specific employees. The fact that the line manager's own bonus will be affected by how well they perform the appraisals should help to reduce the risk of favouritism, and improve the quality of the appraisal process. The fact that the new scheme also sets an expectation for the distribution of bonuses should bring greater transparency to the process. For example, if 50% of a manager's staff receive no bonus (rather than the expected 20%) this could indicate the manager is being too harsh in their assessment of their staff. Having an expectation of the distribution of bonus shares could also mean that forecasting staff costs will be simpler.

However, this scheme does not address the problem that the appraisal categories are vague and do not reflect the KPIs of DS. It also could create a problem, as line managers will give bonuses according to the stated expectation – for example, even where all staff are, in absolute terms, performing brilliantly, only 20% will get the maximum. Also, there is no mention of the scale of the scheme bonuses as there is for Scheme 2, where the maximum bonus available is stated as 50% of basic salary.

Scheme 2

Scheme 2 loses a key benefit of the current scheme in not rewarding in shares; however, cash is an acceptable alternative. Cash may well be a preferred option for the managers as it offers a certain value to them. This form of benefit also reduces the desire to manipulate share prices. It sets standards based on the KPIs and so should lead to greater focus by each employee on the goals of DS. Involvement of both strategic and line management in this process should lead to a better set of measures being used.

It is not clear, however, why five targets are being chosen. This seems an arbitrary figure and it may be more sensible to suggest a range from three to six (the number of strategic KPIs) to be decided by the managers in consultation. The size of the maximum reward seems likely to motivate but the equal weighting for each heading may not be effective. It requires that, say, operating profit margin has the same importance as management retention.

63 Thyme Engine Products

Workbook references. Performance reports are discussed in Chapter 6 of the Workbook, as is the role of the management accounting in providing information for integrated reporting. Target costing, total quality management (TQM) and costs of quality are all discussed in Chapter 11.

Top tips.

Part (a). There is a technical article on ACCA's website (also mentioned in the Workbook) about 'Reports for Performance Management' which highlights four basis criteria which can be used to evaluate an organisation's performance reports:

- **Purpose** – What is the purpose of the report? Does the report provide information which is relevant to the organisation's performance against its mission or objectives?

- **Audience** – Who is the report produced for? Is it appropriate for its audience and their requirements?

- **Information** – What information is needed – financial and non-financial; quantitative and qualitative? Does the report provide the information which is needed to fulfil its purpose and satisfy its audience?

- **Layout** – Does the report make it clear for readers to identify the most important information?

Although you didn't have to use these criteria to answer the requirement, they could have given you a useful framework for answering this question. For example, does the report provide information which is relevant to its objectives and strategies (which are 'very similar' to Thyme's, as described in the first paragraph of the scenario)? Also, Thyme's board need information for 'planning and controlling', so does the report provide information which support both of those aspects of performance management?

Note, however, that the CEO doesn't simply ask you to evaluate the dashboard, but rather to evaluate why it was 'award winning'. Whereas an evaluation of the dashboard would require you to look at its advantages and disadvantages, your focus here should be primarily on its advantages (which have made it award winning).

Also, note that the CEO has mentioned that she thinks 'there may be some useful, specific comments to make about the contents of the dashboard given Thyme's recent problems.' The dashboard in Appendix 1 is for the award-winning company (not Thyme) so an issue to consider here is whether Thyme should include some additional measures on its dashboard in relation to the specific issues it has faced.

Part (b). The fourth paragraph of the scenario tells you that the CEO wants to know 'how integrated reporting might have an impact on the type of information prepared by the company's management accountants.'

As such, a sensible way to approach this question will be to think how the information required for integrated reporting differs from that used in traditional annual reporting – for example, in relation to the 'six capitals'. The management accountant's role will be to provide the information – but, as different information is required what impact might this have on the accountant? For example, will changes be required to the information systems to enable different aspects of performance to be measured?

Part (c). There are two elements to the CEO's request ('calculate...' and 'assess...') and it is vital that you address both of them in your answer.

The requirement is worth 12 marks in total, but the marking guide shows it would be possible to score up to 6 marks for calculations. These should have been relatively easy marks.

However, once you've done the calculations don't just ignore them. Although the CEO hasn't specifically asked you to comment on the cost gap, it would be helpful to think what the implications of it are – in the context of the TQM approach at Thyme. For example, there is currently a cost gap, but this is a new product. As Thyme gains experience in producing it, might its costs per unit come down?

At the same time, think about the key features of the TQM approach – one of which is continuous improvement. How does this link to the idea of closing a cost gap?

Part (d). Although there is only a single question requirement – 'costs of quality' – there are four different elements to what the CEO has asked you to do in the scenario, so to score well here it is important that you address all of these:

- Categorise the quality costs
- Calculate the costs in each category
- Suggest cost areas to be examined
- Evaluate the relative importance of each cost category

The first element here is essentially a test of knowledge. What are the four categories of quality cost? (The final paragraph of the scenario identifies one of these for you – prevention costs – which should help jog your memory as to what the other three categories are.)

The second element should also be relatively straightforward: identifying which category the costs in Appendix 3 relate to, and then calculating the total for that category. Don't overlook the 'Notes' though: the cost of buying higher quality raw materials is also a quality cost, even though it is not included in the list of quality costs identified in the current year.

When answering the third element ('Suggest cost areas to be examined'), it is vital to remember exactly what you have been told in the scenario: '[the CEO] is happy that prevention costs are complete, but is worried some costs for the other three categories are missing, and needs suggestions of cost areas to be examined to identify these missing items.' Consequently, your suggestions should relate to appraisal, internal failure, and external failure; not prevention. One approach here could be to think about the costs which have already been identified in each category, and then think if there are any costs which might be associated with these, but which have not yet been identified. For example, although costs of re-inspection after repairs arising from final assembly testing are included, the costs of those repairs themselves don't appear to be.

When considering the final element of the requirement – the relative importance of each cost category – remember the context of the scenario. Thyme adopts a TQM approach, and one of the key aims of TQM is to get things right first time. Which of the costs of quality is likely to be most important in helping to get things right first time?

Overall. Remember that you have been asked to write a report, so make sure the style and structure of your answer, as well as its tone, is appropriate for a report.

Examining team's comments

Part (a). Similar questions to this have been examined in previous exam and, as such, candidates tended to score relatively well here. However, a significant number of candidates provided very superficial answers; for example, stating that 'there is not a lot of detail in the report'. This could be an advantage or a disadvantage, depending on the users of the report, so it is essential to explain why something is good or bad. Also, this particular question required candidates to focus on the elements of the report that were particularly good, so parts of answers that discussed negative aspects scored very few marks.

Part (b). This question explored the role of the management accountant in providing information for integrated reporting, so it was essential for candidates to relate their answers to integrated reporting. Many candidates did not seem familiar with this type of report, and so discussed – in general terms – changes to the role of the management accountant in recent years. The examining team would like to remind candidates that technical articles are made available on the ACCA website to assist candidates in their studies, and candidates should read these articles. Several of the topics examined in recent exam sittings, including integrated reporting, have been discussed in technical articles.

Part (c). The calculations in this section were performed well by most candidates. However, we would remind candidates to present calculations in a logical order to allow the marking team to award marks for method even if the final answer is incorrect. Good candidates also went on to discuss the results well.

Part (d). Many candidates performed well on the calculations although some were not able to categorise the costs correctly. Also, candidates should pay close attention to all the verbs within a requirement. This part of the question specifically asked for four things (categories, calculate, suggest and evaluate) and candidates' performance would be improved if their answers addressed each of these separately.

Marks

(a) 1 mark per relevant feature of the dashboard which helps to make it award-winning, with additional marks (1 mark per relevant point) for illustrating these features.

Relevant features (and supporting illustrations) include, but are not limited to:

Achievement of the strategies of the business

Breaking down the strategy, and linking to measures in the dashboard

Balanced view

Financial and non-financial; different perspectives; results and determinants; internal and external views

Planning and control

Short and long-term views; forward focus for planning; trends/ budgets for control

Presentation

Brevity; narrative points; link to other strategic issues; eg risks

Specific issues at Thyme not measured in the sample template – up to 3 marks

Total for part (a): up to 15 marks   15

(b) Description of Integrated Reporting – up to 3 marks
Impact on management accountant – up to 6 marks
Total for part (b): up to 6 marks

6

(c) Calculations: 1 mark for each of the following:

Target cost	2,125
Production costs	1,825
Design and development	100
Sales and marketing	500
Target cost gap	300 (12% of current cost)
Current profit margin	$0.075m (or 3%)

Discussion of cost savings – 1 mark
Definition of target costing – 1 mark
Definition of TQM – up to 2 marks
Fit between target costing approach and TQM – up to 6 marks
Maximum for part (c): up to 12 marks

12

(d) Definition of quality costs – up to 2 marks
Calculations: 1 mark for cost in each category (either absolute value or
  % of revenue)

Prevention	$139m	1.21%
Appraisal	$138m	1.20%
Costs of internal failure	$95m	0.83%
Costs of external failure	$279m	2.43%
Total	$651m	5.66%

Discussion of results – up to 2 marks
Identification of other quality costs which appear to be omitted – up to
  6 marks
Relative importance of categories of quality costs – up to 4 marks
Maximum for part (d): up to 13 marks

13

Professional marks – up to 4 marks

4

Total = 50

Report

To: CEO of Thyme

From: Accountant

Date: [today's date]

Subject: Reporting performance and quality issues at Thyme

Introduction

This report analyses the positive features of the award winning dashboard identifying some areas which specifically apply to Thyme. Next, the role of the management accountant in providing information for integrated reporting is explained. Then, the target cost gap for the new engine is calculated and an evaluation is provided of the use of this target cost within the TQM approach. Finally, issues associated with the costs of quality at Thyme are addressed.

(a) **Positive features of the award winning dashboard**

The following are features of the dashboard which will have impressed the assessors' minds when making the award. They are placed in a priority order of most important first, and then there are a few specific comments about the possible use of such a template at Thyme.

Achievement of the objectives and strategies of the business

The critical measure of whether the dashboard is fit for its purpose is whether it answers the question: has the business achieved its key objectives?

The dashboard measures all of the key objectives of the business growth of the firm:

*   Shareholder wealth and returns through EVA™ and TSR; and

*   Growth through revenue and market share growth.

It also measures the strategies used to achieve these results:

*   World-class engineering to design engines through the class leading design specifications;

*   High quality production through fault rates in manufacturing and delivery; and

*   Customer service through those same fault rates and market share (an indirect indicator).

Balanced view

The report presents a balanced view of the business's performance. It deals with various perspectives (shareholders (TSR), customers (market share), internal business (fault rates) and innovation (design position)) which are used in the balanced scorecard approach. This is also achieved using both internal and external data (fault rates and average sector growth). It presents both the results and the determinants of those results by giving financial and non-financial indicators. For example, revenue growth will be driven by the customers' view of product and service, so design and manufacturing quality measures are important. Short- and longer-term measures are given such as profit margin and economic value added.

Planning and control

The dashboard should allow the board to perform both its vital functions in planning and controlling the business. The forecasts for next year (budgets) are given and also, as noted above, there are non-financial determinants of performance such as design and customer service which will drive the future short-term competitive position of the business.

The control activities of the board are served by providing historic trends and also current budget variances. The major headings are provided for under the financial headings with activity measured by revenue, profit by the margin and shareholder wealth by economic value added.

Presentation

The dashboard is kept brief as the board will have an opportunity prior to the board meeting to use it to identify issues requiring further analysis at the meeting. There is a short narrative commentary which deals with the major commercial points arising from the dashboard and also, gives further external market data as context for the figures (eg average sector growth). It is also worth noting that the narrative picks up on strategic issues of risk and opportunity which can be more difficult to capture in numerical form. Hence, the commentary appears appropriate to assist in an annual review of the business.

Specific issues at Thyme

There are certain issues particular to Thyme which may be added to the example dashboard, though if these are deemed short term, then they may not necessarily appear on this main dashboard view. The example dashboard does not show measures of cash flow performance (such as free cash flow generated) nor gearing ratio, although both of these measures would be important for future fund raising. There are no measures associated with governance and ethics which in the light of the bribery scandal may have a higher priority at Thyme. Ethical training costs may give a measure of this area.

(b) **Integrated reporting**

There is no standard format for integrated reporting. However, there are changes in focus of the company's reporting which will require the input of the management accountants of that business. Integrated reporting has a focus on opportunities and risk, how resources are allocated and performance both recent historic and expected in the future. There are six capitals involved in value creation including traditional tangible and financial assets but also including human, intellectual, environmental and social assets.

For the management accountant, these newer forms of capital will require information systems capable of capturing and processing such non-financial measures. The forward-looking nature of such reporting will require more information of a forecast nature (with the accompanying requirement to understand their estimating assumptions). The more strategic view which integrated reporting intends to give also requires reporting on factors which drive long-term performance.

A key part of the integrated report is linking performance to strategic goals and the ability to create value. This will require a less structured and more contingent approach to reporting. In other words, pro-forma reporting must be better tailored to the specific business's situation. However, it is considered a key requirement of such reporting that it is concise and so the management accountant must help to ensure that only the key information is reported.

It can be seen that the dashboard discussed in the above section of this report achieves many of these requirements.

(c) **New jet engine: target costing and TQM**

	$'000
Target cost	2,125 (to give 15% profit margin on a price of $2,500k)
Production costs	1,825
Design and development	100
Sales and marketing	500
Current cost	2,425
Target cost gap	300 (12% of current cost)

The target cost for the new engine is $2.125m and the current estimated cost is $2.425m. Therefore, there is a need to cut costs by 12% to achieve the target profit margin. It is common for the initial costs to be higher than the target cost and for cost savings to be achieved as the product reaches maturity in its lifecycle. However, it should be noted that, even at this higher initial cost, the engine will be still making a small profit per unit (of $0.075m; giving a 3% margin).

Target costing involves setting a selling price based on what will be competitive in the market then deducting a target profit margin to obtain the target cost. An estimate is made of the cost of the engine based on the current design specification. The gap between this cost and the target cost is the target cost gap and opportunities to bridge this gap are sought by amending the product design or cutting costs in production.

Total quality management (TQM) is a management approach which seeks to have no defects in resource or relationship management. It aims to have a culture of continuous improvement in the organisation.

In this new engine project, the TQM philosophy will fit well with the need to cut a relatively small amount of costs (12%) in order to meet the target. The production team will experience a learning curve associated with such a new product, and will make small but frequent improvements as they do so, which should help the required cost savings to be achieved.

Given the size of the cost gap, it does not seem that a major redesign of the engine is required.

(d) **Quality costs**

There are four categories of quality costs:

- **Prevention costs** are costs to prevent the production of engines which fail to meet specifications;

- **Appraisal costs** are costs incurred in inspecting products to ensure that they meet specifications;

- **Costs of internal failure** are costs associated with making good products which are identified as sub-standard before delivery to the customer; and

- **Costs of external failure** are costs associated with making good products which are identified as sub-standard after delivery to the customer.

Working: Costs of quality by category

	$m	
Prevention	139	(= training, 11 + higher quality materials, 92 + maintenance, 36)
Appraisal	138	(= performance testing: 110 + 28)
Costs of internal failure	95	(= re-inspection)
Costs of external failure	279	(= repairs and replacements, 223 + complaint handling, 56)
Total	651	

> **Tutorial note.** The marking guide for this question indicates that if candidates showed the costs in each category as a % of total revenue, rather than $m figures, they also earned the marks available.

Comments on results

The total quality costs are 5.7% of revenue which seems surprisingly low for an organisation which recognises this as a key competitive advantage; notable is the large size of the external failure costs of 2.4%.

Possible other relevant costs

Overall, there are likely to be administrative costs associated with many of these categories and some attribution of overhead should be undertaken beyond the customer complaint handling mentioned.

Appraisal costs include performance testing of final assembly and performance testing of subcomponents from suppliers. There may also be costs associated with inspection of raw materials inward since these make a difference to quality (shown by the higher purchase costs).

Internal failure costs include costs of re-inspection after repairs after final assembly testing. There must also be costs associated with repairing faulty goods identified at final testing and possibly also scrapping failed products. It is possible that there is idle time costs due to work held up by internal identification of faulty products.

External failure costs include customer complaint handling and replacements under warranties. There is also the cost of damage done to Thyme's brand by such problems although many customers will accept that these are inevitable and provided they are infrequent and covered by warranty, they need not be important.

New products such as the new jet engine will likely generate additional failure costs while production methods are optimised.

Relative importance of categories

Given the high cost of external failure and the importance of reputation for Thyme, the most important category is prevention.

It would be appropriate for Thyme with a TQM approach to be spending heavily in this area. This will still need to be combined with warranty spending in order to protect the reputation of Thyme when problems do occur. As prevention succeeds, so the importance of the other categories will decline. It is worrying that external failure costs are more than twice internal failure costs, which suggests that final testing is not identifying a significant number of the faults in production.

64 Fearties

Workbook references. KPIs are discussed in Chapter 2 of the Workbook. Issues relating to non-financial performance indicators are discussed in Chapter 10; Hopwood's management styles are discussed in Chapter 12, as are other strategic human resource management issues (such as setting targets).

Top tips.

Part (a). Although this is a single requirement, the CEO has asked you to do a number of different things in the scenario, in the paragraph under the heading 'Existing KPIs and introduction of the balanced scorecard'. It is important you address all of these points to score well in this part of the question:

- The CEO wants an evaluation of whether the existing KPIs cover the financial perspective of the balanced scorecard

- The CEO believes there is an error in the ROCE calculation in Appendix 1 which you should correct

- The CEO also wants you to recommend, with reasons, two KPIs for each of the other three perspectives of the scorecard (ie six KPIs in total), relating to the key issues facing the business.

In relation to the first of these points, we are told in the second paragraph of the scenario that the Feartie family has tried to manage the business 'to increase profits without excessive risk-taking' and that they are 'dependent on the business through their pay and dividends.' Also, in the paragraph about 'Recent events' we are told that the owners now have a goals of 'increasing growth' by expanding into new countries. So, when evaluating the financial perspective, an important point to consider is how well the existing KPIs enable the board to assess how well the business is achieving these aims.

Although there is a specific instruction to correct an error in the ROCE calculation, you might also want to consider how useful ROCE actually is as a performance measure for a service business like Fearties. In terms of correcting the error itself, what should the ROCE figure in Appendix 1 be, given the financial information in Appendix 2?

In relation to recommending new KPIs, a key part of the instruction here is that the KPIs you recommend should relate 'to the key issues facing the business'. The 'Recent events' section of the scenario highlights these key issues (eg health and safety certification; difficulties in recruiting staff; legal claims). We also know that Fearties has a 'reputation for reliability' so could that be important – for example, in relation to the 'customer' perspective of the scorecard.

Importantly, you are asked to make 'reasoned recommendations' for your indicators. There are a number of possible indicators you could recommend, so the key to scoring well here is in justifying why the indicator you have recommended will help Fearties' board address the issues facing the business.

Part (b). The scenario tells you that Fearties' board has resisted the introduction of customer surveys due to concerns about their ability to measure performance using this method, So, could the board's lack of familiarity with using non-financial performance indicators could be an issue in itself?

There isn't any information in the scenarios specifically about the customer surveys, so you need to draw on your own knowledge here, and one of the key things to remember here is that non-financial data (like customer satisfaction levels) can often be qualitative.

- What are the difficulties in **capturing** qualitative data? How can these be overcome?

- Also, what are the difficulties in **interpreting** customers' feedback in customer surveys? How might these be overcome?

Part (c). The paragraph headed 'Management style' in the scenario clarifies exactly what is required here:

- A brief definition of the three management styles (budget-constrained; profit-conscious; non-accounting)

- An assessment of the existing management style at Fearties

- A justified recommendation for an appropriate approach

The paragraph about targets and appraisals in the scenario provides some useful information for identifying the current management style at Fearties: all the performance targets are financial, for a single financial year, and with bonus payment being dependent on performance against those targets. Which style does this most closely resemble?

Is this style appropriate for Fearties, bearing in mind the business' goals, and the increasing focus on non-financial performance indicators?

A useful approach to this question would be to assess the current style, and then assess the potential advantages and disadvantages of each of the other two styles in turn, before recommending which style you think is most appropriate (based on the advantages and disadvantages you have identified for each of them). The CEO's request doesn't specifically say the approach you recommend can't be the existing style. However, from the context of the request, it is reasonable to assume that the current approach is not the most appropriate, and therefore one of the other two might be more appropriate.

Part (d). The paragraph about 'targets and appraisals' in the scenario tells us that individuals' performance targets are all financial. Will this be appropriate in the context of a balanced scorecard approach?

You could also think more generally here about the characteristics of effective targets. For example, applying the ideas in Fitzgerald & Moon's building block model, what factors could influence the effectiveness of 'standards' or 'rewards' at Fearties?

However, as well as advising about the targets, you have also been asked to advise how they should be used in the appraisal system. In this context, it could be helpful to think about the purpose of appraisals (ie judgement; development). To what extent will targets, and measuring performance against targets, be useful in that context?

Overall. Remember that you have been asked to write a report to the board of Fearties. Is the style and structure of your answer, as well as its tone, appropriate for a board report?

Marking scheme

Marks

(a)   Evaluating financial indicators: revenue growth, operating margin, cash flows generated, dividend growth (long and short term) – Up to 2 marks each

Correcting ROCE calculation; comment on ROCE – up to 3 marks

Comments on change in strategy – up to 2 marks

New indicators – up to 4 marks for each perspective (customer; internal business; innovation and learning). Marks are for justification and discussion of two new indicators for each perspective – up to 12 marks

NB: No marks for naming perspectives.

Total for part (a): up to 20 marks   20

(b)　1 mark per relevant point about problems with measuring and managing performance using non-financial performance indicators

Total for part (b): up to 8 marks　　　　　　　　　　　　　　　　8

(c)　1 mark for definition of each style – up to 3 marks

1 mark for identifying current style

Up to 2 marks for assessing each style (budget-constrained, profit-conscious, non-accounting) in context of the scenario – up to 6 marks

Up to 3 marks for recommending (and justifying) an appropriate style

Total for part (c): up to 10 marks　　　　　　　　　　　　　　10

(d)　U1 mark per relevant point, reflecting:
Balanced scorecard changes
Achievability of target
Controllability of targets
Responsibility for targets
Appraisal process
Total for part (d): up to 8 marks　　　　　　　　　　　　　　8

Professional marks – for style, structure and presentation of report –
Up to 4 marks　　　　　　　　　　　　　　　　　　　　　4

Total = 50

Report

To:　　　　The board of Fearties Security (Fearties)

From:　　　Accountant

Date:　　　[today's date]

Subject:　Performance reporting and management issues

Introduction

This report evaluates the current choice of indicators within the financial perspective of the balanced scorecard and recommends new indicators to cover the additional perspectives of the scorecard. Additionally, it discusses the problems of measuring non-financial indicators. The current management style is evaluated, and a new approach is recommended to match the strategy of the business. Finally, advice is given on the setting and use of targets in staff appraisals.

(a)　**Key performance indicators**

> **Tutorial note.** There are a number of possible KPIs which could be suggested for this scenario. Candidates will be given credit for the KPIs they recommend, based on the justification offered, even if the KPIs are different to the ones included in this suggested solution.

The balanced scorecard has four perspectives: financial, customer, internal business process and innovation and growth. Indicators are needed for each perspective. The indicators suggested here are for the use of the board at a strategic level and not detailed operational management.

Financial perspective

The overall business objective is to grow profit without taking excessive risks. This is focused on the financial aspects of the business and so it is consistent that the current key performance indicators (KPIs) are all financial, being taken or calculated from the accounting information supplied with them. However, they are open to criticism.

The figures provided are the absolute values where it may be more useful to provide the year on year change in order to show growth.

	20X8 $m	20X7 $m	Growth
Revenue	686	659	4.1%
Operating profit	36	34	5.9%
Cash flow from operating activities	64	64	0.0%
Dividends paid	14	13	7.7%

The operating profit figure is less helpful for control purposes than the operating margin which allows for the effect of increased sales activity. The figures above show operating profit improving but, in fact, this just reflects the increased sales, as the operating margin is constant at 5.2%.

The ability to generate cash from operations is one which should indicate if the company is at risk of failure and so it is a valuable measure of risk to the owners.

The dividend growth figure only shows growth for one year, but given the family's long-term involvement in the business, it might be more helpful to have a five-year average of growth, which can be calculated as 7.0%. This smooths out the fact that dividends are often only changed every few years once an increase appears sustainable.

Return on capital employed (ROCE)

The return on capital employed (ROCE) ratio is incorrectly calculated. The ratio calculated in the draft report is the return on equity (profit after tax/equity). This may be useful to a family owned business where share values are critical but it does not reflect the efficiency of the use of capital overall. The correct value for ROCE is 31.3% (operating profit/average capital employed = 36/(21 + 94)). However, this ratio is of limited value to Fearties, as it does not have a significant capital base. The business requires relatively little capital investment as its activities are mainly about the hiring out of its employees' time.

New KPIs

The existing KPIs do not adequately reflect the new plan to grow more rapidly by developing new markets. Figures for revenue growth and operating margin should be broken down as they are unlikely to be similar in the different markets.

Customer perspective

The customer's views are important for growth and so the scores of a customer survey may be used to indicate customer satisfaction. However, as discussed later, there are difficulties in measuring customer satisfaction and so customer retention (which could be measured through the percentage of revenue generated from existing customers) may be a better objective measure.

Reliability is listed as a key selling point, and some investigation may be required to identify on what aspects of the service the customers are basing this view. Possible measures could be the percentage of times that a security team of adequate size and experience are sent to each job, or the number of times when police have to be called to the customer's location (indicating a problem which the Fearties' team could not handle).

Internal business process

The operating margin indicator suggested in the financial perspective will supply useful information about the overall efficiency of internal processes.

Based on the issues facing the company, KPIs for this perspective should reflect employee recruitment and retention, so the average number of unfilled vacancies at the company over the year would be a relevant measure.

The success of the company's training process could be measured by the number and average size of the legal claims against its staff.

Innovation and learning

Training is a key issue for Fearties, so the percentage of staff who are qualified is an appropriate indicator. The time taken for this training and its costs may also be measures of the organisation's ability to learn and improve this process.

The operating margin changes over time which are generated in the new markets entered by Fearties would show the organisation's improvements in these new markets.

Obviously, revenue generated from new services offered would also measure innovation at Fearties. However, there appears to be little appetite for this at present as growth is to be driven from selling existing services in new markets.

(b) **Problems of using non-financial performance indicators**

The problems of using non-financial indicators can stem, at least in part, from management's lack of familiarity with them. This is a particular problem for Fearties given its history of using financial indicators. Such non-financial indicators can have issues in the different areas of recording/processing and then interpreting the information.

Customer satisfaction is a good example of an indicator with such difficulties.

Customer satisfaction is often surveyed and the results are expressed in language. It can be difficult to tell if a complaint which describes service as 'poor' is more or less serious than one which describes service as 'unacceptable'.

The most common way to try to overcome this problem is to turn the data into quantitative data. For example, surveys often use scoring systems to capture data on service. A scoring system will often ask the customer to rank their satisfaction at the service provided on a scale of 1 to 5 with '1' representing 'completely satisfied' and '5' representing 'totally dissatisfied'.

However, the problem remains that such scoring systems are still subjective, and it has often been found that there is a tendency to score toward the middle as people tend to feel uncomfortable using the extreme scores of 5 or 1. However, Fearties may suffer from an over-reaction response as the events it deals with are dramatic. For example, if there was a burglary at a factory it was meant to be guarding, then the loss is all blamed on Fearties' failure and a bad score given.

Also, there is the difficulty in interpreting qualitative data, such as customer satisfaction. It is essentially subjective since it is based on people's opinions. For example, in assessing quality of service, people have different expectations and priorities and so are unlikely to be consistent in their judgements. At Fearties, customer complaints will be driven by such opinions. Some customers may expect there will never be a security incident but this is out of Fearties' control since it is criminal actions which will generate some of these cases.

One way to reduce the effect of subjectivity is to look at trends in performance since the biases in opinion will be present in each individual time period but the trend will show relative changes in satisfaction.

(c) **Management style**

The current style at Fearties would appear to be budget-constrained. The targets set are all financial and are short term in that they are only for the next financial year. This style of management leads to a focus on cost control and often staff are not rewarded if they take actions which will require investment or the foregoing of short-term profit, such as marketing to build a reputation for reliability as an outsourcing partner.

The profit-conscious style evaluates managers on their ability to build long-term profits for the business. This style would appear to suit Fearties' strategic goals, but it does not emphasise non-financial issues such as recruitment and retention. It would not fit with the increased importance of these non-financial factors under the balanced scorecard approach to management.

In the non-accounting style, budgetary information plays a less important part of staff's performance evaluation. It suits an emphasis on quality and on operational factors. It would fit with many of the new non-financial indicators being proposed from the balanced scorecard. However, it may not be strategically suitable for Fearties due to the importance to the family of the financial returns from the business.

Overall, a profit-conscious approach is recommended but one which uses both financial and non-financial indicators from the balanced scorecard to support the long-term financial goals of the company. The profit-conscious style will suit the financial needs of the family and its long-term goal of growth while a supporting non-accounting approach will suit some of the operational arms of the business, for example, dealing with legal compliance and employee issues.

(d)   **Targets and the appraisal process**

The existing system of targets will have to be modified to reflect the new balanced scorecard approach. This will involve the use of new non-financial indicators which will require explanation to the member of staff.

Non-financial targets are subject to the measurement problems noted earlier and, particularly, problems of subjectivity on the assessment of performance may become areas of dispute in appraisal. In order to address this difficulty, a historical analysis should be performed to use as a benchmark for future targets. There is also the possibility that, without such analysis, the targets set are unachievable or else too easy and so lead to unnecessary costs.

It will also be important that targets are controllable and so it will be necessary to review their areas of responsibility to ensure that the new targets reflect the performance of that individual. It will also be important to consider external factors which might require adjustment when considering the final appraisal. An example of this would be if legislation changed requiring higher qualifications for employees and so making recruitment more difficult or training more costly.

Appraisal is the process of collecting and reviewing data on an employee's work which will provide an assessment of their capabilities and potential in order to improve performance, for example, by training. There is a danger that an over-focus on targets leads to a failure to consider helping the employee to advance.

A further issue with the use of targets in appraisal is that what gets measured gets done. This means that the choice of targets is important in focusing the employee on their tasks. The new balanced scorecard approach should assist in creating a broader assessment of the employee's performance and aligning these with the strategy of the business as a whole.

65 Rezillos

Workbook references. Management reports are discussed in Chapter 6 of the Workbook, and issues around mistake and misconceptions in the use of numerical data for performance measurement are also discussed in Chapter 6. Benchmarking is discussed in Chapter 1.

Top tips.

Part (a). Sometimes in APM scenario, when the CEO asks you to do something, there are multiple elements to their request. However, in this case, the scenario (4th paragraph) simply tells you 'The CEO would like an evaluation of the performance reporting system used at the strategic board level.'

Nonetheless, the reference to 'strategic board level' is important when thinking about the criteria which can be used to evaluate an organisation's performance report:

Purpose – What is the purpose of the report? Does the report provide information which is relevant to the organisation's performance against its objectives (ie how effectively is it implementing its strategy?).

Audience – Who is the report produced for? Is it appropriate for its audience and their requirements? (ie Is the report suitable for board members?)

Another important criterion when evaluating reports is layout, and that is also relevant here: is the report well presented; is it easy for readers to find the key information?

However, the main focus of your evaluation here should relate to the 'purpose' of the report. The second paragraph of the scenario details Rezillos' objective: 'to deliver sustainable growth in value to the shareholders by working in partnership with customers to deliver innovative and value-for-money solutions utilising the skills of the highly-trained workforce.' There are a number of different elements in this objective, so a useful approach to your answer would be to assess how well the report provides the board with information about the different aspects of this objective.

Part (b). The CEO has asked you to 'assess the analysts' criticisms of the customer survey' so a useful approach to this question would be to question whether these criticisms are justified. Are there any potential problems or weaknesses in the survey? The scenario also tells us the analysts' criticisms centred on 'the method of calculation, sampling and the disclosures in the press release' so you should try to address all three of these elements: calculation; sampling; disclosures.

The information provided in Appendix 2 should have provided you with some useful clues here, for example:

- The press release says Rezillos has 'performed an extensive survey'. However, only 9 customers were surveyed out of a total of 180. How extensive, or even representative, is this? How were the customers selected?

- 6 of the 9 customers were from Beeland division; with only 1 from Teeland (the division with the biggest revenue). Again, how representative is this?

The key to scoring well in this question is to identify points in Appendix 2 which indicate potential weaknesses in the survey, and then to explain the implications of them.

Part (c) (i). The final paragraph of the scenario tells you that the CEO has decided the three divisions should be benchmarked against each other – in other words, this is an internal benchmarking project. The scenario then goes to identify two things the CEO wants you to do 'initially' – that is, in part (c)(i), rather than in part (c)(ii): :

- Explain the different types of benchmarking

- Provide an evaluation of the usefulness of the type of benchmarking proposed for the divisions (ie internal)

It is important that your answer addresses both parts of this request.

Also, for the second part, note you have been asked for an 'evaluation' of the usefulness of the proposed type of benchmarking, so you should try to consider a balanced assessment of its potential advantages and its drawbacks.

Part (c) (ii). Here, the CEO's request in the final paragraph of the scenario identifies that you need to do three things:

- Complete the benchmarking exercise
- Comment on the metrics used in the benchmarking exercise
- Comment on the results of the benchmarking exercise

The first part of this request should be relatively straightforward: using the data provided to complete the missing figures for Veeland in Appendix 3.

(The 'Notes' in the Appendix tell you how to calculate incident rate, and utilisation of learning and development programme.)

Having calculated the missing figures you then need to comment on the performance metrics used in the exercise. A key issue here is whether the areas of performance being benchmarked are those which are most important to the organisation's success. So, how well do the metrics support the achievement of Rezillos' objective (as stated in the second paragraph of the scenario)?

For the final part of the requirement, you then to comment on the results of the benchmarking exercise itself: how does performance vary between the divisions? To score well here, it is important that you don't simply 'write out' figures from the benchmarking exercise – for example, don't simply say, Beeland has the highest number of face-to-face interactions with its key customers. Instead, try to think about potential reasons for the differences, and the implications of them. For example, what might the differences in face-to-face interactions with customers tell us about the division's marketing strategies, and what might be the implications of this?

More generally are there ways the divisions could improve their performance by learning from others which are performing better than them for a given metric?

Overall. Remember that you have been asked to write a report, so make sure the style and structure of your answer, as well as its tone, is appropriate for a report.

Marking scheme

Marks

(a) 1 mark per relevant point – points must be based on scenario information

Breaking down overall objective and how Rezillos seeks to achieve this – up to 2 marks

Assessment of whether report supports objectives – up to 10 marks

Other points – up to 4 marks

Point could include (but are not limited to): lack of targets; lack of information on capital and liquidity; general presentation (lack of narrative)

Total for part (a): up to 13 marks   13

(b) Comments on average calculations – up to 3 marks
Comments on calculation weightings – up to 2 marks
Comments on sampling issues – up to 6 marks
Summary comments about whether criticism is justified
Total for part (b): up to 9 marks   9

(c) (i) Identify type of benchmarking proposed (internal) – 1 mark
Comments on external benchmarking – up to 3 marks
Comments on functional benchmarking – up to 2 marks

Evaluation of usefulness of internal benchmarking for Rezillos – up to 5 marks

Total for part (c) (i): up to 9 marks   9

(ii) Calculations:
Inventory days – 1 mark
Order book growth – 1 mark
% of revenue from new products introduced in the last three years – 1 mark
Reduction in incident rate – 2 marks
Utilisation of learning and development programme – 1 mark

Comments on choice of metrics – up to 4 marks
Comments on results – up to 10 marks

Total for part (c) (ii): up to 15 marks   15

Professional marks – up to 4 marks   4

Total = 50

Report

To: The Board of Rezillos Engineering (Rezillos)

From: Accountant

Date: [today's date]

Subject: Performance reporting and benchmarking at Rezillos

This report begins by evaluating the current performance report used by the board for their strategic review of the business. Next, the report examines the methodology used in the customer ratings survey in response to criticisms of that survey. Finally, the method of benchmarking to be used for the divisions is evaluated, and the divisional benchmarking exercise is completed and initial conclusions drawn from it.

(a) Performance report for annual board review

The current report has a number of strengths and weaknesses. These will be discussed according to whether the report:

- Measures performance towards the company's overall aims; and
- Is well-presented.

The company's overall objective is to deliver sustainable growth in value to the shareholders, and it aims to achieve this by:

- Working in partnership with customers
- Delivering solutions which are innovative and provide value for money
- Utilising the skills of the highly-trained workforce

Shareholder value – Beginning with the overall objective of Rezillos, the report does not directly measure shareholder value and so does not report its growth despite this being a primary goal of the organisation. This could be done directly by measuring economic value added (EVA™) or total return to shareholders. Also, the report is wholly historical and contains no information about the future prospects necessary to judge whether the growth in shareholder value is sustainable. The current report uses period profits and return on capital employed as its main measures of performance. These can suffer from being short term unlike economic value added.

Non-financial measures – Overall, the report does not give information about the performance of the strategies which are in place to deliver the overall objective. These will require non-financial measures and so do not appear in the report which is dominated by standard accounting information.

Partnership with customers – There is no measure in the report of how the company works with customers. The company does collect data on interaction with customers at a divisional level, although measuring 'working in partnership' is a vague term which should be more accurately defined in order to be measured, possibly by measuring the number of joint product development projects undertaken.

Value for money – An indirect measure of the customer value-for-money is being offered through the gross profit which, when compared to the industry average, gives a partial measure of value but without data on the price/quality mix compared to competitors, it is difficult to be conclusive about this. Revenue growth is given but should be compared to industry growth in order to give an impression of the attractiveness of our offering to the customer.

Innovation – No measure of innovation is offered in the report either in terms of the number of new products or the revenue or profit generated from them. This appears to be an important fault as an engineering firm such as Rezillos will only be viable in the long term if it continues to innovate.

Workforce – There is no information on the training provided to Rezillos' workforce, or their skills, but given the emphasis on innovation and the sector in which Rezillos operates, these appear to be important factors.

There are measures appropriate for these strategies available within the divisions (see the benchmarking exercise later). These could provide easy solutions to many of these gaps.

Divisional performance – The report treats the divisions in the same way as the group, using profit and comparison to industry average margins and budgets as the main assessment tools. This may not be helpful as the divisions are in different markets and so may not be easily comparable. This problem could be solved by providing the targets set for each of the divisions for the major financial indicators.

Liquidity – It is unusual, given the preponderance of financial data in the report, that there is very little about the assets and liabilities of the company or its liquidity. This may be acceptable if the efficiency of capital use and the danger of insolvency are negligible but this appears unlikely as shareholder value is a key measure and the ROCE is quite low.

Presentation – In terms of presentation, the data are clear and in a form which would be easily recognisable to those used to reading accounts. However, it is common to provide a narrative commentary with such a report in order to highlight the key features in the report such as major deviations from target or performance well outside industry norms.

(b)   **Performance report for annual board review**

In a recent analysts' meeting, Rezillos has been questioned about its disclosure that it has an average 7.0 customer rating. The average customer rating is correctly calculated as 7.0 from the sample data. However, there are a number of questions which could be raised over the method of calculation and sampling.

The first issue which might be raised is the definition of 'average' in this context. The method used for the calculation is the arithmetic mean but average can also be considered to be the mode (most common rating) or the median (the middle value of the sample, which here would be the 5th value). Both of these alternative methods of calculation would give the lower value of 6.0 for the rating.

The calculation method does not take into consideration the size of the account. The rating of the large accounts might be considered more important and so given some extra weighting in the calculation.

A larger area of concern would surround the sample selected for the calculation. There are a number of questions to be raised about this:

(i)   A confidence interval and level should be supplied for the rating. If the sample is a small one or the confidence level required is high, then the confidence interval might be shown to be unacceptably large.

(ii)   The method of sampling is not disclosed. Ideally, it should be a random sample.

(iii)   There are various ways in which the sample might be biased:

    (1)   Only customers who are expected to give a favourable response may have been selected.

    (2)   It could be that only the customers who chose to respond are included in which case the sample will often be populated with those at the extremes of opinion on Rezillos' service.

    (3)   The majority of customers in the sample are from Beeland (six of nine) and only one from Teeland. This will not allow the rating to identify divisional performance, which, given each division has responsibility for customer support, may create a bias. In order to do this, random samples from each division should be taken separately.

    (4)   There are only three customers sampled with an above average account size ($20.5m ($3,691m/180)). It is common in such surveys to ensure that all of the major accounts are sampled.

Overall, the criticism appears justified and in future, Rezillos should consider disclosing more detail of the method of sampling and the sample size in order to build trust with the investing community.

(c)   (i)   **Methods of benchmarking**

There are broadly three methods of benchmarking relevant here. The proposed benchmarking exercise is an **internal** one comparing divisions within the same organisation.

The other methods are **external (or competitor) benchmarking** where comparison is drawn with competitors. This is valuable in identifying areas where the other companies demonstrate competitive advantage and also areas for improvement with a similar business. However, although this method can suggest areas where Rezillos can catch up with its major competitors, it will not identify how to gain advantage over these rivals.

At a practical level, the difficulty with this method is obtaining the information and even if a competitor can be persuaded to share information, it will often only give strategic improvements, not operational ones, as such detailed information is unlikely to be in the public domain.

A third method of benchmarking is **functional benchmarking** with a world-class company from another business sector. Rezillos could share detailed operational data without the worry of loss of confidential information directly to a competitor. The difficulty lies in translating lessons learned from one industry to another, so it is often done for generic activities such as logistics. Functional benchmarking against a company from outside Rezillos' industry sector could be challenging as it will require the use of information from another company which will likely use different systems to collect data.

Evaluation of internal benchmarking

The major advantage of internal benchmarking is the ability to obtain detailed operational information and so to share best practice amongst the divisions. This will show the different divisions the advantage of being part of a larger company and assist in integrating them.

This method of benchmarking suffers the drawback that it will often involve non-financial data whose production is often less robust than the financial systems involving subjective judgements. Also, it will not necessarily identify world-beating performance. Its internal focus may lead the company to ignore competitor performance. However, as a one-off exercise to harmonise and improve the divisions' performance, it seems to be suitable for Rezillos now.

(c)   (ii)   **Divisional benchmarking exercise**

The benchmarking has been completed as follows:

	Beeland	Teeland	Veeland
Benchmarking metrics			
Growth of market	8.5%	3.2%	5.0%
Revenue growth	12.5%	3.2%	4.8%
Operating margin	10.6%	12.8%	15.0%
Inventory days	162	162	162
Order book growth	5.2%	5.3%	5.3%
Number of face-to-face interactions with top 10 customers	260	120	40
Percentage of revenue from new products introduced in the last three years	24.9%	29.0%	

	Beeland	Teeland	Veeland
Incident rate (20X8)	1.14	1.13	1.03
Incident rate (20X7)	1.18	1.13	1.18
Reduction in incident rate	3.4%	0.0%	12.7%
Utilisation of learning and development programme	1.20	1.26	0.98

Metrics used

The benchmarking metrics appropriately reflect many of the detailed strategies of the company:

- Order book growth reflects the sustainability of current levels of business;

- Number of face-to-face interactions with top ten customers reflects working in partnership with customers;

- Innovative solutions is measured by percentage of revenue from new products introduced in the last three years; and

- Caring for employees and nurturing their skills is measured by reduction in incident rate and utilisation of learning and development programme.

The major missing piece is the change in shareholder value or profit generated by each division.

Results of the benchmarking exercise

The initial three metrics identify the broad financial performance of each division:

- Beeland is operating in a high growth market and seems to be using lower prices (lower operating margin) and a sales drive (visiting top customers more regularly) in order to push growth above the market rate.

- Teeland operates in a more stable market, but one where the take-up of new products is higher.

- Veeland is growing more slowly than its market, possibly due to higher margins and a weak sales effort (with only a small number of visits to key customers).

So, the divisions apparently operate in markets with different characteristics, but there does appear to be scope to share practices between them in order to improve. Looking at the individual metrics in more detail:

- Inventory days is the same across the divisions, reflecting the new company-wide inventory management system. This indicates that some aspects of integration are working.

- Order book growth is an important measure of the growth and sustainability of profits in the business. All three divisions saw similar order book growth, although Beeland saw higher levels of revenue growth. Beeland visits its key customers much more frequently than the other two divisions (every two weeks on average), so the other divisions might learn from this in terms of increasing the number of interactions they have with their key customers in order to try to increase revenue growth.

- Teeland is seeing the highest proportion of sales of new products but this may reflect the fact that they operate in a more developed market. This could only be controlled by obtaining external data such as industry averages for each country.

- Veeland has shown a significant reduction in safety incidents and its training and operating procedures should be shared with the other divisions in order to see if similar improvement can be replicated there.

- Not surprisingly, the market with the largest proportion of revenue from new products (Teeland) is also the one which makes greatest use of training. The low training score in Veeland may reflect little sales training as the number of sales interactions shows the most dramatic difference of all the metrics.

Mock exams

ACCA Strategic Professional – Options

Advanced Performance Management (APM)

Mock Exam 1

Questions	
Time allowed	3 hours 15 minutes
This exam is divided into two sections	
Section A	This ONE question is compulsory and MUST be attempted
Section B	BOTH questions are compulsory and MUST be attempted

DO NOT OPEN THIS EXAM UNTIL YOU ARE READY TO START
UNDER EXAMINATION CONDITIONS

SECTION A – This ONE question is compulsory and MUST be attempted

Question 1

Company information and mission

Kolmog Hotels (Kolmog) is a large listed chain of branded hotels in Ostland. Its stated mission is: 'to become the No. 1 hotel chain in Ostland, building the strength of the Kolmog brand by consistently delighting customers, investing in employees, delivering innovative products/services and continuously improving performance'. The subsidiary aims of the company are to maximise shareholder value, create a culture of pride in the brand and strengthen the brand loyalty of all stakeholders.

The hotels in the Kolmog chain include a diverse range of buildings and locations serving different customer groups: large conference venues, city centre business hotels and country house hotels for holidays. For reporting purposes, the company has divided itself into the four geographical regions of Ostland, as can be seen in a recent example of the strategic performance report for the company used by the board for its annual review (see Appendix 1). At the operational level, each hotel manager is given an individual budget for their hotel, prepared in the Finance Department, and is judged by performance against budgeted profit.

Strategic changes

Kolmog is planning a strategic change to its current business model. The board has decided to sell many of the hotels in the chain and then rent them back. This is consistent with many other hotel companies which are focusing on the management of their hotels rather than managing a large property portfolio of hotels.

In order to assist this strategic change, the chief executive officer (CEO) is considering introducing the balanced scorecard across Kolmog. He has tasked you, as a management accountant in the head office, to assist him with this work.

The CEO is worried that the BSC might be perceived within the organisation as a management accounting technique that has been derived from the manufacturing sector. In order to assess its use at Kolmog, he has asked you to explain the characteristics that differentiate service businesses from manufacturing ones, using Kolmog to illustrate your points.

Also, before introducing any new performance measurement systems, the CEO wants to assess the current information which is produced for the board (Appendix 1). To assist with this, he has asked you to evaluate the current strategic performance report, and the choice of metrics used.

Balanced scorecard

Senior executives at the head office of Kolmog have drawn up a preliminary list of perspectives and metrics as an outline of the balanced scorecard:

Table 1: Performance metrics for the balanced scorecard

Key strategic perspective	Metric
Strategic financial performance	Financial performance benchmarked to Kolmog's main competitors (share price and return on capital employed)
Customer satisfaction	Customer satisfaction survey scores
Hotel performance against budget	Variance analysis for each hotel
Employee satisfaction	Staff turnover

The CEO has asked you to help him review the preliminary work done on the development of the scorecard in order to ensure that it is consistent with the goal of meeting the strategic objectives of the company by tying operational and strategic performance measurement into a coherent framework. To this end, the CEO has asked you to evaluate the outline Scorecard (Appendix 1), suggesting suitable improvements where appropriate.

The CEO also wants your thoughts about any practical issues arising from introducing the scorecard. Therefore, he asked you to include a section in your report which describes the difficulties in implementing and using the balanced scorecard at Kolmog.

Reward systems

The history of rewards at Kolmog has not been good, with only 1% of staff receiving their maximum possible bonus in previous years, and 75% of staff receiving no bonus. This has led to many complaints that targets set for the reward system are too challenging.

Under a new performance reward system, employee targets are to be derived from the balanced scorecard strategic measures depending on the employee's area of responsibility. The new system is for hotel managers to be given challenging targets based on their hotel's performance against budgeted profit, industry-wide staff turnover and the company's average customer satisfaction scores. The hotel managers will then get up to 30% of their basic salary as a bonus, based on their regional manager's assessment of their performance against these targets.

The CEO wants to use Fitzgerald and Moon's building block model to assess the new system. He is happy with the dimensions of performance but wants your comments on the standards and rewards being applied here. He asked you to explain the purpose of setting targets which are challenging, and then to evaluate the standards and rewards for the hotel managers' performance reward system, using the building block model as the basis for your evaluation.

Required

Write a report to the CEO of Kolmog to respond to his instructions for work on the following areas:

(a)   The characteristics of service businesses   **(5 marks)**

(b)   The current strategic performance report and the choice of performance metrics used

                                                                                               (8 marks)

(c)   Evaluation of the outline balanced scorecard   **(12 marks)**

(d)   The difficulties in implementing and using the balanced scorecard   **(7 marks)**

(e)   Targets, and the managers' performance reward system   **(14 marks)**

Professional marks will be awarded for the format, style and structure of the discussion of your answer.   **(4 marks)**

                                                                                    (Total = 50 marks)

APPENDIX 1

STRATEGIC PERFORMANCE REPORT FOR REVIEW KOLMOG HOTELS YEAR TO 31 MARCH 20X3

	East region $m	West region $m	North region $m	South region $m	Total $m	Total 20X2 $m	As % of revenue for 20X3
Revenue	235	244	313	193	985	926	
Cost of sales	28	30	37	21	116	110	11.78%
Gross profit	207	214	276	172	869	816	
Staff costs	61	65	78	54	258	245	26.19%
Other operating costs							
Hotels	68	70	97	54	289	270	29.34%
Head office					158	150	16.04%
Operating profit	78	79	101	64	164	151	16.60%
Financing costs					78	73	7.92%
Profit before tax					86	78	8.73%

	20X3	20X2	Growth year on year
Capital employed	$1,132m	$1,065m	6.29%
EPS	$1.36	$1.27	7.09%
Share price	$12.34	$11.76	4.93%
ROCE	14.49%	14.18%	

SECTION B – BOTH questions are compulsory and MUST be attempted

Question 2

Framiltone is a food manufacturer based in Ceeland whose objective is to maximise shareholder wealth. Framiltone has two divisions: Dairy Division and Luxury Division. Framiltone began manufacturing dairy foods 20 years ago and Dairy Division, representing 60% of total revenue, is still the larger of Framiltone's two divisions.

Dairy Division

This division manufactures cheeses and milk-based desserts. The market in Ceeland for these products is saturated, with little opportunity for growth. Dairy Division has, however, agreed profitable fixed price agreements to supply all the major supermarket chains in Ceeland for the next three years. The division has also agreed long-term fixed volume and price contracts with suppliers of milk, which is by far the most significant raw material used by the division.

In contrast to Luxury Division, Dairy Division does not operate its own fleet of delivery vehicles, but instead subcontracts this to a third-party distribution company. The terms of the contract provide that the distribution company can pass on some increases in fuel costs to Framiltone. These increases are capped at 0.5% annually and are agreed prior to the finalisation of each year's budget.

Production volumes have shown less than 0.5% growth over the last five years. Dairy Division managers have invested in a modern production plant and its production is known to be the most efficient and consistent in the industry.

Luxury Division

This division was set up two years ago to provide an opportunity for growth which is absent from the dairy foods sector. Luxury Division produces high quality foods using unusual, rare and expensive ingredients, many of which are imported from neighbouring Veeland. The product range changes frequently according to consumer tastes and the availability and price of ingredients. All Luxury Division's products are distributed using its own fleet of delivery vehicles.

Since the company began, Framiltone has used a traditional incremental budgeting process. Annual budgets for each division are set by the company's head office after some consultation with divisional managers, who currently have little experience of setting their own budgets. Performance of each division, and of divisional managers, is appraised against these budgets. For many years, Framiltone managed to achieve the budgets set, but last year managers at Luxury Division complained that they were unable to achieve their budget due to factors beyond their control. A wet growing season in Veeland had reduced the harvest of key ingredients in Luxury's products, significantly increasing their cost. As a result, revenue and gross margins fell sharply and the division failed to achieve its operating profit target for the year.

Framiltone has just appointed a new CEO at the end of Q1 of the current year. He has called you as a Performance Management Expert for your advice.

'In my last job in the retail fashion industry, we used rolling budgets, where the annual budget was updated to reflect the results of every quarter's trading. That gives a more realistic target, providing a better basis on which to appraise divisional performance. Do you think we should use a similar system for all divisions at Framiltone?' he asked.

You have obtained the current year budget for Luxury Division and the division's Q1 actual trading results (Appendix 1) and notes outlining expectations of divisional key costs and revenues for the rest of the year (Appendix 2).

Required

(a) Using the data in the appendices, recalculate the current year budget to the end of the current year and briefly comment on the overall impact of this on the expected operating profit for the year. **(12 marks)**

(b) Evaluate whether a move from traditional incremental budgeting to a system of rolling budgets would be appropriate for Dairy and Luxury Divisions. **(13 marks)**

(Total = 25 marks)

APPENDIX 1

Luxury Division current year budget

	Q1 C$'000	Q2 C$'000	Q3 C$'000	Q4 C$'000	Total C$'000	Q1 actual C$'000
Revenue	10,000	12,000	11,000	7,000	40,000	10,400
Cost of sales	(6,100)	(7,120)	(6,460)	(4,720)	(24,400)	(6,240)
Gross profit	3,900	4,880	4,540	2,280	15,600	4,160
Distribution costs	(600)	(720)	(660)	(420)	(2,400)	(624)
Administration costs	(2,300)	(2,300)	(2,300)	(2,300)	(9,200)	(2,296)
Operating profit	1,000	1,860	1,580	(440)	4,000	1,240

APPENDIX 2

Expected key costs and revenues for remainder of the current year

(1) Sales volumes are expected to be 2% higher each quarter than forecast in the current budget.

(2) Average selling price per unit is expected to increase by 1.5% from the beginning of Q3.

(3) The exchange rate between the Ceeland Dollar (C$) and the Veeland Dollar (V$) is predicted to change at the beginning of Q2 to C$1.00 buys V$1.50. For several years up to the end of Q1, C$1.00 has been equivalent to V$1.40 and this exchange rate has been used when producing the current year budget. Food produced in the Luxury Division is despatched immediately upon production and Framiltone holds minimal inventory. The cost of ingredients imported from Veeland represents 50% of the division's cost of sales and suppliers invoice goods in V$.

(4) The rate of tax levied by the Ceeland Government on the cost of fuel which Luxury uses to power its fleet of delivery vehicles is due to increase from 60%, which it has been for many years, to 63% at the beginning of Q3. 70% of the division's distribution costs are represented by the cost of fuel for delivery vehicles.

(5) The CEO has initiated a programme of overhead cost reductions and savings of 2.5% from the budgeted administration costs are expected from the beginning of Q2. Q3 administration costs are expected to be a further 2.5% lower than in Q2, with a further 2.5% saving in Q4 over the Q3 costs.

Question 3

RM Batteries Co (RMB) is a manufacturer of battery packs. It has expanded rapidly in the last few years under the leadership of its autocratic chairman and chief executive officer, John Smith. Smith is relentlessly optimistic. He likes to get his own way and demands absolute loyalty from all his colleagues.

The company has developed a major new product over the last three years which has necessitated a large investment in new equipment. Smith has stated that this more efficient battery is critical to the future of the business as the company operates in a sector where customers expect constant innovation from their suppliers.

However, the recent share price performance has caused concern at board level and there has been comment in the financial press about the increased gearing and the strain that this expansion is putting on the company. The average share price has been $1.56 (20X8), $1.67 (20X9) and $1.34 (20Y0). There are 450 million shares in issue.

A relevant Z-score model for the industry sector is:

$Z = 1.2X_1 + 1.4X_2 + 3.3X_3 + 0.6X_4 + X_5$

Where:

X_1 is working capital/total assets (WC/TA)

X_2 is retained earnings reserve/total assets (RE/TA)

X_3 is profit before interest and tax/total assets (PBIT/TA)

X_4 is market value of equity/total long-term debt (MVE/total long-term debt)

X_5 is revenue/total assets (Revenue/TA)

A score of more than 3 is considered safe and at below 1.8, the company is at risk of failure in the next two years.

The company's recent financial performance is summarised in Appendix 1. A junior analyst in the company has correctly prepared a spreadsheet calculating the Z-scores, and this is shown in Appendix 2.

Required

(a) Discuss the strengths and weaknesses of quantitative and qualitative models for predicting corporate failure. **(6 marks)**

(b) Comment on the results in the junior analyst's spreadsheet. **(5 marks)**

(c) Identify the qualitative problems that are apparent in the company's structure and performance and explain why these are relevant to possible failure. **(5 marks)**

(d) Critically assess the results of your analysis in parts (b) and (c) alongside details of RMB's recent financial performance and suggest additional data that should be acquired and how it could be used to assess RMB's financial health. **(4 marks)**

(e) Explain the changes that are likely to occur at the maturity and decline stages of the product's life cycle in relation to its selling price and production costs. **(5 marks)**

RMB used a market skimming pricing strategy for its new product at the introduction stage in its life cycle. However, John Smith now believes that the new product has moved into its growth phase, and he is concerned about how long it will be until the product becomes mature.

(Total = 25 marks)

APPENDIX 1

Summary financial information

SUMMARY INCOME STATEMENTS

	20X8 $m	20X9 $m	20Y0 $m
Revenue	1,460	1,560	1,915
Operating costs	1,153	1,279	1,724
Operating profit	307	281	191
Interest	35	74	95
Profit before tax	272	207	96
Tax	87	66	31
Profit for the period	185	141	65

STATEMENTS OF FINANCIAL POSITION

	20X8 $m	20X9 $m	20Y0 $m
Assets			
Non-current assets	1,120	1,778	2,115
Current assets	235	285	341
Total assets	1,355	2,063	2,456
Equity and liabilities			
Share capital	230	230	230
Retained earnings reserve	204	344	410
Long-term borrowings	465	991	1,261
Current liabilities	456	498	555
Total equity and liabilities	1,355	2,063	2,456

APPENDIX 2

Z-score calculations

		20X8	20X9	20Y0
Share price ($)		1.56	1.67	1.34
No. of shares (millions)		450	450	450
Market value of equity ($m)		702	752	603
X_1	WC/TA	−0.163	−0.103	−0.087
X_2	RE/TA	0.151	0.167	0.167
X_3	PBIT/TA	0.227	0.136	0.078
X_4	MVE/Total long-term debt	1.510	0.758	0.478
X_5	Revenue/TA	1.077	0.756	0.780
	Z	2.746	1.770	1.452
Gearing [debt/equity]		107%	173%	197%

Answers

DO NOT TURN THIS PAGE UNTIL YOU HAVE
COMPLETED THE MOCK EXAM

Exam success skills

In any APM exam it will be important to apply good general exam technique by using the six exam success skills identified at the start of the Revision Kit, in the section covering 'essential skills'. These skills are: 1. Case scenario: Managing information; 2. Correct interpretation of requirements; 3. Answer planning: Priorities, structure and logic; 4. Efficient numerical analysis; 5. Effective writing and presentation; and 6. Good time management.

Some examples of how to apply these skills in this exam are provided in the table below.

Skill	Examples
Managing information	It is crucially important to assimilate the information in the question scenario.
	In longer questions, such as the 50 mark question, it is difficult to assimilate information by simply starting at the beginning and read to the end because there is so much information to take in.
	Instead it is sensible to take an **active approach** to reading each question. Read enough of the question to get an idea of the basic scenario and then read the initial requirements so that you understand the first things that you are expected to do with this information.
	For example, in question 1 the lengthy scenario makes a lot more sense if, before reading all of it, you are aware that the first requirements relate to performance reporting for a service business.
Correct Interpretation of requirements	Be careful to interpret the verbs used in the question requirements carefully.
	For example, Q1 part (b) requires you to evaluate the company's current performance report. It is vital that you evaluate the report itself, rather than the company's performance which is shown in the report (a common mistake in the exam).
	Also be careful to identify where a question requirement contains more than one instruction.
	*For example, in Q1 part (e), the question is actually multi-faceted because it is based on a comment from the CEO in the final paragraph of the question. Many candidates will ignore the full extent of the question because the CEO's requirements were **embedded in the main scenario** of the question, as opposed to being in the requirement per se.*
Answer planning	Planning is always important in APM questions, because most of the marks are available for discussion and if your discussion points are not relevant to the scenario then they will not receive any credit.
	As a general rule, you should spend at least 20% of your time, reading the scenario and planning your answer.
Efficient numerical analysis	It is essential that the marker can follow your workings and your logic.
	If you make a mistake early in your calculations that affects your later calculations then the marker will only penalise the error you have made, and not its follow-on impact on other calculations. This means that it is not normally a good use of your time to correct such errors during the exam.

ANSWERS

Skill	Examples
Effective writing and presentation	In APM this is a very important skill. You are often expected to be able to employ **critical analysis**, and this will sometimes mean that you will reject innovative and modern ideas in favour of less exotic tried and tested performance management tools.
	For example, in Q2 part (b) it is perfectly sensible not to recommend rolling budgets in the Dairy Division.
	It is also very important to **relate your points to the scenario** and to the requirement wherever possible.
	For example in Q1 part (b) a key issue is to consider how well the measures are linked to the company's mission – to become the No. 1 hotel chain.
	Relating to the scenario will often require you to apply your theoretical knowledge to the scenario, and here you need to avoid simply repeating a rote-learned technical point.
	However, you **will** be tested on your understanding of the theoretical content of APM and **you will not be able to apply your theoretical knowledge to the scenario if you do not possess a strong understanding of the theories in the first place.**
	For example, in Q1 part (e) it is not possible to apply the building block model to the scenario unless you have a strong understanding of this concept in the first place.
	Finally, in Q1, to score the 4 **professional marks** that are available you should use suitable report headings, an introduction, a logical structure, signposted by the good use of subheadings in the answer, and a clear, concise style.
Good Time Management	The exam is 3 hours 15 minutes long, which translates to 1.95 minutes per mark.
	If you build in an allowance of 20% of your time for assimilating the scenario and planning, this falls to 1.56 minutes per mark (1.95 × 0.8).
	At the beginning of a question, work out the amount of time you should be spending on
	– Planning: for a 25 mark question this will be 1.95 × 25 marks × 20% = 10 minutes. For a 50 mark question this should be about 20 mins.
	– Writing your answer to each requirement: Take the mark allocation and multiply by 1.56 minutes per mark.

Diagnostic

Did you apply these skills when reading, planning, and writing up your answer? Identify the exam success skills where you think you need to improve and capture your thoughts here of what you want to achieve when attempting questions in future.

Question 1

Top tips.

Part (a). Although you have been asked to 'explain' the characteristics, there are only five marks available for this part of the question. So you should keep your explanations relatively brief. There are five key characteristics which differentiate service businesses from manufacturing ones (and five marks available), meaning that there is only one mark available per characteristic. However, don't forget that you need to illustrate how the characteristics relate to Kolmog Hotels. Don't just talk about the characteristics of service businesses in generic terms.

Part (b). The CEO has asked you to evaluate Kolmog's current strategic performance report, and the word 'report' is crucial here. It is vital that you evaluate the **report** and the choice of metrics used in the report, rather than evaluating Kolmog's strategic **performance**.

A key issue to evaluate here is how well the performance report allows Kolmog to assess its performance against its mission. For example, does the report (or the metrics selected in it) help assess Kolmog's performance in relation to it becoming 'the No. 1 hotel chain in Ostland'?

Also think about the 'segmentation' of the report. For example, how useful is it to know how each of the four regions has performed, as opposed to how each type of hotel has performed?

Part (c). One of the key problems with Kolmog's current performance report (which, hopefully, you identified during your evaluation in part (b)) is that the report only includes financial metrics, rather than a range of metrics which can be used to measure performance in relation to the different elements of Kolmog's mission.

By contrast, the different perspectives included in the proposed BSC look at key aspects of non-financial performance as well as financial performance. This should be beneficial for Kolmog.

However, while the idea of introducing a BSC may be a good one, note that the CEO has asked you to 'suggest suitable improvements' to the scorecard where appropriate. So, are there any ways which the proposed metrics could be improved so that the aspects of performance being measured support the mission and objectives more effectively?

Part (d). Your evaluation in part (c) should have highlighted that some of the measures originally proposed for the outline scorecard could be improved. In turn, this should have highlighted one of the main difficulties of implementing the scorecard: choosing what measures to actually include in it.

As Kolmog has not used the scorecard before, selecting appropriate measures and then educating the managers in how to interpret the reported results are likely to be significant challenges in relation to implementing the scorecard.

Part (e). The scenario highlights that 75% of Kolmog's staff have received no bonuses in previous years, and there have been many complaints that the targets are too challenging.

This suggests that the staff don't regard the bonus targets as achievable, and consequently the staff are not motivated to try to achieve them.

Achievability is one of the three key 'standards' identified in the building block model (along with ownership and fairness). Similarly, motivation is one of the three key aspects of 'rewards' identified in the model (along with clarity and controllability).

The key issue in this part of the question is whether the new performance reward system fits with these standards and rewards any better than the old system appeared to. For example, will hotel managers feel they 'own' their performance targets if the budgets are imposed by head office?

Overall. Once again, remember that you have been asked to write a report, so make sure the style and structure of your answer, as a whole, is appropriate for a report. For example, a report should have a short introduction explaining the key issues to be discussed in it.

Marking scheme

Marks

(a) Service industry characteristics – 1 mark per characteristic
(intangibility; inseparability; variability (or heterogeneity); perishability; and no transfer of ownership)
Characteristics must be illustrated in relation to the hotel industry to score the full mark available for each characteristic.

Total for part (a): up to 5 marks

5

(b) For comments on how well the current report enables Kolmog to measure performance against its objectives – 1 mark per point; up to 6 marks

For comments on the choice of measures used in the report – 1 mark per point; up to 6 marks

Total for part (b): up to 8 marks

8

(c) For comments on the outline BSC which has been proposed for Kolmog; evaluating current metrics and suggesting suitable improvements to the scorecard – 1 mark per point, up to 4 marks for each perspective of the scorecard

Other relevant comments about the scorecard – 1 mark per point

Comments must be linked directly to the scorecard proposed for Kolmog, rather than being a generic description of the scorecard.

Total for part (c): up to 12 marks

12

(d) For difficulties in implementing and using the scorecard at Kolmog – 1 mark per point

Again, to score the full marks available difficulties should be linked directly to implementing the scorecard at Kolmog.

Total for part (d): up to 7 marks

7

(e) Explanation of the purpose of setting challenging targets – 1 mark per point;
up to 3 marks. (To score the full 3 marks, the answer must be specifically
relevant to Kolmog.)

Standards – for explaining the criteria of ownership, achievability and
fairness; 1 mark per standard; up to 3 marks

Rewards – for explaining the criteria of clarity, motivation and controllability;
1 mark per reward; up to 3 marks

For comments on the new reward system which has been proposed at
Kolmog – 1 mark per point; up to 7 marks

Total for part (e): up to 14 marks 14

Professional marks – for report headings and introduction, clarity of report,
and language used – Up to 4 marks 4

Total = <u>50</u>

Report

To: CEO Kolmog Hotels

From: Accountant

Date: June 20X3

Subject: **Performance measurement and targets at Kolmog Hotels**

Introduction

This report explains the key characteristics which differentiate service businesses from manufacturing ones, and then evaluates the performance reports and measures which are being used to monitor Kolmog's performance. The report then evaluates the balanced scorecard (BSC) which has been proposed for use at Kolmog, and describes the difficulties which could be associated with using the scorecard.

Finally, the report explains the purpose of setting challenging targets, and uses Fitzgerald and Moon's building block model to evaluate the standards and rewards which are applied to the managers' performance reward system at Kolmog.

(a) Characteristics of service businesses

There are five key characteristics of services that distinguish services from manufacturing.

(1) **Intangibility** – In contrast to manufactured goods which are tangible, physical products, services do not have any substantial material or physical aspects. When a customer books a room in one of Kolmog's hotels, they are not buying a physical product; rather they are buying their overnight accommodation in the hotel.

The fact that Kolmog isn't producing a physical product also helps to explain why its cost of sales (at around 12% of revenue) is much lower than the equivalent figure would be for a manufacturing business.

(2) **Inseparability (or simultaneity)** – Whereas manufactured goods need to be produced before they can be consumed, services are created at the same time as they are consumed. For example, a guest's experience of one of Kolmog's hotels is formed during their stay in the hotel.

(3) **Variability (or heterogeneity)** – One of the key issues which service businesses face is ensuring consistency in the standard of their service. For example, it could be difficult for Kolmog to control the level of service provided to customers by the different hotels in the group, not least because the behaviour of individual staff working in a hotel on any given day will have a significant impact on the level of service which customers receive.

(4)   **Perishability** – Services are innately perishable. If a room is unoccupied (unused) for a day, then the revenue which could have been earned from the room for that day can never be recovered. This explains why room occupancy rates are often used as key performance measures by hotel companies.

(5)   **No transfer of ownership** – When a customer purchases a service, this does not result in a transfer of property to the customer. For example, when a customer buys a car, they become the owner of the car. However, when a guest books a stay at a hotel, they are only buying the right to stay at the hotel for a limited period of time; they do not own the hotel.

(b)   **Current strategic performance report**

Financial information only – The strategic performance report should help the board monitor how well Kolmog is performing in the light of its stated mission.

However, despite the mission highlighting non-financial aspects of performance, the performance report currently includes only financial information. As a result, the report does not provide any indicators of how well Kolmog is performing in relation to the non-financial elements of the mission, such as **customer satisfaction, employee development** or **product innovation**.

Shareholder value – The report covers the subsidiary aim of maximising shareholder value by providing figures for earnings per share (EPS), share price performance and return on capital employed (ROCE), although total shareholder return and economic value added might be better measures than ROCE in this respect.

Importantly, however, maximising shareholder value is only a subsidiary aim, rather than a primary aim of the mission.

Key performance indicators – Hotels often have high levels of operational gearing because many of their costs (such as staff costs and property costs) are fixed. Consequently, their profit levels are likely to be sensitive to relatively small changes in revenue. As a result, hotel chains often view measures such as occupancy rates and revenue per available room as key performance indicators. Kolmog's performance report could be improved by including some key performance indicators like this – particularly indicators which are linked to revenue performance.

Market position – Perhaps the most important aspect of Kolmog's mission is the desire to 'become the No. 1 hotel chain in Ostland'. However, the report does not provide any indication as to how well the chain is performing in this respect, for example by measuring Kolmog's market share.

The absence of any external data is significant in this respect. Not only does it prevent the board from measuring overall market share, it also means it cannot benchmark Kolmog's performance in key performance areas against competitor hotels. For example, although the ratios of staff costs and hotel operating costs are useful, it would also be useful to know how these figures compare to the equivalent ratios for competitor hotels.

Segmental analysis – Although it is useful for the board to have information about how different segments of the chain are performing, breaking down the results into **geographical areas** may not be the most valuable basis of segmentation. For example, if the **mix of hotel types** varies significantly between each region, then simply comparing the performance of the four geographical regions may not be very instructive. In this respect, it may be more useful for the operating results to be broken down by hotel type (for example, conference venues, city centre business hotels, and country house hotels).

Budget figures – Although the individual hotel managers are judged by their hotel's performance against budget, the strategic performance report doesn't show any budget figures. This appears to be a significant weakness in the report. Including budget figures and variances in the report would enable the board to identify any significant deviations in actual performance compared to budget, and take corrective action where necessary.

(c)   **The Balanced Scorecard**

In general terms, the balanced scorecard (BSC) is intended to help a company translate its mission into objectives and measures such that the measures are coherent with, and support, the overall mission. A company can also use the measures in its scorecard to inform its employees about the key drivers of success.

The BSC also highlights the importance of measuring both non-financial performance and financial performance. This could be particularly valuable to Kolmog, given the importance of the non-financial elements in its mission.

Although it may be easier for Kolmog to measure aspects of financial performance than non-financial performance, the long-term success of the hotel chain is likely to depend on how it performs in key non-financial areas. Nevertheless, it remains important to measure financial performance, and the financial perspective of the scorecard highlights this.

Financial perspective

The financial perspective in the outline BSC focuses on measures of strategic financial performance: **share price** and **ROCE**. This fits with the overall objective of maximising shareholder value, although it would be useful to measure **dividend per share** as well as share price in order to reflect **total shareholder return**.

Operational gearing – Although ROCE is often used as a measure of overall performance, the change in Kolmog's business model may make it less suitable as a measure for the company. Once Kolmog has sold and rented back many of its hotels, the business will have a much lower capital base. However, its fixed costs (notably rental costs) will be much higher. Therefore, it may be more appropriate to include a measure such as **operational gearing** in the scorecard.

Revenue growth – It would also seem appropriate to include **revenue growth** as a measure, given Kolmog's stated intention to 'become the No. 1 hotel chain in Ostland'.

Customer perspective

Customer satisfaction survey scores – This measure seems to be appropriate because it is aligned to the mission and the aim of 'consistently delighting customers'.

Brand loyalty – However, measuring customer satisfaction alone does not provide any indication as to whether loyalty to Kolmog's brand is strengthening. In this respect, it would also be useful to measure the number (or proportion) of customers who are repeat customers, as opposed to customers who are staying in a Kolmog hotel for the first time.

Alternatively, it could be useful to measure the value of the revenues (or the proportion of the revenues) which are generated by returning customers, as distinct from customers who are staying in a Kolmog hotel for the first time.

It is not clear from the scenario whether Kolmog has any kind of loyalty card programme. If it does, then a measure based around the number (or value) of bookings from loyalty card customers could also be a useful measure in relation to brand loyalty.

Internal business perspective

Variance analysis – In the outline scorecard, variance analysis (comparing actual performance to budget) for each hotel has been proposed as a measure to support the internal business perspective.

Occupancy rates – In this respect, it will be important for the budgets to include non-financial performance indicators as well as financial ones. As we have already noted, room occupancy rates are a key factor in shaping a hotel's performance, and so should be monitored here alongside financial variances.

However, as we noted in relation to segmental analysis, it is also important to recognise that different business processes or elements of performance may be important in different types of hotel hotels. For example, city centre business hotels may be able to maintain reasonably consistent occupancy rates throughout the year, whereas occupancy rates in the country house hotels are likely to exhibit greater seasonality. Likewise, operating margins in the country house hotels may vary more during the year, because they will still be incurring fixed costs even in months when occupancy rates are low.

Therefore, it may be necessary to adapt the key scorecard measures being used for different types of hotel.

Internal benchmarking – Nonetheless, the performance of individual Kolmog hotels can be compared against others of the same type. Internal benchmarking in this way should enable Kolmog to identify which hotels are performing best, and in turn whether there are any 'best practices' which can be shared between those hotels and others which are not performing so well.

In this way, knowledge sharing between different hotels may help Kolmog to 'continuously improve performance', which is one of the aims of its mission.

Innovation and learning perspective

The innovation and learning perspective of the scorecard should underpin this drive to continuously improve performance. Equally, the measures chosen in relation to the perspective should be ones which encourage the delivery 'of innovative products/services', which again is an aspect of Kolmog's mission.

New products/services – There are not currently any measures proposed which relate to innovation or new products. A measure which could be appropriate here is a measure of the proportion of revenue which is generated from new products or services; for example, any new packages which might be offered by the country house hotels. However, as the hotel industry in general is now a fairly mature industry the scope to deliver innovative products and services may be relatively limited.

Employee satisfaction – As a service business, Kolmog's employees play a particularly important role in delivering customer satisfaction. If the staff in a hotel are happy and motivated this is likely to lead to guests in that hotel enjoying their stay more than if staff were grumpy and unhelpful. The performance metric of staff turnover could give an indication of how satisfied staff are with their jobs. In general, the higher staff turnover rates are, the less satisfied staff are likely to be with their jobs.

Alternatively, instead of using staff turnover as a surrogate for employee satisfaction, Kolmog could perhaps also introduce staff surveys in which staff satisfaction scores could be measured more directly.

No. 1 hotel chain in Ostland – Whichever measures Kolmog finally chooses for its scorecard, it is important to remember the underlying emphasis of the stated mission is 'to become the No. 1 hotel chain in Ostland'. Therefore, wherever possible, Kolmog should seek to benchmark its performance in all of the scorecard areas against its competitors, in order to identify whether or not it is actually achieving this 'No. 1' status.

(d) **Implementing and using the BSC**

The BSC has not been used at Kolmog before, and therefore, as with any new framework, the company could face difficulties as it is introduced for the first time.

Selecting measures – In the previous section of this report we have suggested some alternative measures to the preliminary ones proposed by senior managers at head office. This highlights the first potential difficulty in using the scorecard: selecting which measures to include.

When deciding which measures are the most appropriate to include in Kolmog's scorecard, it is important to include measures which are related to key business processes and activities which add value to the company, not simply those that are easy to measure.

It is also important to remember the scorecard's role in translating strategic measures down to the operational level. So, for example, while there might be an overall measure focusing on customer satisfaction levels, at the operational level this may need to be broken down further into customer satisfaction on the service they received at reception, or the cleanliness and comfort of their room.

The innovation and learning perspective can often be the most difficult to measure directly. However, Kolmog appears to have worked round this problem by selecting measures relating to employee satisfaction.

Equally, it is important not to include too many measures. There is a danger that if the scorecard contains too many measures the impact of them will be reduced as a result of information overload.

Conflicting measures – Some measures in the scorecard may naturally conflict. For example, Kolmog may look to improve customer satisfaction scores by recruiting extra staff in some of its hotels. However, the costs of these staff could adversely affect financial performance in those hotels (at least in the short term).

The board may find it difficult to decide what combination of measures is likely to encourage the best results for Kolmog, but when making such decisions it will be important to look at how well each possible measure helps the company achieve its overall mission.

Interpretation – Even if Kolmog selects an appropriate set of measures for its scorecard they will ultimately only prove valuable to the company if managers can interpret the results of the measures adequately, and use them to initiate appropriate actions to improve performance. If managers have difficulty analysing the figures, or interpreting what the figures are demonstrating, then it will be difficult for the managers to know what actions need to be taken in the light of the results being indicated by the scorecard.

Again, this also reinforces the importance of not including too many measures, in order to avoid information overload.

Management commitment – The scorecard is only likely to be effective if senior managers are committed to using it. If they revert to focusing solely on the financial measures they are used to, then the value of introducing additional (non-financial) measures will be reduced.

In this respect, the proposal to derive employees' targets for the performance reward system to the BSC seems sensible, because it encourages managers and staff to focus on all four perspectives of the scorecard.

(e) **Setting targets**

Challenging targets – When setting targets it is important to find a balance between ones which are too easy (and therefore don't require any effort to achieve) and ones which are too difficult (and are therefore demotivating because staff feel they are unachievable).

In this respect, challenging – or **stretch** – targets provide a middle ground between targets which are too easy and those which are perceived to be unachievable.

This is the balance which Kolmog is trying to find with its new performance reward system.

Unachievable targets – The history of rewards at Kolmog suggests that, in the past, the targets set have been too difficult to achieve. The fact that 75% of staff have received no bonus in previous years suggests that the bonus scheme would not motivate staff because they would never expect to qualify for a bonus.

Standards

In their 'building block' model, Fitzgerald and Moon highlight that in order for performance measures to be effective, employees must view the measures as being **fair** and **achievable**, and the employees must take **ownership** of them.

Achievability – The fact that 75% of the staff have not received a bonus in previous years suggests that Kolmog's reward scheme has historically not been an effective tool for motivating employees. If the staff feel the bonus targets are unachievable, they will only put in the minimum amount of effort they need to keep their jobs, rather than making any extra effort in the hope of receiving some extra reward as a result.

If the new targets are to be more effective in this respect, it is important that they are perceived to be more realistic to achieve.

Ownership – If the performance targets are based on budgets set by the Finance Department, this may also contribute to the sense of staff not accepting the targets and trying to achieve them. In particular, hotel managers' performance should only be judged against factors they can **control**. For example, if there is a downturn in market conditions, there is likely to be a downturn in revenue which managers cannot control.

Fairness – As we noted earlier in relation to segmental analysis, there are likely to be differences in the performance of different types of hotel. The concept of fairness suggests that targets should be adjusted for different types of hotel. For example, targets for city centre hotels should be comparable to each other, but may not be comparable to country house hotels.

Rewards

Rewards are the motivators which encourage employees to work towards the standards set. In order for rewards to be effective, they need to be clear, motivating and controllable.

Clarity – The employees need to be clear about the goals they are working towards.

Motivating – Employees need to be motivated to work towards the targets and in pursuit of the organisation's strategic objectives.

Controllability – Staff should not be held responsible for aspects of performance over which they have no control.

Issues with the proposed system

Ownership – The new system will propose that managers' targets are based on their hotel's performance against budgeted profit. However, if the budgets continue to be set by the head office Finance Department with no input from the managers, then there is likely to be a lack of ownership of the targets. Therefore, hotel managers should be involved in the budget-setting process.

Fairness – Comparing staff turnover against an industry-wide standard may not be fair if managers cannot control staff wages. If wages are set centrally, and are not attractive compared to the wages offered by other hotel chains, staff turnover is likely to be high, and there will be little that managers can do to prevent this. A fairer measure would be to compare the staff turnover for individual hotels against other hotels of the same type within Kolmog.

Aligned to mission – Customer satisfaction is a controllable factor for hotel managers and therefore customer satisfaction scores should be an important element of performance assessment. However, given Kolmog's stated mission 'to become the No. 1 hotel chain' it would be better to compare customer satisfaction scores against the scores achieved by Kolmog's competitors. The current proposal (to measure managers against the internal average) will not directly help Kolmog improve its performance against its competitors.

Clarity – The hotel managers' bonuses will be determined by their regional manager's assessment of their performance against the targets. In order for the reward system to be effective, the regional managers will need to explain the structure of the new scheme (for example, if there are different levels of bonus below the full 30%), and also the factors which will influence their assessment of the hotel managers' performance.

Ultimately, the success of the new scheme will depend on the extent to which it motivates staff and managers to help Kolmog achieve its mission. To do this, the targets will need to be stretching, but also to be perceived as achievable. In this respect, Kolmog should monitor the number of staff receiving bonuses to assess whether more staff are qualifying for some kind of bonus than under the old scheme.

Question 2

Marks

(a) Calculations:
Use of Q1 actual figures as starting point – 1 mark
Revenue: Sales volume increase – 1 mark
Sales price change from Q3 onwards – 1 mark
Cost of sales: Sales volume increase – 1 mark
Exchange rate percentage – 1 mark
Application of exchange rate change – 1 mark
Distribution costs: Sales volume increase – 1 mark
Fuel tax percentage – 1 mark
Application of fuel tax charge – 1 mark
Administration savings – 1 mark
Comments on calculations (impact on operating profit) – up to 2 marks
Total for part (a): up to 12 marks

12

(b) Use of incremental budgeting in the divisions – up to 8 marks
Use of rolling budgeting in the divisions – up to 8 marks
Total for part (b): up to 13 marks

13

Total = 25

(a) Recalculate the budget for Luxury Division to the end of the current year.

	Q1 (Actual) C$'000	Q2 C$'000	Q3 C$'000	Q4 C$'000	Total C$'000
Revenue (W1)	10,400	12,240	11,388	7,247	41,275
Cost of sales (W2)	(6,240)	(7,020)	(6,370)	(4,654)	(24,284)
Gross profit	4,160	5,220	5,018	2,593	16,991
Distribution costs (W3)	(624)	(734)	(682)	(434)	(2,474)
Administration costs (W4)	(2,296)	(2,243)	(2,186)	(2,132)	(8,857)
Operating profit	1,240	2,243	2,150	27	5,660

Recalculating Luxury Division's budget for the year to reflect current conditions gives a more realistic target for the division managers. For the coming year, the effect of this is very significant and represents a much more challenging target for managers as it increases the expected total annual operating profit by 42% (5,660/4,000) over the original budget.

Workings

1 *Revenue*

	Q1 (Actual) C$'000	Q2 C$'000	Q3 C$'000	Q4 C$'000	Total C$'000
Original budget	10,400.0	12,000.0	11,000.0	7,000.0	40,400.0
2% sales volume		240.0	220.0	140.0	600.0
1.5% sales price			168.3	107.1	275.4
Total	10,400.0	12,240.0	11,388.3	7,247.1	41,275.4

2   *Cost of sales*

	Q1 (Actual) C$'000	Q2 C$'000	Q3 C$'000	Q4 C$'000	Total C$'000
Original budget	6,240.0	7,120.0	6,460.0	4,720.0	24,540.0
2% sales volume		142.4	129.2	94.4	366.0
6.67% exchange rate*		(242.2)	(219.7)	(160.6)	(622.5)
Total	6,240.0	7,020.2	6,369.5	4,653.8	24,283.5

*6.67% = 1 − (1.4/1.5), applied to 50% of Cost of sales.

3   *Distribution costs*

	Q1 (Actual) C$'000	Q2 C$'000	Q3 C$'000	Q4 C$'000	Total C$'000
Original budget	624.0	720.0	660.0	420.0	2,424.0
2% sales volume		14.4	13.2	8.4	36.0
1.31% fuel tax increase*			8.8	5.6	14.4
Total	624.0	734.4	682.0	434.0	2,474.4

*1.31% = 70% × (3/160)

4   *Administration costs*

	Q1 (Actual) C$'000	Q2 C$'000	Q3 C$'000	Q4 C$'000	Total C$'000
Original budget	2,296.0	2,300.0	2,300.0	2,300.0	9,196.0
2.5% compound savings		(57.5)	(113.6)	(168.3)	(339.4)
Total	2,296.0	2,242.5	2,186.4	2,131.7	8,856.6

Workings for savings in administration costs

Q2   2,300.0 × 2.5% = 57.5
Q3   57.5 + (2,242.5 × 2.5%) = 113.6
Q4   113.6 + (2,186.40 × 2.5%) = 168.3

(b)   **Incremental budgeting**

This is the type of budgeting which Framiltone currently uses. The starting point of incremental budgeting is usually the previous year's actual performance or budget. This is then updated for any known changes in costs, or for inflation. The budget would normally remain unchanged for the remainder of the year.

Incremental budgeting is suitable for use in organisations which are stable and not undergoing significant changes. This is the case for Dairy Division, which operates in a saturated market and has little opportunity to grow.

Production volumes in Dairy Division have only increased by 0.5% over a full five years, so it is a very stable business. Dairy Division has stability of both revenues and costs. It has long-term fixed cost and volume supply agreements with its supermarket customers. It also has similar fixed contracts with its suppliers of milk, the most significant raw material ingredient used in its products.

Though the third-party distribution company is able to pass on some increases in fuel costs to Dairy Division, these are capped at only 0.5% per year. This is significantly less than the tax increases which will increase Luxury Division's fuel costs after the start of Q3. It appears that Dairy Division has relatively little exposure to rising fuel prices.

Furthermore, these increases are agreed prior to the setting of the current year budget, so there is no need to update these costs on an ongoing basis throughout the year.

As the dairy foods market is saturated and stable, there is little opportunity for the division to incur discretionary costs such as research and development of new products.

Incremental budgeting is only suitable for business where costs are already well controlled. This is because a big disadvantage of incremental budgeting is that it perpetuates inefficient activities by often simply building inflation into previous year results or budgets. It appears that Dairy Division, having been in existence for a relatively long time, does have good cost control as it has a modern production plant and is recognised as having the most efficient production processes in the industry.

Incremental budgeting may, however, build in budget slack. Managers may spend up to their budgeted amounts in one year, so that their budget is not cut the next, which may affect their appraisal and reward in the future. It is unclear whether this is occurring at Dairy Division, though for many years (while Dairy Division was the only division at Framiltone) the budgets set following consultation with divisional managers have just been achieved. This may be consistent with the stability of the division, but could also indicate that budgets were not set at a challenging enough level, even though Dairy Division had the best performance of the two divisions last year.

It is not therefore advisable that rolling budgets are introduced in Dairy Division, as the current incremental process appears satisfactory. This is especially so since divisional managers have little experience of setting their own budgets, and the time and cost of using rolling budgets would exceed the value of them to the division.

Rolling budgets

Rolling budgets are continually updated to reflect current conditions and are usually extended by budgeting for an additional period after the current period, for example, a quarter, has elapsed. That way, the budget always reflects the most up to date trading conditions and best estimates of future costs and revenues, usually for the next four quarters.

Rolling budgets are suitable for businesses which change rapidly or where it is difficult to estimate future revenues and costs.

Luxury Division was only set up two years ago, and is therefore a relatively new business. It also operates in quite a different sector of the industry to that in which Dairy Division operates and where Framiltone has most experience. There is likely to be considerable uncertainty as to future costs and revenues as Framiltone has little direct experience on which to base its forecasts.

Whereas Dairy Division operates in a saturated and stable market, Luxury Division uses rare ingredients which are subject to variations in availability and cost, for example, as a result of poor harvests. There is no indication that Luxury Division has fixed price and volume contracts with its customers or suppliers and is therefore likely to suffer from instability of supply as well as demand resulting from changes in consumer tastes.

The frequent changes in the product range are also likely to make forecasting for a year ahead difficult. The fact that a large proportion of ingredients are imported from Veeland makes costs susceptible to changes in the C$:V$ exchange rates which can quickly make an annual budget out of date, though managers may use methods such as forward contracts to reduce these movements. If managers are appraised on a budget which is out of date or unrealistic, they are likely to give up trying to achieve the budget, which will negatively affect the performance of Framiltone.

Rolling budgets will provide a more accurate basis on which to appraise managers at Luxury Division as they incorporate the best known estimates of future costs and revenues. It can be seen by the recalculation following Q1 results that Luxury Division's revised budgeted operating profit for the year has increased significantly by 42% (5,660/4,000), most of which is due to exchange rate changes. Where costs and revenues are likely to change during the period, rolling budgets give a much more realistic basis on which to appraise divisional performance and appraise and reward divisional managers. Budgets are likely to be achievable, which will motivate managers to try to achieve them.

Though the regular updating of the budget required in rolling budgeting is costly, time consuming and possibly a distraction for divisional managers, it does seem that rolling budgets are more suitable for Luxury Division than the current incremental approach particularly as, being realistic and achievable, they will increase managers' motivation to achieve the budget and so improve the performance of the business.

Question 3

Marking scheme

(a) **Strengths and weaknesses of quantitative and qualitative models for predicting corporate failure**

Quantitative methods such as the Z-score use publicly available financial data to predict whether a firm is likely to fail in the two-year period. The calculation is easy to make using the model but the calculation is only a probability, not an absolute likelihood, so it may need to be used with other data to make a more rounded assessment. It also only gives guidance below the danger level of 1.8 so other scores are difficult to interpret.

Furthermore, the model is based on historical trading patterns of a specific group of companies so a change in trading patterns or a company that falls outside the industry grouping used may find the model inaccurate. There is also a danger that companies in trouble use creative accounting in calculating figures which means where these go into calculations they are unreliable.

Qualitative models attempt to 'fill in the gaps' that quantitative models leave by using in-depth questionnaires but again these have their flaws. For instance, the Argenti A score uses fairly subjective categories to calculate an overall score. These are wide ranging but can be answered subjectively and be open to bias.

(b) **Comment on the results in the junior analyst's spreadsheet**

The Z-score for RMB in 20Y0 is 1.45 which is below the danger level of 1.8 and so suggests a likelihood of insolvency in the next two years. It has fallen over the past three years between 2.746 and 1.45. During this period the variables making up the model have been mostly static or declining. Roughly half the decline in the Z-score arises from variable X_4 (market value of equity/total long term debt) which has fallen from 1.510 to 0.478 or 68%. The bulk of the movement arises from a significant increase in long-term borrowings from $465m to $1,261m because of the investment in new equipment. The average share price has fallen from $1.56 in 20X8 to $1.34 in 20Y0 or 14% in the last year, though it would be useful to see if this is a general market trend and so a comparison with competitor share prices is advisable.

The other variable that has seen most decline is variable X3 (PBIT/TA) falling from 0.227 to 0.078 which reflects a sharp fall in profits ($185m to $65m) and an increase in total assets ($1,355m to $2,456m) thus the company has failed to extract profit from available assets. Maybe this will improve in future periods as revenue from the new investments is earned.

(c) **Qualitative problems in the company's structure and performance and why these are relevant to possible failure**

Using the Argenti A score model, the problems a company is experiencing may be broken down into three broad categories: defects, mistakes made and symptoms of failure. Looking at RMB, defects exhibited are a dominant chief executive officer, a failure to split the chief executive and chairman roles and passive senior management.

Mistakes made by RMB include a reliance on one large project to fuel growth, which is risky and relies on the success of the project. Overtrading as revenue rises is another mistake mainly funded by debt thus gearing has risen from 107% to 197% and interest cover has declined from 8.8 times to 2.0 times. This reliance on debt funding leads to a risk of failure to service debt payments.

Finally symptoms of failure. The information available doesn't reveal these yet but they typically include high turnover, low morale and creative accounting.

(d) **Assess the results of analysis in parts (b) and (c) and state what additional data should be obtained to assess the company's financial health**

The company is still profitable, making $65m of profits in 20Y0. Its revenues are still growing (from $1,560m to $1,915m over the past year) but operating costs have increased by 50% from 20X8 to 20Y0 and interest charges have gone up by $60m over that period. Thus margins have suffered (falling from 21% to 10% operating margin over the period). It is likely at the early stage of the project that costs will be high and revenues low. So a longer-term view needs to be taken before concluding the company is definitely failing.

However, the decline in the margin needs further explanation looking at costs in detail and how these are being controlled.

Finally it would be useful to compare the fall in the share price with the movement in the market to assess whether this is a general trend or reflecting sentiment over RMB's prospects.

(e) **Selling price changes**

Maturity – Sales prices are likely to decrease significantly at the maturity stage. Competitors will have flooded the market with alternative products and RMB is likely to have to reduce its sales prices as a means of sustaining demand for its product and maintaining its market share.

Decline – At the decline stage, demand is likely to fall further, as the product becomes superseded by the next generation of 'new' products. Therefore, price will be lowered further in order to try to attract business sales. RMB may attempt to prolong the life of its product by reducing selling prices significantly at this stage, although such a decision may depend on whether RMB has developed a next generation product of its own.

Prices are also likely to be forced down by over-capacity in the industry. If the selling price becomes too low (so that the product becomes loss making) RMB may decide to stop selling it.

Production cost changes

Total production costs are likely to change with unit sales over the course of the product life cycle. However, the more important changes for RMB will be how unit production costs vary over the life cycle.

Maturity – At the maturity stage, the growth in demand for the product will have slowed significantly. As we have already mentioned, price becomes more sensitive as firms compete with one another to try to increase their share of a static market.

In order to maximise profits, while defending market share, RMB will look to reduce its costs; for example, by automating and standardising production processes as far as possible.

Decline stage – RMB will need to continue to control costs at a low level during the decline phase, to try to retain a positive cash flow for as long as possible despite falling prices and falling demand.

However, as there is unlikely to be any investment in the machinery used to make the product, there could be an increase in costs due to machine breakdowns and inefficiencies.

ACCA Strategic Professional – Options

Advanced Performance Management (APM)

Mock Exam 2

(ACCA Specimen exam)

Questions	
Time allowed	3 hours 15 minutes
This exam is divided into two sections	
Section A	This ONE question is compulsory and MUST be attempted
Section B	BOTH questions are compulsory and MUST be attempted

DO NOT OPEN THIS EXAM UNTIL YOU ARE READY TO START
UNDER EXAMINATION CONDITIONS

SECTION A – This question is compulsory and must be attempted

Question 1

Company information and mission

Iron Chicken (IC) is a multinational business which manufactures commercial building control systems. Building control systems include heating and air-conditioning systems, lighting controls, power and water monitoring and security systems (eg keypad access, alarms and CCTV). IC's manufacturing takes place at a number of factory sites where some products have a long product life and are simple and mass-produced while other products are complex and have a short product life due to changing technologies.

IC's mission statement is 'to create value for shareholders through control products which improve productivity, save energy and increase comfort and safety'.

A new chief executive officer (CEO) has been appointed to address a decline in IC's share price in the last three years. This CEO has identified that the business has grown through acquisition and as a result she stated, 'senior management have focused on making corporate deals and not making control systems'. The CEO has declared that the business must focus on optimising its value generation rather than just getting larger through acquisitions. She has developed an improvement programme for IC.

You are a performance management expert within IC, and the CEO has tasked you with aiding her on four aspects of her improvement programme:

Economic value added (EVA™)

The CEO wants your views on the use of economic value added (EVA™) as the key performance metric at IC. You have been supplied with the current EVA™ calculation (Appendix 1) but there is some doubt about whether the junior management accountant who has done this work was sufficiently trained in the method.

Therefore, the CEO requires you to evaluate its accuracy and the assumptions which form part of the calculation and advise her on your results, providing calculations as needed.

Critical success factors (CSFs) and key performance indicators (KPIs)

The CEO believes that the poor performance of the company can be addressed by ensuring that the mission statement flows down into the performance management of the business. To that end, the following critical success factors (CSFs) and the associated key performance indicators (KPIs) have been identified.

CSF		Associated current KPi
1	Greater staff productivity	Units produced per labour hour
2	Reduction of wastage in production	Power consumed per unit produced
3	Greater innovation of products	Number of new products launched

The CEO wants you to briefly explain a weakness of the current KPI associated with each CSF and then provide a justified alternative KPI.

Improvement projects

In order to improve performance, the CEO plans to implement initiatives associated with 'lean' manufacturing.

Specifically, there are three projects which have been suggested, and the CEO needs your advice on these:

(1)   Move to just-in-time (JIT) manufacturing
(2)   Use Kaizen costing
(3)   Examine the costs of quality in achieving a 'zero defects' approach to manufacturing

The CEO has stated that she needs you to explain what the three improvement projects are, how they will help to meet the CSFs at IC, and also how they will impact the existing three KPIs.

New information system

The CEO is concerned about the implications of the improvement projects for IC's information systems as she feels that the systems are not currently suitable for the plan that she has. The current information systems of the company are based around the functional departments of the business such as manufacturing, marketing, finance and logistics. Each department has developed its own system, although all feed into the finance system which is the main one used for strategic decision making. In order that the department systems can all feed through to the current finance system, these current systems only handle quantitative data. The company is considering the implementation of a new information system. This new system will introduce networking technology in order to bring together all of the departmental systems into a new, single, corporate database. The CEO would like an assessment of the impact of this proposed, new information system on the three improvement projects.

Required

Write a report to the CEO of Iron Chicken to respond to her instructions for work on the following areas:

(a)   The use of economic value added (EVA™) as the key performance metric at IC   **(15 marks)**

(b)   Current key performance indicators   **(6 marks)**

(c)   The three improvement projects   **(15 marks)**

(d)   The impact of the proposed new information system on the three improvement projects
    (10 marks)

Professional marks will be awarded for the format, style and structure of the discussion of your answer.   **(4 marks)**

(Total = 50 marks)

APPENDIX 1

Economic value added	Year ended 30 June 20X5	
	$m	Note
Operating profit	551.4	
Add back: Non-cash expenses	15.1	
Marketing capitalised	23.1	5
Less: Tax	134.8	6
Lost tax relief on interest	24.5	7
Net operating profit after tax (NOPAT)	430.3	
Capital employed		
From the statement of financial position	2,401.0	10
Marketing spend capitalised	23.1	5
Adjusted capital employed	2,424.1	

WACC = (1/2 × 16%) + (1/2 × 6.8%) = 11.4%

EVA™ = NOPAT – (WACC × capital employed) = 154

Assumptions and notes

1	Debt/Equity	100.0%
2	Cost of equity	16.0%
3	Tax rate	30.0%
4	Cost of debt (pre-tax)	6.8%

5   There has been $23.1m spent on marketing each year for the last two years in order to build the brand of IC long term.

6   Tax paid in the year was $130m while the tax charged per the accounts was $134.8m.

7   Interest charged in the period was $81.6m.

Lost tax relief on this interest was 30% × $81.6m.

8   The only research and development spending identified in the last five years was $10m expensed during this year on a new product.

The product has not been launched yet.

9   Capital employed during the period (from the statement of financial position):

	$m
Opening	2,282.0
Change in period	119.0
Closing	2,401.0

SECTION B – BOTH questions are compulsory and MUST be attempted

Question 2

Company and industry background

Culam Mining (Culam) is a mineral ore mining business in the country of Teeland. It owns and operates four mines. A mine takes on average two years to develop before it can produce ore and the revenue from the mine is split (25:75) between selling the ore under fixed price contracts over five years and selling on the spot market. The bulk of the business's production is exported. A mine has an average working life of about 20 years before all the profitable ore is extracted. It then takes a year to decommission the site and return the land to a useable form for agriculture or other developments.

Recent events

One of Culam's foreign competitors surprised the market by becoming insolvent as a result of paying too much to acquire a competitor when the selling price of its minerals dipped as the world economy went into recession. As a result, the Chief Executive Officer (CEO) wanted to know if this was likely to happen to Culam. She had read about the Altman Z-score as a way of predicting corporate failure and had a business analyst prepare a report calculating the Z-score for Culam. The report is summarised in Appendix 1.

The analyst had done what was asked and calculated the score but had not explained what it meant or what action should be taken as a result. Therefore, the CEO has turned to you to help her to make sense of this work and for advice about how to use the information and how Culam should proceed into the future.

Required

(a)   Evaluate both the result of the analyst's calculations and the appropriateness of these two models for Culam.   **(10 marks)**

(b)   Explain the potential effects of a mine's life cycle on Culam's Z-score and the company's probability of failure.   **(7 marks)**

   Note. You should ignore its effect on the Q-score.

(c)   Give four detailed recommendations to reduce the probability of failure of Culam, providing suitable justifications for your advice.   **(8 marks)**

(Total = 25 marks)

APPENDIX 1

Analyst's report (extract)

The Altman Z-score model is:

$$Z = 1.2X_1 + 1.4X_2 + 3.3X_3 + 0.6X_4 + X_5$$

Another quantitative model (Q-score model) has been produced by academics working at Teeland's main university based on recent data from listed companies on the small Teeland Stock Exchange. It is:

$$Q = 1.4X_1 + 3.3X_3 + 0.5X_4 + 1.1X_5 + 1.7X_6$$

Where for both models:

X_1 is working capital/total assets

X_2 is retained earnings reserve/total assets

X_3 is profit before interest and tax/total assets

X_4 is market value of equity/total long-term debt (MVe/total long-term debt)

X_5 is revenue/total assets

X_6 is current assets/current liabilities

Using the most recent figures from Culam's financial statements (year ending September 20X4), Culam's Altman Z-score is 3.5 and its score from the other model (Q) is 3.1.

For both models, a score of more than 3 (for Z or Q) is considered safe and at below 1.8, the company is at risk of failure in the next two years.

Question 3

Company information and mission

Stokeness Engineering's (Stokeness) mission is to provide world-leading, reduced-emission, fuel-efficient power products for the motor industry in order to optimise shareholder returns.

Stokeness has existed for only five years and is owned by its management and venture capitalists (VCs). The management were all engineers who had been working on the basic research associated with new fuel technologies and saw the opportunity to commercialise their expertise. Stokeness is highly regarded in the industry for its advanced, efficient fuel cell designs. As a result, the VCs were eager to invest in Stokeness and have assisted by placing experienced managers into the business to aid the original engineering team.

New product development

Stokeness is developing hydrogen fuel cells for use in powering large motor vehicles such as buses and trucks. They will replace standard petrol/diesel engines. The fuel cells have a clear advantage over these older technologies in having lower carbon dioxide (a greenhouse gas) emissions. The governments of many developed countries are keen to see cuts in such emissions and are supportive of a variety of possible technological solutions to this issue (such as fuel cells, electrical batteries and compressed natural gas).

External business environment

It takes five to ten years to develop a viable product for sale in this motor market. There are a number of companies developing fuel cells but Stokeness is believed to have a two-year lead over them and to be only three years away from commercial launch.

Alternate power technologies, like the hydrogen fuel cells, would be fitted by the major international vehicle manufacturers into their vehicles for sale to their customers. The vehicle manufacturers will need to form a close partnership with any engine producer in order to make their technologies compatible, and this has already begun to happen, with two of the major manufacturers signing deals with other engine makers recently.

A major problem that needs to be overcome with any of these new technologies is that there must be an infrastructure accessible to the end users for refuelling their vehicles (as the petrol station chains do for petrol engine vehicles at present).

Governments have indicated their desire to support the development of such technologies to address environmental issues and to try to establish new, high-value industries in their jurisdiction. They may do this through tax breaks and investment to support the development of the refuelling infrastructure.

Production of Stokeness's fuel cells uses a special membrane that requires rare and expensive elements. Also, it has partnered with two other engineering firms to subcontract the production of certain components in the fuel cell. Stokeness has had to share much of its fuel cell design with these firms in order to overcome certain engineering difficulties.

Also, there are a number of start-up companies developing the other technologies mentioned above, as well as large, existing diesel and petrol engine manufacturers who are constantly reducing the emissions from their existing engines.

The VCs have stressed the need to analyse competition and competitive advantage in order to understand how to make the business profitable in the long term. The chief executive officer (CEO) of Stokeness wants to understand the external business environment and its effect on performance management.

Required

(a)   Using Porter's five forces model, assess the impact of the external business environment on the performance management of Stokeness and give a justified recommendation of one new performance measure for each of the five force areas at Stokeness.   **(16 marks)**

(b)   Discuss how the problems of defining the market in measuring a market share apply for Stokeness.   **(4 marks)**

(c)   Assess the risk appetite of the venture capitalists and discuss how this might impact on performance measurement at Stokeness.   **(5 marks)**

(Total = 25 marks)

Answers

DO NOT TURN THIS PAGE UNTIL YOU HAVE
COMPLETED THE MOCK EXAM

Exam success skills

In any APM exam it will be important to apply good general exam technique by using the six exam success skills identified at the start of the Revision Kit, in the section covering 'essential skills'. These skills are: 1. Case scenario: Managing information; 2. Correct interpretation of requirements; 3. Answer planning: Priorities, structure and logic; 4. Efficient numerical analysis; 5. Effective writing and presentation; and 6. Good time management.

Some examples of how to apply these skills in this exam are provided in the table below.

Skill	Examples
Managing information	It is crucially important to assimilate the information in the question scenario.
	In longer questions, such as the 50 mark question, it is difficult to assimilate information by simply starting at the beginning and read to the end because there is so much information to take in.
	Instead it is sensible to take an **active approach** to reading each question. Read enough of the question to get an idea of the basic scenario and then read the initial requirements so that you understand the first things that you are expected to do with this information.
	For example, in Q1 the lengthy scenario makes a lot more sense if, before reading all of it, you are aware that the first requirements relate to KPIs and economic value added.
Correct Interpretation of requirements	Be careful to interpret the verbs used in the question requirements carefully.
	For example, in Q2 part (c) required four **recommendations** *to reduce Culam's likelihood of failure. Weaker answers focused on the need to* **measure** *different factors (eg non-financial) without indicating what actions to then take to reduce the probability of failure.*
	Also be careful to identify where a question requirement contains more than one instruction.
	For example, in Q3 part (a) the question required the use of Porter's five forces model **and** *a justified recommendation of one new performance measure. Many candidates missed the second aspect to the question.*
Answer planning	Planning is always important in APM questions, because most of the marks are available for discussion and if your discussion points are not relevant to the scenario then they will not receive any credit.
	As a general rule, you should spend at least 20% of your time, reading the scenario and planning your answer.
Efficient numerical analysis	It is essential that the marker can follow your workings and your logic.
	If you make a mistake early in your calculations that affects your later calculations then the marker will only penalise the error you have made, and not its follow-on impact on other calculations. This means that it is not normally a good use of your time to correct such errors during the exam.

Skill	Examples
Effective writing and presentation	In APM this is a very important skill. You are often expected to be able to employ **critical analysis**, and this will sometimes mean that you will reject innovative and modern ideas in favour of less exotic tried and tested performance management tools. It is also very important to **relate your points to the scenario** and to the requirement wherever possible. This means that you will need to apply your theoretical knowledge to the scenario, not simply repeat a technical point as something that you have memorised. However, you will be tested on your understanding of the theoretical content of APM and **you will not be able to apply your theoretical knowledge to the scenario if you do not possess a strong understanding of the theories in the first place.** *For example, in Q2 it is not possible to discuss the Z score model unless you have a strong understanding of this concept in the first place.* **Relating your points to the scenario** does not mean simply repeating the details from the question, but using this information to help to explain the point you are making. *In Q1 part (d) many candidates reiterated the features of the new system that were given in the scenario, but provided little in the way of 'an assessment' of the impact this would have on the projects.* Finally, in Q1, to score the 4 **professional marks** that are available you should use suitable report headings, an introduction, a logical structure, signposted by the good use of subheadings in the answer, and a clear, concise style.
Good Time Management	The exam is 3 hours 15 minutes long, which translates to 1.95 minutes per mark. If you build in an allowance of 20% of your time for assimilating the scenario and planning, this falls to 1.56 minutes per mark (1.95 × 0.8). At the beginning of a question, work out the amount of time you should be spending on – Planning: for a 25 mark question this will be 1.95 × 25 marks × 20% = 10 minutes. For a 50 mark question this should be about 20 mins. – Writing your answer to each requirement: Take the mark allocation and multiply by 1.56 minutes per mark.

Diagnostic

Did you apply these skills when reading, planning, and writing up your answer? Identify the exam success skills where you think you need to improve and capture your thoughts here of what you want to achieve when attempting questions in future.

Question 1

Top tips.

Part (a). The scenario tells you that the CEO wants your views about the use of EVA™ as the key performance metric at IC. However, she doesn't want a general discussion about the merits of EVA™. Instead she wants a specific response to her request about evaluating the accuracy of the calculation and the assumptions used in it.

The fact that the scenario mentions that there are doubts about the junior management accountant's ability to calculate EVA™ should have alerted you to the likelihood that some of the figures in the calculation are wrong. However, this doesn't mean that all of the figures are necessarily wrong.

As such, a sensible approach to this question would be to work through the calculation methodically (line by line) identifying whether each of the current figures is correct or not. Where a figure is incorrect, you then need to adjust the calculation accordingly. In addition – applying your knowledge of the adjustments to operating profit required when calculating net operating profit after tax (NOPAT) – you need to consider if there are any figures which have been (incorrectly) omitted completely.

Part (b). The wording of the CEO's underlying requirement – to explain 'a weakness' and to provide 'a justified alternative' – means that there are a number of possible answers to it. You may have recommended different alternatives to the ones suggested in the solution below, but provided they are relevant (ie they help to measure performance against the CSF) and you have justified your recommendation you would earn the marks available. Nonetheless, to score the marks it is vital that you recommend a KPI (ie something that could be measured), not an alternative CSF.

Importantly, you should not spend too long on this part of the question, as there are only six marks available for it. Given that there are three CSFs, this means there are only two marks for each CSF: one for explaining a weakness of the current KPI associated with it, and one for providing a justified alternative KPI. The instruction in the question to 'briefly explain' is important – you shouldn't waste time giving a detailed explanation, particularly as there is only one mark available per weakness.

Part (c). The short paragraph in the scenario above the three projects – with its reference to 'lean' manufacturing – provides the context for this requirement. In effect, the three projects are ways of (hopefully) making IC's manufacturing 'leaner'.

As the three projects are clearly identified separately, a useful way of tackling the requirement would be to address each project in turn. Then for each project you need to do three things:

- Explain what the project is (ie what are, respectively, just-in-time manufacturing, Kaizen costing, and costs of quality/total quality manufacturing ('zero defects'))

- Explain how the project will help to achieve IC's CSFs (again the reference to 'lean' in the introductory paragraph here could provide a useful pointer here, since eliminating waste (CSF number 2) is one of the key aims of 'lean')

- Explain what impact the project will have on the KPIs

  (Note. Your focus here should be on the levels of performance as measured by the indicators; not on the choice of indicators.)

Note that for the second of the three parts you need to explain 'how' the project will help, whereas in the third you have to explain 'what' the impact will be. The distinction is important, because in some cases – eg in relation to the number of products launched – the projects may not affect the KPI. Make sure you state this, though; saying that the project will not have an impact is a valid answer, and so would earn you a mark.

Part (d). This final paragraph of the scenario describes the new information system. In essence, the new system is an enterprise resource planning system (ERPS) so, in effect, the question is asking how an ERPS would help the three projects.

This part of the question is quite challenging, but, of the three projects, the benefits can perhaps most easily be seen in relation to JIT. For example, in a demand–pull system, with no inventory, sharing information between different departments is likely to be crucial in avoiding stock-outs.

More generally, note that the scenario says that IC's current systems can only handle quantitative data. So, also think about the nature of the information required by the projects. For example, in order to reduce the level of defects, IC will presumably need to know what is causing those defects. But can a system which only handles quantitative data provide that information?

Overall. Remember that you have been asked to write a report, so make sure the style and structure of your answer, as well as its tone, is appropriate for a report.

Examining team's comments. Part (a) asked candidates to 'evaluate the accuracy' of an EVA™ calculation that had been provided. Many candidates spent time discussing the advantages and disadvantages of using EVA™ (such as it being closely related to cash flow) but this was not asked for in the requirement. Although a brief explanation of a model/technique may add some value to an answer, it does not warrant a lengthy discussion – unless this has been specifically asked for.

This type of question – which requires an evaluation of whether or not something is accurate – also requires candidates to do more than simply state whether it is right or wrong. Candidates need to state what is inaccurate, explain what the correct treatment should be, and explain why this is the case.

Worryingly, some students incorrectly interpreted a debt:equity ratio of 100% as meaning that the company was financed entirely by debt, and there was no equity. This is a fundamental error, and one which the marking team was surprised to see at this level.

Part (b) was generally well answered, but answers to part (c) were mixed. Many candidates were limited by the fact that they appear to have little knowledge of Kaizen costing and costs of quality.

Part (d) required an assessment of the impact a new information system would have on the three improvement projects. Many candidates reiterated the features of the new system that were given in the scenario, but provided little in the way of 'an assessment' of the impact this would have on the projects.

For a question like this – requiring an assessment of the information system on the projects – a good answer will identify what the information requirements of each project are and whether or not the new system will meet those requirements. For example, the implementation of initiatives such as just-in-time manufacturing is heavily reliant on an appropriate information system allowing for co-ordination of deliveries and manufacturing schedules in order to meet customer demands.

Marking scheme

Marks

(a) For calculation of corrected EVA™:
1 mark for identifying correct treatment of each of the following and adjusting
as necessary:
- Non-cash expenses
- Marketing expenses
- Research and development
- Tax paid
- Capital employed – opening figure
- WACC
- Economic value added

Maximum for calculation: 7 marks
1 mark per relevant point evaluating the assumptions and advising on the
corrections – up to 10 marks
Total for part (a): up to 15 marks   15

(b)   KPIs for CSFs – up to 2 marks for each CSF
        (1 mark for the weakness of the current KPI; 1 mark for the justified alternative)
        Total for part (b): up to 6 marks   6

(c)   Quality improvement projects
        Definitions and descriptions of the projects – up to 2 marks
        Analysis of the impact of the projects on IC's CSFs and KPIs – up to 6 marks
          per project
        Maximum for part (c): up to 15 marks   15

(d)   New unified database
        Definition and general points – up to 3 marks
        Interaction with each project – up to 3 marks each
        Other comments (eg quantitative vs qualitative information) – up to 3 marks
        Maximum for part (d): up to 10 marks   10

        Professional marks – up to 4 marks   4
                                                                            Total = 50

Report

To	Board of Iron Chicken (IC)
From:	Performance management expert
Date:	[today's date]

Subject: Performance management issues at IC

Introduction

This report evaluates the accuracy and assumptions used in the calculation of EVA™. It then suggests new KPIs for the current CSFs at IC. Finally it considers the impact of three quality improvement projects on these CSFs and a proposed new information system.

(a)   **EVA™**

        Although some elements of it have been performed correctly, there are a number of errors in the existing calculation of EVA™. The correct treatments are described below, and then the corrected EVA™ is calculated.

        Non-cash expenses are correctly added back to profit as such costs are treated as unacceptable accounting adjustments on a cash-based view.

        Marketing activities for long-term benefit are also correctly added back as they generate future value for the business. The prior year marketing expenditure is also added into capital employed.

        Research and development (R&D) expenditure should be added back to profit in the same way that the long-term marketing spending is. (Note. There was no R&D expenditure in the prior year.)

        The **tax cost** in the calculation should be the amount paid, adjusted for lost tax on interest, not the adjusted amount of tax charged in the accounts.

        The **WACC** is incorrectly calculated as it should be based on the post-tax cost of debt.

        The **capital employed** figure should be based on the figure at the start of the year (opening capital employed), not the end of the year.

Economic value added	Year ended 30 June 20X5
	$m
Operating profit	551.4
Add back: Non-cash expenses	15.1
Marketing capitalised	23.1
Research and development	10.0
Less: Tax	130.0
Lost tax relief on interest	24.5
NOPAT	**445.1**
Capital employed	
At 20X5 year start	2,282.0
Marketing spend capitalised from YE 30 June 20X4	23.1
Adjusted capital employed at 20X5 year start	**2,305.1**

WACC = (1/2 × 16%) + (1/2 × 6.8% × (1 − 30%)) = 10.38%

EVA™ = NOPAT − (WACC × Capital employed)

= 445.1 − (2,305.1 × 10.38%) = **$205.8m** (rounded to **$206m**)

The recalculated EVA™ has increased from 154 million to $206m which still indicates a positive position for the company as it adds to shareholder wealth.

In addition to the corrections above, the following assumptions in the calculation require comment:

(1)   There is an implicit assumption that accounting depreciation (included in operating profit) is equivalent to economic depreciation (which should be used for EVA™ calculations). This is questionable generally, although there is no information to allow a more accurate calculation. Also, there is additional marketing spending which will probably have a limited economic life in building the brand. No estimation of this life and the resulting additional economic depreciation has been attempted in the above calculation.

(2)   It has been assumed that no amortisation needs to be charged on the R&D costs since the product has not yet launched. This is in line with the accounting treatment of such items.

(b)   **KPIs for the CSFs**

Greater staff productivity

The current measure of units produced per labour hour does not reflect the skill and effort which goes into producing different units. The products of IC range from complex to simple and so revenue per employee would better reflect the different skill levels involved in production.

Reduction of wastage

The weakness of the existing measure is that it only looks at one cost area of production (power consumption). Inventory (stock) obsolescence will measure the wastage due to technological change which is present in the complex products produced by IC.

Greater innovation of products

Measuring the number of new products launched doesn't reflect the extent to which IC's innovations can become a sustainable source of value for its shareholders. The number of patents filed will reflect greater innovation at IC, but patents also legally protect groups of products. This will represent a stronger measure of innovation than new products launched, since the patent gives legal exclusivity.

> **Tutorial note.** There are many possible acceptable answers to this question. For example, alternatives you could have suggested are:
>
> **Greater staff productivity.** Actual staff hours as a percentage of standard hours for actual production as this would measure staff efficiency in producing a wide range of products.

> **Reduction of wastage.** Input/output analysis of material which looks at the percentage of material purchased which goes into the final product.
>
> **Greater innovation of products.** Percentage of income earned from products which did not exist last year. This will measure the ability of IC to develop successful products. (The existing measure would record unsuccessful products as innovation.)

(c) **Lean manufacturing projects**

The three projects link together as improvements to the quality of the manufacturing process at IC. There are common elements to these projects in the elimination of waste and empowerment of employees which will occur in the long term. In the short term, there may be increased costs due to these disruptive changes.

Just-in-time (JIT) manufacturing

JIT seeks to produce on a pull basis to meet the customers' demands, rather than to produce products for inventory, which then acts as a buffer between production levels and demand. The main impact of JIT is the reduction of inventory which is held. The main enablers for such a system are a need for close links to customers and suppliers in order to predict demand and to quickly supply that demand.

In terms of IC's CSFs, this project will improve productivity as production lines must be made more flexible to meet changes in demand, although it should be noted that there could be a negative impact as constant changes in production lines will require more time to be spent setting up new production runs. It will also help to reduce wastage through losses in inventory as there will be less inventory. It also pushes some of the responsibility for improved quality of components (and reduced wastage) on to suppliers. However, it does not directly impact on product innovation.

The project will not necessarily immediately change any of the existing KPIs as it is about producing the right products at the right time, not necessarily producing more products for any given input, and it does not impact directly on new product launches.

Use Kaizen costing

Kaizen costing aims to reduce current costs of production through continuous improvement. Each period, goals for lower costs are set and then performance monitored against these using variances. At the end of the period, a new lower cost goal is set for the next period. The process also often uses target costing to set the initial planned cost of a product thus incorporating the idea of only producing what the customer values. The purpose is to build into the control of the production process the idea of continuous improvement.

This project has the explicit aim of reducing waste and improving productivity and so is directly linked to the first two CSFs. As a result, it will have an impact on the KPIs which are related to productivity and resource consumption. The project will also require the empowerment of staff to make improvement decisions within their quality circles (teams) and so it may give scope for more innovative thinking. However, this thinking is not aimed at producing new products but at improving the production process, so new product innovation may only be affected indirectly.

Costs of quality and a 'zero defects' approach to manufacturing

Costs of quality can be broken down into four parts:

(1) Prevention costs which occur before or during production and aim to prevent the production of defective products;

(2) Appraisal costs which occur after production and aim to check that products meet quality standards;

(3) Internal failure costs which occur when products are identified as defective before delivery to the customer and so are scrapped or reworked; and

(4) External failure costs which occur when defective products are delivered to the customer.

The 'zero defects' approach is also known as 'total quality management' (TQM). The TQM philosophy is that it is better to spend money on prevention, which involves challenging all aspects of the production process in order to improve and so avoid failure costs.

This project will affect the CSFs relating to improved productivity and waste by reducing defective products, provided that staff time is not adversely affected by aiming for perfection in production. In terms of the KPIs, it may lead to increased time in production but reduced wastage. It will not have a direct impact on power consumption. Again, this project is unlikely to affect the number of new products launched as it focuses on the production process, not product development.

(d)   **New information system**

The move to a single database for the organisation will integrate the subsystems from different functions (such as production and sales). It will require existing systems to be networked and compatible or else be replaced. It will affect overall decision making by improving the visibility of each function's operations to the others and to the strategic decision makers. This shift is often achieved by using an ERPS and a strategic enterprise management system.

The unified database will be critical in achieving the goal of JIT manufacturing as close links between production scheduling and demand forecasts will be required in order to match production runs with demand forecasts/orders. Also, the production schedules will need links to inventory levels in warehousing so that inventory is run down before new production is initiated. As closer communication with suppliers and customers will also be required, some change to existing information systems will be necessary in any case. It may be worthwhile to consider including electronic data interchange (EDI) in the specifications of the new system.

In using Kaizen costing, cross-functional communication will be important. The design team will need to communicate with the production team so that the design is more easily streamlined for production. The financial systems will need to be frequently updated for information from the quality circles as improvements are made. This will affect the Kaizen cost targets which need to be continually monitored and new targets set regularly. Quality circles often involve groups from across the business and so a common information system will facilitate communications amongst them.

The introduction of TQM will require clearer reporting of quality costs to assist in the ongoing motivation of staff, which is often a problem in TQM. Informing the quality teams of the impact that increased prevention costs are having on lowering failure costs will be important in maintaining the push to zero defects. The quality improvements and changes to production processes will need to be communicated across IC's different sites which the new database can facilitate.

The nature of the data used in the current system is quantitative but with the new projects there will be a need to communicate qualitative information, for example, relating to the nature of defects or the new production processes put in place. This will require a fundamental change to existing systems which again motivates the change to a new database.

Question 2

Marks

(a)   For general interpretation of the calculations – 1 mark

For general description of how a quantitative model works – 1 mark per relevant point – up to a maximum of 4 marks

For relevant comments on the problems with the models, in relation to their use at Culam – up to a maximum of 9 marks

Total for part (a): up to 10 marks   10

(b)   For general issues around life cycles and the probability of
     failure – up to 2 marks

     Description of a mine's life cycle (development – production –
     decommissioning) – 1 mark

     For explaining the impact of the life cycle on Culam's Z-score –
     up to 6 marks

     Total for part (b): up to 7 marks   7

(c)   Up to 2 marks for each valid recommendation – 1 mark for the
     improvement being recommended and 1 mark for the
     justification – up to 8 marks

     Possible recommendations include, but are not limited to:

     Increasing size of the business – portfolio effect

     Learn from the mistakes of others – avoid big project failures

     Use of fixed price contracts to avoid volatile commodity prices

     Use of foreign exchange hedging to avoid revenue volatility

     Total for part (c): up to 8 marks   <u>8</u>

                                                 Total = <u>25</u>

(a)   Results of the calculations

In both calculations, Culam's score is greater than the score at which it is considered safe.
Therefore, the models suggest that the company is not at risk of failing in the next two
years. However, the models are only valid for a single point in time, and do not indicate
whether Culam's financial condition is improving or deteriorating.

Moreover, Culam should not place too much confidence in these results because there are
a number of factors which reduce how appropriate the models are for assessing its risk of
failing.

Z-score

Quantitative models use financial ratios to predict the likelihood of business failure and
bankruptcy. Altman's research (from which the Z-score was devised) looked at a range of
variables in relation to companies which failed and which didn't fail. From this, he identified
that the five key indicators of the likely failure – or not – of a company were: liquidity;
profitability; efficiency; leverage; and solvency. These characteristics are represented, in
turn, by the five ratios used to calculate a company's Z-score.

The Z-score model enables analysts to identify companies which share the characteristics
of ones which have previously failed, and are therefore at risk of failing themselves.

However, there are a number of factors which affect the reliability of the Z-score model,
and three of these could significantly reduce its appropriateness for Culam.

Industry characteristics – The model will be most relevant for companies in similar
industries and of similar size to the ones which Altman analysed in his initial research.
Altman's data was primarily collected from the manufacturing sector, whereas Culam is a
mining company. As such, it may not be appropriate to use the model without some
modification to reflect the different financial characteristics of the mining companies
compared to manufacturing companies – for example, their capital intensiveness.

Geographical location – The companies Altman studied were US companies, whereas Culam is based in Teeland. Apart from the fact it only has a small stock exchange, we do not know anything about the economy in Teeland, and therefore how similar or dissimilar it is to the US. However, if, for example, Culam is a developing country, this would reduce the relevance of comparisons based on the US.

Historical context – Altman's research was conducted in the late 1960s, and so the data used in his model is about 50 years old now. The global economy has changed significantly during that time, so it is debatable how relevant the original data is, generally, for companies today.

Q-score

Reliability of model – The Q-score model appears to overcome some of the limitations of the Z-score model – because it is based on recent data, and it relates to local (Teeland) companies rather than US ones.

However, Teeland's stock exchange is only small, which will reduce the sample size from which the academics developed their model. Perhaps more importantly, it is not clear how many companies in Teeland have failed recently; but if this number is small, this means the academics have derived their model from very limited data.

Industry characteristics – It is also not clear what the mix of companies listed on Teeland's stock exchange is like. For example, if the majority of the companies listed on the stock exchange are manufacturing or service companies, then their financial characteristics may not be comparable with Culam's.

Therefore, neither the Z-score nor the Q-score are likely to provide a reliable indicator of Culam's risk of failing. Moreover, given the nature of Culam's business model, its survival could also depend on world commodity prices and foreign exchange rates. However, both models focus only on its internal financial characteristics, rather than looking at any external environmental factors.

(b)   **Impact of mine's life cycle on Z-score**

In total, a mine has a 'life' of 23 years: 2 for its initial development, 20 in production, and 1 for decommissioning.

Development phase – In the first two years, no revenue or profits will be generated, and the mine will require a large amount of capital investment. This investment, coupled with the underlying asset value of the mine and its ore, means that Culam's total assets will be increasing during this period.

X1, X2, X3 and X5 in the Z-score all use 'total assets' as their denominator, meaning that the Z-score will fall during this period, given the absence of any revenue or profit from the mine.

The weightings in the model mean that X3 (PBIT/total assets) has the greatest impact on the overall score; therefore the fact that the mine is not generating any profit during this period could lead to quite a significant reduction in Culam's Z-score.

Production phase – In this phase, the mine will be earning revenues, and hopefully will be profitable.

However, the asset value of the mine will begin to fall, as reserves of the ore begin to be extracted, and as the capital investment begins to be depreciated. Therefore, we would expect the Z-score to be higher during this period.

Decommissioning phase – In this final phase, there will be no revenues, although the value of Culam's assets will also be falling. As such, we could again expect a relatively low Z-score in this phase, although probably not as low as during the initial development phase (because the value of total assets will be lower now).

Life cycle and probability of failure

Since Culam only owns four mines, the phase in which any one mine has reached in its life cycle could have a significant impact on the company's overall Z-score. For example, if two mines are being developed at the same time, then this is likely to lead to a significant reduction in the Z-score.

Although Culam will need to develop new mines to sustain its business as its existing mines reach the end of their lives, the capital investment required during the development phase will make significant demands on its financial resources. As such, the extent of the financial resources which Culam can call on over the life of the mines could be crucial in dictating its survival.

(c)   **Recommendations for reducing the probability of failure**

Increase number of mines – As Culam currently only has four mines, the performance of any single mine will have a significant impact on the company's overall results. For example, if one of the mines proves much less profitable than had been expected, this could potentially threaten the future of the whole group.

If Culam increases the number of mines it owns, this will reduce its dependence on any single mine.

Effective due diligence – However, the recent demise of its competitor highlights that Culam must be careful not to pay too high a price for any new mines it acquires. As such, undertaking suitable due diligence and carrying out detailed risk analysis in advance of acquiring a new mine (or any other significant capital investment) should help reduce the probability of failure.

Securing long-term contracts – Currently, Culam sells 75% of its output on the spot market, and only 25% under long-term fixed price contracts. This mix makes Culam's revenues and cash inflows vulnerable to fluctuations in the commodity prices. However, if Culam increased the proportion of its output it sold under long-term contract this would provide greater certainty over its future revenues.

Hedging – Another way in which Culam could look to reduce risk is by using hedging techniques to reduce the volatility of its revenues and cash flows. As Culam currently sells 75% of its ore on the spot market it could benefit from hedging against a fall in the market prices of its ores.

In addition, the bulk of Culam's production is exported. Assuming that many of Culam's customers will be large industrial companies, it is likely that they will want to use their own currency for buying the ores rather than local currency of Teeland. Therefore, Culam could be vulnerable to fluctuations in foreign exchange risks, since its revenues will be earned in foreign currencies while its costs will be denominated in the local currency of Teeland.

As such, hedging against foreign exchange rate risk could also help to reduce the risk of failure.

Question 3

Top tips.

Part (a). Although this part of the question should offer some relatively easy marks (for analysing the impact the different forces could have on Stokeness), it is important that you realise that the requirement isn't only about the impact of the five forces. You also have to recommend a performance measure for each of the five forces.

This second element of the requirement (recommending new performance measures) requires careful thought. The performance measures need to measure the strength or impact of each of the **five forces** themselves, not primarily different aspects of Stokeness's own performance. So, for example, what would be a suitable measure to indicate the threat of new entrants?

Also, in relation to the first part of the requirement, note that you are asked about the impact of the five forces on **performance management** at Stokeness, not, for example, how the five forces could be used to assess the attractiveness of the industry. In other words, you should be thinking about how Stokeness could use an understanding of the five forces to improve its performance or develop its strategy, rather than simply identifying that a particular force is strong or weak.

Part (b). A key question here is: 'Who are Stokeness's competitors?' Is it competing against all engine manufacturers (including manufacturers of petrol/diesel engines)? Is it competing against suppliers of all the alternative technologies? Or is it only competing against other fuel cell manufacturers?

These questions should highlight the problem Stokeness faces when measuring a market share: unless it has identified its market, how can it measure its share of that market?

Part (c). Even though this part of the question is only worth five marks, in effect there are still two different elements to it: the VCs' risk appetite, and key issues in performance measurement at Stokeness.

Stokeness appears to be a technology start-up company, which suggests the VCs were prepared to accept a relatively high degree of risk by investing in it. Equally, they will expect returns from the company in the future. However, currently, Stokeness is still three years away from a commercial launch. So, for the moment, the key aspects of its performance relate to this pre-launch phase; for example, has Stokeness got sufficient cash to sustain it until it can begin to sell its products? If Stokeness runs out of money before it launches its fuel cells, then there is little chance of it generating any returns for the VCs in future.

Examining team's comments. Part (a) was generally well done, with candidates making good use of the information in the scenario to give useful performance management advice to Stokeness. However, many candidates appeared not to read the second part of the requirement fully: this asked for a **justified** recommendation of **one new** performance measure for each of the five forces. Instead, they simply produced a list of performance measures for each area, often also including market share, meaning that they failed, in three different ways, to answer the question.

Part (b) was poorly answered. Many candidates chose to answer the question 'How do you measure market share' thereby completely missing the point of the question actually set. However, better candidates realised that the definition of market (and hence its size) depended on whether you were talking about hydrogen fuel cells, alternative energy power technologies, or any sort of power unit (including existing petrol/diesel engines).

Similarly, in part (c), many candidates wasted time listing the different possible risk appetites, despite these not being required by the question set. Candidates are reminded that it is vital to read the requirement carefully, and to answer the question asked – not an alternative question of their own creation.

Marks

(a)   For each of Porter's five forces:

Up to 4 marks for performance management implications of the force, and justifying a suitable performance measure

Total for part (a): up to 16 marks

16

(b)   For each valid point made about the problems of defining Stokeness's markets – 1 mark per point

Total for part (b): up to 4 marks

4

(c)   For assessing the risk appetite of the VCs – 1 mark per valid point; up to 2 marks

For assessing the VCs' impact on performance measurement at Stokeness – 1 mark per valid point; up to 3 marks

Total for part (c): up to 5 marks

5

Total = 25

(a)   **Threat of new entrants**

Barriers to entry – The threat of new entrants into the fuel cell market will be determined by the extent of the barriers to entry into the market. The barriers to entry appear to be high, given the technical skills and the length of time required to develop a viable product.

These barriers to entry will be strengthened further by the need to develop a relationship with the vehicle manufacturers who will be the customers for the fuel cells. Even if a potential new entrant develops a viable product, they will not be able to establish themselves in the market unless they can attract any buyers for their product.

Performance measure: Patented revenue – One of the ways in which technology firms can create a barrier to entry into their markets is by registering patents over new products or technologies. In this respect, Stokeness needs to ensure that it obtains patents for new cell designs or technology processes which could provide it with competitive advantage.

A suitable performance measure to use here would be the percentage of revenue which is generated from patented protects. This will indicate the degree to which Stokeness's patents will act as a barrier to entry.

> **Other performance measures:**
>
> **Customer loyalty** – If vehicle manufacturers (customers) are committed to using Stokeness's cells on a long-term basis, this will make it harder for new entrants to join the market.
>
> To this end, it would be useful to measure customer loyalty by looking at the number (and value) of the long-term contracts Stokeness has to supply fuel cells to vehicle manufacturers.
>
> **Ratio of fixed cost to total cost** – This gives an indication of the capital required to develop and produce fuel cell products, and therefore the level of amount of capital a potential new entrant would need to be able to enter the market. If large amounts of capital are required, this could make it harder for new entrants to join the market.

Threat of substitutes

Alternative fuel sources – The existing petrol/diesel engines remain a substitute for Stokeness's products, especially as their manufacturers are reducing the level of carbon dioxide emissions from these engines. Equally, electrical batteries and compressed natural gas products could also be substitutes for the fuel cells.

The petrol/diesel engines still have a number of strengths in the market; in particular, they are the only fuel source for which there is an infrastructure in place which enables end users to refuel their vehicles easily.

Performance measure: Output – The level of threat from substitute products could be measured by analysing the power output of different types of power supply compared to the level of emissions they produce and the cost of producing the power.

The cost of creating different engine types and the price of the fuels required to run them are likely to be very significant in determining the extent to which different types of engine are considered viable by vehicle manufacturers.

Bargaining power of suppliers

Component elements – The membrane which is used to produce the fuel cells requires rare and expensive elements. As a result, the **suppliers' bargaining power is high**. Stokeness's ability to produce the fuel cells will depend on the price and availability of the elements required for the membrane.

In particular, if the supply of these elements is controlled by a small number of suppliers they will be in a particularly strong position to dictate the price of the elements.

Subcontractors – The engineering firms to which Stokeness has subcontracted the production of certain components for the fuel cell also have a high bargaining power because of the knowledge they have gained of Stokeness's products. In this respect, it is important that there is a non-disclosure agreement in place to protect any commercially sensitive details of the products.

The size of the two engineering firms relative to Stokeness is not clear from the scenario, but it is possible that one of them may also consider some kind of forward vertical integration if they feel that Stokeness's products are going to be commercially successful.

Performance measure: Switching cost – The power of the suppliers could be measured by estimating the cost involved in switching to an alternative supplier. This cost could include any penalty fees payable to the existing suppliers, as well as the opportunity cost of lost sales arising as a result of delays incurred in switching supplier. These delays could be quite significant, given the specialist nature of Stokeness's product, which any new suppliers would have to understand, and tailor their processes to, before production could re-commence.

Other performance measures:

Proportion of cost – An alternative measure of the suppliers' bargaining power could be taken as the price of the suppliers' components in relation to the cost of the fuel cell as a whole. Such a measure can give an indication of the importance of the components to the overall fuel cell.

Number of suppliers – It could also be useful to monitor the number of suppliers, because this will indicate the level of competition in that market. If the number of potential suppliers available to Stokeness increases, this could reduce their bargaining power.

Bargaining power of customers

Large manufacturers – Stokeness's customers are manufacturers of large vehicles, such as buses and trucks. It is likely there will only be relatively few of these companies, but they will be quite large, giving them significant bargaining power. Crucially, the manufacturers have a choice of what fuel source to use (for example, fuel cells or standard petrol/diesel engines), and before they agree to use Stokeness's cells they will need to be sure that the cells are compatible with the existing technologies used in the vehicles.

Switching costs – However, once customers have committed to using a particular type of power source, the cost of switching to an alternative source is likely to be high. This may reduce the bargaining power of customers, but only once Stokeness has secured them as customers. In this respect, the fact that Stokeness has a two-year lead over the other companies developing fuel cells could be a significant advantage to it, if it can secure some significant contracts before the competitors have developed their cells.

Given the relative size of Stokeness compared to the manufacturing companies, and the potential importance of the fuel cells in the engine production process, one of the manufacturers might try to acquire Stokeness. However, this might prove to be an attractive option for the venture capitalists, depending on the price offered.

Performance measure: Discounts requested – The level of discount which customers request would provide Stokeness with an indicator of how strong the customers perceive their bargaining power to be. If the customers feel that Stokeness's fuel cells will provide them with a significant competitive advantage, then they will be less likely to press hard for a discount.

Other performance measures:

Switching costs – The costs which a manufacturer would incur to switch from one power source to another could also be used as an indicator of the strength of the bargaining power of customers. The higher these costs are, the less likely a customer will want to switch power source, thereby reducing their bargaining power. Although Stokeness is unlikely to be able to calculate this figure exactly, it should nonetheless be able to make an estimate of it.

Number of alternative suppliers – The number of alternative suppliers which customers could choose from could also affect the customers' bargaining power.

Competitive rivalry

Development advantage – As Stokeness has a two-year lead over the other companies developing fuel cells, the level of existing competition from these companies currently seems low. If Stokeness patents any key technologies it develops, this should help sustain its competitive advantage over its direct competitors.

Moreover, if Stokeness is able to secure contracts with some of the vehicle manufacturers before the other companies have developed their products, this will make it harder for the competitors to break into the market. In turn, this could help reduce the level of competitive rivalry in the industry in the future.

Performance measure: Launch date – Once Stokeness and then the competitors have launched their products, it will be possible to measure the strength of competitive rivalry by analysing market share. Until that point, however, there isn't a 'market' to analyse. Instead, the time until the commercial launch date of a viable fuel cell is a key performance measure. Although it may be difficult to obtain exact information about competitors' expected launch dates, Stokeness should try to monitor these alongside its own.

This measure highlights the importance of avoiding any overruns in the development process, and in delivering a commercially viable product as soon as possible, thereby maintaining Stokeness's competitive advantage over the other companies which are also developing fuel cells.

> **Other performance measures:**
>
> **Partnership agreements** – An alternative measure could be the number of partnership agreements signed, with vehicle manufacturers, or the projected revenues – or volumes – under such agreements.

(b) **Market definition**

The problem of defining the market is a particular issue for Stokeness because there could be some significant variations in the extent of that market.

Overall large vehicle market – In the broadest terms, Stokeness makes power supplies for large commercial vehicles such as buses and trucks. Therefore, its market share could be seen as the number of commercial vehicles powered by Stokeness's fuel cells as a proportion of the total number of commercial vehicles.

However, such a broad definition would include vehicles powered by standard petrol/diesel engines in the overall market, many of which were produced before Stokeness was even formed. If Stokeness wants to measure its share of the entire market on a more comparable basis, it may be preferable to focus on new vehicles only – that is, the proportion of the new vehicles manufactured each year which are powered by Stokeness cells.

Fuel cells – At the other extreme, Stokeness could define its market purely as the market for fuel cells, and therefore measure its performance against other fuel cell makers.

Alternative engine technologies – In between these two extremes, Stokeness might consider itself to be competing in the market for alternative engine technologies (for example, electrical batteries, compressed natural gas).

Because these three markets are so different in size, Stokeness will need to define which one it sees as most important to measure its performance in, so that it can set appropriate market share targets.

(c) **Technology start-up** – Stokeness seems to be a technology start-up company, which suggests that it is a risky company for external investors to invest in. Equally, however, it offers the prospect for high returns if its fuel cell technologies prove successful. Therefore, it appears that the VCs are risk seeking by investing in Stokeness.

However, it appears that the VCs have tried to moderate the level of risk to some degree by placing commercially experienced managers into the business to assist the engineers who founded it. Moreover, because the VCs now have some of their own employees on the management team, this will give them a high degree of influence at Stokeness.

Medium/long-term returns – Given that Stokeness is still three years away from the commercial launch of its cells, the VCs will not begin to see any returns from their investment until the medium to long term. However, the VCs could use net present value calculations, based on projected returns, as a performance measure in this respect.

Cash flow and cash control – In the shorter term, it is vital that Stokeness does not run out of cash while it is still developing its product (and hence not yet generating any revenue from it). Consequently, monitoring actual expenditure against budget and cash outflows will be key performance measures, to ensure that spending is kept under control.

Development targets – Stokeness needs to measure key non-financial aspects of performance as well as financial ones. Crucially, the point at which Stokeness can start selling a commercially viable product and therefore start acquiring customers will have a significant impact on its cash flow and NPV calculations. If the launch of the product falls behind schedule, this will increase the risk of the company running out of cash.

Therefore, it will be important for Stokeness to measure operational progress against key milestones: for example, completing successful test runs of the product.

Customer acquisition – Equally it will be important for Stokeness to sign contracts with customers, in order to secure revenue. Therefore, performance measures showing the number of definite customers signed up and the number of potential leads would also be useful.

ACCA Strategic Professional – Options

Advanced Performance Management (APM)

Mock Exam 3

(ACCA September/December 2019 exam)

Questions	
Time allowed	3 hours 15 minutes
This exam is divided into two sections	
Section A	This ONE question is compulsory and MUST be attempted
Section B	BOTH questions are compulsory and MUST be attempted

DO NOT OPEN THIS EXAM UNTIL YOU ARE READY TO START
UNDER EXAMINATION CONDITIONS

SECTION A – This question is compulsory and must be attempted

Question 1

Exhibit 1: Company information

Arkaig Manufacturing (Arkaig) is a world-leading, listed manufacturer of production machinery for other industries. It has customers in the mining, cement and chemicals sectors and seeks to provide them with the equipment, software and service for their products.

The aim of Arkaig is 'to maximise shareholder wealth by providing world-class, tailored automation solutions, which use technology innovatively, show improved machine downtime and reduced energy consumption for our customers.' This is supported by an entrepreneurial culture among all employees who should 'treat the business as if they owned it'.

Exhibit 2: Strategic internal performance reporting

There has been criticism of the business' current performance reporting by one of the directors at a recent board meeting. However, the chief executive officer (CEO) believes that the reporting system, which he put in place two years ago, is an excellent one.

In preparation for the next board meeting, the CEO needs an evaluation of the current report. As an example, a recent report used by the board for its strategic review is given in Appendix 1. The CEO stressed that it was the report and not the performance of the business which should be evaluated.

Exhibit 3: Economic value added

Another criticism of the performance management of Arkaig was that it lacked an over-arching measure of performance. As a result, the CEO is considering the introduction of economic value added (EVA™) to replace return on capital employed (ROCE) as a principal performance measure. The CEO wants to present this idea at the next board meeting and so needs an illustrative calculation of EVA™ along with a brief explanation of its benefits as a replacement for ROCE. The data in Appendix 2 should be used for the calculation.

Exhibit 4: Performance hierarchy

The earlier work requested focuses on the strategic level of the organisation and the CEO is keen to ensure that the other levels of the organisation (tactical and operational) do not get ignored in this discussion. However, before undertaking any specific work, he wants to make a presentation at the next board meeting. Therefore, he wants you to provide him with a brief description of the nature of the information required for performance measurement at these three different levels and explain how this information is influenced by the extent of planning and controlling activity at each of the levels of the performance hierarchy. He wants examples which would be relevant to Arkaig to illustrate these points in order that the presentation is made more concrete for the directors. He will then prepare the slides for the presentation himself.

Exhibit 5: Value chain

In order to analyse the operational aspects of Arkaig, the CEO has employed a consultant to produce a value chain analysis (Appendix 3). The value chain analysis has highlighted certain critical activities within Arkaig where there was concern about the performance management aspects. The CEO would like you to assess the performance management implications of the consultant's comments on the critical areas identified for Arkaig.

Required

It is now 1 September 20X5.

Write a report to the chief executive officer (CEO) of Arkaig to respond to his instructions for work on the following areas:

(a)	the performance reporting at Arkaig;	(11 marks)
(b)	the introduction of economic value added (EVA™);	(15 marks)
(c)	the information requested on the performance hierarchy; and	(10 marks)
(d)	the value chain analysis prepared by the consultant.	(10 marks)

Professional marks will be awarded for the format, style and structure of the discussion of your answer.

(4 marks)

(Total = 50 marks)

Exhibit 6: APPENDIX 1

Arkaig: Strategic performance report

Year ended 30 June 20X5

	Mining 20X5	Cement 20X5	Chemicals 20X5	Total 20X5	Previous year Total 20X4	Industry average
Orders ($m)	5,204	6,898	5,900	18,002	17,878	
Revenue ($m)	5,100	6,756	5,784	17,640	18,166	
Revenue growth (%)	0	–1.8	–6.5	–2.9		
Net profit ($m)	220	350	302	872	798	
Net profit margin (%)	4.3	5.2	5.2	4.9	4.4	4.6
ROCE (%)	16.1	17.3	17.4	16.8	15.7	15

Commentary:

(1) The company has increased its return on capital employed on the previous year and exceeded the industry benchmark.

(2) Revenue has fallen by 2.9% on the previous year but the order book has grown by 0.7%, indicating sustained sales levels going forward.

(3) The net profit margin has increased to 4.9%, again exceeding the industry benchmark of 4.6%.

(4) The company has continued to emphasise its entrepreneurial culture to its employees.

Exhibit 7: APPENDIX 2

Economic value added

The following details have been gathered for the 20X5 EVA™ calculation:

(1) The operating profit of Arkaig was $3,175m. This includes a depreciation charge of $1,780m.

(2) Amortisation charges of $95m in the year have been incurred.

(3) The corporation tax rate is 25%. Tax of $694m was paid in the year.

(4) The company has spent $90m this year and each year for the previous ten years on long-term brand building.

(5) The economic depreciation for the year is estimated to be $1,907m.

(6) This year and each year for the previous ten years, economic depreciation has included a $10m write-down of the value of brand building.

(7) Research and development expenditure of $705m was incurred in the period leading to an economic asset of $4,233m at the year end.

(8) Interest paid in the period was $213m.

(9) Capital employed during the period (from the statement of financial position):

	$m
Opening	19,404
Change in period	977
Closing	20,381

(10) Cost of capital:

Equity	12.0%
Debt (pre-tax)	3.8%

(11) Gearing: 45% debt/(equity + debt)

Exhibit 8: APPENDIX 3

Value chain analysis

Primary activities:

- Inbound logistics (receiving, handling and storing inputs) – Warehouse and distribution operations are controlled by an old information system which feeds into operations management information.

- Operations – Not a critical area of concern at present.

- Outbound logistics (delivering the product to customers) – Warehouse and distribution operations are controlled by an old information system which is fed from operations management information.

- Marketing and sales – Not a critical area of concern at present.

- After-sales service – This is an important area of revenue generation for Arkaig. However, certain directors are worried about over-focusing on this activity.

Secondary activities:

- Procurement – Not a critical area of concern at present.

- Technology development – Not a critical area of concern at present.

- Human resource management – Arkaig aims to recruit, retain and motivate staff who can fit with its entrepreneurial culture.

- Firm infrastructure (planning, finance, quality control, legal matters) – Not a critical area of concern at present.

Note. The areas noted as not critical do not require comment.

Section B – BOTH questions are compulsory and MUST be attempted

Question 2

Exhibit 1: Company information

Veyatie is a fashion clothing retailer which caters for both male and female customers of all adult age groups. Veyatie has ten retail stores. The company's information systems are basic for a business of its size and focus solely on financial information.

Veyatie's strategic objectives are 'To maximise shareholder wealth by increasing the number of retail stores, making our customers completely satisfied, ensuring our stores are attractive and offering the widest range of fashion clothing in our market.'

The Veyatie board has seen little need for non-financial performance indicators (NFPIs) so far, preferring instead to focus attention on cost control and working capital management. As a result, all senior managers are appraised against targets for operating profit margin, inventory turnover and the current ratio.

Exhibit 2: Customer satisfaction

Following a period of poor financial performance, Veyatie began collecting data on one aspect of non-financial performance, customer satisfaction, as the board had been advised that this is a key driver of financial performance.

The data collection began at the start of Quarter 3 20X3 and there is now data available for two complete years (Appendix 1). Veyatie has found it difficult to interpret this qualitative data and also the trends in this data. Some board members question its usefulness and propose reverting back to reporting just the financial indicators which they are used to.

Veyatie collects this data by asking customers to rate their satisfaction with their visit to the store as they are paying for their items. The scores range from 1 (completely dissatisfied) to 5 (completely satisfied). The mean score is the performance indicator reported to the board and the senior managers. Customers are encouraged to leave a score by having their names entered into a quarterly prize draw to win tickets to major football matches, concerts and amusement parks.

Exhibit 3: Balanced scorecard

A consultant has suggested to the board that the introduction of a balanced scorecard approach may improve business performance, as Veyatie is unlikely to achieve all of its strategic objectives in the near future. The board has already heard what the benefits of the balanced scorecard are, but are sceptical about these.

The board has asked for your advice on the problems of implementing and using the balanced scorecard approach at Veyatie. One aspect of this advice should focus on the selection of suitable performance measures and the consultant has already chosen some performance measures which could be included in a balanced scorecard at Veyatie (Appendix 2). These have been provided to help you illustrate your advice on the problems of using the balanced scorecard.

Note. The board would welcome your advice on how to refine the performance measures as part of your advice on the problems of using and implementing the balanced scorecard, but does not want you to give a detailed evaluation of the advantages and disadvantages of each performance measure, or to suggest completely new measures.

Required

It is now 1 September 20X5.

(a)   Assess the difficulties in using and interpreting the customer satisfaction data at Veyatie.

(10 marks)

(b)   Advise the board as requested of the problems of implementing and using the balanced scorecard approach at Veyatie.

(15 marks)

(Total = 25 marks)

Exhibit 4: APPENDIX 1

Customer satisfaction data

Percentage of customers giving customer satisfaction scores* between 1 and 5

| | | 20X3 | | 20X4 | | | | 20X5 | |
Narrative	Score	Q3	Q4	Q1	Q2	Q3	Q4	Q1	Q2
Completely satisfied	5	5%	5%	50%	5%	5%	0%	5%	45%
Very satisfied	4	10%	5%	0%	14%	15%	5%	20%	1%
Satisfied	3	70%	65%	0%	56%	50%	65%	45%	1%
Somewhat dissatisfied	2	10%	20%	0%	20%	25%	25%	25%	8%
Completely dissatisfied	1	5%	5%	50%	5%	5%	5%	5%	45%
Mean score		3.00	2.85	3.00	2.94	2.90	2.70	2.95	2.93

* Satisfaction scores were collected from a large number of customers when paying for their items.

Exhibit 5: APPENDIX 2

Perspective	Performance measure
Financial	Operating profit margin
	Inventory turnover
	Current ratio
Customer	Customer satisfaction
	Market share
Internal business processes	Stock out percentage[1]
Learning and innovation	Total employee training days[2]

Notes

1   Stock out percentage is the percentage of product lines which are unavailable for sale in each store at the beginning of each trading day.

2   The human resources department already records the total number of employee training days. Employee training covers the three main areas of health and safety training, training in handling customer complaints and training staff to understand the range of products available and how to display them attractively in the store.

Question 3

Exhibit 1: Company information

Daldorn is a manufacturer of heavy steel items. It is funded by a venture capitalist organisation (VC). Following a period of poor performance, the VC has expressed concern that Daldorn's board members are focusing too much on their own interests, while neglecting to adequately measure and manage company performance in respect of other stakeholder groups.

The company has experienced severe cash flow difficulties due to financial losses made on the sale of several new products. These difficulties have been attributed to poor pricing decisions, which were the responsibility of the board and have resulted in many employees losing their jobs.

Exhibit 2: Key stakeholder groups

The VC has identified three key stakeholder groups at Daldorn:

The board

The VC is concerned that due to the past losses made on several new products, the board has become too cautious in their attitude towards potential new projects and, in particular, to the pricing of new products. Given the importance of the board to the success of Daldorn, the VC has recently implemented a new bonus scheme. This is an attempt by the VC to revise the board's appetite for risk and encourage them to take more risks, for example, in deciding on the price of new products. Board members will now receive a very large annual performance-related bonus for Daldorn's achievement of challenging targets set on the financial performance measure of return on capital employed (ROCE).

Employees

The manufacturing process at Daldorn does not require employees to have a high level of skill and so most of the manufacturing employees are relatively low skilled. Other employees in other departments have roles which can require specific skills and qualifications. There is a high level of unemployment in the region where Daldorn is based.

Government and regulators

Daldorn operates in a strict regulatory environment. Daldorn has a good record of compliance, but recently its own scientists have discovered high concentrations of a toxic pollutant, which is a waste product from its own manufacturing processes, in the soil near to its factory.

The VC has asked for your advice on whether Daldorn's existing measures shown in Appendix 1 adequately measure the company's performance in managing the concerns of each of these three key stakeholder groups. You may justify the use of alternative measures, but the VC wants only one measure for each stakeholder group and is not concerned about the potential conflict between measures at this stage. As part of this work, the VC expects you to briefly comment on the power and interest of the three stakeholder groups.

Exhibit 3: Pricing decision

Daldorn is about to launch a new product and needs to determine an appropriate price to charge. The variable cost of each product is uncertain and, hence, there are three possibilities for each demand level. The total contribution of the products at the three possible anticipated levels of demand are shown in Appendix 2.

Exhibit 4: Investment projects

Two new mutually exclusive manufacturing projects, which are totally unconnected to Daldorn, have become available for the VC to invest in. The VC has undertaken many similar investments before and is an almost entirely risk neutral investor.

Two important exogenous (external) variables affecting the net present value (NPV) of the new projects, A and B, are the worldwide demand for steel products and the level of tariffs applied to the import of a key raw material. The probabilities of these two variables are independent. The VC has estimated the probabilities of there being low, medium or high levels of these two variables in Appendix 3, together with an estimate of the expected NPV for project A for each level of demand and tariff. An analyst has already calculated that the overall expected value of project B is $1,347m.

Required

(a) Assess the performance measures shown in Appendix 1 in relation to the three key stakeholder groups as required by the VC. **(9 marks)**

(b) Evaluate which price the board would choose for the new product based on the board's revised attitude to risk and briefly comment on the drawbacks of the decision rule used. **(5 marks)**

(c) Advise the VC which of the two new investment projects it should undertake, including an evaluation of the appropriateness of the numerical technique used. **(11 marks)**

(Total = 25 marks)

Exhibit 5: APPENDIX 1

Stakeholder	Measure
Board	Return on capital employed
Employees	Training costs
Government/regulators	No measure specified

Exhibit 6: APPENDIX 2

Demand, selling price and variable cost for the new product

Demand*	Unit selling price $'000	Unit variable cost $'000	Unit contribution $'000	Total contribution $'000
1,200	75	37	38	45,600
1,200	75	40	35	42,000
1,200	75	50	25	30,000
950	95	37	58	55,100
950	95	40	55	52,250
950	95	50	45	42,750
500	140	37	103	51,500
500	140	40	100	50,000
500	140	50	90	45,000

* Total demand for the whole of the product's anticipated two-year life.

Exhibit 7: APPENDIX 3

Project A – Expected NPV ($ million) for each possible demand level and tariff level combination

		Tariff level		
		High	Medium	Low
	Low	1,200	1,700	1,850
Demand level	Medium	1,000	1,500	1,600
	High	900	1,000	1,100

Project A – Joint probabilities for each possible demand level and tariff level combination

			Tariff level	
		High	Medium	Low
		0.20	0.50	0.30
	Low	0.20	0.04	0.10	0.06
Demand level	Medium	0.50	0.10	0.25	0.15
	High	0.30	0.06	0.15	0.09

Notes

1. The standard deviation of the outcomes for project A has been correctly calculated to be 103 and the standard deviation of the outcomes for project B has been correctly calculated to be 106.

2. An analyst has already calculated that the overall expected value of project B is $1,347m.

Answers

DO NOT TURN THIS PAGE UNTIL YOU HAVE
COMPLETED THE MOCK EXAM

Exam success skills

In any APM exam it will be important to apply good general exam technique by using the six exam success skills identified at the start of the Revision Kit, in the section covering 'essential skills'. These skills are: 1. Case scenario: Managing information; 2. Correct interpretation of requirements; 3. Answer planning: Priorities, structure and logic; 4. Efficient numerical analysis; 5. Effective writing and presentation; and 6. Good time management.

Some examples of how to apply these skills in this exam are provided in the table below.

Skill	Examples
Managing information	It is crucially important to assimilate the information in the question scenario.
	In longer questions, such as the 50 mark question, it is difficult to assimilate information by simply starting at the beginning and read to the end because there is so much information to take in.
	Instead it is sensible to take an **active approach** to reading each question. Read enough of the question to get an idea of the basic scenario and then read the initial requirements so that you understand the first things that you are expected to do with this information.
	For example, in Q1 the lengthy scenario makes a lot more sense if, before reading all of it, you are aware that the first requirements relate to performance reporting and economic value added.
Correct Interpretation of requirements	Be careful to interpret the verbs used in the question requirements carefully.
	Also be careful to identify where a question requirement contains more than one instruction.
	*For example, in Q3 part (c) the question required advice on which project to undertake **and** an evaluation of the techniques used.*
Answer planning	Planning is always important in APM questions, because most of the marks are available for discussion and if your discussion points are not relevant to the scenario then they will not receive any credit.
	As a general rule, you should spend at least 20% of your time, reading the scenario and planning your answer.
Efficient numerical analysis	It is essential that the marker can follow your workings and your logic.
	If you make a mistake early in your calculations that affects your later calculations then the marker will only penalise the error you have made, and not its follow-on impact on other calculations. This means that it is not normally a good use of your time to correct such errors during the exam.

Skill	Examples
Effective writing and presentation	In APM this is a very important skill. You are often expected to be able to employ **critical analysis**, and this will sometimes mean that you will reject innovative and modern ideas in favour of less exotic tried and tested performance management tools.
	It is also very important to **relate your points to the scenario** and to the requirement wherever possible. This means that you will need to apply your theoretical knowledge to the scenario, not simply repeat a technical point as something that you have memorised.
	However, you will be tested on your understanding of the theoretical content of APM and **you will not be able to apply your theoretical knowledge to the scenario if you do not possess a strong understanding of the theories in the first place**.
	For example, in Q1 a strong understanding of EVA is required.
	Relating your points to the scenario does not mean simply repeating the details from the question, but using this information to help to explain the point you are making.
	Finally, in Q1, to score the 4 **professional marks** that are available you should use suitable report headings, an introduction, a logical structure, signposted by the good use of subheadings in the answer, and a clear, concise style.
Good Time Management	The exam is 3 hours 15 minutes long, which translates to 1.95 minutes per mark.
	If you build in an allowance of 20% of your time for assimilating the scenario and planning, this falls to 1.56 minutes per mark (1.95 × 0.8).
	At the beginning of a question, work out the amount of time you should be spending on
	– Planning: for a 25 mark question this will be 1.95 × 25 marks × 20% = 10 minutes. For a 50 mark question this should be about 20 mins.
	– Writing your answer to each requirement: Take the mark allocation and multiply by 1.56 minutes per mark.

Diagnostic

Did you apply these skills when reading, planning, and writing up your answer? Identify the exam success skills where you think you need to improve and capture your thoughts here of what you want to achieve when attempting questions in future.

Question 1

Top tips.

Part (a). This is asking for a general assessment of the current reporting of performance as presented in Appendix 1, which presents a simple financial report for each sector (profit margin and ROCE) plus an overall statement of performance in the previous year and some industry averages.

This is a regularly examined area, and requires a firm understanding of the company's mission and whether the report supports this, in addition to general observations about the presentation, level of detail, and lack of commentary.

Positive remarks and negative remarks would both have been relevant but the lack of measures that directly and clearly support the company's strategy would have meant that the 'critical' points would dominate.

Part (b). This is asking for an evaluation of the replacement of ROCE with EVA using data in Appendix 2 to provide illustrative calculations.

11 of the marks were for calculations; these were mainly straightforward, harder adjustments and easier adjustments were all worth the same marks (1 mark per adjustment) so even if some mistakes were made it was still possible to score well here.

There were also 5 straightforward marks for discussing EVA compared to ROCE.

Part (c). This is asking for a description of the nature of strategic, tactical and operational information required and how this is influenced by planning and control activity; using examples relevant to this company.

Because strategic planning has been covered in part (a) more focus is needed on tactical (planning short-term resource allocation & control) which could include variances and NFIs, and on operational information which could include staff absenteeism and delivery performance. It is important to emphasise the need to link back to the company's mission in the discussion of the performance hierarchy.

Part (d). This requires an assessment of the performance management implications of a value chain analysis given in Appendix 3 which provides four observations using the value chain that require comment (and five observations which are non-critical and don't require comment). These need to be assessed in a practical way (gaining 1 mark per point) and could sensibly highlight interlinkages to other parts of the value chain as that is the main purpose of value chain analysis.

Marks can also be scored for some **brief** observations about the role of the value chain model in performance management (up to 3 marks).

Overall. Remember that you have been asked to write a report, so make sure the style and structure of your answer, as well as its tone, is appropriate for a report.

Examining team's comments.

In part (a) good candidates focussed on the high priority question of whether the report answers the question of whether the company is achieving its objective(s). Weaker answers over-concentrate on minor issues of presentation and often, spend much time suggesting large amounts of additional information which would overload the users without sufficient justification. A decreasing but still notable minority of candidates continue to respond incorrectly to such a requirement with an evaluation of the performance of the company. This demonstrates failure to read the scenario where it was made clear that the CEO wanted the report evaluated and not the performance of the company.

In part (b) many answers solely discussed the benefits and problems of economic value added without the comparison to ROCE and this meant that fewer marks could be awarded.

In part (c), which was generally well done, numerous candidates offered up a performance pyramid analysis of performance management at the company as an answer to this question. This did not directly address the question of the nature of the information for each level and tended only to score marks indirectly. Additionally, a notable minority could not correctly define the tactical and operational levels.

Part (d) was the part of question 1 that was most weakly done by candidates. Only a few candidates could provide a brief general description of the purpose of the value chain analysis and so give context to the consultant's comments. However, candidates were able to discuss broadly the activities identified as critical but often; they did not clearly link to this to the company's circumstances. In particular, candidates did not address the after-sales service issue well. Few seemed to be able to imagine why the directors were concerned about this area.

A significant minority of candidates chose to write about all the possible activities in the value chain despite being told only to address the critical areas identified.

General remarks:

As is now common at APM, those candidates who had practised writing professional answers prior to the examination performed admirably in the presentation area (4 marks). The markers were looking for suitable report headings, an introduction, a logical structure, signposted by the good use of subheadings in the answer, and a clear, concise style. Performance in this area was generally good.

Future candidates should beware that answers that take the form of short bullet point lists are unlikely to be addressing the need to justify suggestions or analyse issues. This is a major fault as most APM questions have the majority of their marks assessing these skills.

Marking scheme

Marks

(a) 1 mark per point – must be based on scenario information

Breaking down mission – up to 2 marks

   eg identify priority of objectives, pick out strategies

Assessment of whether report meets mission – up to 11 marks

   eg Clear statement of inadequacy for mission, addressing elements of the mission, information for relevant decision-making, illustrated by relevant examples

Other points – up to 4 marks

   eg Lack of information in the commentary, data overload, general presentation

Maximum   11

(b) Calculations:

Amortisation		1
Marketing capitalised		1
Research and development capitalised		1
Accounting depreciation	(for replacing with economic depreciation)	1
Tax paid		1
Lost tax relief on interest		1
Capital employed	(for opening figure)	1
Research and development asset		1
Marketing spend capitalised and w/off		1

	Marks
WACC	1
EVA™	1
Comments on result	1
Evaluation of EVA™ versus ROCE – up to 5 marks	
Maximum	15

(c) Each level of the hierarchy – up to 4 marks

    eg explanation of the nature of the information needed, impact of planning and controlling activity and illustrative examples

    Maximum   10

(d) General points on value chain implications and use – up to 3 marks

    Specific points relating to the areas of concern – 1 mark per relevant point

    Inbound logistics
    Outbound logistics
    After-sales service
    Human resource management

    Maximum   10

Professional marks – up to 4 marks   4

                        Total = 50

ANSWERS

Report

To: The CEO of Arkaig Manufacturing (Arkaig)

From: An accountant

Date: September 20X5

Subject: **Performance reporting and management issues at Arkaig**

This report evaluates the current performance report used by the board for strategic review. Next, the use of economic value added (EVA™) at Arkaig is illustrated and its use compared to return on capital employed (ROCE). Then, the differences between performance measurement and management at the different levels of the management hierarchy are discussed with reference to Arkaig. Finally, the implications of a value chain analysis for performance management are assessed.

(a) **Strategic performance reporting**

The current report has a number of strengths and weaknesses. These will be discussed according to whether the report:

- addresses the overall aims of the business;
- contains appropriate information for decision-making; and
- is well-presented.

The primary aim of Arkaig is to maximise shareholder wealth by providing suitable products for its customers. These products should have a number of qualities: be world-class; tailored; use technology innovatively; show improved machine downtime; and reduce energy consumption for customers.

This should be supported by an entrepreneurial culture among the employees.

Overall, the report contains a number of common financial measures but they are only loosely connected to the stated mission.

The following problems are noted about how the report measures the achievement of the mission:

(i) There is no direct measure of shareholder wealth in the report. The overall measure of performance for shareholders is provided through the absolute profit after tax and ROCE. It usefully benchmarks the net profit margin and ROCE with industry averages. However, these measures are only indirectly linked to value. The suggestion to use EVA™ is, therefore, appropriate for Arkaig.

(ii) The supporting pillars of the mission are all qualities of the products produced by Arkaig. The report does not measure any of these individually. There is an indirect measure of customer attitude through the revenue growth figure but without competitor comparison or a market share, it is not possible to draw a conclusion about any of the qualities of the products. These elements relating to the products are difficult to measure overall as they are likely to be dependent on each product line individually. For each in turn:

(1) The 'world class' nature of the offering could be measured by market share or customer survey responses.

(2) The tailored nature of the products could be measured by the cost of individual design for each installation or customer survey responses.

(3) Technological innovation could be measured through comparison of features with the competition or alternatively, by number of industry awards won.

(4) Machine downtime and energy consumption requires specific testing of each product line.

(iii) There is no measure of the employee culture although there is a comment that it is being achieved but this lacks evidence.

The report shows the financial performance by sector as well as in total for the business and the provision of some industry averages is useful in benchmarking performance.

For planning purposes, the lack of external information about customers and competitors makes some of the numbers difficult to interpret. For example, there is no indication whether the fall in revenue is due to general economic conditions or specific faults with Arkaig.

For control purposes, there is previous year information given but not sufficient to establish a trend (which requires at least three years of information). There is no indication of whether the business is meeting its budgets through the provision of variances.

In terms of presentation, the report is clear and it avoids overloading the reader with data. It uses terms which would be easily recognisable to those used to reading accounts. It is helpful that a narrative commentary is provided. However, often the commentary does not go beyond restating the figures in the table. It should provide the significant explanations for each of the major changes commented upon. For example, by stating why the ROCE has exceeded the industry average.

The commentary is an appropriate place to handle the less quantitative aspects of performance such as innovation and employee culture but it does not offer anything substantive. For example, it would be helpful to state what mechanisms are in place to emphasise the entrepreneurial culture (such as percentage of employees who own shares and the total proportion of equity owned by staff).

(b) **Economic value added (EVA™)**

Workings:

	Year ended 30 June 20X5 $m
Economic value added	
Operating profit	3,175
Add back:	
Amortisation	95
Marketing capitalised	90
Research and development capitalised	705
Depreciation	1,780
Less:	
Tax paid	694
Lost tax relief on interest	53
Economic depreciation	1,907
NOPAT	3,191
Capital employed	
At 20X5 year start	19,404
Research and development asset	3,528
Marketing spend capitalised	900
Marketing written-off	(100)
Adjusted capital employed	23,732

WACC = (55% × 12%) + (45% × 3.8% × (1 − 25%))

= 7.88%

EVA™ = NOPAT − (WACC × capital employed)

= 1,321

The business has created $1.32 billion of value in the last year. The net operating profit after tax more than covers the cost of the capital used by the business.

The main benefit to EVA™ is its link to the overall corporate objective of maximising shareholder wealth. ROCE gives a much less direct link to shareholder wealth as it is less cash-like and more tied to the accounting assumptions around producing a profit figure.

The basic test of performance is simple since for EVA™ if it is positive, then the business is generating a return above that required by the providers of finance. ROCE requires a target level to be set usually based on benchmarking to the industry sector and the setting of this target return can be somewhat subjective.

EVA™ encourages investment for the future (for example, in advertising and development) by removing such costs from the performance period and treating them like capital expenditure. This will reduce the dysfunctional temptation for management to engage in some short-term decision-making, which can be a problem with the unadjusted capital employed figure from the financial statements which is used in ROCE. This is particularly relevant to Arkaig, where research and development is a significant activity.

EVA™ is consistent with net present value (NPV) as businesses with an increasing present value will increase EVA™. This will aid communication as NPV is a widely used appraisal measure for businesses.

Overall, however, the better link to shareholder wealth creation and the use of EVA™ in a value-based management framework may make this extra complexity worthwhile for a large entity such as Arkaig.

(c) **Performance hierarchy**

According to Anthony, there are three tiers to decision-making in an organisation and each one has different needs which impact on the performance information which is required.

The strategic level is the one associated with the higher levels of management (such as the board). Strategic performance is measured over longer periods (3–10 years) since this depends on the achievement of the strategies which will enable the achievement of the overall mission of the business. The information will be externally focused requiring information on competitors and markets against which the company's performance can be benchmarked. This information will be used mainly for planning rather than controlling. At this level of the hierarchy, forecasts will be prepared and broad targets will be set for the lower levels of management and their performance measured against these targets. Therefore, information will often be heavily aggregated and qualitative in nature (such as customer attitudes). The board report evaluated above is an illustration of this type of information.

At the tactical level, the middle layer of management will be concerned with shorter term and more detailed objectives (possibly over a quarter or year) than the strategic level. The information will be collected on the deployment of the company's resources and activities on a functional department or business unit level. This information will be used to see that the strategic objectives are being supported by the company's activities. It will contain information to aid some short-term planning but will focus more on assisting this layer of management to control the operations of the business. Much of the information at this level will be internally generated and will be combined with the targets supplied by the strategic level in order to make decisions. For example, generally, the achievement of budget targets or more specifically, the sales and marketing department might be required to report quarterly on changes in the order book in order that the strategic level can forecast future revenue levels.

The operational level focuses on the day-to-day activities of the business ensuring that specific tasks set by the tactical level are achieved. Therefore, information at this level is detailed and task-specific. It will be prepared on a regular basis (often daily or weekly). It will be aimed to assist management at this level in controlling the business in order to achieve its short-term plans (weekly sales or monthly profit targets). There will be little external information needed at this level as there is very little planning activity being carried out.

(d) **Value chain**

The value chain is a model of business integration showing the way that business activities are organised and linked. This model uses activities rather than traditional functional departments (such as finance) to describe the business, emphasising that it is activities which create value and incur costs. The activities are split into two groups: primary ones which the customer interacts with directly and can 'see' the value being created and secondary ones which support the primary activities. The business can then identify how value is created and so focus on improving this through its performance measurement system (for example, the board report).

Another important feature of the value chain is the idea of value creation through a chain linking activities to each other. Therefore, there must be a flow of information between the different activities and across departmental boundaries. In performance management terms, this will affect the information systems which will have to ensure good communication across functional boundaries and also, the job descriptions and reporting hierarchies, as these will have to reflect activities rather than being purely contained within functional areas.

This chain will not stop at the organisation's boundaries as can be seen at Arkaig, where the relationship with suppliers (inbound logistics and procurement) is identified as an area of concern.

A specific area of concern at Arkaig is inbound and outbound logistics where there is an old warehousing and distribution information system. For a business such as Arkaig which aims to use technology innovatively, this could lead to inefficiencies. A state-of-the-art system would be integrated with the production and sales systems and would allow better stock control with fewer errors in picking inventory and reduced obsolescence while improved distribution could lead to faster delivery to customers with reduced costs of transportation.

The concern regarding after-sales service may be due to an inconsistency in having an area which generates a significant amount of revenue but which relates in reality to the failure of reliability of the business' products. It would be important to identify that customers' attitude to product reliability is not affected and that they see this service as necessary (maybe by benchmarking failure rates/machine downtime against competitors).

Although the chain shows human resources as a secondary activity, it is recognised as important to achieving the entrepreneurial culture at Arkaig. This culture can be realised through the reward system where employees are rewarded by share ownership or a share option scheme. Its effect can be measured through improved profitability and increased innovation.

Question 2

Marking scheme

Marks

(a)   1 mark per relevant point covering:
- subjectivity and customer perception
- mean and aggregated data
- incomplete data
- trends and seasonal factors

Maximum

10

(b)   1 mark per point
- problems of selecting measures
- problems of measurement
- the need for balance
- problems of conflicting measures
- need for board and management commitment
- collecting and interpreting data
- information system requirements
- use of illustrative examples from the measures in Appendix 2

Maximum

15

Total = 25

(a) **Subjectivity**

Customers' own assessments of satisfaction are subjective. Different customers could buy the same goods in the same store and at the same time, but still score their satisfaction differently. Different customers may have different expectations of their visit to the store and will attach different levels of importance to different aspects of their visit. Some may place a high importance on being able to move around the store and access goods easily, whereas to others this may be unimportant and would not affect their satisfaction.

Another reason why the data may be misleading is that, when rating their satisfaction, customers may tend to use the middle scores and be reluctant to use the highest and lowest scores. This appears to be the case in the data given where in most quarters customers do not give the scores of 1 or 5.

Aggregated and mean data

The collection of data of a single measure of customer satisfaction does not indicate what aspect of their visit to the store customers are satisfied, or dissatisfied, with. Customers may consider the price, design and quality of the goods, the comfort and layout of the store or the friendliness and product knowledge of the staff when scoring their satisfaction. Without knowing which aspects of their visit customers are satisfied with, it will be hard to know what to do to improve customer satisfaction.

Using the mean score may also make the data hard to interpret. For example, in Quarter 1 20X4, 50% of the customers are completely satisfied (a score of 5) and 50% of the customer are completely dissatisfied (a score of 1). This may be due to an error in collecting or compiling the data, but the mean score of 3 indicates that, overall, customers are satisfied, whereas 50% of them are completely dissatisfied. The calculation of the median or modal score may be preferable because this reduces the distortion to mean scores caused by very high or low scores.

Incomplete data

The data may not represent the views of a wide range of customers. The scores are collected when customers are buying goods at the till. This does not reflect the views of the customers who were so dissatisfied that they did not buy anything.

The prizes offered in the draw to encourage customers to leave the satisfaction score may appeal differently to male and female customers and to customers of different ages. For example, tickets to amusement parks may appeal more to younger customers than to older ones. Using this data as if it represents a wide range of customers' views may be misleading and lead to incorrect decisions being taken.

Identifying trends

Identifying trends is one way of overcoming some of the problems of interpreting the customer data, but it may be difficult to identify trends. In a fashion retailer such as Veyatie, there may be seasonal and short-term or cyclical trends, which make it hard to interpret what the long-term trend is.

In the limited data given, there appears to be a seasonal trend where customer satisfaction is worse in Quarter 4 than in any other quarter in each year. Overall there seems to be a downward trend, with every quarter being worse than the same quarter in the previous year.

(b) **Problems of implementing and using the balanced scorecard**

Selecting measures

Veyatie's strategic objectives are to maximise shareholder wealth by increasing the number of retail stores, making customers completely satisfied, ensuring its stores are attractive and offering the widest range of fashion clothing in the market. Measures must be selected which are congruent with Veyatie's critical success factors (CSFs) and strategic objectives. Though it is unclear what the CSFs are, at least one of the strategic objectives, to increase the number of stores, is not reflected at all in the measures selected. The lack of a suitable measure for this objective could be the reason why Veyatie is unlikely to open new stores in the near future.

BPP
LEARNING
MEDIA

Measures must not be selected just because they are easy to measure. The human resources department already records the total number of employee training days, so this measure could have been selected just because the data is readily available.

The number of days spent on the different types of training is unclear. Though clearly important, staff health and safety training does not directly help Veyatie achieve its strategic objectives. It may simply reflect Veyatie's legal obligations and so would not help gain competitive advantage. It would be better to measure the days spent training staff to understand the range of products available and how to display them attractively in the store, as this directly relates to Veyatie's strategic objectives.

One of the benefits of the balanced scorecard approach is that it presents a holistic view of a business, covering financial and non-financial and internal and external factors. The measures selected do cover all four perspectives of the balanced scorecard, but do not seem to be well balanced as there are more measures in the financial perspective than in each of the other perspectives. Also, most of the measures are internally focused.

The bias towards financial measures may reflect the fact that the board has so far seen little need for non-financial indicators. Financial measures, however, are backwards looking and measure the results of actions taken in the past. It is non-financial factors, such as customer satisfaction, which drive future performance and which will enable Veyatie to achieve its strategic objectives.

Conflicting measures

When selecting measures to use in the balanced scorecard, care must be taken to select measures which do not conflict with each other. Otherwise, without further guidance, managers will not know which measure to focus on, or may simply ignore one measure and focus on another.

Several of the measures selected by the consultant may potentially conflict with one another. For example, in order to achieve a low stock out percentage, Veyatie may have to hold higher levels of inventory which may worsen inventory turnover. This could apply at the overall company level or at individual stores.

The financial measure of operating profit margins conflicts with some of the measures in the other perspectives. The total number of employee training days has been selected to measure the learning and innovation perspective. The cost of this training, at least in the short term, will reduce operating profit margins. Similarly, having a high market share may imply that Veyatie will have to be competitive on price, which will also lower operating profit margins.

Board commitment

If the introduction of the balanced scorecard approach is to be successful, the commitment of the board is essential. Without this, other managers in the business are unlikely to work hard to implement and use the approach.

The board is already sceptical about the benefits of the balanced scorecard. There is the danger that it may simply be abandoned if it is found difficult to use, as was proposed for the collection of customer satisfaction data which was found to be difficult to interpret. The board's apparent disregard of non-financial performance measures is also clearly inconsistent with a successful introduction of the balanced scorecard approach.

Collecting and interpreting data

Interpreting the measures used in the balanced scorecard may be difficult, for example, for qualitative data such as customer satisfaction, which Veyatie has already had difficulties in interpreting. A lack of expertise in interpreting this data, may lead to wrong decisions being made.

The collection and interpretation of the data for the balanced scorecard will take time and resources. There may be staff resistance to the change, though this may be overcome by training in the benefits and use of the balanced scorecard.

Veyatie's information systems are basic for a business of its size and focus just on the use of financial information. They will need to be replaced or upgraded in order to collect and process non-financial and external data required for the balanced scorecard. The cost of implementing and using the balanced scorecard should be compared to the benefits of doing so.

Question 3

Workbook reference. Stakeholder analysis is covered in Chapter 4 of the Workbook. Risk and uncertainty are discussed in Chapter 5.

Top tips.

Part (a). The question scenario added that the analysis in this part of the question should include a brief commentary on the power and influence of the stakeholder and a suggestion of a **single** alternative performance measure.

This means that, for each stakeholder, the answer could logically start with an assessment of the power and interest of the stakeholder, then consider the existing measure and then recommend an alternative (maximum of one measure specified in the question) if appropriate.

This would provide 9 points, which should score full marks if the points are relevant and assuming 1 mark per point.

Part (b). The mark allocation is a clue that a simple approach is required to select a price based on the board's new attitude to risk (ie no longer being overly cautious). A simple maximax approach could therefore be justified here.

Part (c). Because the question tells us that the venture capitalist (to whom we are giving advice in this part of the question) is risk neutral, a sensible approach is therefore to use the detail (including joint probabilities) in Appendix 3 to calculate the expected NPV of the other project and then to use the information on risk and return to debate the relative merits of both projects and to come to a conclusion.

Do not forgot to evaluate the method used (this was worth about half of the marks).

Overall. The main issue with this question is in completing it to time, this is more likely to be achievable if it is planned carefully and not rushed into.

Examining team's comments. In part (a) many candidates wasted time by focussing their answer on performing a jargon-laden, Mendelow analysis when the question requirement focussed on the performance measures appropriate to the stakeholders.

Future candidates should read this question and then test themselves by asking whether they consider a valuable response is either (i) 'keep informed' to one of the stakeholders or (ii) indicate which measures should be used and why for a given stakeholder. If the answer is (ii) then the candidate has grasped the main point of the question.

Part (b) was either done well or badly depending on the basic knowledge of the methods.

In part (c) performance was weak reflecting poor basic knowledge of how to calculate expected values and the appropriate conditions for the use of this method.

Future candidates should ensure that they have learned the whole syllabus of APM as each diet of the examination is going to be a sample test of this knowledge across the whole syllabus.

Marks

(a)   Each stakeholder – 1 mark for power/interest commentary and up to
        3 marks for advice on performance measures.

        Maximum   9

(b)   Justification of maximax approach – 1 mark

        Identifying the maximum contribution of $55,100,000 – 1 mark

        Stating price chosen – 1 mark

        Drawbacks of decision rule – 2 marks

        Maximum   5

(c)   Calculation of expected NPV for Project A – 3 marks

        Comment on indifference or OFR result – 1 mark

        Comment on standard deviation as indication of risk and influence on
        decision – up to 2 marks

        Evaluation of EV method – up to 5 marks

        Comment on further work – up to 2 marks

        Maximum   11

                                                           Total = 25

(a)   **Board**

        The board members are key players who have a high level of power and interest. It is
        important that they understand and approve of Daldorn's strategy. It is vital that they are
        kept motivated in order to drive Daldorn's performance. The VC has recently implemented
        a new reward system, where the board will receive a very large annual performance-
        related bonus for the achievement of targets on return on capital employed (ROCE).

        ROCE may be an appropriate measure as it will be familiar to the board. It does have some
        drawbacks as a performance measure, for example, by discouraging investment in new
        assets. Alternative measures such as economic value added (EVA™) may overcome some of
        these drawbacks.

        Employees

        Employees have a high interest as they depend on the company for their income in an area
        of high unemployment. Most employees are relatively unskilled, and individually have low
        power, as they could be easily replaced. As Daldorn operates in a strict regulatory
        environment, employees' rights are likely to be legally protected which may increase their
        power.

        Employees should be kept informed to prevent them joining forces with more powerful
        stakeholder groups, such as the regulators or trades unions. Training costs are probably
        not a suitable measure for the mostly low-skilled workforce, as the manufacturing process
        does not required a high level of skill. Measures relating to employee productivity may be
        more useful, because, for example, higher productivity may increase their job security.

        Some employees' roles are more highly skilled and, for them, training costs will be a
        suitable measure of how well their skills are increased or maintained. The cost of training
        may not, however, indicate whether the training is appropriate or effective. A more precise
        measure, such as the percentage of employees achieving a particular relevant qualification
        or skill level, may be more appropriate.

Government and regulators

There are currently no measures relating to the government and regulators. As Daldorn operates in a strict regulatory environment, this seems inappropriate as breaches in regulations could lead to fines or loss of reputation.

The government and regulators have a high level of power but low interest. To prevent them becoming key players, they should be kept satisfied. This could be done by introducing measures relating to environmental performance, such as the level of toxic pollutants in the soil close to Daldorn's factory. This would allow Daldorn to take action to reduce the level of pollutants if these approached levels likely to breach environmental regulations.

(b) The board now has very large performance-related bonuses. This will mean that they have a risk seeking attitude to risk, in order to maximise their bonuses. The board would use the 'maximax' decision rule, that is, they would choose the price which maximises the maximum contribution. This price is $95,000 which would give a maximum contribution of $55,100,000.

The main drawback of using the maximax decision rule is that it may encourage the board to take excessive risks, as opposed to their previous attitude which was too cautious. The maximax rule also does not take into account the probabilities of each outcome and these probabilities are difficult to determine.

(c) The VC is an almost entirely risk neutral investor. The expected value (EV) approach is appropriate as they will accept the project with the highest expected NPV.

A problem with the EV approach is that it is a long run average which assumes a decision is repeated many times and is inappropriate for one-off decisions. The EV is unlikely to be the actual outcome of the project.

The VC has undertaken many similar projects and, hence, it would be appropriate to use EV. The estimations of the probabilities and the cost of capital are subjective and could be inaccurate. This would limit the effectiveness of the EV approach. The VC is experienced in estimating these probabilities, which would make the results of the calculation more reliable. The EV calculations for the two projects only consider two important exogenous variables. In practice, there are many different internal and external factors which could affect the NPV of the projects.

The calculations indicate that both projects have the same NPV of $1,347m (W1). As a risk neutral investor, the VC would be indifferent to which project to undertake.

The outcomes of project A have a slightly lower standard deviation (103) than those of project B (106). The spread of possible outcomes is therefore greater for project B, which means that it is riskier. The VC may therefore choose project A. Given that the NPV of the two projects are the same, further work such as sensitivity analysis, or an analysis of the external environment (PEST), could be done to help the VC make their choice.

Working

Expected NPV of Project A*

| | | Tariff | | | |
		High	Med	Low	Total
Demand	Low	48	170	111	329
		(1,200 × 0.04)	(1,700 × 0.10)	(1,850 × 0.06)	
	Med	100	375	240	715
		(1,000 × 0.10)	(1,500 × 0.25)	(1,600 × 0.15)	
	High	54	150	99	303
		(900 × 0.06)	(1,000 × 0.15)	(1,100 × 0.09)	
	Total	202	695	450	1,347

*Assuming the probabilities of the two variables are independent.

ACCA Strategic Professional – Options

Advanced Performance Management (APM)

Mock Exam 4

(Including questions from ACCA Sep/Dec 2020 exam)

Questions	
Time allowed	3 hours 15 minutes
This exam is divided into two sections	
Section A	This ONE question is compulsory and MUST be attempted
Section B	BOTH questions are compulsory and MUST be attempted

DO NOT OPEN THIS EXAM UNTIL YOU ARE READY TO START
UNDER EXAMINATION CONDITIONS

BPP
LEARNING
MEDIA

SECTION A – This question is compulsory and must be attempted

Question 1

Exhibit 1: Organisation information

You are a performance management consultant brought in by the chief executive officer (CEO) of the Department for Internal Affairs (DIA) for the country of Deeland. The department handles, among other areas, the policing of Deeland. The CEO is a government employee reporting to the Minister for Internal Affairs. The Minister for Internal Affairs is an elected politician appointed by the leader of the Deeland government.

The government of Deeland has recently changed and the new Minister for Internal Affairs has instructed the CEO of the DIA to improve the performance of the Deeland Police (DP) by implementing the Minister's new mission statement for DP: 'to protect the community and prevent crime while providing a value for money service.' As part of this implementation, the CEO has identified the following four key areas for action:

(1)   Protecting and supporting those at risk of harm

(2)   Ensuring criminals are caught and brought before the courts

(3)   Achieving long-term sustainable solutions to the causes of crime

(4)   Addressing new forms of crime arising in the virtual world

The new Minister wants general improvement in the first three of these areas, as their political campaign was based around criticism of the previous government's perceived failure on these points. It is widely agreed that in the second area, the major concern is the catching of criminals since, historically, there is a high probability that once caught they are brought before the courts. The third area is being addressed through increased involvement with local communities in order to identify and address the causes of crime. The fourth area of crime in the virtual world (the use of computers to facilitate crime) was hardly addressed under the previous government, and the Minister wants to see the creation of a task force which will develop skills in detection and prosecution of virtual crime.

Exhibit 2: CSFs and KPIs

In a recent meeting with the CEO, the Minister indicated that they felt that the four key areas were too vague and in order to better focus actions, the Minister's adviser has suggested the following critical success factors (CSFs):

(1)   Greater protection and more support for those at risk of harm

(2)   Be better at catching criminals

(3)   Reducing the causes of crime by increased involvement with local communities

(4)   Create a task force to develop skills in detection and prosecution of virtual crime

Initially, the CEO did not see why the four key areas originally given could not be used as CSFs. They want you to provide justifications in light of the Minister's concerns for the changes which the adviser has made to each of these. Then, using the above CSFs, they want you to provide justified recommendations of up to two key performance indicators (KPIs) per CSF in order to measure performance.

In order to help you with the KPIs, the CEO has provided you with a table of data (Appendix 1), which has been used in the past when considering DP's performance. However, you are allowed to suggest new data which would help in measuring performance. The CEO has made it clear that at this stage, no calculations are required.

Exhibit 3: Value for money

Since DP is funded wholly through Deeland's general taxation, the CEO wants to be able to report on whether DP is providing a value for money (VFM) service as required by the new mission statement. They have heard of the 3Es (economy, efficiency and effectiveness) but need an explanation of these three headings and how this links to the work on CSFs and KPIs already requested. Then, they require an evaluation, using the data given in Appendix 1, of whether DP provides such a service. They understand that the evaluation may be limited, as Appendix 1 may not give a data set to perform a full VFM exercise.

Exhibit 4: Non-financial performance indicators

The new Minister has come from a business background into politics and so far, in departmental discussions, they have focused heavily on the financial aspects of running the Department of Internal Affairs. The CEO wants to help the Minister change focus towards using non-financial performance indicators (NFPIs) and so to understand why financial indicators are not particularly useful for public sector organisations such as DP. The CEO wants you to explain this in your report and illustrate your explanation with examples relevant to DP.

Exhibit 5: League tables

The Minister is interested in benchmarking as this was often done during their days in business. As a result, they joined an international initiative for creating a league table of fire service data by sharing information with other nearby countries. The CEO believes that the Minister will want to introduce this idea for DP and so wants an assessment of the use of an international police force performance league table and its link to targets for DP. The CEO is especially concerned about the police officers' reaction to this new idea, as they have a powerful union, which has widespread public support. Therefore, they also needs you to explain how the use of league tables and targets might affect police officers' behaviour.

Required

It is now 1 September 20X5.

Write a report to the CEO of the Department for Internal Affairs to respond to their instructions for work on the following areas:

(a)   The critical success factors and key performance indicators for Deeland Police;   **(16 marks)**
(b)   An evaluation of the value for money service provided;   **(13 marks)**
(c)   The use of non-financial performance indicators;   **(7 marks)**
(d)   The use of league tables in measuring the performance of Deeland Police.   **(10 marks)**

Professional marks will be awarded for the format, style and structure of the discussion of your answer.   **(4 marks)**

(Total = 50 marks)

Exhibit 6: Appendix 1

Deeland Police data for each year ending 30 June

	20X5	20X4	20X3
Population ('000s)	11,880	11,761	11,644
Number of police officers	37,930	38,005	38,400
Number of administrative staff	12,320	12,197	12,075
Number of crimes reported in the year	541,735	530,900	520,282
Number of violent crimes reported in the year	108,347	106,180	104,056
Number of crimes solved in the year	297,954	300,934	303,943
Number of complaints	7,624	7,512	7,483
Response to an incident within the allocated time limit	84%	86%	87%
Cost of the police force for the year ($m)	2,248	2,226	2,203
Staff costs (all staff including police officers) ($m)	2,026	2,103	2,141

Section B – BOTH questions are compulsory and MUST be attempted

Question 2

Exhibit 1: Company information

Clonyard is a private company which sells shoes to adults and children. Clonyard has several retail shops. The mission of Clonyard is 'to satisfy customers by providing footwear of excellent quality for the modern world.' Clonyard has built its reputation on providing footwear to those who have specialist needs in footwear, such as minor medical issues, and Clonyard's staff excel at spending time with customers to determine customers' correct requirements. Clonyard has achieved modest growth over the past five years.

Twelve months ago, Clonyard was the subject of a successful but hostile take-over bid by Elrig, a listed company. Elrig's mission is 'to return value consistently to our shareholders by growing our market share and by offering unrivalled value for money to our customers.'

Elrig's primary motivation for the takeover was to enhance its market share by acquiring a niche operator. In addition, Elrig's directors also believe that there is likely to be consolidation in the industry in the near future and the purchase of Clonyard by Elrig is a reaction to that belief. Having acquired Clonyard, Elrig is keen to retain the Clonyard brand and is also keen to ensure that all aspects of Clonyard's business operations are integrated into those of Elrig.

Exhibit 2: Current situation

Elrig has taken a decision at board level that a similar range of inventory is maintained throughout all Elrig and Clonyard shops. Managers of Clonyard's individual shops are unhappy with this, as this is contrary to the individual specialisms which shop managers were encouraged to develop previously. As a result, several managers have left the business.

In order to help with the integration of Clonyard into Elrig's business, Elrig has ensured that each Clonyard shop will have at least one of Elrig's employees working there. Clonyard's staff have complained that the Elrig members of staff are more focused on ensuring a sale is made than spending the required time with customers. Clonyard staff have also expressed concern about the lack of technical product knowledge of Elrig's staff.

Elrig has retained most of Clonyard's directors. These directors have found it challenging to adjust to Elrig's focus on pursuing market share and recently said, 'It's as though they don't measure anything else. Every report we get is about market share and the message is always that we need more of it, as quickly as possible.'

The chief executive officer (CEO) of Elrig was recently told by a management consultant that Elrig should consider using the McKinsey 7S model to help with the integration of Clonyard into Elrig's operation. The management consultant indicated that they felt that Elrig should only focus on the four soft elements in this model for now.

Exhibit 3: Introduction of an ERPS

Elrig and Clonyard are currently utilising different computer systems. It is therefore difficult for staff at all levels of Elrig's operations to obtain access to Clonyard's performance data. The board of Elrig has complained that any information it receives on Clonyard's operations or performance is too late to enable the board to make decisions. The director of operations for the group, for example, has indicated that they do not see any reports on inventory levels at each Clonyard shop until at least three months into the financial year. They have also indicated that Clonyard shops appear to wait too long for goods to be delivered to them from their suppliers.

The group sales director indicated that the data they receive on Clonyard's monthly financial performance is at least three weeks late. This offers no opportunity to introduce discounted products at an appropriate time, which is a very common sales approach for Elrig.

Elrig's employees in general have expressed concern that Clonyard's computerised information systems are outdated and that Clonyard's employees do not use the computer system as much as they should. For example, it was reported that it is common practice for a Clonyard employee to place an order for inventory over the telephone and not enter the order onto the computer system until after the order has been delivered.

The board of Elrig has decided that it needs real time access to Elrig's overall business operations, including Clonyard, and is considering the purchase of an enterprise resource planning system (ERPS). Further, a director of Elrig has indicated: 'the use of a shared up-to-date information system such as an ERPS will ensure that the Clonyard operation is completely integrated within the Elrig one. The Clonyard employees will also be delighted with the brand new system.'

Required

It is now 1 September 20X5.

(a) Using the soft elements of the McKinsey 7S model, evaluate whether Elrig is properly aligned with Clonyard. **(15 marks)**

(b) Evaluate the introduction of an ERPS into Elrig's overall business, including Clonyard. **(10 marks)**

(Total = 25 marks)

Question 3

Exhibit 1: Background

Roan University (Roan) is based in Teeland, which is a developed country. The government of Teeland has stated that it will cut part of the funding for the university and has made it clear that Roan must develop new replacement income streams. Roan will remain state owned.

Saugh University (Saugh) is based in Deeland, which has a developing economy and which is culturally different to Teeland. Saugh's funding is from the government of Deeland and this funding is secure for the foreseeable future. The government of Deeland has indicated that it wants the university to develop joint ventures and alliances with universities in developed countries.

Roan and Saugh have recently entered into a joint venture to set up a new university in Deeland. The new university is called RS University (RSU). Roan and Saugh each own 50% of the joint venture and a new purpose-built campus has been constructed. RSU will welcome students within three months.

Exhibit 2: Details of the joint venture

Roan and Saugh have established a joint management board (MB) to manage the long-term and short-term operations of RSU. The MB's membership is 50% from each university, plus at least one government representative from Deeland. The MB meets at least three times per annum and the position of chairman on the MB rotates between Roan and Saugh on a meeting-by-meeting basis.

Roan has stated that its aim for the joint venture RSU is 'to internationally expand our provision and lead educational developments in the global arena by enhancing our revenue streams from innovative sources.' Saugh, however, has made it clear that it will view the success of RSU by the quality of the graduates who are produced and by the contribution these graduates make to society.

Saugh is keen that Roan sends as many home-based staff from Teeland to teach at RSU in Deeland as is possible but Roan would prefer to recruit local staff in Deeland to undertake its teaching obligations at RSU. Roan's teaching staff have voiced concerns about the extensive travel involved to teach at RSU and have also indicated that their work at Roan is likely to suffer if they teach at RSU. Specifically, they feel that they would not be able to effectively undertake their teaching duties, research activities or supervision of students at Roan. Negotiations are currently taking place between the teachers' trade union, which Roan's staff belong to, and management at Roan which could result in all Roan's teaching staff refusing to teach at RSU.

Exhibit 3: Public view of the joint venture

There has been some criticism of the joint venture within the local community in Teeland. A parent of one of the students studying at Roan has written, on behalf of a newly-formed public pressure group, to the local newspaper saying,

> All the attention at Roan is on this inappropriate joint venture. My son was told that he could not receive any help or guidance as the staff who could help him were all overseas helping with the development of RSU. His exam results were three weeks late as there was no one there to mark the exams. This is not acceptable. Roan should exist to educate Teeland students primarily. Everything else is secondary.
>
> Membership of the public pressure group is growing.

Exhibit 4: Stakeholder analysis

Roan has undertaken an analysis of its stakeholders using Mendelow's matrix. Part of this work is supplied below, along with the justifications for the categorisation of the three stakeholder groups.

		Level of interest	
		Low	High
Level of power	Low	A	B
	High	C	D

Government of Teeland – the government would be keen to know of any financial problems or difficulties with the joint venture but, generally, it would belong in segment A, so **minimal effort** should be expended.

Roan teachers' trade union – the teachers' trade union's power could be high if it has the backing to recommend to the management of Roan that Roan employees will not travel to or teach at RSU. If Roan can recruit local staff for RSU, the power and interest of the trade union will both be low as there will be little or no need for its involvement. If Roan cannot recruit local staff, then the power and interest of the trade union will both be high and it will fall into Category D of being a **key player**.

Public pressure group in Teeland – the group has a very high level of interest in the joint venture and its power may be determined by its size. If it grows significantly, then its power may become high also. For the present, its power is likely to be low so the group will fall into category B – **kept informed**.

Required

It is now 1 September 20X5.

(a) Discuss the problems that will be encountered in managing and measuring performance in the RSU joint venture. **(16 marks)**

(b) For each of the three stakeholder groups, recommend and justify an appropriate performance measure which could be used by Roan. **(9 marks)**

(Total = 25 marks)

Exhibit 4: Appendix 1

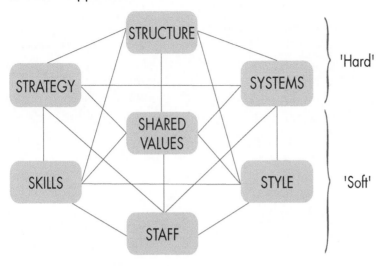

The soft elements are skills, staff, style and shared values.

Answers

DO NOT TURN THIS PAGE UNTIL YOU HAVE
COMPLETED THE MOCK EXAM

Exam success skills

In any APM exam it will be important to apply good general exam technique by using the six exam success skills identified at the start of the Revision Kit, in the section covering 'essential skills'. These skills are: 1. Case scenario: Managing information; 2. Correct interpretation of requirements; 3. Answer planning: Priorities, structure and logic; 4. Efficient numerical analysis; 5. Effective writing and presentation; and 6. Good time management.

Some examples of how to apply these skills in this exam are provided in the table below.

Skill	Examples
Managing information	It is crucially important to assimilate the information in the question scenario.
	In longer questions, such as the 50 mark question, it is difficult to assimilate information by simply starting at the beginning and read to the end because there is so much information to take in.
	Instead it is sensible to take an **active approach** to reading each question. Read enough of the question to get an idea of the basic scenario and then read the initial requirements so that you understand the first things that you are expected to do with this information.
	For example, in Q1 the lengthy scenario makes a lot more sense if, before reading all of it, you are aware that the first requirements relate to KPIs and value for money.
Correct Interpretation of requirements	Be careful to interpret the verbs used in the question requirements carefully.
	*For example, in Q2 part (b) the verb evaluate implies that candidates should assess the positives **and** negatives resulting from the introduction of an ERPS, before coming to a **justified** conclusion.*
	Also be careful to identify where a question requirement contains more than one instruction, **especially in Q1** where the requirements are embedded in the exhibits.
	*For example, in Q1 part (a) the question required justification for making changes to the CSFs **and** justified recommendations of up to two KPIs for each CSF.*
Answer planning	Planning is always important in APM questions, because most of the marks are available for discussion and if your discussion points are not relevant to the scenario then they will not receive any credit.
	As a general rule, you should spend at least 20% of your time, reading the scenario and planning your answer.
Efficient numerical analysis	It is essential that the marker can follow your workings and your logic.
	If you make a mistake early in your calculations that affects your later calculations then the marker will only penalise the error you have made, and not its follow-on impact on other calculations. This means that it is not normally a good use of your time to correct such errors during the exam.

Skill	Examples
Effective writing and presentation	In APM this is a very important skill. You are often expected to be able to employ critical analysis, and this will sometimes mean that you will reject innovative and modern ideas in favour of less exotic tried and tested performance management tools.
	It is also very important to **relate your points to the scenario** and to the requirement wherever possible. This means that you will need to apply your theoretical knowledge to the scenario, not simply repeat a technical point as something that you have memorised.
	However, you will be tested on your understanding of the theoretical content of APM and **you will not be able to apply your theoretical knowledge to the scenario if you do not possess a strong understanding of the theories in the first place**.
	For example, in Q2 it is not possible to discuss the alignment of the two companies with each other without a good understanding of the McKinsey 7S model.
	Finally, in Q1, to score the 4 **professional marks** that are available you should use suitable report headings, an introduction, a logical structure, signposted by the good use of subheadings in the answer, and a clear, concise style.
Good Time Management	The exam is 3 hours 15 minutes long, which translates to 1.95 minutes per mark.
	If you build in an allowance of 20% of your time for assimilating the scenario and planning, this falls to 1.56 minutes per mark (1.95×0.8).
	At the beginning of a question, work out the amount of time you should be spending on
	– Planning: for a 25 mark question this will be 1.95×25 marks $\times 20\% = 10$ minutes. For a 50 mark question this should be about 20 mins.
	– Writing your answer to each requirement: Take the mark allocation and multiply by 1.56 minutes per mark.

Diagnostic

Did you apply these skills when reading, planning, and writing up your answer? Identify the exam success skills where you think you need to improve and capture your thoughts here of what you want to achieve when attempting questions in future.

Question 1

Marking scheme

		Marks

(a) CSFs and KPIs

4 marks for the four CSFs

Up to 4 marks for discussion of KPIs for each area

Max 16

(b) VFM

1 mark for defining each of the 3Es

1 mark for comment on the link to the CSFs/KPIs

1 mark per point – discussing each heading at DP

Max 13

(c) NFPIs

Up to 4 marks for general discussion

Up to 5 marks for examples relevant to DP

Max 7

(d)   **League tables**

Up to 5 marks for general evaluation of league tables

Up to 7 marks for the link of tables to targets and police officer reaction

     Introduction of tables

     Behaviour under the system and sense of accountability

1 mark each for other relevant points

Max <u>10</u>

Professional marks   4

Total = <u>50</u>

Report

To: The CEO, Department of Internal Affairs (DIA)

From: An accountant

Date: 1 September 20X5

Subject: Performance measurement and management at Deeland Police (DP)

This report recommends and justifies critical success factors (CSFs) and key performance indicators (KPIs) for DP based on the four critical areas of performance. DP is then evaluated on the value for money (VFM) provision of its service. The usefulness of non-financial performance indicators (NFPIs) in the public sector is explained. Finally, the use of a league table of police performance and the setting of targets for DP is assessed, with comment on the employee reaction to such a management approach.

(a)   **Critical success factors (CSFs) and key performance indicators (KPIs)**

The CSFs must follow from the four areas which are addressing the overall mission. The four key areas to consider are:

(1)   Protecting and supporting those at risk of harm

(2)   Ensuring criminals are caught and brought before the courts

(3)   Achieving long-term sustainable solutions to the causes of crime

(4)   Addressing new forms of crime arising in the virtual world

The first three areas are on-going in the activities of DP and the Minister wants improvement in each. The adviser's suggested CSFs all appear to be reasonable improvements to manage the Minister's concerns about the vagueness of the key areas as follows:

(1)   Greater protection and more support for those at harm (this is a straight-forward improvement to the existing position in this area)

(2)   Be better at catching criminals (bringing them before the courts does not appear to be critical as it seems to automatically follow)

(3)   Reducing the causes of crime by increased involvement with local communities (improvement using the mechanism suggested)

The fourth area is relatively new, so it will be more in the nature of a separate project to:

(4)   Create a task force to develop skills in detection and prosecution of virtual crime (as desired by the Minister)

The KPIs for the four CSF areas

Area 1

The CSF breaks into two parts – protecting and supporting. There should be a KPI measuring the change in each of these areas:

–   Percentage change year on year of the number of victims of violent crimes, once they are identified as at risk (a register of 'at risk' people would need to be created)

–   Percentage change of staff hours spent with each victim on average in support activities

Neither of these KPIs can currently be measured as the data is not collected. The first point could be indirectly addressed by measuring the number of victims of violent crimes, which should see a fall if those at risk are better protected.

Area 2

This CSF is looking at what is often referred to as the clear-up rate, which is the percentage of crimes where the criminal is caught. The data given allows this to be measured through:

–   The percentage change in the percentage of crimes solved (although care must be taken that 'solved' is not the same as 'criminal caught' as there may be cases where the police know the criminal, but they escape capture)

The second part of bringing the criminal before the courts once caught does not appear to be a critical area needing measurement since this appears to be a low risk possibility. The critical area might be better stated as 'Ensuring crimes are solved and criminals are brought before the courts' since the second part would then be an appropriate area to measure.

Area 3

From the data in Appendix 1, the KPI could be:

–   The percentage change in the total number of crimes in Deeland in the year

The effect of reducing the causes of crime would be to create a long-term trend downwards in this measure. It may be better to use a three-year moving average of the change as a result. However, there may be many factors which cause such changes

including the number of police officers and so the underlying causes of crime may not be accurately measured. The suggested KPI does not capture whether the changes are sustainable in the long term, which will be difficult to do.

Area 4

The KPIs for the fourth area require examination of the number and qualifications of those working on the task force on virtual crime. The data in Appendix 1 is not sufficient to measure this.

KPIs could include:

–   Percentage of roles in the task force filled (this requires that there is a plan for the organisation of a suitable task force, which may be complicated as this is a new area where knowledge of how many staff and what qualifications they should have may not be present)

–   Percentage of virtual crimes reported which are solved (shows the effectiveness of the task force)

(b)   **Value for money (VFM)**

The standard criteria for analysis of the value for money of a service are:

–   Economy – the optimisation of the resources which the organisation has; ensuring the appropriate quality of input resources are obtained at the lowest cost;

–   Efficiency – the optimisation of the process by which inputs are turned into outputs;

–   Effectiveness – how the outputs of the organisation meet its goals.

The 3Es above link to the CSFs and KPIs in the area of effectiveness. The KPIs measure the achievement of the goals of DP and all relate to outcomes rather than processes or inputs in this case.

In order to judge VFM, comparison can be made internally to the historic performance of DP, but it should also be benchmarked against external organisations. The need for external data is also reflected in the desire to benchmark in league tables although no data is given for this here and so the VFM can only be judged against previous years' data.

Considering the situation at DP specifically

Economy could be measured by looking at the cost of buying inputs; the principal input is staff (90.1% of total costs) and so the cost per employee ($40,318) is relevant. This represents a 3.8% reduction on the previous year although it should be noted that the mix of staff is changing with more administrative staff replacing police officers who may be more expensive as they are more qualified. It would be useful to obtain the data on the average police officer salary as they make up 75.5% of the total staff and they are critical to the achievement of outcomes.

As noted above, in order to judge whether this is good or bad, the Department should also compare this to external figures such as the national average wage and, also, the average salary of staff in other police forces in similar countries.

Efficiency can be measured in a number of different ways.

	20X5	20X4	20X3
Solved crimes per police officer	7.855	7.918	7.915
Solved crimes per employee (police officers and admin staff)	5.929	5.994	6.022
Police officers per 1,000 population	3.19	3.23	3.30

The trend in the number of police officers is downward which would suggest improvement. However, the more important outcome is not the resources poured in but the crime results and these show that by decreasing the number of police officers, the number of crimes which each is solving is falling (down 0.8% from 20X3). Performance in this area is therefore poor.

Effectiveness must be measured against DP's goals in its four areas:

(1) Protection and support of those at risk – the percentage of violent crime remains flat over the three years of data at 20% of the total number of crimes reported. This suggests that protection remains broadly unchanged. As noted above, there is no measure of support provided.

(2) Solving crimes – the clear-up rate has fallen from 56.7% to 55.0%. This probably reflects the change in staff mix as police officer numbers have fallen.

(3) Causes of crime – the trend is clearly upwards with an increase of 2% each year over the last two years which may again reflect the falling numbers of police officers in DP.

(4) Virtual crime – as noted above, it is not possible to measure the achievement of the creation of the task force from the data provided.

(c) **Non-financial performance indicators (NFPIs)**

Public sector organisations have a number of differences compared to profit-making entities and these can be partly addressed with the use of non-financial performance indicators.

Overall, DP must consider the use of NFPIs in order to capture the aspects of DP's mission which are fundamentally non-financial and subjective, such as protecting the community.

Lack of profit measure

DP is not expected to make a profit. There is no specific charge for the service to the public and the police are funded through general taxation by the government. The problem with using purely financial measures is that they are, therefore, solely cost measures. If only financial measures are used, then this would mean that positive progress would only be seen in cost reduction. It is likely that this would reduce the quality of the service and so fail to achieve DP's mission.

Multiple objectives

In a profit-making organisation, the goal is clear, however, it is difficult to say with DP which is the single, overriding objective. Therefore, there must be an attempt to balance and so compromise between the different areas which have been set out in order to achieve overall success. DP illustrates this problem in that it has four critical areas, none of which focus on financial goals and can only be measured in non-financial terms.

Difficulty in defining suitable financial measures

Many non-profit-seeking organisations provide services for which it is difficult to define a cost unit. With DP, the cost unit could be cost per crime reported or cost per crime solved or cost per member of the population.

Also, the benefits of the service are mainly non-financial such as a greater feeling of security among the public.

(d)   **League tables**

The use of league tables effectively benchmarks performance and can have a positive effect on behaviour. The sharing of data on performance can indicate areas of best practice and so offers the possibility of improving performance by copying that best practice. Additionally, the use of league tables gives, by the rank in the table, a clear, immediate answer to questions of relative performance.

However, the use of league tables only measures relative performance. The best force in the table could still be producing an unacceptable performance in absolute terms. The different forces in different countries will face different external environments. Each force will have to react to the economic situation in that country and may allocate resources differently according to the priorities of the government of that country. So, it will be difficult to get a single measure, such as the rank in the league table, to balance these competing factors.

This leads on to another area which will prove difficult, which is how to rank the different forces. Usually, there is a scoring system giving points across different areas for each force's performance. The selection of the areas and the weighting given to them within the rank score will affect the position of the different forces. In an example of 'what gets measured, gets done', it may be that the DP management will change their priorities from those given by the DIA to those measured in the rank score and so undermine the alignment of their behaviour with the given mission of DP. Therefore, to be of value to the Minister, the calculation of the rank must encompass the key variables which will drive DP's desired performance.

Therefore, there is a link between league tables and employee behaviour which comes from the setting of targets based on the league table rank.

The impact on the employees includes whether they feel a sense of accountability for the score. If the police officers do not feel that they can affect the rank, then they may ignore it or actively undermine it in public through their union's public statements. This will present the government with difficulty as the police are considered the experts in this area of public policy and their criticism will carry weight with the electorate.

Specifically, the police officers may be demotivated by the league tables if they feel:

(1)   that the league table rank does not reflect the valuable work which they do (for example, in creating the new virtual crime task force); or

(2)   that the rank is driven by factors outside of their control. (For example, the budget for the force may be cut, as appears to be happening with DP, or there may be a link between the number of crimes reported and the economic conditions in Deeland which they do not have power to affect.)

BPP
LEARNING
MEDIA

Question 2

Workbook reference. The 7S model is covered in Chapter 4 and ERPS is covered in Chapter 6 of the Workbook.

Top tips.

Part (a). The appendix to the question presented the 7S model and identified which parts represented soft elements. The candidate was then required to apply the soft elements (staff, skills, style and shared values) to the scenario to illuminate the difficulties in integrating Clonyard.

A good answer required practical comments on these areas, not in overly theoretical terms; 1 mark was available per point.

Part (b). This required an assessment of both the possible advantages and also possible disadvantages of the introduction of an ERPS using the clues provided in the scenario. A good answer would apply a basic understanding of an ERPS to the scenario provided.

Again, to score well this required an extraction of relevant practical information from the scenario to argue against the introduction of ABM (main product is standardised, ignores life cycle etc).

Marking scheme

		Marks
(a)	Skills – up to 3 marks	
	Staff – up to 3 marks	
	Style – up to 3 marks	
	Shared values – up to 6 marks	
	Conclusion – up to 2 marks	
		Max 15
(b)	Advantages of ERPS – up to 5 marks	
	Disadvantages of ERPS – up to 5 marks	
	Conclusion – up to 2 marks	
		Max 10
		Total = 25

(a) **Skills**

With regard to the skills element, it is clear that Clonyard and Elrig train and develop their staff in different ways. Clonyard has placed an emphasis on detailed product knowledge and on ensuring that the individual's needs are met. Such training and development is very much aligned with a company that has a specialist niche. It is also clear that Elrig's focus is less on meeting individual requirements than in pursuing a sale and it is likely that Elrig's staff have been trained and developed more in terms of sales techniques than with regard to product knowledge. This means that the staff from Clonyard have a different skill set and it is clear, from their reaction to the Elrig staff working in Clonyard shops that no attempt has been made to develop the skill set of either group of employees in order to align them with each other.

Staff

It is clear, especially given the point above, that staff are treated in a different way in both organisations. It is also evident from the scenario that Clonyard staff are leaving the organisation. It is likely that staff have been given responsibility for inventory and shop management in Clonyard and that the focus in the company has been on developing the individual to enhance their range of specialist knowledge. Elrig's singular focus on market share would suggest that Elrig's staff are more likely to be trained and developed in the areas of financial performance measures and be aware of costs, margins and the financial implications of the decisions being made. Indeed, the fact that Elrig's staff are seeking to make a sale quickly suggests that they are aware of the cost of the time they spend with each customer and it is likely that there is an ideal time per sale that they will work towards.

Style

Style usually represents the corporate culture of the organisation and it is clear that the cultures are very different within Elrig and Clonyard. The issue of the takeover being hostile in the first instance is perhaps an indicator that the styles of the organisations are very different.

Style is also indicative of how an organisation presents itself to the outside world and again it is clear, through the interactions with customers, which Clonyard would seek to satisfy the customer's specific requirements whereas Elrig would try to sell a product to the customer with the minimum time spent on the transaction. Such a contrast in styles would inevitably be reflected in the customer experience and it may prove to be very damaging for Clonyard if its style is aligned with that of Elrig. Customers may feel that there is no longer any reason to visit Elrig if its main differentiators of individual service, product specialism and time spent with the customer are removed.

Shared values

All of the above elements illustrate that the companies have very different values. The element of shared values should reflect the guiding beliefs of people in the organisation as to why it exists and it is clear in Elrig and Clonyard, even at the level of their mission statements, which they exist for quite different reasons. It is clear that the attitudes and behaviours which reflect these differing strategic approaches are reflected in the differing shared values of the staff in the scenario.

Elrig, for example, expects that it should be able to impose its own business model upon a very different type of business. This is because its underlying objective is that its business only exists to return as much value for shareholders as possible and that the people in the organisation should all be focused on making that happen. There should be no reason, in terms of Elrig's values and beliefs, as to why this structure should not be accepted in Clonyard.

Clonyard's values are very different to this, however, and rely on individuals taking responsibility, and making decisions accordingly; to pursue things which they feel would benefit both the customer experience and Clonyard. Clonyard's lack of pursuit of shareholder value in its mission is reflected in it achieving modest growth, which has most likely ensured that most stakeholders in the organisation have been satisfied.

Each company does appear to have shared values within its own organisation – for example, staff in both Elrig and Clonyard appear to have a set of shared values for the organisation they work for. This makes the alignment of values for the new organisation very difficult. From the scenario, Elrig does not appear to have tried to do anything to help in this regard.

Conclusion

In conclusion, it is clear that there is overlap and interconnectivity between each soft element of the 7S model. Elrig appears to have made no attempt to align these differing elements and as a result there is no sense of shared values, different styles of operation and different skill sets in the respective staff.

The 7S model has been useful in addressing this lack of alignment and provides evidence to Elrig that it must revert to the mission of Clonyard and decide if this now needs to change in the light of the takeover. If not, and as the 7S model has shown, Elrig might be best advised to allow Clonyard to operate as it was doing quite successfully beforehand and consider integration and alignment as a long-term rather than a short-term goal.

(b)   **Advantages**

An ERPS would help alleviate the problems detailed with regard to inventory control in that the current inventory levels would be very clear on the ERPS and any sale would register immediately, thereby showing the effect on the inventory overall. Minimum inventory levels may be set within the ERPS and an order to the supplier automatically triggered when inventory reaches that level. An ERPS will also allow details of the delivery to be tracked and the ERPS will enable staff at the appropriate level to discover how long deliveries are taking and to manage the supplier relationship accordingly.

The discounting of product lines in certain areas is clearly a key part of Elrig's strategy to enhance its market share and the sales manager is correct in that it is impossible to impose this strategy on Clonyard with such old data. An ERPS would ensure that the sales manager has access to immediate sales of each product and could compare this with both planned sales of the product and past sales of the product. The ERPS may also permit the inclusion of some external data which could inform the company of any changes in the market for particular products or distinct product lines. This would certainly enable the sales manager to take real time decisions with regard to which products might be discounted and to what level. The ERPS would be of great benefit to them in this endeavour.

The ERPS, as highlighted above, has the ability to remove the responsibility for the ordering of inventory from the employee and undertake this function based on the minimum inventory levels that have been input. This would certainly solve the problem of Clonyard employees not entering the purchase order into the computer system and would ensure that the relevant people in the organisation are fully aware of the inventory both on order and in store.

Disadvantages

However, the view of the director of Elrig appears to be that they can use the introduction of an ERPS to impose Elrig's strategy on Clonyard and this is something which should be avoided. The strategies of the two companies should be aligned initially and any shared computer system, and the information that it might generate, should be agreed thereafter.

There are other significant potential negative effects of introducing the ERPS based on the director's view. For example, it may further enhance the feeling of alienation that many Clonyard employees appear to be feeling if another system is imposed on them without discussion and agreement. Their motivation would suffer and Clonyard's ability to maintain its position in the market may be affected. This market position is, after all, the main reason for Elrig's purchase of Clonyard in the first place.

There is evidence from the scenario that Clonyard is delaying the information that it offers Elrig as even manual systems could offer more up-to-date data than that detailed by the operations manager and the sales manager. This sub-optimal behavior has perhaps been a reaction by Clonyard staff to the imposition of Elrig's systems. Much as the removal of any sub-optimal behaviour should be encouraged, the introduction of the ERPS without discussion and agreement may enhance those feelings of Elrig imposing its operations upon Clonyard. This stresses again the dangers of introducing a computer system to integrate one company's operations into another and further highlights the need to come to a common approach with regard to the future strategic direction of Clonyard.

It is also naïve of the Elrig director to assume that Clonyard employees will be enthusiastic about the introduction of a new computer system. Aside from the potential negative aspects associated with control that are highlighted above, there is evidence from the scenario that Clonyard employees are not engaging fully with their own computer system. This may be because they have not been properly trained and the prospect of the introduction of a new and much more complex system may be very threatening for them.

Alongside the difficulties associated with the introduction of the ERPS into the Elrig/Clonyard operation, an ERPS has other well-established and more generic disadvantages such as its cost, its difficulty in adapting to the specifics of some individual business operations and the time taken to implement the system.

Overall, the introduction of an ERPS would certainly help with regard to some operational aspects detailed in the scenario. The overall benefits are likely to be much wider than this with, for example, the access to real-time information being very useful to Elrig/Clonyard in their current environment. However, the introduction of the ERPS should not be used as a way of integrating Clonyard within Elrig's operation. This needs to be done at a much more fundamental level where strategic direction is agreed. Using an ERPS to integrate without this agreement first is likely to lead to more problems with regard to integration than it will solve.

Question 3

Workbook reference. The difficulties of managing performance in complex structures is covered in Chapter 14 of the Workbook.

Top tips.

Part (a). This required use of the scenario to look critically at the potential problems. A key challenge here would be to make value-adding comments, rather than simply repeating the information provided i.e. explaining the problem, linking points to each other, judging the potential significance of the issue.

Part (b). Many points could have been made, but the important skill being tested is the ability of the candidate to justify a practical performance measure in the context of a new joint venture.

Marking scheme

		Marks
(a)	1 mark per point	
	Discussion of issues in relation to performance management – up to 9 marks	
	Discussion of issues in relation to performance measurement – up to 9 marks	
		Max 16
(b)	For each stakeholder group:	
	Recommended measure – 1 mark	3
	Justification of the measure – up to 2 marks	6
		9
		Total = 25

(a) **Managing performance**

Establishing common objectives

The initial problem with regard to managing performance in any joint venture is establishing its objectives and goals and the aims of each university for the joint venture of RSU are different.

Roan's main purpose for undertaking the joint venture is to find a new revenue stream. The word profit is not explicitly stated in their view of the joint venture but nevertheless it has to be assumed that Roan is seeking to make a financial return from this and that its focus will be on maximising that return rather than maximising revenue to the disregard of cost. In terms of performance management, therefore, the focus of Roan is likely to be on ensuring that these main goals are met and therefore areas of finance and resource utilisation and consumption are likely to form the core of the management system.

Saugh's main purpose for undertaking the joint venture is to enhance its status within its own country, and perhaps globally, as a renowned institution of learning. The focus for Saugh in terms of how performance of RSU is managed is likely to be on the reputation of Saugh, staff development and the destinations of its graduates.

Developing a joint venture in terms of its financial return and in terms of the contribution that it makes to society may be possible within a performance management framework but it is clear that these aims are contradictory. At a simple level, focusing on the financial aspects can lead to a lack of investment which may damage the quality of the joint venture's provision and, ultimately, the contribution that the graduates of RSU can make to society.

Lack of stable leadership

It is clear from the scenario that the rotational nature of the chairman of the management board (MB) will almost ensure that there is a lack of stable leadership. Unless the universities can agree on a common and mutually acceptable aim, the chairman is likely to be acting more in the interests of their own university than in the interests of the joint venture.

The inclusion of at least one government official from Deeland on the MB may also present problems from the perspective of Roan with regard to performance management. As the current balance of the MB membership is 50:50, the inclusion of representatives from Deeland would clearly tip the balance in favour of Saugh. This is likely to lead to a loss of control for Roan which would clearly have an effect on the manner in which the joint venture is managed in terms of its performance.

Measuring performance

Given the challenging funding environment in Teeland, reflected in the overall view of Roan with regards to what the aim of the joint venture should be, Roan will be focused on the financial return of RSU. This means that Roan would seek to measure traditional financial measures such as return on investment and operating surplus. Roan's focus is likely to be specifically on the fees charged, student numbers, costs incurred and on return on investment overall. The measures that Roan would like to see would therefore relate to fee growth, student numbers and cost reduction. It is not clear how quickly Roan is seeking to achieve a return on the investment but from the scenario it can be assumed, given the cuts to governmental funding, that it would prefer a return to be achieved in the short term as well as over the long term. Roan may therefore be keen to spend a significant amount on advertising, to boost student numbers in the short term, rather than wait for the reputation of RSU to grow by word of mouth.

Saugh appears to be free from any financial constraints, at least in the short term. Its funding is secure and this means that Saugh is unlikely to be interested in assessing the performance of RSU with any traditional financial metrics. As a result, this may place Saugh in direct conflict with Roan with regard to many decisions. For example, Saugh may feel that enhancing classroom technology in RSU is necessary and should be undertaken immediately without understanding that this would represent a significant further investment for Roan.

Saugh will be more focused on the quality of the students that are admitted to RSU, their performance whilst at university and their occupation and perhaps salary level on leaving the university. There is likely to be conflict with Roan with regard to students that are admitted to RSU as Roan will be more focused on recruiting as many students as possible whereas Saugh will be more focused on the grades that these students have achieved either at school or in previous study.

Both universities will be interested in how the students perform at RSU. Roan's reputation would suffer significantly, for example, if it were to accept students who failed its programmes in large numbers. However, Roan will be less focused on the level of excellence achieved by students of RSU than Saugh. Again, this is likely to lead to conflict as Saugh will be motivated to undertake additional investment, be it in terms of staff time in the form of extra classes or through extra resources that are likely to help students achieve higher grades.

Roan is also likely to be interested in how graduates of RSU perform after graduation but it is not as important to them as it is to Saugh. Saugh may therefore be keen to devote significant resource to developing strong links with local industry to ensure that RSU graduates are equipped with the correct skills. Saugh will also want to devote significant resource to monitoring and measuring how the graduates perform after graduation. Saugh may, for example, initiate surveys at various points following graduation at intervals of perhaps one, five and ten years. Given the focus of Roan, it is unlikely to want to devote much by way of resources to such measurement.

As a measure of commitment to the joint venture, Saugh will definitely be motivated to measure how many of Roan's staff will teach at RSU. Saugh may try to impose specific measures here, such as percentage of Roan staff from Teeland teaching on each programme, as it is clear that the involvement of Roan is a critical success factor for Saugh in achieving its aims.

(b) **Government of Teeland**

The government of Teeland is only likely to be interested in the performance of RSU if there is a significant failing. The most obvious examples relate to a financial default through overspend or, potentially, a scandal involving staff of Roan in Deeland whilst working at RSU. It would be impossible to either plan for or meaningfully measure this latter scenario and hence the most likely aspect to be of interest to the government of Teeland is the liquidity of Roan. A simple measure of this, even something as straightforward as the cash surplus of Roan, would confirm to the government of Teeland that Roan is unlikely to go into liquidation.

This measure should be considered alongside the long-term liquidity of Roan and the government would be interested in knowing if Roan had taken on any long-term debt to fund the joint venture and, if so, its overall proportion in Roan's capital structure.

Teachers' trade union

The teachers' trade union would be interested in the number of programmes or courses that are being offered in RSU. The more programmes that are offered, the more likely it is that Roan staff will be required by their employer to teach in Deeland. Fewer courses would increase the possibility that local provision for teaching could be found. However, the more courses that are offered, the less likely it is that the necessary specialism could be found through local provision in a developing country.

Public pressure group

The public pressure group would be interested in how much time is being spent by staff of Roan, perhaps teaching staff in particular rather than those of a higher level of management, in Deeland. The pressure group would like to see this figure probably presented in absolute terms and measured month by month to allow for comparison and trend analysis. The higher this figure becomes the more active the pressure group is likely to become and the more the membership of the pressure group is likely to grow.

Mathematical tables

Present Value Table

Present value of 1 i.e. $(1 + r)^{-n}$

Where   r = discount rate
         n = number of periods until payment

Discount rate (r)

Periods (n)	1%	2%	3%	4%	5%	6%	7%	8%	9%	10%	
1	0.990	0.980	0.971	0.962	0.952	0.943	0.935	0.926	0.917	0.909	1
2	0.980	0.961	0.943	0.925	0.907	0.890	0.873	0.857	0.842	0.826	2
3	0.971	0.942	0.915	0.889	0.864	0.840	0.816	0.794	0.772	0.751	3
4	0.961	0.924	0.888	0.855	0.823	0.792	0.763	0.735	0.708	0.683	4
5	0.951	0.906	0.863	0.822	0.784	0.747	0.713	0.681	0.650	0.621	5
6	0.942	0.888	0.837	0.790	0.746	0.705	0.666	0.630	0.596	0.564	6
7	0.933	0.871	0.813	0.760	0.711	0.665	0.623	0.583	0.547	0.513	7
8	0.923	0.853	0.789	0.731	0.677	0.627	0.582	0.540	0.502	0.467	8
9	0.914	0.837	0.766	0.703	0.645	0.592	0.544	0.500	0.460	0.424	9
10	0.905	0.820	0.744	0.676	0.614	0.558	0.508	0.463	0.422	0.386	10
11	0.896	0.804	0.722	0.650	0.585	0.527	0.475	0.429	0.388	0.350	11
12	0.887	0.788	0.701	0.625	0.557	0.497	0.444	0.397	0.356	0.319	12
13	0.879	0.773	0.681	0.601	0.530	0.469	0.415	0.368	0.326	0.290	13
14	0.870	0.758	0.661	0.577	0.505	0.442	0.388	0.340	0.299	0.263	14
15	0.861	0.743	0.642	0.555	0.481	0.417	0.362	0.315	0.275	0.239	15

(n)	11%	12%	13%	14%	15%	16%	17%	18%	19%	20%	
1	0.901	0.893	0.885	0.877	0.870	0.862	0.855	0.847	0.840	0.833	1
2	0.812	0.797	0.783	0.769	0.756	0.743	0.731	0.718	0.706	0.694	2
3	0.731	0.712	0.693	0.675	0.658	0.641	0.624	0.609	0.593	0.579	3
4	0.659	0.636	0.613	0.592	0.572	0.552	0.534	0.516	0.499	0.482	4
5	0.593	0.567	0.543	0.519	0.497	0.476	0.456	0.437	0.419	0.402	5
6	0.535	0.507	0.480	0.456	0.432	0.410	0.390	0.370	0.352	0.335	6
7	0.482	0.452	0.425	0.400	0.376	0.354	0.333	0.314	0.296	0.279	7
8	0.434	0.404	0.376	0.351	0.327	0.305	0.285	0.266	0.249	0.233	8
9	0.391	0.361	0.333	0.308	0.284	0.263	0.243	0.225	0.209	0.194	9
10	0.352	0.322	0.295	0.270	0.247	0.227	0.208	0.191	0.176	0.162	10
11	0.317	0.287	0.261	0.237	0.215	0.195	0.178	0.162	0.148	0.135	11
12	0.286	0.257	0.231	0.208	0.187	0.168	0.152	0.137	0.124	0.112	12
13	0.258	0.229	0.204	0.182	0.163	0.145	0.130	0.116	0.104	0.093	13
14	0.232	0.205	0.181	0.160	0.141	0.125	0.111	0.099	0.088	0.078	14
15	0.209	0.183	0.160	0.140	0.123	0.108	0.095	0.084	0.079	0.065	15

Annuity Table

Present value of an annuity of 1 i.e. $\dfrac{1-(1+r)^{-n}}{r}$

Where   r = discount rate

            n = number of periods

Discount rate (r)

Periods (n)	1%	2%	3%	4%	5%	6%	7%	8%	9%	10%	
1	0.990	0.980	0.971	0.962	0.952	0.943	0.935	0.926	0.917	0.909	1
2	1.970	1.942	1.913	1.886	1.859	1.833	1.808	1.783	1.759	1.736	2
3	2.941	2.884	2.829	2.775	2.723	2.673	2.624	2.577	2.531	2.487	3
4	3.902	3.808	3.717	3.630	3.546	3.465	3.387	3.312	3.240	3.170	4
5	4.853	4.713	4.580	4.452	4.329	4.212	4.100	3.993	3.890	3.791	5
6	5.795	5.601	5.417	5.242	5.076	4.917	4.767	4.623	4.486	4.355	6
7	6.728	6.472	6.230	6.002	5.786	5.582	5.389	5.206	5.033	4.868	7
8	7.652	7.325	7.020	6.733	6.463	6.210	5.971	5.747	5.535	5.335	8
9	8.566	8.162	7.786	7.435	7.108	6.802	6.515	6.247	5.995	5.759	9
10	9.471	8.983	8.530	8.111	7.722	7.360	7.024	6.710	6.418	6.145	10
11	10.368	9.787	9.253	8.760	8.306	7.887	7.499	7.139	6.805	6.495	11
12	11.255	10.575	9.954	9.385	8.863	8.384	7.943	7.536	7.161	6.814	12
13	12.134	11.348	10.635	9.986	9.394	8.853	8.358	7.904	7.487	7.103	13
14	13.004	12.106	11.296	10.563	9.899	9.295	8.745	8.244	7.786	7.367	14
15	13.865	12.849	11.938	11.118	10.380	9.712	9.108	8.559	8.061	7.606	15

(n)	11%	12%	13%	14%	15%	16%	17%	18%	19%	20%	
1	0.901	0.893	0.885	0.877	0.870	0.862	0.855	0.847	0.840	0.833	1
2	1.713	1.690	1.668	1.647	1.626	1.605	1.585	1.566	1.547	1.528	2
3	2.444	2.402	2.361	2.322	2.283	2.246	2.210	2.174	2.140	2.106	3
4	3.102	3.037	2.974	2.914	2.855	2.798	2.743	2.690	2.639	2.589	4
5	3.696	3.605	3.517	3.433	3.352	3.274	3.199	3.127	3.058	2.991	5
6	4.231	4.111	3.998	3.889	3.784	3.685	3.589	3.498	3.410	3.326	6
7	4.712	4.564	4.423	4.288	4.160	4.039	3.922	3.812	3.706	3.605	7
8	5.146	4.968	4.799	4.639	4.487	4.344	4.207	4.078	3.954	3.837	8
9	5.537	5.328	5.132	4.946	4.772	4.607	4.451	4.303	4.163	4.031	9
10	5.889	5.650	5.426	5.216	5.019	4.833	4.659	4.494	4.339	4.192	10
11	6.207	5.938	5.687	5.453	5.234	5.029	4.836	4.656	4.486	4.327	11
12	6.492	6.194	5.918	5.660	5.421	5.197	4.988	4.793	4.611	4.439	12
13	6.750	6.424	6.122	5.842	5.583	5.342	5.118	4.910	4.715	4.533	13
14	6.982	6.628	6.302	6.002	5.724	5.468	5.229	5.008	4.802	4.611	14
15	7.191	6.811	6.462	6.142	5.847	5.575	5.324	5.092	4.876	4.675	15

Review Form – Advanced Performance Management (02/21)

Name: _____   **Address**: _____

_____

_____

How have you used this Kit?
(Tick one box only)

☐ On its own (book only)

☐ On a BPP in-centre course_____

☐ On a BPP online course

☐ On a course with another college

☐ Other _____

Why did you decide to purchase this Kit?
(Tick one box only)

☐ Have used the Workbook

☐ Have used other BPP products in the past

☐ Recommendation by friend/colleague

☐ Recommendation by a lecturer at college

☐ Saw advertising

☐ Other _____

During the past six months do you recall seeing/receiving any of the following?
(Tick as many boxes as are relevant)

☐ Our advertisement in *Student Accountant*

☐ Our advertisement in *Pass*

☐ Our advertisement in *PQ*

☐ Our brochure with a letter through the post

☐ Our website www.bpp.com

Which (if any) aspects of our advertising do you find useful?
(Tick as many boxes as are relevant)

☐ Prices and publication dates of new editions

☐ Information on product content

☐ Facility to order books

☐ None of the above

Which BPP products have you used?

Workbook   *Other*   ☐

Practice & Revision Kit ☑

Your ratings, comments and suggestions would be appreciated on the following areas.

	Very useful	Useful	Not useful
Passing APM	☐	☐	☐
Questions	☐	☐	☐
Top Tips etc in answers	☐	☐	☐
Content and structure of answers	☐	☐	☐
Mock exam answers	☐	☐	☐

Overall opinion of this Practice & Revision Kit   Excellent ☐   Good ☐   Adequate ☐   Poor ☐

Do you intend to continue using BPP products?
Yes ☐   No ☐

Please visit https://www.bpp.com/request-support to provide your feedback for this material.

Review Form (continued)

TELL US WHAT YOU THINK

Please note any further comments and suggestions/errors below.